Memorial Book of Rokiskis
(Rokiskis, Lithuania)

Translation of
Yisker-bukh fun Rakishok un umgegnt
(Yizkor book of Rakishok and environs)

Edited by: M. Bakalczuk-Felin

Originally Published in Johannesburg, 1952
(Yiddish, 626 pages)

Published by JewishGen Press

An Affiliate of the Museum of Jewish Heritage - A Living Memorial to the Holocaust
New York

Rokishok Yizkor Book

Memorial Book of Rokiskis
(Rokiskis, Lithuania)

Copyright © 2017 by JewishGen, Inc.
All rights reserved.
First Printing: September 2017, Elul 5777

Translation Project Coordinators: Tim Baker assisted by David Sandler
Additional Material: Phil and Aldona Shapiro
Layout: Joel Alpert and Barry Mann
Image Editor: Martha Forsyth
Cover Design: Nili Goldman

This book may not be reproduced, in whole or in part, including illustrations in any form (beyond that copying permitted by Sections 107 and 108 of the U.S. Copyright Law and except by reviewers for public press), without written permission from the publisher.

Published by JewishGen, Inc.
An Affiliate of the Museum of Jewish Heritage
A Living Memorial to the Holocaust
36 Battery Place, New York, NY 10280

"JewishGen, Inc. is not responsible for inaccuracies or omissions in the original work and makes no representations regarding the accuracy of this translation. Digital images of the original book's contents can be seen online at the New York Public Library Web site."

The mission of the JewishGen organization is to produce a translation of the original work and we cannot verify the accuracy of statements or alter facts cited.

Printed in the United States of America by Lightning Source, Inc.

Library of Congress Control Number (LCCN): 2017949409
ISBN: 978-1-939561-58-9 (hard cover: 866 pages, alk. paper)

Cover photograph: 1924 Maccabee Team in Rokiskis.
Photograph is from the South African Jewish Board of Deputies Archive, housed in the Beyachad Building in Johannesburg. Naomi Musiker was the archivist who in 2006 gave Barry Mann permission to scan the image. On the back it states that the photograph was donated by Mrs. Ethel Aarons in 1988.

JewishGen and the Yizkor-Books-in-Print Project

This book has been published by the **Yizkor-Books-in-Print Project,** as part of the **Yizkor Book Project** of **JewishGen, Inc**.

JewishGen, Inc. is a non-profit organization founded in 1987 as a resource for Jewish genealogy. Its website [www.jewishgen.org] serves as an international clearinghouse and resource center to assist individuals who are researching the history of their Jewish families and the places where they lived. JewishGen provides databases, facilitates discussion groups, and coordinates projects relating to Jewish genealogy and the history of the Jewish people. In 2003, JewishGen became an affiliate of the **Museum of Jewish Heritage - A Living Memorial to the Holocaust** in New York.

The **JewishGen Yizkor Book Project** was organized to make more widely known the existence of Yizkor (Memorial) Books written by survivors and former residents of various Jewish communities throughout the world. Later, volunteers connected to the different destroyed communities began cooperating to have these books translated from the original language— usually Hebrew or Yiddish—into English, thus enabling a wider audience to have access to the valuable information contained within them. As each chapter of these books was translated, it was posted on the JewishGen website and made available to the general public.

The **Yizkor-Books-in-Print Project** began in 2011 as an initiative to print and publish Yizkor Books that had been fully translated, so that hard copies would be available for purchase by the descendants of these communities and also by scholars, universities, synagogues, libraries, and museums.

These Yizkor books have been produced almost entirely through the volunteer effort of researchers from around the world, assisted by donations from private individuals. The books are printed and sold at near cost, so as to make them as affordable as possible. Our goal is to make this important genre of Jewish literature and history available in English in book form, so that people can have the personal histories of their ancestral towns on their bookshelves for themselves and for their children and grandchildren.

A list of all published translated Yizkor Books in the project with prices and ordering information can be found at:
http://www.jewishgen.org/Yizkor/ybip.html

Lance Ackerfeld, Yizkor Book Project Manager

Joel Alpert, Yizkor-Book-in-Print Project Coordinator

This book is presented by the
Yizkor Books in Print Project
Project Coordinator: Joel Alpert

Part of the
Yizkor Books Project of JewishGen, Inc.
Project Manager: Lance Ackerfeld

These books have been produced solely through volunteer effort of individuals from around the world. The books are printed and sold at near cost, so as to make them as affordable as possible.

Our goal is to make this history and important genre of Jewish literature available in English in book form so that people can have the near-personal histories of their ancestral towns on their bookshelves for themselves and for their children and grandchildren.

Any donations to the Yizkor Books Project are appreciated.

Please send donations to:
Yizkor Book Project
JewishGen
36 Battery Place
New York, NY 10280

JewishGen, Inc. is an affiliate of the
Museum of Jewish Heritage
A Living Memorial to the Holocaust

Yiddish or Hebrew Title Page of Original Yiddish or Hebrew Book

יזכּור-בּוך

פֿון

ראַקישאָק

און

אומגעגנט

אַרויסגעגעבן פֿון דער ראַקישקער לאַנדסמאַנשאַפֿט אין יאָהאַנעסבורג, דרום אַפֿריקע,

צו איר 40 יאָריקן יוביליי (1912—1952).

רעדאַקטער: מלך באַקאַלטשוק-פֿעלין

פֿרעזידיום — ירחמיאל אַראָנס-אַרש;
א. נח-נחומאָוויץ; שלמה רובין

בור-קאָלעגיע:

מיטגלידער — מענדל מוסקאַט;
ישראל מייקל-מיכאַלעוויץ;
שרה קלאָס; משה קלאַוויר

יאָהאַנעסבורג — 1952 — תשי"ג

Translation of the Title Page of Original Yiddish Book

YIZKOR-BOOK

OF

Rakishok and Environs

issued by

The Rakishker Landsmanschaft of
Johannesburg, South Africa

on the occasion of
the 40th year of its establishment
(1912-1952)

EDITOR:

M. BAKALCZUK-FELIN

Yizkor Book Publishing Council:

PRAESIDIUM:

R. Aarons-Arsch, A. Nach-Nochumovitz, S. Rubin.

MEMBERS:

M. Muskat, I. Michel-Michalewitz, S. Klass, M. Klavier.

Johannesburg, 1952-5713.

Copyright, 1952
by
RAKISHKER LANDSMANSHAFT
Johannesburg, S.A.,

Printed by The Electric Printing Works (Pty.) Ltd.,
15 Error St., New Doornfontein,
Johannesburg, South Africa.

די ראָקישקער לאַנדסמאַנשאַפט

דריקט אויס

איר דאַנק און אַנערקענונג

איר פֿאָרזיצער

ירחמיאל אַראָנס-אַרש,

און זײַן פֿרוי

עטל אַראָנס-אַרש

קאָמיטעט-מיטגליד,

פֿאַר זײערע אַלע אומדערמידלעכע

אַנשטרענגונגען און אַקטיוויטעטן

אויף אַרויסצוגעבן דאָס

„יזכּור-בוך פֿון ראָקישאָק און אומגעגנט"

THE RAKISHKER LANDSMANSCHAFT

express their warm thanks and appreciation

to their Chairman

Mr. R. AARONS

and

Mrs. ETHEL AARONS

(member of the Committee)

for their devoted and tireless efforts in

the publication of the

"Yizkor-Book of Rakishok and Environs."

Introduction to the Published English Translation of the <u>Rokiškis and Environs Yizkor Book</u>

In 1952, the Rakisher Landsmanshaft of Johannesburg published the *Yisker-bukh fun Rakishok un umgegnt* (<u>Yizkor Book of Rakishok and Environs</u>). Since the book was written in Yiddish, its contents were not well known to those who were not familiar with that language.

In the introduction to the 1952 book, M. Rotholz-Kur wrote:

> We, *landsleit*, who were left orphans, decided to write a *yizkor* [memorial] book in order to immortalize our martyrs of the third destruction. This would be a lament on the destruction of Rakishok and when the lamentations were read about the extermination of all of the Jewry in Europe, we would simultaneously read about the death of our *shtetlekh*.
>
> The Rakishok book needs to be found in every one of our houses and be given as an inheritance from generation to generation.
>
> *   *   *
>
> The graves must never be forgotten. We Jews must always remember our martyrs, our victims.
>
> *   *   *
>
> My eyes shed tears and will not be still. Our souls cry over the cruel extermination of millions of Jews and of my home *shtetl*, Rakishok.
>
> -- The *Landsmanschaft* of Rakishok, M. Rotholz-Kur, translated by Gloria Berkenstat Freund, *Rokiškis* and Environs Yizkor Book, pp. 474-475

For many years, a dedicated group of Jewish genealogists, working through the Yizkor Book Project of JewishGen, have provided the means to translate the book, section-by-section, into English. Those English translations have been posted on the Yizkor Book Project's website. Project leaders Joel Alpert and Lance Ackerfeld determined that this printed form of the English translation should be created, supplemented with some additional materials. Most importantly, this printed version contains that names of many of the individuals who were murdered or otherwise persecuted in 1941. In this respect, this book is not only an important reference book regarding the life of the Jewish communities in the Rokiškis region but it also strives to better fulfill the authors' objective of remembering the victims.

Preface

According to some researchers, Rokiškis had one of the oldest Jewish communities in Lithuania. A Vilnius University library manuscript identifies a Jew named Israel Eliashevitch who served as a border customs officer in Rokiškis in 1695. A Rokiškis church record indicates that in 1700 Jews were living in the town under the jurisdiction of the church and paid taxes to the priest.

The Jewish community lived near the site of the old Jewish cemetery until 1730 and then moved to the area of the market square, now called Independence Square. Steadily, the Jewish community grew. In 1784, 21 Jewish families lived in Rokiškis. A century later, in 1885, there were 124 Jewish families. By 1897, 2,067 Jews lived in Rokiškis, constituting 75.5 percent of the town's population. Before the First World War, there were four houses of study and numerous educational, religious, social, and charitable organizations in Rokiškis alone.

Like their counterparts elsewhere in Lithuania, the Jews in the Rokiškis region were engaged primarily in trade and crafts and operated most of the stores and inns. Uniquely, however, the Rokiškis area shtetls had a strong Chasidic influence.

Although many Jews emigrated to the United States, South Africa, and other countries between 1895 and 1939, prior to the Holocaust 3,500 Jews lived in Rokiškis. On June 14, 1941, some Jewish families were arrested by the Soviets and deported to Siberia. A week later, the German invasion and the associated Lithuanian national "Uprising" began a series of events that led to the violent end of centuries of Jewish life in Rokiškis and elsewhere in Lithuania. In July 1941, the Jews of Rokiškis and nearby communities were arrested and taken to temporary detention camps, where they were brutalized and starved. That same month, the three houses of prayer on Synagogue Street, which had been patriotically painted, respectively, in the red, green, and yellow colors of the Lithuanian flag, were plundered and burned to the ground. In August 1941, the Jews were taken to killing places not far from their respective detention camps and murdered *en masse*. This was five months before the infamous Wannsee Conference, where the Nazi regime adopted a general plan to annihilate the Jews of Europe.

The *Rokiškis and Environs* yizkor book was published in Johannesburg in 1952. It was the somber and solemn labor of love and remembrance of individuals who had emigrated to South Africa from the Rokiškis region primarily between the First and Second World Wars and therefore had first-hand memories of the world that had been suddenly and completely destroyed.

As a child, David Solly Sandler saw how the yizkor book "was brought to life" in the dining room of his parents' home in Johannesburg's Mayfair neighborhood. He noted that the woodcut on the book's cover was created by Herman Wald, who designed and sculpted the Holocaust Memorial in the Jewish cemetery in Johannesburg's West Park. With the passage of more than six decades, David wrote in November 2014 that, collectively, "the articles, stories, and memories in the book, more than any other book I have read, tell us about Jewish life in Lithuania as it approached its destruction." With the completion of the translation into English of the *Rokiškis and Environs* yizkor book, this depiction of Jewish life in Lithuania is now accessible to the broader audience of English speakers. It is hoped that the book will, in time, also be translated into Lithuanian.

Acknowledgements

Special thanks to the National Yiddish Book Center in Amherst, Massachusetts and the New York Public Library for supplying the high resolution images used in this book.

Special thanks to the National Yiddish Book Center in Amherst, Massachusetts and the New York Public Library for supplying the high - resolution images used in this book.

Special thanks to Philip Shapiro and his wife Aldona, a native Lithuanian, for collecting and, where necessary, securing the rights to include in this book images, histories, and other information that were not available when this book was published in 1952 but were deemed suitable and desirable to include in a new appendix to this publication.

Thanks to Barry Mann for preparing the Appendix of Shoah Victims from the Rokiskis area whose names appear on the Yad VaShem web site.

Lithuania with Rokiskis indicated

Map by Rachel Kolokoff Hopper

Geopolitical Information:

Alternate names for the town are: Rokiškis [Lithuanian], Rakishki [Russian], Rakishok [Yiddish], Rakiszki [Polish], Rokišķi [Latvian], Rokischken [German], Rokishki, Rakiski, Rakishik, Rekishok, Rokishok, Rokishuk

	Town	District	Province	Country
Before WWI (c. 1900):	Rakishki	Novo-Aleksandrovsk	Kovno	Russian Empire
Between the wars (c. 1930):	Rokiškis	Rokiškis		Lithuania
After WWII (c. 1950):	Rokiškis			Soviet Union
Today (c. 2000):	Rokiš			

Jewish Population in 1900:	2,067 (in 1897), 2,013 (in 1923)
Notes:	Russian: Ракишки. Yiddish: ראָקישאָק In NE Lithuania, 50 miles ENE of Panevėžys, 37 miles W of Daugavpils (Dvinsk), Latvia.

Nearby Jewish Communities:

Panemunėlis 5 miles SW
Obeliai 9 miles ESE
Kamajai 11 miles SSW
Onuškis 12 miles N
Subate, Latvia 13 miles ENE
Jūžintai 13 miles SSE
Pandėlys 15 miles WNW
Neciuniskiai 15 miles S
Aknīste, Latvia 15 miles NNE
Skapiškis 16 miles WSW
Nereta, Latvia 18 miles NW
Suvainiškis 18 miles NW
Dusetos 18 miles SE
Eglaine, Latvia 21 miles E
Svėdasai 21 miles SSW
Kvetkai 22 miles NW
Užpaliai 22 miles S
Antaliepte 23 miles SSE
Šimonys 23 miles SW
Papilys 25 miles WNW
Vyžuonos 26 miles S
Kupiškis 26 miles WSW
Ilūkste, Latvia 28 miles E
Debeikiai 28 miles SSW
Viešintos 30 miles SW

Notes to the Reader:

Within the text the reader will note "{34}" standing ahead of a paragraph. This indicates that the material translated below was on page 34 of the original book. However, when a paragraph was split between two pages in the original book, the marker is placed in this book after the end of the paragraph for ease of reading.

Also please note that all references within the text of the book to page numbers, refer to the page numbers of the original Yizkor Book.

The original book can be seen online at the NY Public Library site:
http://yizkor.nypl.org/index.php?id=2563

A list of this book and all books available in the Yizkor-Book-In-Print Project along with prices is available at:
http://www.jewishgen.org/Yizkor/ybip.html

The appendix at the end of the book contains the list of Rokiskis Shoah Victims that existed on the Yad Vashem web site as of November 23, 2016 when this appendix was prepared. The list on Yad Vashem is continually being updated. It is suggested that the reader access the Yad Vashem web site listed below, and search for people they are interested in, using Rokiskis as the town name and also the last name of the individual.

There is much more information available on this web site, including the Pages of Testimony, etc.

http://yvng.yadvashem.org

Rokishok Yizkor Book

Table of Contents

Preface	M. Bakalczuk-Felin	1
Rakishok Before and After WW I	A. Orelowitz	4
Notes on the Economic Position of the Jews in Rakishok	R. Aarons-Arsh	11
My Shtetl	A. Noach Nachamowitz	17
Peculiarity of Rakishok in the Jewish Lithuania	L. Shalit	34
"Chabad"	Chief Rabbi Professor L. I. Rabinowitz	41
Rakishok and Its Hasidim	B. Stein	45
Jewish National Automony in Lithuania	J. Batnitzky	55
The Lithuanian Shtetl	J. Lestschinsky	60

Reminiscences

Rokishok: A Reflection	Chief Rabbi Professor I. Abrahams	75
Childhood Joys	R. Feldman	79
My Fathers Nigun	S. Rubin	83
Why?	Z. Feldman	91
My Remembrances	Zorach Gafanowitz	95
A Yeminite in Shtetl	B. Sarver	99
Reminiscences of a Socialist in Rakishok	B. I. Kriel	109
Fragments of My Past	R. Arsh	124
We Will Always Remember You	Ahuva Schneiderman-Ruch	134
A Few Words in Place of a Tombstone	N. Meyerowitz-Stein	136
In Everlasting Memory	Bluma Arsh-Lavya	139
My Father, Berchik the Shoykhet	A. Koseff	142
Jews of Rakishok	A. Orelowitz	149
Zalman the Soda-Water Maker	B. I. Kreel	165
Personalities in the Old Home	Ahron-Noakh Nochumowitz	167
Chaye-Sore-Ite Bacher	S. Klass	186
Gite Rubin-Ferman	H. Penn-Lubowitz	188
My Father of Blessed Memory	Meyer Ruch	190
Types of the Old Home	A. Koseff	194

Social Cultural Life and Education Institutions

The Reformed Cheder	M. Katz	200
The Russian Government School	A. Chait	203
The Lithuanian Gymnasium	E. Aarons	205
From My School Years	T. Orlin-Kiel	208
The Beth-Sefer and Pro-gymnasium	A. Josselowitz	216
The Activity of the Kultur-Lige	S. Spevak	218
Concerning the Culture League and its Activities	M. and S. Feldman	221
The Jewish Part in the Left Movement	O. Nochumowitz	225
The Culture League in Rakishok and in Utian	M. Krain	230
Maccabi in Rakishok	R. Arsh	233
Rakishker Maccabi	H. Josselowitz	241
The First Hachshara Kibbutz in Rakishok	Ben Samuel	244
Three Years in Rakishok	Avigdor Ariol-Golumbotzky	245
About the Scout Movement	S. Nanas	248
Leib Jaffe's Visit	A. J.	250
Orphanage	A. Nochumowitz	252
The Society for Visiting the Sick in Rakishok	R. Blacher-Itzikman	257
Jewish Theatre	S. Rubin	260
The People's Bank	M. B.	264

Environs

Abel	I. Michel-Michalewitz	269
My Home Town Kamay	B. M. Hurwitz	291
A Tear in Memory of Kamay	P. Z. Hurwitz	297
Reminiscences of Kamay	Tirza Franklyn-Jaffe	300
A Fair in Kamay	B. Sachs	303

Novo-Alexandrovsk-Exerenay-Zarasay

Reminiscences of the Old Home	N. Sacks, M. Sharp-Saltuper, P. Albert	307
My Birthplace	Jehuda Zwi Ichilcik	315
From My Home Town	I. Dumas	319
My Shtetl Boguslavishok	R. Mechel-Berzak	326
Subat	Rev. M. B. Fisher	329
Ponedel	Berchowitz-Peisachovitz, T. Katz, Jokl Evans	332
From Our Shtetl Dusiat	Ch. M. Kruss-Glussak, N. Blacher	338

Antalept	A. Eydlman, I. Gulis	347
Yuzint; Natzunishok	N. Brinkman	352
My Father Michoel Welve the Farmer	Israel Michalewitz	356
Svisdoshz	Ch. Aires, N. Blacher	358
Sevenishok	D. Katz, R. Shon	367
Anushishok	R. Kramer-Penn	372
Skopishok	M. Gordon	378
Ponemunok	L. Karabelnik	382
My Shtetl Ponemunok	Benzion Joffe	385

Decline and Destruction

My Evidence	M. Rotholz-Kur	390
What I Experienced (My Experiences)	Gisa Levin	398
In Those Days	Herzl Ben-Yehuda	407
The Destruction of Rakishok in Letters	M. Bakalczuk-Felin	412

The Landsmannschaft of Rakishok

Greetings		448
Monograph of Jewish Communities and Towns in Jewish Historiogrophy	Dr. P. Friedman	452
Landsmanschaft of Rakishok: Activities :Rakishker Benevolent Society	M. Rotholz-Kur	469
Notes of the Landsmanschaft of Rakishok	A. Eidelman	559
The Family Manne-Manelewitz	S. Rubin	562
The Thorny Path of the Jewish Immigrant in South Africa	J. M. Sherman	564
In Remembrance		574

Additional Pages

Appendix – Material not included in the original Yizkor Book

Appendix of List of Those Killed in the Holocaust in Rakishok

Partial List of Lithuanian Murderers of the Jews of Rokiskis and its District

Rokishok Yizkor Book

Rokishok Yizkor Book

Preface
by Meilech Bakalczuk

The Yizkor Book to the memory of Rakishsker Jewry and to the communities surrounding it has just been published, eleven years after the annihilation. The pattern of life in Rakishok was similar to that of many small-town Lithuanian Jewries. Here Jews lived as closely-knit, separate units, often discriminated against and not less often in fear. But though there were sufferings there were also tranquil years with their measure of joy. But through all vicissitudes the Jews of the Lithuanian villages held steadfastly to the tenets of the faith and to their spiritual and cultural heritage.

Typical of the Jews' capacity for adjustment, they learnt to adapt themselves to changing circumstances, keeping aflame the hope for better days. Then came Hitler's murderous hordes; and in 1941, in a matter merely of weeks, the Jewish inhabitants of most of the Lithuanian towns and villages were led away like cattle to the slaughter. It was harvest time, and the reaper of death harvested all of Jewish life – the aged, the women, the children – none were spared.

Eleven years have slipped away since the holocaust, but the wounds have not been healed, and while the enormity of the tragedy is difficult to comprehend, there are those in our midst, and many of them, for whom the annihilation was a very personal tragedy in addition to being a Jewish tragedy.

It was, in all probability, this personal factor that partly stimulated the members of the Rakishker Landsleit Society to bring out the Yizkor Book. After all, a book is still the most enduring memorial to a past that has perished. The sponsors of this book set themselves three main tasks when they undertook to issue this tribute to the memory of their brethren in the far-off villages from which they themselves, or their forebears once came. They wanted to reflect the pattern of Jewish life in those villages up to World War II; they wanted to save from oblivion the memory of the ghastly era of Destruction; and finally they wished to place on record the activities of the Rakishker Landsleit in South Africa, during the forty years of the existence of their Society.

To implement these aims required considerable thought and responsibility. Every Jewish community in the old world had its own specific pattern: it virtually possessed individuality, but to convey this was no easy matter, for the simple reason that there are today large gaps in the historical sources which precluded the possibility of rendering a picture of that life in its entirety.

In addition, no real authentic documentation of the last days of Rakishok was possible because there are almost no survivors who could have filled out the record. A very few may have escaped and they may today be in the U.S.S.R., but it was quite impossible to establish contact with them. With regard to the third aim, it was extremely difficult to piece together the story of the activities of the last forty years here from the inadequate minutes in existence today. Despite these difficulties the sponsor thought that the work was worth while, and the Yizkor Book contains important material hitherto unpublished: reminiscences, descriptions of the economic conditions of the various villages and their social and cultural institutions. Humble and poor though most of these Jews were, the material that the Rakishok Society had to sift through disclosed men and women of superb ethical and moral qualities.

The Yizkor book also sheds new light on the forces at work between the two world wars which helped to shape and modernise Jewish national life in the Lithuanian villages. It discloses the social changes which were taking place and the rising consciousness towards our national renaissance, which these people were imbued. Although, as previously mentioned, the compilers were unable to obtain first-hand reports from actual survivors of Rakishok, they were, however, able to secure eyewitness accounts of the destruction, and the merciless cruelties of the Germans and also the Lithuanians. Through documents they were also enabled to trace some of the activities of the Rakishker landsmanschaft, disclosing as they do the wide range of social activities of the old country. These documents reveal, in no small measure, the spiritual and cultural heritage with which we owe to those who perished. In fact, the Yizkor Book, with its illustrations, is an important historical monograph, not only for the Landsleit. It is a contribution to the history of the destroyed Jewish communities of Eastern Europe.

Finally, the Yizkor Book is a human document: a tribute to the simple God-fearing Jews of the villages who lived their lives, simply and genuinely, with those peculiar folk-ways evolved by Jewish Lithuania.

Those who laboured so zealously to bring out this Yizkor Book will be fully compensated if the Yiddish public will find in its pages its intrinsic message, the message of a human and historic document.

Active members of Rokiskis Landsmanshaft, 1932

[Page 7]

Rakishok Before and After World War I
by A. Orelowitz   Translated by Rabbi Ezra Boyarsky

Avraham Orelowitz (May he Rest in Peace)

Between Ponievez and Dvinsk are located the following townships: Subotz, Skopishok, Ponemunok, and Rakishok.

Immediately upon stepping off the train and entering the Rakishok railroad station, one gets the impression that Rakishok is a pulsating Jewish community, characterized by initiative and activity. The town's railroad station with its vibrant and animated crew of taxi and truck drivers, their passengers and cargo, is actually a reflection of the town itself and may be considered a microcosm of Rakishok in its day to day life.

The railroad station also serves as a meeting place where business deals are made and local and world news discussed. In the vicinity of the railroad station are a small number of homes owned and occupied by Jews. Among the families that come to mind are: Zalman the shipping clerk, Baruch the vakzalner (an employee at the railroad station), Zalman Shimshon Shwartzberg and others – all told about fifteen families who were in some way connected with the railroad station.

Connecting to the railroad station with the town of Rakishok is a wide, straight highway which is flanked on both sides by gardens, fields, and long rows of houses predominantly occupied by non-Jews. Towering conspicuously above them is the town's church with its steeple. On the border between Christian and Jewish homes stands the house of Velvele Dimont, the town's notorious informer, whose traitorous acts towards his people have won him infamy and everlasting hate since 1905.

The center of the town is the market place. A wide street cuts through this central area. To the right (of this street) is a road that leads to the count's estate, and to the left, to Yurdzike, a short, rather narrow street connected to Kamayer Street where the town's business center was located. On Kamayer Street were concentrated all the major business enterprises such as the largest textile stores, leather goods shops, as well as the flour storehouses and the warehouses that housed farm machinery. On this street, Hirshe Matizan ran the town's hotel and restaurant – popularly known throughout the region as the "red" building.

Station Terminus Building in Rakishok

In this area, Besl Zamet built a rather large building which was occupied by the town's court, the jail, the post office, and the mayor's residence and office. Singer's Sewing Machine Co. opened a showroom on this street, and when Shteiman decided to open up a store in town, his choice was none other than Kamayer Street near the town's pharmacy.

These stores were known as the "white" stores, and above them were small apartments. In one of these lived Chaim the musician, from whose apartment emanated melodious strains of Jewish folk songs that blended well with the hustle and bustle of the street below and together formed a symphony of Jewish life that became the hallmark of the typical Lithuanian shtetl.

The management of the Folk Bank in 1920
(First row, *right to left*) Bar, Isaac Panitz, Rachmiel Ruch, *Hillel* Eidelson, Meyer Berkovitz, Hertzl Shapiro, Yonah Levin, Yankel Kotn. (Second row, *right to left*) *Moishe* Sher, Chaye-Leah Sitovitz, Chaye Bar, Hinde Katz, Alter *Tzadesh, Choneh Zamet.* Sholem Kalikur. (Back row, *right to left)* Lipovitz, Max Shnoeur, Yudel Meller, Zelik *Tzemachovitz.*

In a house on the corner of Kamayer Street and the market district there resided for as long as anyone could remember Reb Bezalel, the rabbi of Rakishok. On Kamayer Street, in the rear of the newly constructed brick building, owned by Henich Chmelnick, was located the Folk Bank, and opposite stood the Batei Midrashim – the synagogues and houses of study.

As mentioned before, the business center was in close proximity to the market place, and it was there that a large and imposing water pump could be found surrounded by a cement wall. Attached to a chain was a tin can so that passers-by could quench their thirst on a hot, sultry day. At the foot of the pump was a trough, an open receptacle to provide drink for cattle and horses. The board that covered the trough also served as a 'bulletin board" for announcements, messages and information that were of interest and importance to the entire Rakishok community.

Across from the market place stood a large church which was frequented by thousands of farmers from Rakishok and the vicinity. The church's owner was Count Jan Pshezdetzky who spent liberally to beautify the church which was reputed to be the most exquisite religious structure in all of Lithuania.

Large clocks built into the very top of the edifice could be seen from all directions and great distances.

A road from the center of the town extended and led to the estate and residence of the count. During the summer, this stretch of road was a popular meeting place for the shtetl's young people. At a short distance from the road was a brook called "Pruda."

Market Square

Culture and Education

Rakishok, not unlike other Lithuanian shtetlach, was traditionally religious, and immune to modern cultural movements. Orthodox Judaism was by far the predominant spiritual factor that shaped the lifestyle of the Rakishker Jewish community.

The Hasidic movement enjoyed an unusually large following in Rakishok. Three main Hasidic dynasties – the Lubavitcher, Babroisker, and Ladier, and their respective Rebbes, each with his own religious philosophy that characterized his branch of Hasidism – pervaded the spiritual, mundane, and personal lives of their devotees. Each Hasidic group would visit their rebbe during Jewish festivals, especially during the High Holiday season. Being in the presence of their rebbe, listening to his words of wisdom and Divrai Torah, accompanied by old and new melodies, infused them with a renewed zest for life, spiritual enrichment, and optimism. One of the features of Hasidism that accounts for its remarkable appeal to large segments of the Jewish people is a strong sense of cohesiveness among the adherents of the movement. This fraternal attitude also had its practical application. More often than not, affluent hasidim would help their less fortunate brethren financially in the form of Matan B'seser (charity given in secret – a Jewish ethical concept) in order to avoid embarrassment of the recipient.

The Beth Hamidrash (the house of study, usually a part of the synagogue) together with the synagogue itself, served as the spiritual smithy that forged the religious and cultural personality of the Jews.

The educational institutions of Rakishok were the Cheder (traditional religious school) and yeshiva (a school for advanced Talmudic studies). Only boys were enrolled in these schools, while girls received instruction from private teachers. Boys in the 12-14 age bracket who were able to handle the intricate study of the Talmud, left Rakishok for more advanced Talmudic courses offered in larger, out-of-town yeshivas. In those days, the life of a yeshiva student away from his home, parents, and siblings, was, to put it mildly, a difficult one. By and large, the students' parents were of modest means and were unable to completely support their sons in an out-of-town yeshiva. Yet the quest for Jewish religious education at all levels was strong and widespread throughout the Eastern European communities and especially those of Lithuania. Therefore, even the poorest parents made an all-out effort, to the point of self-sacrifice, to bring up sons who achieved the status of B'nai Torah, or Torah scholars.

Several years before the outbreak of World War I, the Haskalah (Jewish Enlightenment movement of the 19th century) began to make inroads into Lithuania, including Rakishok. The spirit of the Haskalah movement – the secular culture – began to percolate throughout the land, especially in the larger cities, and finally infiltrated the shtetlach. As the Haskalah took a firmer foothold in Rakishok, some parents began to provide their children with instruction of a more secular nature, such as Russian and modern Hebrew, in addition to their religious studies.

The children who studied the Bible in the original Hebrew text and Hebrew as a language, developed an interest in reading Hebrew books which, considering the era we are describing, was a phenomenon. If a father was a Makil (an "enlightened" individual) who subscribed to a Hebrew newspaper, that also had a strong influence on the children who, because of their modernized Hebrew studies, also developed an interest in reading a Hebrew newspaper, and eventually a Hebrew novel.

In such a manner, Hebrew in its modern concept and connotation penetrated the minds of the younger generation. In the course of time, small study groups formed that continued to study Hebrew and its literature. As a result of the Haskalah, a new type of Hebrew teacher appeared on the scene who brought the idea of Zionism and Jewish nationalism – the precursor of the state of Israel – and wove it into the socioeconomic fabric of Lithuanian Jewry.

Slowly the Russian language and culture also made its way into the small communities. Russian was the official language of the government. Lithuanian was used in the daily dealings the Jews had with the farmers. The Jews began an intensive study of Russian, and the more "enlightened" younger element read the Russian progressive press as well as Russian literature.

In Rakishok, a Russian government Gymnasia opened – a European school that was equivalent to high school and junior college. Many Jewish children were enrolled in this institution while others studied in gymnasias in Dvinsk and other cities. A few even succeeded in being admitted to universities.

The Jewish gymnasia students wore special uniforms with flashy buttons upon which the provincial townspeople looked with admiration. One of the first Gymnasia students was Zalman Feldman, now a prominent physician in Johannesburg.

In 1910, two young women, Misses Gurevitz and Rabinowitz, opened a four-class Russian Gymnasia for Jewish children in Rakishok. This was a pioneer experiment, undertaken with the purpose of giving Jewish children the opportunity to study Russian in a purely Jewish atmosphere. The pre-gymnasia proved a great success and was filled with students.

In the early years of the 20th century, when the revolutionary movement against the Russian Czar spread in Russia proper and spilled over to the countries ruled by the Czar, many Jewish youths were attracted to its illegal activities and espoused its cause. In 1905 a Jewish revolutionary group was organized in Rakishok which distributed proclamations and organized anti-Czarist demonstrations and rallies. On Sabbath afternoons the Jewish revolutionaries would meet in the Rakisher forest where they were trained in the use of firearms.

The previously mentioned Velvel Dimont was an informer. Together with his two sons he would spy on the revolutionaries and their activities. Several revolutionary activists were banished to Siberia due to the telltale betrayal of Velvel and his sons. At one of the meetings, the Jewish revolutionaries sentenced these despicable and treacherous informers to death.

On Simchas Torah morning when the mosrim (informers) were in the large Beth Hamidrash, they were shot at. The worshiping congregation was panic-stricken, and the informers escaped with light wounds only because the revolutionaries did not want to hit innocent people. Rakishok never erased this tragic episode from her memory. After the war, this notorious family returned to Rakishok. The town then gathered an appreciable number of signatures and petitioned the Lithuanian government to punish the scoundrels. The Lithuanian authorities deported them from Rakishok, never to return.

At the time of the 1905 revolution in Russia, the Yiddish language and culture gained dignity and respectability. The Yiddish press at this juncture, which was primarily headquartered in Warsaw, had many subscribers in Rakishok. The "Moment" and the "Heint" (Today) were the largest newspapers in Czarist Russia. "Der Freint" (The Friend), published in St. Petersburg, was very popular and had a large readership. The Jewish public waited impatiently for B. Yeushson's "Political Letters." He used the endearing pseudonym Itchele Hakatan – Itchele the small one – underscoring his modesty. Sholom

Aleichem's letters from Menachem Mendel to Shaine Shaindel and the humorous stories by Tunkein were at the top of the readers' list.

The young people took a great interest in contempory Yiddish. Often they would gather in private homes to discuss and analyze the various social and national problems as they are entwined in the works of the three Yiddish-Hebrew classicists: Mendele, Sholom Aleichem, and Y.L. Peretz.

The second Russian revolution in 1917 radically changed the economic and spiritual life of the Russian Jews. After World War I, the Jews who returned to Lithuania from Russia were likewise deeply affected by the newly created "world order" and the upheaval it brought in its wake. The young people, who were always ready to carry the torch for new ideas, became active in Rakishok in two distinctly different ideological camps: Zionism and Communism.

The Zionists founded a Tarbus School, while the Leftist group organized a "Culture League" which was instrumental in establishing a Yiddish secular school. They also were the initiators of adult evening classes and a library. The graduates of these schools were admitted to matriculate in the Tarbus, Yavneh, and Kulture League gymnasias. At the same time, many Jewish children were enrolled in Lithuanian secondary schools.

Despite the fact that the secular education institutions drove a wedge into the traditional school system, the orthodox element stood firm by their principles and maintained a Talmud Torah and a large Yeshiva in Rakishok.

The post-war era brought many social changes in Rakishok. For the first time sports clubs and reading circles became a part of the town's landscape and opened a window on the outside world.

Another spin-off of the new, modern times was the role played by the Kehilah (the organized Jewish community) which became the social and political nerve center of the town. One of the tasks of the Kehilah was to levy taxes on the Jewish population to cover the budget that was allocated to maintain the Jewish schools, the orphanage, the religious institutions and the social and cultural societies. The Kehilah was held in high esteem since it was the authoritative body and voice of the entire community.

[Page 19]

Notes on the Economic Position of the Jews in Rakishok

by R. Aarons-Arsch
Translated by Rabbi Boyarsky

Approximately 1,000 to 1,200 Jewish families lived in Rakishok before World War I. This number includes the Jews from the surrounding towns of Radute, Vaksal, Varestzine, and Yurdzike. With these smaller communities was formed what we would call today "greater Rakishok." Due to the excellent railroad connections, Rakishok was in close touch with the main commercial centers such as Kovno, Libave, Dvinsk, Riga, Arlovsk, Warsaw, and St. Petersburg.

Another important factor that contributed to the development and economic stability of the town was the fact that in Rakishok and the surrounding towns such as Ponedel, Birzsh, Subotz, Abel, and Kamay there were longstanding, well-established markets where farmers by the thousands brought products such as flax, seeds, furs, corn, wheat, eggs, butter, poultry, and a variety of fruits and vegetables from their respective villages. The Rakishok merchants would buy these commodities in large quantities and in turn transport them to the above-mentioned larger business centers. The local merchants also utilized the markets to sell the farmers' and villagers' textile goods, hardware, kerosene, etc.

During the winter, Rakishok exported carloads of meat, especially calf meat which was packed in large barrels. In the summer time, Rakishok provided the larger cities with a variety of fruits and berries. During this era (prior to World War I), there was also an intensive lumbar and raw hide trade in which Rakishok's Jewish merchants were engaged.

From the description thus far, it becomes evident that the market place in Rakishok, as in most of the towns in Lithuania, played a key economic role in the lives of the Jews, the majority of whom were small merchants who operated with limited financial resources.

Aside from the merchants, there were many Jewish craftsmen and artisans who engaged in such crafts as shoemaking, tailoring, hat-making, etc. They sold most of their handiwork at the market place. There was also a relatively large number of coachmen, porters, and fish merchants.

Rakishok also had a number of tanneries which produced raw cow hides and leather for all purposes, for footwear, handbags, etc. The tanneries and the sausage factory, whose proprietor was Benjamin Gordon, provided employment for many Jews.

Generally speaking, in comparison to other shtetlach in Lithuania, the Jews of Rakishok were economically in pretty good shape. Most of them owned their own homes, a cow and household goods. Still, as in any community, there were a number of poor people to whose economic distress the townspeople always responded liberally with material aid, tact, and understanding.

In 1905 there existed in Rakishok a credit union society, and a few years prior to World War I, a credit bank was founded by Zalman Adelson. The main purpose of this bank was to give loans to small merchants, poor artisans, and laborers. This bank maintained a high standard, and in return, it enjoyed the community's full measure of trust and confidence. On the eve of the outbreak of the First World War – in 1914 – the Jewish Merchant Bank was established under the directorship of Motel Meller, but it was forced to liquidate its activities because of the war.

At the outbreak of hostilities, a large number of Rakishker Jews left for Russia; a few families moved to Biela Russia (White Russia). Only a fraction of the Jews remained in Rakishok and lived under German occupation. Although the Germans did not subject the remaining Jews in Rakishok to any mistreatment or persecution, the economy suffered a death blow, to the extent that all the former economic prowess the town had attained disappeared.

Immediately after the war, Lithuania fell under Russian rule, but not for long, for soon after, Lithuania, along with the other Baltic states, won her independence and became constitutionally a republic. The fledgling Lithuanian government initially adopted a benign and tolerant attitude towards the Jewish population. Those Jews who had left Rakishok at the outbreak of hostilities gradually returned, and other Jews formerly from other towns in the vicinity settled in Rakishok, so that the population actually increased.

No sooner had life more or less normalized than a Folksbank was opened. The American Joint Committee granted loans for home construction and distributed multifarious aid and relief to the reconstituted community. Gradually the economy improved to the extent that a number of enterprising individuals actually benefited from the war and became affluent, thanks to their ability to adjust to the new economic structure of newly independent Lithuania.

But the government's spirit of tolerance was short-lived. It was replaced by an ultra-reactionary leadership whose objective was to undermine and undercut Jewish business enterprise and initiative. With that motive, taxes were appreciably increased with the overriding goal of hurting Jewish businessmen on whom the government levied extra large taxes. These drastic decrees aimed at the Jews shrank and dramatically worsened the economic circumstances in which the Lithuanian Jews lived. As a result, the younger element began to consider a momentous decision, namely, whether to stay or to leave. At first the number emigrating was minimal, but in the course of time it gained momentum, and thousands of Lithuanian Jews, including an impressive representation from Rakishok left for other parts of the world, among them South Africa.

[Page 22]

Houses on Kamai Street

The non-business (hardware store) of Pesach Ruch and Crone Arsh on Independence Square

The first autobus in Rokiskis

Celebrating the opening of the Hebrew University in Jerusalem in 1925 on Market Square. On the right is the Mebicha Bank.

[Page 26]

The Board of the Loan Society of Artisans
[Also known as the Handworker's Union]
(standing left to right): Hershal Simonovitz, Shimshon Baradovski, F. Levin, Mendel Naumovitz, Nelveh Gomberg;
(sitting left to right): Shual Gulan, Abba-Leib Davidovitz, Yudel Gafanovitz, Chayim-Totteh Lekach, Kuperman

[Page 28]

Monday – a market day in Rokiskis

[Pages 29-42]

My *Shtetl*
A. Noach Nachamowitz
Translated by Gloria Berkenstat Freund
A.

How old is Rakishok? When did Jews begin to settle in Rakishok? – These questions did not interest anyone. It was said in the *shtetl* that the less that was written about we Jews, the better and healthier it was and there was fear that the writings could fall into the hands of gentiles who would use them against the Jews.

The older people of the *shtetl* placed value on oral descriptions, stories from their grandfathers, great grandfathers and great, great grandfathers and not on written documents.

There were two cemeteries in Rakishok: the new and the old cemeteries. The old cemetery lay between two chasms, valleys, overgrown with nettles and between large, many branched trees that hid the headstones on which there was no longer any writing nor sign of a letter. Winds and rains erased the names and families of the deceased people and also the dates of their deaths during the course of years.

Only the talk of the old men, who quoted the talk of their grandfathers and great grandfathers, who told them of how their great great grandfathers would visit the graves of their parents at the old cemetery serves to determine the age of the *shtetl*.

A yard in Rakishok

The age of the great *shul* [synagogue] was also not known in the *shtetl*. In this case, the woven stories and legends created through the years about the *shul* were of use. Grandfathers and great grandfathers would say that when they were children they studied with the rabbi in the great *shul*.

Ozer dalim was engraved with visible letters in the anteroom of the *shul*. From this *gimatria*, the age of the *shul* was determined to have reached 367 years.[1]

"Mesteles" is a village not far from Rakishok. Jews have not lived there for a very, very long time. However, there are signs of a Jewish cemetery, which was construed as testimony that Jews lived there before building in Rakishok began.

However, establishing the age of Rakishok is difficult on the basis of all the evidence because there can be "inaccuracies," perhaps of a few hundred years.

In any case, it has been historically determined that Rakishok is one of the oldest communities in Lithuania.

Rakishok lies on a plain. The plain extends for miles wide. If there is any elevation here, it is in a small area and nearby lies a valley. The entire land of Lithuania that is not mountainous is gifted with flatness.

There were many low huts here in the *shtetl*, which were just a little elevated from ground level. The little house of Haim Yashe, the wagon driver, was like this; the windows and the roof appeared as if almost at ground level.

Arriving through Kameyer Street, the *shtetl* is seen from afar. The church with its high dome jutting out.

On the outskirts of the *shtetl*, peasants live in low and old little houses covered with straw and the stalls are under the same roof as the house. Near each house stand trees with very leafy branches and gardens and in the spring and summer they spread a fragrance over the entire road. The *shtetl* starts at the end of each village with a Jewish shop. This is the best evidence of a Jewish community. There are no gardens, no trees near the Jewish houses because Jews are not interested in planting and cultivating the soil of *gulas* [exile]. The *Tefilat Geshem* [prayer for rain] in praying was meant only for *Eretz-Yisroel*.

Although Rakishok was built without a plan, the houses in the main streets stood symmetrically in one straight line like a row of soldiers. The panorama in the side streets was different, where houses stood in disharmony, without any order.

The main streets were paved earlier. In order to pave the streets, an "order" was issued that every wagon that entered Rakishok must bring 10 paving stones. A barrier was erected at the entrance to the *shtetl* and no wagon was allowed to enter if there were no stones. With such a collective effort, Rakishok was paved.

Rokiskis Yizkor Book 19

The highway was not paved with asphalt and the wheels of a wagon raised a din that woke the street and the people in the houses, announcing that someone had arrived in the *shtetl*, which was very curious to know who the newcomer was, from where the visitor had come and to whom he was coming, improvising various hypotheses. If a peasant arrived, he first encountered the lame Reb Leyzer, or as he was called, Leyzer the *Tsore* [affliction or distress]. He would stop each peasant wagon and ask the peasant if he had something to sell, even though he had not been involved in commerce for a long time, not having any money to conduct business. However, he was a *maven* [expert] about everything. He also was popular among the market peasants, who would often ask about the lame Leyzer.

* * *

Poor and rich people lived in the *shtetl*. Rich and poor houses stood together, one leaning on the other. There stood Feywl Rosenkovitz's large, beautiful house with a glass enclosed veranda, next door a collapsed little house. Besl Zamet's modern house stood next to the houses of Bentshe the tinsmith's and of Yonten, the mechanical engineer, with his workshop, and other houses in which lived several families. Both summer and winter a hill of ash, heaps of broken pots and rags lay near the houses. Every morning, "impurities" were poured out there and after a rain there was terrible mud and the bad smell of a farm.

These unsanitary compounds were common in Rakishok. It was difficult to pass through these courtyards : from Itse the tailor, Khasrial the guard, Bentse Bakser, Yekl Feiwe's[2] and from Tsipa Leah's. A muddy alley that rarely dried up led to the synagogue and served the Jews who went to pray three times a day. Nevertheless, no effort to repair the road or, at least, to lay foot bridges was made.

The marketplace had the place of honor and was the most interesting part of the *shtetl*. Rows of shops extended around the market. The white shops were the property of the count. Two story brick buildings stretched in one line from the pump to the horse market. Nearby stood the brick house of Shteiman, the owner of a grocery shop, and the above mentioned houses of Besl Zamet and Feitl Rosenkovitz. There was a row of red shops, looking like twin houses, on the second side of the market. Next door was the state bank and then the house of Pesakh Ruch where the joint business of Khone Arsh and Pesakh Ruch was located. Opposite, on the other corner, were the jail, the post office, and the office of the police, which threw fear over the *shtetl*.

Monday was the market day in the *shtetl*. On the market day, everyone was very preoccupied; a gold coin, a minute. The movement around the peasant wagons was endless and each person wanted to outwit the other. There was great competition and everyone wanted to earn more because the majority of the Jews in the *shtetl* drew their livelihood for an entire week from this market day.

On a market day, there were no home bodies. Everyone was at the market. Fathers took their sons who were in *kheder* to help. The noise and the hurly burly of the wheels on the cobblestone streets was intense. The shouts of Ezrial Shapiro and of his partner, Notke Gordon, were particularly distinguished in this uproar. One shouted, "*Hayom harath olam* [Today is the Day of Judgment]" and the other corrected: "*Hayom ymod haolem bamishpat* [Today the world will be judged]."

Temporary, special booths would quickly be nailed together on the market day where various goods were sold. The artisans carried around their products to sell in their hands. Wagons stood with baked goods and with various items.

It was very noisy at the horse market. In addition to the curses of the horse traders, loud whinnies were heard from the horses. Fights often broke out. Mende Notke, or "Kozak"[3] as he was nicknamed, was the most competent at the horse market.

The livestock [market] was quieter. The butchers closed transactions without superfluous chatter. The seed and flax merchants considered themselves respectable.

The market only became quiet at night. The peasants departed. The booths were taken apart. When evening fell, the market was empty; only a drunk lay around here or there. The shutters were bolted and the evening prayers were said alone, quickly.

The mood in the *shtetl* was calm in the morning. Merchants and shopkeepers forgave each other as on the eve of *Yom-Kippur*. The ideal *shtetl* way of life continued again in its style and the *shtetl* again received its specific Jewish physiognomy and time was found for prayer with a *minyon* [10 men required for prayer], for reciting a chapter of Psalms and for learning a chapter of *Mishnius* [*Mishnah* – a compilation of writing elaborating on the *Torah*].

* * *

Rakishok always had two rabbis: Reb Betzalel and Reb Shmuel. Each was distinguished by his own supporters. Quarrels often developed between these sides. There were also two *shoyketim* [ritual slaughterers]: Reb Bertsik and Reb Beinish. Reb Bertsik was a Jew and a scholar, full of knowledge and knew the *Talmud* well. He taught *gemara* [rabbinical commentaries on the *Mishnah*] with arduous interpretation, avoiding hairsplitting. Reb Beinish was a quiet person, a man of stately appearance and an affable person to everyone. He was the *mohel* [ritual circumciser] for the *shtetl* and the area. His testament was that after his death, each one whom he has circumcised should light a candle. He had brought the people to the Covenant of Abraham *Avinu* [our father] for three entire generations.

The Lubavitcher Hasidim, who were mainly artisans and small shop owners, belonged to Reb Shmuel's side. Kopl the shoemaker, Itse the tailor, the Ginzburg family were the rabbi's protectors and were ready to battle for the proper respect for their rabbi, who was also a crown rabbi (rabbi in the name of the regime).

On Reb Betzalel's side were Lipe's Sholem, Bentse's Hatse, the Rabinovitch family and the rabbi's own family, which had its own wealthy men.

* * *

There was an old synagogue in Rakishok. There were also houses of study and *minyonim* [groups of at least 10 men required for prayer]; prayers were only said in the synagogue on *Shabbos* during the summer. The synagogue was not heated during the winter and cast a fear. Even Yona, the *shamas* [synagogue official who takes care of day to day affairs] of the synagogue, was afraid to go inside. Before he would go in, he knocked three times with the keys, calling out: "Corpses, ghosts, go to your rest!"

A room was built on to the synagogue, where the board was kept on which the dead were carried. He, Yona the *shamas*, would collect donations for the funeral, calling out with a crying, heartbreaking melody: "*Tzedakah tatzil memaveth* [Charity will save you from death]." The melody alone spread a dread. He would also say that the women should go to the funeral separately from the men, calling out: "Women, move away, move away!"

I heard that years ago Reb Beinish was the *shamas* of the Great Synagogue and on *Shabbos* after *havdalah* [the ceremony at the close of the Sabbath] he would place two pails of water at the exit of the synagogue and would accompany the Jews leaving after prayers with wishes for a good week, a week of good earning. The two pails of water were to assure this.

Simple Jews prayed in the large *Beis-Medrash*: artisans, small shopkeepers, butchers, wagon drivers and ordinary Jews. For many years, the *gabai* was Leah's Bere, who took care of the bathhouse and was a butcher, who furnished meat to the government in Petersburg. He was active in religious-communal life, a person of authority and also one of those involved with the meat tax. He was a very hospitable man. Particularly on *Shabbos* and on holidays, he was the last one to leave the *Beis-Medrash* in order to take home with him emissaries, preachers and poor people who were left waiting for someone to be hospitable to them.

The rich owners prayed in the large *shtibl*, such as Reb Borukh, the railway man, Shaul Bertzik, the railway man, Nakhman's Zalman, Zalman Shimshon, Lipe Shwartzberg, Bentse Rabinovitch from Radute. They prayed later there and because of this it was said that, "Rich men liked to sleep."

There was also a small *shtibl* where the worshippers were Hasidim. They used the familiar form of "you" and took a little whiskey at every opportunity. They celebrated *Shimkhas Torah*[4] with great ardor. The Lubavitcher Rebbe's *yahrzeit* [anniversary of a death] was fervently observed.

* * *

1905. Other winds blew. The most effervescent time in the *shtetl* was in that year. Parents were afraid of their children's entry into the movement.

The Lithuanian Socialist-Revolutionary, Shmeilsky, was located in Rakishok. He organized all of the secret meetings and the police feared him. He organized a revolt in Kamey [Kamai], where the police commissioner was forced to carry the red flag through the streets. He carried on extensive electioneering among the peasants, particularly during market days, when thousands of peasants would come together. He also organized the peasants to demolish the beer and [liquor] monopoly stores.

Shmeilsky called upon the Jewish population to take part in the revolutionary work, frightening them that the *Jode Sistem* [the Black Hundred] intended to stage a pogrom in the *shtetl*, and therefore, they needed to join the S.R. [Socialist Revolutionaries], in order to avoid the danger of a pogrom. The Jewish young people in large part joined the Party.

When a pogrom took place in Dusiat [Dusetos], not far from Rakishok, many Jews then joined the Socialist Revolutionary Party.

The Rakishok police, with the police commissioner at the head, wanted to arrest Shmeilsky, but they could not catch him. The revolutionary movement grew larger and stronger each year. Then a division of dragoons came to the *shtetl* which was billeted in Jewish houses because there were no barracks in Rakishok. These dragoons had the mission of liquidating the revolutionary movement in Rakishok and its surroundings.

* * *

The leader of the firemen's brigade was Talacki, the Christian, who was one of the most distinguished Christian businessmen in the *shtetl*. He had an ironware and agricultural implements shop. He was personally acquainted with all of the Jews in the *shtetl* and helped organize the firemen's brigade that was made up almost entirely of Jews. In addition to the above-mentioned Talacki, Trevize, the Christian, and his son, joined the firemen.

The firemen's inventory consisted of a pump, iron axes, long hoses and rope, pails, brass hats and a brass trumpet, several two-wheeled wagons, on which the water was carried from the wells.

The firemen's brigade did not have its own horse and they took horses from the population. No one was permitted to refuse to give his horse. However, there were cases in which Jewish wagon drivers and village peasants ran away with their horses, not wanting to give them.

It happened very often that it took a long time until the firemen came to put out a fire. This caused much damage. During the last period, a command was issued that each house must have two ladders because of the frequent fires. Two pails of water had to be ready, no straw or hay was permitted to lie in the attic. The firemen had the duty to determine whether their "command" was being followed.

The firemen's brigade would have a *gulyanye* (a celebration [that is usually held outdoors]) once a year to which an orchestra would be brought from Dvinsk. Talacki then organized a march outside the *shtetl*. He himself rode in front on a horse. The other firemen would ride behind him.

In earlier years the *gulyanyes* would be organized in a grove near the train station. The grove would be illuminated with colored paper lanterns that hung from the branches of the trees. A wood pile was also ignited.

A special exercise was introduced for the firemen. A tall tree would be cleared of branches and coated with wax. A flat wooden platform was attached to the tree on which was placed a silver watch, a wurst sausage, a white roll and a bottle of 90 proof spirits. Whoever could climb to the top of the tree and bring it all down won everything as a prize for himself.

Although very few could climb that high, this was an original attraction.

The Rakishok firemen's brigade served the surrounding *shtetlekh*, such as Kamaja, Obeliai, Dusetos, Pandelys and Radute.

* * *

Radute is just one *verst* [.66 of a mile] from Rakishok and numbered just ten Jewish families. To this day I do not know why such a small cluster of Jews separated themselves from Rakishok and built a *shtetl* for themselves. There were so many empty places in Rakishok itself.

I also do not necessarily know why they chose to build Radute in such a place, which looks like a camel with two humps – hill up and hill down – and in the middle there was a valley that is as old as, perhaps, Methuselah, in which there was grey mud in summer and winter.

The road from Rakishok to Radute runs very close to the Lithuanian church and the house of the priest. It was a road of such sadness and created a fear, particularly when the church bells resounded into the surrounding void. At that time, there was a great dread among the Radute Jews who were passing by. That could be why none of the Radute Jews went alone, but collectively.

Radute had its own synagogue, a ritual slaughterer. It did not have its own rabbi, no contract to bake matzoh and also did not have a bathhouse. For these, they had to go to Rakishok.

Therefore Radute was a *shtetl* of wanderers. Radute Jews were seen the entire day until late at night continuously going from Radute to Rakishok and from Rakishok to Radute.

B.

Until the First World War, life proceeded as always, without substantial changes. Everything would pass by inheritance from generation to generation to generation, just as [being a] *Kohan* [priestly class] or a *Levi* [descendants of Aaron and the tribe of Levi] was a matter of inheritance. In this way the children inherited their customs, wealth, lineage and a good name from their parents and also their "spot" in the synagogue. The children followed their father's learning and life experience.

The rabbi was the spiritual leader of the *shtetl*. He not only gave answers to religious questions and judged lawsuits before a rabbinical court, but he also was the authority in the secular community. Rebelling against the rabbi was considered a terrible sin.

The entire *shtetl* was concentrated around the *beis-hamedrash* [synagogue]. That is where one prayed and recited Psalms. The children played mostly within the limits of the synagogue. In 1905, the revolutionaries held their first meetings in the women's section. When Rakishok revolutionary activists needed to shoot the informer, Shimke Dimant, they did it on *Shimkhas Torah* [holiday in the fall when the annual reading of the Torah is concluded and begun again] in the synagogue.

[The people of Rakishok] followed well-worn traditional paths. The young observed the fundamentals of the earlier generation.

Just as in Sholem Aleichem's Kasrilevke,[5] in Rakishok they also remained within the narrow limits of the *shtetl*.

The years of the First World War brought the first great changes. Suddenly Jews were driven out of their generation's long residence. One *prikaz* [order] from Czar Nicholai's uncle created total chaos.

The Jews wandered away from their long-time homes. They ran chaotically from the *shtetlekh* to the farther Russian provinces, running into other elements, with new environments and customs. The social differences that existed earlier in the *shtetl* disappeared during this wandering. The rich men of the *shtetl* became the same as the poorest in social basics. Avraham Itse

Meller, the generation's well known Rakishok rich man, wandered in poverty during the evacuation to Russia and he also needed to go to *YEKAPO* (Committee to Assist Homeless Jews) to ask for support.

During the evacuation, the *shtetl* craftsmen began to look for new economic positions. Each began at the beginning. Rakishok shoemakers, not having brought along their cobbler's forms, began to trade and became successful merchants. Many poor men from Rakishok and poor people became important traders in their new places of residence and the well-to-do became poor. The entire social face changed.

The Russian revolution broke out in 1917. New slogans resounded in the Russian state, such as: "down with the Czar," "down with the oligarchic despotic regime" and "let the revolution live!"

The homeless Jews in Russia welcomed the new order and with great Hasidic bliss they became active in the revolutionary movement that overthrew the Czarist regime and gave them full equal rights and freedom.

The Jews returned to the Lithuanian *shtetlekh* with modern ideas and they brought new ideals to those Jews who had remained living under the German occupation. Each troop transport brought back Jews with a new storm of ideas.

Life changed in every sector. A category of rising wealthy men emerged, who displayed self-confidence compared to the pre-war rich who became impoverished during the war. The newly wealthy, such as Merkel, Kiwke Zamet became the people of authority in the synagogue and bought up the juicy *aliyehs* [more coveted roles] during the reading of the Torah, although internally they still felt a gulf between them and the former rich men in the *shtetl* such as Sholem Milner, etc.

The clothing and the way of life changed and also the communal and cultural conditions in Rakishok. Little by little, the pre-war kind of life disappeared. The clothing became more modern both for women and for men. Girls and women no longer were ashamed to go out in Hasidic Rakishok with low-neck clothing and they danced at weddings, but not quadrilles or traditional wedding dances. Chaim the *klezmer* [musician] with his bandura [plucked stringed instrument] no longer played at weddings and Yashe the *badkhin* [traditional wedding jester] was also not invited to them.

Parties arose. The quarrels among the rabbis, ritual slaughterers and clergymen were minor as compared with the heated polemical discussions that were carried on with strong zealotry among the party members. Even children were drawn into party politics.

The general Zionist organizations were created as well as the *S.Z.* [Social Zionist] party that legally carried out their activities. Jewish youth joined the Zionist parties. The Cultural League was founded; the Lekakh brothers gave fiery speeches about the new era and the social achievements of the Russian revolution. The club of the Cultural League was overflowing with those gathered to hear Khatz and Beinish Kresh, who reported often, propagandizing the idea of freeing all of humanity. Therefore, they stressed that Palestine belongs to the Arab people, who have been there for 2,000 years.

Agudah [Orthodox political party] arose. One of the founders was Avraham, the rabbi, who gave sermons in the synagogue in this style: "Let we fathers be in the synagogue; then our children will be around the synagogue; and if we will be around the synagogue, our children will be *lehavdl* [conjunction used to make a separation, usually between sacred and profane] in prayer." This talk gave rise to creating the *Agudah* whose purpose was also to fight the newly arising parties.

A new modern school system was created. Clubs and Yavne schools [with a stress on both secular and religious education] and a Jewish folks [people's] school of the "Cultural League" opened. The clubs also partly changed. There was more reading and writing and Hebrew books. The young boys in the religious schools were no longer taught until late in the evening. The tinsmith no longer made lanterns for the young boys in the religious schools.

* * *

New states and the Lithuanian Republic arose on the ruins of the Czarist order. The Lithuanian people became independent and began to lead a national life, although the majority of Lithuanians were peasants and the intelligentsia was a very small segment.

The Jewish population would surely have been able to take over the leadership of the Lithuanian government because it lived in the cities and had a very large intelligentsia.

At first, the Lithuanian government actually drew many prominent Jews to nation building. At the peace conference that took place in Moscow, Lithuania chose Dr. Rozenboim, may he rest in peace, to represent the Lithuanian delegation. At that time, there was a curious incident – Dr. Yafa, representative of the Russian delegation, asked Rozenboim the location of the Lithuanian-Polish border. He [Rozenboim] answered that where – in pronunciation – a "sh" changed to an "s," this was Lithuania."

The development of the Lithuanian state took place with amazing speed. The young Lithuanians ran from the villages to the city to take government positions.

A boom – in all areas – also took place among the Jews in Lithuania. There was a Jewish national council and Jewish ministry on Kestutis Street in Kovno. Dr. Rozenboim was elected as the chairman of the national council and Dr. Soloveitchik as the minister of Jewish affairs.

Jewish *kehilus* [organized communities] were created in Lithuania. Elections to the *kehlilus* took place. Heated election campaigns occurred in every Jewish *shtetl* and also in Rakishok. The majority of women, who were religious and God-fearing, voted for *Agudah*. Every Jew was taxed to pay the Jewish community tax. Jews carried on a quarrel with the state.

Folks [people's] banks opened that gave credit to those who needed to repair their houses destroyed during the war and to the handworkers who needed to repair their workshops and also to small merchants.

The *shtetl* took on a different appearance. There was electricity in Rakishok and the gas lamps disappeared.

But this economic boom did not extinguish for a second the national awakening of the Jews. The Zionist movement in Lithuania grew stronger and also in Rakishok. Hilel Idelson was like Mendele's "worker" in the *Takse*.[6] He carried out Zionist education work and asked for contributions on behalf of Zionist investments. The one doing the most Zionist work, Shifra Laufer, was tireless in her Zionist work, stressing at every opportunity that *im ain ani li mi li* [Rambam: If I am not for myself then who will be for me?]. Zionism was spread farther in the *shtetl* and even the Skopishker [rebbe] gave in and also bought a *shekel* [*shekels* were bought as a way of contributing to the Zionist movement].

The majority of *shtetl* youth became thoroughly seized by Zionist thought. Rich children left their homes and enrolled in *haHalutz* [an organization that trained young Jews in preparation for settlement in *Eretz-Yisroel*] and went on *Hakhshara* [Hebrew word meaning preparation – often an agricultural training center] work. Jewish daughters and sons with thin, tall figures and fine chiseled faces [hinting at unfitness for work] joined the *kibbutzim* [collective group] and then emigrated to *Eretz-Yisroel*.

Rakishok sent the first party of *halutzim* [members of *haHalutz*] during the beginning of the Fourth *Aliyah* [fourth wave of immigration to *Eretz-Yisroel* between 1924 and 1928]. The *shtetl* accompanied the *halutzim* with national songs.

* * *

The Russian revolution and the Balfour Declaration brought great spiritual changes. The old basis for Jewish life also began to break apart in the Lithuanian *shtetlekh*. New desires and ideals began to sprout that dominated both the individual and the community.

The idea of a return to Zion was particularly widespread among the Lithuanian Jews who gave substantial contributions to *Keren Ha-yesod* [Foundation Fund – organization supporting the World Zionist Organization's work in *Eretz-Yisroel*], *Keren Kayemet* [Jewish National Fund] and to other Zionist funds. Women also founded a *Keren Hazahov* [Gold Fund], giving jewelry in support of *Eretz-Yisroel*.

The Jews in Lithuania in the service of a republican order faced many anti-Semitic issues that no doubt strengthened Zionism in the Jewish neighborhoods as well as led to their having no connection to the Lithuanian land. It can also be that the folk [community] institutions that sensed the cruel fate of the coming days of destruction also influenced the national consciousness and the Zionist ideals completely dominated the Jewish community in Lithuania.

[Page 33]

Left: A headstone at the old cemetery. Wording: Zion. A woman...(illegible word) Pearl Bat Lei died 18th Kislev Tarsa"ch. Right: A headstone in the new cemetery: Wording: Our Father: Reb Shmaryahu Ben Rav Aharon died 22nd day of Adar Alef Tarp"at

[Page 36]

Volunteer firefighter corps
[Date on photo: 21 August 1927]

[Page 39]

The Maccabee parade commemorating the freeing of Schwartzborden
[who was freed in France]

Fire fighters meeting under open sky celebrating the Balfour Declaration

[Another translation refers to this as a "heated" meeting regarding the Balfour Declaration]

[Page 41]

Keren Kayemet Zionists
[with no identification]
Inscription on photo reads "Rokiskis 18 May 1925"

No group identification; date on photo: Rokiskis, 25 June 1927

(Standing right to left) Rachmiel Ruch, Yosef Caspi, Efraim Grinberg, David Sudavski, Chazrel *Katz*, A. Tzades, Avreml Nachimovitch. *(Seated right to left) Jacob* Givovsky, Hillel Eidelson, Bun, Esther Agents, Choneh Arsh, A. Yoselovitz. [Yosef Caspi, listed here, was principal of the Hebrew school. He was a traitor to the Jews in the German occupation in World War I, but was shot nevertheless. – A. Jermyn]

Translator's Footnotes

1. Each Hebrew letter has a numerical equivalent, its *gimatria*. The numerical value of the letters of the two words *ozer dalim* (which translate as "assists the needy") was used to calculate the age of the synagogue
2. This Yiddish usage indicates that Yekl is Feiwe's son and that Tsipa is Leah's daughter
3. Kozak means Cossack and is Yiddish slang for a strong man
4. The holiday occurring in late September or early October during which the year-long cycle of the reading of the Torah is completed and begun again. The holiday is celebrated with great joy including a procession during which the Torah scrolls are carried around a synagogue
5. Writer Sholem Alecheim's imaginary *shtetl*, in which many of his stories take place
6. A reference to a character in *Takse* [Tax], a work by Mendele Mokher Sforim

[Page 43]

The Peculiarity of Rakishok in Jewish Lithuania
by J. Shalit
Translated by Rae Meltzer

Levy Shalit

Introduction

Sons and daughters of the shtetlach in Europe strive to place gravestones made of words to the memory of their old home place. It is fine, good, and right to do so. Nevertheless, often a thought arises: why this or that shtetl, necessarily? Is our Holocaust a divided one then? In general, can one divide and separate one shtetl from another? Was the life and the Holocaust of all our six million not almost the same? Certainly, the life and death of every Jew was identical in every land. There was no difference for the Jews of Frankfurt, Berlin, Kovno, and Vilna. The life and death of Jews in Poland, Germany, and Lithuania can perhaps be differentiated, but what was the difference between one shtetl and another when such differences did not exist? Perhaps, in nuances and details, but in essence it was the same life and the same tragic fate, the same bottom line.

And yet! The wish of shtetlach Jews to mark and remember their birth place, to express their love for their home place and those who are no longer living, is all understandable. These shtetl monographs will tell the small specifics or the larger episodes that happened in that particular shtetl, giving information for the future historian. The historian of the future will give the larger and complete picture to memorialize the life and Holocaust of East European Jewry. This book about Rakishok will certainly serve as a stone in the future great monument, which will reflect the cutting down of Jewish life, and will stab the heart of the world and the sky above with the horror of our Holocaust.

How is it that in Rakishok, far from the Polish border in the so-called "Lithuanian Siberia," in a land of "Misnagdim," some Chasidim rolled in? Perhaps in this book one will find the answer.

* * *

Pesach Ruch

The Ruch family had a name (i.e. standing) in Rakishok. It was a family of piety, Chasidism, and wealth. The sons, Dovid and Ishker, studied Torah. There is a legend about Pesach Ruch, who was of the first generation. According to the legend, Pesach Ruch was a poor man prior to WWI. During WWI most of the Rakishok Jews were forced to flee Rakishok. Pesach was one of the few who went into hiding in Rakishok until the end of the war. A Polish lord, who owned all of Rakishok, was looking for a place to hide from his enemies. By chance he was helped by the God-fearing poor man Pesach Ruch. Later, the lord bestowed great wealth upon Pesach. Ruch became an even more devout Chasid, and went to fetch his Rabbi and brought him to Rakishok. However, his sons went to the cold "misnagdisher" Yeshiva in Telz.

In the "misnagdisher" Lithuania, many Chasidim were interested in learning. They were referred to as "cold Chasidim". They were expert in the "Gemorah". The Telzer Yeshiva was the most suitable, among all the Yeshivas of Lithuania. In Telz, learning and study was a goal in itself. All the other Yeshivas had various limitations: in Slobodka and in the Kelmer "Talmud Torah," morale was low. In Ponevezh, the Yeshivah was not well established and was surrounded by a big city with all its frightening aspects by Lithuanian standards. Telz was a small, friendly shtetl where the main activity was learning. The measure of a young man's accomplishment was his performance on the "Gemorah". Telzer had very strict standards for piety and for devoutness. The expectation in the Telzer Yeshiva was that one would separate oneself from worldly affairs. For example, Zionism was frowned upon much more in Telzer than in the other nearby Yeshivas. Slobodka and Ponevezh Yeshivas were definitely closer and there was established contact with Kovno; nevertheless the young men of Rakishok went to Telz.

Both Ruch's sons, Dovid and Ishker, and a few others from the Telzer Yeshiva studied "Synyo" while the others studied "Musar". They stood out at Simchas -Torah, Purim, and weddings at the Yeshiva, (when even the cold misnagdim let them-selves go and entered into the revelry). When the Ruch sons danced, they expressed great joy, their singing was jolly and their whole body expressed exaltation. People said it was their Chasidic blood that burst out into their exaltation. They were passionately committed to helping a friend and equally committed to punishing the sinner.

Even in pious and devout Telz new winds were blowing, and the new winds blew right into the Yeshiva. The "chalutzim" were preparing a conference in Telz to be held on the Sabbath. Some of the delegates would travel by train on the Sabbath. A "fanatic" group from the Yeshiva, including the Ruch brothers, gathered stones, determined to stop the conference. The Chasidic blood overcame the "battalions" from the "misnagdisher" Yeshiva boys. The confrontation ended in failure, but the name "Rakishoker Chasidim" became associated with "fanaticism" even in devout and pious Telz.

Rakishok was not a rich shtetl in Lithuania. There were shtetlach that were richer and poorer than Rakishok. In the Gentile population of Lithuania, Rakishok was an out-of-the-way, far-off place, even in the small land of Lithuania. But in the Jewish world of Lithuania, Rakishok was a significant center.

Zionism had a stronghold in Rakishok. The Zionist commitment was deep and strong. Many of the Zionists from Rakishok were the first "chalutzim". One meets them in the oldest "kibbutzim" of Israel. Did their poverty drive the young men and women from Rakishok? Or did the warmth of their Chasidic experience start the flame for their belief in the diaspora? Perhaps it was both.

Rakishok, the largest shtetl in the eastern region of Lithuania, was the spiritual center for the shtetlach of: Ponevezh, Kamai, Abel, Panimunok, Kupishok, and Skopishok. All these shtetlach were provided with Zionist speakers and youth leaders from Rakishok. The Zionist groups of Kovno considered the Rakishok Zionists an independent circle, not a part of Ponevezher circle. In the Zionist organization of Rakishok, the leading group was the Hashomer Hatzair among the youth. Among the older people it was the General Zionist Organization.

Rakishok, among very few other shtetlach, had a leader and personality by the name of Hillel Aidelson, who attended the First Zionist Congress in Basel, Switzerland. Aidelson was intensely committed to the Zionist dream. His every breath was filled with devotion to the Zionist ideal, and his whole life was devoted to Zionism. He never married and did not have a mishpocheh. He was an unusual person. When he walked, his footsteps were very quiet. He was a veterinarian. He used all his intelligence and knowledge to solve Zionist problems. His diaspora dream found all his personal goals in Zionism as well as his ideals and principles. To the Zionist ideals he gave up everything he had: money, health... everything.

In 1937 he attended a youth conference where he was warmly welcomed and greatly honored. But as always, he was very shy. He sat at the head table, an honored guest, but very silent, with downcast eyes, almost ashamed that he was receiving so much attention and honor. Hillel Aidelson was the one who brought the breath and personal messages from Dr. Herzl to Rakishok. He brought the words from the Source. Perhaps this is the reason that Zionism became so strong in Rakishok, much earlier than in other places in the land.

The poverty in Rakishok drove the youth of the town to Zionism, but also to the idealism of building a better world everywhere, and thus redeem the Jewish folk. In the beginning of the 1920's, when Lithuania became independent, nationalism was on the rise, as was Soviet communism. The youth began to cross over the border to the Soviet Union. From Rakishok the Soviet border was close. The youth of Rakishok jumped over the border to Russia – the "New World". Later the border was "hermetically" sealed, and even letters stopped being exchanged. Family members lost touch with one another and were forgotten. The Communists went underground and people were afraid to talk about their friends and relatives who went "over there". In 1939 when the Soviet military invaded Lithuania, Red Army officers and soldiers came into Rakishok and other shtetlach, and people once again recognized the "forgotten ones."

One of the "forgotten" ones was the Rakishoker Jacob Shmuskevitch. In the 1920's he left his father, the Rakishoker butcher, his mother, and his mishpocheh and fled "over there" (i.e. Soviet Russia). When the Soviets occupied Lithuania in 1940, stories about the Rakishok youth Shmuskevitch and his wondrous deeds spread everywhere. The newspapers were full of photographs of him, his mishpocheh, and his house on the street near the railroad where he once lived. The legends about him began almost immediately, even before there was confirmation of his exploits. It seems as if the legends dropped from the sky. With his airplane, Shmuskevitch landed in Rakishok to visit his mishpocheh and his hometown. The new spread like wild fire all over Lithuania. Proudly the Jewish folk hailed "our Yankel (Jacob)!!! Yankel the Rakishoker, a General in the Red Army, Hero of the Finnish (Finland) Front. What a marvelous achievement. Such an honor will ring out all over the Jewish community of Lithuania, and not only in his hometown of Rakishok.

Life is a circle. The end was tied to the beginning. In the years after the First World War, the Lithuanian Jews returned from the Russian diaspora to Lithuania. They came via Abel and Rakishok, returning to their home-towns in Lithuania.

In the first days of the German-Soviet war, many Jews from middle and northern Lithuania moved to the Soviet border via Abel and Rakishok. After 20 years, the Lithuanian Jews were running back to Russia. It was 20 years earlier that they left Russia and returned to their hometowns in Lithuania.

The circle was about to close tightly. The Russian border closed. Close behind was standing the bloody enemy, the German. There was no way to return to one's own hometown, so one was caught in Rakishok. At least one was among Jewish homes. In the marketplace, in the synagogue and school, in every Jewish home, people clung together before the oncoming storm. The German vandals were already in the streets.

It was very crowded in the homes of the Rakishok Jews. Everyone took in strangers who were escaping the Germans. But the crowding did not last long; a week, not more. Then it was crowded in the mass graves. Into the graves they shoveled the Chasidim and the misnagdim, the Zionists and the communists, those who dwelled in Rakishok and those who ran to Rakishok from elsewhere. They are no more.

Closing Words

We all know the enormity of our terrible misfortune; our enormous grief over the Holocaust. Over the graves in the Rakishok orchard, I would like to find a few words of consolation. It is so difficult, so very difficult, to find word of consolation. We do deserve consolation. I force myself to tell you that when I arrived in Johannesburg, wandering around the Jewish quarters, suddenly I saw a sign that read: "Chasidic Beth Hamedresh" (school house/synagogue). I immediately concluded that Jews from Rakishok emigrated to Johannesburg along with other Lithuanian Jews. The Rakishok Jews undoubtedly brought over with them their Chasidism from their old hometown. It must be that here in Africa, as in Lithuania, Rakishok lives on. Let us find a little consolation in those who here in Africa, in Israel, and everywhere in the world carry in their hearts the memory of life in Rakishok, and remember the holy ones and the martyrs. May the holiness of their lives and the martyrdom of their death, strengthen us to march forward and renew our important Jewish future in a better world.

[Page 44-45]

[Page 46]

H. Eidelson
Zionist leader

[Page 48]

JACOB SMUSHKEVICH, at 40, is chief of the Red Army Air Force. He began both his formal schooling and flight training when he was 29, and has twice earned Russia's highest award, Hero of the Soviet Union. A Lithuanian Jew, Smushkevich illustrates the Soviet policy of full racial equality in all spheres of life.

[Page 50]

Chabad
by Rabbi Prof. L. I. Rabinowitz
Translated by Gloria Berkenstat Freund

by Rabbi Prof. L. I. Rabinowitz

Prof. L. I. Rabinowitz is the head rabbi of the Federation of the Synagogues in Transvaal and the head of the *Bet Din* [rabbinical court].

He is Professor of Hebrew in Witwatersrand University and the author of the following books, which were written in English: *The Social Life of the Jews in South Africa*; *Excommunication within the Community*; *From the Depths*; *Soldier of Yehuda*; and *The Mission in the Far East*.

Actually, I was, from a certain point of view, not the right person to write about the Hasidim and even less about Chabad, because my family followed the famous Reb Haim Volozhiner, a follower of the Vilna *Gaon* [genius], whose opposition to the Hasidim, in all forms, and chiefly to the well known Reb Shneur Zalman of Liadi, the founder of Chabad, is well known. Yet although I was shaped as a *mitnagid* [follower of Enlightenment] both by origin and by education, my feeling for Chabad is such that when Rabbi Weinberg, the representative from the Lubavitcher rebbe, was here, I allowed myself to tease him in the following manner: "Even though you are a Hasid, at least you are a Chabadnik."

Reb Haim Vital, the student of Reb Yitzhak Luria, the *Ari HaKadosh* [Translator's note: Ari the Holy; Ari is an acronym for *Adoneinu Rabbeniur Yitzhak* – Our master, our rabbi, Yitzhak] in his book, *Sefer Gilgul HaNefesh* [*Book on Transmigration of the Soul*], presents a remarkable distinction between the Rambam[1] and the Ramban.[2] According to him, it appears that both are descended from the *adam hakodmon* [the original man, i.e. Adam]. However, while the genius of the Ramban comes from the left *peye* [side curl] of Adam that represents intellect and strict judgment, the Ramban's inheritance is from the right *peye* that expresses emotion, tenderness and mercy. This difference was the cause of the first clash between the Hasidim and the *mitsnagdim*.

Yosef Itzhak Schneurson, Lubovitcher Rebbe
The Lubavitcher Rebbe, when he visited Rakishok in 1931

I said above that I was a *mitnagdim* through education. In order to confirm this, I will here describe one incident in my life. I was still a small boy when Hasidism began to have an effect on me. I asked my father if the *Baal Shem Tov*[3] was a great man. His answer was significant. "We can pass judgment as to whether a man is great or not according to the books that he has written. However, given that the *Baal Shem Tov* has not written a book, I cannot tell you."

These simple words were for me the highest level of intellectual supremacy – the extreme rule of intellect over the emotions that were the characteristic trait of the *mitnagdim* against which the Hasidim revolted. Whereas the *mitnagdim* glorified the intellect and considered studying the highest stimulus of piety, the Hasidim made fun of this and focused on ecstatic prayer, and this united them with God through ecstasy and emotions as the level of piety. It is even said that one of the students of the *Baal Shem Tov* is supposed to have said, "Where one studies a great deal, there is no piety."

This Hasidic concept entirely undermined the foundation of Judaism and the *mitnagdim* had to combat this. One could not expect that the Vilna *Gaon*, who had dedicated himself totally to learning for the sake of learning would not react to this heretical "*Torah*," and for the first time in his life, he left the pulpit and threw himself into the feud because the concept of the *mitnagdim* was this, as Reb Ismael had quoted: "There are two verses of the *Torah* that contradict each other and Chabad introduces a third verse that can harmonize the two others."

Since the beginning, Judaism always excelled in the manner in which it harmonized and held an equilibrium between wisdom and awe, between the intellect and the emotions--the study of *Torah* for its own sake is a positive commandment; it does not permit the idea that an ignorant man can be a Hasid. This means that one cannot reach perfection in the faith without the foundation of knowledge. And although it underlines the essence of *Yidishkeit* [Translator's note: Jewishness, also connoting an emotional connection to all things Jewish], it also allows that awe, the emotional approach to G-d, is more important than only the intellectual concept of *Yidishkeit* and G-d: "Wisdom without awe are like someone who has lost the key to his treasure." And Reb Hanina ben Dosa [first century scholar] in *Pirkei Avot* [*Ethics of the Fathers*] characterizes these two concepts in this way: "For those for whom awe comes before wisdom, it will endure. However, if his wisdom has the advantage over awe, his wisdom will not endure."

Reb Shneur Zalman of Liadi, the founder of Chabad, well understood this and built on this foundation. His remarkable system: "It is good that you should believe this and also not release your hand from the other, because he who has fear of G-d, comes to an understanding of both." (*Koyheles – Book of Ecclesiastes*] This was perhaps his motto. He also aspired to place Hasidism on a scholarly foundation and called for belief based on Judaism, instead of a blind belief based on emotions. Therefore, Chabad always excelled with intellectual balance.

Schechter, in his interesting although somewhat superficial treatise about Hasidism, deduced that the pure learning of the *Baal Shem* and of his successor, Reb Ber of Mezherich, degenerated to a cult of *tzadikism* [Translator's note: belief that a *tzadik* or righteous man serves as an intermediary between G-d and man], making the *tzadik* divine. I do not have the opportunity to confirm or to negate his lecture. However, I can confirm one thing, that the degeneration about which he speaks did not affect Chabad. Based firmly on the understanding and information of the *Torah* balanced with the pure belief and ardor of the founder of Hasidism, it always excelled with two traditions – a firm self sacrificing support of *Yidishkeit* and the ardor of a mission fanatic – with which it still excels now. When I visited the Lubavitcher *yeshiva* in New York, I met young men there who had lived their entire lives in Soviet Russia, yet they retained their faith. In the rest of the world as well-- France, South Africa, Australia, Israel--Chabad carries on its Jewish work, "capturing souls" everywhere. It is their firm determination that the light of *Yidishkeit* not be extinguished, given that the future of *Yidishkeit* lies both in knowledge and in belief.

I understand that all Rakishok Jews belong to Chabad.* May their *landsmanschaft* in South Africa derive satisfaction from these exalted and noble Jews.

***Editor's note:** the author's statement here is misleading, perhaps due to the fact that (as far as we know) he was not from Rakishok. While it is true that Rakishok was one of the few towns in Lithuania with a significant Hasidic presence, there were *mitnagdim* as well, as evidenced by the fact that there were two rabbinates in the town, one Hasidic and one *mitnagdim*

Translator's Footnotes

6. Hebrew acronym of Rabbi Moshe ben Maimon or Maimonides
7. Hebrew acronym of Rabbi Moshe ben Nahman Gerondi or Nachmanides
8. Yisroel Ben Eliezer, known as the *Baal Shem Tov* (The Master of the Good Name, was the founder of Hasidism

[Page 53]

Rakishok and Its Hasidim

by B. Stein
(In memory of my father, Moshe Leib, of blessed memory)
Translated by Gloria Berkenstat Freund

Rakishok was considered one of the larger *shtetlekh* [towns] in Lithuania. When I left in 1912 traveling to South Africa, it was thought that the population of the town consisted of 600 families. The percentage of non-Jews in the *shtetl* was very small, so that it had a thoroughly Jewish character. The market day took place every Monday without exception, when the peasants from the surrounding villages would arrive in the *shtetl* to sell their products and buy various things from the Jewish shops. Early in the morning the large marketplace would be filled with harnessed horses, hitched to the peasant wagons. Jewish merchants, both large and small, would walk around among these wagons and bargain with the peasants for the various agricultural products that they had brought with them.

The *shtetl* would lose its quiet and dreaminess on these market days and be captivated by the momentum of the market. The entire *shtetl* was boisterous and boiling like a kettle. At night, when the peasants would leave, the large marketplace emptied and the *shtetl* again would return to its quiet and serenity.

* * *

As is known, Rakishok was the only *shtetl* in all of Lithuania that was completely Hasidic. As far as I know, it is not fully known how it happened that Hasidus captivated the entire Jewish population and completely erased any trace of *Misnagdes* [Orthodox opposition to Hasidus].

The Rakishok Hasidim were divided into three groups based on the rabbis of whom the Hasidim in question were followers. I believe that the largest group consisted of the Lubavitcher Hasidim. The Liadyer Hasidim and the Kapuster Hasidim consisted of much smaller groups. However, the small number of Kapuster Hasidim were the most active and were more typically Hasidic than the others. Of the four houses of prayer in the *shtetl*, the "small *shtibl*" [small synagogue] was under the total influence of the Kapuster Hasidim. There they would study the *Tanya** during *Minkhah* and *Maariv* [afternoon and evening prayer] during the week and on *Shabbos* they repeated Hasidus after the third *Shabbos* meal. The Hasidim there would drink a little whiskey from time to time, as for example, on *Rosh Khodesh* [the start of the new month], at a *yahrzeit* [anniversary of a death] or when a Hasid from a neighboring *shtetl* visited.

*[Translator's note; the principal book of Chabad-Lubavitch Hasidic philosophy written by Rabbi Shneur Zalman of Liady.]

One such Hasid who I still remember very well was Yankl Skopishker. This was the grandfather of the brothers Zalman, Leibl and Yerakhmial Feldman and their sister, Ruchl Zaydl. He was a good friend of my father and when he would come to Rakishok he would visit my father. They would sit with a glass of tea and talk about various matters.

[Page 54]

Yankl Skopishker would come to pray in the *shtibl* in the evening and after the evening prayers he would provide whiskey.

A second such Hasid was Shlomo Skopishker. He moved from Skopishok in around 1910 and settled in Rakishok. As he was an avid Hasid and was well versed in Hasidus, he became one of the prominent Hasidim in Rakishok.

Great revelries would take place at times in the *shtibl* where there would be the feeling of true Hasidic joy.

* * *

A warm relationship to Hasidim and Hasidus was created in me in my young years under the influence of my home in particular and of my *shtetl* in general. My father, Moshe Leibe the *Gemora-melamed* [teacher of the *Gemora* – Talmudic commentaries], was an avid and warm Hasid. He would use his free time mainly to study Hasidus. He studied it himself or with several Hasidim who would come to him on the weeknights and my father would teach the book, *Tanya*, to 10-15 Hasidim in the *shtibl*. On the *Shabbos* nights he would repeat Hasidus for a much larger group. It was apparent to everyone that the teaching of Hasidus was not an obligation to him, but a subject of pleasure. It was the same kind of pleasure that people derive from music or from great literary works. He literally lived in the artistic world that through the generations had produced creative artists. What else were the grandiose, fantastic structures built by Hasidus if not artistic creations? I often think that such people as my father were true followers of and benefited from art. For us, the secular, art is a secondary matter, an addition to life; for them, however, their art was the quintessence of life and what we call reality was a secondary matter to them.

* * *

My warm connection to Hasidus was stronger during my later years when I encountered *Misnagdim* [Orthodox Jews opposed to Hasidus]. The first time was in Dvinsk [Daugavpils] to which I traveled to study after my *Bar-Mitzvah*. There I sensed in the *Misnagdish* synagogues and houses of prayer the large difference between Hasidus and *Misnagdes*. *Misnagdish* houses of prayer appeared cold and gloomy to me, just like the sad *Vhu rachum* ["...and He, being compassionate..."] floating in the air and blowing with cold and sadness. Even the *Lekhu-neraneno* ["Come let us sing"] on Friday night resounded cold and lifeless. I strongly longed then for the "small *shtibl* in my *shtetl* where a certain amount of mystical religious ecstasy and rapture was sensed even in the weekday prayers. Above all, on Friday night the uplift of *Shabbos* actually radiated from the Hasidic faces and a warm joyfulness hovered over the *shtibl*.

[Page 55]

I understood at that time that while the Hasidim and *Misnagdim* believe in the same God and in the same Torah, Hasidus for the Hasidim permeated their very essence and enriched their lives. It became clearer to me in later years. One of the most important things in Hasidus is that one needs to serve God not with fear but with love and that one need be joyful in God's world and [recognize] the possibility that a person can have pleasure from it [God's world] and can make improvements in it. The Hasidic principle of joy did not remain simply a doctrine frozen in the pages of religious books, but penetrated into the heads and hearts of the Hasidim and became the prevailing strength in their personality and character.

The *Mishnagdish* world was gray and gloomy, not only because of the poverty and difficulties of life, but also because of the doctrine of the *Misnagdish* books of moral instruction. They all emphasized that man did not have anything to boast about or to take joy in. They emphasized the insignificance of a person's short life on earth and they disdained the pleasures and joys as something to be renounced. Others books warned that one would have to pay in the next world for every bit of pleasure and joy in this world. They learned that a man must turn away from the world and cry and lament at their own insignificance and sinfulness, at the exile of Israel and the exile of the Divine Presence. Their main goal consisted of a complete negation of everything material, a renunciation of their own self. A man needs to remember that he enters the world with nothing and that he leaves the world with nothing.

Much also is said in Hasidus about the elevated state of consciousness and the nullification of selfhood, but both precepts provide another message. True, the person has to remove his materialism in the world, but there are sparks of sanctity and Godliness hidden in the coarse substance of the world. It is the human task to bring out these sparks from potential to manifestation. The person can show it through worship and good deeds, through human fervor and the human mind, which he can bring to the coarse material world. A person is capable of bringing these sparks of sanctity on every step of his way and he can find a rectification for the inwardness of creation, in the Creation of the world, and through this he becomes a partner with God in the creation of the world. This is a very different kind of removing oneself from the world. Here the person removes himself from the world not to distance himself from it, but to join with it and to reveal the sanctity and Godliness that is buried in it. And as a result, the principle of joy enters here because how can one not celebrate when one receives the gift of such privileges to repair the world and to become a partner of the Creator in the creation of the world.

One understands from this that the Hasidic disdain for material reality was completely different from that of the *Misnagdish*. The latter leads to the denial of one's own self in that the person should completely understand his insignificance and decadence. The Hasidic negation of everything material leads to something completely the opposite. If a person is for himself, with his coarse, egotistical I, with his more rational animal soul banal and fallen, his soul is however at the same time a part of God above and it is a person's task to make known and reveal the sanctity that is hidden in himself. The individual receives an immense importance here in that through worship and good deeds he can unite with the Divine Essence.

[Page 56]

Moshe Leib Shtein

So the dignity that the Hasidic doctrine gives to the person, along with the precept that a person needs to shun sadness and that he needs the opposite, to be full of joy, for his task in the world, this was all mirrored in the Hasidic personalities of our *shtetl*.

* * *

I will try to provide several pictures of Hasidic life at that time in our *shtetl* that still remain clear in my mind despite the 40 years that have passed since I left that life. My father, Moshe Leib, must be the central figure of this picture. This is not because as my father he strongly influenced me and through him I absorbed the spirit of Hasidus from early childhood on, but mainly because he truly was the central figure in the Hasidic life of our *shtetl*, as well as in the area of Hasidic education and in Hasidic society as a whole. He also occupied the central place in Hasidic celebrations and revelries and with a little whiskey he would create an atmosphere of Hasidic excitement and joy among followers of the same rabbi.

[Page 57]

Friday Before the Lighting of the Candles

My mother was busy in the kitchen putting food for *Shabbos* in a warm oven and my father brought the samovar that was already boiling and placed it on the table. Meanwhile he walked through the room and recited *Patakh Eliyahu* [*Eliyahu opened*]. This is a chapter of the *Zohar* that certain Hasidim recite Friday night before the lighting of the candles. His walking back and forth through the room was calm and easy. The light of the spirit poured from his face and he recited the words with pensiveness and restrained spiritual awakening. I, still a young boy, sat still and listened; I, too, became caught up in the enchanted world in which he was engrossed. The magnificence of Friday nights was so strongly etched in my childish imagination and the image in general remains fresh and clear, but also the *Patakh Eliyahu* still remains in my memory. The passage that speaks about God who "encompasses all worlds and permeates all worlds and none can grasp Him" made a particularly strong impression on me. I would translate it into Yiddish: God circles all of the worlds and fills all worlds and no one can comprehend Him. However, I did want to understand it and often thought about it. I then had not heard the word pantheism, but I doubt if my later acquaintance with pantheism brought me more clarity in the matter than the above sentence from the *Zohar*.

* * *

Friday Night in the *Shtibl*

It was light and joyful in the *shtibl*. All of the large lamps were lit and all of the faces and eyes were clear and festive. Jews entered with combed beards and *peyes* [side curls], in black, long, coarse coats with *gartlen* [a belt signifying the separation of the sacred from the profane] and were welcomed with mystical, religious ecstasy and fervor. As if by miracle, all suddenly were freed from the weekday cares and worries and everyone was enveloped by a shared happiness – the luck of possessing a *Shabbos*.

When the welcoming of *Shabbos* ended and the evening prayers were done, everyone wished: good *Shabbos*, good *Shabbos*, good year! – And they left for home.

But several Hasidim remained. While the group recited the evening prayers they [the Hasidim] looked into a religious book; on Friday nights [it was their custom] to recite the evening prayers privately. Avdotya, the [female] water-carrier entered and extinguished the lamps; she only left burning a small lamp that stood on the table where they studied between the afternoon and evening prayers. The lamp cast a weak light over the *shtibl*. The several Hasidim stood in separate corners in the half darkness. My father stood in one corner, Chaim Elye the *shamas* [sexton] stood in another and in the third – Shimshon Nisen. They prayed quietly and calmly at first. However, little by little the praying became warmer and more ecstatic. Everyone became enraptured in their own way, but all of the melodies flowed together in one melody of yearning. They continued to pray quietly, restrained, but the fire of rapture, of the outpouring of the heart was felt in each voice.

[Page 58]

Meanwhile, I sat and listened and I was very irritated that I was still a small boy and could not stand in a corner like the adults and become enraptured along with them.

* * *

Daybreak on *Shabbos*

The voice of my father, of Chaim Elye the *shamas* and Shimshon Nisen reached me behind the oven where my bed was located. For years, both summer and winter, the two Hasidim came at daybreak on *Shabbos* to study Hasidus with my father. Their conversations about various matters while drinking a glass of tea in the other room did not disturb the *Shabbos* calm that ruled over the house. I woke up completely and as the Hasidus instruction began, I became enraptured by the secrets of the spiritual worlds that my father with his deep, hearty voice divulged to Chaim Elye and Shimshon Nisen. I remember that I was almost a *Bar-Mitzvah* boy and I still was concerned with foolishness. I decided that I could no longer be like that. From that day on I became a *ba'al tshuva* [one who repents and becomes more observant]. I fell asleep again, immersed in the magical, mystical world that was created here.

* * *

Shabbos **in the Evening**

My father felt all through *Shabbos* that it was good to live in the world. He had great joy from everything – from prayer, from studying and from the foods of *Shabbos*. However, he had the deepest *Shabbos* pleasure between the afternoon and evening prayers when he recited Hasidus before a group. He was always a man with a stately appearance – with the most beautiful beard, with open, intelligent eyes. But the joy of *Shabbos* lit up his face and shone out from his every gaze when he recited Hasidus after the third *Shabbos* meal. His voice, deep and hearty, conveyed the spiritual pleasure that he felt to the group. Hasidim stood with open mouths and ears and swallowed his words. It was half-dark in the *shtibl*. The weak light from the only lamp that had already burned for 24 hours created a shadow on the group around the table. Soon they would start the weekday evening prayer and the workday [world] would again engulf the *shtibl* and the *shtetl*. But it was still *Shabbos* and my father was occupied with the secrets of the higher spiritual world. He told the group about the influence of the Endless Light that always floods all worlds and gives life and strength to all creatures and things. If the Endless Light would be removed for one second, the world would cease to exist. Everything would crumble and disappear into chaos where it had been before the creation of the world.

He strolled with his listeners to the upper worlds and brought them into the Temple of the Souls. He declared that the souls of people are emanations, revelations from the Endless Light and the task of the souls when they come down to the world below is through prayer and good deeds to redress the imperfections that have fallen into the creative process because of the coarse flesh and to bring to the person the power and unity in the world. The person must rejoice with his missions in the world and, therefore, he must worship with joy and divine love, with devotion and rapture.

[Page 59]

Hasidim stood and nodded in agreement. My father, like a singer with a wonderful voice, took them out of their own narrow, enclosed world and brought them into a freer, limitless world. They felt that one was not simply thrown into the world below. They saw clearly that there is present a narrow connection between this world and the higher spiritual world, between every one's soul and the Endless Light. They felt cheerful and warm because of this.

When it became completely dark outside and someone said the weekday [prayer] "And He, being compassionate," the weekday hardness wrestled with my father's voice whose juicy tenor still hovered in the air and did not want to allow in the authority of the ordinary.*

*[Translator's note: "And He, being compassionate" are the first words of a prayer recited on weeknights.]

* * *

Revelries

The real revelries in the *shtibl* would take place on *Yud-Tes Kislev* [the day that the founder of Chabad Hasidism, Rabbi Schneur Zalman of Liadi, was released from prison, celebrated as the birth of Hasidism], the fifth [Chanukah] candle and *Simkhas Beis Hashoeiva* [celebration of water-drawing held during the intermediate days of *Sukkos* – the Feast of Tabernacles].

Approximately 25 to 30 Hasidim remained after the evening prayers. Chaim Elye, the *shamas*, already had prepared a white tablecloth and he spread it over the table on which they studied between the afternoon and evening prayers. The large lamps were lit and it created a lively mood in the group. My father went from Hasid to Hasid and gathered money for whiskey and food. The richer ones gave up to five or 10 *kopikes* [pennies] each; the poor ones gave up to two or three *kopikes*. He gave the money to Chaim Elye. The latter had already that day prepared everything necessary and had hidden it somewhere in the women's synagogue.

Chaim Elye and one of the Hasidim left for a time and came back loaded with packages. They placed small plates on the table and filled them with cookies and sponge cake. Others busied themselves at the faucet with herring. They washed them and sliced off the skin, cutting them in pieces and laying them on small plates and brought them to the table. The table, now covered with the various foods, took on a holiday appearance. Several Hasidim sat on benches that stood on one side of the table near the wall. Others sat further away from the table and the remainder stood around the table.

A Hasid began to speak:

– Chaim Elye, I did not know that you are such a skillful person. Look at what kind of table you have arranged. But something is missing. I do not know what, but something is missing.

[Page 60]

Chaim Elye acted as if he did not know what.

– What could be lacking? Herring – enough; cookies and sponge cake – enough. Perhaps, roasted ducks?

– A Hasid said, Look at how he feigns ignorance. There is an opinion, Chaim Elye, that when Hasidim come together there is an uncertainty about whether a blessing is recited without performing the related deed, does one make a blessing over certain foods made of grains, without a blessing over certain foods and drinks, except wine. Look at the glasses that are sitting empty and forlorn. They are looking for *tikun* [brandy].*

*[Translator's note: *tikun* is used in Hebrew as a word for brandy. It is more often translated as "redress" and is used here as a play on words.]

– Chaim Elye said, Oh, now I understand. You, of course, mean whiskey. Imagine, I have completely forgotten it.

He walked onto the *bimah* [raised platform in front of the Torah ark in a synagogue], was busy there for a time in a corner and came back to the table with two bottles – "75."*

*[Translator's note: "75" is a reference to the "alcohol proof" of the whiskey. In this case 75 proof.]

Hasidim took small sips [of whiskey] and ate the cookies and herring. It did not take long for the group to become animated and talkative. They joked, they quipped, they provided ingenious ideas and ideas that were related to the mundane conversations of the sages. They had another drop among themselves and another drop.

Shimshon Nisen, as was his habit, was not at the head of the table. He sat on the side. My father suddenly remembered him:

– He called out: Where is Shimshon Nisen? And searched for him with his eyes.

He stood up, looked around for him and found him sitting at the end of the bench.

Shimshon Nisen was tall with a bent back as well as a bent nose. Sitting or standing, he always kept his head lowered. The main characteristic of his figure was being bent over. It reminded one of a picture of a horse that spent the entire day in harness and at night when it stopped for a time, it still stood in harness with a bent, lowered head. As people passed by, a feeling of sympathy and friendship was awakened; they thought that it was time to remove the harness and for it to rest.

My father went over to Shimshon Nisen.

– Why are you sitting on the side, Nisen Shimshon?

When they had a little whiskey, Hasidim would reverse the names, so that Shimshon Nisen became Nisen Shimshin.

– There is no difference where one sits, answered Shimshon Nisen.

– My father called out, ostensibly in anger: Help, what does one do with a *Misnagid*? He carries the exile of Israel and the exile of the Divine Presence on himself.

[Page 61]

He took him by the arm and led him to the table.

– Have you made the blessing, Nisen Shimshon?

– Certainly, of course.

So take another small drink with us, you *Misnagid*!

After finishing his drink, my father said to him: Come, Nisen Shimshon, let us dance. He laid a hand on his [Nisen Shimshon's] shoulder and the dance began. My father sang a Hasidic melody. The others joined and sang along. Nakhum Ber's voice stood out from all of the other voices. Nakhum Ber had a very fine voice, beautiful and he would often pray from the lectern, on *Shabbos* and holidays.

My father encouraged Shimshon Nisen: Lift a foot, Nisen Shimshon. That is the way, that is the way. But it did not help. Even dancing, Shimshon Nisen gave the impression of being in harness.

Meanwhile, other Hasidim joined in and almost all took part in the dance. A familiar warmth grew both in the singing and in the dancing. It filled the entire *shtibl* and embraced the entire group.

Such revelries would often last until late at night.

* * *

The images above were all from *Shabbos* except for the last image that also was not from a usual weekday. It could be thought that there were no weekdays. In truth, there were weekdays and, mostly, they were difficult and bitter days. People toiled and were busy and did not have enough income. Most of them simply did not have enough income, but our Hasidim in the *shtetl* lived for *Shabbos*. The aphorism that the entire world was created only for *Shabbos* was very suited to them. Hasidim would say: what are the weekdays? All the people were busy providing an income, some through commerce, some through trades, some through teaching. There was no distinction. During the weekdays, the world was a weekday one and life was a weekday one. Like ants, *lehavdil* [word used to separate the sacred from the profane] – everything is a race for a livelihood. Only on *Shabbos* does a person truly feel that he lives in the world. God gave the person a *Shabbos* with the additional soul a Jew is said to possess on *Shabbos* so that at least once a week he would be freed from the gray weekdays.

[Page 62]

Jewish National Autonomy in Lithuania
by I. Batnizky
Translated by Gloria Berkenstat Freund

I. Batnizky

The epoch of Jewish national autonomy in Lithuania during the first years of Lithuanian independence at the beginning of the 1920's was short, but spiritually rich, and it can be remembered as the golden era of Lithuanian Jewry. In the course of this brief era, the small Jewish community in Lithuania showed a strong national energy, and the creative national strength of the Lithuanian Jews grew in all areas of life. The 700-year-old tree of Lithuanian Jewry began to bloom and provide juicy and wonderful fruit. South African Jewry very much benefited from this fruit, because the majority of Jewish immigrants, who arrived in South Africa during the time between the two World Wars, were the product of Lithuanian Jewish national education that was an element of Jewish National Autonomy and still remained when autonomy as such had been abolished.

Jewish Lithuania no longer exists. The short time of autonomy looks like a quickly passing episode after the bloody destruction of Lithuania Jewry. Yet it is important that the era of autonomy not be forgotten because it was a clear demonstration of the great potential strengths of Lithuanian Jewry. This intensifies still more our grief over the decline of the nationally vibrant and productive Lithuanian Jewish community with a spiritually rich history of 700 years behind it.

In the following lines I will present a short overview of the rise and destruction of autonomy, which began with great hopes and expectations and ended with bitter disappointments.

After the German defeat in the First World War, in many areas of the former Russia that had been occupied by the Germans, there arose the so-called border states, such as Latvia, Estonia and Lithuania. The concept of "Lithuania" was introduced, a country in its historical boundaries, that is, including also Vilna and Grodno. In such a country, however, the ethnic Lithuanian element made up a minority. Consequently, the Lithuanian politicians tried to draw the national minorities such as the Jews, Poles and White Russians to their side because only with their cooperation could they create the Lithuanian nation in its historical boundaries. Therefore, they promised extensive national autonomy to the minorities. The Poles refused this because, in general, they opposed any Lithuanian nation. They dreamed of a Greater Poland – from sea to sea – that would also incorporate Lithuania. The White Russians and Jews stood on the side of the Lithuanians.

The Jewish leaders, who took an active part in the struggle for Lithuanian independence, had a great vision for themselves. The concept of "Lithuania" in its historical boundaries was identical to the Jewish concept of Lithuania. Such a country would have to be a state of not one nationality but many, and the Jews would be equal partners in the sovereignty of the nation. For the first time in the Jewish history of the last 2,000 years, Jews would become a sovereign nation, as a subject and not an object of the state.

This was the great dream of Dr. Shimshon Rozenboim and the other leaders of Lithuanian Jewry, who stood on the side of the Lithuanians and worked with them for he creation and recognition of the new Lithuanian nation. When further political events did not permit Lithuania to spread out over its historical territory, the Jewish leaders understood that the situation for the Jews would be very different from what they had imagined. However, they fought further for autonomy, but under more difficult conditions, in conditions in which the Lithuanians made up more than 80 percent of the population.

It should be emphasized that the Zionists in all groupings carried the entire load on the autonomy side, from its rise to its downfall. The leftist parties were, in general, oriented towards the Soviet Union and were entirely against the Lithuanian nation. The non-Zionist parties, which were insignificant in number, worked with the Zionists. The heart of Jewish Orthodoxy was full of suspicion and fear for the worldliness of the institutions of autonomy and, therefore, was an uncertain partner of the Zionists in the struggle for autonomy.

Then, when Vilna was occupied by the Bolsheviks, and afterward by the Poles, the Lithuanian government moved to Kovno. It was proposed on the part of the government that the Jews and White Russians take positions in the national government. After deliberations, the Jews decided to occupy the post of Minister for Jewish Matters. The Zionists, at first, held that a minister would have to bear the responsibility for the work of the entire cabinet and would also have to change with every cabinet change. Therefore, they made a proposal of a State Secretary for Jewish Matters, who would carry the responsibility only for his work and would not be subject to any cabinet changes. However, in short, the Lithuanian government insisted on a minister, and this had to be accepted. Dr. M. Soloveitchik entered the government as Minister without Portfolio – for Jewish Matters, on the 2nd of June 1919.

Autonomy took on a public form with the creation of a Jewish Ministry. Thanks to the Jewish Ministry, the democratic *kehilus* [organized Jewish communities] then arose. In the beginning all of the Jewish parties participated in the communities. The left, and among them *Poalei-Zion*, later seceded from the *kehilus*. The left was not represented at the first *kehilus* convention that was called by the Jewish Ministry on the 5th of January, 1920.

A fight between the Zionists and organized Orthodoxy about the substance of autonomy flared up at this convention, with the question being whether it needed to be worldly and nationalist, or religious. In order to prevent the Orthodox from leaving the convention, a compromise was passed and the question about the essence of autonomy was removed from the agenda. A coalition was created of the Zionists and the Orthodox. On the question of the school system it was decided the autonomous administration would not interfere with the program of schools and the freedom of the three existing school movements (*Tarbus, Yavneh* and "Culture League") was recognized. A Jewish National Council was elected at the convention that was the highest democratic organ of organized Lithuanian Jewry.

The political achievements from the rise of the Jewish ministry to the election of the national council were as follows:

1) The insurance for Jews of the widest autonomy through the Lithuanian peace delegation in Paris in August 1919. The was supposed to be the Magna Carta of autonomy, and;

2) The law of the 10th of January, 1920, concerning the *kehilus*, that they have the right to institute a compulsory tax on members.

After the election of the national council, broad, varied activities began in every area of Jewish life. Democratic *kehilus* were organized; a wide network of Hebrew and Yiddish public schools and *gymnazies* [secondary schools] were created; the People's Banks and associations arose that were the economic nerve of the Jewish population. This era was the brightest and most hopeful. Lithuanian Jewry was seen then in its fullest splendor. An ebullient and pulsating Jewish life was sensed everywhere. All of the Jewish students studied in national Jewish schools. At that time, Lithuania was *Eretz-Yisroel* [Palestine] in miniature.

After the second *kehilus* conference that took place on the 14th of February, 1922, in which the leftist parties also took part, a crisis was sensed that was both external and internal. Externally, in the non-Jewish neighborhoods, reactionary sentiments were victorious. It is true that according to the Constitution, the Jewish *Seim* deputies controlled the carrying out of two principles concerning the rights of the national minorities: one principle assured the right of the national minorities to administer their national matters and a principle that the national minorities had the right to tax their members, as well as the right to receive a portion of the government budget for their cultural institutions. However, the Christian democratic majority in the *Seim* did not permit the passage of any laws that would legally strengthen the organs of Jewish autonomy. The mandate of the largest number of deputies of the national minorities was declared void through legal tricks. A. Frydman, whose only purpose was to disrupt everything that was created, was chosen as Minister of Jewish Matters against the will of the Jewish representatives.

Internally, the Orthodox began to sabotage and undermine the institutions of autonomy, arguing that they could not help to build up worldly organs of autonomy. The Orthodox members seceded from the national council and did not take part in the national meeting that was called on the 20th December, 1923, and was elected through general and direct voting.

The newly elected *Seim*, in which the national minority scored a great victory winning 14 delegates, restrained its reactionary character. The attack on the Jewish autonomy on the part of the dominating power was abandoned for a short time. Dr. Sh. Rozenboim was designated as the Minister for Jewish Matters. This was a political maneuver because of the then difficult external situation for Lithuania. The Memel question[1] was then being dealt with in the *felker-bund* [People's Socialist Labor Party] and at that moment no one wanted to disturb relations with the Jews. However, the earlier crisis over autonomy continued.

On the 20th of November, 1923, a Jewish national meeting was called in which the leftist groups took part, but not the Orthodox. The national meeting was the first and, unfortunately, also the last in Lithuania. After the national meeting, a continuous liquidation of autonomy began. The *Seim* rejected the budget for the Jewish Ministry and then the post of Jewish Minister, itself. A decree was issued that forbade writing in the languahes of the national minorities. Litigation was carried out against Dr. Sh. Rozenboim as to why he still called himself the "Jewish Minister." The National Council was dissolved. A law was passed about compulsory rest on Sundays along with a law that did away with the existing democratic Jewish *kehilus*.

In 1926, when the Lithuanian progressive democracy scored a victory in the elections to the Lithuanian *Seim* and formed the leftist government of National and Social Democrats, hope was revived that autonomy would be renewed. However, the government did not last long.

Thus ended the historic experiment of fulfilling national-personal autonomy in Lithuania. After the destruction of autonomy, Lithuania rolled downhill toward the anti-Semitic abyss and, under the leadership of Hitler's beasts, the Germans and the Lithuanians annihilated the entire Jewish population.

Translator's Footnote

1.As a result of the Treaty of Versailles, Memel and its surrounding territory were taken from Germany. Memel was incorporated into Lithuania as a separate autonomous region in 1924

[Page 66]

The Lithuanian Shtetl
by Y. Lestschinsky
Translated by Rae Meltzer

Yaacov Lestschinsky

The Lithuanian shtetl had poverty and need. An historian, Afonsiev, who described the economic life of the region in 1858 said the following:

The Jews live under very crowded conditions. Often several families live in one small room. Uncleanliness inside and outside is the sign of great poverty. Their financial resources are very small. In the morning they eat radishes, onions, garlic, or herring with bread. Those who are a little better off drink tea. Midday they may have soup, fish, or meat and in the evening the same menu. There are workers whose families fast all day until the family wage earner comes home and brings his earnings. (Written Kovno Gubernia (region), St. Petersburg, 1861 page 582.)

These dreadful descriptions are not an exaggeration and can be confirmed in the writing of the Hebrew writer Popernow, who wrote about the Lithuanian shtetl at the same time as the above quote. (Perezhitoya, Vol. II, page 39). The following is a quote from his writing:

The workers and merchants operated with 50 or 100 rubles, barely earning a bitter livelihood. Not finding any opportunity in the shtetl for their skills and professional training, many shtetl dwellers left for unknown places to try to find work. They left their families to the protection of God and to the soft hearts of their neighbors. They were laughed at in the Ukraine and called "Litvaks with their small stomachs" and taunted with the song, " Sunday potatoes, Monday potatoes," and so on.

Lithuanian Jews were very poor, but they did not make peace with their bitter fate and went out in the world to search for ways to earn a living. In the better-off Ukraine, one would meet Lithuanian Jews who were teachers and skilled workers. Lithuanian Jews went far afield to find a livelihood. We know about Litvisheh young people who left for South Africa as early as 1865 and opened the way for thousands of Litvisheh Jews. In the collected books "Budzhtzenost" (1900) we find a very interesting description of the first immigrants from Kovner gubernia. We quote from that source:

The first two Jews from Lithuania, to come to South Africa were two brothers, Shmuel and Elijah. Their family name was Max, from "Nyshtot" (New Town), Kovno Gubernia. Their father was a tailor in a little hamlet and extremely poor. The two boys decided to leave their birthplace and find someplace where they could earn a livelihood. They came to London, where for a time they were tailors, but they decided to look for a better livelihood. They came to London in 1865-66. A London Jew took pity on them and gave them a recommendation to a wholesale business and asked the wholesalers to give them merchandise on credit to be repaid later. They were peddlers, and in two years they learned to speak English well and pass as Englishmen. They heard from friends that in Africa one can make a good living. They went to Cape Town, South Africa, again without a penny. Here they suffered hunger and they did what they did in London, peddled and dragged merchandise on their backs from farm to farm. During this period diamond mines were discovered in Kimberley. Immigrants traveled to Kimberley and the brothers decided to go there. They bought shares in the diamond mine for a low price and soon earned several thousand dollars on their investment. The brothers began speculating with capital, and they made a big financial fortune. They wrote to their brother-in-law in London, whose name was Lewis, and founded the firm of Max and Lewis (or "Louy").

I do not know if this firm still exists. Perhaps in Johannesburg they are more informed about it than I am here in New York. I am interested in describing how Lithuanian Jews were and are still energetic in using their initiative to pursue opportunities. Lithuanian Jews continued to initiate immigration to other places. In the "Report of the Yiddisher" ("Sys" portion of the Second Lithuanian "Sys," 1923-1926) Kovno, 1926, page 63, it states that it is a solid fact that the economic condition of the Jews in Lithuania is much worse than before World War I. I cannot cite here all the data. It is compelling to note that the fearful urge to immigrate pulled entire families to such unknown and far-off lands as Paraguay and Uruguay.

As is well known, the Uruguay Jewish community (about 38,000 souls) is one of the best known, most active, and best organized. One can conclude from reading their newspapers that the leaders in the cultural activities of the community are the Jews from Lithuania. They can be proud of their well-organized, democratic community, and their good network of Yiddish schools. Most of the immigration from Lithuania was from the provinces, from the small shtetlach whose poverty was described in the references mentioned above. We will later document this with statistics.

Until the 1920's, the immigration did not carry a massive character, which is understandable. Not everyone can be as successful as the Max brothers described above. To immigrate one must have financial resources. In the Lithuanian shtetlach, one married young and had many children. In the census of 1897, for the Kovno region, the percentage of children under the age of nine was much higher among Jews than Christians. Especially in the provinces, those with children were very hesitant to immigrate when they had no relatives to go to. When the peasants were given their freedom in 1861, the situation in Russia and in the Kovno region improved somewhat, but there was still severe poverty.

Research carried out in the Lithuanian shtetlach in 1886 gives us important information about the dire situation of the Jews living there, and what a toiling mass of humanity they were. The research was done by the Kovno region committee under A. Dedelov. He writes:

The situation of the workers is a very tragic one. They work from 4-5 in the morning until 9-10 at night. And for all this toil they have only some dry bread and cramped living quarters. They can afford only a bit of meat on the Sabbath and eggs only on holidays, because the prices are very high (16-23¢ per lb.) Even on the Sabbath he can afford only a very limited amount, just barely one half pound for a family of seven souls. (" Atcheri Pa Vaproses Economishsheskoi Yovreiev (Jewish) Russia," S.P. Terburg, 1913, page 30.)

Jews of Rokiskis at the marketplace

The same author describes the dreadful situation of the Jewish horse and wagon drivers, and the Jewish peddlers in the Kovno region. The poor peddlers, who do not have an open stall in the market, go a mile or more from the shtetl, waiting for the peasants who are on their way to the market. They stop these peasants, barter with them, and buy their farm produce. Then they try to sell this farm produce to the families living in the shtetl. Their profit is a miserable 5-10%. That is why the hunger and poverty in their families is so great. They live in dirty and crowded rooms. They have no clothes, only rags on their bodies, and they live a lamentable life.

The situation of the small shop-keeper is not much better. The same author writes:

The life of the small shopkeeper is not one to be envied. He sits all day in the dirty and crowded shop, from dawn to dark, wearing old, worn clothes and searching with his weary eyes for customers.

Of course, there were one or two rich families and about 10 families who were middle-class merchants or owned a business, and made a living. But the majority of peddlers and small storekeepers lived in miserable poverty as described above by the quoted author.

A crisis occurred due either to a poor crop or a fallen market in exporting farm produce. Exports played a major role in the economy of the people and especially so in the livelihoods of the Jewish people who were dependent on trade. In these crises there was widespread hunger in the shtetlach and in the small hamlets where the Jewish people lived. All suffered from hunger. The Russian government took care of the Russian peasants, but did nothing for the starving Jewish people; they were left without resources and had to find a way to take care of themselves. Everything was disorganized.

The catastrophic year of starvation occurred in 1880. In many Jewish communities in the cities and shtetlach the starving Jewish masses, being desperate, accused the community leaders and merchants of causing the widespread hunger. There was a report in the "Voschod" in the year 1880 on pages 1048-1059 by A. Margolis that in the shtetl of Koidanov in Kovno region:

There was a dreadful hunger. The poor class gathered in a sizable mass near the synagogue and attacked those who owned the export businesses. All day and late into the night the starving people roamed the streets, breaking windows and screaming that they will break the bones of the wealthy if they will not take care of their families and prevent their death from starvation." (A. Margolis, Yiddisher Folk Masses in their Struggle Against their Oppressors, Moscow, 1940, p.86.)

The Intensive Growth of the Jewish People in the Shtetlach

In spite of the bitter situation of the Jewish people in the shtetlach in the Kovno region, the Jewish population grew significantly. This was due to several factors. The economic situation of some groups of the Jewish population did improve in the latter half of the 1900's. Germany, the closest neighbor to Kovno, became increasingly industrialized and needed more agricultural produce. The exports from the Kovno region grew. After the peasants gained their freedom, their situation improved. The people in the countryside began to buy more goods from the city and shtetlach. In the shtetl, the shopkeeper's economic situation improved and he was able to hire salespersons and other helpers. A class of skilled craftsmen developed and they employed and trained others. In some of the shtetlach, craft industries developed.

The extended Davidovitch(itz) family in Rokiskis
[no individual names appear]

The growth of the cultural life of the Jewish community had an influence on the shtetl. The Jewish people of the shtetl rubbed their eyes – they came awake, longing for a better life, a richer cultural life, and more freedom. They began receiving letters from America and South Africa with funds and with information about living conditions there. American newspapers managed to get by the censors and were read avidly. People in " Kasrilevke" (shtetlach) began to stir away from the traditional nest and started looking for their luck in the big cities of Russia and in the distant lands across the oceans.

All these developments led to a major decrease in deaths in the Jewish population. The Jewish birthrate was still quite high until World War I. The death rate dropped significantly in the last quarter of the 1800's. The Jewish population in the big cities grew impressively.

A comparison of the Jewish population in several shtetlach, for which there is data for the year 1847 and 1897 demonstrates the remarkable growth of the Jewish population.

Shtetl	1847	1897 (%)	1897 (number)
Zarasai (Novo-Alexsandrovsk)	453	53.0%	3,348
Vidukla (Widzheh)	2,281	68.2%	3,480
Aniksht	1,556	69.7%	2,754
Rakishok	593	75.7%	2,067
Skopishok	282	85.3%	1,010
Dusiat	486	89.0%	1,158
Kamai	453	85.4%	944
TOTAL	6,104		14,761

The Jewish population in the Kovno region more than doubled. No doubt this is related to the intensive industrialization of the region during the last quarter of the 1800's. Under the reign of King Alexander III, who was crowned in 1881, persecution of the Jews in the hamlets (dorf) increased, which forced the Jews to stream to the shtetlach and larger cities. In some shtetlach the growth of the Jewish population was notably high. In Zarasai (Novo-Alexandrovsk) the Jewish population increased seven-fold, in Rakishok three-fold, and in Dusiat more than two-fold.

To consider the total Jewish population of the aforementioned shtetlach, one cannot arrive at a firm number because no data exists on the total Jewish population in these shtetlach before the Holocaust. One can arrive only at an indirect total. In 1937, under the auspices of the Yiddish Folk Bank, a census was taken of the Jewish workers. This census was authentic and truthful. We know that the Jewish workers made up about 35% of all Jews engaged in earning a living. We know that Jewish wage-earners were 33% of the total wage-earners in Lithuania. The situation in the following shtetlach is typical of the other shtetlach in Lithuania.

The Number of Jewish Workers in the Following Shtetlach of Lithuania (The Jewish Handicraft Workers in Lithuania, 1937, Kaunus, 1938)

Shtetl	Number of Workers
Zarasai	82
Vidukla	15
Aniksht	133
Rakishok	101
Skopishok	6
Dusiat	32
Kamai	12
TOTAL	414

Based on the data that one-third of the Jewish population consisted of workers, we arrive at a total population for the previously referred to seven shtetlach of 3,700 souls in 1937. This is one-quarter of the Jewish population in these seven shtetlach in 1897 The data indicates that in 1938 there were 123,000 Jews in Kovner gubernia (region) and more than 212,000 Jews according to census of the Kovner region in 1897. This means that in 1897, Jews were 60% of the total population. In the larger cities, like Kovno, Shavli, and Ponevezh, the Jewish population grew slightly. Where did the Jews in these three largest cities come from? They apparently came from the shtetlach of Kovno gubernia, which lost considerable numbers of Jews. The consequence of this was that there were no longer shtetlach with 75% - 90% Jewish populations. Thus the Yiddish culture that developed in the shtetlach could not be sustained once the demographics of the shtetl changed. Nevertheless, the longing and nostalgia for the shtetl did not diminish because the foundation of the Yiddish lifestyle and culture was the shtetl.

The Lithuanian culture was not as rich or as developed as the Yiddish culture, and did not pull the Jews to assimilate, but the economic and political activity of Lithuania did attract the Jewish population. Perhaps sensing from the discrimination of the majority toward the Jewish minority that they could not expect a promising future in Lithuania, Jews began to emigrate not only to America and South Africa, but also to Israel. No Jewish community sent more " chalutzim" and Hebrew-speakers to Israel than the small Yiddish community of Lithuania.

The Change in the Demographics of the Yiddish Shtetl in Lithuania

There is no doubt that in the last quarter of the 1800's and in the first 14 years of the 1900's, the economic conditions of the Jews in Russia and in the shtetlach of the Kovner region did improve. Generally, the economic conditions in Russia at that time became better, with periodic economic crises and even years of hunger, but the over-all situation had improved. In spite of this, the Jewish emigration from Russia increased. From the Kovner region, between 1897 and 1917, 56,000 souls left the country. The Jewish population naturally increased by 70,000 souls. The net result was that there was hardly any increase in the total Jewish population. The major population increase was in the larger cities, not in the shtetlach.

In 1898, Kovno's Jewish community grew by 8,662 families, which represented 22.9% of the total Jewish population. This was a larger percentage than in neighboring Grodno and Vitebsk, but smaller than in the Vilna region.

One must acknowledge that the concept of "poor man, beggar, pauper" changes with time and circumstances. The poor man of Nicholas I's time was very different from the pauper of the period of the last Nicholas. The concept of "poor man" changed radically. The poor man at the end of the 1800's and the beginning of the 1900's had very little patience and was not very inclined to suffer hunger in silence. He was impudent and bold and demanded help. The days of Linetzki when "a Jew had to eat, but not gorge himself on food," and Mendele's "olive-sized stomach" which was supposed to feed only the soul and not the body – those days were vanishing. Perhaps the strong impetus to emigrate was in part the result of growing appetites for better living conditions. Those who emigrated were often those with energy and initiative. Those who emigrated were not even the poorest, nor the very richest, but those who had a little money and yearned for a life that was a little better than what they had; a life that offered some possibilities and opportunities. Those left behind were the weaker, the poorer, the submissive ones.

The Jewish population fell during the WWI years. According to the data from the Yiddish Statistical Society, 69,000 Jews were expelled from the Kovno region. During WWI the death rate among Jews was high. This, together with the movement of Jews from the Shtetlach to the bigger cities, accounted for the large decline of the Jewish population in the shtetlach. In the 1930's, most of the Jewish youth left the shtetlach, and the percentage of old people in the shtetlach was greater than in the cities. In the 1930's, the Lithuanian Jewish youth were convinced they had no future in Lithuania, and immigration was their only option and hope. The large number of marriages in the shtetlach reflects the reality that a couple could go to Israel on one certificate.

In Rakishok district between 1934-1936, there were 182 births and 155 deaths; i.e., 27 more births than deaths. In the years 1937-39, there were 175 births and 184 deaths, or nine more deaths than births. In the shtetlach, the percent of older people continued to increase.

The Tragic Situation of the Jews in Lithuania – Especially in the Provinces

Evaluating the economic development of the independent Lithuania and the condition of the Jewish population, it is evident without a doubt that Lithuania prospered economically. Its industry increased as did crafts and skilled workers. The Jewish people also gained from this economic growth in the overall economy of Lithuania. But almost from the beginning it became clear that the Jews would be allowed in just so far and no further to the economic " table." The economic and political powers which would allow Jewish access only to the older generation with whom they had practical ties were useful for the Lithuanian majority, and they considered it to be to their advantage to use the superior skills and knowledge of the older Jews for the benefit of the general Lithuanian population. The Jewish youth felt and knew that for them there was no future and no opportunities in Lithuania and therefore they had to emigrate and leave Lithuania.

After WWI, the Jewish refugees wandered back to their hometowns to find chaos and destruction. Nothing was left of their houses or belongings. They had to start over from scratch. The workplaces and shops had been plundered. The Russian money was worthless. The refugees were helped by Jewish relief organizations. In 1923, the refugees in Kovno found themselves in a dreadful situation. They were waiting for the relief organizations to resettle them someplace. They were waiting in barracks where conditions were very unsanitary and the food was horrible. More refugees streamed to the barracks, almost naked and starving. Those who returned to the shtetlach found only devastation. They were starved and feeble and sick. There was no place or medicine to help the sick. Many of the diseases spread among the refugees, and the death rate rose. Epidemics were spreading over the land, especially the dreaded typhus.

Members of the Rakoshker Town Administration with the mayor: Malewitz

After WWI, there was desperate irony, tragedy, and great suffering for the Jews of Lithuania. They had played a significant role in the struggle of Lithuania for its independence. The contribution of the Jewish people to Lithuania's struggle for independence was recognized by the political leaders of Lithuania. This gave the Jews some reason for hope, inasmuch as the Jews had helped Lithuania achieve nationhood, they hoped for justice and equality from the new nation. At the very least they expected that Lithuania would treat the Jews humanely. But the facts proved otherwise. A report by the Jewish section of the second Lithuanian legislature [Sym?] relates the following events of a " blood libel":

The first "blood libel" broke out in the shtetl of Ponidel in 1932. This shtetl was in the Rakishok circle. A Lithuanian shopkeeper planned and initiated the libel. The shopkeeper was a woman who had converted to Christianity from Judaism and married a Lithuanian who was a former petty official. The one accused was the father of the convert. The libel was spread just before the market fair was about to begin; thus the libel spread quickly to a wide circle of the peasant population. The shtetl experienced some very tense, difficult days. The police, fearful of the instigators of the libel, remained aloof and passive.

Thanks to the swift intervention of the Jewish faction of the Legislature (Sym) the central government prevented any excesses. Another entry in the report referred to previously:

In 1924 there were "blood libels" in Mariampol, Shantz, Linkova, and Ayranoleh. In the last two shtetlach, the witnesses upon whom the accusers relied were two young Jewish girls, aged seven and eight. The girls were students in a Lithuanian school and were brought as witness by the instigators of the libel who were the girls' teachers in the Lithuanian school. In both situations, it was the Lithuanian intelligentsia of the small towns that sounded the alarm and protested the libel.

The intervention averted a pogrom on the Jewish population. The Lithuanian intelligentsia of the larger cities were more practical than the peasants in the small towns. The Lithuanians living in the larger cities did not make accusations of blood libels nor commit hurtful acts.

There is an entry in the same report as follows:

In September and October, 1923, Kovno will memorialize the attack on Jewish youth passing through the town by 'chauvinistic' Lithuanian youth, who also defaced synagogues and other Jewish institutions." Further, it is reported that about 20 Jews were wounded, and "on Yom Kippur eve in one of Kovno's synagogues, 25 windows were broken.

Further quotes from the Jewish Section of the Second Lithuanian Legislature (Sym):

The Lithuanian Jews held in their hands the economy, and as the Lithuanians began to move from peasantry to urbanization, they became resentful of the Jews who were already there in positions they coveted. The Lithuanian government used all its power to favor the new merchant class and to discriminate against the Jewish merchant.

The Lithuanian government wanted to wrest commerce from the Jewish entrepreneurs, and also their livelihoods. The government gave million-dollar subsidies to non--Jewish cooperatives, passed laws that made it mandatory for merchants to keep their books in Lithuanian, passed laws that all exams for skilled work must be in Lithuanian, raised taxes on Jews, and held trade fairs and markets on the Sabbath. Thus they weakened and wounded the Jewish community, not just from year to year, but actually from day to day.

The condition and situation of the Jews became ever more tragic. The Jews of the provinces and shtetlach suffered greatly; they felt helpless and hopeless. With the invasion of Hitler and his armies, they felt squeezed, threatened, and faced open brutality and death.

In Lestschinsky's book on the Jews of Lithuania he documents how Jewish people tried to defend themselves and diminish the severity of the economic blows coming from the government and from the organized Lithuanian economic organizations. The gentile enterprises and economy were heavily subsidized from the government treasury, which received a substantial portion from taxes on the Jews.

As far as is known at the time of this writing, the archival material of the Holocaust has not been opened by the government of Lithuania. The archives will not document all attacks of terror because the censor did not report these events. The terror among Lithuanian Jews must have been very great before the onslaught of the Holocaust. The majority of Lithuanians were active participants in the murderous rampages that were organized by the Germans.

The following episodes were reported in the Jewish press ("Folks-Blatt"). Sometimes the news report did not appear until later because it did not become known until the Jewish community intervened with the central government.

1) October 10, 1935: In connection with the attacks on Jews, two Jewish representatives, one of them a member of the Legislature, Mr. Itzkovitsh, and his associate, Mr. Shapira, went to the director of the Interior Department who promised to take strong measures against these actions.

2) December 19, 1935: In the shtetlach Karsh and Varneh, near Telz, there was an anti-Semitic attack by the peasants from the surrounding area. Thirty-three Jews were wounded and one Jew was seriously wounded.

3) January 11, 1936: One of the victims of the pogrom in Varneh on 12/19/35 died. The Jews in the entire region are terrified. Those who led the pogrom are fomenting a wild hatred against the Jewish community.

4) January 16, 1936: A reader of "Paris Today" (a Lithuanian Jew), received a heart-rending letter from the shtetl Varneh where bloody onslaughts upon the Jews of Varneh wounded 30 Jews. The pogrom is described in the letter as follows:

I wrote you this letter a week ago, but could not mail it because of the great unrest here. I write you in the name of all our associates – perhaps something can be done to help us? We are today at the very edge of our reason. We are attacked in the streets and we cannot do anything. The trade fair turned into a battlefield. There were 36 Jews who were wounded. They came from shtetlach around Telz. You know that Jews come to the trade fair to earn a bit of their livelihood. Instead, one got clobbered on his head, and another had his hand broken. Those who were hurt and wounded are in an extremely difficult situation. All the wounded were taken to the hospital. One of the wounded already died. For the past week all the shops have been closed and their doors bolted. People are hungry, but everyone is afraid to go out on the street to shop. Everyone is afraid of these hooligans. Thus, we are in a life-threatening situation, just as if we were in Germany. The police are afraid and no one seems able to calm and control these hooligans who are reigning over us.

5) March 20, 1936: A personal letter received describes the following situation. When the market day ended, some agitators stirred up a drunken rowdy crowd and brought them to the "apteka" (drugstore) of Zelig Rapaport. The agitators convinced this drunken crowd that the body of Veronika Pishvaishkyny is hidden in the apteka and that the Jews killed her. They tore into the apteka and proceeded to ransack and search everywhere. Of course they did not find the corpse. During the search inside the apteka, bricks and stones were hurled from outside and shattered the windows of the "Apteka," as well as the windows of the house next door which belonged to Mr. Soloveichik. The police chased the drunken rabble away and there is supposed to be an inquiry of the guilty ones. We received a report that the apteka and several Jewish houses were demolished.

6) July 22, 1936: The resident of Ausdkalner village, Kretiner Wolost Trokim came to the market on the 16th of July, with his 16-year-old daughter Mariana The girl wandered off somewhere and did not return. Immediately, rumors spread in town that Jews had kidnapped the girl. Irresponsible elements started to foment violence by shouting, " Let's beat up the Jews!" In the evening of July 18, 1936, two gentiles wanted to beat up Jews. They were arrested. Before the arrest, these two hooligans managed to slug a Jew in the face and destroy another's clothes and break 10 windows in Jewish homes. We brought all the latest information to the authorities, but they did not consider the victims important or significant.

The author of these lines. lived through the fear and dread and the heart-stopping fearfulness of the time just before a pogrom was beginning. At any moment one would expect a hard blow on the head. Anyone who has lived through a pogrom, or even the expectation of a pogrom, knows that Jews suffer with their blood and their nerves which are shaken and ruined.

All the pogroms were the prologue to the hate-filled atmosphere that was rising and, in 1939, took on its vengeful, wretched, deadly form. All the subsequent data points to the fact that the enemies of the Jewish people were prepared for mass-murder. Hitler's murderers knew the plan. The Nazis depended on the strength of the Lithuanians who showed from the very beginning that they would take the initiative. When Hitler attacked Russia, they started to murder Jews. The Lithuanians did not wait for the official German commands; they quickly started to murder Jews.

The Occupations of Jewish Workers in the Provincial Shtetlach of Lithuania

In 1937, the Folks-Bank, sponsored a census of all Jewish workers in each of the shtetlach in the Rakishok region. The names of the Jewish correspondents who conducted the census is shown below for each shtetl.

Abel	Tuvi Sher
Autian (Utian)	H. Yoffe
Azshpol	Fraulein Z. Lauffer
Antolept	Frau Sh. Levin-Gershtein
Anikshet	H. Konoich
Anusishok	I. Baranov
Dusiat	D. Shwartz
Wabalnik	G. Stolyer
Wizshun	G. Pipinsky
Widukleh (Widzeh)	Isaac Beker
Widishkis	Chloine Weiner and Honech Pehter
Zarasai (Novo-Alex.)	A. Shtejn
Taragin	F. Aidelman
Salak	I.L. Dovidovitsh
Sviadashits	H. Shachnovitsh
Skopishok	M. Weitz
Ponidel	I. Wengrin
Ponemunok	Frau Lodon-Gerjng
Panemunelis	Fraulein B. Yoffe
Kupishok	Z. Kovensky
Kamai (Comay)	Chaim Anulnik
Rakishok	H. Bosman

Trades and Professional Structure of Workers in a Group of Lithuanian Shtetlach - 1937

	Total	Misc	Watch-Maker	Carpenter	Lock/Tin/Black	Baker	Butcher	Shoe	Tailor/Modiste
Abel	17	5	–	–	–	1	4	3	4
Autian	150	376	5	10	17	13	18	31	19
Azshpol	22	6	–	1	1	4	4	–	6
Antolept	16	1	–	3	4	–	5	1	2
Aniksht	166	74	4	1	9	11	9	42	16
Anusishok	14	1	–	–	–	2	2	4	5
Dusion	32	7	–	–	4	2	6	5	8
Wabalnik	16	3	1	–	2	2	2	3	3
Wizshun	11	–	–	–	–	–	5	1	5
Widukleh	15	8	–	–	–	2	2	–	3
Widishkis	11	–	–	–	–	–	1	–	–
Zarasai	82	16	3	–	8	6	11	12	25
Taragin	23	15	–	1	–	1	2	–	5
Salak	56	10	1	4	7	1	6	13	14
Sviadashits	15	1	–	–	2	1	5	3	3
Skopishok	6	1	–	–	–	–	1	1	3
Ponidel	31	3	–	–	4	1	9	8	6
Ponemunok	2	–	–	–	–	–	2	–	–
Panemunelis	2	–	–	–	–	–	2	–	–
Kupishok	22	11	–	–	3	1	–	5	2
Kamai	12	2	–	–	–	1	3	4	2
Rakishok	101	15	2	1	7	3	24	33	16
TOTAL	812	216	16	21	68	52	123	169	147

Summary of Above Table

Tailors and shoemakers make up almost half of all workers. If we add butchers, we find that those three occupations make up more than half of all Jewish workers. The metal and iron-skilled trades make up only 8% of all workers. These latter are allied to industrial work. The Jewish working population of Rakishok was 101, of which 73 were employed in the following occupations: tailors and seamstresses, 16; butcher, 24. The shtetl of Aution had a more unusual distribution. It had a Jewish working population of 150, of which 68 were employed as tailors, shoemakers, and butchers. They had 17 workers in the iron and metal trades, which was a very high number for the size of the population of Jewish workers. None of the other shtetlach listed in the above chart came anywhere near that number. The closest was Aniksht with nine – just half the number.

[Page 85]

Reminiscences

Rakishok – A Reflection
Chief Rabbi Prof. I. Abrahams
Translated by Rabbi Ezra Boyarsky

Hon. Prof. Israel Abrahams
[Chief Rabbi of Cape Town]

I was born in Vilna, known throughout the Jewish world as Yerushalayim D'Lita – the Jerusalem of Lithuania – due to the fact that Vilna was the cultural and intellectual center of Lithuanian Jewry. My mother of blessed memory was also born in Vilna, but my father of blessed memory was a full-blooded, thoroughbred, Rakishok native. Reb Zecharya Alter, as he was called, and his father, Reb Avroham, and his uncle, Rabbi Katz, the official Rov (spiritual leader) all hailed from Rakishok. This makes me at least a partial landsman of Rakishok. I feel extremely proud of my family connections and through them with the small Lithuanian shtetl, Rakishok, as though I had actually been born there.

Still, you might well ask, why do you feel such an extra special closeness to this town? Firstly, I must admit that I don't recall anything from "der alter heim" (the old country) – neither from Vilna nor from Rakishok. I was only three when my parents with their only son (that's me), left Russia because of the political disturbances and settled in England. A three-year-old can hardly remember anything except stories his parents related to him which consisted for the most part of nostalgic reminiscences and home-spun tales that suffused a flavor that was uniquely characteristic of Jewish life in Lithuania.

It was these stories that fired my imagination, penetrated deeply into my consciousness, and fleshed out events from long ago, as if I had been an eyewitness to them. For example, I was told that when I was only three I told my grandfather with great excitement on the first day of Pesach that I had already dipped twice (at the seder we dip twice, once celery in salt water and a second time moror, bitter herbs in charoses, a mixture of apples, nuts, and almonds, moistened with wine). When my Stroger grandfather asked me, "What did you dip it in?" I proudly responded, "Matzah in chicken soup!" My grandfather smiled and lovingly pinched Yisroel's cheek ... (again, that's me).

I recall a host of such stories, but my unbounded love for Rakishok is not based on these tales. My real pride and admiration is for the tiny Lithuanian "shtetele proper." I actually knew Rakishok and shall never forget her. Once again, you may ask: "How is that possible? You don't remember anything and yet you claim to have intimate knowledge of her. "Yes, my dear friends, this is indeed a riddle and a mystery. And the purpose of my brief article is to uncover the mystery.

My entire youth, from tender childhood till the time I became Rabbi, I was raised in a home that was saturated with traditional Judaism – in an atmosphere that was a veritable carbon copy of Rakishok. The moment one crossed the threshold of our home in London, the capital of the British Empire, one was instantly transported to an entirely different world, to the Jewish East European world, the spiritual repository of the Jewish heart and soul. In my parents' home was reflected, in all its nuances, the life of Rakishok that they had left behind, but only in a physical sense. We spoke Yiddish only, and if perchance an English word slipped through inadvertently, it was "Yiddishized" to such a degree that it was impossible to identify its origin.

Besides the exclusive use of Yiddish, all other aspects of life carried a distinct Rakishok character. The Sabbath Queen occupied center stage and reigned in regal splendor in our home for a full twenty-four hours, from sundown to sundown. The taste of tsholent (a Sabbath dish of meat, potatoes, and vegetables) and the special festival meals that my mother prepared still linger in my mouth. Nor will I ever forget our bookcase that contained all the major Judaic literature: the Talmud, the Shulchan Aruch (the Book of Jewish Codes), the Chabad Tanya and Midrashim. Even conversations on ordinary subjects were laced with Biblical references and scholarly Talmudic discussions.

Judging by material standards, we were admittedly poor, but on a scale of yiras shomayim (piety) and Torah scholarship, my parents were considered wealthy. For the type of person of my father's provincial background who was versed in the various branches of Hasidism and Cabalah (a Jewish mystical philosophy), the problem of earning a living in England posed an insurmountable challenge. My parents had little concern for their own welfare, but for their son's future they had very ambitious plans. In order for their dreams to come true, no sacrifice was too great to have him study in a yeshiva, later in a university, and finally in a rabbinical college where he received smicha--rabbinical ordination. To fully appreciate my parents' joy on this auspicious occasion, one had to be a Rakishoker oneself.

I recall the letter that I received from Rabbi Katz, my great uncle, at the time of my ordination. I also remember the last letter I received from him here in Cape Town. At that time he was over ninety. Shortly after, he passed away and was spared the unspeakable suffering and cruelties perpetuated against our people at the hands of the eternally cursed Nazi beasts. Not long after his demise, his flock which he tended with loving care for so many years, died a martyr's death along with six million of our sainted brothers and sisters during the Holocaust, by far the worst national catastrophe that has befallen the Jewish people in its two thousand year Disasporan existence. Thus ended in fire, blood, and tears the one thousand year chapter of East European Jewry, one of the most fruitful and productive in Jewish history.

Alas, our beloved shtetl is no more, and now belongs to the centuries, but the sweet memories of her will linger on in the hearts and minds of the Rakishker surviving landsleit wherever they may be. Yes, she surely will be remembered as long as the Jewish people do not forget the role the artless Lithuanian small towns played in shaping the collective personality of Eastern European Jewry.

Sisters and Brothers, cherish this Yizkor Book, published by the Rakishker Landsmanshaft, which serves as an everlasting memorial for those who have passed on, but at the same time creates a linkage between them and future generations. And let the world know that Lo Nutcka Hashal shelet – that the chain of Jewish tradition remains unbroken and is ever strong.

The Bet-Sefer "Yavneh" in Rokiskis
[Hebrew Primary School]

[Pages 88-91]

Childhood Joys
by Rachmiel Feldman
Translated by Ken Frieden

Rachmiel Feldman

Rachmiel (Richard) Feldman was born in Skopishok (Skapiskis) in 1897 and, as a young child, moved to Rokiskis. Arrived in Johannesburg in 1910. Attended the Jewish Government School. From 1912-1924 he was active in the South African Assistance Fund for those injured in the war. Together with M. A. Pinkus, he founded the Poalei-Zion (Jewish Socialist Society, later called the Labor Zionist Organization). Visited the Land of Israel in 1924 and in 1928 he visited the Soviet Union as chairman of the South African colonization fund in support of the Yiddish colonization movement in the Ukraine and Crimea.

His activity in the Poalei-Zion movement brought him closer to Yiddish. He gave speeches and wrote articles and stories. In 1935 he published Shvarts und vays (Black and White), a book of stories about South Africa, and in 1945 he published Troyers (Mourners).

He was active in the Jewish Literary Union and helped found the South African Yiddish Cultural Federation.

After 1939 he participated actively in the local political life as a member of the South African Labour Party; after 1943 he represented the Workers' Party in the Transvaal Provincial Council. He contributed diverse articles to English press in South Africa.

[R.Feldman died in 1968.]

There are people who remember well their youthful years, remember their childhood and their experiences, remember the adults and the friends with whom they studied and played.

I'm not one of those "rememberers." My memories of childhood are few in number and foggy.

Perhaps that is because the new way of life in Johannesberg very quickly eclipsed the experiences in Rokiskis; and also because the new homeland accepted me so maternally and warmly, and the transition was painless and without longing.

"Independence Place" in the town square

When a tree is transplanted, its success depends on how young the tree is, how deep its roots have grown, and the quality of the soil into which it is transplanted.

My roots in Lithuanian soil were not deep.

When I was 10 years old, the conflict arose between the cheder, the Jewish school, and the Russian school. It was a mixture of languages—Yiddish at home and in the street, Hebrew in the Jewish school and on the printed page, Russian among the intelligentsia, and Lithuanian at the marketplace and in the village.

As a boy I saw no farther than the shtetl and practical matters. One did not yet think about what one would want to see and what one would want to do.

And yet, and yet, sparks flicker in my memory and light up my childhood years in Rokiskis.

For a long time I have yearned for the joy of the four seasons in Lithuania, with the pleasures of summer and winter, spring and fall. And in general, I have longed for the cornfields that were near our cheder—Moshe of Meshtzansk's cheder—and for the forests that surrounded Rokiskis.

My first written works in English were stimulated by yearning for the Lithuanian fields and forests and for the snow-white winters.

Until this day, when I see large green apples, I recall the early mornings in the late summer in the courtyard of Zalman Nahman, where they would pack apples into crates for export. The smell of the apples woke us up before sunrise, and Zalman Nahman would joke with us about getting out of bed so early.

Even while eating a large, juicy plum, I recall how we used to steal plums from peasant orchards—and how we just barely escaped with our lives and ran away from an angry peasant who was chasing us.

The smell of milk that has been freshly milked is the same everywhere, but in me it always calls forth memories of the Count's courtyard (*dem grafs hoyf*), where we used to go in the summer to get milk that had just been milked. It was a kind of journey to a land of Lords and palaces.

A small selection of flowers and plants grew in and around Rokiskis. In Johannesburg the number of different flowers is vast; and yet to this day I feel closer to the daisy, the nasturtium, and the blue cornflowers than to the beautiful rose, the splendid gladiola, and the exotic strelitzia.

In Swaziland, when I see black children bathing in a stream, and I hear their joyous cries, I recall the joy of bathing in the small "Prudel ." At that time it was an uncommon delight for me, and I was satisfied only after running a few times into it and around the meadow that bordered on the small "Prudel"—in which I once almost drowned.

And when I see a lantern, it recalls the winter nights in the cheder, and the joy of coming home with my own lantern, which rivaled the brightness of the moon and the snowy surroundings.

The joy of the holidays in Rokiskis is unforgettable.

The new year would start on Passover, not on Rosh Hashana, because then the world would be filled with brightness and warmth. By Passover the mud had almost dried, and the trees would clothe themselves again in green.

Who can measure the excitement of the day when our matzah was baked in "Pardiad"—cutting the dough, making punctures in the matzahs, and then the procession home from "Pardiad" with the matzahs.

And that's how it was every holiday, each with its special joy. My holiday would be a bit disturbed because I was the third of three boys in the family, and I always received an older brother's handed-down suit of clothes instead of a new one.

The only gloomy and difficult days I remember are the most tragic—the days when we expected a pogrom in Rokiskis.

There were widespread rumors of pogroms in neighboring towns, and when the "news" arrived that pogromniks were very near and could be expected the next day in Rokiskis, mother decided to leave the shtetl. But where could we go?

For the time being, mother decided to go to the depot—at least we could be near a train station.

There were no carriages to hire. It was as if everything in the shtetl had died out.

For an entire evening we packed, and everyone had prepared a package of the most necessary things.

Very early we went on our way. We didn't go by the main road, because there we could have met the pogromniks. Hence we walked on side streets and through fields. I remember that the path was slippery, and it stretched out endlessly before us.

Zalman Mote Ber's, the father of my aunt Malka Feldman, who lived at the depot, received us in a friendly manner, and in his house we felt safer.

Late at night a storm-wind blew on a broken shutter, and it knocked so strangely and restlessly that we thought that the pogromniks had already arrived.

That time we came through with just a scare. But years later, under Hitler's rule, the Germans—with the help of Lithuanian hooligans—carried out the pogrom that annihilated the Jews of Rokiskis and of all Lithuania.

* * *

Today I see a Rokiskis where every stone and bit of earth in the shtetl is wet with Jewish blood, and one wants to curse the fields that soaked up the blood of our murdered brothers and sisters.

And yet, and yet one remembers the childhood joys, because it is a part of us and of our past.

A picturesque view of a Rokiskis scene, with the Count's dwelling in the background

[Pages 92-98]

My Father's Nigun (Melody)
by Shlomo Rubin
Translated by Kenneth B. Frieden

Many episodes and images have remained in my memory from my childhood years in Rakishok. They become especially vivid now, when I must publish them for my fellow *landslayt* from Rakishok.

My father, Aharon Nathan, was neither a cantor nor a musician, but now and then he would lead the afternoon or evening prayers from the bimah. He had no higher aspirations, because he had no education beyond the *heder*, and at a very young age he had to hitch himself up to the wagon of life.

Yiddish literature was still in its infancy, and seldom did a literary work from the wide world reach us in the shtetl. For this reason, it may be that my father's only reading was Psalms.

I remember how my father used to get up very early, in the winter nights, and boil the little samovar that held 12 cups of water. He would drink tea and read the Psalms with such a touching melody that engraved itself deep inside me.

Regardless of the fact that early-morning sleep was always so sweet and pleasant to me, my father's melody awakened me, and I wanted my father to stretch out his melody into the late morning.

It is too bad that, in those times, there were no collectors of musical folklore in the shtetl. They would have immortalized my father's Psalms melody, and it would have enriched our folk music.

He sang Shabbat songs with the same feeling and abandon—melodies, which I later heard in many homes. To this day it is a mystery to me: where did my father inherit all of these melodies and musical prayer-motifs? I believe that, in other circumstances, he would have been a distinctive Jewish musician.

Good Qualities or Pride

My father was a needy person and always went around looking for acts of kindness. Still, when someone else came to borrow from him, he didn't refuse anyone, and he was willing to go around half of the shtetl to get a loan for another person.

My mother used to reproach him because of this behavior, saying that he did it out of pride or arrogance. My father did not accept her complaints, because he argued that it was better that people looked at him as a rich man than as a pauper—because if they considered him a pauper, it would no longer be possible for him to continue his small fish trade.

Aaron Nissen Rubin
[The socialist fish salesman – he kept good fish for the poor and gave bad fish to the rich – A. Jermyn]

My Father—a Socialist

Friday evening my father had dealings with rich and poor women, who would come to him to buy fish. In these sales he showed his socialist sense of justice.

If a rich woman came to his fish cart to buy the very best carp or pike for Shabbat, he took it out of her hands and placed it under the straw mat, saying that it had already been bought. He would put aside the better fish for poorer women. If he didn't have anyone who wanted the better fish among the poorer buyers, he brought the fish home and would resentfully tell mother about how the well-off women had real nerve: they wanted to buy the best fish. His argument was that poor people also have to eat good fish.

He often engaged in such socialist dealings, also in connection with the young progressive movement that had started among us in the shtetl in 1905.

I remember how, in 1905, a young man was arrested for progressive, revolutionary activity. He came to Rakishok from another city. My father did everything possible to get him out of the policeman's hands. A similar case occurred with a Jewish student, for whom the police were searching in the shtetl in order to arrest him. He was accused of being a revolutionary. The student hid that night at Leah the Tailor's workshop and I disguised him with a beard. My father got a wagon and secretly sent him out of the shtetl in the depths of the night.

My Father's Tears

Every one of us from the earlier generation knows how a synagogue in a small Jewish shtetl looked during the prayers for the Days of Awe. The piety and awe before the Master of the Universe was unimaginable. During prayers, the sighs and groans, tears and cries before the Master of the Universe, resounded in the synagogue—before the God of Judgment. From the women's section we heard crying from every tone and octave.

But it seems to me that no one cried like my father. One felt that it was torn from the deepest cells in his heart—the pain that had collected in him during an entire year. As after a big storm, the lament and bitterness burst out of him, overflowing the boundaries of his "I." He would break into such a strong gush of tears that my pen is incapable of describing it. The cantor would interrupt his devout outcries for a while and wait until my father calmed down, just as he would wait during prayers while the rabbi or another respectable person continued the Standing Benediction.

Until today, I wonder where my father acquired such strong religiosity and fear of God. He wasn't one to put on a big show of piety. His behavior was secular: he cut his beard short and never went to a religious study session. He didn't even know the meaning of the Hebrew prayers. In order to understand the meaning, he would have to look at the Yiddish translation of a Torah, a Tanakh, or a prayer book. His belief and awe before the Throne of Glory was, presumably, deeply engraved in his heart.

The Slap

I delivered the first and last slap of my life in my youth. This happened because of the following event.

In 1912-13, a teacher came to our town Rakishok. I don't recall his name. It seems to me that later he became a well-known poet. In Rakishok this teacher was already writing poems, which he used to read aloud to us. Incidentally, I hardly understood the meaning of his writings. Still, he assured us that these were poetic creations that would someday be published.

Thanks to his initiative and the assistance of Shmuel Leyb Matizon, the teacher Yosl Stein, Khonen Meler, and yours truly, a library was created in the shtetl—which at the time was illegal. The library was located in a side street, in an attic room, and young boys and girls zealously read the works of Mendele, Sholem Aleichem, I. L. Peretz, D. Frishman, and Sholem Asch.

We would also come to know young authors—thanks to the journal *The Jewish World*, which appeared at Kletzkin's publishing house. For us, the writer and poet "Der Nister" was a mysterious type, and we used to discuss his works among ourselves for a long time.

There were lots of readers then, and one didn't do it to show off, but rather there was a powerful hunger for Yiddish books, which gave us great intellectual pleasure.

We, the readers of the library, would get together at the shop of Feygetshke Yakum Meyers. We bought beans, lemonade, and chocolate there, and meanwhile we carried on heated discussions about the books we read.

Feygetshke was a quiet and contemplative girl. One of her friends once became upset because she wasn't given a book. In her excitement she said: "I'm going to report you to the police...." We were all terrified by her words. Quickly we moved the library to another apartment.

It was a winter night. While I was carrying part of the books from the library, I met the girl who had threatened to report us to the police. I became very excited and gave her a flaming slap to the cheek.

"Feygetshke"
Ikus Mayers Abramovitz

Revolutionary Youth

The reign of terror by the Czarist police was so far-reaching, that one had to use great caution even reading a book or discussing it.

In those years I belonged to the group called "Malienkaya Grupe Sotzialistov Revolutzionarov" (Youth Group for Socialist Revolutionaries). On Shabbat we, the youth, would come together at the house of Sheyne the teacher. She was a teacher of writing and reading Yiddish. She also sold lemonade and beans. We paid her on Shabbat and she gave us change.

She was tall, with gray hair. She gave lessons about Socialism and gave advice on how to conspire to carry out the revolutionary activities. She inspired us and gave us to understand that we were the first people [literally, "swallows"] to spread socialism on the Jewish street.

It seemed to us that Sheyne the teacher came from another planet. With taste and confidence she read aloud to us Sholem Aleichem's "Uncle Pinie and Aunt Reyze." While doing this she explained every word and sentence and praised Sholem Aleichem's story as a great work of political propaganda, directed against the Russo-Japanese War in 1904.

A new world opened up to us. Her commentaries made clear to us that writers don't just write, but that every writer and poet has his intentions and ideas. We came to understand that we, as readers, had to penetrate every word and line the author had written.

To this day, Sheyne the teacher is an enigmatic type: who was she and where did she come from to our shtetl?

The Itinerant Preacher

As to every Jewish shtetl in Lithuania, there also came to us, in Rakishok, itinerant preachers. For the most part they traveled on foot, and now and then, along the way, they hitched a ride with either a Jewish or a non-Jewish coach.

They held their sermons during the day on Saturday, and in rare cases also on Sunday. Small announcements or flyers would be stuck to the doors of the houses and synagogues, after this fashion: "Tomorrow a Preacher [maggid] will Deliver a Sermon."

A sermon was successful if it was held in a simple, folksy style, which was familiar to the average person. Almost no one would tolerate moralistic speeches.

I remember a tall, thin preacher, with a small beard and a big nose. He was vivacious, with shining eyes, and definitely no weakling. It was a wonder to me that he had become a preacher.

I loved preachers' sermons, even when I became older and had very little to do with the House of Study. I especially liked to hear the preacher mentioned above. His sermons were ornamented stories that had a moral. The following story of his is, to this day, engraved in my mind.

Once an old landowner passed the property of a young landowner. He was astounded to see the young landowner holding a stick in his hand and hitting a white hen, because in all his life he had never seen such a thing as punishing a hen. He knew that people hit cats, dogs, but not hens.

On account of this, the old landowner went to the young landowner and asked him: What happened with your hen? What was her transgression? To this he received the answer: "Don't you see that the hen is muddy? For a half hour already, she has been sitting and rolling in the sand, and so I wanted to knock the dust off her."

From this the preacher drew the following moral of the story, in his own particular melody: "This white, innocent hen, dear people, is like your innocent children. All of God's creatures pick up dust, and just as with the hen there comes a time when she feels the dust on her and shakes it off, so it is with your innocent children. For as long as they are young, they crawl around in sand and dust. When they become older and bigger, they shake off this dust—that is, the wildness, which they had taken on. You, dear friends, have seen this reality for yourselves. A boy is wild, like a really impudent lad, and suddenly you are surprised to see that he is becoming a complete person, with respect. Therefore, dear friends, you will not get rid of the 'dust' by beating your children. You must not act like the young landowner. A time will come when your children will themselves cast off the bad manners and behaviors."

The "Banker"

In Rakishok there were extremely poor people among the Jewish population. It sometimes happened that an established man or woman did not have the possibility of giving alms to a poor man, not even a groschen [a small denominator coin].

In those times there was a Jewish man who thought up a way to help poor people, who were dragging themselves from one city to the next and begging door-to-door. He made a stamp and small pieces of cardboard. Equivalent to every coin was a cardboard piece of a different size and shape. The stamp bore the name of a charitable organization or another name.

These stamped cardboard pieces were given to poor people, who redeemed them in the poorhouse, five for a kopeck, or sold them to market women, four for a kopeck. Every Jewish woman could, in this way, distribute the four pieces among four poor people.

There was also a "Banker" who bought these pieces, and this became a source of income for him.

Gloomy Thoughts

Often I am disturbed by dark thoughts, thoughts about the problem of animals and human beings. These thoughts were nourished by reflexes from childhood years in the city of my birth, Rakishok.

I remember how, at the end of the winter, the snow melted and in some places bits of earth started to show. In the shtetl one could already get around without a sled, but outside the shtetl, traveling to the train station, one still had to use a sled, when the snow barely covered the earth.

Once I saw a sled arrive from the side of the church. The two horses were dragging the sled with all of their might. From overexertion they were almost lying on the ground. After that sled there was a yellow Jewish coachman with his miserable horse. The wretched horse dragged the sled with all of his might and the coachman helped him pull it. Despite all of the exertions of the horse and the coachman, the sled didn't budge. It remained a short distance from a snowy area.

That coachman and horse wanted to reach that showy patch. But the sled wouldn't move. The coachman went into a rage and tried hitting his exhausted horse. He hit him mercilessly with his whip. He begged him with entreaties and yelled with load curses. The coachman hit him incessantly, but it didn't help. A white steam rose from the horse and finally the horse fell in its harness. Then the coachman hit him angrily and the whip handle struck the horse's head, from which flowed a stream of blood, which colored the earth.

I was then a little boy and didn't have the courage to stand up for the mute creature. With me were also adults who watched this and were silent.

When I became older and had already seen many horrors in life, there always hovered before me the image of that miserable horse, which sowed in me the first seeds of pessimism.

[Page 99]

Why? Various Memories
by Zalman Feldman
Translated by Mathilda Mendelow, born Ginsberg

Skopishok the small Shtetl where I was born, was found in a distant backward corner of Lithuania, a land that was reigned by a despotic and dark regime. Apart from the two churches, a couple of two-toned wooden structures, the houses and shacks were small and dilapidated, not much better than the crude dwellings of the gentiles of the surrounding towns. The streets were naked and gray; muddy when it rained and dusty when it was dry, but in my wanderings in later years I seldom found a more beautiful and more colorful community than one that was my Shtetl.

On the west side of the Shtetl were two large lakes that seemed to reach to the horizon. Hazardous pine forests surrounded the Shtetl on the South-east. There were lakes with their beautiful water lilies and Irises. The glamorous sunsets reflected in the waters of the lakes in all sorts of colors and forms and walks in the woods were accompanied by the quiet rustling of the trees, the squirrels that jumped around in the branches and the pleasant smells of the pines and berries, black, blue and red. All this together left a deep impression as did the orchards full of apples, pears, plums nuts and cherries. But still, life in Skopishok was hard. I was too young then to understand why, but I felt that it was bound up with the tax collector, who ruled the Shtetl with an iron hand ("blackjack). My mother once told me that apart from the tax that he used to demand from the town's citizens one still had to give him something under the lap, otherwise, one dared not, so-to-say, even sneeze. "But why does one not drive him out?" I wanted to know. One can't do anything my mother declared, behind him stands the mighty tzar regime. In Skopishok, André was the regime.

There was such poverty there, corruption and a feeling of fearfulness within oneself that my father, an unassuming, withdrawn and unusually honest person realized that in this tyrannic land there could not be a future for his family. He left this land when I was still a young child to look for his fortune in a far-off land.

When I, the eldest of 4 had to go to cheder, my mother a beautiful and hearty personality took herself and family across to Rokishok – that was a change in comparison to Skopishok.

In certain ways Rokishok resembled my birth Shtetl. Rokishok was also surrounded by water and forests but still it was not my own Shtetl. In comparison to Skopishok lakes, Rokishok lakes looked like puddles and the water was not crystal clear. The Rokeshoker lakes were not adorned with water lilies or irises. The waters of the greatest lake section were stagnant and almost the whole year round were covered with foam. On its isolated island stood a dilapidated mill, also the forest was not so accessible and inviting, but in this the guilty ones were the count and his guards.

Rokishok apart from that had the oldest police with three policemen who ruled over the Shtetl like André over Skopishok and it also had, as an extra, the count on whose ground the Shtetl was standing. To him also belonged the lakes and the forest around the Shtetl. His palace stood at the furthest end of the middle division.

Almost no one ever saw the count or his castle. The vicious dogs and the more vicious guards saw to it that no one ever went there. Therefore, perhaps people spoke about the fabulous riches that were in the palace, rare antique furniture, golden plates and expensive decoration. But the opportunity to see the count arose soon after we arrived in the Shtetl. The Rokishoker inhabitants got to know that the count had married a highly aristocratic woman of noble birth, a princess was coming home with him!

The Rokishokers on whom the tax payments were heavy thought that if they arranged a warm welcome for their boss, their chief would become amenable to lighten their tax burden.

The day of his arrival was declared a holiday in the Shtetl. All in their best clothing came to greet the count and his wife, the princess. Expensive arrangements of flowers and plants were placed in many locations and at every gate the count was stopped and given bread and salt according to tradition. The city orchestra in beautiful uniforms marched in front of his cart and played certain military marches and the princess was given bouquets arranged of the most beautiful flowers that were found growing in the district.

It was an unforgettable day in the life of the Rokishokers and thereafter they spoke about it for a long time. They were sure that this would help them out of the heavy burden that they found themselves in, but their hopes were dashed and the princess showed herself to be more unfriendly than the count. She marked the Jews of the Shtetl as the dirt of the earth.

Two incidents from that time left a deep mark on my childhood and helped without a doubt to form life's outlook. I together with other children on a hot summers' day went to bathe in the shallow waters of the smallest section of the lake. We were not in the water for long when we were alerted that the count's guards were coming – we ran out of the water and ran fast across the field leaving our clothes at the lake. The guards caught other children and hit them. I missed their whip and ran naked and crying through the Shtetl to my mother, with only my hat, that I managed to grab, on my head. Several weeks later the count's guards caught my younger brother who was not yet 5 years old, and who was picking berries and beat him badly.

To my questions why we were handled like this, my mother found no better answer than to say that the forest and the lakes belonged to the count.

"Did the count plant the trees and fill the lakes with water?" I remember I asked my mother. "No my child," she answered "God did all that!" I did not leave it at that and asked, "Why did God then give such beautiful things to such a bad person?" My mother tried to soothe me saying "The lakes, the forests and the ground on which the Shtetl stands, the count probably inherited from his father or grandfather."

One night I dreamt that the count came to my mother and demanded the air that she and the children breathed. He complained that just as everything that is on the ground and under the ground belonged to him, so the air was also his; besides that, it was still horrible that he and the princess should breathe the same air as us, the people of lower standing.

The impression of the dream was so strong on my young mind, that for many years I walked about afraid that there might be a few people who would declare a monopoly on the air, as they did with the ground, the rivers, the lakes and everything that found itself under their control.

Another incident that came about several years later ingrained itself on my memory. One winter's day, when everything was lying under snow, Rakishok was alarmed, a rumor spread around that wild blood-thirsty peasants with choppers, long knives, hay forks and swords were descending on the Shtetl with intent to kill the Jews and to rob their homes. Knowledge of pogroms which came from elsewhere wherein hundreds of people had been eliminated became known a few weeks before in the Shtetl. Now these wild barbarians had come closer to us and we had, if possible, to save ourselves. It would not have helped to go to the government for help because it was known that not only did the pogroms happen with the knowledge of the government but it was also known that agents of the government took part in them. My grandfather who fortuitously was in the city wanted my mother and the children to go to friends near the station about 3 miles away. I have never forgotten what it was like to "schlep" 3 miles with my baby sister in my arms. To my question why the peasants came to kill us, my mother did not answer. All she said was "When you will get older you will understand the world better my child."

The pogrom wave in Rokishok is over but the perception of what the pogrom shenanigans have done in other cities I got from people, who themselves lived through them and from photos that appeared in newspapers and journals. Babies with chopped off heads, men with burned beards, eyes torn out, the sex organs mutilated; pictures of pregnant women, the fetuses torn out and the bellies filled with straw. Why did they do this! How could they do such things? Were the questions that filled my mind. Questions that did not allow rest, disturbed sleep; questions that demanded answers, but there was no answer.

Even my grandfather, a person, a patriarch with long white beard with a lot of wisdom and knowledge, did not have an answer. He used the old formula "It is God's will, a punishment for our sins." And when I got him into a corner and demanded why God desired such wild barbarity and what sins the little children did, he could only say that no one could answer that "Truly no person understands God's ways and intentions."

* * *

The years have passed with unusual hurry – years of storm and urgency of mighty battles and wars, of rivers of blood and oceans of tears. The temptations and experiences of a generation have packed themselves into a trunk (chest).

With the end of the second world war the curtain lifted over the lowest and most terrible picture of cold blooded murders in human history. Six Million Jews – men, women and children were eliminated with such cold blooded brutality that it shook even this generation which is used to brutality. In this so-to say world pogrom, not one community no matter how small, not one iota, not one came out free of the bloody Nazi hands as the masses of graves of Skopishok and Rokishok bear quiet witness.

Unwillingly the old question of "why" is torn from ones heart when the tragedy of Skopishok and Rokishok became known. But the question remains as incomplete as before. Continuously reminding me of my Grandfather's answer – "No minds of humans understand God's intentions and ways."

[Pages 103-105]

My Remembrances
by Zorach Gafanowitz
Translated by Gloria Berkenstat Freund

Z. Gafanowitz
[He moved from Latvia to Rakishok because
the Jewish population where he came from was only
30 families – A.Jermyn]

I traveled to Rakishok as a nine-year-old child. Previously we lived in Aizkraukle (Courland), where my father was a *shochet* (ritual slaughterer). Aizkraukle was a settlement of 30 Jewish families. A *melamed* (religious teacher) for the children was brought from Yakobstat or from Rakishok.

My father, of blessed memory, thought about sending me to study in Rakishok because we had family there: my aunt Pesa-Liba and my uncle Zelig, the son of Yisroel, of blessed memory.

I arrived with a wagon driver who was traveling to Rakishok for a market. I intended to live with my aunt Pesa-Liba, who was a very righteous woman. My uncle, Zelig Yisrael, spent the summer teaching (that is how it was in Rakishok-- in winter one would trade or make flax, and in summer, a teacher), so I lived and studied with him, and from this *cheder* (school) I remember episodes.

I remember how among the young boys in the *chederim* (schools), it was the fashion to hold wars: one *cheder* against another. Our *cheder* against Moishe Meshtsanski's *cheder*. Upon hearing that a new *cheder* boy had come from Aizkraukle, the students from Moishe Meshtsanski's *cheder* declared war against the young boys in Zelig Yisrael's *cheder*. I was very frightened because in Aizkraukle we were not accustomed to such things. However, with my luck, this "war" did not happen.

I remember many people from that time, among them the Rabbi, Reb Asher, who was a person of stately appearance and Rabbi Reb Betzalel and the peculiar Bertzik the *shochet* (ritual slaughterer), who was a great scholar.

I remember that every Friday after noon the firefighters marched through the town and we young boys ran after the commander, Bera Laya's son Shneior, from Kamaier Street. They would march through the market with brass hats and come into a courtyard, where the commander would ingeniously climb onto the roof and begin sprinkling with a water hose. For we young boys this was a happy spectacle.

After this, *Shabbos* came quickly. There was the great and the middle-sized *Beit Hamidresh* (synagogue) where the Rakishoker aristocrats *davened* (prayed), such as Abraham Meller and others. The Hasidim *davened* in the small *shtibl* (small prayer house), as did my uncle Zelig.

* * *

After I studied for several terms in the Rakishoker *cheder*, I left Rakishok to go to my parents. When I was in Rakishok I was just 11 or 12 years old. I only came to Rakishok from Lubavitch for the second time for conscription by the Czar's army. [The author's meaning here is not entirely clear. -Trans. and Ed.] My uncle was already in Africa and my aunt of blessed memory and my sisters and brother also moved to Rakishok. We lived with Leiba Pakgrund in an apartment.

Rabbi Reb Asher no longer lived in Rakishok and his successor was his son-in-law Rabbi Reb Shmuel Levitan, who is now in America. He was a student from the Lubavitcher *yeshiva*. Rakishok was already divided into factions: Shmuel's side, and Beltzalel's side. Bobruisker' Hasidim, at the head of whom stood Reb Shlomoh Skopishker, and Lubavitcher Hasidim. Among the Bobruisker Hasidim were people with sharp minds, such as: Zalman Shamshim, Haim Elihu the *Shamas* (rabbi's assistant) and Reb Shlomoh Skopishker, who would preach about *Hasidus* all day *Shabbos*, in the small *shtibl*.

The Lubavitcher Hasidim concentrated around Rabbi Reb Shmuel. The closest intimates of Rabbi Reb Shmuel were Pesakh's son Arszik, (Ninzenburg), Mendl Milner (known as Mendl the Turk), Haim Moishe Gen,

Yudl the shinglemaker, Mendel the shoemaker, Yisroel Leib Snieg, and Welvel's son Mendel.

Every *Shabbos* both Rabbis would study in the *Beit Midrash*: Reb Beltzalel at his table and Reb Shmuel at his table. The others who did not belong to the two factions, the so called neutral people, sat in the middle of the *Beit Midrash* on a bench and listened with one ear to the talk of Reb Beltzalel and with the other ear to Reb Shmuel's sermon.

Rabbi Reb Shmuel had a dependable *minyon* (ten men required for prayer) in his home. The *gabai* was Pesakh's son Arszik. At the late afternoon *Shabbos* meal, Lubavitch melodies would be sung so sweetly that they would be suffused into everyone's heart.

* * *

With the passage of time, relations between the various factions were greatly aggravated because of the matter of the Kazyaner Rabbinate. Each side wanted to appropriate for itself the Kazyaner Rabbinate that received an income from controlling the metrical books (vital record books) and from the sale of yeast. Rabbi Shmuel's side triumphed. He was led in a great parade in a circular procession with the Torah scrolls in the synagogue and all of his supporters celebrated the great victory. But with all of their disputes, they were all kind and dear Jews.

At the same time Rabbi Reb Shmuel founded a *yeshiva* in Rakishok. Among the *yeshiva* students were: Itze Gecel Tzindler, Yankl Wingrin, Moishke Shtern, Welvke Pakgrund, Ahrke Noach-Noachumowitz, Leibke Pawalitz, Gelcer, Shual Bacher, my brother Itze-Yankele, who is now is South Africa. This *yeshiva* existed until the First World War. Reb Shmuel the Rabbi and his family evacuated themselves to Russia. My family also left Rakishok and during the course of the First World War we lived in Tambower, Bawer *gubernia* (province), Russia.

In 1921, I, with my wife Matla and daughter Hana Sara, came back to Rakishok, passing through the quarantine in the neighboring town of Abel. I found Rakishok then in a different garb: with new merchants, stores and upstarts made rich by the war.

Coming then from Russia, I, too, began to trade. I produced synthetic honey and half the town began to be occupied with producing synthetic honey. Tailors laid down their scissors and irons and cooked honey. The competition was great.

There were no longer quarrels among the factions. Other winds began to blow. The war with its experiences had leveled the divisions. Only during voting would a struggle emerge and again there were factions: the *Agudah* and the Zionists. Reb Shmuel Aba Snieg was leader of *Agudah* and Yerachmeil Ruk was leader of the Zionists.

Reb Ber Zalkind then founded a large *yeshiva* in a beautiful building and the town provided for the *yeshiva* students. The head of the *yeshiva* was Reb Moishle.

* * *

In 1928 I arrived in South Africa. A few years later I brought my family, thanks to the material help of the Rakishoker *landsleit* organization that lent me money for this purpose, for which I am thankful to this day.

Everyone knows what became of all of the Jews in Rakishok. With the help of the Lithuanian peasants, everyone was annihilated, among them my family and also my sister Sara-Rashel, with her husband Yitzhak Hurwitz and their children.

In South Africa I also lived through a great loss: my oldest son, Pinkhas (Pinka) tragically perished in the last World War in El Alamein on the 12th of Av, 5702, 26th of July 1942, in a battle with the Nazi army.

His memory and the memory of my annihilated family and of all the ruthlessly annihilated Rakishoker Jews is for me unforgettable and holy.

Pinkhas "Pinkie" Gafanovitz
[as young soldier]

[Pages 106-114]

A Yemenite in Shtetl
(Memories of a Rakishoker)
by Berl Sarver (Tel Aviv)
Translated by Gloria Berkenstat Freund

White, blue smoke from the chimneys meanders up to the cloudy, winter heaven. Houses stand as if huddled together. A white, downy snow is strewn on the sloped roofs and covers them as if with *erev-Shabbos* [eve of Shabbat] tablecloths. Young boys pursue each other with reddened faces and ears and barely notice the partly or completely worried faces of the aged Jewish men and women.

The frost cracks, sleighs travel hitched to skinny peasant horses, which spread the sound of lonely bells. On Monday, peasants come to the market, wrapped and rolled up in cloths, the children coming back from *kheder* [religious elementary school] with the earflaps of their hats pulled down. Their clear, small voices resonate through the long "New Street."

Night falls: strange and yet full of promising stars that light up the sky; their shine distant, hazy; their glance barely a gesture to the distant Milky Way. And if one of them "falls down," girls in love murmur, "Good luck!"

This was a curious winter: hungry wolves from the surrounding distant forests smelled Jewish foods in the fresh snow. Sometimes they desired a look – what kind of face does Rakishok have in winter – and they came near.

Yekl, the *melamed* [religious school teacher], said this himself. The other day he went out "for what is natural" near his house. He noticed that some kind of "a strange dog" was coming toward him from beyond the fence. Its look was "suspicious" - make up your mind; you are a dog, look, do what you need to do – and run away! But you are looking for so long, and, in addition, with a turned head – you are surely a wolf!

Later, when Reb Yekl quickly ran into the vestibule, he heard a long drawn out howl that bore into all of his limbs and ran through his soul – and then Reb Yekl was convinced that there was no doubt – it was a wolf! But he could not understand one thing – why did it look at him so long?

This is how Reb Yekl described it on *Shabbos Noakh* [the Sabbath on which the Torah portion entitled *Noakh* – Noah – is read] in the *grynem minyon* [green *minyon* – a *minyon* is 10 men needed for prayer]. Rakishok had three *minyonim* in addition to the *misnagid* [opponents of Hasidism] synagogue – the green, yellow and red. They stood in one row on the same street, and each color recalled a third of the flag introduced by the Lithuanian Republic.

Each *minyon*, as well as the *misnagid* synagogue, is a chapter in itself – and calls for perhaps an entire book – but in short we will say that the scholars prayed in the yellow *minion*, and therefore, Reb Yekl the *melamed*, who thought of himself as a scholar and was also thought to be a scholar by others, would come there.

* * *

For a long time there was nothing new in the *shtetl*. The world there carried on in the old way: Bertsik Zalkind's *Talmud-Torah* [religious school for poor boys], Reb Moshe Sidrer's *yeshiva* and the Hebrew public school stood on the same spot. It was said that in spring the recruits would not break any Jewish window panes because Dr. Soloveitchik achieved American recognition for Lithuania – *de jure* [literally "concerning the law" – in principle]. And now there would probably be no thumps in the People's Bank because it was being said that the means had been found to distribute to the smaller banks. Non-Jews would push the Jews out of the flax and seed trade, but would they succeed, the peasant heads? There was also time to think about hiring a shepherd to drive the cows to Radute. The winter was still severe. Meanwhile, red bilberries and cabbage were being placed in the barrels.

And once, on one bright winter day, the *shtetl* was stirred up by a sensation: a strange dark Jew, with burning dark eyes, a red hat on his small head, with *peyes* [side curls], twisted and long like little snakes – and with two large valises – got off in the *shtetl* at the train station. He had been brought by "Ezrial the beard" (he was called that in the *shtetl* because of his beautiful, long beard and he had once been envied for having the merit of bringing the Lubavitcher Rebbe, of blessed memory, to Rakishok).

A winter scene in Rokiskis

Rokiskis Yizkor Book 101

"Who saw the Turk?" women asked one another, tapping a chicken on Monday at the market, or two neighbors drawing a pail of water at the wells.

"Why do you think he is a Turk?" asked another one.

"Because he wears a red hat, he is a Turk?"

"So, what then is he? Perhaps a Jew?"

"Certainly, he is a Jew; he speaks *Loshn Koydesh* [holy tongue – the Hebrew language]!"

"It is said that he is one of the red Jews from the *Hore-Khoysekh.*"[1] "Why do you think that such a Jew would in fact come to Rakishok?"

"Who knows? Perhaps he was told that the Rakishokers are charitable people!"

"And with whom do I think this Jew – this Turk – lodges?"

"Certainly with Nusen the *shoykhet* [ritual slaughterer]!"

"Is that so? And the daughters certainly pamper him!"

"Is he then unmarried?"

"God forbid! Apparently, a "punished" Jew. But is it relevant to say?"

"*Hakhroses-orkhrim*!" [Commandment to provide hospitality to a stranger, particularly on *Shabbos*]

So the *shtetl* had something to talk about – and the snow continued to fall on the horse and wagon, and on the red hat of the dark, little Jew, until he was swallowed in the half darkness of the apartment of Nusen the *shoykhet*.

* * *

On a soft sofa in a separate room sat Reb Yitzhak Khyun, a Jew from *Eretz-Yisroel* who had moved there from Yemen. And now he was in Rakishok.

He sat wrapped in a large shawl and his teeth chattered from the cold. A curious look came over him as to where he was in the world. He looked at the drapes, the portraits on the walls, the almost flaxen colored beard of his host, the short sleeves of his daughters, and the strange frost patterns on the window panes with his naïve, half-wild look. Curiously, he considered the new world into which he had fallen. He was a little afraid of it. The *shoykhet* and his family, a family of Jewish people in the far, flat area of Lithuania, a land of level-headed, stubborn *Klumpes* [Lithuanians] stood around him no less astonished.

Amazed, they looked at the thin Jew from *Teymen* [Yemen], and I think the *shoykhet* thought that the *Yosifon* [10th century book of Jewish history based on the works of Josephus] mentioned this land of the past.

"Six days a week the Sambatyon River[2] cooks and boils and throws giant stones up to heaven."

"Sambatyon, Sambatyon, how long will you boil; and Jews, how long will you continue to rage?" "But *Shabbos* comes, it stops boiling and seething. A calm controls its cloudy ripples, and then it can be crossed on foot."

Looking at Reb Yitzhak Khyun, this little story ran through Nusen the *shoykhet*'s thoughts.

How many years had he lived in Duksht [Dûkŏtas], Swiadashts [Svedasai] and Rakishok and in how many *yeshivas* had he lingered and in how many slaughterhouses had he trudged and had the honor of being a Jew from "those parts." And now he had someone like this in his house? God's wonder!

Some kind of Jew, a trifle, who spoke only the holy language [Hebrew], even during the week![3] (Cold, cold, the Lord should take pity on him because here he was dying from the cold.) A hospitable smile spread from the lips of the owner of the house and he answered him equally with a [Hebrew] verse: "You will not die because you will live." His daughters took pride in their father's Hebrew. And little by little, they entered a wider conversation. First of all, the guest announced that he was a "sufferer." He was not accustomed to all of the foods that the Ashkenazim [western Jews] eat.

And he stated another plea: while he was still in this country where the frost was a mortal danger, here was a Jew, a Torah scholar. But who would preserve his health so that he could serve the Creator?

His pleas were listened to with respect and then a talkative bearded mouth opened and the person began to speak. What did he speak about and what did he not speak about?

– About the distant, very distant Land of Yemen, about Sana'a, Chaban and the *Hatser Mavet* [Court of the Dead, possible reference to a cemetery]. Yes, there is such a place in the world that is called the *Hatser Mavet* - that is, the "Court of the Dead." There one is afflicted by heat and dust, with the salty earth and illnesses. And Jews also cry there.

He said, "Not in every place in Yemen are Jews poor and oppressed in the same number. There are places where the *Ishmaelim* [Arabs] take into consideration the *skhus oves* [accumulated merits of ancestors] of the *Am hakhasav* (the people of the writing or book, meaning the Torah), but there mainly is a bitter fate – and he stressed, very, very different from you in Lietuva [Lithuania in the Lithuanian language] – and more than you can imagine. Oh, the bitter exile of Yemen, when will we finally be redeemed from there? With you in Lietuva, I am equal with all men. Perhaps many injustices are done to you, but no one humiliates you – but with us in poor, unfortunate Yemen – Oh, my God - alas and alack – Jewish Yemenites are taken to be converted, heaven preserve us. We have to give respect to the *Ishlmaelim*; we have to yield the way, we may not ride on a beast because only the leaders can have the honor to ride on a horse or on a donkey, but not the impure Jews – the heretics (who deny the prophet Mohammed). Jews have to go on foot and on the pavement. Oh, how difficult and bitter is exile and the coming of *Moshiekh* [the redemption] is taking so long, so many generations! Why does God not want *Moshiekh* to come? We have had need of him for so long!"

He spoke this way with his throaty expression – people were barely able to understand him. Reb Nusen somehow understood him, and this was thanks to his long years of soaking in the Jewish books that were published in *Loshn Koydesh*.

"The *Torah* brings the distant closer," the *shoykhet* thought. "The language is a bridge to understanding," thought his well-educated daughters.

* * *

Reb Yitzhak Khyun sat in the *shoykhet's* house and asked *kashes* [questions]. The *shoykhet* would say of this with a joke that Sambatyon could not answer these *kashes*.

The women are an unlucky people. A Jew brings a part of *Eretz-Yisroel* with him to Rakishok, and not one Jewish woman, except for the *shoykhet's* daughters, has yet had the honor to see him. That is, there is no talk here of looking at someone who is a "good looking man," but he is someone from *Eretz-Yisroel* and also from Yemen!

The men, for their part, took pleasure in him. That is, he was no great, eminent man, but (speaking among themselves) when could Rakishok expect learned men, distinguished scholars, except for such individuals? And he understood a bit of *gemara*.

The *yungatshes* [rascals] said that the *Evrit* [modern Hebrew] comes from him passably, spoken through the nose and not according to the correct grammar. (Then they began to see, after the first enchantment was over.)

The main critics were the youth from *Tarbut* [network of Hebrew language, secular schools] and the *Yavne pro-gymnazie* [religious Zionist school that prepared students to enter the *gymnazie*] and the students from the *Beis Sefer* [school] with Klumial's students occupied in the mastery of Hebrew. The *HaShomer-HaTzair* [Socialist-Zionist youth movement] were interested in the person. He was living evidence for what was happening in the life of the "land of Israel," although they did not believe that all Jews there wore a beard and *peyes*.

Reb Nusen the *shoykhet*, Yekl the *melamed,* and others who were able to grab a conversation and study with him (after the frost fell, Reb Yitzhak Khyun began to go to the "yellow *minyon*" for prayer), supported him completely and took his side. "To what is this relevant?" they said to the *yungatshes.* "You mean then apparently that your Spanish is the right expression of the Holy Tongue? We can only say to you that you break your heads with your *pasekh* [Hebrew vowel signifying an "a" after a consonant] like those Jews who think that in German everything is with a *pasekh*, for example: *Di Levana sheint* [the moon shines] and *di kala veynt* [the bride cries], and so on, but in truth the Yemeni Jews speak the true *Evrit* because not every *komets* [Hebrew vowel sign signifying an "o" after a consonant] is a *pasekh*, and there is a *komets gadal* and a *komets katan*."[4]

Thus declared Yekl the *melamed,* and the group of *yungatshes* winked at each other. "Right away he will want to tell stories about the wolf in *Evrit* with the Ashkenazi *havore* (pronunciation)."

Meanwhile the "scholars" occupied themselves with Reb Yitzhak round and round in a Torah discussion about matters of *shmita* [leaving the land fallow every seven years] in the *Eretz Yisroel* of the present. Why does Yemen not observe the *Takanot haRem"a* [religious rulings by Rabbi Moshe Isserles] in matters of *shmita?* And they found that all of his answers were sustained and connected with "*mikama mekomot*" ["from several places"] and with a considerable amount of ability.

His wonder ascended, and it is pertinent to say that Jews still study everywhere!

* * *

Christmas came closer. The pious gentiles began to prepare, one with a little pig, one with a gift to the priest. In addition, in the middle of town in the market square, on the left, the *abratina* (tea house); on the right, a variety of Jewish haberdashery and manufacturing shops. At the corner of this square, the Catholic Church with its sharp contours appeared in the clouds and broke into the blueness of the sky. The pointy cupola, arrogant to the wintry clouds, lifted its heroic copper ornaments - crosses formed in sharp-cornered Gothic style.

From the first night on, a month before Christmas, the dull drumming over the invisible sheet metal of the church was heard. Each drum pinched a weak heart; with each ring of the bell scores of echoes poured out, derived from metal, proudly swinging. Here they woke, and here again they were on the verge of being lulled to sleep as with a cradle. Sure of themselves, unctuous and calm, and immediately again alarming and threatening – the sounds of the bells over the bent, seemingly frightened Jewish roofs.

And it seems as if each ring of the giant, massive church clock mourns Jewish life in the land of the gentiles. The threatening ring still shakes a little; it wrestles still in the night with invisible strength, until it discharges vibrations and becomes silent. Will this threatening-sleepy ringing awake them again? Will it constantly bring shudders to Jewish hearts?

After a rooster crows, another answers him, and all flow into one boring chicken melody up to the dawning grey sky - another day announced by the crowing of a rooster over the still existing Jewish Rakishok.

Rokiskis Yizkor Book 105

* * *

The *Shabbos* night, for which Reb Yitzhak Khyun long waited, finally came. The Jew from *Eretz-Yizroel* would speak today before the "group." At his right hand stood ready a pale and tall young man in the jacket of a *gymnazie* [secondary school] student. His feminine, carved mouth smiled at his friends around him. It was said that he often came to Nusen the *shoykhet*'s house – probably to see one of his daughters.

This young man with a knowledge of Hebrew had to translate Khyun's sermons from Hebrew to Yiddish. Reb Khona Arsh was intoxicated with the possibility that the older Jew with a grey beard and *peyes* would give an entire sermon in the holy language. When, for example, a Zionist speaker came from the *Keren-Kaymet* [Jewish National Fund], he thought, the *Agudanikes* [members of Orthodox non-Zionist political party] would not even admit him. Contemptible tailors would shout: "Yiddish, Yiddish," because Khona Arsh – it should be known that he was a liberal man, he made sure to wear a beautiful, always clean suit, his beard always trimmed – was a universal Zionist according to his beliefs. He always hated those called "extremists," but instead took the middle way with people and with politics. But in relation to *Evrit* he was romantically disposed and a very terrible extremist, and it evidently was seen in the personal victory this *Shabbos* night at Khona's.

It cannot be said that the heart of the young *gymnazie* student did not beat like a dove in a cage without an *eyenhore* [evil eye], seeing before him a large "group" of people. But he tried not to show it, because from the "women's section" his mother looked out from one side, and not far away, the *shoykhet*'s middle daughter. This young man found himself in the crossfire of two kinds of looks. His mother's eyes were velvety, calmly deep, and although a little sad, a luster of former joy sparkled in their pupils. And there a little further, the girl's blue-green eyes seemed kindly, and yet audacious and a little deriding.

Khyun wrapped himself in a wide Turkish *talis* and drew it over his red hat with the fringe. The "crowd" turned forward, like an effervescent sea of waves.

From the neighboring *shtetl* Abel [Obeliai], a few people came out of curiosity to look at the "Turkish" Jew. Gedalyah-Velve, the crazy one, came running with them. He invaded the "red synagogue" like a whirlwind. His black cherry-eyes smiled with that good natured, dull expression and yet very humanely. Thus he smiled with his eyes, and half hoarse, he spoke through his nose.

"A Jew like a Turk, a Turk like a Jew! He will speak, he will speak Hebrew! *Evrit*, a new language, *Evrit* and really a language – *Loshn Koydesh, Lokshn* [noodle] *Koydesh*. Ha, ha, ha! Where is the rabbi's tie? Why does he not wear a tie; it is not nice without a tie! You think I am crazy; I say to you that I am entirely not crazy, because a father proves successful in a son."

The *yungatshes* rolled with laughter. The older people were angry and tried to send him out, but he was a stubborn Jew and did not allow it.

"Who will understand him?" he suddenly exclaimed. "Aha! Freydka, daughter of Nusen the *shoykhet*. For a daughter is like a father.

"*Sha, sha* [quiet], get out of here you *sheygets* [non-Jewish boy]!" Reb Yekl screamed at him. But Nusen the *shoykhet* hinted that things should be calm. Little by little Gedalyah-Velve became quiet.

Khyun began: "Dear brothers, our brethren in Israel! From far, very far lands I came to you! As the verse states: 'And came the whirlwinds of the south,' the storm of exile also brought me here. This is the storm also of the *oyses hazman* (signs of the time). Our sages said: 'The son of David shall not come until money has vanished from the purse.' (Moshiach [descended from the "son of David"] will not come until the penny does not end up in the pocket [until poverty is widespread]). I see that with you, thank God, it is not such, and therefore," he added with a smile, "you delay the redemption. But it is different with the Jews in Yemen. Their poverty is flagrant." He spoke more about Jewish troubles around the world and mainly in Yemen. He ended with verses from the *Tanakh* [Bible] which pass on the word of the revival of Zion: "Just as we see now eye to eye that a new light begins to shine in our old-new fatherland, Jews are there colonizing little by little and building, but we must strengthen and help them."

He himself had come because of *haskhnoses-kale* [community arrangements for marrying poor and orphaned girls] and he actually spoke about his daughter. But is the *mitzvah* smaller because of this? At the same time, he would honestly transfer [the money] and give a receipt for each amount that the *kehile* would give him for the poor people of the holy cities of the fatherland.

With a trembling, but clear voice, the 19-year-old *gymnazie* student translated his words and plunged himself in the dreams of Zion, and also added his [own words].

The audience listened with sympathy. Reb Khona Arsh listened very closely and was pleased. But there was trouble that in emphasizing the moments about *Eretz-Yisroel*, the *gymnazie* student forgot about Khyun's private matter – about *haskhnoses-kale*! He emphasized the point of *tzadekah* [charity] for *Eretz-Yizroel*.

Suddenly, something bizarre happened: Reb Yitzhak Khyun assumed such a tiger-like pose towards the *gymnazie* student (Itsek's son, Berke), that even Gedalyah-Velve, the crazy one, was afraid.

The "*khokhem's*" [usually translated as sage, but used ironically here] eyes were shining strangely wild, and there twinkled in them that strange fire of a desert man, or perhaps a wild peasant at the Monday market.

Nusen's daughter, Freydka, the middle daughter, became pale, and Itsik's daughter, Henya Eidl – the mother of the *gymnazie* student – wrung her hands. The audience was amazed. The *gymnazie* student himself blinked his eyes in surprise and, perhaps also fear, and instinctively took a step back.

Meanwhile, Reb Yitzhak Khyun burst out: "Why did you not say that the main income needs to go to *haskhnoses-kale*; why did you hide this thing from them?"[5] The people murmured in astonishment, in the manner in which a wind traveling over much greenery murmurs. Others called out: "Understand? Does he then understand Yiddish?" It is unnecessary to say that a bit of "exoticness" fell away immediately from the Eastern man, Reb Yitzhak Khyun, who seemed to understand Yiddish as "a *nash brat*" [a regular fellow], so that his Yemen Jewishness became a little paler and his body curled up to the size of an ordinary little Jew.

From a practical standpoint, the collection was not affected. On the contrary, a number of the group, and among them also Khona Arsh, heartily laughed at the entire incident.

How a young man forgets himself and thinks that he is the speaker! The student explained and immediately proceeded to *talmatshen* (to translate) the point about *haskhones-kale,* and the Yemenite's blinking eyes calmed a little. In his heart, Itsek's son, Berke, thought that perhaps he was a little confused because his mother and his bride had looked out at him from the women's section.

And then Reb Yitzhak Khyun again was permeated with warm talk of consolation for the Jewish people. Among others, he described for them the "night of the bells," and how he survived them.

"May God have mercy," he argued, "for indeed exile is here, too! This is how I spoke to myself in the thick darkness of my room with the 'sage' Nusen, hearing Esau's bell [the gentile's bell]. And this is what I asked: How long is your beauty in captivity and your magnificence [Israel's] in the hands of the enemy?[5] But Esau's bell desecrated my prayer."

"Wake up, dear brothers, wake up! Your exile is actually easier. That is, they do not spit in your face and do not convert your children; they do not chase you from the sidewalk. But little brothers, if we have to consider everything as a favor, it is an exile here!"

"Therefore, Jews, stand up to help *Eretz-Yisroel*, the place of the Royal Palace. New rays [of light] shine out from there; our young people, may they be blessed, soak the land with their sweat and blood. Each piece of earth there is dear to them, as the godly poet, Reb Yehuda haLevi, wrote: 'The clods of your earth are sweeter to me than honey.' "[5]

"And to my pious brothers, I say: do not think, dear ones, that this is, God forbid, hurrying the end of the exile before the time,[5] because the land is here, and its emptiness awaits all Jews who can and will come here, and also the Lithuania Jews whose Judaism is so strongly persevered among them. If you only want to!"

And a new light shone on them. There was a great delight.

* * *

The "community" listened, but not everyone agreed, and later they were not able to follow the message that spoke of the "rising sun of redemption." Alas, not everyone was affected by this new spirit that the "Red Jew" had left behind in the shtetl. Alas, not everyone was saved from the desolate bloody days and lost lives.

But, listening to the preaching of the "Red Jew" and to similar preachers, many of their children left for there [*Eretz-Yisroel*], and are building anew the disrupted life of the past generation in the personality of their very worthy, strong and freedom loving children – native born Israelis, or *Sabras*. [*Sabra* (cactus) is the name given to native-born Israelis in recognition of their tenaciousness in living in a desert climate, as does the cactus].

1. The term "red Jews" has many meanings and often has an anti-Semitic connotation. It can refer to the Lost Tribes of Israel who were thought to live beyond the *Hore-Khoyshekh* – the legendary mountain of darkness..
2. The Sambatyon River is a legendary river of stones beyond which the 10 Lost Tribes of Israel are believed to have been exiled.
3. Hebrew, the holy language, was usually reserved for the synagogue. The language used by most Jews in Lithuania in their daily lives was Yiddish.
4. This paragraph is commenting about the different dialects or pronunciations of Yiddish and Hebrew. The *komets gadol* is transliterated as an "a" and the *komets katan* is transliterated as an "o."
5. This question appears in Hebrew and is followed by the Yiddish translation in parenthesis.

[Page 115]

Reminiscences of a Socialist in Rakishok

by Buim Yidel Kreel

Translated by Lillian Dubb and Sadie Forman

Chasidic Rakishok

During the first Russian Revolution of 1902 to 1905, the Jewish masses in the little towns and shtetlach became inspired with revolutionary ideals. The bad economic conditions, and the tradition-bound lives of the Jews in Tsarist Russia, were among the reasons for this to happen. In Rakishok, revolutionary groups were active, some of whom were influenced by the Jewish workers parties from Dvinsk.

Dvinsk already had a big textile industry, such as the well-known factories of Natanson, Zaks, and Griliches. These factories employed hundreds of workers including workers from Rakishok. Rakishok also had small factories which employed a few thousand workers.

The call to freedom and struggle was answered by the workers in the small workshops as well. A barrier to the spread of revolutionary ideas was the Chasidic groups, who were hide-bound to their traditional way of life. It is well-known that Rakishok was a stronghold of Chasidim.

From North to South, we were surrounded by the spires of churches and cathedrals. In the East stood a beautiful Roman-Catholic cathedral with a spire hundreds of feet high, on the apex of which was a steel cross point which earthed lightning. On the West side, there was a Russian cathedral with many crosses.

The religious attitude to the revolutionaries was negative – they were antagonistic. At that time, it was viewed as a disgrace to be a tradesman. Religious study was the acceptable life. There was also a negative attitude to Zionist movements. The following example will illustrate this:

In Rakishok, there was a well-known Chasid called Zalman Yossel Rubens. He was a reader of the Torah and a respected person. He became a Zionist. The Chasidim were suspicious of him and no one spoke to him. He was barred from reading from the Torah, a formidable sanction. A short time later he died, and the Chasidim regarded his death as payment for his sin of Zionism.

The Chasidim were outraged when the brothers Mendel and Label Rabkin who were members of the Enlightened Movement opened a Hebrew school where modern secular Hebrew was taught.

Under the influence of the Russian revolution, a number of Zionist groups were formed by the children of Chasidim. They became friendly with the workers` groups in the town, and participated in their activities. The stormy years of the revolution broke down the hold of the Chasidim over the community and there was more interest in secular and cultural activities.

The so-called cream of the Chasid community, their intelligentsia became increasingly drawn into the socio-political world.

As a result, a number of different political groupings were formed, such as Zionists, Zionist-Socialists, Hapoael-Zion, Socialist Revolutionaries and the Bund. The Zionist-Socialist Party was founded by Matilda Mathieson, and by a socialist worker called Schwartzberg. Matilda Mathieson was the daughter of a Chasid who prayed in a Chasidic shtiebel. She would lecture on various ideologies in the Jewish section, such as Zionism, Socialism, Territorialism[1] and others. She also led discussion groups that developed from the lectures. These meetings were held in private houses, in special study houses and also in the surrounding woods.

From these study groups, nationalist and revolutionary parties emerged. When the discussions became heated they led to quarrels and the voice of the Beadle would rise above them and he would chase them from the venue shouting, "Get out of here; these are Holy places."

The topics discussed at these gatherings were regarded with great seriousness. Apart from the philosophical, they also discussed concrete, practical matters such as how to achieve an eight-hour working day and how to organise strikes in order to achieve improved working conditions.

At these meetings, the agenda would have been set previously by the Central Committee members who had experience in various strategies of the struggle. These meetings were often held in secret because Tsarist agents were sent to spy on the meetings. Because of this nothing was written down and only general books were available. For example, there were books of poetry and prose by writers such as Dovid Edelshtam, Morris Rosenveld, Morris Venshevsky, Abraham Reisen, Sorah Reisen, Emile Zola and other classical writers, such as Mendele Kliatcha. These books were read and analysed from a socialist and revolutionary perspective.

At that time, revolutionary tracts were printed on wrapping paper and they would pass from hand-to-hand. On the thinnest cigarette papers were printed pleas, the history of revolutionary movements and Victor Chernov's "The Agrarian Question and Revolutionary Territorialism." Afterwards, the members would get together and discuss the relevant problems printed on these illegal pamphlets.

Stormy Days

I recall an incident in those stormy days. A member of the Socialist Revolutionary Group, Shimke Dimant, became a spy. The Socialist Party discussed the problem of spies and following the policy of the Central Committee in Riga, they were ordered to eliminate Shimke. The lot fell to two people to carry out the job, one of whom was a tailor whose parents were Chasidim.

The deed was to take place in the Great Synagogue on the Sabbath while the congregation was at prayer. When the two revolutionaries approached him to charge him with betraying the Party for being a spy, he drew his knife to stab the tailor, son of the Chasid, but the tailor preempted the attack by firing his revolver and merely wounded Shimke. The turmoil and chaos in the Shul was tremendous and terrifying and the entire congregation turned their passionate anger on the accusers.

In no time, a posse of policemen arrived on the scene and forbade anyone to leave the shul. However the two revolutionaries escaped before the police arrived. They escaped through the priest's gate and fled to a small fenced-off wood near the shul which was close to the Rudomer Forest.

As they ran, one of them fell, but the tailor did not leave his comrade behind. Lifting him up, and with the revolver in one hand he stood poised to face the police. Fortunately, the one who fell got up and with all his strength he struggled on until they reached the Jewish village in Rudomer.

A poor Jewish woman recognised their danger and hid them in her attic, filled with new-mown hay. She then went away from the house, leaving her children playing peacefully in the garden. The police arrived and asked the children if they had seen two men running away. The eldest daughter kept her cool and told them that two people had run into the forest. The two men heard the police talking to the girl and decided that they would rather kill themselves than be caught by the police.

The police charged into the forest like wild dogs after them and by good fortune, they were saved from death.

Meanwhile, in Rakishok people were being arrested and sent to Siberia. Yoske's brother Arke and a plumber died in Siberia. Mika-Itcha Leibes and another two were freed in 1917 at the time of the February Revolution.

I was also wanted by the police at that time. My aunt hid me until I made my escape to Dvinsk.

"My Brother, who shot (upon) Shimke Dimentn"
[Spy in the Socialist organization – A. Jermyn]

A Yeshiva Bocher

Dvinsk was a town well-known to me. I had studied at a Yeshiva there. There were two Yeshivas in Dvinsk. One was known as Hurwitz's Yeshiva which consisted of three sections. Reb Simcha taught the beginners *Matchilim*. Reb Yachel Yehuda took the older students and Reb Yomtov worked with the rabbinic students.

The second Yeshiva was a Chasidic school - Wittenberg's Yeshiva, whose principal was Reb Yehoshe Arsch. In addition, my grandparents lived in Dvinsk and they were like my own beloved parents. My Zeida was a poor man. His livelihood was from his two cows and he made a living from the dairy products yielded by these two cows.

At first, I studied in the beginner's Yeshiva, with Yehuda and afterwards I moved up to Wittenberg's. The principal, Reb Arsch, was an extremely strict man and exacted great diligence from his students, but I had a zest for learning.

A Yiddish teacher, Soloviov, was recommended to me and we began to study Russian. He prepared me for entrance to the second level of the Russian secular school. I had a strong yearning to learn more of the outside world beyond the parochial, but without neglecting my Chasidic studies. In time, I had my own pupils among the workers. They would ask me to explain the difficult passages in the illegal booklets.

Soloviov advised me to leave the Yeshiva and to enter the Dvinsk Technikon where one could receive free meals. As a student at the technical college, I soon became a member of the Student Socialist Movement. I was appointed to the group responsible for improving the standard of the food in the kitchen. Soon the students were able to have their say in the running of the kitchen. I graduated from this "Three Classics School" with honours.

Dvinsk and The Bund

In Dvinsk, I became a member of the Bund. There were a number of professional organisations and worker's unions in Dvinsk at that time. I really wanted to share my knowledge of the process of government deriving from the Constitution and Parliament, the voting system and how the franchise was exercised.

My first practical experience in the field was to address an audience of two thousand who had to make a decision for all specialist building workers, such as the plumbers, painters, carpenters and bricklayers to unite into a large, single union. In a state of feverish anxiety, I prepared a draft document of how this should come about.

My appeal had an unexpected result. The proposal for the union was unanimously accepted. This event inspired me to further revolutionary activity. I helped to distribute a highly illegal pamphlet of revolutionary songs, "The Vow" by Sh. Anski and songs such as "The Salty Sea of Human Tears," and "How long, how long will we still be slaves," and others. These songs were sung with resounding echoes in Natanson's button factory. Passers-by would stop in their tracks to listen to the enthusiastic singing of the workers.

In the first days of Pesach in 1905, I took part in a conference of the Bund in Ponevezh. The sittings were stopped for afternoon and evening prayers. Twenty-five delegates attended and the subjects for discussion at the conference were how to conduct propaganda, how to distribute literature, how to organise strikes, and the organisation of workers' meetings.

A tall, intelligent young man, one of the stewards, walked up and down and around the hall, and emphasised that we were not to write anything down. We were to remember the resolutions and the decisions made at the conference and to memorize them carefully so that we could report the conference accurately to our members in the Ponevezh region.

Group photo of exiles in East Kulos
(first row right to left) "Machlin"
(second row right to left): wife and husband Prokopyevitch

On the third day of the Pesach week, the delegates went home peacefully. They were inspired and felt energised to commit themselves to achieving the aims of the Conference and to further their ideals.

My desire to study was intense. I traveled to Vilna, but was unable to enrol at the Teachers' Seminar because I was from the Kovno Guberniya (province) and not a local from Vilna. Disappointed, I left Vilna and returned to Riga.

In Riga, I found an open cultural umbrella organisation called Carmel. This was a progressive body under whose roof were a variety of groups and people. There were Latvians, Lithuanians, Estonians, Germans of every political left-wing colour, such as Social Democrats and Bundists. Carmel was a central meeting place for all committed activists.

Later, a Federation of the different parties, called the Soviet developed. I was co-opted on the Soviet as an assistant secretary. Drs. Scheinfeld and Hirschfeld were very active members of the Soviet (Not long ago, before I started writing these memories, I was grief-stricken to hear that Dr. Scheinfeld and his whole family were killed by the Latvian - Hitler regime).

In the Soviet, I had the opportunity to meet interesting Socialist theorists. I also had a group of students to whom I gave classes and explained the democratic developments in our Jewish history, such as the Sanhedrin, that gathered together traditional regulations uniting Jews who were scattered over the four corners of the earth. We also discussed the Karl Marx Manifesto. I taught my students that religion in the first period of its development, as presented in the religious texts, was progressive and democratic.

From that time of my teaching, I remember the Bundist, Abraham Chofetz, a student from the Kiev Polytechnic. He was a strongly committed comrade of the Party. Despite his tubercular pallor, he gave the last ounce of his strength to the Party. His learned lectures and theoretical analyses were a treasure house of knowledge and culture.

Unlike Chofetz, a school friend, Julius, who doubted our sincerity, turned himself over to the secret police and blackened the names of about ten members of the Bund, including mine. One of my friends, Auerbach and I were taken to a police cell and then transported to the Riga prison, where we met our eight other comrades who had been arrested. After questioning, we were released.

Earlier, I was taken for questioning to the "Centralka." They tortured us badly. Terrible screams, groans and cries could be heard from every cell. We remained in the Riga "Centralka" and were prosecuted. We attempted to send coded messages to the other political prisoners. For six months, we were kept in the prison. People from the Socialist Party brought us food - we had butter, cheese, cigarettes and even chocolates. No private visitors were allowed to see us apart from family members.

Exile to the Volog District in Siberia Begins

One day, I was visited by a woman who said she told the police that she was my fiancée. She told me that the verdict of the case was that we were sentenced to the Vologda District for three years. She comforted me with the assurance that the Party would do everything they could for us. And so it was.

The morning came when we were told to get ready for the journey. We marched all the way to the station under police escort and in the train we were guarded by armed soldiers. From Riga, they sent us to Petersburg. In the Petersburg jail, we were locked up with a few criminals. We were then sent to Vologda. The Vologda jail, a wooden two-storied building looked more like a shul than a prison. There was one room with large windows and strong metal grilles. On one wall was a poster with instructions for the gaolers and on the opposite wall, names of those who had been there before us. We also added our names to the list.

From Vologda we were taken to Viatke. On the station at Viatke we noticed a huge van, guarded by police and soldiers with swords held in their hands. Sitting in the van were a woman and a man dressed in expensive furs. We discovered that they were the famous revolutionaries, Tcheidza and his wife. He had been released and she was taking him home.

The Viatke jail was in a long dark, dirty cellar with mice and bugs. Political and criminal prisoners were put together in the same cells. After a period we were taken in convoy on a wagon drawn by four or six horses. The guards had guns and every few minutes we heard them loading their guns. We did about

40 versts[2] a day. We rested in villages along the way, in places which had been prearranged by our gaolers. There was one room for the soldiers and a long, fenced-off back room with iron bars and barbed wire was for us, the prisoners. We slept on straw on the floor. At every rest place a new convoy took over.

About 100 miles from Viatke our treatment improved. They allowed us to walk because we had become stiff from the long hours of sitting. The convoy leader began to speak to us. When we got to Yarensk the soldiers allowed us to buy food from the peasants - yellow cheese, butter and herring. There was no bread, except for a type of village cake called *yarushnikas*.

Winter, With a Guitar

Winter came. We arrived at Ust-Saisiyalsk prison where we were much more comfortable. Although the prison room was not large, it was heated and the guard was friendly. For small change, he brought us food - warm prison soup.

In the middle of the room, stood a long table and we could sit there. Two new comrades, a man and a woman joined us. He was a Russian from Moscow, an artist. A warder brought him a guitar and we spent a jolly evening. He imitated a man who had drunk too much vodka.

We all laughed and the warders standing by the large kerosene lamps were also amused.

From Ust-Saisiyalsk we travelled to Ust-Kulas which had a climate that covered the land in frost all year round.

This was our destination. Here we received money from the Bund in Riga. We needed the money for warm clothes. And, we met other Bundists from Vilna – Yezierski, and Machlin who was a friendly man. Machlin's logical lectures on world problems and literature were scientific and erudite.

Machlin, Auerbach and Leibchik

Machlin was a tall broad-shouldered chap with a beard, and his looks reminded me of the well-known Zionist Dr. Chaim Weitzman. The comrades in his cell and the Christian neighbours, nicknamed Machlin "Your Holiness."

In that far-away place, we had a library and received illegal pamphlets. Machlin used to read us matters of interest. I also remember, Comrade Alexander, who was an interesting person. He was a Russian from Moscow where he was secretary of a cooperative. He was an expert in different social problems. He formed a group that studied the history of English industry. I shared a room with Leibchik Popliak, a comrade from Riga. My friend comrade Auerbach was with me all the time.

Chaver Auerbach was released before me. His parents requested that he be freed. Chaver Leibchik received information from the Party telling him to escape. Leibchik disappeared one night, thanks to a woman who ran Kuzbazier's business that exported butter, oil, fish, sardines, furs, and dairy products, and a small river-craft for the use of the customers. The business owner's son had arranged for Leibchik to escape on the boat with a passport saying that he was a customer. So he got away.

Once the police arrived and knocked on my door, but I did not open up. They forced an entry and I was then sent to East Saisiyalsk because they suspected that I was spreading socialist propaganda and illegal literature.

In East Saisiyalsk, I met another deported family. One of them was comrade Kramer, a student in the medical faculty. He was a most interesting person. To this day, I can recall his intelligent face in all its particulars.

Later, I was sent back to East Kulas, and given new quarters. I shared a living area with a family, Prokopievich. All my free time, I spent with my friend Machlin. We bought a small boat in partnership and in the mornings we would go down the river Kulas which had a very narrow entry. It stretched out and became very wide while at the same time the current became stronger and stronger. One day, when Machlin and I reached the middle of the river, the boat almost overturned.

During this time of my exile, we received a sum of 8 roubles from the state every month. We also got a basic allowance for our winter clothing. In addition, I received money from the Riga organisation and friendly letters from Lena Popliak.

Amnesty

After 18 months were up, I was notified that because of the 300-year celebrations of the Romanov dynasty, we had been granted amnesty.

The police guarded us until we reached Vologda, and there we were released. With happy hearts and train tickets in our pockets, we traveled to our separate homes.

Pesach time in Rakishok. The melting snow, with its accompanying mud, lay heavy on our hearts, only the anticipation of Pesach lightened our spirits. On the threshold, we were met with tears of joy at our homecoming by our families.

After Pesach and the Amnesty celebrations, the old system reared its ugly head once more. Freedom's short spell in Rakishok District was short-lived. I received letters from other friends in East Kulas. Many of those released comrades who had not been able to get home so quickly, were rearrested.

A Short Time After My Release, I Married

In a little village, Zabeshik, a few versts from my shtetl, I met my wife, Malke Levine. I was resting there after my ordeal in exile. A few weeks passed and my father arrived early on a Sunday. He was pale and frightened. With trembling lips he told me "My child you must leave here immediately. You cannot return to our shtetl. The police are looking for you. They turned our house upside-down trying to find you. They questioned me and your mother as to your whereabouts. When they didn't find anything they went to look for you in the Chasidic shtibel. They surrounded the minion and called out our family name. I managed to get out, but they told me that they were looking for Bunim Yidel and not Yankel Baruch." After this news, by the next morning I was already in Tavrik.

It was December, 1912. I crossed the border into Germany. From there, I traveled to sunny South Africa and arrived in Cape Town. My wife and baby son came many months later.

South African Soil and Politics

I arrived on African soil having endured 18 months in Tsarist jails. From the small jail in Riga, I had journeyed to the furthest reaches of the Vologda region. Viatka, Valanda, Yorensk, East Saisiyalsk and East Kulas. It seemed that South Africa was a land of political freedom, a paradise, compared with despotic Russia. I was overjoyed to be in South Africa.

I soon became interested in the political climate of South Africa, and particularly the Socialist movement. My brother Lazar, who lived in Cape Town, welcomed me with great hospitality. Thanks to him, I met my Socialist friends, Joe Pick, Goldblatt and others. It turned out, Goldblatt had lived in the same neighbourhood in Dvinsk as my grandparents and he immediately recognised me.

At that time there was a Social Democratic Federation in Cape Town whose members were for the most part English. Their premises were in Shortmarket Street not far from where I worked in my uncle's business. The hall was very light and airy and could hold 100 people. Meetings were held there often and all political subjects were discussed. I remember the following people who were on the Committee of this organisation: the Chairman McManus, Harrison, Connolly, Stewart, Driberg, Lemmon and others. There were a few Jewish members in the organisation. Aside from Pick and Goldblatt there was Walt, Baskin, Jacobson, Schumann, the three Gamsu sisters and myself.

**Bunen-Aidel Kril, his son Israel,
and his wife Malkah, 1913**

**Members of the Socialist Federation
including members of the Yiddish Group of the Socialist Federation**
(standing left to right) Davidov, Valt, Shuman, Slos, Goldblat, Baskin, B. A. Kril;
(seated left to right): Boyarski, Lapitzki, Berman, Sosnovitz, Mak(monis), Lemon

Members of the Socialist Federation
(top row standing) English sailors sympathetic to the Socialist Federation;
(next row standing, right to left) Pick, Shuman, Goldblat, Berman, Lapat, Kril;
(seated right to left): R.-L. Harrison, Kanoli, Andrusch, Dreiberg
(second row right to left): wife and husband Prokopyevitch

The lectures and discussions were held in English and comrade Pick would translate for me into Yiddish. There was a good and friendly atmosphere at the meeting. The other members were very interested in me, and I was able to participate in the discussions in Yiddish which was translated into English.

Yiddish Section of the Social Democratic Federation

A short time later a few of us, including Pick, Schumann, Goldblatt and I decided to organise a Yiddish section of the Federation. Pick, an energetic initiator with ambitions to rise in the organisation, called a meeting of the Yiddish members. A Yiddish section was formed and a committee of eight was appointed. I was also elected on to the committee. Pick was elected Chairman and Walt Secretary.

There were twenty members in the Yiddish Section including Turok, Slom and Rudovsky. Slom later emigrated to America to study medicine. I remember that the first cycle of lectures was held in Yiddish and the subject was the Russian Revolutionary Movement. These lectures attracted about 50 people each time they were held. After each lecture there were lively and interesting discussions. I spoke about democracy and mentioned that the Sanhedrin was based on democratic principles. The Yiddish Section grew from strength to strength. Many interesting meetings were held. Comrade Slom lectured on scientific matters as well as party dynamics. Comrade Pick spoke about Trades Unions and comrade Davidoff talked about politics. My brother Lazar discussed literature and I spoke about political economy and the growth of the working class movements.

There was a great need for Yiddish books. Most of the comrades who were invited were too poor to import Yiddish books. The committee itself was too limited and too impoverished to buy books. Nevertheless we managed to collect some books from friends who lent them to us. These were books by Morris Vinshevsky, Avrom Reizin, Dovid Edelschtadt, Sholom Aleichem, Mendele as well as Y. L. Peretz, Perets, Stolensky, etc. These books also led to many discussions. A great attraction was the ad-hoc debates and all were encouraged to participate in the discussion. These evenings were full-houses.

Thirst for Knowledge

I had a great thirst for knowledge that I had inherited from my father. I remember once when he had spoken to me, trembling. "I myself took you to Rabbi Yachiel Yehuda's Yeshiva. After that you passed into the Wittenberg's Chasidic Yeshiva. How much sweat and tears did this cost me. I am now going to the head of the Lubavitch, and if you don't come with me and enter this Yeshiva, I will cut you off so that you will never receive anything from me - no shoes or clothes - you will have to fend for yourself in your goyisha world."

Even though these words had come from another world-view, they still encouraged me to enrich my soul with ever more education. Coming to South Africa reawakened in me a need to be educated. I had a great desire to pursue scholarship. My comrades referred me to an elderly professor, Palmer, who was at Cape Town University. I studied with him with great enthusiasm for 5 months. I read the works of Aaron Hill, *Before Adam*, Jack London as well as *Uncle Tom's Cabin*, William Morris' poetry, Ruskin's political economics and Karl Marx's *Das Kapital.*

I was soon able to participate at the Social Democratic Federation meetings in English, and was also able to write short reports. But because of material needs I had to drag myself away from my studies with the professor. When I brought my wife and child out of the old country, I had to work much more to make a home for them.

In spite of my limitations, I made the time to read and to participate in the activities of the Federation that had developed into an intense cultural-political centre. All our meetings were well attended. New members, for example Fox, Joffe, and the Bayer brothers, enrolled. Some of the Jewish members reverted to the original section as they felt that we had become too left and one of them, Stewart, exposed his anti-semitism. It's true that he was chosen from the Federation but we no longer trusted him. This was the main reason for the Yiddish section to move to other premises in Plein Street

International Socialist League (ISL)

In mid-1915 I met the well-known Socialist, S.P. Bunting, who was the editor of *The International* a journal published by the International Socialist League (ISL), of which I was a member. He gave me the opportunity to write a number of articles. This encouraged me to write for the South African Worker, where one of my articles was published. I continued to write for the Yiddish section as well.

At one of the Yiddish Section meetings, we decided to open up a Yiddish Sunday school for children. The more progressive members of the Jewish community wanted such a school for their children and this became the first secular Jewish school in South Africa. The teachers at that school were Berman, Pick, Davidov and, at the beginning, I also taught there.

Davidov and Berman organised a choir at the school and they often held concerts when the children performed. I particularly remember a young girl, Rosa Rudovsky, who sang a song by Rosenveld so beautifully.

Johannesburg

After wandering around various towns in South Africa, we finally made the family home in Johannesburg, where I became an active member of the International Socialist League and the Jewish Workers' Club.

At that time, Sylvia Pankhurst, the suffragette who (unlike her mother and sister) fought in the War-on-War League against the First World War, edited 'The Workers' Dreadnought' in England. The newspaper focused on the struggle of the working class in Britain and elsewhere and was eagerly awaited and read by us regularly.

I always remained firm to the ideals of socialism and, to this day, I am committed to these ideals with all my heart and soul.

1. Territorialism was the term describing Jews in Europe and Russia who were debating the idea of having a single Jewish territory, not necessarily in Israel, but very possible in Russia after the revolution. The example of Birobijan established later in the USSR was regarded as a Jewish territory.
2. One Verst is approximately three-quarters of one mile.

[Page 131]

Fragments of My Past
by Ralph Arsh (Yerachmiel Aarons-Arsh)
Translated by Mathilda Mendelow, born Ginsberg

I inhaled the Zionist redemption ideal when I was still in my parents' home. My father truly knew whole works of Yiddish and Hebrew literature by heart. He was a grammarian and had a great knowledge of the Bible. He studied Holy writings together with a group in synagogue. He was the leader of all the most religious congregations – first in Sviadests and then in Rakishok. To him, his first duty was love of Zion and love of Israel. That was the most important essential in his life.

My mother was an intelligent woman. Her greatest pleasure was to read books. I grew up in an atmosphere of enlightenment and love of our nation. Yiddish and Hebrew journals and newspapers used to arrive in our home. When I was only two years old, I used to look at the photos in the books and newspapers and I knew the names of the writers.

The childhood years planted within me an energy and desire to be independent in my path. Still, long before there were preparatory agricultural centers for training in Lithuania I obtained a training in agriculture from a peasant whose name was Poepelis. He lived in a village whose name was Trumpantze, at the Lithuanian border. A lake divided the border from the Latvian wilderness. The town's inhabitants were mixed, about half were Russian peasants and half Lithuanian peasants and a few Polish families. Although, at first the work of the peasant was difficult for me and the living style strange, I wanted to reach my goal to learn how to plough, plant and reap.

More than once I used to long for books and journals and especially for more Jews. I was also bored during the autumn days and nights when it rained continuously and the mud was more than knee deep. When I learned all about farming and knew all about country life, I wrote to the Pioneering Center in Kovno telling them that I wanted to go to Israel as an immigrant. The Pioneering Center answered me that I was too young and that I should wait.

A new spirit entered within me. As a stop gap, I left for Palatage where the first Lithuanian Kibbutz was situated, since I did not work and I could do the agricultural work well. The head of the kibbutz was Zisle – I later met him at the Ein Harod.

The first Litvisher (Lithuanian) Kibbutz in Palestine (Koidan)
(first row, standing left to right) "Zisle", Director of the Kibbutz;
(first row seated) I. Arsh [others in photo not identified]

Because I became ill at the Kibbutz, I left for home in Rakishok. For a few weeks I walked around the Rakishok streets without a goal and empty handed. Often I used to go to the Zionist offices and I started reading Jewish books.

As I did not get a positive answer from the Pioneering Center, I wanted to work for a prince who called himself Kazlov, but my father got me a job in Kovno at a German firm where I worked for a year and a half. My older brother Melech was also in Kovno at the time. He was in his last semester of the teachers' qualification. My Aunt Mira (may she rest in peace) was also studying medicine in Kovno at that time.

Although I worked hard at this German firm, I still had time to study Hebrew and to read books. At the same time I did not stop obstinately and stubbornly demanding a certificate from the Pioneering Center. Even though I was already 17 years old and considered from all sides to be ready as an immigrant to Palestine, the Center did not hasten to answer my numerous requests. But one day someone told me a secret that if I was prepared to cover the expenses of the journey for a comrade they would give me a certificate.

It was not easy for me to put such a proposition to my father, but still I wrote a letter about this to my parents. I was greatly amazed when I received a letter from my father that he was prepared to give me the expenses of the journey for a second comrade so that I should be able to go.

In 1925 I went to Israel. At that time an excursion was organized to the opening of Jerusalem University and a group of pioneers came along with us. We went by train through Berlin and Belgium to Marseilles. At the boat we met two young people from Poland who wanted to emigrate, but they had no certificates and no tickets for passage. We pioneers found a way so that they would be able to come along. They came aboard carrying our luggage and we emptied two large baskets in which they hid until the documents were checked. Thereafter they walked around the boat free as birds! Each time they checked the documents we hid them in the baskets.

The ship was an old one, built to carry goods and cattle feed. The air was choking. There were two double-storied bunks in fourth class. People were ill and those from the upper bunks used to vomit on to the heads of those who slept in the lower bunks. The food was bad. We were fed potatoes and at each meal we received only one sardine.

Excursion from Lithuania to Jerusalem for inauguration of the Jerusalem University
[Ship and individuals not identified; date not shown]

In the third class the food and the quarters were better. We arrived in Alexandria and several passengers disembarked and continued the journey by train to Eretz Israel. The rest of us continued by boat to Beirut. There I together with the two illegal passengers from Poland got off the ship to explore the city. They did not return to the boat and when we arrived in Jaffa they were already waiting for us!

We arrived on shore in small boats. My joy was immensely great standing on Israeli soil. We passed through the port and were immediately transferred to the immigration center which looked like barracks where I felt very unhappy. The representatives of the transition association came to receive the new comrades and on the third day I joined a company going to Petach Tikva. There in the Kibbutz I felt at home. I was able to work the land. I knew how to plough, sow and use the scythe. I also knew how to deal with cattle and horses. In other words I was a useful pioneer. In the Spring of 1925 our group settled on our own piece of ground known as the Third Hill. When I was in Israel in 1950 they celebrated the 25th anniversary of the Kibbutz. As I looked out I could not believe that human hands could do so much.

In the beginning our Kibbutz was in a terrible condition. The Petach Tikva superiors did not want to establish Jewish Workers. They hired workers at three piasters a day. Our daily wage at that time was 15 piasters. Overall they looked upon us with open hate and our way of living was strange and not understandable to them. The colonists did not like the fact that girls and boys were together in the Kibbutz. The area folks looked upon us askance and believed us to be heretics. Because of their antagonistic and bad behavior we took on contract labor and we earned only 4.3 piasters per day!

The Kibbutz had 200 souls and there was work only for a few tens of people. The rest were busy with household and farm administration. I remember how we were hungry. For many weeks we lived on watery soup which had a little oil in it. Bread was frugal. Still, in spite of the bad position we were in, we danced the Hora, sang a lot and we had lectures and discussions. The greatest personalities in the settlement came to us to give us lectures. Ben Gurion used to visit our Kibbutz, as did Chaim Arlozov, Z. Ruvashov, Professor Chaim Weitzman, Nachum Salkalov and many others. I also remember the visit of Rubin Breinen while he was still a Zionist enthusiast.

Tel Aviv was fourteen kilometers from Petach Tikva and we used to walk to Tel Aviv on Shabbat. I often visited the immigration center there. In Tel Aviv I met with Rakishoker pioneers and my friends Aaron (Nachamowitz) and Nachum Louis Kopelowitz.

Today, I particularly remember two experiences from my visits to Tel Aviv. Arriving on Shabbat in Tel Aviv, I was very hungry. I thought when I arrived in the immigration center they would think that I was a new immigrant and they would give me food. I sat down at the table. They immediately realized I was not a new immigrant and they told me to leave the table at once.

The first Chalutzim of Rokiskis in Israel
(seated right to left) Nahum Kapelovitz, Shimson Dekar;
(standing right to left) unknown chalutz from "Exyerene" (sp?),
A. Nahumovitz, Rachel Fine, Nahum Shuster, Rachmiel Arsh

The second episode also occurred in Tel Aviv on a Shabbat. I was walking on Alenavi Street and smoked a cigarette. A Jew with a fine beard met me saying "Son, what have you got against me?" For the moment I did not understand his meaning, I did not know what he wanted of me and I said to him "Uncle, you have a complaint, but you don't know me!" He answered me in saying, "I really do mean you. If you slapped my face it would not hurt me as much as it hurts me to see a Jewish boy with a cigarette in his mouth on Saturday afternoon in Tel Aviv." This was the last time I smoked openly on a Shabbat in the streets of Tel Aviv.

Since there was not much work in the Kibbutz four friends and I went through the land from Dan to Ber Sheba. When we returned to the Kibbutz I heard that they were going to drain the swamps at Migdal. A group of Lithuanian Jews had settled near the town of Saba which is 12 kilometers by road from Petach Tikva. The Keren Kayemeth demanded that each Kibbutz should send several workers. I joined the group that had to dry out the swamps at Migdal. The work was difficult. We had to dig in mountains up to the Yarkon River. We stood in swamps up to our belts. The heat was terrible – the chamsin (hot desert wind) used to draw the marrow from ones bones. Often we drank the filthy water from the swamps because of thirst and treated unripe watermelon as dessert.

"Harvest Time" – R. Arsh
[others in photo not identified]

After three months work I became ill with malaria . I did not want to give up and went to work with a high fever although no one forced me to do so. I developed dysentery from eating unripe watermelons and was sent to the hospital in a terrible condition where I wrestled with death. After I left the hospital I was weak and the Kibbutz gave me light work – to guard a field at night against jackals. They built a booth on four stakes and gave me a tin with which I had to frighten the jackals. I again had a malaria attack and when a friend brought me food I was lying down with a high fever and the whole field of watermelons had been eaten up!

My friend Noah Nachomowitz wrote a letter to my father that I was ill with malaria. My father sent fifteen pounds. The doctors advised me to leave the land. The hospital also helped with expenses and in Spring 1927 I left the land on a French boat.

I went through a lot of misery until I arrived in Kovno. I delivered a letter from the hospital to the Pioneer Center. The letter stated that because of a severe illness I left the land. I borrowed money from an acquaintance for a ticket home. At that time my father had many business divisions. The iron business went well so he started the wood trade, a credit bank and he built the first iron factory in Rakishok. It was easy for me to get a position in one of my father's businesses, but I hoped that as soon as my health improved I would return to the land of Israel.

The Pioneer Center in Kovno sent me to Memel as an instructor. I worked in Memel for the whole summer until the middle of the Christian holiday on the eve of New Year. After I returned from Memel I decided to complete my studies. My teacher, David Sudafski gave me private lessons and within about four months I was examined in Rakishok, and passed a full course of the pre-college requirements in Hebrew with a good grade. In Rakishok I was a member of Maccabi. It did not take long before I took over the managing of the library which I enriched with tens of books.

In 1927 I met my wife and after military service I got married on Lag Baomer in 1929 in Sviadoshz. My parents, my grandfather Joshua and my wife's parents, my grandfather Moshe Jacob and grandmother Beila Ethel and close friends were guests at the wedding.

Chalutzim at the tobacco plantation, training to be farmers to go to Israel
R. Arsh [others in photo not identified]

The chuppah ceremony took place at the home of my grandfather Moshe Jacob (the Cohen) Farber (may he rest in peace). Shortly after the wedding around Shavuoth we left for South Africa. My wife's brother sent us the necessary documents and seventy pounds to leave the country. Although my urge to go to the land of Israel was great, I feared that possibly I would have another bout of malaria and so I agreed to go to South Africa. My father was against my leaving because he wanted me to join his business since he already felt his age.

On arriving in South Africa I was greatly disappointed. My brother-in-law Ephraim Swartsberg was earning ten pounds a month and the rest of the friends of my wife's family showed little interest in our position.

With the help of my wife's friends I opened a small business. The first six to seven years were difficult. My wife and I worked from early morning till late at night so that there no time to spend with cultural and soulful activities. My only reading was the "Forward – The American Jewish Voice" from Kovno and the local Jewish Press.

Time does not stand still and goes its way in anguish and happiness. The arrival of the second World War weighed heavily on me. I was then the father of three children. My wife understood my broken mood and my thoughts, but she spoke very little to me about it, being unwilling to touch the wound in my heart.

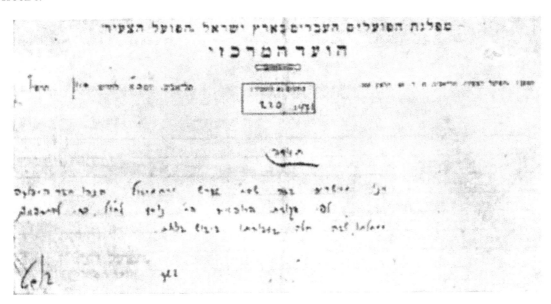

Mifleget Hapoalim Ha'ivrim b'Eretz Israel "Hapoel Hatza'ir" Hava'ad Hamerkazi

One fine day, walking in the street, I saw a line of people standing at the city hall waiting to sign on for war. I could not restrain myself and also stood in line. I arrived inside and signed on to go to war of my own free will. After signing on they gave me military clothing. When I arrived home my wife was shocked by my deed, but I explained that if we lost the war they would in any case eliminate us Jews. It was therefore better to die fighting. If Hitler lost, our children would be able to freely live their lives in the world and they would be proud of my deed.

A few days later I left for the military camp. I was in the war for six years. My only desire was to see Germany destroyed and to live to avenge the spilt blood. As frightful as war was in the desert, I had the opportunity to be in Israel often and to help the Jewish Brigade that was near our depot. On Rosh Hashanah 1945 I returned home in peace. Letters arrived from my brothers who wrote about the gruesome killings of the Jews in Rakishok and Lithuania and in Europe. In spite of there being an act to help the remnant refugee community, I found a need to help the leftover living Jews of Rakishok and the surrounding area. At the beginning of 1946 I helped to establish the Rakishok Aid Society. In certain places packets were sent out to countrymen and financial aid was sent to Israel for new immigrants.

Galiel Mamel, 1927
[the framed photo is of Mamel]
Second row from the top, seated second from left: noted Yiddish writer and poet Noah Itzhak Gotlieb.
The first from the right is "Habibah" who is lyrically included in his poems and songs.
[No row is indicated to identify this individual precisely]

Group of Jewish soldiers in the Lithuanian army

But the deep sorrow after the Holocaust of the Jews in Europe does not let me rest and I experienced the deep need for a monument for Rakishok and its neighboring shtetlach in the form of a Yizkor Book. I spoke about this plan to my friends Abraham Oralowitz (may he rest is peace) and to Shlomo Rubin and Aaron Nachomowitz. They also agreed with my idea to immortalize our old homes in a Yizkor Book of Rakishok and its Environs. May this Yizkor Book of Rakishok and its Environs truly be an immortal monument for our present and future generations.

I. Arsh, Staff Sgt. in South African Army

[Page 142]

We Will Remember You Forever

by Ahuva Schneiderman-Ruch

Translated by Rae Meltzer

The Zionist Youth Organization of Rokiskis

I am reminded of my shtetl Rakishok, before my immigration to Israel. I remember her wide streets and her narrow streets. Although Rakishok did not produce any writers, artists or musicians, nevertheless, the shtetl had good, ordinary Jews, with Jewish hearts, who always dreamed of their own homeland and were not lucky enough to see the great miracle of the birth of our homeland in Israel.

I remember the active Zionists in Rakishok; Hillel Eidelson (Brash) whom we called "The Grandfather". [See biographical sketch and photo of Hillel Eidelson on p. 46.] Without Grandfather Hillel Eidelson no meeting of the "Keren Kimes," "Keren Hisod," or other Zionist organization would begin. He also joined with us in the hora dance. I remember the Zionist "minyon" with our own "cantor," that good Jew and Zionist, Alhonen Arsh, may he rest in peace.

It was all so loving, dear, and holy. Mostly, the whole shtetl believed in Zionism. We had a "Kibbutz" organization, "Hapoel" organization, which was not only interested in sports, but also in cultural affairs, and we also had our own library. The Zionist organization brought new life into the shtetl. On the street one heard Hebrew spoken freely. A new generation was growing up and looking for a way to establish a Jewish homeland.

Only a small number had the resources to make aliyah to Israel. The Holocaust horror forced many Jews to seek a haven in Israel, where there are 110 families from Rakishok. Some are members of kibbutzim, a large group are workers who participate in all the work of the country. We in Israel remember the Rakishoker martyrs. We will never forget them. Our people will forever remember the German murderers and the bestial atrocities they committed upon our people.

[Page 145]

Personalities and Types

A Few Words in Place of a Tombstone

(My Father, Rabbi Abraham Myerowitz)

by N. Meyerowitz-Stein (Nachamel Stein)

Translated by Rabbi Boyarsky

My father, Rabbi Abraham Myerowitz, was a son-in-law of Rabbi Bezalel o.b.m., and serves as the rabbi of the township Skimiahn. He hailed from Karelitz, located in the province of Minsk, and studied in the Mir, Wolozin, and Slabodka yeshivas.

I recall as a child when we returned to Rakishok from Russia, we were welcomed back by the townspeople with flowers, love, and honor. My father was a wise man and no stranger to world affairs, and his command of Russian and German which he acquired on his own, broadened his horizon beyond the boundaries of Rakishok.

Frequently he was called to Ponevez to sit on a rabbinical arbitration board to help resolve disputes between litigants. He was also one of the original founders of the Rakishok Folkbank and served as its director. Many Rakishok landsleit now living in South Africa surely remember the bank loans he approved for them.

My father was a Misnaged--an opponent of Hasidism--but by no means a fanatic, and was considered to be a "modern" person in accordance with the socio-religious standards of that time. His Zionist orientation led him to join the Mizrachi--the National Religious Party--within the Zionist movement. He often appeared as speaker at their meetings and political rallies. Because of these activities, he was less popular in the ultra-orthodox Agudas Yisroel circles.

At a rabbinical conference held in Ponevez, my father issued a warning that we were sorely mistaken in thinking that Hitler's objective was confined to the destruction of the German Jews. He declared that this was an ominous signal for the entire Jewish population in Europe. This raised a volley of criticism among the Agudah delegates. Unfortunately, his admonition fell on deaf ears, and he met his death with the rest of the illustrious Lithuanian Jewry Al Kidush Hashem--in martyrdom.

I know that my father had immigration papers for America, but my mother, Asne Rivka o.b.m., refused to emigrate, leaving behind the older children. In 1928, my father was the rabbi of Abel, and remained there till the very end. According to eyewitnesses, he was found dead from a fired shot on the highway to Abel, in the early days of the German-Russian war.

Rabbi Bezalel Katz   **Hon. Rabbi Avrum Meyerovitz**

Rabbi Betzalel Katz with Lithuanian President Smetana at the dedication of the newly-built station in Rokiskis

The Rokiskis people meet Pres. Smetana on Komeyer Street near the School

[Pages 149-151]

In Everlasting Memory

by Bluma Arsh-Lavya, Israel

Translated by Gloria Berkenstat Freund

Khona Arsh

H. and Nechema-Liba Arsh with their daughter Blumeh-Liba Arsh

The name of my father, Khona Arsh, was well known in Rakishok and in its vicinity and in distant cities and towns in Lithuania. He was descended from a very important family in Dvinsk. His father, Yehoshua Arsh, was the famous head of the yeshiva in Dvinsk, previously of Witenberg's and later in the Lubavitcher yeshiva. After the First World War until his death, he was the *dayan* [rabbinic judge] in Dvinsk.

Khona was his parents' oldest son and was raised in an environment of *Torah* and study.

There was a wonderful Jewish intelligentsia in Dvinsk that was permeated with the most beautiful ideas. Interest in worldly culture was strong among the young people and Khona Arsh and his brothers also were inspired to learn the Russian language and to enter a *gymnasia* [secular high school].

The Zionist movement captured Khona during his early years and he was very active in it. The greatest experience for him was when Dr. Theodor Herzl traveled with his mission to Russia. He was also at the reception that the Vilna Jews held in honor of Dr. T. Herzl, when he visited Vilna.

The Zionist ideal was holy and dear to him and he was devoted to it his entire life. His dream and wish was to settle permanently in *Eretz-Yisroel*.

Joshua Arsh (Lubavitcher)   **Moiseh-Jacob (The Wise) Farber**

He married a daughter of an esteemed merchant in Sviadoshits at age 23. There he opened a small iron business and he lived there with his family until the First World War.

During the First World War, he and his family evacuated to Russia, where he remained for seven years living through the turbulent times of the war and the revolutionary years.

In 1922 he returned to Rakishok with his family. His eldest daughter, Ruchl, remained in Moscow.

He succeeded in building up a large iron business with Pesakh Rukh and greatly strengthened his economic position.

However, the Zionist movement filled his spiritual essence. He was active in all of the institutions and societies in the *shtetl*, one of the most prominent workers. He also was active in the area of the educational system, as an active member of *Tarbus* [Translator's note: *Tarbus* promoted secular Zionist education taught in the Hebrew language].

He contributed as if a rich man to all of the funds and he received emissaries from *Eretz-Yisroel* with great hospitality, looking at each as a herald... Khona Arsh's house was the center of Zionist-communal work in Rakishok.

He had an elevated Jewish soul, and with deep love he did everything that he could on behalf of the Jewish people and on behalf of *Eretz-Yisroel*.

He was slim and handsome, and a person of stately appearance internally and externally. It was not without reason that he was revered in Zionist Lithuania.

My mother, Nekhame-Liba Arsh, helped him in his communal-Zionist work. Her father, Moshe Yakov haKohan Farber, was a very great scholar and a pious man and the greatest aristocratic man in Sviadoshits. (He died this year in Jerusalem at the age of 97.)

As a young woman, my mother frequently attended the Russian school and was a skillful business woman in my father's cut-goods business.

After her marriage, she helped her husband run his business.

She was a logical person, with deep understanding and energy, and was very truthful in her actions. She very much liked to read and tried to give her children a good education.

They perished together cruelly at the hands of the Hitlerist devils in 1941, with the entire Rakishok Jewish community.

May their names and memory be blessed!

[Pages 152-157]

My Father, Berchik the *Shoykhet*

by Avraham Koseff

Translated by Gloria Berkenstat Freund

The Jewish temperament, impatient and stubborn, led to arguments, to unreasonable hatred in many cities and *shtetlekh* [towns] not so passionate about personal matters, although this aspect was also present – as it was about *kehile* [organized Jewish community] matters; a *gabbai* [person who assists in running of synagogue], a *khazan* [cantor], a *shoykhet* and so on. Each side wanted the rabbi, the *shoykhet* [ritual slaughterr], etc. in the *shtetl* to be his. Rakishok possessed two rabbis; each rabbi had his supporters. The *shoykhetim* had their sides, too. However, the supporters of the rabbis themselves split because of the *shoykhetim* and the supporters of the *shoykhetim* were divided over the rabbis. Consequently, the result was that the entire *kehile* was divided and torn apart into groups and factions.

Hon. Gaon Saul Vilkomirer

My grandfather, Zorukh, was one of the *shoykhetim* in Rakishok. He probably hoped that his only son, Berchik, would inherit his position as *shoykhet* when he, Zorukh, would die. However, his only son was a great prankster. He climbed on fences, roofs and trees the entire day up until the age of 14 or 15. Therefore, his father had great sorrow when he saw that his only son was not inclined to follow in his path. He did not study and did not want to study. As a result, my grandfather beat him because he did not want to raise a peasant.

However, Berchik turned 15 and a great change took place in the spoiled young boy. Quietly, he took a few rubles out of his father's drawer and ran away to the Wilkomirer Rabbi and *gaon* [Torah genius], Reb Shual, who was their relative. There he threw himself into studying and later became a brilliant student and beloved by Reb Shual.

It should be understood that my grandfather was very happy. His hope that his son would take over his position moved him to advise my father that he should study slaughtering and the laws of kosher slaughtering. Thus, after my grandfather's death, my father became one of the Rakishok *shoykhetim*.

Berchik the *shoykhet* was well known both in Rakishok and in the surrounding area as a great scholar, whose mastery of and resourcefulness in the Talmud and the commentaries was great and deep. Outwardly he had a disheveled beard, a wide square forehead and restless eyes that looked out from under an angry brow. His forehead was wrinkled from constant deep thought. However, I often saw a smile on his face, as with an innocent child. Even his anger appeared to me as the squinted whim of a child.

Bertzik the "Shochet" (Butcher)

The quarrels which broke out during the later years led to Rakishok having three or four *shoykhetim*. This hurt my father greatly. There were even people who blamed him and said that he was the cause of the quarrels because, although my father was the son of a devoted Hasid, he was not very devoted to Hasidus. He was undecided about becoming a follower of a Hasidic Rebbe and could not bear the Hasidic indifference to *Halakah* [the Jewish laws dealing with all aspects of life] with which his thoughts were always occupied. Therefore, many Hasidim were his strong opponents, but he did not pay attention to this. He went on his own path. He treated everyone with impartiality. He was convinced of his correctness and stubbornly defended it because one cannot play on two fiddles at once [hold two opinions at the same time]. Even his enemies had respect for his firmness. He did not look for any honors nor did he wear a *shtreimlekh* [fur hat worn by Hasidim]; he was satisfied with his fate that had made him take over the tenure of his father. At the end I was told the after the First World War, when the people from Rakishok came back to their homes and did not find Reb Berchik, his greatest opponents regretted the loss of their *shoykhet*, Reb Berchik.

The library of Bertzik; the Shochet's wife Chaiye Kosef

He would wake up in the middle of the night to study, but it was almost day, and studying during the day was often interrupted because of business. Therefore, his jumbled books had to be left alone. The days and the nights were too short and time could not be borrowed. By nature, he was impetuous and impatient and he did not have time and any interest in other matters, only for studying. Even when lying in bed, resting on his arm and wanting to rest, his face was strained, concentrating and suddenly he would spring up, take out a book, page through it and again sit and study. In the synagogue, when he prayed, he did not have the patience to wait until the person leading the prayer finished. He was the first to finish and threw impatient looks at the worshiper as to why he took so long. However, on *Shabbosim* [Sabbaths]. and holidays, when he would recite the Torah before the congregation, his impatience would disappear. A sedateness and tenderness would then reign over him, as with an old grandfather who was having a good time with his grandchildren. He would try to bring his listener to him. He spoke with the greatest simplicity, explained things so that they could understand and comprehend what he was saying to them and his face beamed with satisfaction when he felt that the congregation had absorbed his talk.

He was very rigorous with concerning piety for himself and among others. When it came to unfamiliar interests, he was lenient. Therefore, the butchers in the slaughter house, although they were afraid of him because he was strict with them, requested that he inspect their cattle because he could spend a great deal of time studying an adhesion on the lungs in order to declare the cow kosher because an unkosher cow was a great loss for a butcher.

He disliked taking the time to talk about everyday things with those around him in the *shtetl*. However, he loved to spend time with the young men who would come from the *yeshivus*, and with people who had visited foreign lands, if they were a little involved with dissent from the religious norm. He loved to carry on philosophic conversations with young men. He was acquainted with the old Greek philosophy; he studied "The Guide to the Perplexed," the *Khazari* [*Kitab al Khazari* by Yehuda ha-Levi] and similar books, although the very pious frowned upon them. The young people considered it an honor to visit Reb Berchik.

My father was frail. He traveled abroad often because of his weak health. He also used these journeys of his to alleviate his suffering to acquire old books. As a result, he had visited all of the historical centers of Torah. Returning, he brought old books, rare books. When he received such a book, the satisfaction would radiate from his eyes. He was so joyous when he found, and brought with him from abroad, a first edition of *Sheylus Vatshuves* [book of rabbinical analysis of questions of religious law] by the *Rashba* [Rabbi Shlomoh ben Aderet] and other books from abroad. (The mentioned publication by the *Rashba* was printed in 1545 and in now with his son-in-law, Mr. Yitzhak Padowicz [Johannesburg]). It is said that at the outbreak of the First World

War, when everyone in Lithuania was evacuated, he was the last one to leave Rakishok because he did not want to go without his books, which he needed to pack in sacks. He had a great treasury of books. Because of this, his trip into deep Russia was slow. He wandered aimlessly at each train station longer than the other homeless. Only a small portion of his books are in Johannesburg. His Talmud and other books, on whose edges he wrote his comments, remained in Latvia. He certainly intended to publish these comments, which surely would have stood out in the rabbinical literature.

My father remained in written contact with the famous Rogatchover *gaon* – the Hasidic rabbi of Dvinsk. When I went to study in the Witenberg *yeshiva*, my father told me that I should visit the Rogatchover *gaon* and extend a greeting from him. I remember the visit. It was dark in the first room where the old *shamas* [synagogue sexton] with a grey-yellowed little beard sat and napped over a book. He woke up and immediately led me into a bright and homey room where books were spread on the tables. Two dark eyes, blazing like diamonds, looked out from under a large forehead. With his face looking like a large parchment, the *gaon* sat in a long velvet jacket. Upon learning that I came from Rakishok, he immediately asked me: "How is Reb Berchik?"

Facsimile of Reb Bertsik's (the ritual slaughterer) writing titled "Questions and Answers"

We children have letters that the Rogatchover wrote with great respect to my father. My father had several students; one, Reb Zelig Rakishker, later became the head of the Lomza *yeshiva*. A second, Reb Shmuel Aba Snieg, became a famous rabbi and leader, and is now the chief rabbi in Munich, Germany.

When one of the students would come from the *yeshiva* bringing a letter from the head of the *yeshiva* stating that he was not showing any interest and was not making progress, my father would not punish or reproach him. He only asked him, what kind of employment would he chose for himself, because education did not have to have a purpose, it had to emanate from an internal need, like eating or drinking.

Learning for him was life, and life for him meant studying Torah. Jews would hope to die with the *vide* [confessions of sins] on their lips. I believe my father died with Torah on his lips.

He died at the age of 65, may the memory of a righteous person be blessed.

Reb Shmuel Levitan

Editor's Note: Reuben Ruch notes that the photo also contains the future Lubavitcher Rebbe, *Menachem Mendel Schneerson, seated at the center of table.*]

Shmuel Levitan and the Lubavitcher Rebbe

[Page 158]

Jews of Rakishok

by Avraham Orelowitz

Translated by Gloria Berkenstat Freund

Reb Shlomoh Skopishker

Rabbi Shloime Skopisher

I begin with my father and why not? May a son erect a *matseyveh* for his father: Let the following writing be his bright memorial.

My father, Shlomoh Orelowitz, may he rest in peace, or as he was called: Reb Shlomoh Orelowitz, Reb Shlomoh Skopishker and, also, Reb Shlomoh, Zelig's son, was the most popular person in the entire area and was known as a great, learned man and the most enraptured Hasid in all of Poland.

During his childhood he studied in the *yeshiva* of the Kopuster Rebbes. He was acquainted with many Hasidim. After his marriage, a great Hasid attracted him to his businesses and he was employed as one who sells on commission in Kenigsberg [Konigsberg]. Later, he settled in Skopishok [Skapiskis] because of family opportunities and opened a yard goods store there. From that time he received the name, "Reb Shlomoh, the Skopishker" although he had to call himself Reb Shlomoh Orelowitz. This alone confirms his great, esteemed position in the *shtetl* [town] that bestowed the name, "Skopishker."

He was tall with broad shoulders. However, by nature, he was very humble and would always hold his head down.

Twice a year he traveled to his rebbe to hear the mysteries of the Torah, to listen to Hasidus [the teachings of the Hasidic rabbis] from the mouth of the rebbe. Before his departure, he took *kvitlekh** from almost everyone in the *shtetl* to bring to the rebbe. When he arrived at the rebbe's for the Days of Awe [the period including *Rosh Hashanah* and *Yom Kippur*], he stayed until after *Simchat Torah*. His power of memory was noteworthy. He remembered every innovation, word and melody.

[Translator's note: A kvitl is a piece of paper on which a person writes a request for prayer from the rebbe for such things as a good marriage partner for a child or the conception of a child by a barren couple. Kvitlekh is the plural form.]

In 1919, my father and the family moved to Rakishok [Rokiskis] and opened a haberdashery shop. Our house became the central gathering place for all Hasidim. Every Hasidic guest, Hasidic messenger who would come to Rakishok found lodging with Reb Shlomoh Skopishker. This was the address for our own Hasidim and for other Hasidim.

Every *Shabbos*, between *minkhah* and *maariv* [the afternoon and evening prayers], he celebrated *shalosh seudot* [third *Shabbos* meal] and told all the Hasidim and worldly people about the rebbe and he did not forget to pass on the rebbe's new melodies. Then one went to the *Beis-Midrash* [house of study and prayer].

It was already dark in the *Beis-Midrash*. The shadows fell on the eastern wall. This was the right time for Hasidus. He was the one to speak of Hasidus. Everyone sat quietly and listened word by word.

I relate only one thought about Hasidus that he would often repeat for a circle of Hasidic friends:

"Hasidus is not spoken hurriedly; Hasidus is said under one's breath, because then it can be more thought through; Hasidus has a *neshome yeseyre* [the additional soul a Jew possesses on *Shabbos*], that includes a Godly part, and it has a melody! Hasidus needs to climb gradually from "underneath," step by step and one must go slowly on the steps, not jump over them because a mortal can be injured; Hasidus teaches how to love one another and to serve God because of love; knowledge is not everything, the Torah seeks man's heart, and so on."

In such a manner Reb Shlomoh Skopishker held his Hasidic audience, who felt that he was leading them away to the higher worlds, suspended.

Although it was already late and the time had passed when the *maariv* prayers should have been said, the Skopishker did not rush; he still floated in the heavens.

The *Shamas* lit the candles very late and the weekly "*vehoo rachoom* [He is forgiving – first two words of prayer of supplication recited on Mondays and Thursdays at the end of the morning prayers]" was heard.

In a volume of short stories by Alter Epshtein that was published in America, there are passages about my father, who in his youth when he lived in Ponemunok was known as Zelig's Shlomoh [Zelig's son]. I will here pass on the following essays of text, word by word:

"A circle of people stands at the Eastern Wall around Zelig's Shlomoh, a tall, thin, pale young man with a long, thin neck and with large black eyes and with a hoarse voice, deliberately, with respect, he tells of the wonderful things that happened to him, "upon my word." And the crowd around him stands as if enchanted, holding their breath.

"And a dangerously sick person came to him. The doctors had given up on his life. And no one knew how sick he was. Even the professors in foreign countries failed to guess. As soon as Zelig's Shlomoh looked at him, at saying hello, he said immediately: 'Go home and God will help you.' 'But, Rebbe, I cannot stand on my feet,' the sick man argued. 'It does not matter, God will help you, have faith,' the rebbe said to him – and what do you think, on *Sukkous*, the same Jew came, healthy, strong, unrecognizable. What do you think of that? – And his face shone like the sun.

"The congregation heaves a sigh. Everyone feels a deep longing in his heart. As if tongs were drawing them there, to the distant *shtetl* that had been wrapped in holiness for many generations and if only once in a lifetime to look at him; to hear *Torah* from his own mouth. The *shtetl* stands before the eyes; it calls and winks; and everyone decides that if God would only give health and earnings, one must go there for *yom-tov*. "In addition to the stories, Shlomoh brought new melodies from the rebbe of a kind that had not been heard in our locality. These are the melodies that are sung every *Shabbos* at the Rebbe's table at the third *Shabbos* meal.

"And the time came that night crept up and a sadness invaded and it began to gnaw at the soul; they began to ask Shlomoh to sing. He was obstinate; he was embarrassed. However, the congregation did not yield because time would not stand still. It would be dark, impenetrable and crowded in a minute. It was clearly seen that *Shabbos* was giving way like smoke. A weak glimmer was seen on the market. There day was wrestling with night, *Shabbos* with the week. Finally, Shlomoh gave in. He coughed, moved his thin hand over his face and began.

"A loud shout tore out of his chest and the entire *minyon* [prayer group] shivered. All became silent, holding their breath. Those reciting Psalms also became quiet; they knew that this was important...and again a scream, strong and powerful was carried through the air and it seemed that it would again become *Shabbos*, become light. The week was frightened, shivered and lowered its hands.

"The congregation sang along with rapture, with fervor. All the voices flowed together, mixed, one woven into the other and they became one voice, one melody. And a love, a joyfulness was heard in the singing. And it appeared as if everything, the Torah ark, the walls, the old forest and the heavens were singing; everything sang the sacred, strange melody.

"And from on high, from the women's section of the *shul*, an old woman sneaked out her head. She labored to penetrate the darkness with her weak eyes and to look at her consolation, her treasure, and tears of joys rolled over her old cheeks. How many tears did she shed at that time, when her child roamed from home among strangers and, alas, suffered from hunger. Who saw her tears? However, thanks to God, she lived to see her source of pride. Here where he was now.

"And the melody rolled, turned and twisted higher and higher. The congregation cried and shook and snapped their fingers. There was a joy, the eyes shone and gleamed with faith, with enthusiasm."

My father was a very sociable man and he would be an arbitrator in various disputes. I remember such a case:

Two merchants once came to him about a forest dispute. He received a handshake agreement from both that they would implement his decision.

One insulted the other, he stopped them, saying: "Whereas, if you are not on good terms only because of money matters, then why do you insult each other?

He reconciled them and the two merchants became good friends. Several times a rabbinical position was proposed to my father. However, he did not accept because of modesty. He was beloved in Rakishok and in the area, esteemed by old and young.

Shlomoh's Son, Shabtai

My brother, Shabtai Orelowitch, was well known in the Slabodker *yeshiva* as "Shabtai Rakishker" and in Rakishok as "Shabtai, Shlomoh's" [Shlomoh's son]. I stayed with him in the same quarters when he studied in Slabodka. Yeshiva boys would come to him often in the evening and it was the greatest pleasure for me to be in this environment. Discussions were often held about Yiddish, Hebrew and Russian literature and various problems of the Jewish people and matters of importance were discussed.

During the years of the First World War, Shabtai evacuated to Krementzug with the Slabodka *yeshiva*. He was a teacher for a time in a *shtetl* in Mahilver [Mikalavas] *gubernia*.

He married in Panevezys upon returning from the evacuation and became very beloved and esteemed by everyone in the city.

He perished with his wife, Lipsze Zelbowitch, and his children and with the entire Jewish community, *al kiddush hashem* ["in the sanctification of God's name," as a martyr] at the hands of the Nazi hangmen.

The Rabbi Reb Zelig Orelowitch

Rabbi Reb Zelig Orelowitch

My brother, the rabbi Zelig Orelowitch, was the last rabbi in Rakishok and was known by the name, "Zelig Shlomoh's" [Sholomoh's son, Zelig] or "Shlomoh Skopishker's son."

He studied in a *yeshiva* as a young child and was a very industrious person in the style of H. N. Bialik's *HaMatmid* [the poem, *The Talmud Student*]. He was also gifted with a dynamic spirit and with a strong will. He took part in the "revolutions" that would break out in the *yeshivus* against the leaders and supervisors.

The first *yeshiva* in which he began to study was in Kupishok [Kupiskis]. There he ate his meals and had his lodgings with a wagon driver. Later, he studied in Panevesz [Panevezys], Bobroisk and in Slabodka-Kovno.

In the Slabodker *yeshiva*, he rebelled against supervision that was too dictatorial and severe and persecuted those students who read secular books. Zelig Orelowitch, too, was marked by the supervisor as one who read heretical books, and after a talk with the director of the *yeshiva*, he left the Slabodker *yeshiva* and went to study in the Mirer *yeshiva* with which he was satisfied. The head of the *yeshiva* in Mir, Reb Alya Brukh, took a more moderate course and did not scrutinize so carefully if a student read a worldly book.

He moved to Vilna during the First World War, where he lived under German occupation. We did not receive any news about Zelig for a long time. Then he informed us through the Red Cross that he was in Vilna.

In 1918, Zelig was in Poltawa, where the Mirer *yeshiva* was located. By chance, I was also in Poltawa, and when I met him, he made a strange impression on me. He sat, in the evening, with other young men from the *yeshiva* and almost all of them were covered with long beards and made gestures as if crippled. They made themselves appear as cripples and sick in order not to be mobilized in the Russian army. He, Zelig, also wore a long beard and was dressed in a pair of military shoes and in a paper suit.

The civil war began in Russia. There was turbulence in Poltawa. We moved to the *shtetl* Kaupos [Kaupyay], Mohilever *gubernia* [province]. Then he left for Mahilev where he gave a lesson in Torah to a great crowd.

However, Zelig was thirsty for knowledge. Returning to Rakoshik, he corresponded with Professor, Reb Haim Heler of Berlin, and left to study in Germany. He studied for four years at the *Beis Midrash Elyon* in Berlin and earned the title, Doctor of Philosophy.

After returning to Rakishok from Berlin, he was a teacher in the Hebrew *pre-gymnazie* for a short time and then he was hired as the director of the Yavne Gymnazie in Kovno. He was the head of Reb Asher Nisen's *Yeshiva* in Shavl [Siauliai] for a short time.

He married Roza Snieg and settled in Rakishok. At that time, he was invited to become a rabbi in Sweden and he was also offered a rabbinical position in Johannesburg.

After Rabbi Betzalel's death, he became the rabbi in Rakishok. The Soviet regime was then in Lithuania and the rabbinical seat was not a good economic position. Yet, he accepted the Rakishok rabbinate.

He perished *al kiddush Hashem* [as a martyr; sanctifying God's name] along with his wife, Roza, and his son, Moshele and with all of the Jews from Rakishok and the area. It was reported that the Germans permitted him to speak to the Jews who stood near the open pits. He spoke for two hours until the Germans interrupted his speech with a volley of shooting.

He was the last Rabbi in Rakishok and perished with all of the Jews on the Inquisition pyre of animal-like Nazism.

The Rabbi, Reb Zelig Rukh

Hon. Rabbi Zelig and Micha der Rokiskiser

Rabbi Reb Zelig Orelowitch

The Rabbi, Reb Zelig Rukh was a very interesting and remarkable figure. He was given the title, the Rabbi, the *Gaon* [genius of the Torah and Talmud] Reb Zelig Rukh.

His father, Reb Mikha the Rakishetsiker, was the lessee of an estate in the village of Rakishetsik and was known as a fine Jew.

Reb Mikha gave his son a religious upbringing and sent him to study in the great *yeshivus*. He, the Rabbi, Reb Zelig, also studied at the Slabodker *yeshiva* where many other Rokishker young men studied. He excelled with his great diligence and erudition.

The Rabbi, Reb Zelig was a great authority in the rabbinical world and was the head of the Lomza *yeshiva*.

The entire Rakishok area was proud of its follow townsman, the Rabbi, the *Gaon*, Reb Zelig Rukh.

He perished at the hands of the Nazi hangmen in Lomza.

The Rabbi, Reb Asher

The Rabbi, Reb Asher was an old man and weak, with a grey beard. He, for the most part, sat alone in his house and was little involved in city matters. At the end of his life, he dedicated his entire time to study and to writing a *sefer* [religious book] about religious questions and answers. His house became full of his religious books and published works that his daughter sent away to cities and *shtetlekh*.

He was a great authority in the scholarly-rabbinical world.

After he died, his rabbinical seat was taken by his son-in-law, Reb Shmuel, who is now in New York and occupies an eminent place in the Lubavitch *yeshiva* there and in Lubavitch Hasidic circles.

Reb Moshel, the Head of the *Yeshiva*

Reb Moshel was the head of the *yeshiva* in Rakishok. He was short, with an emaciated face and small pointed beard and, in addition, he was a hunchback... he was dressed in a suit coat and hat that were always dusty.

He was a sage and great aristocrat. It was a pleasure to talk to him and when he would scratch the end of his beard, there was a premonition that he would soon utter a pearl of wisdom. He was a great scholar in the scholarly world and wisdom and learning shone from his eyes.

Reb Shmuel Aba Snieg

Reb Shmuel Aba Snieg studied in the Slabodker *yeshiva* with his younger brother, Itze Lozer. It was said in the *shtetl*: Shmuel Aba was growing into a great scholar and a sage and would be a great *gaon b'Yisroel* [brilliant man of the Jewish people].

He and his brother mentioned above were very beloved in the *shtetl*. Rakishok was proud of both brothers who were later modern, intelligent young men and were friendly with religious and non-religious elements, with Hasidim and scholars.

In later years Shmuel Aba Snieg became "Reb Shmuel Aba Snieg." He devoted himself to communal work and was chairman several times of the *Vaad Kehile* [Communal Council] and of the People's Bank. He would also study a page of *gemara* with a group in the synagogue.

At the time of the independent Lithuanian state, Reb Shmuel Aba was nominated as the chief rabbi of the Lithuanian army and was awarded the rank of colonel. He was respected and esteemed by both the Jewish and by the Lithuanian populations. He often worked in the Lithuanian press and was a constant co-worker in the Lithuanian army newspaper. Everyone marveled at the fact that Shmuel Aba had learned to write so beautifully in Lithuanian, even better than many Lithuanian journalists.

Reb Shmuel Aba Snieg survived the cruel Hitler years. His wife perished. In a letter from Munich, Germany, dated March 16, 1942*, he wrote that he was chairman of the *Vad Agudas Kharevim* [Council of Union Friends] in the American zone. He also wrote that he intended to settle in Israel.

[Translator's note: the year 1942 is a mistake as the war had not ended and the American zone was not in existence until after the war ended.]

The Eidelson Family

Hilel, Zalman and Hana belonged to the Eidelson family. They all wrote a heroic chapter in the cultural-communal life of Rakishok. Zalman Eidelson had organizational abilities and was an educated person. He spoke Yiddish and Russian well and he administered the most important institutions. He alone founded and led the town library and then created the Jewish Bank, which was the only organized Jewish credit institution in Rakishok and in the vicinity. He also organized the firefighters' brigade.

Hana Eidelson (Shadur) was very active in all communal organizations of the town. She dedicated much energy to the Rakishok orphanage that was also a central institution for the area.

Hilel was a unique person. He was chairman of the Zionist Party, of the *kehile*, of *Maccabi* [Jewish sports organization], chairman of the orphans house, of the *halutzim* [agricultural pioneers] organization, was also one of the founders of the town library and loan office. He was the axis around which the entire cultural-communal work in Rakishok turned.

He was very active in the refugee committee at the time of the First World War. He traveled across the cities of Russia in order to make arrangements for homeless Jews. He always excelled in his communal work.

Not every city in Lithuania had a person such as Hilel Eidelson. He was an idealist starting from his youngest age. He was also a vegetarian and remained one until the end of his life.

He held socialist beliefs and lived very modestly and was poor. He had a few rooms on a side street that were appropriately furnished.

Hilel Eidelson gave up the idea of getting married and devoted himself entirely to communal work in Rakishok and served the Zionist ideal with ardor and great devotion.

Yeheil Zamet

Yeheil Zamet was then perhaps the only student in the *shtetl* who studied at the Berliner University. He was a great attraction when he came down to Rakishok in a uniform. Everyone would stop to look at the handsome student clothing with great wonder. It was an honor for a simple person to meet him. Young girls would be interested in making his acquaintance.

When he received the title of Engineer in Berlin, he settled in Rakishok and served in his profession in the Rakishok city hall.

Later Yeheil Zamet devoted himself to communal work and was active in the *kehile*, in the city managing committee and in the People's Bank.

He was also the leader of the Zionist-Socialist Party in Rakishok.

Reb Efroim

Reb Efroim was a blacksmith and would work in the smithy all day, standing at the anvil in a leather apron. He held his pincers in which there was a long piece of iron in one hand and with the other hand he drew up and down on the bellows. At the same time, fiery sparks flew on all sides.

He was very professional at shoeing horses. He would approach the craft as a dance. He stroked the horse's mane before and then he would begin filing the hoof with a file.

The horse looked foolishly with his large horse eyes and calmly gazed into Reb Efroim's eyes.

Coming home from the forge, he changed into other clothing and went to the *Beis haMidrash*.

He was a Jew and a scholar, and would sit at a long table and study with a group. He then looked like another person, as if the divine presence had rested on him.

In later years, he devoted himself to communal work and was also the *gabbai* [lay person who assists at the reading of the Torah] of the large *Beis haMidrash*.

Reb Yankl-Hirshe

Reb Yankl-Hirshe was a wagon driver and yet the town gave him the name, Reb Yankl-Hirshe the Baal Shem Tov ["Master of the Good Name," the founder of Hasidism].

At dawn, in the dark, he would drive passengers to the train station. During the day he carried various loads to the train and from the train.

However, he was a man who was happy with his luck, although he worked hard. He had to carry full sacks and chests on his back every day.

When he came home tired and weary in the evening, he would sit down and study a chapter of *Mishnah* and recite a chapter of Psalms.

I had the occasion to travel with Reb Yankl-Hirshe to and from the train station. Seeing how other wagon drivers passed Reb Yankl-Hirshe's wagon, I once asked him why he does not whip his horse so that it would go faster. He answered this: "The horse is also a creature and my partner; we both work together and it is a pity on him. I hold the whip, but I do not flog him with it because the Most High in heaven is also concerned. He would punish me for every sin; I would no longer be in the world."

Because of his behavior, Reb Yankl-Hirshe was crowned with the title, Reb Yankl-Hirshe Baal Shem Tov.

The Brothers

There were three brothers in Rakishok who were called "*bnei Zysa*" [sons of Zysa] and they lived in Jurdzike.

The three brothers were peddlers, common Jews. However, they could be distinguished from other toiling *shtetl* Jews in that they lived a collective life: they bought the same clothing, shoes and led the same way of life. They also traveled to the same rebbe.

The *Bnei Zysa* were Lodzer Hasidim and would travel to their rebbe several times a year and tithed part of their earnings to him.

I remember that before they traveled to the rebbe they would come to my father so that he could calculate how much they had to tithe to the rebbe including every penny from their earnings in the course of an entire year.

Reb Haim Elya

Haim Elya, the *shamas* [rabbi's assistant] of the small prayer house was short with a large yellow beard. In as much as it was accepted that a blond was an angry person, it was also the same with Haim Elya. The proprietors in the *shtetl* would shake before him because when he was irritated, he shook like a *lulav** and would rebuke them and the *gabbai* [lay person who assists with Torah readings and other synagogue tasks].

Translator's note: group of three species of leaves which are shaken together with the esrog [citron] during Sukkos [Feast of the Tabernacles that occurs during the month of October].

However, everyone knew that Reb Haim Elya was a Jew who was capable of studying and was a great Hasid who was esteemed in the high circles of the Hasidic world.

Erev Yom Kippur [on the eve of *Yom Kippur*] he would stand by the large table in the small prayer house near the door with a wide strap in his hand and would administer *malkus* [39 soft lashes received as a reminder of the need to seek repentance and forgiveness for any committed sins] . He did this with his heart and with his conscience; he would only administer the strap for the sake of appearance.

Once an esteemed proprietor who had insulted Haim Elya said during the *malkus*: "*Nu*, now you can get even with me." He answered that: "If you think that way, I will not administer any *malkus*. On my part, I forgave you a long time ago."

In addition to being the shamas, Reb Haim Elya had an additional source of income. He would make wine for *kiddush* and for Passover. I once came to him in his small house to buy wine. He was then in the cellar with a candle. I went down to him in the cellar. There stood small and large casks of wine. The cellar was a real wine factory, with glass tubes.

I was curious and wanted to touch a tube and as a result I turned over a bottle of wine. I was very afraid that Reb Haim Elya would tear me to pieces. However, he immediately noticed my fear and assured me that no one would know of my shame and he would not tell my parents about this.

I was no longer angry with Reb Haim Elya after this act.

Reb Haim Elya had two sons: Leib and Dovidl. They studied at the Babroisker *yeshiva* and when they would come home for *yom-tov*, Haim Elya drew great pride from his children.

Leib was a pious Jew and Dovidl had a love of looking into a secular book and also shaved his beard. He, Dovidl, had a sweet voice and when Hasidim would come together, they asked him to sing.

He was a wonderful singer and Haim Elya, the *shamas*, took pride in his Hasidic melodies. He also had great pleasure from Leib, who later became a rabbi.

There were still more notable personalities and types in Rakishok who I have not mentioned. I have certainly not meant to wrong them, but the run of years has erased many memories. Therefore, at the end of my work, I will at least describe a Rakishok *Shabbos* – between *Minkhah* and *Maariv* [afternoon and evening prayers]. Perhaps this will serve as a partial supplement.*

*This description was published in the *Afrikaner Yidishe Zeitung* [*African Yiddish Newspaper*] several years ago.

"Here goes Reb Betzalel, the rabbi with a black coat over his shoulders, strolling with his son-in-law, Reb Avraham. Behind them is Reb Moshe Leib the *malamed* [teacher] with Haim Yitzhak Klumel. "

"The *gabbai* of the *Beis haMidrash*, Reb Bera, Leah's son, Shamai Welwe the ropemaker, Mendl the shoemaker, Itsche the tailor and others are seen going from Kovner Street. Men are sitting on Yankl the quilter's stoop and talking. The entire street is full of people who are drawn to the courtyard to stroll. From Jurdzike and Neye Streets, people can be seen from the marketplace near the pump."

"Avraham Itse Meller and his wife sit in the attic, looking down on the strolling crowd and catch a word with several passersby."

"People sit on all of the bridges, old and young. Young men and women stand near Nusen Dubin's house and talk."

"The boulevard is full of people. Others stroll from the boulevard to the courtyard and all passersby convey an expansive *gut-Shabbos* to each other. Everyone is dressed up in their *Shabbos* clothing and is in a very elevated mood."

"The air is so sweet and cozy; it seems as if the fields and trees are accompanying the Jewish crowd on its *Shabbos* stroll."

"Young men and women walk in the courtyard where the trees on each side of the road come together as if they were a tunnel. They feel as if no one sees them and they hold hands. Young friends see this and point their fingers, look – he is holding her hand."

"Near the large synagogue, people are in motion and gather in the synagogue and other stand and talk. Young people chase each other and make a racket. Above, on the stairs, it can be seen that Sura, the *rebbitzen*, and other women are going to the women's section of the synagogue. And here comes the rabbi and everyone enters the synagogue."

"Jews are sitting and talking in every corner of the synagogue. It is dark and the talk is of the large markets in Kamaj [Kamajai], Ponidel and Abel [Obeliai], about the great bargains that were bought there and how many eggs the peddlers gathered in the village this week."

"In one corner all deplore the great misfortune that befell Haim Beynish the butcher with the large ox that he bought this week; it had an adhesion on its lungs and was therefore not kosher – and, it is a pity, he lost money and the hypothesis is that the peasant knew that the ox had swallowed a nail and thus he sold it so cheaply.

Sabbath after lunch

"Reb Yankl-Hirshe Baal Shem Tov sits in another corner of the small synagogue. He was a wagon driver. But he is called Reb Yankl-Hirshe Baal Shem Tov. All of the merchants trusted him with their money for transporting their goods from the trains. It is said that he would often make an error and gave the merchants more money then he had been given. The Baal Shem Tov sits with a Book of Psalms in his hand, melodiously reciting the Psalms and rocking. Reb Elyakim Meir stands near him, leaning with his head against the wall, his hands turned over his head and whispers. No one knows what he is saying there. It is said that he speaks to the angels."

"Suddenly a bang on the table is heard; the rabbi is going to speak. And it becomes quiet. Everyone gathers around the table and everyone perks up their ears to hear the stories the rabbi is going to tell from the *Midrash* [commentaries on biblical verses]."

"A little later Shmuel the coachman sits in a corner and takes a delicious nap. The week was so difficult and he dreams so enjoyably here in the synagogue. A gang of jokers move inconspicuously and push a can of snuff under his nose – he sneezes and has such a fit of sneezing and the rabbi must stop speaking because of the great uproar."

"When the rabbi finishes speaking about the *Midrash*, Kopl the shoemaker goes onto the *bima* [lectern], bangs on the table and cries out: *Ashrei temimei derekh* [Happy are those who walk in the righteous path]. The entire congregation says verse after verse. Others sing the verses so that it melts the heart."

"It is already very dark in the small synagogue, so that they cannot see each other. At the door in a small corner stand friends and they fool around, shove, carry on, and, meanwhile, a towel is twisted together and thrown into the heating oven. There is a tumult, a cry and the first to call out – "Rascals, get out of the synagogue!" – is Hilel's son Bentsa, who himself threw the towel."

"In the central part of the synagogue Bertsik Zalkind sits near a table and reads for a group. The *shochet* [ritual slaughterer] sits at a second table and reads for another group. It looks as if they are partners in the business of teaching. They do not compete for listeners. One does not shout over the other; if one wants to, he sits at the other table – it is not a competition."

"Betzalel Kaplan sits in the antechamber of the synagogue with others around him and they talk politics, tell stories and ordinary witticisms."

"In a house opposite the central part of the synagogue Hasidim gather together from a *shtibl* [small prayer house] to have the final *Shabbos* meal. Reb Moshe Leib the *malamed*, Haim Yitzhak Klumel, Haim Elya the *shamas* and his son, Shimshon Nisen the *malamed*, Zalman Shimshon Shwartsberg, Mende Milner, Ahron Zelig and Shlomoh the butcher, Reb Nakhum Ber and a few arriving *yeshiva* students, Shmuel Aba Snieg and his brother, Itse-Lazar, Zelig and Shabtai, Leibe and Dovid-Shlomoh's son, Khatskl Garbuz and others arrive. They talk and they take a little whisky at the final *Shabbos* meal. Fish and cookies are arranged on the table. They eat and talk about various Hasids and Hasidus and what is happening with the rabbi, may he be healthy. They tell about how the rich man from Petersburg, Ziamke Levin, had danced a Hasidic dance with Shimshon Nisen the *malamed* on *yud-tes Kislev** and the next morning Ziamke came to Shimshon Nisen, knocked on his door and said to him, – 'I am leaving soon and I do not know if we will, God willing, see each other again. Be well. And I have an interest-free loan of 25 rubles for you – be well!"

*Translator's note: yud-tes Kislev, the 19th day of the Hebrew month Kislev. Rabbi Shneur Zalman, the Alter Rebbe, the founder of Chabad Hasidism was released from a Russian prison on this date in 1798.

" – Shimshon Nisen pleaded with him, 'Good heavens, Reb Zalman, how can I take the money from you? My entire income is from the small amount of beans that my wife cooks and sells in the *chederim* [religious elementary schools]. So, from where will I find the money to give back to you?"

" – Ziamke scolded him, 'Do not be a fool, do you want to become a partner of Satan the accuser; I could not sleep the entire night and I wrestled with Satan and barely convinced him that I should give you an interest-free loan of 25 rubles. Now you come and agree with Satan. I tell you, Shimshon Nisen, no resurrection of the dead and no repentance will help you."

"Pitifully, Shimshon Nisen was very frightened and took the 25 rubles and shook Ziamke's hand and said to him: 'Ziamke, you say I have an agreement with Satan. I say that you have made an agreement with the Almighty. Go in health and God grant you another year [of life]!'"

"As it got dark, Dovidl was asked to sing the new melodies that he had just brought from Bobroisk. As the congregation came to life singing, it seemed as if the angels were dancing around the house. Everyone's face radiated with joy and notes were sucked, turned and twisted with such sweetness that the hearts would melt with longing."

"Shimshon Nisen the *malamed* sat in a corner on a chair and snapped his fingers, his head cast up and with an earnest face looked far, far into the sky. It was as if he was asking for mercy from the stars in the sky with his eyes, that they not rush to come and disturb the holy *Shabbos* until dusk."

"After the singing the congregation stands up and enters a smaller room. There Shlomoh Skopishker repeats Hasidus for the group."

"Leibl's son, Bertsik, sits in a corner and learns *Mishnah* by heart...he pulls his red handkerchief from his chest pocket in which a can of snuff is wrapped, opens the lid and pinches a bit of snuff. He sniffs it and gives the can to the others."

"When Shlomoh Skopishker and the others enter the *shtibl*, everyone sits down around the table. It becomes quiet and everyone goes around on tip toe, so as, God forbid, not to disrupt. When Shlomoh repeats the Hasidus, he lays a spark in every word, a spark from himself, from the rebbe, may he be in good health, so that it radiates as from a burning fire and everyone feels as if in a sweet dream. When Shlomoh discourses about Hasidus and floats in the highest worlds, it can be seen, even at dusk, how Mende Milner holds the point of his beard bitten between his lips, as if he would draw in a sweet honey. "

"Reb Moshe Leib the *malamed* sits in thought. His forehead is wrinkled and he smoothes his white beard. Borukh the railway station worker holds his head to the side and his hat turned to the side. As if he had traveled from a large market day. Haim Elya the *shamas* has his head on the table and his beard appears pasted to the table as if he cannot tear it away. In the darkness, more heads moving around in the other, higher world, such as Meir the shoemaker, Shimshon Nisen the *malamed*, Haim Elya the *shamas* and Zalman Shimshon Shwartsberg, are seen all around the synagogue, going around arm in arm with the heavenly angels."

"As Shlomoh Skopishker ends the repetition of Hasidus, a bang is heard on the lectern and Shlomoh the butcher cries out with a sad melody: He is merciful and will forgive, and everyone's heart becomes gloomy. Everyone begins to think about tomorrow's promissory notes, about a new interest-free loan and about the small bit of flour and barley that his wife is concerned about buying. "They think about the week and its worries.""

[Page 172]

Zalman the Soda Water Maker

by Bunim Yidel Kreel

Translated by Nathan Snyder

Zalman the soda water maker was an immensely pious and ardent Chasid. He was by nature a quiet, gentle and good hearted Jew. He was loved by all of the town's people and highly respected by the Chasidim. He was slender of build and the work at the soda machine had made his chest concave and his back hunched, his shoulders rounded. It was difficult work for him to make the soda water. He did it with his last strength. And he earned his livelihood with the sweat of his brow.

His house was opposite the small Chasidic *shtiebel*. A great window with clear glass panes looked out right opposite the *shtiebel*, as if it could observe the comings and goings of the Chasidim, going three times a day to give account to the Creator of the Universe.

Zalman the soda water maker is among the earliest of those going to the shtiebel to pray. From a side door of his house, with a bowed back, he goes out into the cold fresh dawn, meeting up with other Chasidim.

Zalman the soda water maker led the prayers during the Days of Awe for the Morning and Additional Services. This was his prerogative.

Zalman the soda water maker poured out his heart and feelings before the pulpit for the community of Israel. And, at twilight, he used to sing out vigorous Chasidic melodies for groups of Chasidim.

With bowed heads, bent to the earth, the Chasidim hurried to the shtiebel. The small yellow blue flames, giving off a subdued glow from the rows of large wax tallow candles which threw a pale grey light over the small room's walls.

Like white snow covered trees in a thick forest, on a quiet winter's day, so the Chasidim appear in the shtiebel with their snow white prayer-robes. And like a snow white swan, Zalman the soda water maker, the prayer leader, shone out in his white robe.

The panes in the prayer room are covered with a cloudy film, the air is heavy and smells of fat and paraffin from the candles. However, the quiet groans of Zalman's prayers cut through the thick atmosphere.

Zalman's open-hearted soulful groans and sighs are not for himself, but rather for all Israel. He ignores his sick heart, the care of which he entrusts to Divine Providence.

The "Unetaneh toykef," the "Let us now relate the strength" prayer is the essence of all prayers. He puts his last ounce of strength into it. He prays with all of his very being, preparing for the Day of Judgment. The entire congregation is aroused by the outpouring of his soul. With a quiet murmuring, he cries out, "who shall live and who shall die." Just as a still calm breeze moves the young branches of a tree, so he has whispers the words "Who shall live and who shall die."

But now, his voice raises itself to higher octaves. The crowd of praying people is swept forward and a great cry of lament, a sobbing breaks forth from everyone including the "Women's Gallery."

With outstretched arms, reaching to the Gates of Heaven, wrapped in a white prayer robe, as a gigantic eagle with mighty wings, Zalman stands, his entire body stretched out, the words resounding out: "WHO BY STRANGLING, WHO BY STONING."

The noise and lament in the room becomes stronger and stronger. All the more it turns into a trembling, shaking the prayer books and the cry flows with strength, striving to reach the very Throne of Glory.

It once happened that Zalman the soda water maker fell in a faint as he led the Yom Kippur service. A cold sweat covered his forehead and a dark cloud seemed to dim his eyes which lost their shine.

He fell helpless into a faint in the middle of "Let us tell how utterly." The crowd tried to revive him. He came to himself. However, in a few days, he gave up his soul, and closed his eyes forever.

The town made him a great honorable funeral the next day. Big and small accompanied into eternal rest, Zalman the soda water man, who was a great Chasidic Jew, with a good heart and exalted soul.

[Pages 174-189]

Personalities in the Old Home

("Warm Images")

by Ahron-Noakh Nochumowitz

Translated by Gloria Berkenstat Freund

Various strongly characteristic and unique *shtetl* [town] types run through my memory. I will sketch several of them with my modest pen, indicating their main traits.

Reb Bertsik Zalkind

Reb Bertsik Zalkind was a clever man, a Hasid and a scholar; he knew the Torah well and was a preacher. He received ordination as a rabbi in his early youth, was a substantial merchant and a philanthropist, a sympathetic and a modern Jew. He would be neatly and cleanly dressed. He was a short and very mobile person. There was a dynamic communal strength in him that stimulated him to do all communal work with love and passion.

After the First World War he took on the mission of building a *Talmud Torah* [school for poor boys]. Knowing that Rakishok was not financially able to build a large building, he traveled around all of the surrounding *shtetlekh* selling *kletser* [wooden blocks] – asking every Jew to buy a block and his name would be written on the block in the *Talmud Torah* building. If someone was not able to buy a block, he could purchase a table, a bench, prayer tables and so on. A plan to guarantee the budgets of the *Talmud Torah* also occurred to him. He went to the leather manufacturers – the Nurok brothers in Shavl, to Kovno and Ponevesz and persuaded them to provide monthly support for the *T.T.* [*Talmud Torah*].

He then opened a *yeshiva*. Both institutions exist thanks to his energy. He gave up all of his private commercial activity because of his communal work.

Reb Bertsik Zalkind was a jewel in Rakishok.

Reb Moshe-Yankl

The fathers in the *shtetl* did not remember when Reb Moshe-Yankl became the *shamas* [rabbi's assistant] of the *beis-medrash* [house of study or synagogue] and the grandfathers believed that because the years are a gift from God, a man's age may not be counted. Therefore, the city did not know how old the *shamas* was or how old his wife was.

Reb Moshe-Yankl and his wife lived in a small room that was built onto the large *beis-medrash*. There were a couple of beds, a small closet, a table spread with a tablecloth, a couple of seats. There was also a reading stand, because a *minyon* [ten men required for prayer] prayed there, if there were many *yahrzeitn* [plural of *yahrzeit* – anniversary of a death]. That the wife of the *shamas* sewed, cooked and was busy with her household did not disturb the worshippers. She, the wife of the *shamas*, did not fail to answer "amen" and would stand with all of the worshippers during the *kdushe* [prayer of sanctification].

She knew what prayers must be said. Many times she would help the person reciting the prayers. She also helped her husband in his duties as a *shamas*: lit the *yahrzeit* candle, cleaned the *beis-medrash* and sold *hesheynus* [five willow branches beaten on the floor on *Hoshanna Rabba* at the conclusion of the Feast of Tabernacles or *Sukkos* to symbolize the elimination of sin and as a prayer for rain.], etc.

Reb Moshe-Yankl also was a *bel-koyre* [Torah reader], blew the *shofar* [ram's horn], read the *megilah* [the Book of Esther read on Purim] and also led the morning service on the Days of Awe [Rosh Hashanah and Yom Kippur].

He would not have enough income from this work. God blessed him that he was born to a father who was a *kohan* [descendent of the high priests]. He had income because he had the right to redeem* all first born sons in the *shtetl*.

*[Translator's note: The *kohan* performs the ritual of *pidyon haben* – redemption of the son – which releases the first born son of his obligation to serve in the Holy Temple in Jerusalem. The commandment to do so is found in Exodus 13:13 – "And you shall redeem every human firstborn among your sons." The ritual is still observed although the Temple no longer exists.]

By nature Reb Moshe-Yankl was a modest Jew, a calm person, who did not drive away the children when they would play and run around the lectern and *bimah* [pulpit] – on the contrary, he said let the children play – yet, when he would need to go to a *pidyon haben*, he became another person. He dressed up as for a holiday – put on the new gabardine, a new hat – and acted respectful, as he would say: I, Moshe-Yankl, am a *kohan* [priestly class] and being a *kohan* is a noble inheritance to me.

He looked majestic on arriving at a *pidyon haben* and he immediately went over to the first-born son – to the child – taking him in his arms. He went straight to the door with the child, saying: "Thank God, I will have an assistant in my work as a *shamas* in my old age."

Rokiskis Yizkor Book 169

Those in attendance turned to Reb Moshe-Yankl: "Why are you in a hurry; let us make a blessing in honor of the first born and eat some cake with whiskey, cookies with herring." After a little haggling, Reb Moshe-Yankl permitted himself to be persuaded; he had a drink and made a blessing, one cup after the other. Meanwhile, one of the guests joined in: "Reb Moshe-Yankl, what can you do with the first born? Who will give him a bath, watch him, you are so busy with your work as a *shamas*?"

– "No, Jews" – answered Reb Moshe-Yankl – "an honor belongs to the *kohan*. The child is mine."

Meanwhile, the child cried.

"So, how much will you give me for the child? – I want 10,000 rubles ransom money."

Meanwhile, the child was given to his mother so that she could nurse him while they came to terms with the *kohan*.

They gave Moshe-Yankl a packet for his wife: cookies, herring, cake – and several pennies for him

With this, the spectacle of the *pidyon haben* ended.

Kopl the Shoemaker

Kopl the shoemaker was a toiler. He made a living from shoemaking. However, he was a respectable artisan. He would enter all of the respectable houses and knew about everything that happened in the *shtetl*. At work he would sit in a *yarmulke* [skullcap] and draw the shoemaker's thread accompanied by a melody from the Days of Awe.

On *Shabbas* night, he would recite Psalms in the *Beis-Medrash* aloud, with ecstasy.

He would always find time to mix in all of the *kehile* [religious community] matters of the *shtetl*. Nothing started and ended without Kopl, who thought of himself as a representative of the working masses.

He had great interest in *kehile* matters. If they wanted to raise the community tax on candles and yeast, he went onto the *bimah* [elevated platform in a synagogue from which the Torah is read] and banged the table, crying out: "I am stopping the reading of the Torah because it is a great sin to raise the community tax from which the poor people will suffer the most. Let the rich men pay more; then it will not be necessary to raise the community tax."

The rich proprietors as well as the gentle young people were not happy with Kopl's dictating. But Kopl did not give any consideration to this at all. He would react immediately when someone opposed what he said: "I am a toiler!"

This was his slogan. Everyone knew that Kopl was correct because he sincerely and with great stubbornness defended the interests of the poor segment in the *shtetl*.

Leibl's Son, Bertzik

Leibl's son, Bertzik, was one of the oldest and finest Jews in Rakishok. He also belonged to the class of Jews who lived the years given by God. It was evident that [God] had generously given him years [of life].

Leibl's son, Bertzik was an independent person into deep old age and earned his own livelihood. He was a peddler and would drag himself through the villages with a basket of goods on his back or a sack on his shoulders. He no longer went to the distant villages because, first, his feet no longer served him, and secondly, he wanted to *daven Maariv* [pray at the daily evening service] with a *minyon* [10 men needed to be present for prayer].

His children wanted to provide his means of support so he could sit in his home. Yet he refused to accept the offer from his children because he said as follows: "As long as I can still earn for myself, I will not depend on anyone, not even my children."

He became accustomed to the way of life of a peddler. On the road, he would sit down and study a chapter of *Mishnius* [*Mishnah* – compilation of the oral laws of the Torah]. The Jews of Rakishok, traveling to the market, knew well that somewhere at the edge of the road, Reb Bertzik, Leibl's son, had to be sitting and studying. They would specially stop and look for him in order to bring him home.

Leibl's son, Bertzik, was mainly known as an "exorcizer" or "charmer." He exorcized "skin fungi," a "fear," a "woman in childbirth" who was having difficulty with the birth, a "rose" [red areas of pigment on the body, often on the face] and an "evil eye" and also "toothaches." For a "skin fungus" and a "rose", he would take a blue paper and pour "potato starch" on it and bind it around, saying a prayer of incantation at the same time. For toothaches, he would stick his finger in the mouth on the sick tooth and also say his "incantation." For other illnesses he would take a kerchief from the patient, "exorcize" it and then ask that [the patient] be bound with the kerchief on the condition that one could not speak at the same time.

It was said that his "exorcisms" helped more than those of other "charmers" and his name was known even among non-Jews. Peasants from the villages would even come to the *shtetl* to ask where is the Jewish "[quack] doctor" who exorcises.

He was esteemed and respected by Jews and non-Jews.

* * *

It should be understood that the best day in the life of Reb Bertzik, son of Leibl, was *Shabbos*. He would love *Shabbos* – from *Minkhah* to *Maariv* [the afternoon and evening prayers] – he would sit in a corner of the synagogue and from his lips would flow a chapter of Psalms or a chapter of *Mishnius*.

It was said in Rakishok that he could recite the entire *Mishnius* with Rashi commentaries.

Reb Bertzik Laible's

Aba-Bertzik Kruk

Aba-Bertzik Kruk of Varescine, a village that is 6 k.m. from Rakishok and is on the way to Abel, was known in Lithuania and even in the cities and *shtetlekh* of Russia. It was said of him that he took as his goal to compete with Petersburg.

A few *minyonim* [10 men required for prayer] lived in Varescine, and were all agricultural workers. It was actually a Jewish village and their way of life was also pastoral. The Jews would plow there and cut wheat, and they would pray to God for rain, that He water their fields.

The Varesciner Jews would not entrust a strange *bel-tefilah* [the cantor or man who prays for the congregation at the lectern] to recite the *Geshem-tal* prayer [prayer for rain]. Only one of their own representatives of the *kehile* poured out his prayer to God that He should send rain in time.

As well as working as agricultural workers, they also traded with neighboring peasants. They were influential people. Their economic influence was expressed mainly in that they would buy articles from the peasants, not in taking the goods to the market. They sold directly to wholesale dealers who would come directly to them in the village.

Although the Jewish community in the village was so small, they were divided among Hasidim and *misnagdim* [opponents of Hasidism]. There was also a *kheder* [religious elementary school for young boys]. Parents sent their older children to study in Rakishok.

There were esteemed men of means in Varescine such as Lipe the Varesciner, the Seitvitch family, Shimshon Shvartsberg and the Kruk family.

Aba-Bertsik Kruk of Varescine was particularly popular.

* * *

Aba-Bertsik Kruk was a follower of the Enlightenment, who knew the Russian, Polish, German languages. Thanks to his acquaintance with languages, he was appointed by the Czarist regime as the *staroste* [village chief] of the village and was entrusted with having the state stamp of the House of Romanov.

In addition to being the village *staroste*, he was occupied with the legal profession. He wrote petitions for the peasants and he was permitted in court to defend his clients. All of his court appearances were successful.

Because of this he was esteemed and well known in the area, but he became well liked chiefly because of owning the stamp. This was his importance. With the stamp, he could make Jewish young men older and younger in order to avoid going to serve "*Fonya* [Russia]."

Rakoshiker and Jews from the neighboring *shtetlekh* would often go to Varescine to seek help from Bertsik Kruk.

As a result, although only a few dozen Jewish families lived there, "those registered as citizens" of Varescine numbered in the hundreds. Even Jews in Russia were included in the metricals [birth, marriage and death records] of Varescine. The Varescine stamp encompassed Jews from near and far.

In the course of time the governor in Kovno learned of the various machinations with the stamp and sought all means with which to discredit Aba-Bertsik Kruk and searched for an opportunity to invalidate him as the *staroste* and he entrusted this mission to the baliff.

One day, Aba-Bertsik Kruk received an *ukase* [proclamation of the Czarist government] from the baliff; he should appear at this office and bring the stamp of the village chief.

Learning of this, Aba-Bertsik Kruk immediately went to consult his rabbi. Then a miracle from God occurred and, on the same day, the baliff died, when he, Aba-Bertsik Kruk, was with the rabbi.

Several days later, Aba-Bertsik Kruk was arrested with the severe accusation that he was responsible for the death of the baliff. He was taken away in a procession of convicts, put in chains in the Kovno jail.

Right after the arrest, Sheina-Ete, his wife, who was a great woman of valor, left for the train and left for Petersburg in order to present herself to high society and attain an audience with the Czar in person.

In Petersburg, she rushed around the street that led to the Czarskoie Selo Palace for several days; finally she waited for the moment when the Czar and his retinue passed by. She then fell near the Czar's carriage. The Czar stopped the carriage and she delivered a "petition" to him.

Several days later, Aba-Bertzik Kruk was freed and was again the *staroste* in Varescine into his deep old age.

* * *

The day arrived when Aba-Bertzik did not feel well and declared that his days were numbered. He called his wife and all of his children to his bed, saying to them that death was not difficult for him, because a person is only dust at the end.

But it was difficult for him to part with the stamp, which had done so many favors for our brethren the House of Israel. He gave this stamp to his son and told him that he should endeavor to have the regime choose him as the *staroste*.

It happened after Aba-Bertzik's death that Mendl, Aba-Bertzik's son, was chosen as the *staroste* of the village of Varescine. However, his mother, Sheina-Ete, who had experience with this work, supervised the stamp and books.

After the First World War, the refugees returned from the evacuation, and since the papers and the metrical books had mostly been destroyed during the war, they needed birth certificates. Then the Varescine stamp was put to much use. Previously, it had competed with Petersburg and in the time of the Lithuanian Republic, it competed with Kovno.

This Varescine stamp was then a renowned object in all of Lithuania and the connection to the name Aba-Bertzik Kruk was not forgotten.

Eliakim Meir (Ikum Meir) – the *Lamed-Vovnik**

* [Translator's note: a *lamed-vovnik* is one of the 36 righteous men said to hold up the world.]

Reb Eliakim Meir, or as he was called, "Ikum Meir," was crowned with the nickname, the *lamed-vovnik*. He was a quiet one, spoke very rarely even to his own family. He would speak few words to his own wife, not looking at her face. He said speaking brought idle words.

Summer and winter he would wear a winter coat bound with a *gartl** on his hips. He was seen running to the *mikhvah* [ritual bath] very early and then to the synagogue. He said that to serve the Lord one must be swift as a deer. He moved into a corner in the synagogue, close to the door and prayed under his breath. He never prayed in a group. From the synagogue he went with leisurely steps, because "one cannot run from a synagogue."

*[Translator's note: a *gartl* is a cloth belt worn by pious men. It symbolically separates the sacred from the profane.]

He spent the entire day occupied with study and prayer, mainly reading the *musar-seforim* [books of moral instruction]. His wife and children took care of earning a living and he took care of the world to come.

His wife, Lifshe, had a small shop with rolls, cookies and candies. Most of her clients were *kheder-yinglekh* [young boys attending religious elementary schools]. Every morning he would tell his wife: "remember, do not fool the children" [i.e. do not overcharge them].

Erev Yom-Kippur [on the eve of Yom Kippur], he was the first to go to the *shamas* [synagogue official who assists the rabbi] to be given a symbolic whipping in atonement of his sins [*shlogn malkes*] and at the same time to ask that he be whipped more strongly.

Monday and Thursday were fast days for him. On *Tisha b'Av* he would stick himself with conifer cones in order to bring himself humility so that he could live in the *Shekhinah* in exile.*

*[Translator's note: the 9th of the month of *Av* – July or August – a fast day commemorating the destruction of the First and Second Temples in Jerusalem; the *Shekhinah* is the manifestation of God which has descended to dwell among men.]

Zalman Pesakh – the *Moshiakh* [the Redeemer]

Zalman Pesakh left his children only one inheritance – the nickname *MOSHIAKH*. How does a mortal man come to such a nickname?

From his earliest youth, Zalman Pesakh knew that his fate was to be a *nawenadnik*, that is, a peddler: going through the villages with a pack of goods and selling them among the peasants. While still young and, later a young man, Zalman Pesakh would drag himself from village to village on foot, bringing home a measure of rice, a sheep skin, etc. from what he earned as his poor livelihood and looked at saving a little money for buying a horse and wagon as a challenge. He first bought a wagon without wheels.

Meanwhile, it happened that a Jew died and left a daughter and a white horse. The *shtetl* interpreted this as God given because the horse was just right for Zalman Pesakh's wagon and the daughter was a match for Zalman Pesakh. That which lacked wheels – the *shtetl* would provide.

And so it was. Zalman Pesakh no longer went through the villages on foot. He was married and had reins in his hands. Although the wheels that the *kehile* gave him at his wedding did not fit. Still when a wheel is round, by chance, it must turn.

Zalman Pesakh was poor before the wedding and after the wedding he remained a pauper. But he had a great deal of faith; the *Reboynu Shel Oylam* [God] would not forsake him, particularly now that he was married.

After an entire week wandering through the villages, he would return home before the lighting of the *Shabbos* candles, bringing a few chickens, potatoes, a fur pelt and a little grain. The white horse barely moved from exertion and the wheels squeaked so that the women hearing the squeaking knew that it was late and they soon would have to bless the candles.

The legends tell that *Moshiakh* will come on a white horse before the blessing of the candles. When the women heard the squeaking of Zalman Pesakh's small wagon and saw his white horse, the idea snuck into their minds that perhaps he was the *Moshiakh* and this was the proof: he always came on Friday right before the blessing of the candles.

In such a manner, he was given the nickname: *MOSHIAKH*.

Feytl's son, Itse Avrahamchik – the *Lekhu Neraneno**

*[Translator's note: O come let us rejoice... First words of a chapter of Psalms sung on the eve of Shabbos.]

Feytl's son, Itse Avrahamchik, inherited the name from his father and grandfather. This was his only inheritance. In addition to his own name, he had three names and, therefore, he was given another nickname by the *shtetl*: the *Lekhu Neraneno*.

This is a nickname that he legitimately and honestly earned.

He loved to pray at the cantor's reading stand and particularly for the welcoming of *Shabbos*. He had great joy when he said, "Come let us rejoice." He would for the sake of their blessed memory think of a *yarhrzeit* [anniversary of a death] of one of his relatives which fell on Friday evening, so that he could pray in front of the cantor's reader's stand.

Feytl's son, Itse Avrahamchik, dealt with orchards, that is, he bought the fruit from the trees when they were not yet ripe. He and his entire family would live in a cabin in the orchard during the summer. During the winter they lived in the *shtetl* and sold the fruit.

One year he succeeded in leasing the "priest's orchard," which was well known for having the the best apples and pears. Because he guarded the orchard from thieves, he also welcomed the *Shabbos* there and sang *Lekhu Neraneno* with ecstasy and with a sweet melody.

The priest passed by one night and heard his melody. The priest called to him and asked – what kind of prayer is it? Itse Avrahamchik said that this is a special prayer to meet the *Shabbos* queen.

On that night he received the right to the priest's orchard. Because of *Lekhu Neraneno* the priest would not rent his orchard to anyone else; Feytl's son, Itse Avrahamchik, then received the nickname – the *Lekhu Neraneno.*

Shmuel-Itse the Tailor

When Shmuel-Itse the tailor reached the age of 90, he prepared to go on his way, because how long can a man receive the gift of years? Each day he anticipated going to the world to come.

In the synagogue he once heard from his rabbi the story of King David and how in his deep old age he constantly sat in his study in order that the Angel of Death would have no power over him. Therefore, Shmuel-Itse wanted to do the same thing and, as he could not study, he would recite Psalms. But his problem was that his eyes were dim and he could not recite Psalms and he did not remember them by heart.

An idea flew through his head of how to drive away the Angel of Death. As he had an *arbe confes* [undergarment worn by pious Jews with *tsitses* – fringes – on four corners] knitted of thin wool, the *tsitses* would drive him away.

Therefore, he was often seen actually holding the *tsitses* stiff in his hand in order to drive away the Angel of Death.

Shmuel Itze the Tailor

* * *

It happened that on the eve of Passover, he felt very ill. The *Khevre Kadishe* [burial society] sat near his bed, watching for Shmuel-Itse's last breath.

Here he asked that his wife, Malka, be called to him. He asked her to bring a half bottle of *nayntsiker* [90 proof whiskey]. Shmuel-Itse braced himself and had a drink with the members of the *Khevre Kadishe*. At the same time, he said to Malka that she should change her jacket in order not to *reysn krie** on her new jacket. He turned to the *Khevre Kadishe* with a request that his cane by placed on his grave as a headstone because it not only served as something to lean on, but also for taking measurements when sewing garments for his customers. The cane was actually full of notches and signs; it would be a witness in the world to come that he, Shmuel-Itse, the tailor, never measured too much and did not profit from the remnants of his customer's cloth.

*[Translator's note: The act of tearing one's garment as a sign of mourning. This is done by the closest relatives of the deceased.]

Then he asked everyone to leave, except the *shoykhet* [ritual slaughterer] whom he asked to carry out the sofa in order that it would be used as his *taare bret* [board on which the dead are laid for ritual cleansing before burial].

Then he fainted. He began to die and closed his eyes forever.

Yoshe the Bricklayer

Yoshe the Bricklayer

Yoshe the bricklayer was famous in Rakishok and in the neighboring area as a great expert in building ovens.* His ovens would not "smoke" and they joked that even wet wood would burn in his ovens.

*[Translator's note: Ovens were built for heating as well as baking.]

He would construct the ovens himself, without an assistant. It was said that he specifically did not hire any workers so that no one would learn the "secret" of how he built the ovens. Only his wife, Mere, would help him with his work. She would mix the lime, carry bricks and help him. It was said in the *shtetl* that Mere could make as good an oven as Yoshe.

They were both industrious people as well as thrifty, amassing one penny to the next. Everyone in Rakishok knew that Yoshe would convert the saved money for a sacred purpose, but it was not known for what *dvar mitzvah* [fulfillment of a religious obligation].

One day, large and small in the *shtetl* saw how Yoshe was in deep conversation with the scribe. Then it was assumed that he would give a *Sefer Torah** to the synagogue.

Rokiskis Yizkor Book   179

*[Translator's note: A *Sefer Torah* is a parchment scroll on which the Torah is handwritten by a scribe. It is considered a great *mitzvah* – a good act – to donate a *Sefer Torah* or to participate in its creation.]

Yoshe invited the entire *shtetl* to the celebration, which took place in the synagogue, on the day on which the *Sefer Torah* was completed. When the crowd arrived, it was noticed that Yoshe was a little upset and that his wife, Mere, was not in the synagogue.

There was then a surprise for everyone. No one knew what had happened. Then it became clear that a dispute had arisen between Yoshe and his wife, Mere, who demanded half of the world to come for the *mitzvah* of donating a *Sefer Torah*. She did not want it anyway else but that he give her a *tekies kaf* [striking of hands as a pledge of an obligation], at the open Ark, with a *minyon* [10 men] as witnesses that she would have an equal portion of the *mitzvah* in the next world.

She asserted and stipulated that she had toiled as much for the *Sefer Torah* as had he, Yoshe, and she had mixed lime, carried bricks and done all kinds of heavy work and an equal portion of the world to come was surely also hers. However, Yoshe did not want to give in, saying, "A trifle, to give half of the world to come to a woman!"

The crowd intervened in this dispute between husband and wife. The rabbi and the property owners also sought a reconciliation between them.

In the end they reconciled in this way: Yoshe had to give his wife, Mere, half of the *mitzvah* of donating a *Sefer Torah* to the synagogue; in addition to this, Yoshe gave the synagogue a portion of the Aramaic Talmud and this *mitzvah* was exclusively on Yoshe's account.

Mere accepted this judgment and she also came to the synagogue.

A great, joyous celebration took place then and the entire *shtetl* celebrated with Yoshe and Mere.

Family photo of Shmuel Itze the Tailor

Welwe the Tailor

Welwe the tailor was not satisfied with prayers for the destroyed Temple in Jerusalem and did not want to wait for the time of *Moshiakh* [the arrival of the redeemer].

On one beautiful morning, Welwe packed his scissors and needles, his *Shabbos* clothing and other trifles and decided to go to *Eretz-Yisroel*. The words of his son as well as the arguments of the rabbi that the redemption had not yet happened and it was not yet time to go to *Eretz-Yisroel* did not help. He was stubborn and no one could stop him.

A long time passed and Rakishok and its environs had not heard from Welwe; Welwe was lost.

One morning Welwe appeared in the *shtetl*, arriving smeared and muddied and with a large sack on his pack. He had brought soil from *Eretz-Yisroel*.

Itse Yankl the Candlemaker

Rakishok had a small tallow candle factory. The "manufacturer" was named Yankl the candlemaker. His candles did not turn out even with one size and width.

He was also the town book seller. He only sold *Khumishim* [Five Books of the Torah] and *Musar-Seforim* [works on ethics], but not books of the *Haskhalah* [Enlightenment]. His wife made certain that in their small shop there would not be had, God forbid, any heretical books.

She was very pious and the *firzogeryn* [woman who reads the prayers to other women] in the woman's section of the synagogue and entering the house of prayer, she would first sing a prayer in an undertone with a great fear of God: "*Riboynu Shel Oylem* [Ruler of the world], I, Rywka, Your servant, am here and Your slave, Itse Yankl is finishing the cooking of candles and will come; Your third servant, our only son, Shmuelke, is still asleep and will also come soon.

Yoshe the Policeman

There were three cantonists [conscripts in the Russian army who were required to serve for 25 years] who were called Yoshe the soldier, Dovid the soldier, Moshe the soldier. They carried the nickname "soldier" until their deaths.

Yoshe the soldier received another nickname: "Yoshe the policeman." He was a policeman in the Czarist police. He had a commanding figure, was wide shouldered with a jutting, healthy chest and with a wide combed beard. Compared to the remaining *shtetl* Jews with bent backs and sunken chests, his distinguished appearance was as if he had come from another part of the earth.

It happened that the governor, Vyravkyn, traveled through Rakishok and noticed the Jewish policeman, Yoshe; he dismissed him immediately. The words of the police commissioner that Yoshe had been a Nikolayevsky soldier* did not help.

*[Translator's note: A soldier who had served under Czar Nikolai I for 25 years.]

Yoshe the policeman had to take off his uniform. Although the *shtetl* gave him the position of lamplighter, the nickname "Yoshe the policeman" remained with him for his entire life.

My Mother

My mother was an economical woman, lived very frugally. First, because she simply did not have much. Secondly, my mother knew that a Jewish daughter lived a modest life and is not someone who squanders.

She would plant her own potatoes on a section of a field rented from a peasant; the potatoes had to last for the entire year.

The day when my mother went to the field to plant the potatoes was a holiday for us children. Then we did not go to *kheder* [religious school] and would go with our mother who would also ask her neighbors to help her. Picking the potatoes was also a holiday for us.

We would pour the potatoes picked from the field into a large pit, cover them well with straw and cover it again so that it would not freeze during the course of the winter.

My mother had her medicines and remedies for illnesses. She healed us children with the most primitive ways:

For whopping cough, our mother healed us by taking us to a stall and having us inhale the smell of the fresh manure or by passing near a river where braided trees grew, through which we had to pass. In addition to this, our mother believed drinking urine was a remedy or she would take us through a house where there were two doors. We needed to go in through the front door and go out through the back door.

For her part, our mother was not passive. She would fast on Mondays and Thursdays on behalf of our health.

She had great fear of an *ayin hore* [evil eye]. She would often carry out an exorcism of an *ayin hore* that for her was similar to a remedy for a toothache.

When she cleaned the house for the *yom-tovim* [holidays], my mother would not permit the spider webs to be taken down off the walls because she would use them to stop the blood when we children would cut our hands.

She was very pious. Every day she had a question to ask the rabbi, although yesterday's question was the same as today's.

Once the chief of police of the *shtetl* compiled a report about my grandmother about why she did not keep the farm yard clean. My grandmother had to pay a fine or sit in a dungeon. Then my mother took the "crime" on herself and went to jail for my grandmother.

It fell that she had to sit for three days: Friday, *Shabbos* and Sunday. On Friday, we children brought two pillows, a quilt, the *Shabbos cholent* [stew], two candlesticks for blessing the candles, her *sheitl* [wig worn by pious married women], her *Shabbos* dress and also her *Tseno Ureno* [woman's prayer book] to our mother in the dungeon. On *Shabbos* we stood on the other side of the fence and watched how our mother sat dressed in her *sheitl*, in her *Shabbos* dress and read the *Tseno Ureno* with much religious ecstasy and feeling.

* * *

The *Shekhinah* hovered in our house on *Shabbos*. It was entirely holy in our poor apartment.

Sadness fell on the third *Shabbos* meal; the beloved holy *Shabbos* was leaving. Our father was coming from the synagogue and we would finish the last *challah* [braided bread eaten on *Shabbos*] that our mother had left.

The sun went down gradually and was about to set. The weekdays were coming with their concerns about earning a living.

It was becoming dark in the room. Our mother stood near the window and directed her eyes to heaven, waiting for the first star. Her face ringed with creases and tormented by cares; she would soon have to knead bread so that it lasted for the entire week. The shoes of one child needed to be repaired and a second child had clothes that needed mending.

A star appeared in the sky, after it – a second, a third. My father recited *havdalah* [the prayer concluding *Shabbos*] with innumerable words, in order that the *Shabbos* would be drawn out longer and my mother's lips murmured: O, God of Avraham, of Yitzhak and Yakov...

We, children, counted the seconds, the minutes and waited with impatience for the fire and candles to be lit and it would become light!

Slova the Wife of the Tanner

The *shtetl* could not do without Slova, the wife of the tanner. She was a server at weddings and very efficient at baking and cooking; mainly, she had a reputation for her *gefilte fish*. On the eve of *Shabbos* she was very preoccupied, providing all of the poor in Rakishok with *challah*, fish and so on. She would collect donations for buying an outfit for a poor bride.

Slova was a tone-setter at celebrations. She would dance the entire day from the bride's house to the synagogue and also at the wedding in honor of the bride.

It was not a real celebration without Slova.

Slova was also the tone-setter at a funeral. She heartrendingly mourned the deceased and she was a great artist in this role.

She also could change her tone and role. Here she came from a funeral and she could immediately change into her *Shabbos* garment and go dancing at a wedding.

Slova, the wife of the tanner, was *Sore bas Toyvim** in Rakishok in miniature.

*[Translator's note: *Sore bas Toyvim* is a legendary figure who assists women and children.]

Zelda-Mine

Who taught Zelda-Mine how to write? No one knows. She also did not tell anyone. This became of great use when she remained a widow.

She became the women's *Malamed* [teacher in a religious school] in Rakishok and even had her own *kheder* [religious school for young children] where girls and young wives would learn to write in Yiddish from her. In addition to this she wrote letters for all of the African wives, whose husbands were in Africa. Zelda-Mine did not need people to tell her what to write. She knew the husbands and wives when they were still children and knew well what women can write to men.

Her income from writing letters was not large. It was said about her that she was a lucky writer: money always resulted from her letters. When a check would arrive she would receive an extra fee.

Ruchl-Leah – the *Bobe* [grandmother]

All of the *kheder* boys called Ruchl-Leah, the *Bobe*. It could be that she got this name because she was already an old woman, perhaps the oldest in Rakishok or because she carried around beans [*bob* in Yiddish] to sell.

She had many competitors because other women would carry around beans to sell. But we, *kheder* boys would only buy from her for these reasons: First, her measure was larger than with other bean sellers and, secondly, she gave credit which she never jotted down because she was illiterate.

Yet we did not wrong her and always paid the debts--none of us wanted to be tempted by such a sin for fear of the burning *gehenom* [hell] with the iron horseman.

Many times when the *Bobe* would see her debtors passing by and not buying any beans, she would call them to her and ask why they were not buying any beans. When they told her that they do not want any new debts, she would ask them if they were going to *kheder*. If she received the answer: "Definitely we are going to *kheder*," she would take a full pile of beans and give it to each debtor without cost.

The *Bobe* had many such cases. To this day this matter is puzzling to me and it is a great mystery: How did the *Bobe* get the money to carry on her "business?"

Nahum-Moses and Rochel-Leah Peres

Yechiel Rotman and Sara-Riva Levin

[Page 190]

Chaye-Sore-Ite Bacher

by S. Klass

Translated by Sam Lichtenstein

The wife of Yitzchak (Alter) Bacher was an unusually righteous woman. She was born in an area of farms and forests on the outskirts of Rokiskis, Lithuania. Despite the fact that during her early married life she lived in poor economic circumstances and various weather conditions, she went from house to house collecting donations for the poor families.

When she became widowed, she spent much of her time collecting donations for the purpose of helping poor brides with the necessities for their wedding preparations. In 1929 she immigrated to South Africa together with her five children to join her sons, Saul and Koppel. Her useful communal capability further directed her to collect donations with which she sent parcels to her birthplace and surrounding places for needy families.

I remember one early morning in Johannesburg a sudden knock on the door. Sarah Bacher brought two letters in hand. I directed her to a chair. She had just received two letters from Rokiskis, one from a young married woman wanting to join her husband in South Africa, the other from a young bride wanting to come to her future husband. Neither of them had money for travel expenses. I endeavored to persuade her that the weather was bad and that we should delay the trip for another day, but she was not prepared to accept it, demanding that we must obtain the money from some people.

We took a tramcar, which took us to the end stop. There we went by another tramcar to Kensington and traveled to the last "stop." Suddenly a heavy rain came down. We then ran to a tree for shelter. The uphill climb left us breathless. When we reached the house of the Rokisker family, the lady of the house gave us a handsome donation for that purpose. From there we went to other homes, and none refused. On that day alone we collected 50 pounds. Within several days Chaya-Sarah-Ita Bacher collected 175 pounds, which she sent to Rokiskis to the interested persons, who quickly came to South Africa.

She had done all her work in South Africa devotedly. Many women are thankful for her efforts, which has enabled them to escape the Nazi persecution and to come to South Africa.

[No caption]

She has performed all her work alone, without any help from committees or societies, and with great dedication. No wonder her name is valued greatly by Rokishker Jews.

In the presence of her sons, daughters, sons-in-law, daughters-in-law and grandchildren she departed on the 28 September 1943.

Yitzchak (Alter) Bacher

Yitzchak (Alter) Bacher was born on a farm near Salok. In his youth he learned tailoring. After he married he immigrated to America.

He was not happy with the American way of life and longed for the religious way in his hometown.

When he saved up some dollars he returned home and opened a little shop in Radute on the outskirts of Rokiskis. At the time of the First World War Yitzchak settled in Rokiskis.

Unfortunately, in 1923 he died suddenly when he was in his forties. He was a good-hearted Yid, whose pleasure was to do good deeds and to help others in time of distress.

[Pages 192-193]

Gite Rubin-Ferman

by Chana Penn-Lubowitz

Translated by Gloria Berkenstat Freund

Gita Rubin Ferman

Gite Rubin-Ferman, the sister of our fellow townsman, Shlomo Rubin, was raised in a communal atmosphere. While still in Rakishok she was an active worker in *Lines haTzedek* [organization that provided medical needs and nightly care for the sick poor], in *Gemiles Khesed* [interest free loans] and in other communal institutions.

With great love, she transplanted her communal work to her new home, America. Today, she occupies a very respected position in Jewish communal life in Philadelphia. She is the general secretary of the Federation of the Lithuanian Jews in Philadelphia. She is also active in the field of organizing summer colonies for the Jewish children. She organizes Hope, the children's camp, in Philadelphia every year.

Gita Rubin Ferman and R. Rubinstein

The above mentioned Federation was founded in 1937 and her original activity was to send help to those suffering from need in the old home.

After the Second World War, the Federation extended its aid work, sending thousands of food and clothing packages to the survivors in the camps and in Israel.

Thanks to the initiative of Gite Rubin-Ferman the idea to build houses in Israel for the homeless Lithuanian immigrants developed at the Federation.

In October 1951, Gite Rubin-Ferman traveled to Israel with Mr. and Mrs. Shulman, active members of the Federation, and with Mr. and Mrs. Epstein, in order to bring the project to fruition. A contract was agreed to with the building company, Raska-Israel Corporation.

The work to build a Lithuanian colony called *Shechunat Lita* [the Lithuanian quarter or neighborhood] began on the 2nd of December 1951. The work went ahead with full force thanks to the energetic Gite Rubin-Ferman.

The Lithuania Federation of Philadelphia is a people's organization and consists of ordinary people. Gite Rubin-Ferman is a meritorious woman of the people who remains devoted to the ideals of communal work, which she absorbed in our hometown, Rakishok.

[Page 194]

My Father of Blessed Memory: Biographical Notes on the Lomza Rosh Hayeshiva, Rabbi Yehoshua Zelig Ruch, O.B.M.

by his son, Meyer Ruch, Johannesburg, SA

Translated by Rabbi Ezra Boyarsky

On the map, Rakishok, a small town in Lithuania, was difficult to locate. However, in the rabbinical-yeshiva world, Rakishok was famous due to the fact that it was the birthplace of my father, Reb Zelig Rakishker, born 1879 to Michel and his wife Pere o.b.m, plain, ordinary but honest folks.

Very few details of his early childhood are known to us except that when he reached adolescence, his strong personality traits began to manifest themselves. He was gripped by an insatiable desire to study Torah, unusual for a boy his age, even in those times. Already as a bar mitzvah boy he showed signs of greatness, and his fame as an illuy--a child prodigy--was acknowledged with pride by the entire community.

The very next week, after he had a serious discussion with his father as to whether to continue on a Torah course or begin planning for a more pragmatic career, he left Rakishok for the world-renowned Slabodka Yeshiva. The distance in miles between Rakishok and Slabodka, a suburb of Kovno, is a relatively short one, but in matters of Jewish Weltanschaung, they were worlds apart. Rakishok was considered to be a fortress of the Lubavitch branch of the Hasidic movement in Lithuania. Hasidism, of which Lubavitch is an integral part, did not stress the pre-eminence of Torah study in its broader connotation, when it first formulated the basic principles upon which its ideology rests. Not that it put Torah study on the back burner, but rather it argued that proficiency in Talmud alone should not be the ultimate goal. Character building and developing a positive attitude toward one's fellow men were equally important. Slabodka, on the other hand, being the recognized Torah center of Lithuania, championed Talmudic erudition as the highest achievement that a yeshiva student should strive to attain.

When the dean of the Slabodka Yeshiva, Rabbi Nata Hirsh Finkel, known as Der Alter, examined the newly arrived student from Rakishok, he was deeply impressed by his knowledge and acumen. As already mentioned, Rakishok was a bastion of the Chabad brand of Hasidism, and Der Alter couldn't help wondering why the young prodigy was drawn to Slabodka in preference to a Lubavitch institution more in line with his upbringing.

The Rakishoker yeshiva bocher got so engrossed in his studies that he seldom took time to visit his family in Rakishok. Another reason that kept my father in Slabodka was that the dean, Rabbi Finkel, found in him a staunch supporter for his pioneer work to introduce a new subject to the Lithuanian yeshivas--Musar. Musar is the 19th-20th century Jewish religious movement which stresses moral and ethical edification. Rabbi Finkel's motive in expanding the yeshiva curriculum to include Musar was to produce scholars not only equipped with extensive Talmudic knowledge but men also possessed of high moral fiber, for these students were to be the future community leaders either as rabbis or as learned laymen.

Ever since childhood, Zelig Rakishker was brought up in a Lubavitch atmosphere and imbibed its moral teachings, and therefore he was no stranger to Musar, which explains why he became one of the dean's most devoted followers in his endeavors to popularize the Musar movement.

At this time the mystery as to why Zelig chose Slabodka began to unravel. Now it became clear to Rabbi Finkel that what the Rakishker prodigy sought was a synthesis of Chabad and Slobodka.

Some of the other Rosh Hayeshivos (deans) opposed Rabbi Finkel's Musar idea, arguing that making Musar an integral part of the regular yeshiva program would interfere with the Talmudic studies which require much concentration, and would defeat the very purpose for which these higher Jewish educational institutions were founded. However, in spite of the strong opposition, in the course of time, this issue also won many proponents in the yeshiva community, resulting in the formation of two mutually contending camps. Gradually the dispute grew into a conflagration, with the main frontlines positioned in the Telz and Mire yeshivas. Rabbi Finkel felt that since he was basically the cause of the uproar, it was his moral duty to douse the fires of controversy and mediate a peaceful solution.

Now Der Alter was faced with the difficult task of selecting a qualified emissary whom he could entrust with executing this extremely important assignment. As you may have guessed, Der Alter's choice for this mission was none other than Zelig Rakishker. Reb Zelig spent several months in Ponevez and Mir respectively, and succeeded in calming the raging conflict. His fame as a Talmudic scholar extended far beyond the precincts of Slabodka. The Torah prestige that he personified with his charming personality played a major role in winning over the opponents. No wonder then that Rabbi Eliezer Shulowitz, known as Reb Lazer Lomzer, chose Zelig to be his son-in-law, and simultaneously appointed him to the position as Lomzer Rosh Hayeshiva.

At the outbreak of World War I, when my father and family were evacuated deeper into Russia, a large number of his students of the Lomza yeshiva went along and stayed with him in the town of Priluki near Poltava for the duration of the war. Here in Priluki, under the most adverse circumstances brought on by the war, my father's paternal devotion and concern for his students revealed the high quality of his character.

At the end of the war, many yeshiva students from Minsk, Kiev, Charkov, and other cities joined Zelig in his return to Lomza. This was not unexpected, for my father's students also felt warmly towards him, and regarded the yeshiva as their home. On the way back to Lomza, my father stopped for a short stay in his birthplace, Rakishok, and visited his brother Reb Pesach and family.

The glorious period of the Lomza yeshiva began with the end of World War I. When the displaced Jews returned to their homes and life normalized again, the quest for advanced Torah education increased rather than decreased as is usually the case in unsettled times. Hundreds of students from distant parts of Poland and Lithuania flocked to the Lomza yeshiva either to begin or to resume their studies disrupted by the war. Because of this increase in the student body, the main lecture hall of the yeshiva could not accommodate such a large number, and so the synagogue magnanimously opened its doors for the student overflow. Other communities reacted in like manner in similar situations. For the Lomza Jews who helped maintain the yeshiva, this was another occasion to demonstrate their high regard for the Rosh Hayeshiva who, in a manner of speaking, had put their city on the map.

In his later years, my father's father-in-law made aliya to Eretz Yisroel, and there founded a branch of the Lomza yeshiva in Petach Tikvah. My father followed, bringing with him fifty of his best students for the opening of the branch, and remained there to serve as its first Rosh Hayeshiva. But despite his boundless love for the land of Israel and his enthusiasm for the yishuv (the Jewish settlement), he was impelled to return to his students in Lomza.

In the thirties, when Poland experienced an economic depression, the yeshiva's finances were seriously affected. At this juncture, my father decided to go to South Africa for the purpose of collecting sufficient funds to keep the yeshiva functioning until the economy improved. He undertook the trip primarily because he felt that, as head of the yeshiva, it was his moral responsibility to do all in his power to safeguard the yeshiva's financial stability. By temperament, the task he undertook was out of character for him. Rabbi Cahanman, the world-renowned Rabbi of Ponevez, characterized him best when he said: "The Lomza Rosh Hayeshiva lacks the ability to make money. His virtues stand in his way." Yet, according to my father, he accomplished far more than others in South Africa. Upon his return to Lomza he said: "Thank God my trip was successful. I influenced one Jewish man to put on teffilin and another to keep his store closed on the Sabbath...." He won people over with his impeccable honesty and naivete. A Jewish man in

Johannesburg told me that "to this day I keep my store closed on Shabbos Shuva--the Sabbath between Rosh Hashanah and Yom Kippur--in memory of your father."

A few years prior to the outbreak of World War II, his health began to fail. He ignored the doctors orders not to deliver any lectures or to continue bearing the heavy burden of the yeshiva. Eight months later he suffered a heart attack and became weaker by the day. When the Germans entered Lomza in September 1939, their first "order of business" was to cut off the beards of all jews. When they were done with this contemptible act on my father, he said to them, "danke sehr"--thank you very much. I am certain that this was the only ironic thank you he ever uttered.

A few days later when Lomza was taken by the Russians, he had the opportunity to escape with his family to Lithuania where living conditions were still relatively normal, but he categorically refused to leave as long as a number of his students were unable to join him. No amount of pleading by his family and students were of any avail--he remained steadfast in his resolution to stay on as sole guardian of the now empty Torah citadel which the Russians converted into a tailor shop. They then hermetically sealed the Polish-Lithuanian border. Several months later, prior to the wholesale slaughter of Europe's Jewry at the hands of the eternally cursed Nazis, a group of his closest and most loyal students jeopardized their lives and brought their teacher and his family to Vilna.

Old and physically broken, he paid his final visit to Rakishok. The town of his birth, though now impoverished and on the brink of destruction, tendered her favorite son an enthusiastic welcome. His stay in Rakishok was a brief one, and he returned to Vilna to be with his students who died martyrs' deaths together with their teacher, and of whom it may be said: "The beloved and dear in their lives were even in their death not parted." (Samuel II , Chapter 1, Verse 23).

[Pages 198-202]

Types of the Old Home

By A. Koseff

Translated by Gloria Berkenstat Freund

Nusan, Reitze's Son

Nusan, the son of Reitze, was a water carrier in Rakishok and was our water carrier, too. That is probably why I remember him clearly, more clearly than my childhood friends.

He was tall and firmly built, with strong arms and hands with long fingers that would hang down like swinging branches of a water tree (weeping willow). His back was already a little bent from the many full pails of water that he would carry day after day for his customers. He never cheated his customers. The pails were always full to overflowing.

His eyes – dark, quiet, dreamy – mirrored the wells from which he would draw the water. His nose was as if carved, and his full lips, round, always with the moistness of desire. He had a short black beard, a little smaller than the beard of Jesus.

I remember how he would stand for hours without the slightest movement, just as the water in the well. It seemed as if he looked into his own world, which was hidden from us.

At times his rasping bass voice would thunder out of his long neck with its protruding Adam's apple, shaking his slender body and causing it to shudder.

Nusan Reitze's son, took each expression of friendship to his heart-felt soul and paid it back with the full warmth of his soul and heart and with his entire strength.

He did not have any friends and was lonely, but he felt a closeness to "Tzimtzervises," the *Shabbos goy* (the non-Jew who does required work that a Jew cannot do on *Shabbos* or holidays), when Tzimtzervises would play his fiddle. After the playing, Nusan, Reitze's son, stood as if forged to the earth. However, suddenly, as if guilty, he would hurry on his way. It was not nice for him to befriend "a thief and, in addition, a non-Jew!"

It happened that Nusan also would sing in the house or on the street without rhyme or reason. When he had the desire to do so, he would call out his song in what was always a monotone.

The scoundrels approached him with care when they mockingly asked him to sing. Then, as if frozen, he would stand in one spot and, in the blink of an eye, he would look deep into his own world. For long moments he would move his feet heavily and clumsily, like a bear, as if absorbing air through them. In such cases, one had to beg for a long time and push Nusan until he woke up from his dreamy world. Then he would suddenly have an awakened smile on his face and spreading his feet, he would, automatically, earnestly cry out in his bass voice:

"A bear stands on the street

with a ring in his nose;

thus goes the bear with the ring in his nose;

a foot here and a foot there;

carrying water is difficult."

The singing resounded swiftly through the strained, swollen, long throat. This was a good game and joke for the friendly pranksters and even for the passersby.

Nusan, Reitze's son, came into our house often and was devoted to us. During the week he would bring a multitude of pails of water from the well behind the church, knowing that these full pails of water were good for brewing tea. And when he succeeded in bringing full pails, his face would be covered with perspiration. Quietly he would place the pails of water on the ground, and say with satisfaction: "Well, Heika, two full pails of water brought from behind the church!" A satisfied rattling laugh accompanied his words. He would receive for this a slice of bread with butter or juice. And every Thursday, he received a piece of meat with *shmaltz* (rendered chicken fat), which he would bring to his mother Reitze for *Shabbos*.

Nusan's mother, Reitze, was a short, squat woman, quiet and bashful. She would go around the houses gathering donations. It did not matter if the donation was a *groshen* or a note or a crust of bread, she would softly and calmly visit only the houses where her bashful wish of good morning might bring something.

Earning a livelihood was difficult and bitter for her son, the water carrier. During the winter when his income was larger, the days were bitter cold and his hands were frozen like the iron pails. During the summer there was competition for Nusan's livelihood. Parents would call their children, the brats who played in the dusty streets, and say, "Meirke, Joske, bring a small pail of water from Shmuel the shoemaker's well!"

However, the long summer days were deadly dangerous for Nusan, when we, a bunch of clowns from *cheder* (religious school), would meet him during our playtime carrying many pails full of water. It did not help that he wanted to avoid us. He would hurry by us with careful steps and with frightened eyes he would look after us, careful that his pails remained full. He would shake, when we small brats, attacked him and wanted to dirty his water by spitting into the pails. Although, by nature, he was unassuming and was thankful for the smallest sign of friendship, a small storm of rage would spurt from him at the smallest hint that we wanted to dirty his water.

With foam from his mouth and with the roar of a slaughtered ox, he would then rip out stones from the cobblestone pavement and throw them at us. But he would see to it that the stones did not hit us. Thus – through shouting and roaring – he threw a fear in us, until we took to our heels. When he chased us away, his lowered hands always were filled with stones and a wheezing smile would appear on his dusty lips. His eyes shone joyously with his great victory over his assailants and with joy that his pails of water remained clean.

This was a great sports contest for us, the sect of clowns. However, *erev Shabbos* (the eve of *Shabbos*) was care-filled for the woman who waited for water in order to brew the hot tea for *Shabbos*.

Nusan strongly esteemed *Shabbos*. Every *Shabbos* he would wash and would put on a clean suit of clothes made of inferior fabric that he had outgrown and, like the polished candlesticks, his face shone.

He had great respect for the village's teachers. He behaved with great humility and reverence toward the teachers. He knew all the educators and the extent of their learning. He had his own measurement specifications for evaluating each according to his own "Nusanish" notion: Reb Yehezkeil knows twelve parts of the *Talmud*, eight and a half of the *Mishnah* and three of the second part of the *Shulkhan Arukh* (the book of rules for living a pious Jewish life); Reb Nisen knows three part of the *Talmud*, seven of the *Mishnah* and half of the *Tanya*; but Reb Yisroel knows hundreds of parts of the *Talmud*, two hundred of the *Mishnah* with hundreds from the second part of the *Shulkhan Arukh*, much of *Chai Odom* and more from the *Shlukhan Arukh* and so on. The closets and shelves around the wall, fully packed with *seforim* (religious books), such as Nusan had not seen elsewhere, influenced his evaluation of Reb Dov Yisroel's learnedness. This was the measure according to which he would make evaluations.

And when he was asked: "Well, Nusan, how much does the Rabbi Reb Shmuel know?" After earnest thought, with an earnest smile, he would say: "The Rabbi Reb Shmuel must know more *Gemara* (commentaries on the *Mishnah*)."

He also had levels thought out for the wives of the educators according to their piety. For example, he would say: "Yehezkeil's wife Sara knows ten parts of the *Tsene Urene* (Yiddish book of Bible stories for women) and ten Yiddish prayers. But to the other women for whom he had a special respect, he would add that they also know a fourth or half of the *Khumish* (the prayer book).

When he sensed that one of the educators showed a sympathetic feeling toward him, he would shuffle toward him, with his long feet, with restrained steps and with a servile humility he would pat his back and tell the teacher his evaluation of his good education. Thus he would conduct himself with the wives and, giving them a pat, with great respect he measured the level of their knowledge. Thus he wheezed a smile, swallowing it in his Adam's apple and long throat.

Nusan, Reitze's son, was an honest and quiet person. His heart drew him to a homey quietness and calmness, where people are kind. He would find his redress in a sad singing sanctity in the synagogue at twilight.

Elya and Bethsheba

We had in our town Elya, a kind of friend of Nusan. Both occupied the same corner near the oven in the large synagogue. Elya could drive his fist into a face if someone called him by his nickname. His work was to help the *shammus* of the large synagogue, where he stayed. However, Elya was so lazy that he did not always take care of the wood and water for the synagogue. The *shammus*, an old man, had enough vexations. From *Shabbos* to *Shabbos*, the floor of the synagogue was covered with muddy sand.

It was murmured in town that in the evening he befriends the crazy Bethsheba. Bethsheba, with her pack, made her home in the women's section of the synagogue, on the other side of the railing in the synagogue. In her young years, it was said, she gave birth to a child each year and she would beat the baby to death, near the priest's little river, in the same clear transparent water where we children would splash in damp pants in the river.

Elya would go around with a string around his waist over his dirty *gartl* (belt worn during prayer). His chest was stuffed day and night with rags, the opposite of Nusen.

"Tzimtzerevizes"

Tzimtzerevises was the *Shabbos goy* in Rakishok.

The name "Tzimtzervizes" was, in truth, a nickname. I believe scarcely any of us knew his actual name. The nickname was given to him because he was constantly squeaking on his fiddle. Young boys and girls would run after him and yell "Tzimtzervizes! Tzimtzervizes!" They actually meant to say, "Squeak, fiddle, squeak, squeak, fiddle!"

Tzimtzervizes spoke Yiddish. His Yiddish was better than the peasant language spoken by the Jews. For weeks and months he would drag around the town without any work. He knew all of the Jews, and from them, cunningly he would receive food in order to still his hunger. He would receive his holiday meals on market day at the market, always at the corner of the *monopol* (concession with exclusive right to sell an item such as salt or vodka), among the gathered peasants, where the concession's customers would jump around like fireworks.

He was a thief and would have to be led away from the entrance way. It was difficult to get along with him. His peasant blood would draw him to his village and, during the summer, his soul would long for green grass, for birds and for summer nights, and in winter days he longed for a little dance and a flirtation with a full-bosomed village *shiksa* (gentile woman). He would then be lost, where nature itself sings and where the melody is spun from the silence of the night.

On Friday nights, it was necessary to run to faraway neighbors to catch the *Shabbos goy* from the next street and, indeed, that cost a double portion of *challah* (braided egg bread traditionally served on *Shabbos*).

Tzimtzervizes would go through the streets in town familiarly with hopping steps, and on his face, with the small pointed eyes and pointed nose, a smile always shone. His face paled at the sight of the scoundrels and he patted his fiddle that rested against his chest, under a homemade cloak. He said in Yiddish that, "he loved his fiddle more, for example, than the priest."

He knew all of the Jews in the town, calling them by their first names: Pinya, Haimke, Panye Berkish and so forth.

If, while marching across the *shtetl*, he met someone who greeted him with a smile of familiarity, he would tenderly take out his fiddle from his chest and scratch out peasant dances and sad, longing gypsy melodies. And very often the melodies suited the mood of the listener.

When finished playing, he shoved his fiddle back against his chest and, with his pointed laughing face, he marched back to the center of the *shtetl* – to the pump at the marketplace.

Peasants traveled there together and they met others who stopped at the pump to give water to their horses. People went by the pump to the neighboring booths to buy small batches of bagels, and if this passerby was a familiar face, he would beg and receive a nice portion of the sweet bagels.

But if it was empty around the pump, he would hop across the marketplace to the street corner near Shmienern's wall, where the "petty bourgeois council" was. Peasants from neighboring villages would stop by the street corner in order to visit the "petty bourgeois" and discuss their military conscription and other matters.

Or sometimes one could meet at the corner Hilel Mesztzansker, one of the town intelligencia and a bit of a clown, too. Hilel would let himself be fooled out of a kopek for a little fun.

The rich man Iser's tavern stood along the road, where one could buy a glass of liquor or a half bottle of beer for a few kopeks. The environment of tavern noise, mixed with the sharp smell of liquor, strongly affected "Tzimtzerevizes'" fiddle, and with heart and soul it played its best.

[Pages 205-206]

Social Cultural Life and Education Institutions

The Modernized Cheder

by Moshe Katz

Translated by Ken Frieden

Moishe Katz

I was educated at yeshivas and, already in my early years, I absorbed the ideals of the Jewish Enlightenment. My life was permeated by the idea of national rebirth, by the Zionist ideal. Many of my friends and acquaintances were among the Enlightenment writers of the time. At the same time, I defended the principles of our faith and religion. I was both a believer and a follower of the Enlightenment.

For a few years after getting married I lived in Kurland (Courland), where I was a teacher (*melamed*) in a cheder. But I taught using a new approach and method, in the spirit of my national-religious views. I instructed grammar, Tanakh, Hebrew, and fragments of our Hebrew literature, following the system of teaching Hebrew in Hebrew.

Because of the law that Lithuanian inhabitants were not permitted to live in Kurland, my residence there was not legal. But one day the Czarist regime issued a harsh order that everyone who was from Lithuania had to leave Kurland within a couple hours. Then we, a few families, were forced to leave Kurland, and my family and I traveled to Rokiskis.

That was in 1912. On the basis of an initiative by a couple of wealthy men with Zionist leanings, I founded a modernized cheder. A few of the householders in Rokiskis viewed my accomplishment with suspicion. The work was not so easy, especially in a shtetl where the Enlightenment had not yet penetrated deeply.

School children and teacher, June 1927

In a back room, at the home of Treyne Zelbavitsh, I set up my modernized cheder. There were four school benches; four pupils sat on each bench. I taught them until six in the evening, using a modern method. The order of studies was: Hebrew, Tanakh, a page of Gemara, preparations for bar mitzvah, arithmetic, Yiddish, and a little Russian. The children made quick progress in their studies. If at the outset their parents had a hesitant attitude toward the modernized cheder, they later became strong supporters of it, on the basis of the children's successes.

The arrival of the First World War interrupted studies in the modernized cheder. Many of the Jews in Rokiskis were evacuated. Afterward the Germans opened an obligatory school, and there I taught the Hebrew studies.

After the war, Bertsik Zalkinds opened a Talmud-Torah (elementary school) in which I was the head rabbi. With the help of Peysekh Rokh and several other wealthy men, a hall was built for the Talmud-Torah. I then also taught Gemara to students in the Rokiskis Yeshiva. At the same time I was cantor and prayer-leader. I had a pretty voice and in leading prayers I was a success.

Nevertheless, I was drawn to my modernized cheder, and to this end I built a house of my own. But at the time there was already a large school in Rokiskis, and my income from the modernized cheder was not enough to make ends meet.

Because of this I had the thought of emigrating to South Africa. I knew that in Africa one should also know how to be a kosher butcher, and so I studied kosher slaughtering. During the month of Elul—during the Days of Awe—I learned that trade.

In 1928 I left Rokiskis and came to South Africa. My first position—as "Reverend"—was in Offerton. Over the past 17 years I have been in Braamfontein in the position of Rabbi, kosher slaughterer, cantor, and teacher.

I now have an honorable income and, no evil eye, a large family. But it is hard for me to forget the dear shtetl Rokiskis. In my memory, Rokiskis is associated with the years when I taught children in the modernized cheder. I remember everything vividly from that time, and also the dear and diligent pupils from that period in Rokiskis.

[Page 207]

The Russian Government School

by Asne Chiat

Translated by Rabbi Ezra Boyarsky

Asneh Hit

Admission to the Russian Government School was hard to come by, but a rich father and a dose of good luck helped. I was very jealous of the children who studied there. Every morning when I saw the Christian and the few Jewish children walking to the government school, I admit I was filled with envy.

One day I gathered enough courage and appealed to my father to make every effort possible to have me admitted to the Russian school. My father submitted an application at the school office and began looking for a "lobbyist" to intercede on my behalf.

The director of the shkola (school) was the town's "pope" (priest). My father, my cousin Malka Davidowitz and I first went to the head teacher of the school. He was a fine Russian gentleman, but he advised us to see the "pope" first concerning the matter. My father did not hesitate for one moment, and the three of us went to see the priest-director. I recall that at the entrance, a domestic called the priest, and my father bowed and kissed his hand as was the custom. Upon his inquiring as to the purpose of our visit, my father replied that he hoped the priest would be magnanimous and grant us admission to the school. The director did not reject our request out of hand, but told us to go to the headmaster to be examined, at which time he too would be present.

We were taken to a classroom where the examination took place. The "pope" was not satisfied with the results of the entrance examination, and advised us that the head teacher would prepare us for another try. The teacher agreed to tutor us after school hours, and my father promised to pay him well for his efforts. We used to come to the school at three o'clock in the afternoon to receive instruction, and applied ourselves with zeal and diligence to our studies. The teacher also encouraged us and led us to believe that our prospects of being accepted at the school were good.

At the end of the month we were examined a second time by the assistant director. We were sure that we had passed with flying colors, and were confident that we would finally be accepted. But how bitterly disappointed we were when the priest-director informed us, in a dispassionate and matter-of-fact way that the quota for Jewish students had been filled, and that he therefore could not accept us to study at the shkola. I went home embittered, dejected, and depressed, and in my heart I harbored a deep hatred for the anti-Semitic Czarist regime.

Instead of studying, which was my first choice, I got a job as a store clerk, and my dream to obtain an education remained just that, an unfulfilled dream.

Chaim Hit (died in Israeli War)

[Page 209]

The Lithuanian Gymnasium

by Ethel Aarons-Arsh

Translated by Rabbi Ezra Boyarsky

The first school that I attended was the German Zwangshul--the compulsory school--that was opened in Rakishok and lasted for the duration of the First World War. At first it was difficult for us children to learn German, but in time we got used to it.

Leibe Klingman, a tall, lean young man, was our German instructor. He was a good-natured person, and we respected him. Everybody in town admired his knowledge of the German language. Frequently he would also teach us Yiddish and Hebrew songs. The student body consisted exclusively of Jewish children, and therefore the German authorities engaged a special teacher for Jewish subjects. The town's Hebrew teacher, Moshe Katz, taught the Yiddish and Hebrew courses. When the Germans left Lithuania, the Zwangshul was closed.

After the war was over, we had to contend with a babel of languages. When the Germans left Rakishok, the Russians took their place, and along with them came the Rakishok Jews who had been evacuated to Russia. Most of the children of the evacuees spoke Russian, and some of the adults engaged in teaching Russian privately. They prepared Jewish children for the Russian Gymnasia in Ponevez.

The Russians' stay was short because before long the Lithuanian Republic was established. Soon after, Lithuanian schools were opened and we, the Jewish children, began to study Lithuanian--a third foreign language.

The Lithuanian gymnasia was housed in a building located on the corner of Market Place and Neyer Street. At first the Jews looked upon the Lithuanian schools and the gymnasia in particular with a great deal of skepticism. The Jews had their own reason for this attitude: they believed that there was a good chance the Russians might return and restore the former Russian school system. Therefore, Jewish parents made every effort to enroll their children in the Ponevez Russian gymnasia.

It was during this post-war era that a Hebrew progymnasia was opened, and a network of Tarbus schools was established in Lithuania. With the issuance of the Balfour Declaration in November 1917, the Zionist movement burgeoned, and Jewish Nationalism won many followers. This national awakening motivated the majority of Jewish parents to send their children to the Tarbus institutions, the focus of which were the Hebrew language and the Zionist-national ideology. The religious sector sent their children to Talmud Torahs and Chedorim. I and several of my friends who studied in the German Zwangshul, but whose parents lacked the financial means for tuition in the Russian Ponevez gymnasia, enrolled in the Lithuanian gymnasia.

Two-story building that housed the Lithuanian Gymnasia in Rokiskis

In the early years, it was relatively easy to be admitted to the Lithuanian gymnasia. At that time, Lithuania did not have enough textbooks in the Lithuanian language, and therefore the instructors were forced to use Russian textbooks of which there was no shortage. The teacher who prepared me for the Lithuanian gymnasia was a non-Jewish Lithuanian woman.

For a time, many out-of-town students came to the Rakishok Lithuanian gymnasia which acquired a reputation as one of the best secondary schools in Lithuania. Its teaching staff was of a very high caliber. Some of them were brought in from outside the country.

As is known, during the honeymoon years there was hardly a trace of anti-Semitism in the fledgling Lithuanian republic. The non-Jewish teachers did not in any way discriminate against the Jewish students. On the contrary, they admired and respected them for their ability and diligence, as on average, they far outstripped their Christian classmates. The Jewish students were excused from writing on the Sabbath. Their Christian fellow students would provide them with the day's assignment and lecture notes. In many cases, their non-Jewish classmates would carry their textbooks for them on the Sabbath if they came from strictly observant homes. (Carrying any article in the public domain is forbidden on the Sabbath according to Jewish law). Also, no examinations were scheduled on the Sabbath.

Students in the Lithuanian Gymnasia

It once happened that a newly appointed teacher did schedule an examination to take place on the Sabbath. The non-Jewish students staged a protest and stood solidly behind their Jewish comrades. On account of their show of solidarity and refusal to appear for the examination, the director had no choice and apologized publicly for the incident.

In the course of time it became more difficult for Jews to matriculate in the Lithuanian gymnasia. Firstly, the school administration stiffened the entrance requirements by demanding of the students a more thorough knowledge of the Lithuanian language. Secondly, Lithuanian chauvinism began to appear on the political horizon, and many non-Jewish teachers became members of clerically dominated chauvinistic organizations. The former friendly and mutually tolerant relationship between the Jewish and Christian students gradually deteriorated as a result of the winds of chauvinism that were sweeping through the new republic.

Notwithstanding the newly existing circumstances and unfriendly atmosphere, a considerable number of Jewish students managed to complete their gymnasia education and continued their studies in various universities in and outside of Lithuania. Many distinguished themselves by their active community service and leadership positions in Eretz Yisroel, in Lithuania, and in other lands of Jewish dispersion.

[Page 212]

From My School Years

by Tybeh Orlin-Kiel

Translated by Rae Meltzer

My mother, Riveh Kiel, settled in Rakishok at the time of the First World-War, when the Germans occupied Lithuania. We lived with Sara-Lahn Reznikovits (may she rest in peace) in her house.

To this day, although many years have passed, Rakishok is still beloved and dear to me. I remember Rakishok in various periods, during the German occupation and the First World War, and also the German compulsory school where I was a student.

The Germans opened compulsory schools. The school for Jewish children had three classes, all held in one room. The school teacher, Leon Klingman, was a kind, mild. and good person. However, he was unable to maintain discipline in the classroom. He was particularly inept in disciplining the boys. I remember that he had a stick with which he hit the boys, but once the students stole his stick and flung it in the nearby stream.

Fear and dread came over us when the German school inspector came to the class. It happened that a student from the third class committed a transgression and he received lashes. If the punished student did not want to return to school, he was brought back to school by the police. Although this German school inspector was very severe and strict and hit the girls in the compulsory school for Gentile children, we Jewish girls never received a slap from him. They gave us milk in the compulsory German school. Often the milk was burned and spoiled, but we absolutely had to drink it any way. There was also a school doctor who supervised our health and gave us injections against typhus, which was widespread at that time.

The Germans put great importance on the sanitation of the shtetl, and when the typhus epidemic was spreading quickly, they shaved off the beards of certain Jews. I remember that Bereh-Leah's went about with a red hand-kerchief tied around his face because the Germans cut off his beard, and without a beard he was ashamed to be seen.

School children in the German (compulsory) school

Once the Crown Prince arrived in Rakishok, and the shtetl made a great, festive welcome! Beautiful gates were built and decked with flowers. The Christian leader met the Crown Prince with bread and salt by the church. To make a "distinction between the sacred and profane" (Lehavdl), our Rabbi, (Blessed Be His Name) met the Crown Prince by the Red Beth Hamigdash (small synagogue). All of us school children participated in the parade for the Crown Prince. We were all dressed in white pinafores (aprons) and my sister Zinah presented the Guest with a crown of flowers.

World War I: greeting the German Crown Prince in Rokiskis

A Sunday Concert in Rokiskis

Germans in marketplace

    The Germans of that time already exhibited their brutal actions and deeds. They were also cruel to the French prisoners-of-war, who found themselves in Rakishok. The French prisoners slept in the barracks at night and during the day they were forced to do very hard labor. Behind our dwelling was a large garden where the French prisoners dug the sand which was necessary for use in building tracks for the small train that ran from the shtetl to the train station. The French prisoners suffered terribly from hunger, and we children would steal bread to give to them. We had to be extremely careful, because if the Germans noticed that we were giving them bread, the Germans would cruelly punish the French prisoners. There were some good German guards who looked the other way while we were giving the French prisoners food.

The French were in Rakishok for a whole year. I remember one murderous event when the German guard shot a French prisoner just because he did not pull the wheelbarrow with sand fast enough. I heard a story that once a French prisoner chased a frog hoping to catch and eat it to still his hunger pains. For that he was instantly killed by a German soldier.

After the Germans evacuated Rakishok, cheders were organized in the community. The Bolsheviks came and later the Lithuanians. It was at that time that the Tarbus- School was founded. In the beginning there were three classes. Two teachers named Goldapt and Yudelevitz from Kovno were engaged. Chanah Yackobson was also a teacher in the school.

Many Jewish students from the German Compulsory School became students in the Tarbus- School, including myself. All of us diligently attacked our studies, just like people who have been very thirsty and suddenly get water. Our interest was captured by the beauty and enchantment of the stories in the Hebrew reader, the gymnasium exercise books, and especially the Hebrew songs. The first Hebrew song that our teacher Yudelevitz taught us was H.N. Bialik's "Al-Hatsfur". Children's concerts were often organized and performed. The first "Spectacular" performed by the children was held in the "Arbatina."

Our school had a garden where many varieties of plants and flowers grew. We schoolchildren tended the garden, even during school vacations. We loved the school and the teachers in the school. The teachers Yudelevitz and Goldapt left Rakishok, and it was extremely difficult to find replacements for them. Rakishok looked diligently for replacements, but it was very hard to find teachers as good as Yudelevitz and Goldapt. After a time, Hoftsovitsh was engaged as a teacher. He was a weird, queer, and strange person, who used to speak more Russian than Yiddish. In both summer and winter he went around in a large, grey, warm coat. He did not know much Hebrew and he could not discipline the students. Initially he came to Rakishok alone and later he brought his wife. It became apparent that she was a Christian woman.

Tarbus School [primary school]

The parents and the Board of Directors of the School began to discuss measures for getting rid of this teacher. After very long negotiations, he was given 300 "Lit" and he left. In his place came the sorrowful and famous Kaspi, who always left a blot behind. When the teacher Hoftsovitsh bade us farewell, he told the Board members in anger: "You got rid of me for just 300 Lit, but you will not get rid of this gentleman Kaspi for any amount of money." His words in this regard proved to be correct.

Kaspi had a very pale face, with white hands and two piercing eyes which looked deeply into your soul. His hair was always disheveled. He was a troubled, anxious, and restless person, and this made us fear and mistrust him. He was our chorus director. If any one made the slightest mistake while singing, he might slap that student very hard. I remember one incident when a student said to Kaspi, "You dog, you," and ran out of class and never came back. Kaspi assembled all the students and asked them what kind of punishment should be meted out to this student. All the students remained absolutely silent because of their fear and dread of Kaspi. Finally one older student spoke up and said: "The one who calls the teacher 'dog' is a bigger dog than the teacher." Kaspi became enraged. He tied the student up and put him in a basket as punishment for his "chutzpadik" answer.

Kaspi brought a teacher from Kovno named Glambatzki, who now lives in Israel. In the beginning all of us mistrusted him, but little by little, as we got to know him, he became beloved by all the students. He used to tell us the history of the Jewish people, sing songs with us and tell us stories. To each of us he was more like an older brother than an official teacher.

The Teachers

The Hashomer Ha'tzair

In those school years, the youth of the shtetl became active, and often lecturers would come from Kovno to our shtetl to talk about Eretz Israel. A popular person in the shtetl was Moishe Vesterman (honored be his name). He was a bookkeeper and perished in the Kovno ghetto. He sang beautifully. He recruited members for a new organization called "Hashomer Ha'tzair" [the Young Guardians]. Our teacher Glambatzki was also active in this organization. At first they would not let us young people join the organization, but after persistent pleading, we were finally permitted to join. Uniforms were made for us and we became active members of "Hashomer Ha'tzair."

The Rakishoker "Hashomer Ha'tzair" was well organized and disciplined. At our gatherings, called "kibbutzim," we were exposed to various literary works and the ideal of devotion to Eretz Israel. Often we would get together outdoors on the boulevard for gymnastic exercises. We also organized outings in nearby fields and forests, where we sang Zionist songs, or we heard readings of literary works and published articles from the Zionist organization.

Rakishok had a strong Zionist organization. I remember when the writer L. Yaffeh was coming to Rakishok, the whole shtetl prepared feverishly for his arrival. Pesach Ruch obtained a carriage with two horses from the Count, and everyone in the shtetl, from the smallest to the tallest, went to greet L. Yaffeh. At the station L. Yaffeh was greeted with cheers and ovations. The parade from the train was led by the Count's carriage, with L. Yaffeh at the head. Then came the Maccabi, marching in straight rows. They were followed by the Hasomer Ha'tzair. The streets were overflowing with people. There were also Gentile people in the crowd. The Gentiles said in Lithuanian: "The Yiddish Kaiser has come!"

Tarbus School

Our water-carrier, Urshuleh, was standing in the crowd and crying. When she was asked why she was crying, she would answer: "How can I **not** cry? The Yiddish Kaiser will take all the Jews away with him. I won't have any customers for my water, and I will die of hunger!"

That evening we had a huge banquet in the new Talmud Torah building. The entire shtetl was invited to this event and a large sum of money was raised for "Keren-Hesud."

After L. Yaffee's visit, the first "Keren-Kimes-Pushkes" (the blue and white little cans which were used to collect funds for building Israel) were distributed in Rakishok. We of the Hashomer-Ha'tzair would empty the pushkes and turn in the money to the adults.

Rakishok had a beautiful youth group and the shtetl was the cultural center for the entire region. From Kovno, Zionist speakers often came to Rakishok. Among them I remember A. Freedman, who is now the Israeli Consul in Czechoslovakia, and also Dr. Berger, who later became the director of the Hebrew Gymnasium in Shoval [Shavli?], a shtetl near Rakishok.

But good times don't last long! The sky over Rakishok clouded over and darkened. The teacher Glambatzki received an order from the government to leave Lithuania within 24 hours! (There was a strong suspicion that Kaspi reported him to the government.) We students and the young people cried and were mournful because we were losing such a good teacher and a bright, capable community activist. Glambatzki left for Kovno. He was permitted to live in Rakishok for only one year.

The beloved shtetl became too confining for me; the air became heavy and oppressive. In the face of the reactionary Lithuanian government, the youth began to leave Rakishok and Lithuania forever. After Glambatzki left Rakishok, the work of Hashomer was led without the former fervent enthusiasm. I left for Kovno to study. I waited impatiently for school vacation, because I was very homesick for Rakishok.

To this day, Rakishok has remained holy and precious, and all the landsleit, wherever they find themselves, are beloved and dear to me. The happiest day in my life will be when I can see my former home, which is the source of my beautiful childhood dreams. Who knew so intimately the big forest and the cornfields, the little fast-running river, as we children did? We used to tease the butcher Epshtein Brune's, where we took water for boiling our Sabbath tea, and the priest's orchard from which we were chased by the watchman.

Many, many years have gone by. Nevertheless, I remember every detail--every particular. Who could have foreseen that the same earth that was so carefree in our childhood would be soaked with the blood of our brothers and sisters--our friends from the beloved Rakishok Jewish community? From time to time I leaf through my memories and the photographs of my Rakishok album. From every page of my album, I feel a great sadness, a powerful black terror about our immense tragedy and catastrophe. It seems to me that all the photographs in my album are crying and moaning because that which was will never, never be again.

Hashomer Hatza'ir Rokiskis, 18 June 1927

[Page 220]

The Beth Sefer and Progymnasium

by Abraham Josselowitz

Translated by Rabbi Ezra Boyarsky

Among the several educational institutions in Rakishok that played an important role in shaping the cultural character of the youth were the Tarbus Public School and the Progymnasium. Both institutions were recognized by the Lithuanian government which also supplied them with laboratory equipment and musical instruments. Both schools shared the same building and classroom facilities.

The syllabus was pitched at a very high level, with Hebrew as the medium of instruction. Evidence of the success enjoyed by both schools was their large enrollment and excellent academic results. As indicated above, both schools wielded an enormous influence on the students by implanting in them a strong love for the Hebrew language and the Jewish national holidays: Hanukah, Chamisha Asar, Beshevat, and Lag Ba Omer (33rd day in the counting of the Omer). This type of Jewish education produced an entire generation of Jewish nationalists.

Quite frequently the student body would arrange concerts which attracted large audiences and received enthusiastic accolades for their performances. The faculty was very active in the social and cultural spheres, and participated in all the projects sponsored by the Keren Hayesod, Keren Kayemes Leyisroel (Jewish National Fund), Maccabi Club, Bet Hayesomim (Orphanage) and Vaad Hatarbus--the Tarbus Committee.

In time, adult evening courses were organized for the study of modern Hebrew, natural science, and a host of other courses of an academic nature. The science courses included laboratory experiments.

The teaching staff of all these institutions often delivered public lectures and endeavored to interest the parents in various sports activities. Due to their initiative, a parents' association was organized which arranged football matches with the teaching staff. Some of the teachers excelled as gymnasts.

During my time, the teaching staff of the Tarbus Bet Sefer consisted of the following: Y. Kaspi, Principal, A. Yoselowitz, and D. Sudarsky. In the

Progymnasia, the following served on the faculty: Y. Zamet, Principal, Y. Kaspi, D. Sudarsky, A. Yoselowitz, Mr. and Mrs. Greenberg, and F. Greenstein. Besides them, two non-Jewish teachers also taught in these schools, one for Lithuanian and the other arts and crafts.

I end this account with a painful feeling of nostalgia for those happy days of my youth, and for my never-to-be-forgotten birthplace, Rakishok.

Teachers and school children

Performance by young schoolchildren with teacher A. Yoselevitz

[Page 222]

The Activity of the Kultur-Lige

Sarah Spevak

Translated by Rabbi Ezra Boyarsky (deceased)

The "Kultur-Lige" which was founded in 1919 occupied a prominent position in Rakishok. The young working class, the tailors, shoemakers, carpenters, and other artisans derived great joy from the establishment of the Kultur-Liege. Many of them had just returned from the larger Russian cities where intensive political and socio-cultural activity was part of the Russian landscape. The Russian Revolution instilled in them a new social awareness. It enriched their thinking and ignited their quest for freedom and culture.

After World War I, Rakishok was, roughly speaking, divided into two socio-economic classes: the upper-middle class and the working class, and there was very little social contact between the two. The returned workers found life in Rakishok extremely monotonous and boring. The town had no library, and social life was almost non-existent. For this reason, there was much enthusiasm when Meyer Nahum Katz, a pale-looking young man, issued a call to the workers and to all who had a desire to expand their knowledge, to meet at his home.

On a Sabbath afternoon, with great anticipation, we gathered in Meyer Katz' attic home. Everyone's attention was focused on the pale young man who surveyed the assemblage in uncanny silence. Gradually his paleness assumed a rosy color, and he began addressing us. "Comrades and Friends..." From the very beginning, we sensed an affinity with this young man. He continued, saying that a few weeks before, a Jewish organization called the "Kultur-Lige" had been established in Kovno, and that it was our duty to establish a branch in Rakishok. This organization's task should be to disseminate knowledge among the Jewish workers who, due to the economic hardship of their parents, had been deprived of a broader education.

We listened to his lecture with undivided attention, and in response to his question as to who among us participated in any political or cultural activities, half the group raised their hands. I was among them. A committee was chosen which immediately went to work. It rented a spacious house which served a dual purpose: to house a Yiddish Folkshul and to have a suitable place for meetings.

Key committees were appointed to get the Lige's activities going. A special Library Committee was formed to collect Yiddish books from local donors. The committee also ordered books from the Lige's headquarters in Kovno. The opening of the library was a great event, and soon after the Yiddish Folkshul was established, as well as evening courses for adults. Meyer Nahum Katz became the director of the school and chairman of the parent organization-- the Kultur-Lige. He worked for the cause with love and devotion, and received full cooperation from the two idealistic teachers, Ida Dectar and Mr. Shapiro.

The student enrollment of the Yiddish school consisted largely of the poorest economic strata in town. The children applied themselves to their studies with exceptional diligence, and this was reflected in the children's concerts and stage performances that the school arranged.

I vividly recall one balmy sunny erev Shavuos (Shavuot eve) when the children went on an outing to the nearby forest. The boys and girls marched jubilantly, with radiant faces, through Kamayer Street under the watchful eyes of their teachers. Throughout the march, the townspeople came out of their houses and listened enraptured to the chilren's sweet resounding voices as they sang special songs in honor of the Shavuos holiday. Such outings were frequently arranged for the students of the Yiddish school.

The Folkshul and the Lige's other cultural activities enjoyed much popularity, and both ventures made great progress in a relatively short time. As a result of the rapid growth and development of the school, the two famous educators, Helena Chatzkeles and Mr. Abramson, came to Rakishok to evaluate the educational achievements of the institution. They did not have enough words of praise for the director, the teachers, and for the children's accomplishments.

Under the leadership and initiative of Shlomo Rubin, now a long time resident of South Africa, a dramatic club was formed which met on Friday evenings and at which literary and artistic programs were presented. This club also proved an enormous success. The audiences consisted, by and large, of young working class people, and of some of the more worldly individuals who had begun to show an interest in our work. More evening classes were added upon request, and these were usually followed by a public lecture or some appropriate entertainment.

In 1923, just when the Kultur-Lige was in full bloom, the Lithuanian government closed it down. Only the Folkshul was allowed to continue. In 1928, the school was also shut down, not by the government, but because of inadequate funds and the inability to obtain competent teachers. Nevertheless, the social, cultural, and political work continued. The idealism that had fueled the fire in the hearts of the Kultur-Lige workers was not extinguished. The progressive members of the working class continued their political work despite hostile and adverse conditions.

School children and teachers Eda Kektor and Engel

The Yiddish Folk School Outing on Lag B'Omer Holiday 5-8-1928

[Page 225]

Concerning the Culture League and its Activities

by Michal and Shlomo Feldman
Translated by Gloria Berkenstat Freund

The Culture League in Rakishok comprised an important chapter in the history of the cultural-communal work in Rakishok. Thanks to the initiative of Meir Nachum Katz and Berta Abramovitz, the Culture League was created in 1919. The founding committee members were the following: Meir Nakhum Katz (chairman), Sura Spivak, Berta Abramovitz, Ida Dektor, Leah Madur, Ester Ogins, Shlomo Shimeonovitz, Yankl Maron, Beinish Kres and Feibush Sinior.

The central organization of the Culture League was in Kovna. Sura Tsarfas was very active in the central organization and came especially to Rakishok to help with the work there, giving methodical instructions.

The following activities were noted in the program of the Culture League – to open a public school with instruction in Yiddish, evening courses for adults and to found a library; to create a dramatic section and a literary circle; the creation of a sports organization and a sports circle for young people that was given the name, *Wanderfoygl* [migratory bird].

First, a Jewish public school was opened in a house on Jurdojke. It was divided into five grades with 75 students. The teachers at various times were: Ingl, Shapiro, Hitlshtein, Lap, Chiene Mordekhailevitz, Reznik and Ida Dektor. The first school director was Meir Nakhum Katz; the second was Ida Dektor.

The school children were from the poorest strata in Rakishok. In addition to secular subjects, they were taught Yiddish and Jewish history.

The school was a member of the Kovno school headquarters, which was headed by Helena Khatzkeles, Engineer Abramson and the above-mentioned Mrs. Tsarfas.

The school budget was covered by activities, flower days, and taxation. A small subsidy would be received from time to time from the school administration.

Rokiskis Yiddish Evening School, 3 March 1928

The attitude towards the Jewish school on the part of the Zionist-Hebraist element was distant, not satisfactory and the Hebrew teachers showed a negative attitude to the Jewish public school. There were also difficulties created in receiving the school subsidy. The Rabbi, Reb Betzalel, once demanded that the teachers from the Jewish school take exams as to whether they knew a page of *gemara* [Talmudic rabbinic commentaries on the oral law]. Such a demand made it difficult for the Jewish school to receive a state subsidy.

Yet, with the greatest efforts, the school existed until 1928, even after the closing of the Culture League.

During the same time period that the Jewish public school existed, evening courses for adults were held regarding Yiddish, Jewish history, and political economy. A cycle of lectures about the French Revolution was also held.

The teachers at the Jewish public school also taught the evening courses and lectured on various subjects.

During the period when the Culture League was legal, a library of 1,800 books also existed on its premises. It received a great number of books from People's Relief in America. The library was located on the premises of the Jewish public school. A subscriber needed to give a security deposit of five *lit* [*lita* – Lithuanian currency] and pay one *lit* a month.

When the Culture League was closed, the police confiscated all of the books from the library, transferred them to the "jurisdiction" of the Jewish *kehile* [organized Jewish community].

There was a literary circle at the Culture League and a good dramatic section. During the literary evenings, works of writers were discussed and evening classes organized.

The teachers from the public school and also Sh. Rubin and Leah Sadur led the drama section. For a time there was a talented artist who came to the *shtetl* from Kovno. I do not remember his family name because he was always called by the "mysterious" name, "Shmerele." He was a gifted man who also gave interesting lectures and could dramatize various literary works well in a condensed manner. He staged *Tevye der Milkhiker* [*Tevye the Milkman*] very successfully, presenting Tevye's doubts about God in an outstanding manner.

The motto for the Culture League's dramatic section was "We want and will be." The section performed the following plays: *Der Dorf Yingl* [*The Village Youth*] of L. [Leon] Kobrin; *Der Mishpukhe* [*The Family*] of H.D. [Hersh Dovid] Nomberg, Sholem Aleichem's *Tevye der Milkhiker*, *Tsezeyt un Tseshpreyt* [*Scattered Far and Wide*], and others.

Arrests took place during the closure of the Culture League. Arrested were: Meir Yakov Katz, Ida Dektor, Henya Abramovitz, Beinish Kres, Portnoy and Sura Spivak.

In March-April of 1924, Ida Dektor was freed on bail and came to Rakishok. Before she left Rakishok, she wanted to leave behind a group that would revive the work of the Culture League and even carry it on illegally. She entrusted this work to Chaim Elia Abramovitz.

Chaim Elia Abramovitz took over this responsible work and drew together another few active comrades to help. The activity was carried out illegally. Moshe Birger of Ponevezh [Panevezys], who helped carry on the work, also often came to Rakishok. Comrades from Rakishok met secretly with Ponevezher activists from the leftist movement and also with Christian comrades.

Secret party cells were created to carry on political activities. Such illegal cells were organized in Ponedel [Pandëlys], Sevenishok [Suvainiskis] and in many villages.

Soloman German, Hirshl Abramovitz and Aba Leib Davidovitz founded the society *Libhober fun Wisn* [Lovers of Knowledge], and received the confiscated books from the *kehile*. A sports organization with a soccer section, a ping-pong section, and so on, was active before the society was founded. Within a short time, interesting cultural-communal activity developed again. A journal produced by hectography [gelatin duplication] was also published with the name, *Kultur un Wisn* [*Culture and Knowledge*] and there was often a wall newspaper.

Active Members of Sports Organization

With the growth of [reactionary feelings], the sports organization and also the library were closed. All books were sealed in boxes and sent to Kovno to the address of Helena Khatzkeles.

The illegal political activity, however, did not end, despite the regime's persecutions. Widespread political work was carried out in secret. Several active comrades, such as Dovid-Itske Dunai, Shlomoke Shimeonovitz and others, were arrested for this illegal activity. Active comrades remained who did further work with great self-sacrifice until the Second World War.

The Jewish Part in the Left Movement

O. Nochumovitz

Translated by Rabbi Ezra Boyarsky

The Jewish masses in Rakishok and environs who sympathized or actively participated in the Leftist Movement clustered around the Culture League which was synonymous with revolutionary and progressive activities. This was also the case in larger and smaller towns throughout Lithuania. Most progressive elements in the Jewish communities found an ideological comparability with the Culture League.

The Culture League in Rakishok was founded in 1919, and carried on a varied program of activities until 1923. The Lithuanian government detected the radicalism of the League, and as a result, it was closed down, its library confiscated, and a number of its most active members were arrested. Still, radicals of the town regrouped and on May 1, 1924, distributed proclamations in Yiddish and Lithuanian, and issued a call to the populace to rise up against the reactionary forces.

Both Jews and Lithuanians alike were greatly surprised at what the Rakishok activists dared to do. Nobody could imagine that while their own leaders were still in jail, the rank and file would carry on the political and revolutionary work. Many of the former members of the Culture League who had become inactive because of the arrests, now resumed their active participation. Not only that, but the League gained new members who became extremely active in our progressive leftist movement.

"Mohr" was organized illegally. The task of this organization was to help those who were serving time as political prisoners. The library was started to function again, and in 1924 when the October Revolution (May 1st) was celebrated, circulars and illegal literature were distributed not only among the Rakishok Jews and those in the vicinity, but among the farms and villages, thereby creating closer contact with the radical elements of the Lithuanian rural population.

Besides the political activities, there was an unusually strong striving to resume the former social and cultural activities, and since the Culture League was outlawed, we organized a sports club which functioned as such, but which also continued the interrupted social and cultural functions of the Culture League. The newly created sports club was allowed to exist under the same legal provisions as did the sports organizations in Kovno and elsewhere.

In Rakishok the club rented a large facility adjacent to a big field which the club used as a training ground for a variety of sports events. It also arranged concerts, lectures, a "living newspaper," and produced a number of plays. The newly acquired facility became the second home for the entire leftist movement.

Arke Nachumovits

Young men of sports organization

Later on a society was founded called the "Lovers of Knowledge." Included in the steering committee of the new organization were representatives who championed the importance of Yiddish as a language, its literature, etc. They were known as "Yiddishisten." Other members of the committee were people who were cleared by the government before they could serve as officers in any capacity. At this time the library was allowed to reopen, and the confiscated books were returned.

It was during the Grinus government that the newly established society and sports club experienced a period of growth. At that time, the club moved to more spacious quarters and acquired a lot of athletic and calisthenics equipment. Many football matches were local and outside teams took place in Rakishok and in neighboring towns. Rakishok's poorer elements were especially proud of the sports club, and through their participation in the various club activities, their self-esteem was raised.

The blossoming of the club lasted until the political upheaval that occurred when the Smetana government came to power. Smetana closed the sports organization, and the club's activities, including the social and cultural events, were now conducted illegally. Arrests were frequent. Among those who were arrested was Gitel Gordon who spent a few years in prison. When she was released, she became even more active in the leftist, radical movement. She was joined by Ida Weiner.

Rokiskis sports organization

Right up to the outbreak of the Second World War, the members of the former Culture League and the sports organization carried on the political work undercover despite the danger involved. I will now mention some of the more active members of the movement: Hayam Elie Abramovitz was an employee in a store and a former yeshiva student. He was an excellent lecturer and possessed a strong character. he organized a union of business employees in Rakishok after the Smetana regime came to power. Due to the political persecutions, he and his wife Chaye-Rive escaped to the Soviet Union.

Yankel Himelshein was a teacher in the Yiddish Folk School and an outstanding lecturer. He was chosen as a representative of the Yiddish Workers' Caucus to the Yiddish National Convention in Lithuania. After he was arrested in Kovno, he was released on bail. He then returned to Rakishok resuming his active role in the movement. He and his wife also escaped to the Soviet Union.

Boruch Lekach was one of the most active and inspiring workers for the sports organization. He served as co-editor of the **Passover** humorous paper. At present he resides in the Soviet Union.

Boruch Lekach

Moseh Amdur was quite a character. He was by nature a very quiet and unassuming person. He hardly ever spoke to anyone. Still, strange as it may seem, he was one of the most fervent activists of the Rakishker leftist movement. His job involved delivering goods from wholesalers to the markets in the surrounding towns. This gave him an excellent opportunity to make contact with people who were on the same political wavelength. Among the wares in his delivery car he would hide illegal literature which he distributed in the villages on the way to and from Rakishok. When the police got wind of his "underground" activities, they staked him out, raided his warehouse barn, and found a large quantity of illegal circulars and brochures. Fortunately, he was not home at the time. When he was notified, he immediately took off. The Smetana police announced a reward of 1,000 Lit. for his head. Moshe Amdur escaped to the Soviet Union, but a short while later, he returned to Lithuania in order to resume his political propaganda.

He was again arrested by the Lithuanian secret police, but he categorically denied that he was Moshe Amdur. The police brought him to Rakishok for identification, but both his father and his young sister disclaimed any relationship to him. The father said that this was not his son, and the sister said that this was not her brother. He was sentenced to a long prison term, but the Smetana regime, in reviewing his case, concluded that since Moshe Amdur was a key revolutionary activist, they would exchange him for a Lithuanian prisoner held by the Soviet Union.

Moshe's father was the "official" grave digger in Rakishok. For a long period of time he hid illegal literature and also our library in the cemetery. Despite the fact that this was fraught with danger, he took that chance, and what's more, he refused any remuneration, even though he was extremely poor.

Chaim-Elya Abramovits and his wife Chaye-Riva

Rokiskis cemetery caretaker

[Page 234]

The Culture League in Rakishok and in Utian

by Moshe Krain

Translated by Gloria Berkenstat Freund

We publish a report by Moshe Krain about the "Culture League" in Rakishok and in Utian that was printed under the pseudonym "Mohican" in *Undzer Weg* [*Our Way*] of November 1921, published by the *Poalei-Zion* [Marxist Zionist] Party in Johannesburg

Moshe Krain was an active cultural worker in Johannesburg. He visited Lithuania in 1921. He died in 1933

* * *

And now I want to point to the work that was carried out by the Culture League in two small *shtetlekh* [towns], Rakishok and Utian. This will illustrate the cultural position of the Jewish workers, because only they can be members of the Culture League."

First Rakishok:

The budget of the Rakishok Culture League is 30,000 marks (almost the budget of our literary union) and consists of 40 members. A public school exists at the Culture League at which 90 children study. There is a kindergarten and a school kitchen located at the school. Last year, during the winter, evening courses functioned with 67 attendees. The Culture League possesses a library of 200 books and 85 subscribers and also a dramatic section that carried out many performances. A choir exists in the section. The Culture League also publishes a hectographic [gelatin duplication] journal, *Kultur un Wisn* [*Culture and Learning*]

Utian

Yankl der Shmid [Yankl the Blacksmith], Di Nevole [The Infamy], Der Shtumer [The Silent One], Got fun Nekomeh [God of Vengence], and Der Pushte Kretchme [The Empty Inn]

Now several general figures: 1,651 children and teaching personnel of 52 in the 15 schools (the writer probably means in all of Lithuania). In addition, there exists one (1) Folks-University, two kindergartens and two orphanages. The number of members in the courses for adults is 713, teachers – 44. Only four (4) schools are subsidized by the local kehile [organized Jewish community]. Subjects: three (3) languages: Yiddish, Lithuanian, Hebrew. In the older classes: geography, history, natural sciences, mathematics, handwork. In the courses for adults there is also the teaching of political economy, literature and cultural history

"Mohican"

Monument of Dr. Janus Basanowiczois

Note regarding photo of Memorial to Jonas Basanavicius.

At the large marketplace in Rakishok, where all of the businesses were concentrated, stands this memorial that records Lithuanian independence. The liberation of the Lithuanian people is portrayed by a statue on one side of the memorial and on the other side is the bust of Doctor Jonas Basanavicius, the veteran of Lithuanian culture who lived during the years 1851-1927.

When the Lithuanian Seim President in 1923 forbid the Jewish Seim deputies to give speeches in the Seim in Yiddish and when the Lithuanian Fascists smeared Yiddish signs with tar, and the police in many *shtetlekh* [towns] forbid the public to use the Yiddish language, Dr. Jonas Basanavicius sent a protest letter to the *Yidishe Shtime* [*Yiddish Voice*], dated the 12th of August, 1924, where he sharply condemned the scandalous deeds of the Lithuanian Fascists.

[Page 236]

Maccabi in Rakishok

by R. Arsch
Translated by Rae Meltzer

Farband (association), 8 April 1926

Maccabi members practicing sport

The founding of the Maccabi organization in Lithuania and in Rakishok goes back to the period after World War I when the Zionist ideology, after the Balfour Declaration, captured the attention of the Jewish people of Lithuania. The majority of Jewish young people accepted Zionism as the only option for the Jewish people, and the Maccabi slogan, "A heathy spirit in a healthy body," was immediately appealing to Jewish youth, which stimulated organization of the sport group Maccabi. As with most Jewish organizations, they were first of all founded in the larger cities. Initially the Maccabi was organized in Kovno, then in Shavli, Ponevezh, and other cities and shtetlach.

In 1922 the Ponevezher Maccabi delegated instructions to Rakishok to organize a Maccabi organization. The youth of Rakishok responded with great joy and friendship to the leaders of the Ponevezher Maccabi and their recommendation to form a Maccabi organization in Rakishok. A committee was formed in which all the factions of the Zionist organization participated: "Ts. S. Hatadut," General Zionists, and "S. T. S." The location was first in Aaron-Jacob, the ritual slaughterer's, house on Kamaier street, and later in Shomer's house. [Translator's note: these acronyms are transliterations from the Yiddish. English has no equivalent letter for the "ts" in Yiddish, which is the first letter in the Yiddish word for "Zionist." The text does not identify what the "S" stands for. The other transliterated words are from Hebrew and stand for various Zionist organizations whose purpose was to raise funds to help build a Jewish homeland in Israel.]

Maccabi sport members

The match between Kupiskis and Rokiskis

First Rokiskis Men Maccabi, 13 Feb. 1926

The most active members of the Zionist Party (Ts. S.) demonstrated great effort and enthusiasm for organizing the Maccabi in Rakishok. The Ts. S. had their own meeting place, where almost all of the Rakishok Zionist youth would assemble. The Zionists had a "Lecture Circle" and invited lecturers from Kovno, Ponevezh, and Shavli. Often there were meetings held with speakers and judges of literary work. We also had a Yiddish library and the Zionist party members were represented on all the boards of Zionist organizations that raised funds to build and support Israel ("Keren-Kimes," "Keren Hesud," and "Kehillah V'Kadumeh"). All the Zionist youth immediately joined the Maccabi sports organization, which stimulated other youth to follow their example. The Zionist party gave authority of their library into the hands of the Maccabi.

In the beginning of the Maccabi organization, all the factions worked harmoniously. Everyone was amazed at the success of the Maccabi, which brought inspiration and a new spirit to the youth. It also brought a new psychological awareness to the older Jewish people, who for generations had neglected the individual's physical development. The older generation had believed that sport was not in keeping with Yiddish values and tradition. With great energy and enthusiastic spirit, the young men and women threw themselves into the work of Maccabi when they came back from their evacuation into Russia. We learned to play football, lift weights, perform various athletic and gymnastic exercises and work-outs. We participated in various energetic and fiery parades and demonstrations.

The first friends of the Maccabi, who built the foundation for the Rakishok Maccabi, were as follows: Hillel Eidelson, Libke Itzikman, Sara-Dinah Abramovits, Henye Blum, Hanah Bun, Nison Berkovits, Zelig Gen, Benimke Geltser, Rochel Vingrin, Hanah Zamet, Roza Han, Arkeh Han, Giskeh Levin, Moishe Levin, Ephrim Lang, Shmerke Loibavits, Chaim Loibavits, Yankel Levin, Boruch Leker, Shifreh Loifer, Yoskeh Meyerovits, Heyeh Reizkeh Panevesh, Israel Panevesh, Ezra Tsuckerman, Alser Tsodes, Elya Kopelovits, Itzhak Klingman, Leah Kur, Shaul Kur, Itzhak Kark, Yosif Kark, Abba Rubin, Brider Ribak, Moishe Rozenkavits, Arke Shmuskovits, Feivkeh Shmilg, Ephrim Shwartsberg, Irachmial Shmuskovits, and Moishe Shmilg.

Rokiskis Maccabi, 28 Feb. 1925

The Maccabi organization grew to more than 100 friends, men, and women of Rakishok.

The relationship between the different parties in the Maccabi organization became strained, because each party sought to win members from the Maccabi into their own party. This became a bone of contention to such an extent that it almost led to a split in the Maccabi organization. An extraordinary meeting was called at which time it was decided that a member of the Maccabi could not belong to a political party. The Zionist members consequently left the Maccabi organization and took their library with them.

Maccabi, Rokiskis, 19 June 1925

The exit of the Zionist members did not result in any visible devisiveness in the Maccabi. In time, new members joined the Maccabi, especially graduates from the Hebrew School System, from the Tarbus School, and from the Tarbus Pro-Gymnasia, who had already received a Nationalistic Hebrew education. The growth of the Maccabi did not slow down, but actually became stronger and grew in membership. A new library was also opened.

Often there were sport competitions with other Maccabi branches from nearby and distant shtetlach. There were also competitions with Lithuanian sport organizations, and with sport organizations from the "Artiker [?] Culture League."

In addition to sports, Maccabi organized various recreational, entertainment, and cultural activities. Maccabi offered evening courses in Hebrew and Jewish history, with classes taught by Shifra Loifer, Kaspi, Yoseh Levits (now a teacher in South Africa), Abigdur Glambatski, Vesterman, and Sudovski. There was also a Literary Section that organized literary readings and literary criticism. The literary criticism events were very popular. I remember the literary critique event about "Bontshe Shweig," a classic story by I.L. Peretz. I was supposed to be the prosecutor, and Israel Panevesh was the defender. Before the event, Israel Panevesh changed places with me, and I became the defender and he the prosecutor.

Maccabi, 13 Jan. 1926

Group not identified

Women's Section of Maccabi

The literary judgement of "Saul and Samuel" also drew a large audience of a couple hundred people. Twelve men of standing were the judges. Sitting on the platform were Abraham Meyerovits, my father H. Arsch, Abraham Itzhak Meler, Harmits, Yehiel Zamat, Givovski, and others. Hillel Aidelson played the part of Samuel (Shmuel) and I took the part King Saul. Kaspi defended Samuel and the teacher Sudovski defended King Saul. An interesting "trial and judgement" also took place about H. N. Bialik's "Hamasmid."

The organized lectures offered by Maccabi were on various subjects and themes. After the lectures there were always lively discussions.

The dramatic section of the Maccabi was very dedicated. The director of the dramatic section was Israel Panevesh, who was himself a very gifted actor, with a fine voice and great talent in recitation. He directed many plays, with the major actors being: Hannah Pats, Israel Panevesh, Teibe Kiel, Hennach Shneiderman, Loibeh Veger, Leeba Ruch, Gittel Agins, Tuveh Ruch, Berl Ruch, Aaron Nahumovits, and the author of these lines.

In addition to dramatic presentations, the group also put on many musical evenings for the community. The MACCABI had their own orchestra under the conduction of Hyvis Berzon, who was a very talented violinist, and Abraham Kur, who was a fine clarinet player. The members of the orchestra ensemble were: the brothers Yudel and Motel German, who were famous violinists in

Lithuania, Judith Shwartzberg, who played the balalaika, and Tsarkeh Levin, who grew up to become one of the outstanding violin artists in the Baltic lands. There were other outstanding musicians, but regretfully I do not remember their names. The income from the drama section's performances were utilized to benefit the Maccabi Library.

Upon my return from Israel in 1920, I took over responsibility for the Maccabi Library in Rakishok and became vice-president of this organization. I became associated with publishing organizations in Kovno and Riga, and published good books. We published books by Tolstoy, Dostoevsky, Chekhov, Turgenev, and other writers, as well as French, German, English, and American authors.

In the course of the two years that I was responsible for the affairs of the library, we increased the holdings by several hundred books, and the circle of readers grew larger. The library had its rules and regulations, among which were fees for taking out books. A reader was charged 5 "Lit" for a library card and 1½ "Lit" per month for using the Library.

The Maccabi organization was led by Abba Rubin, a brother of our landsman Shloime Rubin. Shifra Loifer, a strong activist, taught Hebrew to the Maccabi members and inspired them with her fiery Zionist spirit. A beautiful chapter of rearing the youth in the Zionist, nationalist spirit was written and accomplished by the Maccabi organization in Rakishok.

In 1933-34, the Rakishok youth became interested in the "Chalutz" (Zionist Pioneers), and a Zionist youth movement known as "Hanuer-Hatsoini" was started.

Ten score Maccabi friends emigrated, but the dedication to the Maccabi organization did not falter. To this day, though many years have passed, not one of us Maccabi friends will ever forget the Rakishok Maccabi. The Maccabi gave our generation a nationalist, modern upbringing of enormous meaning to us.

[Page 243]

Rakishker Maccabi

by H. Josselowitz

Translated by Rabbi Ezra Boyarsky

It was during the "Golden Age" of Lithuanian Jewry – when a network of educational institutions such as "Tarbus, "Yavne," Yiddish Folkshulen, and the Hebrew gymnasias became the hallmark of Lithuanian Jews – that the Maccabi sports clubs sprang up throughout the country. There was hardly a Jewish community, large or small, that did not have a Maccabi sports organization. And how so many sports instructors and skillful gymnasts suddenly appeared on the scene was a mystery to me. Yet I did not dwell too long on solving the mystery. What concerned me more at the time was whether I would also some day attain the skill to qualify as a gymnast.

Sample membership card for the Maccabi sports and gymnastics organization in Lithuania
Unidentifed portrait, probably of gthe person named on the Maccabi card

When I first saw a young Jewish fellow lift an eighty-pound weight with one hand, it awakened in me a feeling of great pride to perceive that Jews possessed physical strength alongside intellectual acumen. However, I also became jealous of the young man, and resolved to take up bodybuilding so as to be able to exhibit a similar physical prowess. After a short while, I achieved my goal.

In proportion to the size of Rakishok's Jewish community, the local Maccabi organization was quite large. Rakishok was fortunate in having many young people in good physical shape who were the building blocks of the Rakishok Maccabi branch, recognized as one of the best in Lithuania. It should be mentioned that all the training exercises, instructions, etc., were conducted entirely in Hebrew.

Abba Rubin, President of Rokiskis Maccabi

For a short time there was also an "older group" composed of young married adults, teachers who were on the staffs of the Tarbus school and the Hebrew gymnasia. These proved to be good soccer players and excellent "kickers" to whom a paraphrase of the well-known Biblical verse may be applied: The voice is Jacob's voice but the feet are the feet of Esau.

Besides the physical aspect, the Maccabi organization offered a rich cultural program consisting of lectures, poetry readings, etc. The town was virtually brimming with physical and cultural energy.

During my three-year residence in Rakishok, the community provided me with a wide variety of activities. I would like to acknowledge the outstanding work rendered by Hillel Idelson who contributed his time and talents to the community on all fronts, and to express my gratitude to Ada Rubin who, as president of Maccabi, was greatly responsible for its success.

Unfortunately, no trace remains of those golden years, and who knows whose cursed feet now tread the turf of the Maccabi athletic field in Rakishok. Our only consolation is that our youth will rebuild our historical homeland, Eretz Yisroel, and provide a secure home and happy future for our nation.

[Page 245]

The First Hachshara [Pioneering] Kibbutz in Rakishok

by Ben Samuel
Translated by Mathilda Mendelow, born Ginsberg

The general Zionist group "B" had a central committee that established Kibbutzim. They established a Kibbutz in Rokishok in 1933 – 1934. Initially the Kibbutz had six persons and was located in a house not far from the hospital. The leader of the Kibbutz was comrade Lazer. He studied in Vienna in the theological seminary and was a good speaker. He is now in Israel.

I was delegated to the Rokishok Kibbutz by the Kovno officer. No one in Lithuania had such a person as Hillel Idelson. He greeted us on arrival with a warm "Shalom Alechem!" I remember that he was always dressed poorly, even with torn shoes. He lived in a side street, and he had only a large table and a poor bed in his room. But he was a great and lusty idealist. He gave a lot of his time to our Kibbutz and thanks to him the Kibbutz progressed.

When the Kibbutz became larger, they rented a facility for us at Nachman the Shochet. We opened a kindergarten on our Kibbutz for our locality. The Kibbutz busied itself with cultural work. Through us we spread the "Jewish Voice" of Kovno and other Zionist publications and we were constantly involved in many of the Rokishoker societies.

First kibbutz in Rokiskis

[Page 246]

Three Years in Rokishok

by Avigdor Ariel Glombotzki

Translated by Mathilda Mendelow, born Ginsberg

Three years of my life I spent in Rokishok. During the above remembered time I became very close to the Lithuanian Hasidic Shtetl. In the long years that I have spent in far away lands I longed very much for the poor Litvak community, for the loving plain warm hearted Jews and for the exciting youth with whom I spent my whole time. Even now after 20 years and after all the gruesome experiences that happened to my brothers and sisters on the Lithuanian soil, the memory of the Shtetl and its Hassidim, mitnagdim, non-believers, rich owners and the horrible poverty is very near to me.

Unidentified group photo, but probably a Scout group

Each part of the year had its own beauty – the spring flowers, the flower-filled summer, also the cold of autumn and the very sharp cold winters. During the great catastrophe, in the various places where I have been, I was followed by the lonely stillness of the Rokishoker streets, be it in the Kamier main street or be it in the side streets, be it in the city market that used to be lively during the time of the Jews – especially during the winter flax market when flax merchants from the surrounding cities and shtetlag and a multitude of peasants or gentiles from the surrounding area used to come.

I spent from 1922 to 1925 in Rokishok being a teacher in the Hebrew School. The school drew most children from all levels: children of well-to-do homes, children of workers, religions and from certain free Zionist rings.

During the above remembered years there was a revival of Hebrew over the whole of Lithuania. The Jewish youth in the Shtetl studied with zest. One prepared oneself to enter Jewish Colleges. They strived to get into the lists of the "Halutzim" so as to pass a qualification and leave for Israel.

Then I established the Jewish Scout movement of Rokishok. This was even from the land organization which had divisions in cities and Shtetls, the organization did above all include the scholars of the Hebrew School. During this time the Jewish Scholars of the local Lithuanian College and even the scholars of the agricultural school joined us of the working youth, who had no schooling. The students devoted themselves with "life and limb" to this goal. A youth club was organized, where talks, plays and gatherings were arranged.

A group of Scouts in Rokiskis

Rokiskis "Hasherah-Kibbutz" of future immigrants to Israel

On Saturdays and yomtovim (holidays) they used to organize collective walks and outings in the area on foot. In summer, during vacation months we arranged summer camps in the forest. We lived collectively, and enjoyed the lap of free nature very much.

Our youth movement during that time was the only Jewish Youth movement in Rokishok. It had a great influence on the children and youth of the town. With Chassidic fervor, and support of Chassidic Chabad it had a great influence on the youth organization which produced an ethical, normal and friendly relationship between one another and normalized a lot of the relationships between children and parents.

My personal influence on the children was great and parents used to threaten disobedient children with "I'm going immediately to Avigdor." The following friends also worked well for the good of the organization: –

Moshe Weisman (May his memory be a blessing)

Shifra Leifer (May her memory be a blessing) and

Abie Rubin

The following youth also excelled and helped:

Henick Patz

Sarah Patz

Tybie Kil

Rivka Nochomowitz and others

[Pages 249-250]

About the Scout Movement

by Shulamit Nanas, Israel

Translated by Gloria Berkenstat Freund

I have already been here [in *Eretz-Yisroel*] for 22 years and much is erased from my memory. But, like a dream of the infinitely distant past, an early morning in our Rakishok comes to life. Here, I think, Vilner Street comes to life, along with the house of the *Rosh haYeshiva* [head of the religious school], Reb Josef Yitzhak Klein.

Scouts in Rokiskis

Just now the morning bloomed and the energetic *tsofe* [female scout] from the scout troop approached the house. She carefully, quietly opened the shutter of the room in which I slept, as we had agreed. I was ready, having opened the bolt that closed the window during the evening before going to sleep.

I sprang out of the window so that my father would not notice. I had to lead a group (meeting) of my "scout" collective that would take place in the city garden, where 10-12 year-old girls would come together. Although I was only a few years older than them, the responsibility had been placed on me

A scout program was carried out that included: frank discussions with remarks on all sides; characteristic games; singing songs and conversations about the native land [*Eretz-Yisroel*] that always had blue skies and a strong shining sun.

I was admonished more than once by my father upon returning home that my conduct was not appropriate for the daughter of the head of a yeshiva. Yes, dear father--he did not know that this was the fruit of his own seedlings that he had planted in my child's soul with his *gemara* [discussions on the Talmud] melodies. Then, in the evenings and nights, when he would sit studying the *gemara* words of "*Amora* Reb Akiva" [plural: *Amoraim* – 3rd to 6th century rabbinic sages], and the melodies would pour out into my heart and fill little corners of my soul and carry it far over the seas to the far and beloved land where the *Tannaim* [2nd and 3rd century rabbinic sages].

I remember so clearly and distinctly a *Shabbos* night when the weekly meeting of the entire troop would take place. The club was on Vilner Street. At first, the head of the troop was Moshe Vesterman, and later, Avigdor Glambatsky. I still feel the enthusiasm when an interesting subject would bring out a mighty singing of various national songs that stirred and demanded their due. Each word had its particular charm and tang. We sang: "Rest, rest our dear friend, sleep there eternally – we like you will sacrifice ourselves for our nation." I felt a readiness to be ready for everything and I trembled with my entire being for the Judea mountains. After our program ended, we all marched along dark Vilner Street, but our spirits were in ferment – we were enriched with encouragement and hope.

Yes, that holy mood that came over us all cannot be forgotten. Those memories of our scout movement are engraved deeply, deeply in my soul.

Hashomer Hatzair Hebrew Scout Organization in Rokiskis

[Page 251]

Leib Jaffe's Visit

(To his illustrious memory)

by A.Y.

Translated by Gloria Berkenstat Freund

When the great poet, Leib Jaffe (may he rest in peace) was in Lithuania, among the few cities and *shtetlekh* [towns] he visited was Rakishok. We began to prepare several days in advance to make a fine *kaboles ponem* [welcome] for him. The Count of the *shtetl* was asked for the loan of his carriage and horses; a small orchestra was obtained, and at the designated "hour" everyone was at the train station.

When he got off the train, he received a very fine reception from people standing along the entire road to the *shtetl*. All of the teachers and the students from the school and *pro-gymnazie* [school that prepares students to enter the *gymnazie* - secondary school] marched in straight lines and accompanied by members of various organizations and committees, as well as Christians who were just curious to see the Jew who was being given so much "respect" with the Count's carriage and orchestra music, as appropriate for a king.

An official welcome was held for him on Makabi Square. Various organizations and institutions gave greetings, as well as teachers from the school and the *pro-gymnazie*. Then members of *Makabi* demonstrated various sports feats. Thus, the first half of the day went by. In the evening there was a banquet for him in the auditorium of the *Talmud Torah* [religious primary school usually for poor boys] which was decorated with flags. A picture of a large lion with the inscription, "The lion roared, who will not fear," hung on one wall.

Before his arrival in Rakishok he was extolled as inspiring people with his speaking. This interested me very much, so at the banquet when he spoke, I looked him in the eyes for the entire time to see his carriage and movements and this is a picture of his manner of speaking: he stood straight, closed his eyes, spoke not too high, not too low, and describing (or better, speaking), painted as if with a paint brush various pictures that drew one to hear his every word as if to a magnet. Thus looking at him, one felt as if hypnotized and this was the power of his speaking, not storming--"without an uproar"--and it was for good reason that he earned the respect that he received all over.

When he would come to speak, a great sum of money would be collected. Several years ago, when I read about his tragic death during an explosion at the Jewish Agency building, something pulled at the strings of my heart as from a hidden instrument and all of the above mentioned images passed by as if alive. His memory will always remain in my heart, as well as with everyone who was present at his arrival in Rakishok.

[Pages 252-256]

Orphanage

by A. Nochumowitz

Translated by Gloria Berkenstat Freund

Right after the end of the war [World War I], all of the homeless began to return from Russia and the Jews from the surrounding *shtetlekh* [towns] also settled in Rakishok. It was time to found an orphanage.

Many widows and orphans were found among the returning Rakishok Jews and there were also orphans from the surrounding villages and *shtetlekh*. Rakishok was plundered during the war and very poor, and the Jews were not able to support the large number of orphans* in Rakishok.

Chanah Shadur

*[Translator's note: In Yiddish, an orphan can be a child who has lost one or both parents.]

A delegation consisting of Shifra Laufer, Hilel Eidelson, and Shmuel Aba Snieg went to Kovno to request help from the American Joint [Distribution Committee] to found an orphanage in Rakishok. After long negotiations it was decided that the Joint would equally, in partnership with the *shtetl*, support the orphanage.

Rokiskis Yizkor Book 253

After the return of the delegation, there was success in renting a house in Jurdzike on the road to Radute. It was a large building, in which plays had been presented earlier. Although it was far from the *shtetl*, the orphanage was opened there because a better house could not be found.

A meeting was called of all Rakishok Jews before the orphanage opened and the necessity of an orphanage institution in the *shtetl* was clarified for them. And they turned to every Jew among the assembled and told them that they were obliged to tax themselves with what they could [afford] so that this important institution could exist.

A committee was chosen at the general meeting which proceeded to this work. All orphaned boys and girls from the age of five to 13 were registered and clothing and shoes were received from the Joint to clothe them because the children were dressed in sacks, in torn garments and went around barefoot.

The chosen women's committee took upon itself the task of permanently providing clothing and footwear for the children. A shoemaker was hired who would sew and repair the children's shoes.

A doctor was also hired to heal the sick orphans.

A teacher came from Kovno so that she could teach the children who had studied in a school or in a *kheder* [religious primary school] and to help prepare the lectures.

The older children were placed with artisans. There were orphans who were much older who could not be placed in the institution and places were rented for them in private houses where they would eat and have a place to sleep. The Orphan Committee paid for them.

The orphanage turned into an exemplary institution in a very short time. The name "Rakishok Orphanage" became renowned. Children began to arrive from distant towns. Moshe Kac's house was rented when the premises became too small to take in so many children. Later, they bought their own building across from the market.

The children also received good care; they were taught and educated in the national spirit. The girls were taught sewing, knitting, and various hand work. The children took part in gymnastics and various sports workouts.

Chanah Shadur with orphans

The Orphanage Building, 1927

Board of Orphanage

The following people who gave a great deal of time and effort on behalf of the orphanage should be remembered: Hilel Eidelson, the father of the orphans; Hilel Eidelson's sister, Chana Shadur, household director; Shifra Laufer, secretary; and the writer of these lines, manager of the orphanage.

The orphanage numbered more than 80 children during my time and existed until the destruction of Rakishok.

Flower day to raise funds for the orphange

Invitation card of the Rakishok Orphanage

Invitation

The Managing Committee of the Rakishok ORPHANAGE has the honor
To invite you to

The Traditional Entertainment Evening,
That will take place

SHIMKHAS TORAH, Sunday evening 6 o'clock

In the house of the Orphanage.

A wind orchestra will play that evening, with various entertainments
And a buffet.

Until 2 o'clock at night.

The importance of our institution insures us of your attendance.

With great respect

The Managing Committee   **Printed by A. Y. Meller, Rakishok**

[Pages 257-259]

The Society for Visiting the Sick in Rakishok (Rakishoker Linas-haTzedek)

by Rywke Blacher-Itzikman

Translated by Gloria Berkenstat Freund

When the evacuated Rakishok Jews returned from Russia after the First World War, it immediately became apparent that an aid organization such as a Linas-haTzedek [society for visiting the sick] was a necessity.

Aid Society "Linat Hatzedek"

The hospital for the poor in Rakishok was overflowing with sick, crippled and paralyzed people, including patients from surrounding towns. The poor and sick lay in the houses of prayer. Jewish women helped in every way, but there was no organized administration that would do the aid work.

The work was urgent. Irle Rubin, the mother of our esteemed landsman [person from the same town], A. Rubin of Johannesburg, and her daughter Gitl, took the initiative to found a Linas-haTzedek in Rakishok.

Members of Aid Society

Drama Section of "Maccabi"

The strongly devoted Jewish community worker, Irle Rubin, called the first meeting in her home, at which a committee of the Linas-haTzedek was created. In addition to Irle Rubin and her daughter, Gitl, the committee chosen included: Sure Pines, Chana Yakobson, Chana Lubovitz, Rywka Itzikman, Sime Milner and Gnendl Maitovitz.

The first task of the committee was to create a means of [raising] money. They immediately began to solicit members. The city responded warmly and sincerely supported the Linas-haTzedek. Almost all of the young girls in the city took part in the work.

From the very beginning, order was created in the hospital: it was cleaned, beds and mattresses were brought for the sick and they were provided food. The paralyzed people were fed by hand and they were cared for with love and devotion. Then the Linas-haTzedek took over the care of the most needy families, secretly helping impoverished men. Poor women giving birth were cared for, provided with food and with the first clothing for their new born child.

In 1926, the Linas-haTzedek rented a house and created a birthing institution in Rakishok. This attempt was made in a modest way. Only two beds were provided. When a poor woman needed to give birth, she was brought there and provided medical help and all necessities.

The Linas-haTzedek also helped the poor passing through, who had no place to turn. There was a case where a Jew from outside the city came to the synagogue and became ill there. Our Rakishok young girls tended to him for many months and took care of him. The sick were also provided kosher food.

The Linas-haTzedek existed until the death of the Rakishok Jewish kehile [organized Jewish community]. Many of the active Linas-haTzedek workers are now in South Africa and when Rakishok landsleit [people from the same town] come together, the meritorious activities of the Rakishok Linas-haTzedek is remembered at every opportunity with love and acknowledgement.

[Page 260]

Jewish Theatre

by Shlomo Rubin
Translated by Rabbi Ezra Boyarsky

I am not in a position to offer a detailed description of the development of the Yiddish theatre in Rakishok. I recall that as a child of ten, I thought of an idea as to how to entertain the wedding guests after the musicians had already left and the young people danced, but without music. So I sang and acted out a folk song that was popular in those days. The song dealt with an elderly man who was isolated in a foreign land away from his family who had abandoned him. I dressed up in old, long clothes and assumed the role of the old man. This was my debut as an actor. At that age I had no idea what theatre was all about. As a matter of fact, I did not even know that such a thing existed in the world.

Yiddish Theater

A short while later there came to Rakishok a dramatic director from Warsaw who, with the cooperation of some interested townspeople, produced a play in the hall of the fire department. I went to see the play and, as was then the custom, dancing followed the end of the performance. I mingled with the dancing couples, hoping to bump into the performing artists, but no such luck. My ambition was to meet real flesh and blood artists face to face, and to experience the feeling of what it is like to actually stand on the stage.

The play "Frighten Shaindel"

A few years later, a wonderful theatre company came to Rakishok. The director chose some local talent, including me, and together with the actors he brought, we successfully performed a number of plays. I played the part of the matchmaker in the play "Hertzele Meyuchos." To this day I remember the poke I received from the "mekhutn" (son-in-law's or daughter-in-law's father). In those days the theatre performances were more realistic--a poke was actually a poke, and a slap was a slap.

The theatre fascinated me, so I decided to produce a play in a private home, and for this I chose "Mit Dem Shrum" (With the Current) by the well-known Yiddish author, Sholom Ash. I was also instrumental in establishing a small amateur theatre and musical group. One of the performances was: "Oh, You Tiny Little Candles"--a reference to the Hanukah lights. I gave my little sister a part in the play.

We followed this up with one-act plays by the famous humorist author Sholom Aleichem. Admission was free, and we always had a full house. Those who could not find room inside stood on the window sills. We enlivened the town, and enjoyed the popularity and the acclaim of the viewers.

Years later, we put on plays from the repertoire of the famous playwright, Y. Gordin. With the passage of time, new business enterprises were opened in our town and Rakishok experienced a period of growth. A bank was opened which necessitated the importation of bookkeepers from larger cities. Some of the newcomers also had a passion to perform in Yiddish theatre, and their enthusiasm gave Rakishok a shot in the arm. This brought intensive theatre activity, and the theatre was now moved to a large auditorium with a real stage where we could have stage scenery, props, and decorations.

The Rokiskis Art Lover Association with the play "The Truth of Life" in 1926

In 1915 I was mobilized and served in the Russian army. At the end of 1922, I returned home and brought with me many plays from the Russian theatre where I worked as a make-up artist. Rakishok received me with open arms, and I found in the theatre there a wide range of activity. We concentrated on plays and dramas by Sholom Aleichem, Yaakov Gordin, D. Pinsky, and Yud Leib Peretz. It became clear to us that through the medium of the theatre, we could disseminate Yiddish culture: every performance made a cultural impact on the audience and brought joy to the town. Throughout, we maintained a high standard, and our repertoire contained only the best creations of the Yiddish classicists. We never considered literary trash.

I left for South Africa, but the Yiddish theatre continued to function in Rakishok. According to the reports I received in 1928, there were several dramatic groups with talented actors who performed under a collective directorship. Evidently, each group wanted to preserve its own character. Some of the actors belonged to the Culture League which at that time was illegal.

I regret that I do not have precise details concerning the Rakishok Yiddish Theatre, which occupied a respectable position in the communal and cultural life of the town.

The Rokiskis Art Lover Association with the play "Yekel the Coachman", 8 Nov. 1930

[Pages 264-268]

The People's Bank

by M. B.
Translated by Gloria Berkenstat Freund

Pursuant to an unpublished book about "the Jewish People's Bank in Lithuania," in which there is information collected by the inspectors from the Jewish banking system – B. Entelis and Y. Borvin – during the course of the 21st of December 1926 to the 28th of February, 1927, we learn about the Rakishok People's Bank and several important figures among the Jews in Rakishok.

The Folk Bank

The inspection report begins with the following introduction:

"Rakishok (the name of the train station is the same name) counts 2,013 souls in the number of its Jewish population.*)

The main pursuit of the Jewish population is the usual small trade and as artisans; the flax and seed trade (export) particularly developed here.

Before the war [World War One] a Jewish loan and savings fund functioned here that failed with the start of the war; the present People's Bank was founded in July 1920 (according to the initiative of the national council) and includes in its circle of activity, in addition to Rakishok itself, several surrounding towns: Abele [Obeliai] (10 members), Kamay (7 members), Ponedel [Pandėlys] (6 members), Anisishak [Anèiðkis] and Panemunok [Panemunëlis], and so on (7 members).

A Jewish "Society for Mutual Credit" also exists here."

According to the Rakishok bank report, which was put together by the above mentioned inspectors – on the 10th of March, 1927, we learn the following:

"The Rakishok People's Bank numbered 464 members whose professional standing was the following: tradesmen-204; artisans-123; merchants and industrialists-44; agricultural workers and gardeners-6; workers and wagon drivers-25; employees-25; independent professionals-37."

Management and staff of the Rokiskis Yiddish Folk Bank, 1929

Fifteen Christians were also included in the Rakishok general membership.

The People's Bank in Rakishok provided long term and short term loans.

Long term loans were given the debtor for up to 500 lit, terms – to six months with further prolonged charges – 15% a year; (partly as a pledge). An exception of no pledge was made for the Rakishok Artisans Union that paid 10% yearly – under the guarantee of a private promissory note.

Short term loans were given on one account, in a sum up to 5,000 lit; interest 24% yearly; terms – up to three months; guarantee – promissory note in a deposit bond.

In the course of 26 years were distributed:

Long-term loan in the sum of 59,576 lit;

Short-term loans in the sum of 224,516 lit.

In addition to loans, the bank carried out various collections and cashier operations both in cash and with cargo, took deposits and it figured in the typical credit for those who emigrated to South Africa. The bank report provides the following version:

"The bank still gives in several cases a great deal of specific credit, namely: it buys a check for 35 pounds (the minimum that an emigrant needs to possess according to certain decrees) for this or that person, who emigrates from here to Africa, taking for it a promissory note, guaranteed by another local person. Thus, for example, at the moment of the inspection, the shown sum (35 pounds – 1,729 lit) was charged to the account of a certain Mr. Sher, a relative of someone who traveled to Africa."

The People's Bank had its own building, the worth of which was (according to its [bank] balance) – 36,908 lit.

It had its own statute that was registered on the 23rd of June, 1920.

The system also had, among other items, an item concerning the size of fee that was 10 lit and also the maximum credit to one member – in the sum of 5,000 lit.

The leadership of the bank consisted of: a council (nine people), a managing committee (three people) and an audit commission of three people.

The personnel of the bank consisted of:

Bookkeeper Mr. German with a salary of 400 lit;

Treasurer Mr. Milner with a salary of 300 lit;

Assistant bookkeeper Mr. Lipovitz with a monthly salary of 300 lit;

Secretary Mr. Bar with a monthly salary of 300 lit;

Clerk Mr. Idelson with a monthly salary of 200 lit;

Courier with a monthly salary of 125 lit.

The bank's balances up to the 1st of January, 1927, were the following:

Passive		Passive	
Cash for Immediate Disbursements	17,687 lit	Cash for Immediate Disbursements	17,687 lit
Reserve and other capital	51,600 lit	Reserve and other capital	51,600 lit
Deposits	51,543 lit	Deposits	51,543 lit
Savings Deposits	2,630 lit	Savings Deposits	2,630 lit
Credit from Central Bank:		Credit from Central Bank:	
Bonds	60,000 lit	Bonds	60,000 lit
Renewals	56,000 lit	Renewals	56,000 lit
Current Accounts	91,495 lit	Current Accounts	91,495 lit
Promissory Note-Credit	35,280 lit	Promissory Note-Credit	35,280 lit
Installment Payments	3,466 lit	Installment Payments	3,466 lit
Drafts	74,214 lit	Drafts	74,214 lit
Committed Amounts	375,053 lit	Committed Amounts	375,053 lit
Payments Repaid	18,604 lit	Payments Repaid	18,604 lit
Miscellaneous	18,969 lit	Miscellaneous	18,969 lit
Sum Total	**870,788 lit**	**Sum Total**	**870,788 lit**

There are a series of statements about the general performance and instructions from Inspector B. Entielis which also characterize the economic crisis in the *shtetl* at that time and it is therefore worthwhile to publish several:

"Excluding the 'Recurring Expenses' about which inadequate movement is noticed here in the extensions that are widely applied, only old debts are recorded here. Debts of around 112,000 lit (40% of the long and short term loans), among which the bank itself counts up to the present moment, 40,000 lit, as entirely lost.

"All hopeless debts (including also long term debts) to be terminated (disbursed at approximate dates) and the terms that will be established need the approximate sums to be strictly observed.

"No loans can be given out without a determined term and, at that, the long term loans must be given out to be repaid in installments (and not all at once).

"Credit should not be given to the same person simultaneously with various accounts (such as running accounts, discounts, renewed amounts and so on), as is now done in the bank and is a factor in that several people actually owe very significant amounts.

"The collection process needs to be taken care of accurately.

"The disbursed collected freight without the backing of security money (guarantees) cannot be practiced further in what is an immoderate manner.

"The fictitious loans and deposit accounts must no longer be carried."

All of the conclusions in the bank report provide evidence that the Jewish economic situation in the *shtetl* and its surroundings was at that time not a good one and the Jewish merchant did not stand on a firm foundation.

* According to a letter from YIVO, with the signature of Mark Yoweliner, dated the 24th of May, 1951 and addressed to Sh. Rubin, secretary of the *Landsleit* Union of Rakishok and Surroundings, the following information is presented:

"In the *Evreiskaya Entsiclopediya* (Russian), published by Brockhaus and Efron, Petersburg, vol. 13, column 298, there is a note about Rakishok that we present here in Yiddish translation:
"Rakishok, Kovno *Gubernia*, Novoaleks County. According to the Census of 1847, 'the Rakishok Jewish community' (*kehile?*) consisted of 593 souls. According to the enumeration of 1897 there were 2,736 residents in Rakishok. Of them 2,067 Jews."

[Page 271]

Environs

Abel
(Obeliai, Lithuania)

55°56' 25°48'

by I. Michel-Michalewitz
Translated by Nathan Summer

My birth town Abel is a sister "shtetl" from Rakishok and from the neighboring towns, and has also a history of various events and episodes of interesting personalities and most typical characters too. This town possessed a spirited Jewish living style and a very active social environment.

To my regret, I can only share some minor points of the Jewish social activities in Abel from the beginning of the twentieth century until the end of the First World War years; and since the establishment of the Lithuanian Republic. With this work of mine I intend in my humble way to put a written monument in memory of the tragic onslaught against the Jews of our town. Let my words be an eternal memorial of my hometown, Abel.

Abel had a train station on Libauer-Romner train-highway, from where many trains have stretched to two different directions: to Dvinsk and to the towns of Rakishok, Ponieviezh, Radviliski, and others. This was the first train station on Lithuanian territory, the key to all of Lithuania.

There was always on the Abeler station a sort of bright atmosphere. The train auditorium was always full of business people and tourists, women who were very visible selling all sorts of their produce, including fresh-baked bagels, cookies, and cakes; also they were peddling all sorts of fruits, such as apples, pears, and plums. The coachmen were going around in working clothes and ropes around their hips, and in their hands a whip, calling on the surrounding people, men and women, to ride with them! At various times, because of a passenger, they exchanged their whips. The train station was also a central place for the neighboring towns and villages like Dusiat, Alexandrovno, Krevne, Subotch, and others.

From the station to town, it was about two kilometers along a wide highway. From both sides of the highway during the summer months there were beautiful gardens, lawns, and fields. Near the town grew beautiful wild flowers that twisted toward a stone fence nearby to the town of Subotch.

Nearby the town there was a fleeting and narrow, deep river that gushed down to the area of the Stashunzer Forest. At the entrance to town there stood impertinent the white painted church with a gray shingle roof. On the wall of the church, facing the town, there could be seen sculptures symbolizing divine beings, and from the top of the edifice we have seen in reflection of the sun, bronze crosses.

And after that we have seen long lines of Jewish homes that led to the marketplace, to the pharmacy and to a very old monument that was considered to be the central place of the town, from where they used to advise the population of the town of various orders and new laws. From this place, you could see in two different directions--one that led to the large court orchard that was well known for its assortment of fruit and especially for its spring water that gushed from a wood pipe. People suffering from poor eyesight used to come to wash their eyes there, hoping to find a cure and relief from its pains and aches.

From the above-mentioned court orchard, a swampy area led to the brewery, which for many years produced and marketed all sorts of liquors and beverages to many central cities of Russia. From the dregs and refuse of the beverages they used to feed gulls so that they became tremendously large and wild. They were hardly able to move as they gained a lot of weight. Through their noses they used to fasten a copper ring, and they also attached a long chain that a number of people used to lead them for safety reasons. The people of the market area were very much in fear when they used to walk with these wild animals. Mothers immediately made sure that their children were put to safety.

A second group from the stone monument led to the length of the town, through the bridge passing Berzig, the under-brick layer; left close to the homes of Yosel Shapiro, Israel Chayes, Beyne Itze the blacksmith, and Bere Mote the gravedigger, was leading to a muddy road to the Stashunzer Forest.

A narrow trail was winding through Velvele the farmer's house and joined the wide Antenasher Highway, which from its right side we found the beautiful pine forest which during the summer time was filled with nuts, wild strawberries, gooseberries, and other berries. This beautiful forest was also a resort place. In 1905 there were many secret revolutionary meetings held there.

There was also the Antenasher River that bordered with the creek, which sent its streams to the Abeler River, near the street of the House of Prayer. In this street there were bungalows in which were housed Beile Cheikels the midwife and also Sara Leah the widow. Higher down on a hill we were able to see the homes of Shmuel the sexton, Hirsl Nachman the tailor, and Zuse, the teacher of a "cheder." Further down the street there was the new House of Study--and close to it was the old sunken synagogue, where Jews used to gather during the high holidays for prayer services.

On the other side of the street lived the families of Tzivieh the bagel baker, Abraham Moshe the butcher, Heshel the shoemaker, and Frume Baruchs the matzah baker.

Through a narrow street, past Ethel the baker's garden, you entered the main street of the town, which was a central place of most larger stores, and business people like: Itzik Zak, the forest businessman; Zalman Mehler's liquor store; Abraham Teztzis; Itze Zelig's seltzer factory; Leibe the barkeeper; Abraham Tirzes' general store; Elie the Moskvers' manufacturing business; Sarah and Elie Leyzer's general store; Leibe der Lange's stores of flax; Israel-Itze and Yose-Abela, fruit dealers.

In the near proximity, there was the only Chasidic synagogue in town, an old wooden building, with a patched-up shingle roof, where they had an attached ladder leading to the chimney. From all three sides we were able to see three large carved windows. In a narrow corridor, led from one side to a special examining room where the rabbis had for years their own place, and from another side of the corridor, leading to the main synagogue.

When one observes the edifice in its entirety--the long benches around the walls, the large tables by the sides, the shelves of prayer books, the beautiful bimah (platform) close to the door, the ark with the old faded curtain, the torn yellowed holy books that protruded from the book shelves, and the sunset that sends its last rays toward the ark where the holy scrolls are kept--some mystic reflections will remain with you forever.

Economic Status

The majority of Abeler Jews were considered declassified, without any specific trade or profession. There were many without thinking of earning a living; there were some who considered themselves as brokers, small-time dealers of anything; and a large segment of the Jewish population just doing nothing, with the hope that God would help them. Most of them made their livelihood depending on the one market day of the week on Thursday. Peasants from nearby villages used to bring their produce on that day to market. On that day, most Jews of the town were quite active. They used to rise very early that day. First they used to hastily do the morning prayers and leave for the marketplace with faith in their hearts, meeting the gentile peasants on their way.

The shopkeepers used to put up their tables with their wares like: leather, men and women's clothing, all sorts of utensils, dishes, etc. Among the many shopkeepers, they used to compete with each other quite loudly, which led to insulting each other. Although they didn't really hate each other, most of them were worried that if they didn't sell enough, they would not be able to meet the week's expenses. That's why most of them were trying to run ahead with their wares towards the potential peasant buyers.

The marketplace in Abel

From the nearby towns, like Rakishok, Subotch, and Dusiat, arrived many established business merchants that used to buy from the peasants flax, seeds, geese, and cows. Only on the day of the market gathering did the town really become very active and lively. Everyone had hopes on that day to make sure they would be able to make expenses for the week ahead. But on ordinary days, Abel was considered to be a sloppy and dead town. No wonder in Abel and nearby towns they used to call people in the town "Abeler ghosts." Once in awhile we used to see a peasant come into town to buy a bottle of gasoline, herring, and other small things. All merchants were looking at the peasant, perhaps because he would stop at their place to buy something. Not too many people of Abel were experienced laborers. There were only a handful of them: a shoemaker, a few tailors, a bricklayer, a watch repairman, and a couple of glaziers. There were also butchers, including: Henech, Abraham Moishe, Berzia the Strapyker, Shalom der Schwarzer, Shmuel Alexandrover, and Saul Klas. They were very experienced and specialists in their trade. The town also had a few fine bakers, such as: Leyo Rachmiels, Zivieh the bagel baker, and Etil Yoses.

Many were the gardeners, the so-called orchard renters, like: Bereh Motte, Hirshe Gross, and Yoseh Abales. They were only occupied with this sort of business. They exported first-class fruit to Warsaw, Lodz, Riga, and other places. There were also some business dealers that were well known as the flax merchants-- Leibe Zakshtein, Berzik Friedman, and Yudel the Pakrevner-- who dealt in a more commercial manner. They had their own storehouses where they had to keep and clean the flax. The better kind they exported to Preisen. The same dealers were also handling special kinds of seeds, which they transported to an oil factory in Dvinsk. The small dealers used to buy from them flax and seeds for a certain percentage.

In town there were two forest dealers: Itzik Zak and Leibe the forester. They led large commercial dealings with other countries and they lived quite comfortably. They were considered progressive and observed a secular Jewish lifestyle. Itzik participated in various social endeavors. For a long time, he was on the ritual committee of the Chasidic synagogue.

Itzik sent his children to study in universities. His older son, Israel, was studying in the famous Petersburg University and received a diploma in building engineering. His second son studied law and later became a prosecutor in Ponevezh. Itzik Zak's wife, Yente, was a very devoted wife and mother, and very pious in her religious beliefs. She was always helping indigent families. I remember that once when Yente came to an impoverished home to visit a sick person, she brought with her a dish with jam. I also remember when a poor shoemaker asked Itzik the little money that he owed him for fixing his shoes, Itzik looked at his pocket and answered the shoemaker, "You will excuse me, I just haven't got the few kopeks that I owe you with me." Yente, listening to her husband, took out a five-ruble coin, gave it to the shoemaker, and asked him to take out as much as her husband owed him and give her change. She criticized her husband a little for not paying the workman in time.

As a rule, the more affluent people seemed to look down on the working people. They seemed to have kept themselves to a sort of higher standard than the poor hardworking people. They kept themselves with pride of their inherited beautiful homes that their parents left them, and with their better economic position.

Social Cultural Events

Until the First World War, Abel's cultural life was quite backward. There was the lack of a cultural environment, where the youthful elements had no chance of advancement. Only some individuals from time to time left Abel and went to larger cities, where they had an opportunity to pick up some secular knowledge.

In our Jewish community of about 300 people, the rabbis had the greatest influence. The parents were religious zealots and were very much afraid that their children shouldn't forsake the right path.

The children were sent to "chadurin" (religious Jewish schools) that were mostly kept in crowded, dark, and filthy rooms. The so-called "teachers" did not take care of the children in a kind and loving manner. For the slightest misbehavior, a child was punished in a very vicious way. Abraham-Itze the Hunchback, the melamed (teacher), was a very unkindly person. His entire "cheder" schoolroom consisted of a long table, embraced with some benches. Close to the stove, he put up a bed separated with a linen curtain. This was his bedroom, and the "cheder" children used to spread their mostly patched-up clothing there. The crowdedness in this cluttered room was unbearable. Abraham-Itze was of medium height, with a long hunched nose, and a disheveled beard and head of hair. He had a short body with long legs that moved pretty fast from one child to another. He had a leather whip and if a child made some remark that he didn't like, he would whip the child and he didn't care on what part of the body his whip landed.

Worse were the winter months, when the cruel frosts entered the impoverished homes of the so-called "schools" where the children-students were very uncomfortable and freezing until late into the evening. The "melamdim" (teachers) were underpaid and were barely able to have a decent livelihood, and surely they were not able to heat the iron stoves properly.

Aba, the Talmudic teacher, had a much better relationship with his young students. First, those young Talmudic students came from better, more affluent homes, and the teacher was well compensated, financially. This teacher was known as a great Talmudic scholar, and a student of his really became very knowledgeable. He had a very disciplined and tactical relationship with his students. Aba the scholar-teacher had a comfortable livelihood from his teaching and did not have to depend on side jobs outside of his profession.

For many years Abel did not have a formal community that would care and try to improve its educational institutions among its Jewish populations. They had a group of ringleaders, like Leibe the tall one, Leibe the coachman, Yankel the Yakres (the dearth), Itzik Zak, and Zalman Mehler. These men moved to take positions of leadership. They were more dedicated to all sorts of quarrels among them rather than productive work towards educational goals.

In the shtetl there were "Chasidim" and "Misnagdim" (opponents to the more orthodox Chasidim). The split among them was very partisan. A "Chasid" would never think of entering a synagogue of his opponents, and a "Misnagid" felt the same way about the "Chasidim," although they pray to the same God. The split among these groups were of such magnitude that at various times it led to violent engagements of insulting each other and even attacking each other physically.

During the winter months, when a biting harsh wind would dance through town in a very devastating manner, and there was a snowstorm that blocked and covered all streets and highways and byways of transportation, the low-built houses with straw roofs were covered with tons of snow and the window panes were beautifully painted with flowers and figures of frost. Most people were under the impression that these devastating snowstorms would stay with them forever and never end. On those days when the impudent winds and frost came through our town, the worshipers in the houses of prayer were very much upset and angry and couldn't find anything to keep them happy and proud. At that time, the only warm-hearted individual was the stately appearance of Shmuel the goat, who brought the worshipers a mood of consolation and joy through his snuffbox of tobacco.

Chasidic Synagogue in Abel

Most synagogues in town during these hard winter months were seldom heated because of the shortage of firewood. The worshipers were very upset and angry because the two prominent forest merchants did not provide them with wood to keep the houses of worship warm and comfortable. They told them to stay home and not dare to come to the synagogue because of their being stingy to provide the poor people with heat during the nasty and cold winter storms.

Now some influential individuals of the Jewish community brought with them a novel idea how to get money to be able to provide the houses of worship with heat. They asked the sextons to announce in all synagogues that every worshiper would contribute as much as he can for buying wood to heat the ovens. Every one of the assembled worshipers was asked to leave their little prayer shawls overnight and by bringing five kopeks, the shawls would be given back to them for the morning service. In this sort of novel manner, they collected some money to purchase firewood.

In the "Misnagdim" synagogue, Rabbi Chaim Nasan was the rabbi for a long time. He lived in a little crowded apartment with three small windows in the Beth Medrish (the house of study) through which you were able to see the town's bathhouse, near the running brook and some nearby areas of the town. The Jewish community was not able to pay the rabbi a living wage. They gave him some kopeks from chicken "schite" (slaughter) and from yeast sales. From all this, he was barely able to make a poor living to support his family. The rabbi was a very God-fearing man, and because of poverty stricken circumstances, he was constantly searching to improve his material position.

Being a very knowledgeable preacher and speaker, he asked his leaders of the synagogue, since it was very hard for him and his family to maintain any living standard, to allow him to travel to nearby towns to deliver lectures. The trustees of the synagogue had no other choice but to allow him his demand. Rabbi Chaim Nasan began touring the neighboring towns and cities. On his way, he met a young rabbi who just came out of a yeshiva (academy). The young rabbi told him that he was married to a daughter of a very rich merchant. Rabbi Nasan told him that perhaps he would accept his position for a certain sum of money. The young rabbi accepted his offer and he gave Rabbi Nasan a large sum to allow him to take his rabbinic position in the synagogue that Rabbi Nasan was leaving. Rabbi Chaim Nasan now had enough money to go to America with his family. Before he left the town, the synagogue arranged a farewell party for him and his family. One of the members of the committee wished him to go in peace and now we can say about him, using a biblical quote: "Now you are a man of the world."

The very young rabbi took over the former rabbi's position, and he became very popular among the people in Abel. They called him lovingly, the "red-haired Rabbi." He really was a man with great ability. In his sermons, he showed great Torah knowledge and wisdom, and the town was entirely under his influence. He managed to arrange all the expenses and finances of the synagogue on a solid basis. There was enough money to cover all outgoing expenses and enough to provide the edifice with firewood for the cold winter months. After a few years of serving the Abel population, he too left for the United States.

Under Czarist Russia, Abel had only one public school. There was no high school, so most well-to-do Jews sent their children to larger cities to get a better education--cities like Kovno, Dvinsk, and Petersburg. The only Russian public school in Abel could be found on the side where the administrative office was located, not far from the house of Aba the melamed's house. The classes in public school were quite often interrupted. They were not too steadfast. During the summer months they would keep them entirely closed, for the reason that the children were mostly used at their homes because of the coming Christian holidays, where the children were busy feeding the pigs, cows, and geese. The schools did not have too many Jewish children in the public school because they only allowed about five percent of the Jewish population. Besides, you needed some protection from the higher officials. If for some reason a Jewish family was not favorably liked by some official, their children were not accepted.

Later, many parents sent their children to private teachers, but there were not many teachers that had command of the Russian language. There was an exception--Sarah of Moscow. She happened to be the only Russian language teacher in Abel, an only daughter.

The firefighters of Abel

At that time in Russia, "socialism"--which was very popular but illegal--was transferred to smaller towns and villages in Lithuania. The Lithuanian towns were very inspired by the revolutionary movement, but they were very much in need of intellectual leaders. Also, at the time, Abel was very much aware of the revolutionary mood. In Antenasher Forest, which was also known as a resort place, tourists used to come during the summer months from the surrounding towns for vacation and rest. Among them was one young man by the name of Boris. That was his pseudonym. His real name, no one knew. This fellow Boris was delegated by the revolutionary Central Committee to organize the youth of the town. He rented a room from Sarah Karabuz and told her that he was a professional Russian teacher. He taught those children that were not accepted in the public school On Saturdays, he used to take them on a hike to the Antenasher Forest, where he read stories to them and led discussions, especially on social justice issues. The brothers of those kids were also interested in the teacher's taking a hike to the forest and his reading and discussing issues that they paid much attention to. The youths were very inspired and hypnotized by his lectures. They were very much ready to revolt against the Czarist despots and to free the Jewish people and humanity from this Czarist regime. As a result of the illegal gatherings by Boris, Abel had a considerably large revolutionary circle in the small factories and workshops that regulated the working hours of the day. If an owner objected to some of these regulations, they told him that he was playing with fire.

All the illegal meetings were held in the forests. The group of revolutionaries dressed themselves as peddlers that go to villages to sell some products. Sometimes they spoke to the peasants about the hard times they endured under the Czarist regime. At the head of the Freedom Committee were two very capable men--Shmuel Itzke and Motke, sons of Beres Notes, the cotton maker. Before they became involved in social issues, they were students of the Dvinsker Yeshiva. They became very dedicated to the coming revolution with all their heart and strength.

In 1905, before the uprising, they were in contact with the "Sabatcher" comrades, and together they planned an uprising in the area. The first insurrection appeared in the marketplace. There was a very large stone on which they placed a red flag and they used it as a platform for the speakers. The peasants came to the market area to pay attention and listen to the speakers.

Beres' sons, Shmuel Itzke and Motke, were the main speakers that, with their aggressive speeches, aroused most of the attended crowd against the Czarist regime. The Lithuanian writer from the town's administrative office, Chutzke, was known to be a very able orator. He ended his speeches with the slogan: "Let's revolt--the time has come!"

The speeches had such a great influence on those that participated at the gathering that they reacted by running down to the various government offices, burned and destroyed papers, documents, and pictures that were related to Czar Nicolai and the House of Romanov.

With great courage, the peasants of Abel broke into the Monopol storage of vodka and whiskey and they were drinking without a stop. It broke into a stampede, and police started to arrive and tried to disperse the crowd, but they were afraid for their own lives and they started to run away.

A division of Cossacks was housed in a government brewery. Immediately they came running down to the area of great turmoil and were running into the crowd with their horses and swinging bayonets. The peasants resisted, but they were weak against an armed militia. There were many victims that had to be hospitalized and many lost their lives. Most of them disappeared into the fields. The Lithuanian writer and orator, Chutzke, was killed in the stampede, and the sons of Beres ran into the town's bathhouse and managed to hide themselves and save their lives.

The police were looking for them. A peasant by the name of Tarashi, who lived on the other side of the river and was one of those that hated Jews, was helping the police to find them and others whom he called the conspirators against government. But as for the sons of Beres, they were not able to find them.

The lake in Abel

When the situation in town had settled down somewhat, some friends had prepared women's apparel for Beres' sons, in which they escaped to some unknown area in town. A fisher boat waited for them at the river and brought them to the other side of the river, and they escaped to the popular pine forest.

For a long time, no one heard anything from them. Their parents and close friends for a long time did not know their fate. One morning when Yose, the sexton from the "Misnagdim" synagogue was delivering the mail (he was also the mailman), he delivered a letter to Beres with foreign postage. The letter was from their sons in America. A gush of happy tears ran through Beres' face. There was celebration and joy by their parents and their friends.

In their letters that they had written to their parents and close friends, they complained that they were missing the active life of Abel, and fate had brought them to a land where they were not able to live according to their ideals and aspirations. In their letters of later years, they wrote that they got involved in scientific studies, and they became medical doctors, and they were very much respected in American medical circles.

Among the revolutionaries of 1905 were also: Eidel Zakshtein, Chaye's son, and Yankel Snieg. Because of persecution by Czarist Russia, they emigrated to foreign countries. Yankel Snieg at the time emigrated to Africa. He died the fourteenth of April 1952. He was very much involved and dedicated to the Rakishker Society. In recognition of his dedication and hard work, the Society honored him to be a lifelong president. He was president until the end of his life.

Years passed on. Until the First World War, the face of the town had not changed much. The Russian revolution of 1905 was crushed by strong armed forces and by large hordes of Cossacks. It appeared the year 1914. War had erupted. The turmoil was unheard of. Most people felt desperate and depressed. People did not know what to do--run away to some far away village, or to leave Russia. It was hard to leave, to part, from the very little that they had accumulated over the years. But the command of Nicolai Nicolieavitch-- the Czar's uncle, that Jews had to be deported from the front lines, ended all hesitations and suspicions.

People felt bad and not too well under the created situation. The peasants spread rumors that Jews were spies. "Karusia," the water porter, with her "lover," reported to the Police Commissioner that they had seen a German airplane land at Velvele the Lessees' backyard; and that Velvele had packed the plane with butter, cheese, and milk. The Commissioner believed them, calling Velvele every day to be investigated. The Jews of the town were observing it, and they understood that these were meaningless spy reports that could be made against them. Therefore, they decided to evacuate to Russia.

The Jews were running to the villages to buy horses to be able to leave fast enough. They were, at the time, afraid to travel in the trains, because the Cossacks killed Jews and raped women. More than three-quarters of the Jewish population evacuated themselves. Only one-quarter remained in town, hiding themselves in their homes and in the cellars. My father also bought two large horses and loaded a wagon with the most needed things that he sent away with the first transport to Dvinsk. A day later, my father came back to town and took the rest of the things and family, and left empty and hollow walls.

We were four of us: my parents, my brothers and myself. I remember I was sitting zipped in a warm fur coat, riding through muddy roads, and a cold nasty wind was blowing from the fields and forest. My father was very restless. At sunset, father said that the red-radiant stripes in heaven are the witness to tremendous shedding of blood. In Novo Alexanderovsk, they dragged young people to dig trenches. My father put a dress on me so that they wouldn't grab me for work. We got tired of dragging our horse and wagon endlessly, so we decided to go back to Abel.

The German cavalry came galloping into town, The Jews that remained started coming out of their hiding places. We started to adjust ourselves to the German government. They began to establish a civil administration, with a Jewish mayor, whose name was Moishe Zakshtein. They arranged forced labor. The mayor, Moishe Sakshtein, was running around the streets every day, wearing special-fit trousers and boots, holding a long leather whip. With the passing of days, the Jewish mayor became more demanding, even using the whip against friends and elderly Jews. The local forced-labor was not too rugged, but some Jews were sent to special work camps, and I was among them. We had many hardships there; it was really bad. With brutal regulations, the Germans were treating us. They did not feed us well, and they even used to beat us with wooden sticks, and they also gave us the most unbearable hard-working conditions, like unloading railroad cars with rails, laying them out, and screwing them together. We also had to load some railroad cars with rocks, and also did ground digging. The work camp stretched a Russian "viorst" (equal to 0.66 of our mile) which was fenced around with heavy barbed wire. The exit tower was heavily armed from both sides.

It was impossible to exist in the camp. I was looking for a way to free myself from this slave camp. One early morning, I went to a doctor and complained that I was sick. He examined me and in an angry voice shouted: "Farfluchte Yude" (Damn Jew). I will make you real sick." He started to beat me with a stick. Under a strict vigilant guard they sent me back to the slave-camp. Looking at my failure, I was earnestly thinking of running away. It was the time of the Jewish holiday weeks (Shavuot) and we had a deluge that flooded the camp. Vicious winds were blowing all around us. At that time, I decided to get away from this evil place. It was two o'clock during a very dark night. Me and two of my friends slowly opened the door from the barracks and listened to the steps of the guard. We ran over to the toilet that was close to the fence, and we separated some of the barbed wires to create an opening. We managed to get away to a nearby forest with our last strength. From there we got to our homes.

Jews endured hard and bitter times in our town under the German occupation. We suffered great deprivation under the so-called tolerant Willhelm's heel.

The First World War came to an end, and the Germans left Lithuania. It was the beginning of a new era. Homeless Jews deep down in Russia started returning to their former homes. At the brewery building, the Lithuanian government started a quarantine that reflected the tragic events of the Jewish people. The quarantine was fenced around with hard barbed wire, and a military guard was there day and night. The treatment of the Lithuanian government towards the returning Jews was far from friendly. Every one of them was being investigated. They were looking, thinking perhaps that they would find some "communist" cell among them. Any intervention on their part did not help. Many months passed by until they freed all Jews from being quarantined. The sanitary condition was also very bad. There was a breakout of an epidemic of typhoid that spread to all barracks around the brewery.

The Drama Circle

From right standing: Chaya Sarah Gordon, Horovitz, Yankel Kaplan, Chana Friedman, and Moishe Klavir. From right sitting: Fannie Klas, Horovitz, Bacia Friedman, Riva Yoselevitz, and Elie Klas.

The Jewish National Committee of Kovno started its own effective medical help to stop the epidemic outbreak. Many Jews at the town's quarantine at Abel lost their lives and were buried at the old cemetery of Abel.

All Jews that came from their evacuation brought with them a different spirit, a more creative spirit for culture and progress. Before the Lithuanian government had reconstructed themselves, the town was administered by a Soviet regime. The Jewish youth was very active in a Soviet board. They organized a fire department, a civil administration, and a town militia. The Soviet board opened the first cooperative at Zalman Meiler's house. This was of great help to the Jewish population, which was poverty stricken and now able to buy produce and other articles for reasonable, stable prices.

In 1920 they organized a Culture League. The initiators were: Israel Zak, Benjamin Zak, Heske Zakshtein, and Moishke Zakshtein. The work was conducted with great enthusiasm. The club-local was always packed with young people at the time when there was a recitation or lecture by our writers and poets. The lecturers were: Benjamin Zak and Yankl Zweigarn. But the older members of the Culture League did not have any interest in getting closer to the younger friends and did not get their attention. The younger people separated themselves from the elderly group and organized a new culture league under the name "Youth Center." Among the leaders were: Moishe Klavir, David Halpern, Nachemka Feitels, and Chaye Sara Gordon. They organized a library and evening courses. The teachers of the evening courses were: Chanah Friedman, Yankl Zweigarn and David Halpern. Almost all of the youth in town joined the "youth group."

The Scouts in Abel

In 1923 the "Culture League" was closed by the Lithuanian government, as they suspected them to be "left" oriented. In its place, they organized a Jewish folk-library, which became the town's cultural center. They also organized a drama circle under the name "The Dramatic Section part of the Abeler Jewish library." The first amateurs were: Bashke Friedman, Moishe Klavir, Nachemke Feitels, Baruch Elke Feitels, Shmuel Bams, Chaneke Friedman, Rivke Malies, and Yisraelke Michalewitch who for a time directed some of the plays and also participated in serious roles. The plays were held mostly in a barrack that the Germans put up during the war years at Itze Zelig's garden. The income from the shows was used for the library expenses.

For a short time the library was enriched with Yiddish and Hebrew books that were able to culturally enrich a larger Jewish population than Abel had at that time. Abel had no Yiddish school. They opened a "Tarbut school" (Hebrew language school) under the leadership of Michal Kuperman. At first, he was the only teacher and director, but later the National Board sent in some teachers from Kovno. It also opened a Lithuanian language school in the old monopole building, and Jewish children were obligated to learn the Lithuanian language.

The first convention of "Chalutzim" (Pioneers) from Rakishok and vicinity that was held in Abel

In 1923, a Jewish communal board was formally organized that had to oversee all Jewish events in town. The first board members were: Leibe Zakshtein, Zalman Mehler, Baruch Kadish, and others. From year to year, the spiritual and cultural life greatly progressed. It formed a strong National Jewish movement. Among the youth groups, there was a splitting into different views and aspirations. There were such groups as: Tsofim (Scouts), Social Zionists, Young Zionists, General Zionists, and Chalutzim (Pioneers). The most active of the groups was the (Chalutzim) Pioneers. Most of them went to various farms to prepare themselves to be fit for work in Israel. The heads of the Chalutzim were: Lipke Friedman, Ziamke Friedman, Baruch Elke Klas, Moyshe Klavir, and Mayerke Klavir. They were very dedicated and created a strong Chalutzim movement.

Since the time that the Lithuanian government adopted a reactionary attitude towards the Jews and they abolished the Jewish National Board, the youthful elements became very discouraged and felt that under that government they could not expect great things to happen in future endeavors. The time became ripe to emigrate. They began to emigrate to various foreign countries. Only a small group of the youth remained until the beginning of the Second World War, and was actively involved in communal and cultural endeavors that were part of life.

The continuation of Jewish life was shattered with the coming of the Germans. A black dead curtain was covered over the Jews in Abel that had lived a more progressive life. The bestial Nazis in the first days of occupation destroyed many of the small Jewish towns and, likewise, Abel that counted about 300 families.

Abel is close to the Lithuanian border and is 60 viorst from Dvinsk, and fell the first victim from the German invasion. In haste, the Jews took with them the little they possessed and ran. Families with small children were at nights in muddy fields and on roads, hoping to find some alternative. But the German parachutists and the Lithuanian fascists attacked them on the roads whenever they found them. The chapters of the Psalms that the elderly people were uttering as prayers didn't help. Wild Lithuanian peasants, led by the Germans, attacked them on the roads and in town. From the panicky condition in the nearby towns, most of them started running in great fear to Abel. There, together with the Jews in Abel, they were all taken to the Antenasher Forest where they were in a gruesome way tortured to death.

A devastating storm has destroyed the generations-old town of Abel, with its roots. In the deep ground of our brothers graves lie our parents, brothers and sisters, relatives, and all our dear ones--our kind and sincere Jews of Abel who were in a vicious way snuffed out by the wicked Nazis and fascist Latvians. With deep sorrow and pain we must remember our killed martyrs. That was their will.

Characters of Abeler Jews

Elieyuhu Gordon

When Elieyuhu Gordon came to Abel, the people named him "The Moskver." A long time before the Japanese war, he lived illegally in Moscow. He was a merchant, a very wise man, and a great Talmudic scholar. He saw to it that his children got an education in a religious Judaic spirit.

The brutal Czarist government released a decree against those that had no "living right" in Moscow, and must leave the city by a certain date. The police immediately notified all those that at the given date, they must leave; otherwise they would be arrested. A lot of Jews were forced out of the city, and among them Elieyuhu Gordon. Fate brought Elieyuhu Gordon to the town of Abel. At first, it was very hard for him to adjust to a small muddy town. With the passage of time, he adjusted himself to the town and its people. Especially being a very sympathetic person, he gained many friends and during the years he endured in the town of Abel. He became one of the well-known personalities of the town.

One daughter, Chaye Sarah, became a Russian teacher and the second daughter, Dobre, opened a dry goods store that within time did very well. He himself used to assemble all the freight bills by the merchants and made the payments at the train office. He earned a certain percentage for his endeavor.

In the evenings, "Reb Elieyuhu" spent most of his time looking into some Talmudic books. He was a Chasid outwardly and inwardly. He wore a beautiful Chasidic garment with a silk belt and his gray-white patriarchal beard gave him that Chasidic charm. Years passed on, but his hatred against Czarist Russia remained with him, because of their vicious decree against the Jews who were forced to leave the large cities. When the Japanese war broke out, he was of the opinion that Russia would lose, because Nicolai was a weakling, had a head of an ox, and glass eyes of an idiot. Later, when Russia lost the war to Japan, Reb Elieyuhu Gordon, or as he was called, "Elieyuhu the Moskver," was in "seventh heaven," and among groups of Jews he said that he had foreseen the downfall of Russia as a result of their King Nicolai "who is a weakling, an idiot, and has glass eyes."

Mendl Klatzkin

Mendl Klatzkin was known in Abel as "Mendl the Attorney." He was a son of a Rabbi. His father had a position as a Rabbi in the town of Anishishok, but Mendl did not follow the rabbinic position of his father. He was fascinated by the enlightenment movement of those days. During the daytime hours, his father taught him Talmudic scriptures. During the night hours, Mendl used to isolate himself without anyone knowing that he was reading secular books.

Against his father's wishes, he visited a Russian high school and also entered a jurisprudence faculty to study law, but he did not accomplish his goal. He later married Zalman Meller's daughter and moved to Abel, interrupting his studies. Yet, his town crowned him with the name, "Mendl the Attorney." First, he looked like a lawyer, and resembled the well-known Gruzenberg, who defended the accused Beilis. He used to help people when they were in need of a lawyer. For some reason, he had some influence on the local administration.

It once happened that Mendl the "attorney" wanted to fool Reb Elieyuhu the Moskver on the first of April, so he sent him the following telegram: "I, the imperialist of the country of Russia, happened by incident to look through the protocols of the decree of Moscow, and not finding any accusation against you, I allow you at present to settle in Moscow or any other city beyond the Pale of Assignment to Jews. With friendly greetings, Nicolai Romanov."

Elieyuhu, listening to the message, was so ecstatic, that he ran among Jewish circles and told them: "Well Jews! What are you saying now? Is it possible that Nicolai, the ox head himself, should for me abolish the decree? It really could have happened by such a tyrant, that he is now being repentant, which I consider a miracle from the Almighty."

The news spread like a storm throughout the town. Leibe the sexton from the synagogue of the "Misnagdim," a Jew with all sorts of assumptions, thought it was perhaps a signal that better times are coming for our people. The "fire fighters" were not so sure about the telegram. People working in various places stopped working and came to the streets; women at the street corners started gossiping. The whole town of Abel went on wheels. Most people thought it was a second miracle of Purim.

Israel Chiyois

Israel Chiyois was a hard working man, a very honest and good human being. His eyes always smiled in a friendly way, expressing love to everyone. As a rule, he was a quiet and easygoing man, and seldom did he speak in a loud voice with the exception of the evening services, or when he was reciting the Psalms. In a high voice, he started the Psalms prayers so that everyone understood that he had a hidden strength. Also, in the bathhouse he raised his voice. He was the only massager, and he considered that to be his trade. He used his strength to bring his clients up to the higher benches, where the steam was hotter, and with his hard brush and soap he used to massage his people.

From the bathhouse, he used to leave sweaty, and during the biggest snowfall he used to roll in the snow to cool himself.

The Almighty has endowed him with good health and a strong body. Friday, before the beginning of the Sabbath, he went around town with his horse and wagon delivering sand to Jewish homes to spread on the floors. It happened sometimes, when the wagon went into a thick muddy area and his horse was unable to move the wagon, that Israel went down from his wagon and used his arms to push it; and, when the horse began to feel his helping hands, they were able to get out of the dense mud.

There was talk in the town that Israel Chiyois was freed from serving in the Russian army as a result of pulling several teeth from his mouth using a pair of pliers. He used to be a heavy eater. In one meal, he was able to finish a five-pound black bread with a few herring, holding the head of the herring in one hand and the tail in the other hand. After that he guzzled down 10 glasses of water.

I remember once coming into Israel's house, which was at the end of the town neighboring with Bertzig's house, next to the road and in the vicinity that led to the Stashuntzer forest. He was at that time lubricating the wheels of his wagon. Coming into his house, he took a large radish and cut it into pieces and put some salt on it. His wife, the short-grown Chaya, served him a large plate of soup, and she threw in hard pieces of bread. After such a meal, he said the meal blessing and kissed the door mezuzah and took a sack on his head and went out to harness his horse and wagon. He had a lot of trades, but he was still a poor man. But on Saturday he still found a challah on his table.

Although his was a poor material life, in his home there was contentment, and they had a strong faith in the Almighty. He lived to an old age. The last time I saw him, he was already a very old man. I asked him, how do you feel Reb Israel? His answer was: "Oh, my son, times have changed. There is no more the years of the past, when for my streng th the ground under me was trembling. Now, I tremble against the earth."

An Abel family: Nacham Zeligman and his wife, and two sons, Shimon and Heshke.

The Drama Circle. From right standing: Chaya Sarah Gordon, Horovitz, Yankel Kaplan, Chana Friedman, and Moishe Klavir. From right sitting: Fannie Klas, Horovitz, Bacia Friedman, Riva Yoselevitz, and Elie Klas.

[Pages 292 - 295]

My Hometown Kamay[*]
(Kamajai, Lithuania)

55°49' N 25°30'

by Binyamin-Michel Hurwitz
Translated by Gloria Berkenstat Freund

Benjamin Michel Hurwitz

Kamay is a distance of 22 km from Rakishok (Rokiskis) and 12 km from Ponemunok; 17 km from Sviadashits, from Uzpaliai 24 km and from Dusiat 28 km. There is a river that flows into the Vilye, and nearby flows Lake Petrastzik and the wide and beautiful Lake Saol. A beautiful landscape spreads out around the *shtetl*, with large and thick forests, which are ringed by the villages of Ruzh, Navar and others.

The Jews farmed the lakes and they alone caught the fish, which gave them a livelihood. The fishermen Moishe and Zundel were particularly well known.

Before the First World War, 65 Jewish families were counted in Kamay. Trade was in Jewish hands--there was not one Christian shop. There were very few craftsmen, only two blacksmiths, 2-3 tailors, two shoemakers, two glaziers, and two shingle-makers. There was one Christian wigmaker. None of the craftsmen were experts. For the most part, when one wanted to have a proper garment made, he traveled to Rakishok, which was sort of a metropolis compared to Kamay.

There were peddlers and a few local merchants. Several supplied eggs to Riga. There were a couple of inns. *Klezmorim* (musicians) were brought from Rakishok for weddings. The mail was handled by a Jew.

There were no doctors in the *shtetl*, but there was a *feldsher* (barber-surgeon), who was named Chaim Shalom. He would give a diagnosis of catarrh (inflamed mucous membranes) for every illness. He later became Kamay's official rabbi. He would make the remedies for the sick himself. This caused resentment with the pharmacist in town, Yoshe Ber Garber, the Meshtzanker. [Translator's note: Meshtzanker is a derogatory or ironic use of the Slavic word which denotes a resident of a city as opposed to one who lives in a village. In this case it implies one who gives himself the air of someone who lives in the big city, but actually is just one of the "plain folk."]

It happened that Yoshe Ber denounced Haim Shalom to the government and he was arrested. However, Haim Shalom was a Jew, a *tzadek* (righteous man) and very distinguished in Kamay. A stir was created in the entire town and in the end, he was freed. Both the Jews and the Christians were infuriated by Yoshe Ber and this forced him to emigrate to America. After his departure, a Lithuanian took over the pharmacy.

The shopkeepers and craftsmen waited for the market and the annual fair. If the fair fell on a *Shabbos*, it was postponed to another day of the week. The peasants from the town and the surrounding areas were also concerned that the annual fair not take place on a day when the Jews would be unable to trade.

Only a few Jews were rich. The remainder was a poor mass of people. The greatest paupers were Leibe-Mote and Shlomoh Glezer.

Poverty was great in Kamay because of the frequent fires. The fires would occur because flax was made in the houses. The largest fire occurred in 1915. Almost the entire *shtetl* [burned] down. The poor who lost property did not have a roof over their heads. The neighboring towns such as Rakishok and others immediately sent help for the suffering Jews.

There was a time when one lived in great fear of a pogrom, mainly at the time of military conscriptions. The gentile recruits would get drunk and break Jewish windowpanes.

Once, in such uneasy days, a young Jew shot from an attic and hit a gentile child. There was a great panic in the town. All of the authorities from Rakishok came together to investigate, but the guilty one vanished.

It happened that three village gentiles came to Kamay, in order to carry out a pogrom in the town. The Jews called out the Cossacks, who drove away the peasants.

Half of the [people in the] *shtetl* were Chasidim and half were *Misnagdim* (opponents of Chasidism). There were 2 *shuls* and 1 large *shul*, in which there was *davening* only on the Days of Awe. For years the large *shul* was unfinished: without a ceiling and without a floor.

The *Misnagdim* Rabbi was Reb Leizer Luft. He gave lessons in *Talmud* and had a kind of *Yeshiva* in which 30 children [from outside of Kamay] studied, who "*habn gegesn tayg.*" [Translator's note: were invited to residents' homes for a day of meals.] The Birzer Rebbe, Reb Yitzhak Agulnik, studied at this Kamayer *Yeshiva* during his early years.

Before Leizer Luft, Rabbi Elihu Gordon sat in the rabbinical chair. Rabbi Gordon's son, Hirshe Leib, now lives in America and writes often for the weekly periodical, "*Der Amerikaner*" ("The American").

Later, Rabbi Leizer Luft's successor was his brother-in-law, Yisroel Zisel Dvartz, who is now a bank officer in Israel. The successor to Rabbi Yisroel Zisel Dwartz was the Rabbi Reb Meir Fein. He is now in America. Rabbi Leib Tiger, who perished at the hands of the Hitleristic hangmen, was the town rabbi in the final years.

The Chasidic rabbi for a long time was the old man Reb Leib. There were two *shoykhetim* (ritual slaughterers): Abraham Leib on the Chasidic side and Shlomoh – from the *Misnagdim* (opponents of Chasidism). Later the *shoykhetim* were Efrayim Zilber and Benzion Shkliar. There were often quarrels among the Chasidim.

I remember there often occurred an appeal because there was no money to buy wood. One was wont to take away the *talisim* (prayer shawls) during the *Shabbos* prayers, in order to coerce contributions for wood and for repairs for the *shul*, or *lhavdl* (Translator's note: word used to separate something sacred from something profane) the bathhouse.

There were *chederim* (religious schools), *Bes Medroshim* (synagogues), a *Chevra Kadisha* (burial society). The principle workers of the *Chevra Kadisha* were: Zorah Elihu Zilber and Kaleb Sapozhnik. They would take pledges of burial money. The *melamdim* (teachers) of the *chederim* included: Manish, Leizer-Zalman, Bencie, Hirshe. Manish was a *Gemara-melamed* (teacher of the *Gemara* – the discussions on the Talmud), and when he died, all of the shops were closed. Leizer-Zalman was a sort of modern *melamed*.

Magidim (preachers) would often come to the *shtetl*. It is recalled how a *magid* came and gave a *drosh* (sermon) at random to the world, without a *tefilin* (phylacteries) strap and without any content, and at the end he called out: "Gentlemen, I planted cucumbers and they did not grow, and now I preach because I have to make a living."

The words of the *magid* moved everyone and everyone contributed to him, in order to help him.

Although there were simple people in the *shtetl*, they made an effort to educate their children. Simple Jews had fine children, *Bney Torah* (scholars). Even the bathhouse attendant had a son who was a scholar.

Kamayer Jews woke up at dawn in order to go to *shul*. Leizer the Kamayer, who was called the *Tilim-Yid* (the Jew who said Psalms) because he could say nothing more than Psalms, was known in the area. At the end, he lived in Rakishok, and one would meet him saying Psalms in the street or in his home.

Good hearted Jews lived in Kamay. They helped each other with interest-free loans. There were pious women who would go out among the houses with baskets to help make *Shabbos* for the poor people. On Passover, no Jew would receive his matzoh from the matzoh bakery until he had paid his alms to provide Passover needs for the poor.

The school in Kamay

There was barely any modern cultural-communal life before the First World War. Just like Sholem Aleichem's hero Zeidl, in Kasrilevka, there was one subscriber in the shtetl to *Hatzfire*. [A Hebrew periodical published in Warsaw from 1862 to 1931.] His name was Pesakh Shreier, who had the nickname, "*Der Meshugener*" (the crazy one). There was a small library in the home of Barukh Hurvitz. And there was a group of Zionists. Yisroel Ziel Dwartz traveled as a delegate from Mizrachi [a religious Zionist organization] to the Zionist Congress, and when he returned, he brought with him from the outside a "thermos." This was a surprising invention for Kamay.

The revolution in 1905 also made a mark in Kamay. The leader of the revolutionary movement in the *shtetl* was a Christian, Shmeiski Yurnish, who was a seminarian and later abandoned his religious studies.

I remember how in 1905 Shmeiski Yurnish led a large meeting at the market. Three red flags were hung in the center of the market. A great mob came together, and the Czarist Police Commissioner and three guards were surrounded by the revolutionaries, and they were forced to remove their police hats and to hold the red flag.

Later, a punishment battalion of Cossacks arrived. There was panic in the *shtetl*. The Cossacks chased after Shmeiski Yurnish, but he disappeared. The anger [of the police] was let out on his small wooden house, which was demolished by a cannon.

Shmeiski Yurgin then ran away to Switzerland and returned when the Lithuanians established their regime. He was a school administrator and a great friend of Smetana. He was later shot by Smetana's opponents.

In 1915, the Jews left Kamay because of the proximity of the Russian-German front. Only 10 Jewish families remained in their homes. They were sent to forced labor at the Rokiskis train station.

The years of the Lithuanian Republic, after the war, were marked with very intensive cultural activity; there existed a school for manners with 60 students. The [female] teacher was Yeruzalim, a Shavler girl. – Parents sent their children to study in Ponevezh and Vilkomir.

The town's carriers of culture were Haim Asher Zilber, Binyamin Michel Hurvitz, Efrayim Zilber, Benzion Shklar, Gershon Farber, Tabakhowitz (?) and others.

Later a large library opened and Zionist pioneer activity was carried out.

There are no precise details about the Holocaust in Kamay. My cousin, Elke Beier, ran from the *shtetl* at the last hour before the Germans arrived. She reported how the Lithuanian rowdies and devils had – before the arrival of the Germans – caused vexation and humiliation for the Jews and killed several Jews, too.

* I express my heartfelt thank you to Mrs. Mariashke-Palavin for this information.

[Pages 297 - 298]

A Tear in Memory of Kamay

by Peretz-Zev Hurwitz
Translated by Gloria Berkenstat Freund

Peretz Zev Hurwitz

Kamay was a Jewish *shtetl* (town), like hundreds of *shtetlech* in Jewish Lithuania.

Just as in other *shtetlech*, there were two sides [to the dispute over Judaism] in Kamay: *Chasidim* and *Misnagdim* (opponents of *Chasidism*). The *Chasidim* had their house of study, rabbi and *shochet* (ritual slaughterer) and the *Misnagdim*, too, had their clergy and prayer house, as well as a large *shul* (synagogue) in which little doves and little birds settled. Reb Leibtzik, of blessed memory, a Lubavitcher *Chasid*, was the rabbi of the *Chasidim*. He was a *tzadek gomer* [Translator's note: completely holy] and shook off all the burdens of this world.

The *shochet*, Reb Abraham Leib Atlas, of blessed memory, was an aristocratic Jew, whose son lives in America and has a position with the Reform Seminary in Cincinnati.

The *Shamas* [synagogue sexton] Reb Hirshe was a good Jew [Translator's note: literally, a good person]. Fine people were: Shimeon Smatkin, Shmuel [the son of Mendl, Welwe the son of Mend], Zalman the son of Shmuel, Yosef Ber the pharmacist, Haim Shalom the *feldsher* (old-time barber surgeon), Zelig the shopkeeper who sold hides, Pesakh Agulnik, Reb Leizer Zalman and many others.

I remember that the *misnagdim* had several rabbis. Reb Bunim Camekh, of blessed memory, whose son occupies a very distinguished place among the Orthodox in America, was from the old generation.

When the Rabbi Reb Bunim Tzamekh settled in Dusiat, the rabbinical chair was taken by Rabbi Elihu Gordon of Vidz, of blessed memory, who was a scholar and a preacher, too. He wrote many *seforim* (religious books). His two sons and two daughters are in America. One son, Dr. Hirsh Leib Gordon, is a well-known and learned doctor and the other son, Yakov Dov, occupies a rabbinical chair.

After Rabbi Elihu Gordon settled in Vilna, a young man from the Telzer *Yeshiva* (religious school of higher learning), Reb Eliezer Luft, of blessed memory, who was a great scholar and a God-fearing person, substituted for him. He was an adherent of the educational school of thought that influenced me, because I was his student.

In my time, the *Misnagdim shochet* was Reb Shlomoh – a scholar and God-fearing man. His son and daughter are in America, not far from New York.

The sextons were: Reb Mordekhai, of blessed memory, and Reb Naftala Hertz, of blessed memory. Reb Naftala Hertz was a fine *bel tfila* (person who leads the prayers). His two children are in Baltimore.

The proprietors of Kamay were: Leizer Shira Rives and his brothers Mendl and Noakh and several other families.

There were dear and sincere Jews in Kamay. The old ones died and the young generations were born. Thus was the succession of the world.

Later the younger generation spread over the world and a large number are found in South Africa, Canada and America.

Though the *shtetl* was a small one, it had much charm.

A large marketplace was in the middle of the *shtetl* and four streets stretched from it: *Shul* Street, Mil (Mill) Street, Brik (Bridge) Street and Meszczanski Street.

The tavern stood in the middle of the market like a large well-to-do proprietress.

Each street had its assignment. The *Shul* Street served to go to *daven* (pray), as well as, God forbid, to a funeral; the Bridge Street for traveling to Rakishok and to larger cities; going on Friday to the bathhouse, to stroll on *Shabbos* to Tzipuke's Forest and to the Bar Forest to gather berries, and in winter the children skated; the Mill Street for fetching water or to wash laundry in the river; Meszczanski Street – to travel to Pomenunok – to the train station, from which one traveled to Africa and America.

No trace of Kamay remains. It all perished and was erased. The survivors are spread over the entire world, where they must continue Jewish life in the Diaspora and to help build a new life in the Land of *Yisroel*.

Am Yisroel Khai! (The Jewish People Live!)

[Pages 299 - 301]

Reminiscensces of Kamay

by Tirza Franklyn-Yaffa

Translated by Gloria Berkenstat Freund

At 12 years of age, I left Kamay with my mother and sister to emigrate to South Africa. This was a Thursday in December 1938. Almost all of the Jews in the *shtetl* accompanied us to the train station. Although there was a frost outside, they all waited until we left, wishing us warm blessings – an easy trip and a safe arrival in faraway South Africa.

I remember how a woman from Natzunisk especially came to send a greeting to her friends in Africa, not knowing their name and address.

Jewish children in Kamay

My remembrances of my birthplace, Kamay, are very foggy. Yet, I remember several Kamayer Jews clearly, such as:

Efrayim the *shochet* (ritual slaughterer) slaughtered poultry and was a *melamed* (teacher), too. The students respected him greatly. The c*heder* (religious school) was across from our school, and the young *kheder* boys would run around on the little hills of garbage, which stuck out like the humps [of a hunchback];

There was another *shochet*, who was named Bentzil. He had a store, and slaughtering was a sideline for him;

The rabbi in the *shtetl*, Yehuda Leib, was a very young man, the son of a rabbi. His income came from the selling of yeast, and he received a percent of the community tax. In school, he taught us the Jewish customs and prayers. His wife was a religiously advanced *rebbitzin* (rabbi's wife) and already wore a modern *sheitl* (wig);

The *gabai* (sexton, assistant to the rabbi) of the *shul* was Aba Kil. He was a cripple, limping. I knew his daughters Sheina and Henya very well. Henya was married and had a beautiful two-year old son, Leizer Dovidl. He wore a blue woolen coat. The second daughter, Sheina, got married in Rakishok and had a dry goods store. I heard that she survived, and her brother, Ruvin, perished in the war;

I remember Moishe the *Shamas* (synagogue caretaker) and his family.

Survivors of the family of Yosel and Feiga Levin, after their return from the evacuation to Russia

More than anything else I remember the Kamayer school. We were approximately 50 male and female students. It was a preparatory school with five classes. The chief teacher was Yankele Khrit of Dusiat.

I was a student in the fourth class. The curriculum consisted of the subjects: modern Hebrew, Hebrew grammar, Jewish history, nature studies, Jewish customs and prayers, the Lithuanian language and the history of Lithuania, singing and gymnastics.

We had a beautiful school choir and we often gave performances. It was a joyous life with carefree years as children.

We children really loved the *yom-tovim* (religious holidays). Every *yom-tov* had its beauty and power of attraction.

Few Jews survived the immense and difficult catastrophe of our people.

I will list several Jews who eluded the Hitleristic harsh decrees:

Yosel and Feiga Levin, with their daughter Zelda and son-in-law Yakov, and a younger daughter Shulamit and son Mantcik; Yosel's mother-in-law with her young daughters, Pesele and with a mother and two brothers (a third brother was killed);

Berl-Leib Brikman, with his children: Beilke, Manuhahke, and Zeldele;

Aba Kil's daughter and her family;

Gershon the "Preparer" (quilter) and his wife and their family;

Elya – Itsl's daughter and her husband and family;

Yisroelke Zilber, a son of Haim Asher Zilber and a family of 11 people;

Saul and Lese Goldes;

Itzke Tudrus, who returned to Kamay after the war;

My uncle Yosel-Levin and his family.

These people and families saved themselves from death by escaping to Russia. On the eve of the arrival of the Germans, they left the *shtetl* and succeeded in running away to the Soviet Union.

However, the rest of the Jews remained in Kamay. It hurts my heart that shortly after our departure for South Africa, all of the good and pious Kamayer Jews who did nothing bad to anyone perished so tragically at the hands of the Hitlerist Fascists.

[Pages 302 - 305]

A Fair in Kamay

by B. Sachs

Translated by Gloria Berkenstat Freund

B. Sachs: well-known journalist and writer

The marketplace occupied the place of honor in the *shtetl* and was widely spread out, dominating the neighboring alleys and streets. The houses and shops that surrounded it on all sides seemed to appear humble and shrunken out of fear and regard for the great number of peasants who would come to Kamay on market days to sell their village wares and, at the same time, buy the goods they needed.

The villagers and the Kamayer traders carried out a vibrant market trade during the middle of the week. However, there was an even greater event with even more excitement when a fair would come to Kamay.

Kamay sparkled and the idyllic Jewish *shtetl* quickly changed its garb, its face. On a fair day, peasants [male and female] from the vicinity, near and far, would convene, even from villages that were 30 *versts* from Kamay. [Translater's note: a *verst* equals two-thirds of a mile.] The *shtetl* would be crammed with peasants, butchers, horse traders whose racket echoed strong and far.

The Kamayer shopkeepers did not sleep the night before a fair and were busy sorting the various articles for the next day. They sorted each article with deliberation, order and zest, so that they would tempt the customers. The various goods truly stuck out of the shelves like ripe stalks in a cornfield.

My mother was busy at the oven the entire night, baking iced and tasty cookies and bagels. She was determined that her baked goods would be the best and they were of all flavors in order to tease the nostrils, the appetite, of the fair guests. A great fire smoldered in the oven and she spread the hot glowing coals symmetrically with a poker. She rapidly began kneading the dough, which already had risen above the edges of the kneading trough, which was wrapped with old quilts.

At Rikl's "China" teahouse, they were awake at night preparing for tomorrow's income. The pot-belly copper samovar was scoured and cleaned so that it functioned well. Dozens of glasses with bowls, plates of herring; containers of whisky were secretly prepared...

Was it any wonder that the fair brought such cheerfulness and activity to Kamay? The poor *shtetl* waited for weeks for the fair, since on the day of the fair the poor Jews found it easier to earn rubles. The hope of a good income gave them courage, and worrying Jewish faces radiated with the appearance of a bright morning.

The peasants, too, prepared for the road during the night. Each of them considered which cattle they should sell, either the one with the turned up nose or the anxious cow, which pig and ox and how many measures of rye and which poultry. They cleaned the legs of the cattle with straw and they fed them potatoes and barley.

During the night before the fair they did not sleep, and before the cock crowed, all of the sleds were filled with wheat, eggs, chickens, etc. Cows and calves, oxen, pigs and goats were firmly tied to the harnesses with ropes and they went silently after the peasants in their coarse brown woolen coats and in heavy pelts, step after step. Peasant women in their sandals and high-healed shoes, with wicker baskets in their hands, wrapped with red woolen shawls and in wide petticoats and in linen aprons, which were adorned with red borders of knitting wool, prudently and compliantly followed, as in a caravan. When dawn began to break, the pace accelerated and the horses and livestock were driven with spirit, in order to arrive at the great Kamayer fair in time.

The buying and selling between the Kamay merchants and the peasants began at the turns in the road and at the edge of the *shtetl*. Jewish traders waited in advance and they immediately made a connection. Arguing, bargaining, gesturing with their hands and swearing all the false oaths in the world. Bickering started that was louder than the squealing of the pigs and the quacking of the chickens and geese.

The congestion and screaming in the market place grew greater and greater and among the Jewish market traders, Yankel the prankster distinguished himself in the tumult by telling a spicy story about Africa and the black Africans who reached 60 feet in height and had only one eye in their forehead. Although the ice-frosty snow tugged at the fur-wearing peasant who clapped one booted foot to the other in order to warm himself, the story of Africa and of the frightening African snakes and scorpions held him.

The fair was spread out on all the streets and alleys, on all of the *shtetl's* rows and courts. Many poor people and beggars swarmed around and there were street musicians and blind village troubadours who begged and repeated monotonous heartbreaking melodies, one after the other, on all kinds of instruments, from a barrel organ to a whistle.

These melodies drew clusters of peasants and also tall Aleksei, the proprietor of the brickyard that was located 6 *verst* from Kamay. Aleksei pushed apart the surrounding peasants with his fists, made a place for himself and began to dance the *kazatska* with authentic peasant-like rage so that the ground shook. His high spirits exhilarated the remaining peasants, who strongly applauded him, drowning out the heartbreaking melodies of the troubadours and the street musicians.

Aleksei was considered the strongest peasant in the area, and all would shake in deadly fear of him. He loved to march in with his gang of peasants to the thicket of the fair and everyone would give way for him. He would be avoided particularly when he was as drunk as Lot.

Jews sold whisky surreptitiously. Hanaka, a short woman was involved in that, too. She would bribe the Russian officer (policeman) so that he would pretend ignorance.

She was afraid to sell whisky to Aleksei, because when he became drunk, he created a scandal and with his feet he knocked down Hanaka's door, cursing her with ugly words, asking why she would not sell him more and more whisky.

Because of this she took care not to sell Aleksei any vodka.

Although Aleksei's wife was of short stature with flaxen hair and blue eyes, she had power over him and when she would see him drunk, she would slap his face. Then he meekly pulled his fur cap over his eyes and shuffled away from the thicket of the fair in the direction of the bridge, accompanied by the loud whistling and laughter of the peasants.

There were many colorful incidents during the fair. There was no absence of scuffles and in the courtyards lay around many drunk peasants who drooled and wheezed wildly and crazily.

Only when evening fell did the excitement diminish. For the most part, the peasants departed.

But in Rikl's "China" the peasants drank vodka in public, singing folksongs, accompanied by a harmonica.

The peasants' horses stood tied to the "China's" fence and rummaged in the snow and gasped from boredom and tiredness. On the ground, near the wagons, one could notice a drunk peasant lying on the filthy snow, with a naked, disheveled chest, gesticulating drunkenly and babbling chopped up, unintelligible talk.

Only when the Russian police officer appeared late in the evening, around eleven o'clock, did "China" become empty of peasants. Drunk peasants left the teahouse, shaking at the order of the policeman, and among the clods of snow, they barely found their way to the harnessed horses.

The horses moved from the spot and the sounds of the bells merged with the notes of the melodies from the intoxicated peasants in the sleds, who lay there like lambs.

Because they feared the drunken curses, the Jews closed their shutters and firmly bolted their doors. The earnings for the day were counted and recounted by the light of a smoking lamp or a tallow candle.

Children were not yet asleep either, their sleep disturbed by the excitement of the tumultuous day. They told each other of interesting episodes during the passing of the day, and they drooled with enthusiasm, especially when they spoke about Hirshke the fisherman, who had fought with six Lithuanian peasants in the market and how he bloodied each of them.

Hirshke's strength teased their childish fantasies and, with the distant echo of the bells of the parting peasants and the quiet sound of the counting of the coins, they fell asleep on the hard floor, dreaming of Hirshke, the strongest Jew in the *shtetl*....

[Page 306]

Novo-Alexandrovsk-Exerenay-Zarasay

Reminiscences of the Old Home
(Zarasai, Lithuania)

55°44' N 26°15'

By Nisn Sacks, Moyshe Sharp-Saltuper, and Pinye Albert

Translated by Harry Abramowitz

Until the First World War, Novoalexandrovsk was the administrative town of Rakishok and many other villages and settlements. When Alexander III traveled with his entourage from Moscow to Kovno, he renamed the town "Novoalexandrovsk." [6]

Since the time of the Lithuanian king Gedimin, the town had been called Ezros. "Ezros" is a Lithuanian word that signifies "lakes." Because of the tsarist tendency to Russianize, they changed the name from Ezros to Novoalexandrovsk. In honor of the above-mentioned Czar Alexander III, a monument was erected to stand for generations in memory of his visit. It was a pole of cast iron – about 50 feet high – and on the top there was the Russian eagle. After WWI, when the Lithuanians took over Lithuania (1918), they renamed the town "Ezhereni" (Ezeranai). Later, in the 1930s, they renamed the town "Zarasai."

The scenery of Novoalexandrovsk is remarkably beautiful. Besides the lakes, there are also forests. The beauty of the surroundings was compared to the beauty of Switzerland. It was not for nothing that president Smetona called the town and its surroundings "The Lithuanian Switzerland." But in Lithuania our native town was known as "The Lithuanian Siberia," because it was colder there than elsewhere in the country. People used to come there during the winter to skate on the frozen lakes.

No caption. On photograph: Ezerenai [photographer: M. Botvimika]

Novoalexandrovsk was very near to the border of Latvia - only a few versts - and Dvinsk was only 24 versts away. Through the town of Novoalexandrovsk there was a chaussée [road], which led on one side to Utian and on the other side to Dvinsk. This road led also to the little towns of Solok, Dusiat, Ushpol and Taragin. The Polish border was also near, only 14 km away. The Tormond railway station was the Lithuanian-Polish border at the time of Poland's liberation.

Under czarist rule, the population of the town was about 5,000. The Jewish citizens numbered about 2,500. In the town there also lived Poles, Lithuanians and "staroveries" ("old believers"), who were Orthodox Christians.

The Jewish inhabitants lived mainly in the center of the town, in the main streets. There the homes of the shopkeepers adjoined their shops. The Jews settled on the main street, on the chaussée, where there were also inns, near the butchers' shops on the Aristocratic street, on the Tailor street, in the little suburb of Petranishek, downhill near the lake, in Saltupa, beyond the bridge.

The Jews tried to earn a living in many ways. That's why they had various incomes. There were a considerable number of shopkeepers, merchants, colporteurs [book sellers], wagon-drivers and tradesmen: blacksmiths, carpenters, shoemakers, tailors, makers of felt boots and others. There were also a number of seamstresses, who made ready-to-wear clothes, which they supplied to the shopkeepers. In the town and surroundings Dovid the Tandetnik was known for the ready-to-wear ladies' coats he made. There were Jewish fishmongers and fishermen who would catch fish in the lakes. Yoyne Zisl Lonshteyn had a permit to catch fish in one lake. The biggest shop-keepers were Artshik Tsimerman, Leybe Mikhoels, Yisroel Troyb, Leybe

Glikman, Meyer Leyzer Plat, who had a grocery shop as well as a bottle store, because he was a merchant of the first guild. The widow Broyman, with her two sons and daughters, managed a big enterprise. They sold galoshes and groceries, and also had a refreshment shop.

The following merchants were also known: Bertshik Shteyman, Boris Daytsh, who traded in flax and grain; Yerakhmiel Levin, Shloyme Fligl, Avrom Okun, who were timber-merchants; Avrom Tshertkover, who was reckoned a well-to-do man. He possessed 10 desatins of land (1 desatina = 2.7 acres). The island and the lake were his property, and he tried to build a datcha [country house] there.

A street in Novo-Alexandrovsk

The market was the main source of earnings. Big market-days were Tuesdays and Fridays. On Sundays, there was intensive trading with the farmers who used to come to town from the villages. Two big fairs were arranged yearly: one in winter and one in summer. The fair lasted a couple of days. Trade took place in flax, ladder [??] and pigs' bristles, and agricultural products. There were also gentile traders who had stands and sold bread and various fatty items. The "Starovery" dealt in groceries. The Jewish traders did their trade with the aristocracy, who were mainly Polish.

Before World War I, Novoalexandrovsk was considered to be a progressive trading town. Unrest used to break out at the time of military mobilization, which was carried out in Novoalexandrovsk since it was the administrative town of the surrounding lands. Newly mobilized soldiers came from little towns and villages throughout the district. With the newly mobilized, the parents, brothers and sisters also came to town. Newly mobilized drunken Christians would walk unsteadily all over the town, frightening the Jewish population. The newly mobilized Jews obviously did not willingly agree to serve with these gentiles. Jewish parents accompanied their children to the mobilization commissions with sighs and cries.

The year 1905, during the Russian revolution, was a restless period. During this period, the Jewish Bund and Social Revolutionary parties played an active part against the Czar's regime. In Novoalexandrovsk, the Russian officials and the police threatened the Jewish inhabitants with pogroms.

Parade of firemen on Vilkomirer Street in Ezerenai

An important revolutionary of those days was a man named Motl, whose family name we do not remember. He once got up on the "bima" in the synagogue demanding that there should be no prayer for the Czar. He unfolded a red flag, saying, "This flag will remove the bloody Czar Nicholas II." Once Motl and the cobbler Meyer Krut organized a demonstration on a Saturday afternoon. They marched all along the chaussée singing revolutionary songs in Russian and Yiddish. Half of the Jewish population took part in that demonstration.

A meeting was arranged in Shteyman's orchard. The main speaker was Mine (Motl's sister), who was a seamstress. At that meeting the speakers were both Jews and non-Jews. Mine held a red flag and asked the demonstrators, "How long will Jews live only in specially designed areas like ghettos and not be allowed even to travel to Moscow?" In the middle of the meeting mounted police came and hit those assembled with special whips. They beat the demonstrators very severely. A couple of hundred were arrested. But the revolutionary youth were not intimidated and they continued to arrange meetings.

Arke, the son of Alter the Baker, once called for a meeting on the Island. Police came and arrested Arke. They led him to prison with a cracked skull. It was at the time of the Beylis case and times were generally restless. The Jews were having a very difficult time. Rumours spread that the Christian Russian population wanted to make a pogrom on the Jewish inhabitants. The leader of the pogrom makers was the Starover Semyon Kholopov. No pogrom, however, took place at that time, because the pristav (the head of the Russian administration of the gubernia) Popov was successfully bribed to stop it.

The hospital in Novo-Alexandrovsk

At all times the Jews strived for their children to get a good Jewish education.

Up to World War I, this education was purely religious. Only after World War I the Jewish education in the shtetl was in the spirit of Zionism and the national-religious foundations were established. Before World War I, there were absolutely no modern schools, either in Yiddish or Hebrew. There were only cheders. There were the following cheder teachers: Bertsik Maklaner, the Talmud teacher, who after World War I became a rabbi; Yisroel-Meir Ikhiltshik, whose son, Yehude-Tsvi Ikhiltshik, is a well-known musician who has for years lived in Johannesburg; Avrom-Moshe Ikhiltshik; Yoshe Ikhitshik; and the Hebrew teacher Moyshe Leyb.

There were some exceptions, with a few Jewish children who studied in the Russian schools, in "Yevreyskoye utshilishtshe" (Jewish school), and in the three classes "gorodskoye utshilishtshe" (town/state school). Apart from the above-mentioned teachers, there were also Itse der Taytsh ("Itskhak the German"), who taught his pupils to write, and Khaye the letter-writer, who wrote letters and addresses for girls and women whose husbands or fiancés had emigrated. There was also a Talmud Torah school. The teachers of the Talmud Torah were Note Shvabski, Mikhoel Leyb and Yisroel Meir Ikhiltshik, who also taught in Talmud Torah. The Talmud Torah was managed by Khaim Levin, who afterwards emigrated to the United States. Lipe the Shoykhet took his place.

Of observant religious Jews there were always many and the synagogues were full of praying Jews. There was the "Groyse Shul" (big synagogue), the Chassidic shtibl (small synagogue) - the "Red Minyan," the Groyser Beys-Medresh (the large synagogue), the Chassidic "Green Minyan," the synagogue on the slopes of the hill, called "Toliker" (in the valley); and the Tailors' Synagogue. Naftali Vayts was the recognized "bal-tfile" [prayer leader] of the town.

Before World War I, Novoalexandrovsk had two rabbis: an Chassidic rabbi called "More Tsedek," and Rabbi Burshteyn. After World War I, the rabbi's chair was occupied by Elyohu Reznik. A long time ago the rabbi of the town had been the famous "gaon" (scholar) Rafoel Shapiro, who was the rabbi and the head of Volozhiner Yeshiva.

The congregation ("kehila") looked after the religious requirements of the population, and also the health and welfare of Jews. The congregation had a "bikkur-cholim" (sick society) under the management of Zalman the Paramedic and Leybe Mikhols. There was also a hospital. The chief doctor was Doctor Bukont, a Lithuanian who was a good surgeon. There were also Jewish doctors: Doctor Pik, the dentist, Miss Mistroyb, and there was Doctor Loyne, a German. During the czarist regime there was also "meshtshanske uprave" (administration of the town or local community management), the head of which was Avrom Moyshe Tsimerman. The military rabbi was Ayzik Yafo.

The outbreak of World War I ruined the established Jewish positions and the community organization. Because they feared the approaching front, the Jews abandoned their houses, leaving everything in the care of the Almighty. They went far away, to Russia. The Jews of Novoalexandrovsk left during the war for places such as Penze, Saratov, Nizhni-Novgorod, Kazan, Yelyets, Simperaol, and for the Caucasus region.

In 1919 the Jews of Novoalexandrovsk started to return home. The journey home was very difficult and lasted a long time. The journey from Penze to Dvinsk took three months. When the Jewish refugees returned to Novoalexandrovsk, they found their possessions had been looted and their homes severely damaged. Only the synagogue buildings were not ruined, because the German army had converted them into stables for their horses.

It was only in 1920-22 that larger groups of Jews began to return to Novoalexandrovsk. But a considerable portion of Novoalexandrovsk Jews remained in Russia, and the number of Jews in Novoalexandrovsk was noticeably and considerably diminished.

Headstone for the annihilated of Zarasai District

The decrease of Jews in Ezhereni is referred to in the book "Lite" that appeared under the editorship of M. Sudarski, Uriah Katsenelbogn and Y. Kisin. Before World War I, the population of Ezhereni was 9,000; after the return of the Jews it was less than half that number, namely 4,200.

According to the statistical table dated 1st January 1927 prepared by Y. Barvein and B. Entelis, inspectors of the central committee of the Yiddish Folk Bank in Kaunas, we see the decrease of the Jewish population in Novoalexandrovsk . At that time there were 1,329 Jews constituting 284 families; members of the Bank numbered 325.

We learn from the above-mentioned table that the People's Bank in Novoalexandrovsk /Ezhereni was founded in 1920. At that time, just after the First World War, the number of Jews was 880 and the number of families 176. The Bank also served the surrounding villages. After the war, the administrative area of Novoalexandrovsk was diminished. A number of villages remained in part of Poland, and Dvinsk (Dinaburg) was cut off. New administrative centres arose in Rakiskis and Utian. The fact that Novoalexandrovsk had no railway station also hindered the development of the economy.

In Novoalexandrovsk trade dropped to a minimum and the poorer peasants around were greatly impoverished, deriving their nourishment mainly from dairy products. In other Lithuanian towns and villages there was a very active reconstruction process, while this was entirely lacking in Novoalexandrovsk.

Nonetheless, after the First World War, a cultural and economic life began in Ezherieni. Because of the impact of the Russian Revolution and the Balfour Declaration, education and social life were modernized.

Under the direction of Ya'akov Mushel, a Hebrew primary school also opened. There being no Hebrew middle-school, many Jewish children attended the local Lithuanian Commerce High School. A Maccabi organization was established. There was also a drama society, of which Leybe and Khaye (Chaya?) Tsimerman, Mulye Tsimerman, Khaye (Chaya?) Shulman and Rivka Berkovitsh were members. There was a library and a Zionist-Socialist party formed. A Linat-Hatsedek, or place for people without shelter, was established. A branch of the Folk Bank was established under the management of Azriel Fitel, Zalman Levit, Rabbi Eliyahu Reznik and Leyb Melnik. Before the war, the director of the Credit Bank was Yudel Shteyn, and the book-keeper Leyb Gilbert. The "Joint" (American Joint Distribution Committee) also sent subsidies to the Folk Bank to assist people to repair their houses and guesthouses (Hakhnoseth Orkhim).

Towards the end of the 1920s, the emigration of Jews from Ezhereni increased. The main emigrants were the young, and they went to Brazil, South Africa, South America and Palestine.

According to Rabbi Efraim Oshri's book "Khurban Lite", Ezhereni-Novoalexandrovsk was among the last places in Lithuania that was occupied by the Germans. The Germans also brought Jews from the surrounding villages; they locked them up in the synagogues, and later took them, together with the local Jews, to the nearest forest where they killed them all.

After the liberation in 1945, a monument for the 8,000 Jews massacred was erected there. Also, after the Holocaust, some letters were received from countrymen who survived the destruction. They wrote to say that they found Novoalexandrovsk totally *Juden rein*.

[Pages 314-316]

My Birthplace

By Jehuda Zwi Ichilcik
Translated by Gloria Berkenstat Freund

Yehuda-Tzvi Eikhilczik

My birthplace is Nova-Alexandrovsk (Ezereni). I studied there in a *cheder* and at age six, with the help of my father, I made a fiddle out of a small sieve and the strings out of hair from a tail. A few years later, my father took me to Mikhal the *klezmer* (musician), who taught me to play the fiddle and the clarinet.

I became widely known in Nova-Alexandrovsk as a gifted fiddle player and the rabbi would even invite me to play at the celebration during the intermediate days of *Sukkos*.

Nova-Alexandrovsk was not a large city. Its population numbered about six thousand souls. The Jews lived in the center of the town and the Lithuanians and "Old Believers" (Orthodox Russians), whom the Jews called "*Fonyes*" (the Yiddish word for Russia or Russians), lived on the edges.

There were orchards, gardens and beautiful lakes. Nova-Alexandrovsk was considered one of the most beautiful spas in Lithuania.

During Czarist times Novo-Alexandrovsk was a district city, with a bailiff [or district police chief –Ed.] at the head. The Jews were very poor; only a few Jews had an easy life. The majority of the Jews were without a definite occupation. A poor income was drawn from the Tuesday market days, when Jews would walk among the peasants selling their packs of pig hair, a calf and produce.

Zalman Feldsher (old-time barber-surgeon)   Yisrael-Meir the Melamed (Teacher)

The end of winter in Novo-Alekxandrovsk

Jews traded in fish, along with grains and cows. The butchers did not wait for the customers to come to their butcher shops to buy--they would carry baskets of meat to their customers.

There were craftsmen: tailors, shoemakers, tinsmiths, tar makers, and so forth.

There was great poverty among the Jews in Novo-Alexandrovsk. My father was poor. He was an enlightened man and was occupied with teaching.

He was a *Talmud-Torah* teacher and every Friday he simply would have to go to collect *kopeks*, and he never was able to gather together his salary of three rubles a week. Only for *Shabbos*, my mother would buy the head of a calf. She would divide the meat among the children and leave the bones for herself and my father to suck on.

I remember how my father Yizrael-Meir, of blessed memory, would send me with a *kopek* on *Shabbos* night to buy *kvas* for *havdalah* (the ceremony at the close of *Shabbos*). But he would tell me that I should spend half a *kopek* and leave the second for another week. The *kvas* seller would record on the wall that he should give me a portion of *kvas* without cost on the coming *Shabbos* night for *havdalah*. The *kvas*, alas, was made from the crusts of black bread, and was very sour, like the sourness of the mood of the coming gray week with its worries.

However, great artists came out of Novo-Alexandrovsk such as Yudl Pen – a great painter and academician. He died in Russia during the Bolshevik regime which buried him with a great parade at government expense. Great singers, players, conductors and composers also came out of my birthplace. It is most certain that the beautiful landscape affected and influenced their artistic souls.

There was also a small aristocratic class. The so-called "aristocrats" were "advocates" who [did not have academic credentials] and wrote petitions for the peasants on market day. They were my wife's father, Zalman the *Feldsher*, who graduated from a school for *feldshers* and whom the Jews called Zalman the lucky man; the advocate Gordon (my wife's uncle); advocate Bendet, advocate Fridland; advocate Yerkhmeil Berman, who later became a judge in Utian; Dr. Moishe Berman, who was the head of the Lithuanian Red Cross; and several people from the merchant class.

At age eleven I walked a distance of 50 miles to the Wizer *Yeshiva* to study. Later I studied in the Dvinsker *Yeshiva*. Then I left for the wider world where, thanks to my talent, I became the conductor of the orchestra of Nikolai's uncle, "Prince Altenburgsky." I came home to visit every few years.

In 1921 I returned to Lithuania. The Lithuanian government was then a young one that expressed liberalism toward the Jews. A short time later, anti-Semitism began to grow which pushed me to emigrate to South Africa.

I have been in South Africa ever since. Now I think back on Novo-Alexandrovsk and her Jews, who although they lived in poverty, were very elevated in their simplicity, in their popularity, and in their honesty and their habits.

[Page 317]

From My Home Town

By Yitskhok Dumas

Translated by Harry Abramowitz

A classic joke is told about my home town, Novoalexandrovsk-Ezhereni-Zarasai. Many years ago my home town was called Ezros because of the majestic lakes (Ozeres) that surrounded the town. But when the grand highway from St. Petersburg to Warsaw was completed, the Czar himself, Alexander III, passed through Ezros to Novoalexandrovsk and was so taken with the natural beauty surrounding the town that he ordered the name to be changed from Ezros to Novoalexandrovsk, after his own name. The citizens, Lithuanian peasants, Jews and Poles, received an additional command that anyone who dared to call the town Ezros would be caned. It happened that a *Yishuvnik*, an isolated agricultural settler, came to the town to observe the anniversary of a death (of an acquaintance?) . He prayed at the prayer-stand in front of the Ark, and when he came to the part *"ezras avoyseynu"* (the help of our fathers), he was too frightened to say the words and instead said "Novoalexandrovsk *avoyseynu.*"

When the Lithuanians got their independence they quickly changed the name of the town to Ezhereni, and in the year preceding the Second World War the Lithuanians changed the name of the town to Zarasai. Thus my hometown was blessed with three names. But for the most part the town was called Ezhereni, and the Jews generally called it Ezhereni.

Ezhereni was known as the Switzerland of Lithuania and I maintain that this honourable title is well-deserved. The town was situated on a mountainous peninsula surrounded on all sides with majestic lakes that spread out over a large area.

In the town itself there were two big parks and a beautiful boulevard. In one of the parks there was a monument with a large Russian eagle on top in honour of Alexander III. People used to call this monument the cast-iron post. This park had many trees of all kinds, flowers and glades. On Saturdays and other holidays people would come to the park to get some fresh air and children used to play on the steps of the cast-iron post.

The streets of Ezhzereni were cobbled. Ezhzereni had no muddy streets because the rainwater was drained down to the lake.

A beautiful corner on God's earth, as if painted, was the Ostror (island). People used to come to the island by small boats, and there were picnics and various other entertainments. The young enjoyed themselves and were happy there. Even the cemetery was a peninsula and when there was a burial, those with a sense of humor said, "The corpse is being taken to a *datcha*."

Around the town there were many pine and birch forests. Near every Jewish house there was a garden. Jews had their own orchards and gardens, which made their lives easier economically, and because of that, poverty in our town was not as great as in other smaller towns.

Jews had many brick and stone buildings. The row of shops belonged exclusively to the richer Jewish shopkeepers. There was a big two-floor stone building, where on the ground floor there were big shops and above it, dwellings.

Before the First World War, Novoalexandrovsk, as it was then called, was the administrative center of a very large area, and the following little towns belonged to it: Dusiat, Antalept, Abel, Rakishok, Vidzh, and others. Under the government of Lithuania, Ezhereni lost half of its former towns. A large part fell under the government of Poland. Rakishok then became the administrative center of its surroundings, including other little towns like Abel.

In general, Ezhereni lost a great deal after World War One, being the most remote part of Lithuania, and cut off from Dvinsk. Before World War One, there was considerable commercial activity between Ezhereni and Dvinsk. Finding itself only four versts from Dvinsk, the citizens of Ezhereni were permitted to go to Dvinsk with a permit instead of a proper passport. Even though the connection with Dvinsk was not entirely cut off, normal commercial activity between the two towns could not continue.

The population of the town consisted of Jews, Lithuanians, Poles and Russians. That is why anti-Semitism was not strong in Ezhereni: the Poles hated the Lithuanians, and the Russians hated both groups. Thus they left the Jews alone. As far as I know, there were no fights between Jews and Christians.

Before World War One, the economic position of the Jews was generally satisfactory. There were many rich merchants and some of them were "merchants of the first guild" who conducted trade all over the world.

There was a richer class and a poorer class. The richer Jews lived on the chaussée [road], on Sodover Street, around the commercial center, where the shops were. The poor Jews lived down the hill, near the lakes. The Poles lived in Saltupe, and the Russians near the factory.

Jews traded with peasants and with neighboring villages. The craftsmen had their own workplaces. The wagon-drivers used to take goods and passengers to Dvinsk and to surrounding villages. The shopkeepers dealt in haberdashery, manufactured articles, hardware and colonial articles. The richest man of the town was Israel Traub. He had a big wool and textile business and was respected by Jews and Christians.

The whole week the shopkeepers stood in their shops, waiting for customers, and having no business they discussed politics and town affairs. But on market-days peasants came from all the surrounding areas, and Jewish shopkeepers and craftsmen would bustle around, engrossed in their business. There were separate sections for timber, hay, cattle and horses. The horse-traders and the butchers were the main bidders at the horse and cattle markets. There were butchers who did a big trade, transporting fish and meat to Dvinsk and other towns.

The annual fair was very noisy. Merchants and peasants came from near and far to this fair.

Novoalexandrovsk had no industry, but there were several lumberjacks who had sawmills behind the town. These Jewish economic enterprises were ruined during World War One.

On the outbreak of World War One, the Novoalexandrovsk Jews were sent far away into Russia. Only from 1918-20 did these refugees return to their homeland and start to rebuild their economic life. Gradually trade with the peasants and with the nearest villages and little towns became normalized. Shopkeepers again opened their shops and craftsmen rebuilt their workshops. Fishermen took leases for fishing on the lakes and occupied themselves with fishing, and with God's help, when there was a good year, profits were very satisfactory.

Nonetheless, the pre-war economic position was very much better. After the war, many families lived only on the support they received from the United States and South Africa.

The religious life of the Jews did not differ from that which existed in other Jewish towns and villages at that time. Before World War One, when the numbers of Jewish inhabitants in Novoalexandrovsk was much greater than after the War, the Jews built six synagogues: the large Beth Midrash, the main synagogue built of brick and stone, which was used only in summer because in wintertime one could not warm up such a big, tall place; the tailors' Beth Midrash; the Beth Midrash down the hill, and the two Chassidic synagogues. These synagogues were always filled with people praying.

In the last years the head of the Jewish community there was Rav Eliyohu Reznik, of blessed memory, and the ritual slaughterers of poultry and livestock were Yosef Litvin and Pinkhos Shteyn. Before World War One, the Chassidim had their own rabbi, whom they called Moyre-Tsedek.

The Enlightenment Cheder in Ezhereni in the 1920s

There were cheders and a more enlightened cheder called the Cheder Methukan. This enlightened cheder was managed by Chaim Williamowsky and Shlomo Pelz. After WWI, a school was established and Chaim Williamowsky went over to teach in the school, working together with the other two teachers, Moyshe Mushel and Yasman.

But the cheders continued to exist even after the school was founded. Reb Ben-Zion Lyubatsky, who was both learned in the Torah as well as an enlightened person, had his own cheder. Also well-known was the cheder of Chaim Mordechai Abramowitz, or as they called him, Chaim-Motte the "bord," because of his long beard. He was an Chassid and before World War Two he emigrated to Palestine. Mr. Avroham-Yoshe Ichilchick was also well-known as a Hebrew scholar who distinguished himself with his beautiful handwriting. Children of rich parents were his pupils. Many of the pupils of the cheders and schools now live in South Africa.

The pupils of the Hebrew school were, after entrance examinations, enrolled in the Lithuanian gymnasium because there was no Hebrew high school. The more well-to-do parents sent their children to study in Kaunas and in other towns. Many of the children who studied in the cheders afterwards went on to study in the Yeshivoth of Manevezys, Slobodka, etc.

After World War One, various youth movements were started. The Zionist-oriented youth were active in and around the Maccabi organization, and the

Jewish youth who were left-inclined belonged to "Y.A.K" (Jewish Athletic Club). The Maccabi movement had a very good team of football players, and matches were organized with the surrounding little towns. Teams even used to come from Dvinsk, making their way on bicycles to play with the local Maccabis. On such occasions this was quite a holiday in Ezhereni. Shopkeepers closed their shops, hastening to see the match. The Maccabi members used to organize tournaments and beautiful gymnastic exercises. The "Y.A.K." also had a good football team and a dramatic circle, which quite often put on Yiddish plays that were much enjoyed by the spectators.

In the 1920s there arose a Chalutz movement, and many young people emigrated to Palestine. The youth saw no future for themselves in their impoverished hometown and took many roads. Some went to Palestine, South Africa, Argentina and other countries.

To finish, I shall mention the local fire brigade which consisted mainly of Jews. The chief of the brigade was Abrasha Rosenberg. All brigade members wore uniforms with shining brass helmets. The fire-brigade had their own musical band. On the occasion of official parades, like Lithuanian Independence Day, the fire brigade used to march with the military units led by Abrasha Rosenberg. (Later he emigrated to South Africa and died a short time ago in Cape Town.)

Maccabis in Ezhereni

No caption (Elementary School)

This was my little hometown. A community of Jews lived there, more or less satisfied with its fate, trusting in God. They married off their children and built homes--some better ones, some worse. All enjoyed the surrounding lakes and forests, until the savage Nazi plague arrived and killed all the Jews.

Ezhereni did not produce any great men. As far as I know, only eight persons were known throughout Lithuania. These included the sole Jewish judge, Yerachmiel Berman, who was a judge in Utian, and his brother, Dr. Moshe Berman, who was the head of the Jewish Hospital in Kaunas in the last few years before World War Two. He, together with other doctors, Benjamin Zacharin, Zvi Elkem, Rosa Golach and Leyb Feldshteyn, organized courses in Kaunas for Jewish partisans and ghetto fighters to enable them to give first aid.

All the Jews of Ezhereni were dear, hearty, plain Jews with crystal-clear souls.

Only a few Ezhereni Jews managed to save their lives. According to the latest information only seven or eight Jewish families live there now, Joseph Grinman amongst them.

This is the terrible tragic history of my hometown Ezhereni.

6. According to my research, before the town was named after Alexander III, it was known by several names, "Oziera", "Ozera", "Ezherena" and even in plain Yiddish "Ozeres." This new name of Novoalexandrovsk was proposed to Alexander III to honour his visit on his way to Kovna, because various kings had given similar names to various towns. "Novoalexandrovsk" was a somewhat pretentious name for a very little town with no railway to the outside world, because the Slav ending "-ovsk" usually signified a town of some importance, either as a communication center or because of its large population or industry. None of these could be attributed to Novoalexandrovsk.

The tombstone of the 8,000 Jews of Ezhereni and surroundings

[Page 324]

My Shtetl Boguslavishok
(Bagaslaviškis, Lithuania)

55°05' 24°46'

By Raisel Michel-Berzak

Translated by Helen Mitnick

Reizel Meikel-Berzak

My shtetl Boguslavishok was small, and it was far from a train station, it was between Vilna and Kovno.

Around my shtetl were many farms and valleys, in the spring and summer everything was fresh and green, until today these things are still fresh in my memory about the vast expanse around my shtetl.

Rokiskis Yizkor Book 327

The adjoining small shtetlekh were called Shirvint, Musnik and Gelvan. My shtetl was close to Gelvan by about 5 miles. There they had a library with a good assortment of books, also a section of dramas. Boguslavishok was far from the cultural area, so our young people stayed close to Gelvan.

At our shtetl we didn't even have a house of prayer, only an old classroom. The slaughterer was also the Hebrew teacher, who taught the children the alphabet, and then how to pray.

Wealthy parents sent their children to Vilkomir High School. The students would come home on holidays. They also held meetings on Zionism, Socialism, and other literary topics. From time to time they would have lectures.

About sixty families lived in Boguslavishok. We didn't have a regular Rabbi because our shtetl had no means of supporting him and his family. There was a "Kazianer" rabbi by the name of Avraham Pik. He was a great scholar. Our shtetl did not have a doctor, so they called the local priest who helped with the physicals and put up cups and also leeches, or applied hot bricks for stomach pains and lung disease.

Our shtetl was the same as all the shtetlekh around us; it was hard for Jewish people to make a living. Also during the Lithuanian leadership the situation didn't improve, and when the cooperatives opened, the situation of the Jewish people got worse. We also had small merchants, hard working laborers, one tailor and several shoe repairers.

All our people were honest, hard working, simple, but the hard work did not alter their goodness for each other. Till this day I remember the good deeds of our people. Moishe Yosel, Avrum Shimsons, and Hirshke Burshtyn were the drivers of the horses and wagons in Boguslavishok.

The bad economic situation and poverty got worse, so that it created an emigration from our shtetl, especially for the young. The elderly remained in place, dependent on God and the generosity of their children who had left to improve their life. Waiting for their help, the Jewish population got smaller in Boguslavishok. The Jews in town lived so very poor, waiting for better times, and also the hour when they could leave to join their children in their new homes. But the Nazis stopped all hope and all dreams of a better day. They all perished from the German enemy.

Many years have passed since I left my shtetl, but I still have many memories, pictures of my shtetl and my beloved sweet home. I remember my mother being very busy on Friday, and her mild face lit up always when she had the greatest joy over lighting the Sabbath candles, and from the shining brass candlesticks that would light up her face, and were spread over the white Sabbath tablecloth, the floor with sand shining as a sign that Sabbath has arrived and the weekly worries have vanished.

From the small window that overlooked the holy Temple, we could see the gray-haired shammash, Yahuda, who was waiting for the congregants to come and honor the Sabbath. The sun is setting and the congregation is already there in shul, at the pulpit was my father in his Sabbath robe, deep in prayer. On the faces glimmers the soul of Sabbath. When the shoemaker, Shimin Yosel, stands at the pulpit to honor the Sabbath with his glorious tone, all the Jews join in with great joy and delight.

Boguslavishok had dear Sabbaths and good-hearted people.

[Page 327]

Subat
(Subate, Latvia)

56°01' N, 25°54'

By Rev. M. B. Fisher

Translated by Yona Fisher

Reb M. B. Fisher

Subate was divided by a lake (ozere) as though there were two towns. There were two different rabbis, different shochtim, teachers, and Beit Midrashim. The eastern part of the town was the more significant in respect of the commercial center. The rich (gevrim) also resided in the eastern part close to the Market Square. The well-known wealthy of the town were the Factors, Abrahamson, Mariengeburg, Rubanenko, and others. It was a quiet Jewish town. With the exception of Monday, the market day, one rarely saw a strange person. The majority of the town was occupied with labor and transport. There were also "Luftmenschen" and retailers. There was no shortage of "Karabelnickers" who used to leave with a heavy pack on their shoulders from early Monday till Friday and traverse through the villages and farms.

Reb Avigdor Lempert z"l (of blessed memory)

The surroundings of Subate were extraordinarily beautiful and healthy. The lake, which was to be found in the middle of the town, added much to the beauty of the town. It used to attract many visitors who enjoyed the summer months.

From the year 1915, when Subate was occupied by the Germans, we were totally cut off from Courland. At that stage Rakishok was the nearest center with which we were connected commercially and which influenced us spiritually. Teachers, cantors, and orators were brought from there. Generally we were influenced by the Lithuanian Jewish Renaissance. We also made adjustments to the modernization of our education and established national culture organizations according to the Lithuanian style.

Our old rabbi, Hagaon Rabbi Moshe Zacher, was known as "Gadol Batorah." I once heard from the Rogevitscher Gaon, Joseph Rogen, that Moshe could "lernen." Our well-known Chazan was Avraham Yitzchak Katzevitz (the shochet from Abel in Lithuania), a type of "Berele Chagi." He also served Rakishok with his beautiful davening.

After the First World War a modern Hebrew School was organized via the brothers Cohen (currently residing in Johannesburg) and the son of the shochet, Israel, was the principal. Our school produced a large number of Hebrew speaking pupils. Israel (Katzevitz) was a fine "Maskil" with unique pedagogic abilities and was caught up somewhat excessively in the Haskalah movement. His initiative led to a well-organized Zionist organization and also a theatrical group.

In this theatrical group, Pearl the "rebbes" wife with her natural talent, proved to be outstanding. She was also the first female member of our democratic community. The chairman was our last Rabbi, Hagaon Yaacov Epstein (nephew of Gaon Rabbi Moshe Epstein, Rosh Yeshiva of Hebron).

Gershon-Velve the Shochet (ritual slaughterer) with his wife Sara-Chana

As far as the existence of genuine Judaism in the Jewish street was concerned, it is worth remembering a certain incident. A well-known shopkeeper who conducted classes in Meshniot on Saturday and Sunday had a liking for the Omed (bimah) and was a very pleasant davener without payment. When it became known that his two sons, students at the Lithuanian Gymnasium, were writing on Shabbat, he was no longer permitted to approach the Omed.

May the above sentences remain as a memorial to our most beloved and dear holy ones (Kedoshim) who lived a true Jewish life and raised their holy souls (Al Kiddush Hashem). May their blood be avenged.

[Page 331]

Ponedel
(Pandėlys, Lithuania)

56°01' 25°13'

By R.H. Berchowitz-Peisachovitz, T. Katz, Jokl Evans

Donated by Lois Feldman Clausen

Translated from the Yiddish by Paul Silbert

Ponedel lies on the road from Rakishok to Birz. Before the First World War it was a muddy and neglected little town.

Ponedel is surrounded by the little towns of Suavenshki, Anushishok, Ponimunok, Skupishok and Papel. It is 28 kilometres from Rakishok.

The marketplace in Ponedel

Around Ponedel there is a chain of villages.

The centre was the market square. From Rakishok you used to come in through Main Street, which stretched as far as the market. A large and beautiful House of Prayer stood on the market square, as well as the shops and the shopkeepers' residences.

To the right from the market square stretched Railway Street. Ponedel had only a narrow-gauge railway which the Germans constructed at the time of the First World War. The narrow-gauge railway linked Ponedel with Skopishok and Suavenishok.

To the left from the market square--the vital nerve-centre of the little town--was Pazelayker Street, which led to Suavenishok. From there stretched the Birz road, which led to Kvetki and Papel [and] as far as Birz.

On Synagogue Street was found the synagogue courtyard, where were located the house of study, the synagogue, the prayer room and the deacons' synagogue, and the poorhouse, into which poor people used to be admitted. On Bath Street there was the ritual bath.

Ponedel had no river [it was located on a hill overlooking the river Oposhta] or lake: there was only a muddy tank for rainwater in the market square.

The landscape around Ponedel was very beautiful in appearance. It had many orchards and gardens and the houses stood in the midst of greenery.

Before the First World War Ponedel belonged to the Novo-Alexandrovsk District. After the war Ponedel was attached to the Rakishok District.

The population numbered approximately 150 Jewish families and 50-60 Christian families. The total number was estimated at approximately 2500 souls. The Christians of the little town were all Lithuanian peasants who supported themselves by agricultural labour, having their own fields and pastures.

The Jews gained their livelihood from the market. There used to be two annual fairs. Jews were shopkeepers, traders and artisans, the latter following such trades as cobbler, tailor, shinglemaker, tinsmith, hatmaker, butcher and wigmaker. There was also a pair of Jewish herdsmen. One of the herdsmen was called Leybke Yudels.

The largest businesses were: the draper's shop of Shimon Zuse, who had three educated daughters; Itzik Pinkushevitz's draper's shop; Khaim Flax's drapery business; Khaim-Leyb's drapery shop; Yisrael Zalevetzki's shoe store and Zalman Pinkushevitz's hardware store.

The following had food or grocery stores: Mendel Zak; Bebe Yoses; Rokhl-Leya, Khaim-Ber's daughter; [and] Getzl Mizrach. Fayve-Yose-Itze Ekdes had a restaurant. Shneur Flax was a flax dealer. Sara-Breyne was a baker. There were peddlers and several teamsters.

[No caption] "Maccabi" written on photo

Ponedel Jews were all Chassidim. The rabbi, before the First World War, was Rabbi Moyshe Ogins, a very learned man and a fine human being, who was greatly beloved in the little town and the surrounding area. Two of his daughters are now in Israel and one in Johannesburg. His son, at the time when the Germans entered the town, hid at the [parish] priest's. The priest turned to the Christian Dr. Straus to assist him in saving the rabbi's son, but Dr. Straus betrayed the rabbi's son to the Germans, who killed him and the priest.

After Rabbi Moyshe Ogins died, the rabbinical chair was taken by Rabbi Itzik Dubov, who is now in America. Afterwards the rabbi was Rabbi Yitzhak of Riga.

A very fine personality was the ritual slaughterer Zalman Rabinovitz. He was a good Jew and a very learned man. The entire town respected him. After his death he was succeeded by his son, Artshik Rabinovitz, who was a modern Jew and for that reason had many opponents. The son was rescued [presumably by friendly Lithuanians] and is now living in Vilna.

Ponedel had many teachers. The best-known were: Zalman Skeyster--a teacher of Gemara; Avraham-Leyb; Yishaya-Bere; Yisroel; Mayer-Tuvya; Moyshele and Khaim Tepper, now in Cape Town.

The prayer leaders were: Leybe-Bere the Bookseller, Moyshe Gershons, and Shmuel-Rafoel.

Among the important householders in Ponedel were reckoned: Moyshe Yisroels; Hirshe-Mote; Yose-Itze Ekdes; Shimon Grimbla; Yitkhak Pinkushevitz.

[No caption] "Histadrut" written on photo

In 1915, when the Russian Army retreated, Cossacks rode into Ponedel. They called on the old rabbi and gave him the order that the town [ie. the Jewish population] had to be evacuated within 24 hours. Seized by a great panic, everyone fled from Ponedel, but the Germans captured Ponedel and the immediate area so quickly that many returned. A great number of Ponedel Jews were evacuated deep into Russia and came back in 1920-1922.

The town, during the course of the war, was reduced to ruins. The returning Jews lay about in the synagogue and poorhouse and wherever they were able to find shelter.

Thanks to assistance from the Joint [American Jewish Joint Distribution Committee] and from relatives overseas, Ponedel quickly rebuilt itself and acquired a modern appearance. The Lithuanian authorities had the streets paved. Trade ties were revived, mainly with Rakishok. The tax on artisans was increased [by the Lithuanian government]. This was a high tax for the little tailors, who now had to face competition from their Christian colleagues.

A People's Bank [cooperative bank] was founded. The president was Shmuel Pinkushevitz; Henekh Kark was secretary.

The economic life of Ponedel greatly improved with more secure times, but the heavy tax burden on the Jewish population impoverished the Jewish shopkeepers and artisans.

The town received a final blow with the removal of the shops from the market square--the most important source of livelihood for many Jews. The order to clear the market square of shops was supposedly for purely aesthetic reasons--to beautify the town--but it was in harmony with the "patriotic" struggle of the Lithuanian cooperatives to drive Jewish shopkeepers out of their positions.

Regardless of the various political-economic phases in Jewish Lithuania, Jewish organisations revived in our home town. Various factions of the Zionist Movement distinguished themselves as did the "Aguda" [ancestor of the ultra-Orthodox Israeli religious party of that name], the "Tiferet Bachurim" [evidently an Orthodox youth movement], and there was also a left-wing movement.

Branches of "Maccabi" [the Jewish sports association] and "HaShomer HaTzair" [a left-wing Zionist youth movement] and a "Khalutz" [Pioneer] group were created.

The Ponedel "Maccabi" numbered over 100 members, and had a soccer section [the Yiddish text includes a team photo], a dramatic circle, and a library. There were shows, lectures and other cultural activities. The leaders of Maccabi were Velve Herring and Henekh Kark.

The "HaShomer HaTzair" was a good scouting organization which occupied itself in preparing pioneers for emigration to the Land of Israel.

The left-wing movement was very active. The "Culture League" was founded in 1922. The founders and leaders of the "Culture League" were Yose Hak, Ratner the teacher, the teacher Libe Yikir, and Yankl Fabrikovitz. The "Culture League" in Ponedel set up a Jewish People's School where the language of instruction was Yiddish. The school was recognized by the government, which used to pay the teachers and also provided a Lithuanian [language] teacher. The Jewish People's School was on a very high [academic] level, and even when the "Culture League" was closed down, the Jewish People's School continued to exist.

In the "Culture League" there was an active dramatic section. The actors were Itzke Katz, Yose Hak, Khilke Hak, Sarke Hak, Khaim Hak and the teacher Ratner. The dramatic section used to bring in outside acting troupes. The income went for the library, which numbered 1000 books.

At the time that Smetona became president [after the right-wing military coup of December 1926] and the Reaction grew strong, the "Culture League" was closed. The members, out of fear of the authorities, burned the library.

But this did not halt the political activity of the "Culture League". After the closing of the "Culture League" an association was created called "Sport" under which [political] work was resumed although it met with persecution on the part of the authorities. Once Khanke and Yokhanon were arrested--a brother and sister. They were taken away to Ponemune [Ponemunilis] and the members of Ponedel "Sport", with Toybe Evens at their head, maintained contact with the arrested comrades and sent them parcels with food and necessary items.

Due to the fanaticism of the Aguda people [ultra-Orthodox], Ponedel did not have a Hebrew People's School. The parents who wanted to give their children a [secular] Hebrew education, sent their children to Rakishok, where there was a large Hebrew school. Ponedel did not even have a "Yavneh" [Religious Zionist] School.

In general, Ponedel had a fine and active youth. Many young people from Ponedel are today found in Africa, Argentina, Brazil and in Israel. They emigrated because their own little town had become narrow for them and hard to survive in both economically and spiritually.

There are no details [known] about the death of Ponedel at the hands of the German terrorists [on August 25, 1941]. But it is said that the Germans, together with the Lithuanian peasants, drove all the Jews together into the market square and BURNED THEM ALIVE to the musical accompaniment of a German [military] band.

[Page 336]

From Our Shtetl Dusiat
(Dusetos, Lithuania)

55045' 25051'

By Chaya Malka Kruss-Glussak and Nachum Blacher

Translated by Hedva Scop, Henia Sneh and Haim Katz

Edited by Sara Weiss-Slep

The shtetl goes by various names: Dusiat - in Russian, Dusetos in Lithuanian, and the Jews called the shtetl Dusat-Dushat. The shtetl itself is situated between Rokiskis (Rokishok), Utena (Utian) and Novo-Alexandrovsk (Ezerenai/Zarasai). The natural surroundings were quite beautiful. Pine forests, a lake and a river surrounded the village. Green fields and gardens bloomed extensively during the spring and summer. The suburb Padustelis (Podusiat) served as a summer holiday resort ("dacha") for the people from the neighboring townlets.

A lake separated Dusetos from a courtyard ("heyf") belonging to a Polish landowner ("poritz"). The lake was called the "Courtyard Lake," and could be crossed by means of a wooden boat, run by Yosse Gafanovitch.

In the winter, the lake would freeze over totally, and one could travel across the ice. There was a local saying that the lake had to claim a victim each year. In the early spring and in the autumn everything was covered in thick black mud. Anyone walking in galoshes or travelling by wagon would sink deeply into it.

The three main streets converged on the market place. There were only a few houses between the square and the lake, as well as the Chassidic synagogue. The market place spanned an area of four acres and there were a few shops on all sides of the square. Almost all the shops had dwelling places above, accessed by an outside staircase.

The street facing the lake was called Maskevitcher-Gasse and ran in the direction of the Christian townlet Padustelis. Off to the right was the Skinaiker forest. Past the forest was a road that led to Antaliepte (Antalept) and Utena. On the left via Deguciai one could access the road running to Novo-Alexandrovsk.

The Hashomer Hatzair in Dusetos

Pupils of the Tarbut elementary school, 1927

From the market place, on the left side of the lake was "Unter-Brik-Gasse" (Under-the-Bridge Road) leading to Uzpaliai (Ushpol) and Rokiskis. The road followed the course of the Perkailus river, and hence the name, "Unter-Brik-Gasse." The church and residence of the local priest were situated at the end of this road.

To the left of the square was Milner-Gasse, and at the end on a hillock was a windmill. The sails of the mill were visible from our window. From the direction in which the sails rotated, we could tell which way the wind was blowing. The miller was Elya Yoffe, a tall, handsome and scholarly Jew. Everyone in the shtetl was very fond of him.

The public bathhouse was at the end of Milner-Gasse. For many years Leib-Itze Scop maintained it. In his later years he immigrated to South Africa where he lived out the rest of his life in a quieter fashion.

Between Milner-Gasse and Maskevitcher-Gasse stood both the large synagogue (Beth Hamidrash - shul) and the smaller prayer house. Behind the large synagogue was the well where all the inhabitants would draw their water. Over and above the well, Dusetos had two springs, which served to quench one's thirst during the hot summer days. On Shabbos eves, the Jews would draw water to prepare tea for the Shabbos. The "Shabbos goy" Mazeleniche would take the clay vessels from those waiting on line and fill them up with the sparkling water.

The only streets in the shtetl were those mentioned above. Between the wooden houses, one could see a couple of red brick houses owned by the Jews who were more comfortably off. There was no electricity, but because of the straw roofs of the Christian houses, Dusetos was "illuminated" more than once.

A large fire broke out in 1905. A couple of horse thieves set alight a building in the vicinity of the bath-house, and the fire spread to Milner-Gasse. Many of the homes of the non-Jews were burnt and the "poyerim" (peasants) waited for an opportunity to settle the score with the Jews. An air of unrest filled the shtetl and the Jews feared that this would lead to a pogrom. The youth formed themselves into self-defense league, and were joined by those from Salakas (Salok) and Novo-Alexandrovsk.

The danger of the outbreak of a pogrom was greatest on Sundays and Wednesdays, the latter being market day. Many peasants would come to the market from the surrounding area.

One Sunday, a pogrom did indeed erupt. The Christians, on their way out of church, started attacking the Jews. Members of the self-defense league held out bravely against the rioting, but the counter-attack was tough. The pogromists broke into Jewish houses and stores, smashed the windowpanes and stole what they could. The Jews barricaded themselves in the cellars and in the women's section of the synagogue. The league managed to fire a few shots before retreating. Itze Barron, who had a shop in the market place, crouched on the stairs with a handgun and fired at the angry "poyerim". After he ran out of bullets, the rioters pulled him down the stairs and beat him over the head.

**Sara-Leah Shein, the old lady (midwife) in town.
She died at the old age of 99.**

Rochel-Leah Poritz lived nearby Itze Barron. Rochel-Leah was blonde and looked like a Christian. She donned the local apparel and ran over to the priest's house. She found him inside the church and cried out to him: "Just know that you are responsible for today's events in the shtetl, whether it be in the name of G-d or in the name of the authorities. One man has already died, and who knows how many more will fall!" The priest heeded her words and ordered the bell-ringer to sound the bells. When the rioters heard the ringing, they took it as a call to come to church. The priest implored them to stop the pogrom.

The authorities in Novo-Alexandrovsk were informed, and they sent a Cossack company who managed to drive the rioters away and restrained the leaders in chains.

R. To L.: Rachel Blacher (now in South Africa), Henye Slep (killed in World War II), Yoel Zeif (in Israel), Hava Shub and Noah Paretz (killed in World War II)

R. to L.: Standing: Gershon Baron (killed in Partisan camps); Michah Baron (in Israel); Gitte Baron (killed in WWII); Eliyahu Paretz; Yehudah Baron (killed in WWII); Yosef Baron (killed in Partisan battles); Alter Baron; Esther Baron; Eliyahu Baron (killed as a Partisan).

Among the peasant leaders were: Venezindes, Barzdes, Kaitkes, Pakalnes and others. They were indicted, convicted and sent to prison. The Cossacks remained in Dusetos for an extended duration. They set up quarters at Maishe-Leib's house. When things calmed down, they were called up, and off they went. Thanks to the very brave Jewish woman, Rochel-Leah, the shtetl and its inhabitants were saved.

In 1908, a further pogrom almost erupted. The Dusetos resident Yoel, bought a cow in Kriaunos, about 6 miles from Dusetos. Apparently he managed to convince the owner that the cow was barren. But the owner soon found out that the cow was with calf. He sought Yoel out at home and threatened to kill him. The news of the incident spread like wildfire. The self-defense league intervened and persuaded Yoel to back down from his previous claim. For a long time people in the shtetl continued to live in fear of the outbreak of a pogrom.

In 1910 another large fire raged. Almost all of Dusetos was burnt down. Of the few surviving buildings were the Hassidic synagogue, and the homes of Itze Mashiah and Henech Kahath. It is hard to describe the tragedy. Men, women and children, including the elderly, were gathered on the muddy banks of the river. Everyone had lost their homes and all their possessions. Children wept heart-breaking tears, but no one paid any attention to them. Everyone's spirit was broken. News reached the surroundings towns and villages and soon people started arriving, bringing with them food and clothing. They also managed to gather a large sum of money in donations. With aid coming in from America and Africa, work on rebuilding the shtetl commenced. The large synagogue was reconstructed. By 1912, the building was completed.

There were some 200 Jewish families in Dusetos. According to the supervisor book ("Ispektzia Buch") of the Folks Bank of January 16th, 1927, 704 souls were accounted for. Side by side the Jews lived about 100 Gentiles, who were Christians and of Lithuanian origin. Many Jews became retailers and artisans. Some earned their living by working the land on plots they leased. There were thirty Jewish-owned stores, the largest being that of Rochel-Leah Poritz, Bertchik Levit and Chaim-Leib Adelman, Henech Kahath and the wife of Eber. Eber was an advocate, a wise man who was also well versed in the Torah and an exemplary scholar.

The longest row of stores was opposite the lake and belonged to the Levit clan who were known as the "Yuzinter" (those who hailed from Yuzint - Juzintai). They were very learned and somewhat proud folk.

Wednesdays were market days. This was the only day of the week that the Jews could make a living. Fairs were held twice a year and they were quite a spectacle.

During the WWI, Dusetos traded with Daugavpils (Dvinsk) by means of oxcart. There was no railway station in Dusetos. The closest railway station was Obeliai (Abel). During the war, a few traveled by rail, but most people traveled by horse.

A pioneer on a preparatory kibbutz in Rokiskis

In Dusetos, like in the other prevalently Jewish townlets, there were peddlers, shoemakers, tailors, smiths and other tradesmen, and also butchers. There was only one furrier and one wood joiner (carpenter). Abba "Der Ilgishiler" was the only carpenter in the shtetl. In later years he went blind, however he continued to work at his trade. Lozer was the local potter. His wares were sold both at the local market and at those of towns and shtetlach in the area. Another admirable person was Dr. Druyan who went to Israel. Meir Tzirlin was a learned man who traded in tailoring cloth, and then parted for America. Abba Shlomovitz, the son of the late Reverend Shlomovitz, went off to Johannesburg where he wrote several books.

The richest and most well to do families other than the Levits, were Moshe-Leib Ziev who ran a tavern where both guests and government officials would stay, Chaim-Leib Adelman and Emmanuel Slep.

The shtetl was proud to have Torah scholars who would serve as readers in the synagogue services. Rabbi Noteleh Zilber officiated until his passing before WWI. His son (Rabbi Eliezer Silver) is a well-known rabbi in the States. Dusetos had 5-6 "cheders," one at a high level. The teachers were learned men: Alter Shein; Moshe Paseler who was also a writer; Moshe Karpelas; Moshe-Elya; Leib-Itze; the Gemora teacher Avram-Moshe; another Gemora teacher Shaul; and Chaim-Leib. The rebbe of the higher "cheder" was Yechiel Garber and was renowned for his Hebrew teachings.

Before WWI, besides studying in "cheder," Jewish children attended the Russian folkschool. From Dusetos, emerged honorable Jews and outstanding personalities. Among them was Soreh-Leah Shein who lived to the ripe old age of 99. She made a living by practicing cupping and leeching. She served both as nurse and midwife. She had a cure for every illness. Other interesting personalities were: Chaim-Aharon Shein the pharmacist and son-in-law to the rabbi; Zovl was the male nurse. A fine human being was Shaul-Dovid Shubb, the slaughterer. He was a serious scholar.

Mordechai Yoffe in the book "Lithuania," edited by Dr. Mendel Sudarsky, Oriah Katzenellenbogen and Y. Kissin, wrote in length about Reb. Shaul-Dovid:

"He was handsome, erudite and bright, and modern. One does not have enough fingers on one's hand to count all his good qualities. People could trust him and had respect for him. If asked a question, he would give an answer; if asked for advice he would give it. He was always willing to add a few good words. If there was a dispute, he would mediate. If there was a "simcha," he would participate. If someone was in trouble, he would help. How could it be otherwise?

While mediating, he would lean back in his armchair as if at the Pesach Seder, listening calmly to each of the sides, and looking for the best way of reaching an agreement."

Characters worth mentioning are: Reb Eliyahu Aharon the Torah reader on Shabbos; Henech Kahath and the rebel Hirsche Rubin's. He was always in dire straits, living in poverty and hunger. He always had a grudge against everybody.

Others deserving of mention are: Elya, the son of Soreh-Mira, with his kindness and compassion for others; Pinyah the painter with his respect for learning, even though he himself could not read enough to daven; Itzikel Esak, otherwise known as "Itzikel the Bricklayer," who was a pauper; Leibele "Nye Rosh" ("Hands Off" in Russian) whose nickname was inspired by an incident where he had tried to take a pumpkin from a peasant's wagon, and the peasant had warned him fiercely not to touch the wares.

WWI changed Dusetos. There was not one military force that did not pass through. From the cannon fire in the distance, they thought the Russians were preparing to march on the town. Just as they started packing their belongings, the Germans arrived and all the inhabitants remained at home. Even before the appearance of the Germans, a group of refugees had come from Vilnius (Vilna). The Dusetos Jews received the Vilnius Jews warmly and openly.

In the period after the war, the Jews of Dusetos had managed to make ends meet. The stores were open and the merchants would travel to Panavezys (Ponevez) to order to purchase merchandise. Most of the trade took place amongst the closest villages, both in buying and selling.

The economic situation in Dusetos had not changed much since the war.

After Daugavpils was incorporated into Latvia and trade increased with Rokiskis (since Panevezys was too far away), the shtetl became unrecognizable both culturally and spiritually.

The Balfour Declaration brought with it a new national spirit. The old "cheder" went out of fashion. Instead it became a culture school. The headmaster was Hillel Schwartz, and the teachers were Yudel Slep and Leibtzik Gordon. Berl Levit taught night classes for the adults and was in charge of the teaching staff. He went to Johannesburg afterwards. A Maccabi organization was established numbering 50 members. A library was opened and the newly–formed dramatic circle put on some shows. There was also an active Zionist group.

In 1924, a Jewish national bank was opened. The managers were David Schwartz and Yossel Poritz. There were 152 clients, drawing from various skills and professions: 53 tradesmen; 78 storekeepers and merchants; 4 gardeners; 8 builders and foremen; 2 clerks; 7 free and other professions. The bank also included the neighboring Antaliepte in its activities.

Dusetos followed the "Mitnaggedim" stream.

During this period, there was a minister who was responsible for Jewish affairs in Lithuania, and an elected committee ran the affairs in the shtetl.

There was also a left-wing movement in Dusetos. Amidst the shtetl-dwellers were some prominent figures. One of the Levit family (Dr. Yeshayahu Levit) went to study in Germany, where he read for a doctorate in Philosophy, and when he came for a visit, a banquet was given in his honor.(He died suddenly in Vilnius 1940).

Yisrael Joffer (Yoffe) who wrote for the Kaunas (Kovno) publication "De Yiddishe Shtieme" (The Yiddish Voice) and Mordechai Yoffe the poet and writer who went on to Canada, both hailed from Dusetos.

The inhabitants of Dusetos were in touch with the Jews of Salakas and Antaliepte, as well as Deguciai some 17 miles away.

May their memory be blessed!

Antalepte
(Antaliepte, Lithuania)

55°40' 25°51'

By Arye Eydlman and Yitskhok Gulis (Geli)

Translated by Dr. Khane–Faygl (Anita) Turtlebaub

Translation commissioned by Debra Rade, in memory of her beloved grandfather, Rev. Lazar Rade, z"l, who emigrated from Antaliepte with his wife and son in 1922 to Chicago, and in memory of the families who remained.

Antalept [as it was known in Yiddish – currently referred to as Antaliepte] was a typical small village in Lite[7] and was part of Novo–Alexandrovsk Province. It was 10 Russian viorst[8] from Dusiat and six viorst from the Dvinsk–Vilna highway. The train station closest to it was Utian. There were few villages nearby, and the majority of the peasants sold their wares in the market towns of Novo–Alexandrovk–Ezhereni and Rokishok. The [economic] situation of the Jewish shopkeepers and artisans in Antalept was quite difficult, because business and commerce bypassed Antalept.

The only important source of livelihood was the local monastery, where approximately 100 nuns lived. It was a Greek Orthodox monastery, whose mission was to proselytize and spread Greek Orthodox beliefs among the Catholic Lithuanians and Poles. The shopkeepers, artisans, masons, and builders all benefited from the monastery, since the monastery building was frequently being repaired.

[Page 347]

The Jewish population was poor, and Antalept did not have a weekly market day or annual fair like other towns.

The town had 80 Jewish families–about 400 souls. There were 10 shopkeepers, including Nakhum Levin, who had a well–known fabric store. His children were Moyshe Levin, Leyzer Levin, and Rabbi Berl Levin. Yome the shopkeeper was also well–known, with a big store that sold flour.

A group of Antalepter Halutzim (pioneers) before their aliyah (emigration) to Eretz-Yizrael

There were a few craftsmen, including three or four shoemakers, two or three bricklayers, one tanner, and Lipe the tailor. There was no manufacturing to speak of other than one brush factory. But there were a lot of peddlers.

The circumstances of the Jews under German occupation during the First World War were very bad. As soon as the Germans entered [the town], the nuns of the monastery fled, and the German staff was quartered there. Practically all the Jews stayed and did not escape deeper into Russia. Only two Jewish families left their homes and wandered off into the Russian provinces.

* * *

The Jews were religious, as was the case in all the Jewish towns of Lite, and Antalept was known for its rabbis. The rabbis lived in poverty, and their [meager] incomes were derived from the sale of yeast, shmura–matzo[9], etrogs[10], and other articles necessary for religious observance. This was their only source of income.

The reason for Antalept's great reputation in the rabbinic world was the fact that in the second half of the 19th century, Rabbi Yudl of Antalept, of blessed memory, was the Chief Rabbi. In addition to his greatness in Torah [learning], he was also a sage and very good with people. He was renown throughout the surrounding areas, and he was invited from far away to arbitrate and resolve complicated matters before a Torah court. When the local rabbi of Novo–Alexandrovsk passed away and a substitute could not be found quickly, Rabbi Yudl did not want to take the position permanently because of his age. But Antalept lent Rabbi Yudl for two years to lead the Jewish community of Novo–Alexsandrovsk.

The Melamed (teacher) Itze-Bencie, in the military during the First World War

[Page 348]

Rabbi Yudl was a great Torah scholar, and came from a long line of great Vilna and Shidvint rabbis. After his death, his son–in–law, Rabbi Dovid Nakhum Kovnat, was selected to take his place, but seeing that there was opposition to his appointment in town, he resigned on his own and settled in Balavsk, Latvia. He was the rabbi there for several years and was beloved by the whole Jewish population.

Another rabbi in Antalept was Rabbi Zalman Tuvia Tarkovits, who was killed in the "Ninth Fort" in Kovno, along with his son, Rabbi Khaim Shimshon, who was the author of the book, Dvar HaKhaim [Words of Life]. He was a grandson of [the author of] Shem HaGdolim HaKhodesh HaShlishi [Names of Great Torah Scholars in the Third Month]. Reb Chaim Zalman also had a phenomenal memory, just like his grandfather, Reb Moyshe Markovits, and was well known in the yeshiva world as a great Torah scholar.

In The Destruction of Lite by Rabbi Efraim Oshrey, there are many noteworthy details about Reb Moyshe Markovits, who was just a simple Jew, a shoemaker by trade, who did not even know how to write. Nevertheless, he published his wonderful historical book about the lives and work of the Lithuanian rabbis over the course of hundreds of years.

In the above–mentioned book, the following appears about Reb Moyhe Markovits, of blessed memory:

"His memory was phenomenal. He never forgot anything. He always carried a book with him, and from his bootleg he would take out a pencil and ask someone to write down what he said. He was a person of medium height with a tangled beard. His whole face was covered. Only his eyes and nose could be seen on his face. He lived in poverty and hunger, because he was busy with his religious books and neglected his shoemaking. His wife would say that, "the book is my angel of death. Ever since he started writing, hunger has moved into my house." He published the two volumes of Names of Great Scholar in the Third Month before his death. He died in Gorud at the age of 81".

* * *

After the First World War, Jewish life was somewhat altered. [Ed: the text reads "Second" World War, but from the context, the author clearly was referring to the First World War.] The upbringing of children was modernized. Some parents sent their children to other cities to learn. Even before the Czarist regime, Jewish children were learning in the "National School," which was several viorsts from Antalept.

[Page 349]

There were several cheders in Antalept. Dovid Hirsh Geli, the father of Yitskhok Gulis (Geli), taught Gemora[11] to his students. He also taught them to write Russian, as well as Hebrew and Tanakh[12]. Itse–Bentsye was a good teacher. He was also the one who read from the Torah.

In the 1920s and 1930s, the young people began to leave Antalept for economic reasons and because the town had no prospects. Many of the young people immigrated to Palestine.

The Gemora Melamed [the Gemora (commentary on Talmud) teacher] Dovid-Hirsh Geli

Translator's Footnotes

7. Lite refers to the area of Lithuania, Latvia, and Estonia.
8. A measure of distance formerly used in Russia approximately equivalent to .66 of a mile.
9. Specially guarded matzo.
10. Citrons used on the holiday of Sukkot.
11. Commentary on the Torah.
12. A Hebrew acronym for Torah, Prophets, and Writings.

Yuzint; Natzunishok
(Jūžintai, Lithuania)

55047' 25041'

By Natan Brinkman

Translated by Gloria Berkenstat Freund

Jews In the Villages
A. Yuzint

Yuzint was actually more a village than a town that numbered approximately 60-70 families and, all told, there were 12-13 Jewish households. The Jews were occupied as shopkeepers and craftsmen. The Lithuanian population was exclusively engaged in agriculture.

This large village had a church that drew neighboring peasants, who would come to offer their prayers and at the same time to buy all the needed articles from the Jewish shops. In as much as Yuzint did not have a weekly market, Sunday was the biggest sales day, both for the shopkeepers and the craftsmen. Yearly markets would take place, for which the Jews and the Christians waited impatiently. The yearly market was the biggest event in Yuzint.

Life was easy and quiet. Yuzint stood on the banks of a large lake, surrounded by fields and meadows. Relations with the Lithuanian population were very satisfactory. Yuzint did not have a school or *Beis-Midrash* (synagogue), no *shochet* (ritual slaughterer) and no rabbi, either. Therefore, Yuzint had a respectable Jew, a great scholar, Reb Abraham-Hirshe Levit. As a young man, he studied in *yeshivus* (religious schools) and had rabbinical certification. He passed judgment occasionally on religious questions when the opportunity arose. He did not want to be an official rabbi. He ran large businesses and owned several houses. He was esteemed throughout the area and was also known as a good chess player.

A regular *minyon* (ten men necessary for prayer) was organized in one of Reb Abraham-Hirshe's houses. The men prayed in one half of a room and in the second half – the women.

Naftali Saposznik, the shoemaker, prayed in front of the lectern during the week, but on *Shabbosim* (Sabbaths) and *yom-tovim* (holidays) Abraham-Hirshe Levit prayed at the lectern.

Although it was said that Reb Abraham-Hirshe had experience with *shita* (ritual slaughter of animals), he did not engage in this. Almost all of the Jews in the town were butchers; a *shoykhet* from Kamay was brought for both poultry and sheep and cattle or they were brought for slaughter to Kamay, which was 12 kilometers from Yuzint.

Chaim-Yudel Brikman and his wife Hinda-Matla

There was a respected businessman in the town, Haim-Yudl Brikman, who had seven sons and three daughters. He had a shop and was a butcher. Mainly, he leased fields from the surrounding peasants and he, together with his family, worked the land.

Haim-Yudl, would bring a *malamed* (religious teacher) for his children. The remaining children from Yuzint would study with him, too. In the 30's, Yakov Blakher, the brother of Nukhem Blakher, who is in Johannesburg, was the *shoykhet* and *malamed* in Yuzint.

In the 1920's, a modern teacher was brought to Yuzint who would teach the children Hebrew and other worldly subjects. Several children would travel to Rokishak to study, which was 27 kilometers from us.

Rokishak was the center, the county seat, and the train station, too, We would often travel to Rokishak on various occasions to take care of certain formalities at the government offices, to doctors and to buy goods. Rokishak was a metropolis for Yuzint and Kamay – a city.

After the First World War things changed and Jewish life was partly modernized, principally because the parents made efforts to give more education to their children, who would study in Rokishak and other places. The children would come to Yuzint for *yom-tov* and for vacations, bringing with them new thoughts, aspirations and new ideas.

"*Di Yidishe Shtime*" ("The Jewish Voice") would be received from Kovno and there were subscriptions to books in the libraries of neighboring towns. Meetings would take place at which various problems were discussed.

Yuzint was principally disposed to Zionism and young people went to *hakshara* (agricultural training) and then emigrated to *Eretz-Yisroel*; first people traveled to America and then to South Africa and later, they primarily emigrated to *Eretz-Yisroel*.

It is not precisely known where the Jews of Yuzint perished. It is told that many years ago, the gentiles became drunk and began to break Jewish windows until they reached the house of Haim-Yudl Brikman. My grandfather, Yitzhak Brikman was still alive then and he went outside with a piece of iron and so battered several peasants that they remained angry. One of the peasants who was left crippled swore that if not him, his children or his grandchildren would take vengeance on the Jews.

In the course of the last fifty years, the family would remember that talk and it is a guess that the family did actually kill all of the Yuzint Jews.

The following Jews lived in Yuzint.

Three Saposznik brothers and their families, who were shoemakers. One Saposznik son is in Africa. Here he calls himself Levy. The same family had a son Yehosha-Yehuda, who studied in the Telcer *Yeshiva* and received rabbinical ordination and was known as a great Talmudic student; the family of Itze Khatz, he was a tailor and a butcher; the family of Nisen Marglis – a tailor and a farmer; the family of Alter Rabi – a shopkeeper; the family of Meir Yafa – a shopkeeper; the family of Ruven Bedek, who had a tractor; the family of Mendel Visakaiski, who received support from his children in his old age and would sit in the *shul* reciting Psalms day and night; the family of Shlomoh Meller, whose daughters Kajla and Grunya are now in Israel.

The above-mentioned Abraham-Hirshe Levit and his wife lived in Yuzint until the Second World War.

Everyone was killed by the bloody assassins and the small Jewish settlement in Yuzint was torn out by its roots, as if it had never existed.

B. Natzunishok

Between Yuzint, Kamay and Sviadoshz was the Jewish village, Natzunishok. It was a typical Jewish village of Jewish agricultural workers.

Fifteen families lived in this village. They had their own *Beis-Midrash* (synagogue), a *cheder*(religious primary school) for teaching the children. Reb Leib was the rabbi, *shochet* (ritual slaughterer) and *melamed* (religious teacher) in the town. He was already in his sixties and still had to serve Yuzint, too, which was six kilometers from Natzunishok. The Jews of Natzunishok lived a *frumen* (pious) way of life, and during the *Shabbosim* (Sabbaths) and *yom-tov* (holiday) days the small settlement lived with a typical Jewish Sabbath festiveness.

The life of the Jews in the village of Natzunishok was poor. They farmed the land in a primitive way, with skinny horses and wretched equipment. In addition, they thought about business. They bought a calf and pig hair and sold it at the market in the neighboring towns. Because of this, they neglected the economy of their fields, although the earth was the best in the area and each family had about 10-15 hectares of land.

In the course of time the Jews began to sell their land because of the poor livelihood and because their children began to befriend the Lithuanians in the neighboring villages, leading to the problem of protecting them from intermarriage. Also, the parceling out of the land in Lithuania had begun and there was pressure from the peasants to settle on the farms. The Jews did not want to agree to this kind of life, because they would not be able to live their lives as Jews.

The first to sell his land was Abraham the Natzunishoker, although he, as an exception, had maintained the economy of his farm and had lived abundantly from it. He was the *gabai* (trustee) in the *shul* and the peace-maker in the town. He and his family emigrated to America.

Later, the remaining Jews began to sell their land and thus the Jewish village of Natzunishok was liquidated. It could be that this was the hand of Supreme Providence, because the majority of Natzunishokers survived the great catastrophe of the Jewish people.

[Pages 354 - 355]

My Father Michoel Welve the Farmer
By Israel Michalewitz
Translated by Gloria Berkenstat Freund

My father, Michoel-Welve, lived on the land that belonged to the "Stirnishok" Court for many years – the estate of a count. He and his family lived in a brick house that stood on the shore of Lake Dusiat. Spring and summer, this house was submerged in greenery and blossoms. In the winter, the building stood as if orphaned and was exposed to winds, blizzards and snow.

Michoel-Welve was valued by the Count and in the neighboring villages. He owned cows and cattle, leased fields and would buy flax, seeds and grains from the peasants.

Income was abundant and my father and my mother Nehamah had great confidence in the Creator of the world.

During the winter evenings and in the early hours, my father sat and studied a page of *Gemera*. For his children he brought a *melamed* (religious teacher) named Mudrus who also knew the tradition of *shkhite* (kosher slaughtering of animals). This teacher was one of the household, like a member of the family.

The *mitzvah* of hospitality to strangers on *Shabbos* was maintained both by my father and by my mother. The house was open for all those passing through, for peddlers, village Jews, for fishermen who spread nets in the lake, waiting to catch fish. All were treated with great friendship and hospitality.

However these quiet, idyllic years were interrupted by the despotic Czarist regime, which published a decree that Jews must not live on the land. This hurt my father's endeavors and the Count interceded so that an exception was made in the case of the honest Jew, Michoel-Welve Michalewitz.

My father's passive rebellion did not help either; he would rarely be at home, thinking that the police could not throw out his wife and children if he were not there.

My mother and the children would remain alone in the house. Her sleep was disturbed by every rustle and even the tick-tock of the clock would make her afraid that the Czarist police were coming.

Her fear was justified. One night the commissar of police came with guards, who violently hurled out everything from the house, all the chattel, and drove my mother and children outside.

My mother tried to protest against this calumny. However, the commissar and the guards did not let her speak, screaming at her: "*proklyataya zhidovka* (damn Jew)."

My father came in the morning and found his wife and children, sitting on the grass by the lake.

After, my father and his family were sent out of Stirnishok and he was ruined economically. For a time, we wandered in various villages, until my father and the family settled in the village of Barshen. There, my father again began to trade in flax and seeds, but in the end, the business was not successful and he was an impoverished man, a great pauper. My father began seeking a new home and he and his household settled in Abel. In addition, my parents had great heartache and sorrow over the death of their only daughter, Rivele.

My father spent bitter and difficult years of poverty in Abel. Our apartment was under the same roof as the bathhouse. This house was a ruin and the walls were damp.

Then on Friday night the table was covered and *Shabbosdike* (Sabbath) repose sparkled from every corner. The two brass candlesticks gleamed and the flames brought cheer to carry us through the week of cares.

Many *Shabbosim* (Sabbaths), as Kh. N. Bialik says in his song, "We had no meat, no *challah*, no fish for *Shabbos*" – however, *Shabbos* was *Shabbos*. My father made *kiddish* with a dull knife over coarse black bark bread, and sang the *Shabbos* songs so sweetly, that hope for a better time radiated on my mother's careworn face.

The better time did not come. My mother became ill and breathed out her soul in the hospital in Panevesz. My father awaited the savage Hitlerist assault hat killed him and the family with the entire Abeler Jewish community.

[Page 356]

Sviadoshz
(Svėdasai, Lithuania)

55°41' N, 25°22'

By Haikel Ayresh and Nachom Blacher

Translated by Batami Hertzbach

Translator's Note : I dedicate my efforts in translating this work to the memory of my mother's family who lived and lost their lives in Sviadoshz. My mother Celia Peres Yewlow, one of only three known survivors of the town, lost her father, Yosef Lazer Peres, listed below as Yossi - Hirsh Yankel's, her mother, Henne Rochel, their two sons Yankel and Sholom and their daughter Ester.

* * * * * * * *

Sviadoshz was an idyllic, beautiful small Jewish town. The town was nestled between two large lakes, birch and pine woods, drenched in greenery and reflected on the lakes' waters.

Four straight rows of houses stood around all four sides of the market square, from which meandering streets led to the neighboring villages: Paloikishok, Slabe-Si-Le, Narunte, Lepe-Gire (Ester Malka Jacobson's inn stood in between Narunte and Lepe-Gire), Boten, Vikantzi, Naialitshi and Poirishik, where Yankel Zavisher lived for many years.

Nearby, there were many small Jewish towns. The closest Jewish communities were Vizhon, Oshpole, Kamai and Davink. Sviadoshz was located between Aniksht, Utian and Rakishok The nearest train station was in Ponemunak, 30 kilometers from Sviadoshz.

Our beloved hometown had a quaintly beautiful landscape. It was so quaint and attractive and its Jewish population was so exalted that it seemed a perfect fit in the beautiful natural panorama.

Moshe-Yaakov Hacohen Farber

All the Jews of Sviadoshz were literate and knowledgeable in the Bible. There were practically no Jews who could not read at least a chapter in the Mishnah. Each man, at the conclusion of the workday, came to the synagogue to study a portion of the Talmud, a page of Gomorrah or to say prayers with the greatest intent of opening up his heart and soul.

In brief, there were Hasidim and Mitnagdim. In fact, in Sviadoshz the Hasidim were great scholars. In Sviadoshz all the Hasidim were Chabadnikers and they sent their children to study in Liubavitz. There were two synagogues: a Mitnagdic one and a Hasidic one. Lazar Blacher was the gabbai (warden of the synagogue) of the Mitnagdic synagogue and Sheftel Kaplan was the gabbai of the Hasidic synagogue.

Although the Hasidim and the Mitnagdim both had separate houses of prayer, yet they had only one rabbi and one shochet (ritual slaughterer). The Rabbi would pray one week in the Hasidic shul and one week in the Mitnagdic shul.

Sviadoshz had great teachers. The best scholars in town were Zalman Neimark and Moishe Yakov haCohen Farber. They would interview the potential Rabbi before he even arrived in Sviadoshz to assume the position of Rabbi. If the above mentioned authorities said that the Rabbi was in fact a qualified scholar, their word would in effect be the final recommendation indicating that the Rabbi should be accepted as the spiritual leader of Sviadoshz.

From the right: Mantzik Berman, Chaikel Eyresh and Nachum Blacher

Before the First World War Reb A. Klatzkin was the religious leader of the Jewish community in Sviadoshz. He was a respected and renowned authority in Lithuania. Reb Joseph Halevi was the Rabbi after World War I. The shochet in Sviadoshz was also a notable scholar. Noshem Freedman was the shochet up until the First World War. He was also the Gomorrah teacher in the town. Following World War I he became the shochet in Rakishok.

There weren't any organized societies in Sviadoshz until 1914. Jewish children were raised in a religious and nationalistic spirit. There were religious schools. The teachers included the above-mentioned Noshem the Shochet, Yudel Uzshpaler, Abba-Elie and Aaron Yitzik. There was also a Russian elementary school where several Jewish children studied, most of whom were girls.

No one seemed to notice the lack of organized administrative societies or parties in Sviadoshz, yet a dynamic and modern life pulsated there. The above mentioned Zalman Neimark and Moishe Yacov Farber, who were the most prosperous Jews in town, had son-in-laws who were enlightened scholars who brought a new spirit into the community right at the beginning of the present century.

Moishe Jacob Farber, a Lubavitcher Hasid, would voluntarily tithe money from his own earnings to help pay the tuition fees for a cheder. He had a large fabric shop. He selected a young man from Dvinsk to marry his daughter, Hannah Arsh. The son-in-law taught torah to the people. He wrote newspapers and books. Since he was well-versed in the torah and a secular teacher, he was able to gather a circle of young people around himself. In spite of being a Hasidic Jew, Moishe Jacob Farber permitted his daughter, Miss Farber, to study medicine and then to practice in Rakishok. Her husband, Dr. Gendelman, was the dentist. They both, along with their children, committed suicide, when the Germans arrived in Rakishok.

Zalman Neimark, or as he was also known, Zalman the innkeeper, had a large hardware store and a roadhouse. His three sons-in-law were handsome, fine young men. The oldest son-in-law, Koifman Neimark, was a scholar and an adherent of the enlightenment. He helped raise the intellectual level of the town. The other two son-in-laws, Laibe and Gershon, were also scholars. After World War I Leibe became the head of the Yeshiva in Slabodke.

Zalman Neimark's son, Shabtai, was the Rabbi in Rogeve. Zalman's brother, Elia Neimark, was a scholar and his son, Shloime Neimark, was a lecturer in South Africa at Johannesburg University and is now a delegate in the UN as an economic advisor.

Leibe Moishe Epstein was a distinguished, proprietor and a scholar. His son Chaim Joseph was a great scholar and the son-in-law of Moishe Yacov Farber. Furthermore, Moishe Jacob's son-in-law, Rueben Rubenstein, was the former editor of "The Jewish Voice" in Kovno.

It is important to mention Toviah haCohen Kaplan and his son, Sheftel Kaplan, who was the town baker. Toviah had respectable sons-in-law. Toviah's son-in-law, Moishe Ayresh had two sons in South Africa, Haikel and Yitzhak. Leibe Wolfson was another one of Toviah's sons-in-law. He was educated, a very good chess player and a worldly, modern Jew.

Hirshe Kaplan Berger was a man of the people and a joker. He would deliver the merchandise from Dvinsk for the businessmen of Sviadoshz.

Bertzik Gafanovitz, or Bertzik the Tanner, was a respectable man. He was a good student and an intelligent man. Two of his sons now live in Capetown and another son lives in Israel.

The cantor for the High Holy Days in the Mitnaggedic synagogue was Zalman Berman, or Zalman from Tzik. He had a beautiful voice. He dealt with lumber and merchandise. He was a very hospitable man who would invite poor people home for the Sabbath or the holidays.

There were original and unique characters amongst the Jews. Mates the Shoemaker was a pauper but a man of exceptional integrity; Abba Blacher was an extremely forthright man and a hard worker. Shmuel Simanovitz was known as Shmuel haCohen. His sons were respectable young men and actively took part in all the social activities in town.

We could enumerate each family house by house, because each one of the Jewish families in Sviadoshz was praiseworthy, admirable and commendable. Sviadoshz included over 60 Jewish families. They were all good, decent people and lest we forget them, we will perpetuate them in our memorial book as much as we can remember, as much as we can name:

Hannah Arsh	Fievke the Smith Herish
Moishe Ayresh	Noshem Vilkis
Aaron Yitzak the Rabbi	Shmuel Vineberg
Bere from Azubal	Velve Vineberg
Itche-Pesach the peddler	Peretz and Hene-Ite Vineberg
Efraim the peddler	Leibe Wolfson
Osher the Shamos	Velve the Shopkeeper
Moishe Blacher	Leibush from Zavish
Abba Blacher	Reb Yosef Halevi
Rofel Berzan	Yossi - Hirsh Yankel's
Zalman Berman	Mates the Shoemaker
Baruch Brom	Shmuel Segal
Hirshe Kopel Berger	Zalman Neimark the Innkeeper
Lazar Henesh Blacher	Meyer-Hirshel Neimark
Bertzik Gafanovitz the tanner	Aaron Itche Neimark
Hannah,shoemaker Gafanovitz	Elia Neimark

Ure-Leib Neimark

Dubre and her daughter Chaya-
Gittel Neimark

Michel Neimark

Sara-Esther Neimark

Shmuel haCohen Simonovitz

Mende Segal

Eidel Sklader

Rachel-Leah Swarin

Leibe Moishe Epstein

Chaim-Yosef Epstein

Lazar Padovitz

Artshik Payes

Moishe Yacov Farber

Chaim Itche Fulman

Noshem Freedman the Shochet

Liba the mailman

Koifman Neimark

Shloime the Smith

Hirsh Tarnagel

The Jews lived around the market place and along the neighboring streets. There was a well in the market place and the entire community drew their water from it. All the land in Sviadoshz was part of the landlord's court and in the course of many years the Jews bought the ground which became their communal property. Before World War One the town was part of Vilkomir County. A sheriff from Aniksht governed Sviadoshz.

In 1915 as the war's front drew near, the Jews of Sviadoshz fled fearing the imminent combat that would occur close to their town because the German/Russian positions were, in fact, at the little lake three viorst [1] outside Sviadoshz. For seven weeks the position of the front remained the same and during this period the Jews abandoned their established homes and fled to Russia: to Kalatz in Varanez Province, to Rostov, Penze, Astrahan. Only a few families in the flight stopped in Sventzion, where they waited out the war.

In 1920 all the Jews of Sviadoshz returned to their homes, except for 10 families who remained in Russia. It is notable that only a few houses were destroyed during this period. The good relations that were enjoyed between the Jews and Christians in Sviadoshz confirm this. Even the priest in Sviadoshz always maintained warm relations with the Jewish population.

A typical letter written by a boy living in South Africa to his uncle Itzik (Yitzhak) Ayresh in Sviadoshz written several years before the war.

Dear Uncle Itzik Leib Bayel!

May good fortune always follow you. You should know that we are all well, thank God, and anticipate nothing worse to come. Also I can write to you that I go to school and I am now in fourth grade and I am a good student. Gita is in first grade and she is a good student. She is good in Hebrew. And she is very good at singing and dancing. Tebele runs around in the streets. My little brother, Lifale is in a shtayalke.[2] Furthermore I would like to ask you to send a little scarf. A new suit was sewn for me. Send me the scarf for Passover if you could. Also everyone sends regards. Be well.

From me your nephew Leibe Pakabitz

The youth went off to study. They were thirsty for knowledge. In general Jewish life in Sviadoshz flowed serenely. Each person was satisfied with his lot in life, with his own individual means. Each individual Jewish family had a small house, a garden, and its own sense of worth. Thick and vast forests stretched out around and around their town and the Jews believed in the Master of the Universe, that He would protect them from all evil. Their faith in the One above was great, and with much devotion and religious fervor they took great care to be observant in their religious lifestyle.

The social-economic situation of the Jews in Sviadoshz was the same as in all small towns in Lithuania. Approximately 30% if the Jewish population earned their living as shopkeepers. A large proportion were peddlers; others were ferrymen, orchard keepers, craftsmen, several flax merchants, a few lumber dealers. Montzic Berman was a lumber dealer. Yacov Shtolov was the town pharmacist. Hirshe-Kopel was the exporter.

Also, fairs were held twice a year. Gentiles from the surrounding villages and dealers from the neighboring towns would gather together.

*****

The Germans, along with the help of the Lithuanians, left neither a remembrance nor a trace of the Jews of Sviadoshz. There are, however, Sviadoshzer Jews in South Africa, America, Argentina and Israel and, of course, in other lands. In brief it is estimated that there are approximately 10 families in Israel, 20 families in South Africa, 50 families in America, 8 families in Argentina.

We, the remaining Jews of Sviadoshz, must continue the beautiful traditions and the high morals of our beloved and admired town of Sviadoshz. The memory of Sviadoshz and its entire sincere and simple community, which was comprised of religious, observant and honorable Jews, must be held sacred and dear to all. May their memory live on forever!

13. Russian measure of distance equal to .66 mile
14. a wood contraption for toddlers. It is a cross between a modern day walker and a playpen. Stationary and sitting low to the ground, it holds a standing child upright around the chest and under the arms so that the child's legs and feet are free to move around

[Pages 362-365]

Sevenishok
(Suvainiškis, Lithuania)

56°10' 25°17'

By Dovid Katz and Yerakhmial Shon

Translated by Gloria Berkenstat Freund

Sevenishok or Suaveniski is a small *shtetl* that lies very close to the Lithuanian- Latvian border. A small river, Naret, which divides Lithuania from Latland, flows between the Nareter Court and Sevenishok. Sevenishok is found on the Lithuanian side and on the Latvian side lies the Nareter Court, which belonged to Count Shivalov, one of the richest landowners in Latland-Kurland.

The Nareter Court took up a vast area. The Nareter Market, which was six *versts* [Translator's note: two-thirds of a mile – an old Russian measurement] from Sevenishok, was very well known. The Nareter market was the largest in Kurland. Tens of thousands of peasant wagons would come riding together. Although there were only three houses, the largest merchants in Lithuania and Kurland would arrive there on market day every Wednesday. After the First World War a small *shtetl* was built around the Nareter market.

There was also a court on the Lithuanian side, which belonged to Count Kamarawski. The soil of Sevenishok was his property, too.

A large village with 90 Christian families was a neighbor of Sevenishok. A long street, the Radunker Street, went up to the marketplace. The market was quadrangular, and a large church stood there.

The market was inhabited by Jews who had their shops and apartments there. There was only one brick house in Sevenishok. Elya Prazer was the proprietor of the brick building with an inn and shop in it. Around the marketplace were the shops of Lotzef's dried produce and manufacturing business, Zisl Shon's dried goods; Gershon Bedek's food shop, Elya Bedek's inn, Ben-Zion Gershuni's inn and grocery-haberdashery business. Gerhsuni was the *gabai* (synagogue warden and assistant to the rabbi) of the *shtetl*. He was a great scholar. An important merchant was Nusen Halshtein, who had eight employees working for him.

Sitting: Moishe Shon, with his wife; Standing: Leizer Shon (killed in the First World War); Yerachmiel Shon (now in Johannesburg)

The border street led from the right of the marketplace, which led up to the bridge – the border point between Lithuania and Latland. Another small street meandered near Gershon Bedek's shop.

The *shtetl* numbered 60 Jewish families. There were merchants who traded in furs, grains, forests, cattle and so on. The mill in the *shtetl* belonged to the Zif brothers. Haim Leib Shon was one of the richest merchants. There were several craftsmen. The men's tailor, Mikhal Gafanowitz, was well-known, as was Mrs. Ruchel Lewin, who sewed men's clothing.

Before the First World War, when no border existed between Lithuania and Latvia, the Jews of the *shtetl* drew most of their income from the Nareter permanent market day. Although Sevenishok also had a market on Thursdays, it did not have any great significance. The larger Nareter market prevented the Sevenishok market from developing.

A group of sportsmen in Sevenishok

Katz Family in Sevenishok: Motel Katz, Misha Katz, Sara-Ethel Katz, Yudel Katz

There was no train traffic from Sevenishok to Nareter. The Germans built a railway spur during the First World War, which joined Ponedel with Sevenishok. Naret, however, had a railway line that led to Kreizberg and Riga. A large highway ran through Sevenishok and Naret to Riga. Before the First World War, thousands of wagons traveled through Sevenishok and Naret, laden with fruit, grains and furs. Horses, cattle and oxen would be driven by way of the highway.

When an order was issued that the Jews could not live in Kurland, the Jews would live in Sevenishok and trade in Kurland. There were several settlers, such as Moishe Shon and Haim Yankel the "Settler," who lived legally on the Kurland side; however, they were considered Sevenishok Jews.

It was a quiet and peaceful life before the First World War.

During the First World War, the Jews of Sevenishok were driven out. Only two families took a risk and remained living on the spot: the families of Yankel-Matathias Shon and of Itze-Moten. When the evacuees returned during the 1920's, everything was broken. The properties were plundered and the houses abandoned.

The *shtetl* was divided in two parts, and on crossing the bridge to Latvia, it was necessary to have a "pass." Then Sevenishok again began to be built up with the help of the "Joint" (the Joint Distribution Committee) and relatives across the sea. Craftsmen began to establish workshops, and shopkeepers opened their businesses. Sevenishoker Jews were members of the Rakishok People's Bank, which gave them short-term and long-term loans.

There was smuggling across the border, and many Jews from Sevenishok were engaged in smuggling. The county seat of Sevenishok was Rakishok.

Culturally and socially, Sevenishok – before the First World War – was poor; she did not even have a rabbi. Nusen Khalshtein brought a rabbi on the eve of the First World War. However, during the war, when the expulsion of the Sevenishok Jews took place, he was also driven out and he did not return to Sevenishok. After the war, the Rakishok *rosh-yeshiva* (head of the religious school) Reb Abraham-Mikhal, who was a talented person and a preacher, was the rabbi in Sevenishok.

There were several *khederim* (religious schools) in Sevenishok. The better teachers were: Haim-Itze, Haim-Henekh, and Moishe-Hirshe. The *shochet* (ritual slaughterer) Reb Mendl was very esteemed in the *shtetl*. After the war, Reb Moishe was the *shochet*. The *shammus* (synagogue caretaker), Reb Shlomoh, was a fine Jew. He *davened* (prayed) in front of the pulpit and was versed in books.

After the war, a "Tarbus" school opened. [Translator's note: a type of Hebrew school that existed between the two world wars.] The first teacher was Dovid Sudavski who after this was a teacher in Rakishok. A second teacher was Gafanowitz, who came from Ponevezh. The school in Sevenishok numbered 40 students. It was the great aspiration of the parents to give their children an education. Parents sent their children to study in the *yeshiva* in Rakishok and to the Lithuanian *gimnazie* there. Haim-Motke Gafanowitz ended up as a barrister.

Di Yidische Shtime (The Jewish Voice) and the *Folksblat* would come to the *shtetl* from Kovno. A sports organization was created.

Because of the hopelessness of a better future in Lithuania, the young began to emigrate. Here, in South Africa are found the following Sevenishoker Jews: Sheike and Yerakhmial Gurman – née Kutzgal; Shlomoh Kres; Mikhal Gershuni; Yerakhmial Shon; Henek Gafanowitz; Leibe-Leizer Gafanowitz; Dovid Katz and Mrs. Nowitz, and also others.

The great annihilation killed all the Jews of Sevenishok. Not one soul remained of them. We did not know of any refugees from the Holocaust. We learned, however, that all of the Sevenishoker Jews were taken together to Tarutzer Forest and forced to dig out large pits into which they were hurled and shot. Many were buried alive.

No one remained in Sevenishok, but there lives in each of us a longing for our old home, and an eternal sorrow and pain haunts us.

[Page 366]

Anushishok
(Onuškis, Lithuania)

56°08' 25°32'

Translated by Aviva Kraemer

The small town [shtetl] Anushishok, or, as it is also called, Oniskis, is located close to the border of Courland. [In 1918 Courland was incorporated into Latvia] In the vicinity is the little town of Akniste, and Rakishok [Rokiskis] is 21 kilometers away. In actual fact there were in Lithuania two small towns with the very same name. One was on the Lithuanian-Polish border, and the other on the Lithuanian-Latvian border.

Before the First World War, when no border existed between Lithuania and Courland, one would pass by Anushishok when traveling from Rakishok to Jakobstadt [Jekobpils in Latvia].

The shtetl Anushishok, on the Lithuanian-Latvian border, is surrounded by large, dense forests; and 2 versts [equal to approximately .66 of a mile] from Anushishok there is a beautiful lake.

Anushishok's land belonged to the Polish count Kamar, and the Jews of the town paid a tribute for their properties. The more prosperous among them gradually bought out the land. The houses were all made of wood, except for the tavern, a large brick building, which belonged to the Polish count until a Jew by the name of Fein bought it from him. Later, the priest purchased the building and the first cooperative was established in it.

There was a large round market-place with a water pump in the middle from which the whole town drew water. All the main stores surrounded the market-place. A long road led from the market-place to the village and from there wound its way through Juodupe to Rakishok.

Before the First World War there were 60 or 70 Jewish families in Anushishok. As the shtetl was near the border of Courland, the Jewish inhabitants made a living by trading with the Latvians, and the Jewish artisans supplied the wares ordered by them. There was an extensive trade in horses and cattle and there was a big fair on market-day which took place every Thursday. Since Anushishok had a large church, which stood on a hill to the right of the market-place, hundreds of peasants would arrive in their carts every Sunday for church services, and the Jews would profit from their presence.

There were some big businesses in Anushishok. The best-known shopkeepers and merchants were: Leibe Grintuch who had a dry-goods store and traded in furs; Shlomo Fein who owned a big wholesale store of clothing, hardware, agricultural machines, enamel ware, galoshes; Shmuel Penn who owned a textile store; Yitzchak-Moshe Penn who had a textile store; Menachem-Mendel Penn, the owner of a clothing store, a dying plant, a hosiery plant, and who in addition was also a furrier; Yankel Kanelowitz who had a clothing store; Kaplan who had a clothing and haberdashery store; Velve-Bere Fein a timber merchant; Tzepaikin, a miller; Abba Zuckerman, a merchant whose business was in Elze-Muze (Courland), but was an inhabitant of Anushishok and who loved to lead the prayers in the synagogue even though his Hebrew-reading was not very good.

In general, the Jews made their living from shopkeeping, but there were also various artisans, butchers, peddlers, gardeners, and horse traders.

Until the First World War the economic situation in Anushishok was quite good. Parents raised their children in the spirit of Jewish tradition and observance, in the typically traditional way of life, although the Haskalah [Jewish Enlightenment] had already begun to have an influence at the beginning of the twentieth century, and newspapers and journals began to appear in the town.

There were a few cheders [Hebrew schools]. The most distinguished teacher was Beinish Belek, a Jewish scholar. His son Leib Belek was a well-known leader of the British Labor Party, and his second son, Ben Zion Belek, was the leader of the leftist movement in Lithuania. I remember other teachers, but cannot recall their names. The shochet [ritual slaughterer] was Shalom-Reuven Gordon, the grandson of the Skopiszki rabbi. He was known throughout the region for his learning and wisdom.

There were both Chasidim [adherents of a Jewish religious movement founded in the 18th century in Eastern Europe, devoted to particular rabbis and generally stressing pious devotion and ecstasy more than learning] and Mitnagdim [the opponents of the Chasidim within Jewish Orthodoxy] in the shtetl. There was a big Chasidic synagogue, and the Mitnagdim had their own prayer and study house.

When the First World War broke out and the front drew closer, the Jews of Anushishok began to pack their wagons. I was just a little girl, and was placed in the wagon beside my uncle, Shmuel Penn. The battle came ever closer, and my father did not manage to pack everything and therefore remained at home under the German occupation. So it was as though I had become an orphan.

We traveled for six weeks in the ox-drawn wagon until we arrived in Kaplancy in the Vitebsk province. From there we went to Kursk. I only returned to my home and family in 1921.

In 1921-1922 Anushishok Jews began to return from Russia. However, many of them remained in Russia, among them the Grintuch family and my uncles Shmuel Penn and Yitzchak-Moshe Penn. Those who returned found the town destroyed and plundered.

The great revolutionary and martyr Hirsh Lekert, who was hung in May 1902 by the Czarist hangmen. Holy is his memory!

The new border between Lithuania and Latvia was disastrous for my hometown. Trade with the Latvians ceased as merchandise could no longer be transported to Latvia.

The post-war youth, returning from military service, from the front, looked around desperately and saw that there were no prospects. An emigration of the youth began. Elderly people, who lived from the support sent by their children, remained in the shtetl.

Anushishok Jews, in their new lands of immigration, were throughout the years closely connected to their old home, helping not only parents and friends, but also the communal institutions in the shtetl.

Thus few Jews remained in Anushishok after the War. They dispersed, as Shalom Aleichem says: some to Lisi and some to Strisi. They settled in Kovno and in Rakishok, and they also emigrated to their children who were already overseas. The remaining Jewish families lived under the impact of the new era. The little town was caught up in the Zionist ideal and the Jews sent their children to Hebrew schools in Rakishok, Vilkomir and Kovno. Jewish children also learned in the gymnasium in Anushishok.

The Rabbi, the Gaon [genius, brilliant man] Abraham-Dov Popel z"l (of blessed memory)

Anushishok was a very small town, but was nevertheless well-known because of the personalities who had lived there.

The Revolution years from 1902-1905 brought forth new ideas and trends. An active revolutionary circle was established from which emerged the famous revolutionary and martyr, Hirsch Lekert, who, in May 1902 in Vilna, shot the provincial governor, Von Wahl. Lekert was illiterate, a shoemaker by trade, but he had a beautiful soul, a pure heart, a strong feeling for honesty and freedom. He was a very lively young man and Anushishok Jews remember him to this day. The shot that he fired reverberated throughout Russia, especially in the Pale of Settlement [the area assigned to the Jews in Czarist Russia]. He went proudly to the gallows as befits a hero who took revenge for the injustices done to his people. Soon after this event, a number of Anushishok Jews were arrested.

Anushishok was known for its rabbis. At the beginning of the 20th century the rabbi of the town was Rabbi Klatzkin, who later became the Rabbi in Swiadoscz [Svedasai?]. His son played a significant role in establishing the national council and was later the rabbi in Rasssein [Raseiniai] and Livoi [Laviai?].

The name Rabbi Avraham Dov Popel was renowned and acclaimed. He was the son-in-law of Avraham Penn, the wealthiest Jew in the shtetl.

Avraham Dov Popel was a great scholar and when he was still very young he was ordained by the greatest rabbis of his time. He studied mainly at the Eishishik [Eisiskes] Yeshiva, and he was known as a prodigy. When Rabbi Klatzkin left to become the rabbi in Swiadoscz, Rabbi Popel became the rabbi of Anushishok, despite the fact that his uncle, a brother of his father-in-law, was against his candidacy because he was a Mitnaged..

Rabbi Avraham Dov Popel was one of the finest personalities in Jewish Lithuania. Apart from his scholarship, he was a lover of peace and often served as a mediator in disputes between individuals and groups. He was also an eminent orator with a strong power of elucidation.

Before the First World War [in 1905], he became the rabbi of Mariampol. He was one of the leaders of Lithuanian Jewry and was vice-chairman of the national council and one of the builders of national autonomy, chairman of Agudat Israel and vice-chairman of the Yavne schools in Lithuania.

Rabbi Popel was also a representative in the Sejm [the Lithuanian parliament] and was famous for his speech in parliament against capital punishment, which was reported in the world press and, in particular, the press in the United States.

Even though Rabbi Popel was one of the pillars of the Aguda, he nevertheless always supported fund-raising for Eretz Yisrael [Palestine].

Rabbi Avraham Dov Popel died on the 4th of Shevat in 1923 at the age of 53. He left a wife and children. His wife Rachel died in the Shavl ghetto; his son Arieh, [who was doing his doctorate in chemistry in Belgium] was deported from France to a concentration camp where he perished. His daughter Henia died in a concentration camp. His daughter, Rivka Wilkov, lives in Johannesburg with her husband and daughter. [In 1962 they immigrated to Israel where Rivka Wilkov died in 1994. Her daughter, Aviva Wilkov Kraemer at present lives most of the year in Chicago and part of the year in Israel.]

After Rabbi Popel left Anushishok, Rabbi Kadesh became the rabbi of the shtetl.

In South Africa there are about 25 families of Anushishok origin. Amongst them are the following: three brothers Katz who have a clothing factory; Joseph Penn [deceased]; Berel Penn; Julius Penn [deceased]; Yitzhak Moshe Penn [deceased] and his sons Wolf [deceased], Abraham, and Dr. Aaron Penn; Kruz; Shulman; Tuvia Glass; Harry Miller; Yudel Tzupeikin.

The Anushishok Jews, wherever they are now settled, hold sacred the memory of the Jews of their idyllic, beautiful shtetl, who perished in Rakishok together with the Jews of Rakishok.

In Anushishok there is an old tombstone on which is inscribed that it was erected over 150 years ago. This proves that the Jewish settlement in the shtetl was not new. And now, nothing is left of the Jewish presence, as though it had never existed.

[Rachel (Ray) Kramer (Penn), who wrote this chapter on Anushishok, lived in Johannesburg for many years and then for a number of years in Cape Town. Her two daughters and their families are now living in Australia. Her sister, Raina Zemel, and brother, Berel (Barney) Penn are still living in Johannesburg.]

[Page 370]

Skopishok
(Skapiškis, Lithuania)

55°53' 25°12'

by Mendel Gordon

Translated from the Yiddish by Abraham Zygielbaum and edited by Lennard Thal

Itze-Yankel, teacher in Skopichek, Chaim Grinberg, textile merchant in Skopichek

Before World War I, 50 Jewish families lived in Skopishok (approximately 200 souls). The Lithuanian population there was substantial. Skopishok had four main streets: Koloveyer Street, Ponedeler Street, the Tzigayner (Gypsy) Street, and the street called "Yene Shtetl" ("the other shtetl"). Jews were concentrated in the center of the shtetl adjacent to the marketplace. They were mainly tradesmen and merchants. Among the more important merchants were Ortchik Fein, Zalman-Moteh, and Shlomo Orlovitz who resided in Skopishok for many years. There were some peddlers called "Karabelniki" (men who carried their wares, often just odds and ends, to nearby towns). There were also some artisans including Abe-Leib the tailor; Shimon the tailor; Noteh the Tailor; Micha the shoemaker; Elkona the shoemaker. There was also an extensive flax trade. These included Israel Gordon; the writer of these lines (Mendel Gordon); Ya'akov Feldman (the grandfather of the brothers Feldman in Johannesburg); Leslie Feldman and Abraham Feldman. These flax merchants, as well as other merchants, also traded in seeds. Until World War I, trading was done with Novo Alexandrovsk (New Alexandria) the regional city, and with Dvinsk. After World War I, the merchants of Skopishok traded with Kibard, situated near the Lithuanian-German border, and with Kovno. Jews also traded in forest products and were lessors of lakes (presumably with water and/or fishing rights). There was a large, dense forest around Skopishok and two beautiful lakes were owned by the city.

Yehoshua Turetsky, a scholar in Skopichek.

The relationship with Christian Lithuanians was good. There were no pogroms. I remember one event which caused panic in the town, but it did not develop into an attack on the Jews. The following took place. Two peasant women from the village of Srubishok came to the place of Shimon the tailor to comb the wool. It happened to be just before Passover. Shimon went out to the market and left the two women villagers inside his house. They became frightened by Shimon's sudden departure and were seized by the thought that the only reason he had left so suddenly was to summon other Jews with long beards to kill them in order to use their blood for matzos for Passover which was approaching. Terror-stricken, the two women broke into the market-place shouting, "gevalt! gevalt!" It was the day of the fair in the town and the peasants attending the fair gathered together, ready to fight. Panic broke out as people sensed the possibility of a pogrom. My wife, Fraidl, quickly ran to the Catholic priest, a Lithuanian, and pleaded with him to go quickly and calmly to pacify the peasants given the imminent danger of a bloodbath. The priest summoned the Christians to the church by ringing the church bells and there he appeased them by explaining how groundless and stupid the women's accusations had been.

During World War I, some families evacuated into Russia because Skopishok was too close to the front lines. Jews of Skopishok settled temporarily in Yeletz and Bobroisk. In 1921 most returned to Skopishok, but some did not. In general, the Jewish population became smaller, shrinking to 25 families after the war. The young people began to emigrate, particularly when the economic situation worsened. The government opened Lithuanian co-operatives (stores owned by the authorities which sold goods at lower prices). The Lithuanian Prime Minister Tubelis threatened that he would fill the Nieman River with Jewish blood. My children Itzhak, Moshe, Zalman, and Chaim emigrated to South Africa. Until 1937 I lived in Skopishok.

The regional city was Rakishok. There was little change in the life of the shtetl. Everything went on according to the old ways and fashion. There was no "folkshul," and no library. From time to time the young people organized an amateur theatrical performance. There were two wooden synagogue, one Chasidic and one Mitnagdic. The Chasidim were followers of Kapist (Kapister Chasidim). Before World War I, the Rav of Skopishok was Rabbi Azriel Gordon. Subsequently this post was occupied by Rav Reb Mendel. The religious teachers (Melamdim) were Zalman-Itzeh and Itzeh-Yankel. The schochet's name was Nacham.

After the Holocaust my wife received a letter from her brother Mosheke Gafinowitz. He wrote about the destruction of Skopishok and how he escaped to the partisans in the forest. He came back to the shtetl as soon as the Red Army liberated Lithuania. He wrote that the structures remained intact but that the Jewish cemetery had been demolished. He became horrified and nearly went insane when he saw all the Jewish houses without even one living Jewish soul: doors open, houses empty. He couldn't linger on in Skopishok and left for Vilna where a group of Jewish survivors had settled.

In the picture: Families from Skopichek and Panamunak after the wedding in Skopichek

[Page 374]

Ponemunok
(Panėmunelis, Lithuania)

55°55' 25°29'

by L. Karabelnik

Translated by Lucas Bruyn

L. Karabelnik

Ah, my poor ruined little town! But though it was small, smaller than the other shtetlach in the vicinity, it was privileged by having a railway station. On the big wall-maps in Russia and in the Baltics, Ponemunok was marked by the icon for "relay center." Ponemunok played a bigger role in commerce than Kamay, Ponedel, and Skopishok. The inhabitants of these townlets had to come to Ponemunok's rail station whenever they had to take trips, whether they traveled in-country, abroad, or overseas. Coachmen driving shopkeepers and merchants used to come to collect deliveries of goods or to send off fruits and other agricultural produce.

Before the First World War, Ponemunok had a Jewish population of about 200 souls. Probably because of the rail station the townlet had increased rapidly in size. You must realize that during the reign of the Czar there were no borders between Russia, Latvia, and Poland, and there was a far-reaching network of trade with cities and localities in Russia. No doubt the presence of the railway station attracted people who wanted to ease the struggle for a livelihood by settling down there.

Ezra Karabelnik

Apart from the railway station, Ponemunok is surrounded by a fine landscape and the river Nemulenim, a subsidiary of the Nemunas, lends a particular charm to the town. That river certainly was one of the main attractions for the youth of the town--we all have lots of memories connected with that stream running through the city.

After the Great Fire [see "My Shtetl Ponemunok," by Ben Zion Joffe] and after the expulsion of the Jews of Ponemunok during WWI, the Jewish community of Ponemunok diminished considerably and only 22 Jewish families remained, all living around the railway station, while the Lithuanian community numbered about 60 families. The Jews busied themselves trying to make ends meet.

After the death of the only Jewish tailor, Segal, there were no more craftsmen in Ponemunok. They were tradesmen, shopkeepers, peddlers [karabelnik-krumer], and farmers. The few affluent families took care of the poor in the shtetl, giving them matzah during Pesach and meting out an irregular income to them. They lived in peace with each other and they helped each other out with interest-free loans.

Because the community was so small, there was no resident medical doctor. The Jewish apothecary, Olkin, who lived in the center of the town, used to bring over a doctor from Ponevezh twice a week. There was only a Christian barber-surgeon living in town and in urgent cases they had to ride to Rakishok for doctors. After the war Rakishok, 16 kilometers from Ponemunok, became the capital of our district.

In my time Ponemunok did not have a Rabbi either. There was a young yeshivah student from Telz who officially registered as Rabbi of Ponemunok in order to have grounds for exemption from military service. He only came down to the shtetl in the evening, in order to satisfy the authorities. The prayer and study-house was a simple wooden one, with a modest ark and a lectern without any carvings. Only on Shabbes and during the High Holy Days did the prayer house have an occasional minyan of worshipers. On weekdays there would seldom be a minyan if it were not for someone's yahrzeit. At first, Yoyne Karabelnik was gabbai (caretaker), and after he died the position was taken over by his brother Ezra Karabelnik.

All people of the shtetl were Chasidim, and the tradition followed in praying was the Sefard style. Only the members of the Karabelnik family were Mitnagdim. Sometimes when the gabbai Karabelnik went up to the lectern for prayer and recited the "Yatzmah Purkanei" from the Kaddish or a "Barukh She'amar" as "Hodu," a tumult would arise in the benches [shtenders], but it never became an outright shouting match.

Parents took care to give their children an education. For many years the shochet Avrom Epstein was the only teacher [melamed] in Ponemunok. He was a man with a long beard that reached down to his waist. He was thirsty for knowledge and he was well-read, mainly in astronomy. His pupils in the cheder loved him because of his mild and friendly behavior towards them.

After the death of Mr. Avrom Eliezer, Vilenski from Nayshtat became shochet and chazzan.

There was a Lithuanian "Volkshul" in Ponemunok where some Jewish children went; young men went away to a yeshivah or a "gymnasium" [classical grammar school]. For some time they had an imported female teacher of Hebrew and general studies in Ponemunok. She taught Hebrew with the Sephardic pronunciation [havore], which clashed with the Ashkenazic style taught in cheder.

****

I left Ponemunok in 1936. A quiet and idyllic life formed the heartbeat of the shtetl. The only dynamic force was the railway station. Nothing special ever happened; no changes took place, and there was no social activity. The paupers occupied themselves only with the battle for survival and the well-to-do people were not active in the community either. Maybe the small number of Jewish inhabitants in Ponemunok were simply not interested in showing any initiative in the field of social activity.

A great social upheaval took hold of Ponemunok when the writer of these lines "sold shekalim" [shekels--collected fees for the Zionist organization] and then called for a general meeting, during which I urged for a vote to elect the delegates to the 19th Zionist Congress, for a certain Zionist party. For the people of the shtetl it would be the first Zionist Congress, because they had never been involved in the activities of the Zionist movement.

Ponemunok did not produce any famous people. Leibe Levin was the only "utsjoni Yivrei" (erudite Jew).

The whole community of Ponemunok somehow did not have much cohesion, especially after the First World War. This becomes evident from the fact that there was no Jewish cemetery. They used to bury their dead in Kamay, 11 verst [1 verst is .66 of a mile] from Ponemunok. It could be that the Jewish inhabitants of Ponemunok had a premonition that in the end the Jewish community of Ponemunok would be rooted out, as indeed happened during the days of Hitler's reign, may his name be blotted out.

[Page 377]

My Shtetl Ponemunok

By Ben Zion Joffe

Translated from the Yiddish by Lucas Bruyn

It is many years ago now that I left Ponemunok. I have been forty years in South Africa. My father, Chaim David Joffe, may he rest in peace, initially traveled to Africa alone and later brought over his family.

With the passing of time spent in South Africa, under influence of the changed living conditions of the new country, the memories of my old home have faded out. But although many things have unfortunately become nebulous, still, to this very day, shreds of reminiscences, images, and figures from those distant years in the shtetl of my birth still run through my mind. This is all the more so since the great destruction [khurbm] of the East European Jews in general and the annihilation of my town Ponemunok in particular.

I do not know when a Jewish community was first established in Ponemunok, but the story in the town went that Jews started to settle there with the building of the railroad. Before that time it used to be a kind of farm [folvark], under the estate [hoyf--court] of Ponemunok, the property of count Shvintetski. The fact that the church did not stand in town, but rather on the estate, bears witness to this.

Ponemunok was surrounded by large woods, fields, and meadows. Along the town stretches a dense forest and a small river named the Nemunelim cuts through it. (In Lithuanian, Nemunelim means Little Nieman). [The river Jara, a subsidiary of the Shventoji/Swenta.]

Zalman-Itze Misrakh

To this very day I am puzzled why the Central Railway Board of Czarist Russia chose Ponemunok for the site of a new railway station--one even bigger than that of Rakishok. [The reason might be that before the railroad was built, Ponemunok was on the main road between Dvinsk and Libau, while Rakishok was not.]

Trains used to halt in Ponemunok for a solid half hour, and there was a canteen in the waiting room. While the train was standing at the platform, passengers would alight to eat and drink there.

Ponemunok's railway station served all small towns and villages in the region. The towns Sviyadosht, Kamay, Skopishok and Ponedel, as well as dozens of villages, exported their agricultural products, cattle, and timber through PonemunokÕs railway station. Thousands of farmers would deliver logs at the station for further transportation by train, and these would lay in wide circles around the station. At the beginning of the geese season they would drive flocks of geese towards the station and the noise of the gaggle would be deafening. At the end of summer they would bring whole strings of carts full of fruit to be exported to many places.

Every Thursday there was a big market, and the marketplace was in the center of town. You could also find shops there with living quarters above, as well as some brick buildings. Big merchants from Russia and Germany used to come down to the market of Ponemunok. In my time the town counted about 60 Jewish families, and almost all of them were in commerce. There were big merchants and small traders. There were almost no craftsmen--only one shoemaker, a tailor, and a blacksmith.

Panemunak Yiddish youth at the Nemunelis River. Right to left: Leah Beralski, Lyuba Kavalski, Vita Karabelnik, Beila Yaffa and Moishe Karabelnik

Thanks to the railway station--and also thanks to the fact that the post office of Ponemunok served the surrounding towns and villages--the economical development of Ponemunok went well. There were several wholesale businesses. The owner of the biggest wholesale store was Zalman Itze Mizrekh. You could say of him that he united religion, cleverness, and wealth in one person. In his shop you could find anything, from a needle to a threshing machine.

A big lumber merchant was Shmuel Avirer (Karabelnik). He kept a roadside inn. He was a man of high morals, and always the first when it came to helping out someone or doing someone a favor. When it happened that someone fell ill during the night--Ponemunok did not have a doctor, only a Christian barber-surgeon [feldsher]--they would run to Shmuel the Avirer and he would immediately harness his horse and deliver the patient to Rakishok himself. He was always ready to give a loan, to offer hospitality, to help out an orphan getting married, or to assist a widow.

Yoyne Karabelnik had a good name in the region. He had a textile business and was a timber merchant. He owned a two-story brick building.

Malatski was a man of Talmudic learning and the owner of a big business. Moyshe Arn, the butcher, was a good and fine person.

My father, Chaim David Joffe was a real man of the people, always lively and in good cheer, clever and witty. He brought his plain Yiddish personality along to South Africa and spent a lot of time on community affairs. For 40 years he was a member of the Rakishok Society and other Jewish institutions.

In my time there were two prayer houses: one Chasidic and the other Mitnagdic. Most Jews were Chasidim; the wealthy ones were Mitnagdim. Yitzhok-Moyshe, the son of the Rabbi of Ponedel, was the [Mitnagdic] Rabbi. [TranslatorÕs note: the author is not clear if Yitzhok-Moyshe was Mitnagdic or Chasidic, but the text reads "rov" rather than "rebbe," generally indicating a Mitnagdic rabbi. It may be that he served both synagogues.] He was a man of great Talmudic learning and an exceptionally capable person. He was also in big business [groyse miskhorim] and he did not make a living from his rabbinate. Moreover, he was a great singer [bal-menagn], the chazzan [cantor] in the Chasidic synagogue, a preacher [bal-droshn], and in general a man of stately appearance [a hadres ponemdiker yid].

I think that Avrom was the shochet [ritual slaughterer]. He was a modern man, not only learned in the Talmud, but also an adherent of the Haskalah [Jewish Enlightenment] movement, who spoke Russian and Polish well. He gave his children a secular education.

Shmerl the shames [beadle] was an interesting character. He always said the morning prayers, blew the ram's horn in the synagogue, and was the reader of the Torah. He also used to write out the addresses for women whose husbands were overseas.

In the Mitnagdic shul, Zalman Itze Mizrekh was the chazzan.

Ponemunok as I remember it had several cheders. The teacher of Gemara was Bertstik. The well- to-do families used to send their children to study at the yeshivah of Ponevezh. I also remember a strange man who had 22 children.

****

I don't remember any special events in Ponemunok. There was a bit of commotion in 1905 when they killed a member of the secret police in Ponemunok. My brother Itse Berk and his friend Nefl [?] Naftali were accused of shooting him. They soon escaped to America, were they live until this very day.

Around the turn of the century there was a great fire, and the whole shtetl burned down. Before long, however, the shtetl was rebuilt with a new bathhouse [merkhets].

Up until the First World War the Jews of Ponemunok lived in comfort and contentment. After the war the economic situation of Ponemunok went downhill. Rakishok became the governmental seat of the region and competed with Ponemunok. The business of the whole region centered on Rakishok.

There never was a cemetery in Ponemunok, giving rise to the joke that this was why the Jews of Ponemunok lived to a ripe old age.

The Jews of Ponemunok, together with those of Rakishok, were all murdered. May this account keep alive forever the memory of my home town, Ponemunok.

The great annihilation killed all the Jews of Sevenishok. Not one soul remained of them. We did not know of any refugees from the Holocaust. We learned, however, that all of the Sevenishoker Jews were taken together to Tarutzer Forest and forced to dig out large pits into which they were hurled and shot. Many were buried alive.

No one remained in Sevenishok, but there lives in each of us a longing for our old home, and an eternal sorrow and pain haunts us.

[Page 383]

Decline and Destructon

My Evidence

by Bryna Rotholz-Kur

Translated by Rae Meltzer

Names and family of my parents: Jacob Hirsh and Sara Kur
Education: Finished the 6th class "YVNAH" (Hebrew Folk School)
Graduate of the Lithuanian Government Gymnasia in Rakishok
Residence: Rakishok (until World War II)
Where did I save myself: the Soviet Union
Current residence: Paarl, Cape Province, South Africa

Bryna Rotholz-Kur

Until June 15, 1940, Lithuania was an independent republic. Then the Soviet military power came into Lithuania and also into Rakishok. I remember a Sunday. I was then barely 16 years old. Students were on vacation and so no classes met. Together with my girlfriends we went out to watch the long line of Soviet tanks. The Count Jan Pshedzetski of Rakishok, was waiting for the Soviet garrison.

No excesses occurred during entry of the Soviet power into Rakishok. There was complete order. However, our social and communal life changed. All business were immediately nationalized. The merchandise from the stores was concentrated in cooperatives. From early morning until late at night, customers stood in line in order to buy things from the cooperatives. Rumors spread that the Soviets had an enormous shortage of produce and of manufactured goods. Because of these rumors there was an intense rush and violent emergency to get to the cooperatives.

From the palace of Count Pszedetzki – in the noble's building – where the Germans detained the Jews of Rokiskis and vicinity; the Jews were led to graves, to slaughter

The rich strata and the ordinary Jewish citizens as well as the Christian population was opposed to and unhappy with the invasion of the Russian army. The strongest resistance to the new Soviet power was based on the Soviet policy of nationalization of private businesses and came especially from mercantile enterprises that were fairly large. There was strong opposition to the Soviet policy against free trade. There was a severe scarcity of everything.

The majority of the youth in the shtetl were excited and even inspired by the coming of the Soviet power to our shtetl. But at Succoth time, we were ordered to exchange our Lithuanian money for Soviet money. This aroused a strong dissatisfaction towards the Soviets. The Soviets were strict and stern, and everyone was fearful to express even verbal objections and criticisms of Soviet orders. Even the Lithuanians were frightened and did not show or express displeasure and objections. In spite of these strict orders from the Soviets, the Jewish population felt more secure under the protection of the Soviets. No one feared the excesses of the former Lithuanian government.

In the last years of the Lithuanian Republic, the anti-Semitism in Lithuania became very pronounced. A boycott was organized against Jewish merchants and other businesses. There was agitation against Jews and pamphlets were distributed telling Christians not to patronize Jewish merchants or buy Jewish goods. Leaflets were distributed reviling the Jews and insulting them by calling them "ethnics." The Jewish people in Lithuania saw threatening signs that black, perilous days were coming for Lithuanian Jews. For this reason, they were pleased with the Soviet power in one respect-- that the Soviets opposed anti-Semitism.

The Jewish population in Rakishok grew. A stream of Polish Jews and Poles also immigrated to Rakishok. The Jews of Rakishok helped the Jewish refugees and immigrants with much concern and devotion. They helped them with housing, clothing, and footwear.

Life in Rakishok became more normal. People became acclimated to the existing Soviet government. There was unrest and worry about the possibility of war between the Soviets and Germany. In secret, everyone spoke about this possibility with great anxiety. In the last months before the German-Soviet War, one actually saw large multitudes of military personnel marching in the direction of the German border. This was an actual, factual signal that the peace between the Soviets and the Germans was on a very shaky foundation. However, no one expected or believed that war would break out so fast and so violently.

On the 22nd of June, 1941, Kovno was bombed by the Germans. This disastrous news spread like wildfire and lightening. No one believed that war had broken out between the Germans and the Soviets. On the same day, at seven o'clock in the morning, my older brother, Henech, who was a mechanic in the Russian "compartay" [Communist Party?] told us that indeed it was true, that war had broken out between the Germans and the Soviets. At twelve o'clock the Russian Foreign Minister, Commissar M. Molotov, announced that the Germans had attacked Lithuania and other Soviet borders. He said in his statement that every citizen must help the Soviet Union defeat Fascism.

On Monday, June 23, 1941, a German airplane was sighted over Rakishok, but there was no bombing. The same day, at five o'clock in the afternoon, another plane was sighted, but Rakishok was not bombed. The day before we had already seen wounded Soviet soldiers being brought from the Soviet-German border. On the roads there were Lithuanian partisans who shot the Russian soldiers. They hung banners on the posts and the national Lithuanian flags. Their banners were inscribed with anti-Soviet and anti-Semitic slogans. Many Jews who were on the regular roads and on the unpaved roads of Rakishok were killed by the Lithuanian partisans.

The Soviet government in Lithuania was not able to control the panic and at the same time liquidate the Lithuanian partisan organization. I know only these facts: four Lithuanian partisans were caught by the Soviets and condemned to be hung on the telegraph- poles. Other Lithuanian partisans came and freed them before they were dead. I also know that Mishkeh Rotman shot a Lithuanian partisan, Patrim. These nominal measures could not liquidate the Lithuanian-fascist-partisan organization. It was like a drop in the ocean. The Lithuanian partisans multiplied quickly with every passing hour.

On Wednesday, June 25, 1941, at four o'clock in the afternoon, dreadful panic erupted in the shtetl. We saw how the Soviet "Compartay" was leaving Rakishok. My brother was also getting ready to leave with members of the "Partay". Everybody came running to us to find out the details of the catastrophic situation. The Jewish population was deadly frightened of the Germans. All the persecutions and the death penalties that befell the Jews of Poland were reaching Rakishok. The whole shtetl was ready to flee.

People began to run with horses and wagons, with bicycles and on foot. Almost half of the Jews of Rakishok fled. Ninety-nine (99%) of the youth fled. Everyone ran in the direction of Abel, Subot, Dvinsk, and the Lithuanian-Soviet border. On the border stood the Lithuanian soldiers, who would not let the fleeing Jews cross the border. They said to the Jews: "Go fight in your land." They said the same to the Rakishok "Compartay." There was every reason to think that the Lithuanian soldiers were deliberately trying to provoke the fleeing Rakishok Jews.

The fleeing Jews and the Soviet officials as well as the "Compartay" were forced to turn back to Rakishok. On the road they were encircled by Lithuanian soldiers who shot at them and threw grenades. A battle developed, which lasted two-and-a-half hours and there were dead and wounded. The Soviet government condemned to death three Lithuanian partisans who were between 20-25 years old. They were immediately shot.

The Lithuanian driver of the "Compartay" ran away during the battle to the Lithuanian partisans. My younger brother, Michal, took over the automobile and became the driver of the "Compartay." The battle-field overflowed with Jewish dead and wounded and their property was strewn around everywhere.

We found three wounded Jews from Abel--two Jews were lying in one grave and another Jew in a second grave. We thought that one of them might be Hon. Abraham Meyerovitsh from Abel and two other Jews from Abel. They were shot by Lithuanian partisans. In Vorestsineh, six kilometers from Rakishok, there was a large grouping of partisans who shot at us. We got to Rakishok at eleven o'clock and the situation was very dangerous. Between Abel and Subot there were German sentries who were shooting the returning Rakishok Jews who had fled earlier.

The panic rose from minute to minute and from twelve o'clock to one o'clock in the afternoon, all the Soviet officials--the police, the NKVD, and the "Compartay"--were just taking a last breath before pulling out of Rakishok. The only way of escape was by way of Anikshot-Kurland. All those who fled toward Abel were killed by the Germans and the Lithuanian partisans. My parents perished fleeing to Abel. The Komeyer Jews, Brikman and Shtein, were the only ones lucky enough to save themselves while fleeing to Abel.

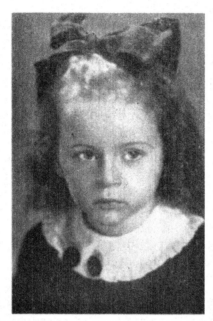 

Top right: Chaya Ita Schwartzberg poisoned herself (to avoid capture by the Nazis). Top left: Yordina, the young daughter of Miriam Farbereite and Henok Gandelman who poisoned themselves (to avoid capture).

Bottom right: Yankel Kark. He represented the detained Jews before the Germans. Bottom left: Dr. Miriam Farbereite Gandelman provided the poison to her children, husband, and Chaya Ita Schwartzberg

The Bube (grandmother) Chaya-Zipe Kur; sitting center – the father, Yakov-Hirsh Kur, and last in this row – the mother Sara Kur. The remaining [people] in the photograph are children of Yakov-Hirsh and Sara Kur.

I fled through Anikshot, where the border was open. We went through Jacobshtot to Rezshitseh, about 500 kilometers. Then we pushed toward Velikeh-Luki-Apatsk. For 90 kilometers we struggled on through a swamp. From there we rode troop trains. For 22 days we rode on the troop train toward Kazan. We were distributed among the villages and "kolkhoz," where I found my three brothers. Along with myself, my sister and her child escaped also. Because of the continuous German conquests, we rode deeper and deeper into the Soviet interior until we reached Uzbekistan, where we found a community near the Iranian border. It was there that we remained throughout the war.

In November 1945 I returned to Vilna. It was Succoth time. Rakishok had been liberated in 1944. Shloime Kagan was the first Jew to get back to Rakishok. He participated in the struggle of the Lithuanian division that was formed in the U.S.S.R. (Soviet Union) in the town of Gorki, January 20, 1943. The majority in this division were Jews, amongst whom there were many Rakishok young men. They included: Laibke Ribak, Poli Ruch, Boruch Kruk, Berke Kur, Shayarke Levin, Shmulke Rif, Shloime Kagan, Abraham Kagan, Hershl Abramovitsh (who reached the rank of Major), Laibl Yakubovits (who reached the rank of Lieutenant), Rueben Levy (Lieutenant), Marek Etengaf, whose father, Dr. Etengaf, accompanied the echelon of those forced to go to Siberia which included the following families: Ruch, Fanya Levin, all the brothers Meller, and Yonkel Klingman with his family. In the Lithuanian army the following served: Laib Shoib, Tsimeh, the Rabbi's son, Itzhak Shrubinski, the brothers Oiyershans, and others. It is known to me that Motl Klug, Hirshl Harmets, Kopl the orphan, one of the brothers Oiyershan, and Motl Shub perished in the war. Yudel Vyner died in the Soviet army in Japan. One of the most severe invalids among the survivors was Laibl Ruch. Those young Jewish men of Rakishok who were in the Lithuanian division were loyal and fought bravely and heroically in the area of "Klaipedo" (Memel) and were the first to fight their way back to Lithuania. The Rakishok youth told me the above details and much more information about the death and destruction of our Rakishok Jews.

The Germans came into Rakishok through Komayer Street. The speedy arrival of the Germans came at eleven o'clock in the morning. Jacob Jacobson was peeping through his window and he was immediately shot and killed by a German soldier. He was the first Jewish corpse. The second corpse was Kasriel Shomer, who was shot as he was walking back from Jacobson's funeral. Then the Jewish community turned around and went back to the cemetery to hold a second funeral. Immediately after their march into Rakishok, the Germans assembled the men and encircled them at "Lordship's red stable wall." The women and children were forced to flee to Antenasheh. Children up to the age of eight were kept with the women.

The Germans forced the Jews to do back-breaking work such as finishing the paving of the highway, which through Jewish forced labor was extended to the marketplace over the "red minyon." [Amanda's note: The "Red Minyon" means "The Red Shul". There were several Shuls In Rakishok identified by color- our family went to the Green Shul. I remember my aunt telling me about this.]

In addition to hard-labor the Jews were beaten, tortured and stabbed with spears.

The Germans forced the Jews to do inhumane, exhausting, heavy labor, and in addition they bullied, baited, and drove them under a hail of punches and kicks to the river "Prud" and back.

The local Rakishok gentile population did not show any sympathy to the Jews.

The sadistic perpetrators of the pogrom among the Christian population of Rakishok were the following: the tailor Bronislov who had said, "Yiddish blood must be spread on my hands." Andrushka, who all her life worked with Jews, even spoke Yiddish very well, and worked for the bagel-baker Rachmiel Ruch. In those Hitler days she was the worst assassin. Pytrenas, who was the commander of the police and watched over Jews in the "red (outside) wall." Before the entry of the Soviet army in 1944, Pytrenas was shot and killed. A

Rokiskis Yizkor Book 397

second police assassin was Antsenas, who worked until the war in "Stsukas Auto-Garage" and was in hiding in 1946, in the woods in the vicinity of Rakishok.

Later, the Jews were cruelly tortured for several weeks before the men were shot and murdered on August 10, 1941. The women were shot and murdered on August 20, 1941. Before the Jews were led out to be shot, they were told that they were being sent to work in Smolensk and vicinity. The driver, Janos, from the Lord's estate, helped the Germans lead the Jews to their place of execution. All Jews were brought to a place behind "Boyar," and before all were shot, Hon. Zelig Orelowitz turned to the Jews and directed them not to resist, but instead to "sacrifice one's life in martyrdom for the name of the Lord" (Muser Nefesh Tsein El Kiddush Hashem).

Fifty-eight hundred (5,800) Jews, in 5-7 "brother" graves (mass graves) are buried there in the above-mentioned PLACE. Those buried there include Jews from Rakishok and nearby shtetlach: Abel, Kamai, Ponidel, Suvianishok, and Raduteh.

Before the execution, the following committed suicide by taking poison: the apothecary, Mishl Sher, together with his family; the doctor/dentist Henuch Gandelman and his wife; Dr. Miriam Farberyteh-Gandelman, and their two children. Dr. Farberyteh-Gandelman, an aunt of Yrachmiel Arons (Arsh), administered injections of morphine to her husband, the dentist/doctor Henuch Gandelman, her two children, and also Chyeh-Eyten Shwartzberg, a sister of Etl Arons (Arsh). At the home of "advocat"-Trivski, while the Germans were entering Rakishok, there was a banquet. Then because of a conflict in which their son was involved in a lawsuit with a Lithuanian Communist, the Germans shot Trivski and his son. Also, Nechama Jacobson was charged by the Germans as a Communist. She was unmercifully tortured in the Rakishok jail until she was shot.

On the basis of the information gathered through Shloime Kagan and through my brother who was also in Rakishok after the Liberation, there was a short period of five weeks that the Jews of Rakishok lived under the power of the Germans. During that time a "Judenrat" was formed of Reznikovits and Jacob Kark.

After the execution of the Jews, the Germans confiscated all Jewish property and put it in Besel Zamets' "moyer" [perhaps it means "stable"] and in the red minyon and sold it for negligible prices. There were those who ran away or escaped before and during the execution. They included: Henkeh Yafeh, a dedicated member of Maccabi, whose husband was Yser Kapelovits. She hid in a village with the Christian family, Dohdes. This family informed the Germans about her and they shot her while she was walking. Berl Shlossberg, at age 55, saved himself on the Aryan side [?]. He did not wish to talk about the details of the "Churban" (Holocaust).

Those who were in Rakishok after the Liberation told us that the shtetl remained whole. The bombs did not damage or destroy any buildings. Only the railroad station and a few houses near the church were damaged. All the houses remained standing in their places. Only the synagogue/school, the "green minyon," the "red minyon," YVNAH Hebrew Folk School, and several houses on Vilner Street were pilfered and distributed by the peasants and the Germans. Also, the Old Synagogue was pilfered and distributed. The Jewish youth of Rakishok wanted to accuse the peasant at whose place was found the wood from the Old Synagogue, but it is not known whether they did so. Generally over the shtetl hovered a sense of horror, dread, and terror--a "churban." Peasants live in the former Jewish houses. The area of Comay Street and Urdzikeh Street looks like a village, and the view is of gardens and fields and plains that stretch far into the distance. [Translator's note: "village" is used here in contrast to "shtetl." A "village" is a small rural hamlet and is called a "dorf" in Yiddish, whereas "shtetl" is a town, more like a small city. Before the "churban," Rakishok was definitely a small town (shtetl) and was reduced to the level of a ("dorf") rural village after the Holocaust.]

Thanks to the intervention of the Jewish youth of Rakishok, seventeen pogrom-assassins were shot while the Soviets were in power.

[Page 391]

What I Experienced

by Gisa Levin

Translated by Mathilda Mendelow

Until 1940 I lived in Rokishok. When the Soviets came to Lithuania I moved to Kovno, although the rich Jews were complaining to be under the might of Russia, it was better under them than under the Germans. I worked in Kovno in a large military business. During the day I worked and at night I studied.

Gise Levin

The Russian Government had opened university courses for adults in Kovno. The Russian teachers told us that the Germans were their greatest foes and that they were preparing for war with Hitler's land.

By June 22, 1941 at 4 am Kovno was bombarded and the radio announcer announced that the German - Russian war had started. The Jews started their exodus to the boundaries of Russia, but the Lithuanian partisans stopped them and killed the departing Jewish and Soviet Russian workers. They tore away the railway tracks and mined the roads. They were afraid of the Lithuanian partisans and they turned back. Besides this there were the bombers of the Germans. All the roads were monitored. The Lithuanians did the same in other cities and towns. They accused the Jews of shooting Lithuanians. They searched for arms and arrested Jews and killed them and stole all their belongings. They accused Jews that they were shooting Lithuanians. On Wednesday June 25, 1941 the Germans entered Kovno with a big parade, grand marching, with the nazi flag.

With great fear and in greatest trepidation, the returning Jews came into the city from their retreats. They feared that the Germans would see them walking and they would shoot them then and there. In a fearful positions, Jews walked with their wives and children, carrying small children. They all looked like shadows and not live people...

Within 5 weeks of the arrival of the Germans there was a Ghetto. Both Lithuanians and Germans treated Jews sadistically - not only once was the revolver over my heart - Christians saved my life once - A Lithuanian captain, obviously a Democratic Person helped me to hide until I ran away from the Lithuanians and Nazis.

Once the Lithuanian partisans took me to a house where we had to clean and work. They laughed at me and forced me to sing Russian songs and they maligned the Jews, and they were the worst outcasts of all times. [They claimed that]the Jews were all communists, e.g. when the Communists came the Jews met them with bouquets of flowers.

We had to wear the shameful yellow patch. I was a blond and did not look typically Jewish and therefore I often went from the Ghetto to the city without the shameful patch. An unusual tale of happenings an tortures started in the Ghetto. In the Ghetto everyone was forced to work both old and young - in airports or in the fields. Also, the German SS were present in the Ghetto. During the day one had to work and at night were fearful because they used to take people away from their homes. I have been alone without family and afraid of death. More than once I have been close to death and was one of the 12,000 that were to go to the 9th fort. [*Translator's note: I believe this was a dilapidated fort where inhabitants were placed before they were all shot. There is now a Russian monument on the site to commemorate the events at this location]*. I was able to avoid death by escaping from the small Ghetto, where I was, as it was being liquidated, to the larger Ghetto.

Fresh in my memory are the gruesome happenings of Ghetto living and also the following terrible episodes. – The Germans once surrounded the Jewish hospital with coal throwers and burned the sick, the Doctors, nurses and all personnel. Another terrible order was that all those living in the Ghetto had to gather together on October 28, 1941 in the morning at a place for registration. No one was to go to work that day. No one was allowed to stay home. Even old and sick adults and children had to gather there. The order stated that all those who stayed in their homes would be shot.

All Jews understood what it meant - On October 28, 1941 at 6 am, after another sleepless night, people were forced to go the big open plaza in the Ghetto. It was a misty cold morning and a darkness surrounded the enclosure of the Ghetto. Fathers, mothers and children in diapers, children in mothers' arms, old and sick, young and strong walked to the place with heads down. Each one bemoaned his fate and the cries and screams of the confused Jews enclosed the place as though they were sentenced to death - about 30,000 Jews....

In an unusual order the German rogues came, the German police, the Gestapo leaders and the Lithuanian bandits searched the Jews' homes to check if somebody was not left behind and at the same time to take Jewish belongings. The whole Ghetto was surrounded by a strong patrol from that night onwards. Quietly and with resignation the 30,000 Jews stood and waited to see what these sadists would do with them. Here in the blink of an eye the whole company felt as if an electric shock passed though them. The Gestapo appeared amongst the rows of Jews and they started sorting people to right and to left, to left and right. While families were disrupted, the cruel ones tore the children from their parents and parents from their children, sisters from brothers and brothers from sisters. A whole day the Jews were on this place. The Gestapo and the Lithuanians behaved like the greatest evil. A human pen has not the strength to describe this whole gruesome human tragic picture. Till 6:00pm 12,000 Jews were sorted to die.

Jews on forced labor under Nazi domination. Top left: a work duty card from Kovner Ghetto

The following morning they were sent to the 9th Fort in the Kovno area, children in their prams or children in their parents' arms, old people and ill ones were shot the same day.

Life in the Kovno Ghetto was gruesome and hard. In great suffering were the ones living, who were left in the Kovno ghetto until 1944.

1944 - The Russians neared and the Jews of the Kovno Ghetto were transported to the concentration camps and death camps - the men in Dachau and the women in Stuthof. Many stayed in the bunkers. I was one who was sent to Stuthof. I was there for five weeks. From Stuthof the German death needs took us, 5,000 women by boat to Elvinger near Danzig. There we were digging trenches 4.5 meters wide and 3 meters deep. German guards were standing and kept watch over us. We worked naked bedraggled and unshod and hungry. As the front neared Danzig we were transported further.

Jewish children who perished in Kovner Ghetto

There was no place anymore where to take us. The Russian army strafed the Nazi foe. Still they chased us from place to place and the weaker ones they shot. One whole Jewish group was completely shot, In Proast, Danzig there were concentrated thousands of Jewish women who were in a terrible condition, hungry, bedraggled and unshod- their clothes and bodies were riddled with millions and millions of lice.

The group I was in marched deeper into Germany - without direction and without a road. It was winter in 1945 we walked in deep snow and wished we were dead. Eighteen days we walked. The Hungarian Jewish girls could not keep up with us so they were lashed and tortured and many of them were shot. One evening we left to sleep over in a forest far from a city and people. There we found a barn with straw and mushrooms. We were hungry and we started looking for kernels in the straw. We eat what we found and became ill. We stayed there several days. A typhoid epidemic broke out amongst us. In the same barn in a hole we placed the typhoid sick. 500 women were with us and also a few French and Russian prisoners of war with us along with a few Poles. Every day 20 to 30 died. For a few days they did not feed us. Then they gave us blue water with a few wheat kernels and potatoes. The roof of the barn was full of holes. It was heart breaking to see how we huddled together even to dead people who were amongst us.

Suddenly one night there was a tumult. We thought they were going to burn us, but 500 new women arrived from Stuthof. They were sick and had been walking a few weeks. Amongst these women I met my cousin Rivka Kramer from Rokishok.

That night I left the barn. The hunger was great and I decided to go and look for a piece of bread, and if they shot me on the road, it would be a relief. My ideal was then to at least eat a piece of bread before death. Thus I ran to a village. I then heard a battle around me. The noise was of the artillery and a strong light flickered around my eyes, but still I ran towards the village.

I ran into a village called Hina, there was frost on either side and I saw rows of Soviet tanks coming. I cried with joy. The Russian soldier who saw how I looked ran out of the tanks saying (in Russian, oldie don't cry) and soon gave me food. They brought me to a house and I grabbed food and looked for clothing for myself. I was dressed in torn rags. I found German men's' civilian clothing. Soon other women ran into the same house and started looking for food and clothing. It was as if wild creatures were released from a cage. I then once again met Rivka Kramer, she already had typhoid.

The Russian soldiers told us not to linger in the town because soon there would be a great battle with the foe. Soon we went further away from the front. We were in Leonberg for several days and after that we were told to go further away from the front.

Many fell on the roads from weakness. I stayed with my cousin Rivka Kramer, she was very ill. With us was a Frenchman who had transport and now and then they transported Rivka. Mostly I dragged her with me. The whole company used to go forward and she and I were left alone along the roads. Still we managed somehow to get to Warsaw.

In the city there was not a single Jew - only on entering Prague we found a few Jews and also the Jewish Committee. We slept on the floor of the Jewish Committee. Most Jews were from Russia and a few living [remnants] of the German camps. The Jewish committee gave us portions of bread every day.

In Warsaw we found out many concentration camp women were in Bialystok, so Rivka Kramer and I also drove to Bialystok. The Jewish Committee was located on Minsker Street. It was a two- story building and there were also many Poles - men and women. The Jewish Committee helped us with food. My cousin Rivka Kramer was ill. The doctors did not think she would live. Many women went back to Kovno. I did not want to go to Lithuania because I did not want to see the ruined home.

Rivka was married. She kept asking me to find out about her husband who had been in Dachau. I and another girl from Anushish asked about her husband who had been in Dachau. It was another girl from Anushish, Bekkie who looked after Rivka. Many miles we dragged her to baths. The Jewish Committee was not interested in her condition. A Russian Jewish doctor found that one had to amputate her leg because it had blood poison. We begged the Red Cross that she should be taken to hospital. The doctors there found that she had Pemphigus [Gum cancer?] in her mouth and her teeth fell out. She did not look human, only like a monkey.

Murdered concentration camp inmates. The Nazi butchers did not have time to make a bonfire of the murdered.

On May 5, 1945 she died in hospital. The Jewish Committee promised us that they would bury her. At the time I worked in a textile factory. Seeing that several days had passed and she was still lying there, I once more came to the Jewish Committee and they gave transport and I and the girl from Anushish and more women whom I paid from my last Zlotys, took her to the Bialystok cemetery.

The road to the Bialystok cemetery was full of danger because of the unrest of the Polish opportunists, anti-Semitic groups who made pogroms against the Jews. The grave had already been dug by hired hands of the Jewish Committee and we the four women placed her in her grave and covered it and as a headstone we brought two large square black polished stones.

When I was in Kovno Ghetto I and some other Rokishoker Jews in Kovno, sent Christians to find out what had happened to the Rokishoker Jews. >From Kovno to Rokishok is about 300 kilometers. With our last financial resources we tried to find out what had happened to our closest. One messenger came and told us that he found the two Gurvics brothers lying dead in a forest. A Christian told us she noted on the road two Jewish boys named Jacovwitz and when they saw her they started running deep into the forest. She also told that Rokishoker Jews were killed in Viziofnke within six weeks after the Germans arrived in Rokishok. Before that all Rokishokers were held in a camp Antinoske.

From right to left: Rifka Kremer; Roza Kremer, now in Johannesburg; the third – unknown.

We also had news of Joffee, an apostate Jew, who was later brought to us in Kovno Ghetto and later died in a concentration camp. He gave us the following tales:

a) In the home of Shlomo Friedman in Abel there was hospital where Jewish doctors practiced - Gundelman and his wife Farbereite.

b) One Saturday they assured all Rokishoker Jews that they were being brought across to Soverinshok and there they would work for themselves on land until the end of the war. The Jews knew it was a lie. Gundelman and his wife and children poisoned themselves. Chaia Ita Swartzberg also poisoned herself. On the Monday morning they saw how Jews were chased out of Rokishok and many Jews were shot on the road.

c) Joffee once was sitting at home together with his family, when a Christian came to him and asked him that he should come to her house to exchange something for a lamb. He did not want to go but in the end he was persuaded and left with her. The Christian took him to a stable and he saw a two wheel cart. She lifted the seat of the cart and he saw his cousin Mishke inside. Joffee started crying. Mishke, the Christian and Joffee came to the house and Mishke told the following story:-

He and six others decided to run away from the place of execution, this Christian hid them all. Two Poles in Abel and Panimunik knew about it and helped her with food for the Jews. Also the apostate wife of an actionary knew about this story and she also helped the Christian with food for the hidden Jews.

The apostate Christian told them that two hidden Jews in her house had died and she buried them in her yard and when freer times will come she will then deliver the dead to a cemetery in Israel.

He, Joffee had since that time helped the gentile woman with products, but he asked Mishke that he should not come to his home, because the Germans had their eyes on him. He showed himself very little in the open.

How Joffee related the tale about the hidden Jews thus:- All were caught, a few of them ran away, and those left were taken to the Rokishok jail where they were shot.

In Bialystok I wanted to get in touch with my brothers in South Africa. I remembered the address of my brother Jacob Levin from Cape Town and from a woman friend , Mrs. Kark of Germiston. I sent off two postcards, in which I wrote with my heart's blood about this, that I find myself in Bialystok and I had lost everything.

After a short while there was an order that either one takes the Polish citizenship or returns to ones home. I knew I had no one at home and I had no one to go to and I did not want to become a Polish citizen. I did not know the polish language and above all I wanted to tear myself away from this gruesome sadness, from a place that saw so much spilled Jewish blood.

I went to the forger who gave me false papers of a Greek Jewish woman and with other such "Greek" Jews we wondered through borders and lands - Czechoslovakia, Hungary, Rumania till Austria. In Austria, in the Lintz communication center I wrote letters to Russia. To my great luck I received a letter from my younger brother Shaierke Levin. He wrote me of his own happenings and from his having been in Rokishok. He did not stay there long because to look at the desolation he wrote, one could go mad. He settled in Vilna and married a Jewish girl from Memel.

He told me in detail of what had happened to him during the war. He ran away from Rokishok on the eve of the arrival of the Germans. He and my second brother Samuel Levin dragged themselves to Riga and from there deeper into Russia. They joined the army, and later in the Lithuanian Division, Shaierke worked for a captain who also kept Samuel near him. Once when Shaierke was away on a commando raid, the captain sent Samuel to the front to Auriel Where he died. Shaierke also wrote to me from Vilna that my postcards arrived at my brothers in South Africa and that they were looking for me. I then contacted my brothers in South Africa who brought me to them in South Africa.

My pen and patience are not in a position to relate all the Nazi atrocities and the great pain which I suffer through this gruesome ordeal of my unforgettable dear parents, sisters and brothers who died through the Hitler murderers. My Mother, Sara-Fruma, my father Mendel Levin, my older sister Faiga and her husband Jacob and their two little children, Pearl and Lazar, my brothers Louis and Samuel and my youngest sister Hanna.

Through various happenings and through a long time of anguish and death dangers I breathed my life.

Translated by Mathilda Mendelow, born Ginsberg. Her dear parents brought their young family safely from Rokishok, home of her great grandparents, via Russia, to a safe haven in South Africa during the First World War. Her parents taught her, amongst other things to speak Yiddish for which she is very grateful.

[Page 401]

In Those Days

by Herzl Ben-Yehuda

Translated by Rabbi Ezra Boyarsky

In June 1941 the Germans suddenly attacked Lithuania. The Russians then withdrew from their border positions, accompanied by Lithuanian partisan heavy shelling. In addition, the Lithuanian Fascist populace fired on the retreating Red Army and the escaping Jews from rooftops, churches, etc.

We immediately realized the danger we were in , but it became more real upon hearing Hitler spew his poison-saturated diatribes: "Lithuanians, we are about to wind up the expulsion of the Russians from your homeland!" "We are liberating you and it is your duty to murder all the Jews, because Lithuania must become Judenrein!"

Upon hearing these bestial words, thousands upon thousands of Kovno Jews left their homes and set out in the direction of the Soviet Union. My wife, our infant son, and I joined the refugees. On my back I carried two heavy packs, and I held my son Shmuelik in my arms. My wife Chanele trudged along dragging a heavy suitcase.

We walked on in a state of hopelessness and despair. Although the situation was extremely critical, without any hope of survival, still our pace somehow gained momentum in order to reach the border of the Soviet Union. In the course of a few days we covered approximately 40 kilometers. Unfortunately, we were overtaken by the Germans who forced us to return to Kovno. The civilian Germans whom we met on the way advised us to commit suicide rather than return, for as they said, any Jew who enters Kovno is shot on the spot. These words made it clear that we were standing on the brink of death. Our hearts were pained beyond description, not over our fate, but for our two-year-old son. In a circuitous way, through side streets and alleys, we reentered Kovno. The Germans issued a "cease fire" order not to shoot anymore, and we all returned to our homes.

Chana-Elinke Kremer: the bright memory of my wife Chana-Elinke – a daughter of Shmuel Hirsh and Ida Kremer and a grandchild of Bere-Leah's – and my little son, Shmulinke, who tragically were annihilated by the Nazi hangmen.

A few weeks later we were ordered to wear a yellow Mogen Dovid (Jewish star) badge sewn on our clothes, and the entire Jewish community was moved to Slabodka (a suburb of Kovno) where the Kovno ghetto was located. In the Kovno ghetto there were also some Rakishker Jews who stayed close together and were devoted to one another even under the extremely adverse conditions of the ghetto. It was not at all unusual that after a cruel and savage decree was issued against the ghetto population, the Rakishok Jews immediately began to seek out their landsleit to raise their morale and help in a material way to the extent that this was possible.

Besides myself, my wife Chanele (a granddaughter of Bere Leah's from Rakishok) and our son, the following Rakishker Jews were with us in the Kovno ghetto: Rivka Kramer and husband; Mosher Wasserman and wife; Rivka (Reznikowitz), Idke Baradovsky, her husband, and small child; Idke's brother; Esterke Baradovsky and her younger sister; Faniske Berkowitz (Samet) with her two small daughters; the two Simelewitz sisters; Nise Levin; Rivka Epstein, Zalke Nafanowitz (son of the shamesh--synagogue sexton). There are a number of other Jews from Rakishok who were with us in the ghetto whose names I regrettably do not remember.

Bere-Leah: Chana-Elinke's grandfather

The Rakishker Jews in the Kovno ghetto demonstrated an unusual sense of mutual responsibility and devotion. Collectively, they formed a model of unity in a time of extreme adversity. My home was the main meeting place for our townspeople, and was frequented by them on a daily basis.

Somehow, the Rakishker families adjusted themselves to the ghetto economic conditions, Fanishke Berkowitz, with her two small children, was not that fortunate. Her husband had been shot even before the creation of the ghetto. The Rakishker families extended a helping hand to her and to a number of other families in similar circumstances.

In 1943 the number of Rakishker Jews in the Kovno ghetto decreased. Several of them escaped and joined the partisans in the forests. Rivka Epstein, who was a professional nurse, also joined a partisan group and showed great heroism. Ziamke Baradovsky was also a partisan. He met a hero's death in the Kazlaveruder forests. His contribution to the partisan resistance movement was prominently recorded in the periodical, "From the Last Destruction," which was published by the Central Historical Commission of the liberated Jews in Germany, and edited by the well-known educator and historian Israel Kaplan. In this periodical we are told that Baradovsky was among the first partisans who tried to make contact with the Russian parachutists in the forests. He met a hero's death in a fierce struggle with the Germans.

My tragically killed son Shmulinke was snatched from us during one of the German-organized raids on children. Rivka and Moshe Wasserman were also robbed of their son, Chayiml. Most of the time the children were left alone in the house unsupervised while we parents were away working. Chana-Elinke would always instruct our little boy either to play inside or close to the house. Every day we would wait impatiently for the work to end and hurry home to see him. But one day when we came home from work our little boy was not there, and we never saw him again. The German murderers staked out an opportune moment to round up the innocent Jewish children in the ghetto and transport them to the death camps.

Neighbors told us that during the confusion that ensued, our child was taken by a young couple who hid him in the attic, but the German beasts searched the house and found him. Upon seeing the approaching Germans through the window, our little son took the sandwiches we had left him for lunch, put on his little coat, and then the sub-human Germans led him away to the slaughter. His heart-rending crying for his mother an father did not arouse a ripple of mercy in the hearts of the savage Germans. Our child was only three-and-a-half years old and already he knew all the ghetto songs. He was a delightful, intelligent child, and until the last days of my life I shall not forget him.

Early in 1944 the Germans were forced to retreat, but they did not forget to take along the surviving Jewish slaves. At first there were many Jews who succeeded in hiding in underground bunkers, but in the end they were detected, and few actually escaped the German claws. Among those who were caught in the underground hideaway were the above-mentioned Estherke Baradovsky and husband.

The Jewish men and women whom the Germans took with them in the transport trains to Germany were separated from each other. I was also then separated from my beloved and unforgettable Chanele. Of the large Rakishok group, only a few survived.

This is only a very brief account of the indescribable tortures which the Jews, men, women, and children suffered at the hands of the eternally cursed Nazis.

Hitleristic demons bully the Jews

[Pages 405-430]

The Destruction of Rakishok in Letters

by M. Bakalczuk-Felin

Translated by Rabbi Ezra Boyarsky and Gloria Berkenstat Freund

The published works about the Holocaust in Rakishok and vicinity provide a narrow basis for a description of all the various German persecutions of the Jews leading to the days of slaughter and also the tragic, dramatic situations in the face of the executions. Both the collection of testimony from B. Rotholtz and the descriptions of Gita Levin and Hershl Ben-Yehuda tell of Rakishok's destruction through personal experiences plus facts that were heard of, so to say, from rumors and reverberations.

For the most part, little material remained from our Jewish shtetlach, which were devoured with lightning speed by the Hitlerist pestilence and slaughtered by the Nazi hangmen in the first weeks of the German-Fascist occupation. Only a few individuals, two or three people from a Jewish community, were saved from slaughter by a miracle, and sometimes not even this. What happened to the Jews was as if the earth had suddenly opened, swallowing them in its vicera, or as in the age of the flood.

The German plan of a lightning victory was closely bound with the plan for the complete physical annihilation of the Jewish population in Europe. If the interval of time from July to almost the end of 1942 was the era of the greatest extermination according to scope and area and according to the number of victims, the start of the most brutal extermination took place in July-August 1941. This was the clearest signal of a massive annihilation of the Jews.

For those Jews who were assembled in various barracks during the first days of occupation and isolated, it was unbelievable that they would actually be killed. Still more, they relied on the fairness of the world and the ethical human feelings that would spurt in the German hearts in the last moments before their execution. That is perhaps why there were no attempts to escape from the [barracks] and that is how almost all perished, leaving few traces.

Only individual Jews kept their bearings in this situation. In Rakishok, Doctor Gandelman and his wife, the dyer, and Chaya-Ita Shartzberg recognized the hopeless condition and poisoned their children and then themselves. Certain similar suicide actions occurred in other shtetlach. However, it was hidden and there was no one who would talk about it.

Because of the dwindling base of material, I found a substantial need because of the situation to publish a bintl brief [bundle of letters] that will throw a spotlight on the tragic circumstances and situations of those days. These letters will certainly be an important contribution to the Holocaust subject matter and particularly to the Holocaust in Rakishok and the surrounding area.

Abraham Ginzburg as [a member of the] Red Army

The returning Jews described the evacuation of their ruined homes with heart-rending direct words and with Jobian tragedy and absorbed all of the news and rumors about the various phases of martyrdom, describing the confused escape to Russia and the Lithuanian partisans who lay in wait for them on every road and detour, and also about the extermination.

I publish the letters that were addressed to friends and to the Rakishoker landmanschaft from various people, both direct witnesses and those who gathered all of the information, rumors and echoes, and place them in print without linguistic improvement; let the letters themselves speak of the great tragic epic, of the dreadful Third Destruction whose "beginning" was started immediately after the first day of occupation by the murderous Vandals of the 20th Century. [Translator's note: this refers to the destruction of the First and Second Temples in Jerusalem.]

A Letter from Riva Epshtein

On the 4th of October 1944, Riva Epshtein, a Rakishok girl, described her own tragedy and [the tragedy] of the people to Yitzhak Ginsburg, in Johannesburg.

Dear Friend!

Of course, you will be surprised that I am writing to you. If not for chance that led me to travel with your little brother, Abraham, I certainly would not have written to you, because I would not have had your address. Thus, by chance, I remained alive during the terrible war years, when our European Jewry was marked for destruction. So by chance, I met your small, weak Abrahamle, as a soldier, in Shavl [Šauliai].

However, he is no longer small. He is much taller than you and for a year he had been fighting the enemy. You will never understand even a little of what I have survived to meet him. No human fantasy can imagine what I have survived.

However, in the time when we all suffered together, it was easier. The great tragedy first began for those who survived. It is already three months since I was freed by the heroic Red Army. However, five minutes do not pass that I can forget our collective loss: the loss of my parents, brothers and sister who perished through *Kiddush haShem* [died in the sanctification of God's name; died as Jewish martyrs].

I traveled to Rakishok and at least wanted to find a small photograph of my parents, brothers and sister and, even this, our "dear neighbors" did not find it necessary to hide. Understand, not a sign remained of Jewish things, of Jewish belongings, that this was once a Jewish place.

It was not necessary to hide things, but a small photograph, if it remained with the living, this did not interest them. Therefore, they say, they could be punished. Shooting Jews—neighbors--with whom they lived for years in friendship, shooting and torturing Jewish women and innocent Jewish children, throwing them alive into pits – of this they had no fear.

However, the punishment will come for them. Innocent spilled blood calls for revenge and revenge must come. My dear friend, you can be proud that you were not in Lithuania and even prouder that you will never be in Lithuania. For me, it is a shame that I have lived with neighbors, friends and comrades and did not know that on a beautiful day they would slaughter my parents, brothers and sisters, my people, and only because we are Jews.

But my fate was different. I worked as a nurse in the Kovner Hospital and, when the war broke out, I no longer had time to escape to the Soviet Union.

And thus I remained in the Kovner Ghetto for two years. During that time tens of thousands of Kovner Jews were shot before my eyes; tens of thousands of foreign Jews; Jews from Germany, Belgium and from other lands. This all took place in Kovno in the Ninth Fort [one of a series of fortifications that encircled Kovno].

I escaped to the forest from the Kovno Ghetto where I joined the Red partisan detachment (division). I was there and fought the enemy until the arrival of the Red Army.

I write this letter to you having already been freed. The yellow patches that we wore in the ghetto, I no longer wear. I walk equally with everyone on the sidewalk, look everyone right in the eye and I have no fear of my own shadow.

However, my tragedy begins here. I do not know what I lived for, and I am tortured day and night by all of the frightening images.

My situation – I do not mean in the material sense – is terrible. Loneliness is a terrible feeling. The material side does not interest me because I have no interest in living. On the whole, I am not thankful for my fate – that I survived. How it goes, it goes. If I could free myself from my terrible moods I would not be lost. I have a trade, work; I will always earn my bread. And that which interested me before the war, I am too apathetic to have an interest in. Today, the important things are missing from life. I am missing blood, blood, blood! I alone remained from such a family!

* * *

The writer of the letter, Riva Epshtein, was in the Kovner Ghetto and escaped to the partisan woods, where she saved herself. She survived much torture and many threats of death that "no human fantasy can imagine."

Although she was freed and no longer wears the yellow patch and has no fear of her own shadow, she is in a vise of terrible apparitions that persecute her and "five minutes do not pass that she is able to forget the loss of her parents, brothers and sisters." She is not satisfied with life and is not thankful that she survived.

She ends her letter with an elegiac exclamation: "I am missing blood, blood, blood! I alone remained from such a family!"

The letter is a faithful mirror of her mood of despair and resignation.

A Letter from Liba Kur to Malya Wittz

All of my dear ones together! I received this letter that you wrote to me on the 23rd of May. Yes, dear Malya, I was very happy to receive a letter written by you because this is the best for me, to receive a letter. As I alone remain of everyone, it can be imagined how it affects a person. But what can we do; it is already decreed. I am very happy that you write me out of everyone.

Dear Malya, you ask me to write everything that I know of the dear lost ones. It turns out to be very difficult for me because I know that you will receive no joy from this and, also, it will greatly increase your pain. But, as you ask, I will do it:

When the bloody war began on the 22nd of June 1941, we already freely knew what was in store for us. The anguish was very terrible. People began running to one another, but no one knew what to do or when. All of our friends came together and we began to talk and cry: do we run from Rakishok or do we remain? Uncle Itze and Aunt Chaya immediately said that what God will give, that's what will be. They will not run from Rakishok. The Germans will not do anything to them. Only Rokhka packed a package and took both children and left on foot because there were no longer any horses and we could still travel by train. We were so mixed up that we did not know what to do. Rokhka and both children left for the border with Abel because everyone ran in the same direction. And the uncle and aunt remained in the house and I, running to the same border, met Rokhka and came to the border. However, everyone was turned away. She said to me, "Libka, take the things I am carrying from me, because I cannot go further." Her feet and the feet of both children were very swollen. And it is difficult for me to describe to you. I did not take the little package from her because my life was also in the balance. I will not describe everything to you because I have so much to write that I get dizzy. Rokhha came back to Rakishok alone and the Germans entered two days later and you must have heard of their treatment [of the Jews].

As far as the Christians tell it, before they killed the Jews, they tortured them so much. All of the Rakishok Jews were driven together into the court where the Count had lived. They were held there without food, and the cries of hunger from the children and of the mothers were unbearable. In addition, they would be driven completely naked into a fenced off area and cut with whips on their naked bodies. Thus the Jews were held for six weeks. Naturally, many of the children and adults died there as a result of their treatment. During the sixth week they were taken away to a place near Baiar, that is, eight kilometers from Rakishok, and there were already four large holes dug out. And the gangsters were already there with tractors that would drown out the voices of the Jews. The people were placed in rows of 20 and were shot with one bullet so that they were alive because a bullet only reaches one person, not 20.

Dear Malya, what I write to you here is just a tiny part. The terrible pains that were inflicted on them, I cannot describe. In this way, 5,000 (five thousand) Rakishoker Jews were in the four holes and no one remained, only those who went to Russia and survived. Among the 5,000 Jews lie my dearly beloved mother, father, Chayala and her husband and two children, my uncle Itze, my aunt Chaya and the unlucky Rokhka and her two children and, also, our remaining friends.

My heart is wrung. I would write, but I have no one to whom to write. I alone remain of everyone. My only consolation is when I take the photograph of my mother and my father in my hand and through it I become a little lighter for a while, but not for long. Thus we live from day to day.

So, Malinka, this is enough of this.

Remain healthy and strong as I wish you, your distant cousin Libka Kur.

The above noted, Liba Kur, also wrote a second letter, dated the 17th of July 1948 to her cousin, Asna Hit, with the following content:

Dear cousin Asna and your husband and children, may you always be happy!

You ask me about everyone – the dear lost ones, that I should write to you with details about everyone. Yes, dear Asna, I know about everyone, but when I just think about them, it becomes very difficult for me. Disregarding this, I must take the strength and write to you so that you will know and now I write and I will not repeat it again because neither you nor I have the strength. You ask about our aunt; I will describe how she perished. I should write everything about this, but I can only tell you this:

Three months before the dark war, our aunt left for Kovno to go to Saraka because Saraka held an important position. She was an important person. She could be relied on. She would often appear in the newspapers because she would excel in her good work. In a word, it would have been an honor to remain alive with her. But, alas, when the war broke out, on Sunday, at four o'clock in the morning, that is on the 22nd of June '41, Saraka went to work; but she could no longer get there. She was forcibly placed in a car to travel far from Lithuania to Russia. She strongly argued; she did not want to go, thinking that Aunt Toyba Riva remained. But nothing helped and she left. But she could not rest. From the car she was placed on a train and when the train would stop, she would run around to see if her mother [was on the train] because she always imagined that her mother would not stay without her and she, too, went after her. And so at each stop she looked to see if her mother was traveling.

But Saraka lost her life in one unlucky moment. The train in which she was traveling stopped. She did not take notice of anything or hear what people were saying to her. She ran around to a spot further from the station and, suddenly, a bomb fell and hit her and it immediately decapitated her and she lost both legs.

Yes, dear Asna, she would have lived if she had not run out to the stations. But, unfortunately, that was her destiny.

Our aunt remained in her room in Kovno with the thought that Saraka would come from work and they both would think about what to do, and in thinking this, she lost her life because in time Hitler's murderers took Kovno. And she was destined to perish together with all of the Jews. She was burned with thousands of Jews in the second group at the green mountain in Kovno. The screams of the people were unbearable. The city was enveloped in smoke and as horrible as it was, it is as horrible for me to describe because I am unable to continue to write. In a word: they both lost their lives through a terrible death.

It is also terrible to write about Chashka and her husband and child. They were all obliterated alive with my dear parents, sister and her family and all of our dear friends. Oh, how terribly I would scream and not stop if I would meet one of my close ones because this all presses on my heart and I will never stop thinking of their terrible death.

Heika and her family perished in Dvinsk. It was no better for her than for us.

In a word, dear cousin Asna, our dear close ones no longer remain for us, only the memory that once every one had a family that was so loved and dear and now we remain alone like a stone without anyone.

Your devoted, Liba Kur.

* * *

Both of Liba Kur's letters to her cousins, Malya and Asna, are direct and powerfully heartrendingly written. She writes with great effort because it is very difficult for her to write about the Holocaust of the Jews and "my heart is wrung."

She describes important events and reports many details that were not known.

In the letter, she described how the slave labor continued and how the Germans applied the most sadistic tortures to their slaves – the Jews. She brings out the fact that the Germans placed tractors to drown out the screams and shrieks of the Jews and how 20 Jews were placed in a row and they were shot with one bullet.

The description of Saraka is very tragic, how she could not rest in the train and ran around on every station to see if her mother was on the train. She lost her young life because of her devotion to her mother.

Liba Kur also presents information about the death of family members and their names, ending almost with similar elegiac words as the writer of the first letter: "Our dear close ones no longer remain for us." "And now we remain alone like a stone without anyone."

A Letter from Rajza Kark

Rajza Kark, in an undated letter to a friend in S. A. [South Africa], writes:

Today I received your first letter. Your letter, with your devotion, reminds me of the past and refreshed the great wound that does not heal because it is the kind of wound that no person can imagine; to remain alone from such a family, knowing that such young people and children must lay in large holes that the gangsters made for them with such inhumanity. They came to their deaths in such difficulties. I cannot remember anything of what I was told by the Jews who I met in Rakishok.

I was sick when I escaped from Rakishok. The gangsters held Malka and Fajgetshka in prison for 20 days and before that severely tortured them. The rest were with all of the Jews in the camp. All of the Jews were brought from the smaller shtetlach. And I must write to you that it was a terrible death: half were buried alive, together with the dead.

Yes, dear, everyone in our family perished, except for me who has survived. They were driven out in a wagon and only I remained in the house until everyone left the city. But the misfortune was that they apparently went to Dvinsk and we went a little on foot and a little with someone who would take us into an auto. And thus we, I and my husband, left Hitler's paws and survived.

You ask about the date of the slaughter. It is difficult to say, although there were local helpers, but then they could not kill everyone in one day and, therefore, we do not know exactly. In any case, after the period from the beginning of August 1941 to the 20th, there were no Jews in Rakishok. Only one remained who had been hidden by a Christian. If you remember, there was Berl Shlosberg, the brother-in-law of Ester Leah the dressmaker, the husband of Sara Beila. He remained the only Jew and he explains that the Rakishok Jews were driven to Abel and they were killed on the 10th and 12th of August.

From Yurdzike, I and the deaf one's [son], Shimkin Beigl, survived. There is no one else and from all of Rakishok, everyone can be gathered together into a small group. That is the fate of the Jews of Rakishok. The same as all of the remaining cities and shtetlach, through which Hitler's gangsters marched with their bloody paws.

As you see, we never believed such devastation would leave us all alone, without friends from such a family and good friends.

You are like my own mother and sister. I will end because my daughter is asking why I am crying. She is still too young to tell her about this, that she, too, once had a grandmother and aunts and uncles and that there was one such as Hitler in the world.

Write to me about how you are living, about your health.

From me, your friend who wishes you luck, Rajza Krak

* * *

Rajza Krak "left Hitler's paws" thanks to her successful escape to Russia.

Returning from the evacuation, she learned of the slaughter in Rakishok from the beginning of August 1941 until the 20th and that, with the exception of Shlosberg who had been hidden by a Christian, there were no longer any Jews in Rakishok.

She ends the letter with motifs of loneliness: "As you see, we never believed such devastation would leave us all alone, without friends from such a family and good friends."

A Letter from Yudel Meller
Dated 10.08.47

I happen to have come across a letter you wrote in which you seek some information about the Rakishker Jews who escaped the German carnage and survived the Holocaust.

I feel I must first give you some facts about myself. My name is Yudel Meller, Avraham Yitzhak Meller's son. My family and I are among the few Rakishker Jews who survived. All my brothers, Shmuel, Motel, and Chonye, together with my uncles, aunts, cousins, and their families were killed at the hands of the blood-thirsty German murderers and their Lithuanian collaborators. At present, my wife and I, together with our son and daughter, live in Vilna. During the war I was in the Soviet Union. Upon my return, I visited Rakishok, but found nobody. The sub-human Germans brutally tortured the Jews, pillaged their possessions, and then killed them in cold blood.

This house survived in Rokiskis, undamaged. The photograph is from before the war. From the right: Chaya Dektar, her mother Toyba Dektar and her sister Lyuba Dektar.

After the war, this family returned to Rokiskis from the evacuation to Russia. From left to right: Ida Dektar, her child and her sister Chaya. Standing is Ida Dektar's husband, Yakov.

On the road to Anushishok, at a spot about five kilometers from Rakishok, I found a massive grave where the remains of our beloved and never to be forgotten family members and fellow Jews are interred.

Now we must start from scratch again to build a new life. Understandably, this is not easy after our devastating and ravaging war experiences.

With kindest regards, Y. Meller

A Letter from Maya to her Brothers and Sisters

Dear Brothers and Sisters,

How are you all feeling? How are you all getting along? How come you haven't written for such a long time?

As you probably already know, my first husband passed away. But life must go on. I met Zalman Gordon, Meyer's friend, and since he too remained alone, we got married. For some time his father lived in Rakishok. My husband was mobilized, sent to the front, and was wounded. But now, thank God, he feels fine.

We started a new life and are slowly getting back on track. We have a little boy. His name is Grisha and tomorrow is his birthday. He will be two years old.

Tisha B'Av, the ninth day of the Jewish month of Av, is a day of fasting and mourning in commemoration of the destruction of the First and Second Temples in Jerusalem. It is customary to visit the graves of family members on this day. We--that is, all Rakishker Holocaust survivors--hired a car and went to visit our parents' graves on Tisha B'Av. Our dear and beloved ones are interred in seven large pits near a grove located five kilometers from Rakishok on the road to Visiumke. Each pit measured four meters long and two meters wide. A sudden, uncanny apprehension seized us as we tremblingly approached the mass graves. It seemed as if the trees around were vying with each other to tell us of the cruelties and atrocities that our parents, relatives, and indeed all the Jews of Rakishok endured before they were led to the pits where their noble lives were snuffed out. Brokenhearted and crying incessantly, we visited all the pits, not knowing in which pit our parents were interred.

August 15 marks the sixth *yahrzeit* of their death. We made a dugout surrounding the cemetery for purposes of identification.

Yours, Maya

A Letter from Leah Shamer
Dated 08.09.47

(This letter was addressed to the Rakishok landsmanshaft.)

We have heard a lot about you, and we are very grateful for your warm response. The writer of this letter is Shamer's youngest daughter who worked as a teacher in the Rakishok kindergarten. Many waters have passed under the bridge since those idyllic and peaceful days. Our *shtetl* Rakishok is empty, without a trace of a Jewish child, and our homes lie in ruins.

When I came to Rakishok for the first time since I returned from the Soviet Union, I was overcome by an uncanny fear and seized by a gnawing pain. Lost in my thoughts and in a maze of flashbacks, I was wondering, "Where are my neighbors, Bentzie Baksir the shoemaker, Mendel and Ronyie the bakers, and all whom I loved like family? Where are they and why do they not come out to greet me?" Frightened goyim looked at me as though I were a specter risen from the billowing smoke of the crematoria.

Feigning innocence, the Lithuanian goyim described in detail and with an eerie precision how our sainted parents were tortured. Their chilling nonchalance caused me untold anguish as did the unmistakable glee in their eyes.

Now a few facts about myself. I met my sister Chvolyie and my brother Shmuel Yonoson in Russia, and now we all live together in Vilna. My only sister is ill with tuberculosis, and her sickness is of great concern and an awful blow to us. Whatever financial aid we receive from you is very much appreciated. It helps us to alleviate our suffering and gradually to normalize our lives.

As soon as I obtained your address, I decided to get in touch with you. I feel an intimacy and a close kinship with Rakishker Jews. I wish you a happy year, success in all your endeavors, and good tidings to all of you.

With kindest regards, Leah Shamer

A Letter from Ruchl Gor

Ruchl Gor, the wife of the author of "Holocaust of Jewish Kovno," Josef Gor, writes a letter from Munich to Sara Klas, Johannesburg.

We provide only the most important excerpts from the letter that is dated the 16th July 1948:

Dear friend Sara and husband!

Your letter of the 28th June has been received. I was very surprised by your friendship. You were correct when you wrote that, perhaps, I would not know who was writing to me because I would not remember you from home. I remember your cousin, Leiba Spiwak, very well. It is possible that if I saw a picture of you, I would remember. Time has passed with much trouble and pain.

Now I will write a little about me:

In 1932 I married a man who comes from a small shtetl, Kron, near Kovno. You have surely not heard about this shtetl. He studied, worked and always lived in Kovno. I was a nurse and until the war I worked in the Kovner Jewish Hospital. My husband was a teacher by profession. However, he worked for the Kovner newspaper, *Folksblat*, during the last years. Our life was good.

In 1941, immediately after the outbreak of war, I gave birth to a daughter. We were already in the Kovno Ghetto. The child was named Gitele. The trouble, need and pain we suffered in the Kovno Ghetto cannot be described.

In 1944, after I had hidden the child from the murderers in an attic during the search for children in the Kovno Ghetto, I gave the child to Christians in the city. A nun took her from me and hid her.

Several months later when the Russians were already near Kovno, the Germans drove us toward Germany. On the way, not far from the German border, still in Lithuania, my husband and I jumped out of the moving train (the 12th of July 1944) and hid in a field of rye and in holes for 20 days, until the Russians took that area and we were liberated.

Upon our return to Kovno, we immediately ran to look for our child. We found the child and then we were the happiest people in the world. Later, when the Jews began to leave Kovno to go to Poland and further on from there, we also went with the stream, not wanting to remain alone and forlorn on the graves of those closest to us.

We had a very difficult trip from Kovno to Germany. We lay around in various dirty camps without a shirt on our back and without money. We stole across the border through mountains and valleys until we arrived in Austria. There I became sick with typhoid fever and lay in an Austrian hospital for five weeks.

My husband and child were in a camp where they received little food. When I left the hospital very weakened, we stole across the border to Germany in order to reach the area where more Lithuanian Jews lived. There we did meet many Lithuanian Jews from the Kovno Ghetto who were very well known to us, and they helped stand us on our feet. However, how does the saying go: "When it comes to life, one must die." Our child was exhausted by such a trip. She became infected on the way and arriving in Germany, she became sick with brain fever. We did everything we could to save our only child, but it did not help, and in December 1945, the child died. You can imagine our great pain and grief at losing our only child who suffered so much in her four and a half year life. We were so broken and wretched that we cannot to this day recover from the great misfortune that we encountered.

Yes, my dear, it turns out that the cup of tears was not full for us.

Of my family, only my two brothers, Leizer 27 and Efriom 21, survived. They both escaped Rakishok for Russia two days before the Germans took Rakishok. Leyzer married and has a daughter who was given the name of our mother, Chaya, may she rest in peace, and he now lives in Vilna. He is a hat maker. My younger brother, Efriom, came here, left for Eretz Yisroel and was on the ship, "Exodus 1947," if you read about it. He left again and has been in Eretz Yisroel since the month of April. They suffered enough during the war. Efriom lost an eye in Russia. Now he only sees with one eye. Ryfka and Sara Beilka were in the Kovno Ghetto and survived. They know that I am in Germany. Chasya-Beilka was in the Kovno Ghetto. I helped her a great deal. I do not deserve any thanks. She is my cousin and this was my duty. However, our vexation is great, because we protected her from all of the deportations and, at the end just before the liberation, she perished, and not one of their family survived. At the end, she married a young man from Rakishok, Gafanowitch, the son of the *shamas* [sexton], and they both hid in the cellar of a house. The Germans set the entire ghetto on fire and they were burned in the cellar. A terrible death. We also hid in an attic. However, at the last moment, we went out by ourselves and traveled on the transport to Germany. On the way, as I have already written, we succeeded in jumping from the train and survived.

My best greeting, Ruchl Gor

* * *

Ruchl Gor and her husband were in the Kovno Ghetto. They successfully hid their child with a Christian and they themselves escaped from a transport while the train took them and other Jews to crematoria.

Both the hiding of their daughter and their jump from the train were uncommon experiences.

She also writes about the happy meeting with their little daughter and how the blind fate of death persecuted their little daughter who died during their wanderings.

Ruchl Gor also gives details of her family, both those who perished and, may they live long, those who survived.

Kovner Ghetto in flames and smoke

A Letter from Shafir Efriom (Israel)

(In a letter from the 14th November 1950) Shafir writes to Yerakhmiel Aronsarsh:

A hearty thank you to the Rakishok landsleit committee for the material help that you decided to give me. Everything that I have received is very useful to me. Let us hope that better times will come and no help will be needed.

Mrs. Klas asked me to write everything I know about the Holocaust of the Rakishok Jews. After the war I was in Rakishok for one week. This was in July 1946. I experienced so much from that time until now that one event causes me to forget the next one: *aliyah bet* [clandestine immigration to Palestine during the period 1920 to 1948] on the ship, "Exodus Europe," the struggle in the country and so on.

What I know are details that I think you already know about. Nevertheless, I will write what I know.

As the Christians describe it, the Jews were killed in August 1941. Eight thousand Jews were killed in Rakishok and vicinity, as many refugees who had run from the Germans remained in Rakishok because the Latvian border was in dispute and they could not run any further. Not many people were able to save themselves because they did not have the wherewithal to travel. Specific details that I learned from the Christians I have already forgotten.

Rokiskis Yizkor Book   427

They were killed near the Gilincer Woods. Before they were killed, they were assembled in the Count's courtyard that was enclosed by barbed wire. All 8,000 were placed into two large holes.

The synagogues were burned. All of the personal property was looted by the Christians and a large part of what the bandits had gathered, they sold for trivial amounts. Christians from neighboring villages moved into the Jewish houses.

Now, after the war, only a few Jewish families live in Rakishok: Nakhum Sabl, Hirshl Bin, Mikhal the Kamayer [from Kamajai] and also several families from the smaller shtetlach who have settled in Rakishiok. For the most part, they settled in Vilna.

Hirshl Bin and my brother, Leizka, collected 500 rubles from each surviving Rakishok family to erect a *matzeivah* [headstone] and fence in the area.

In my eyes, all of Rakishok looks like a cemetery. Quiet, silent, as if everyone had died.

Whoever one speaks to among the gentiles contends that they are all good and religious; there are no guilty ones. Each declares that he helped; this one brought bread, this one something else, and so on. And when one comes into their rooms, there one sees it filled with Jewish property, clothes, furniture and other things.

I will stop writing. Writing about myself is very difficult. It makes my head hurt and I cannot concentrate on my thoughts. Ask more questions--perhaps it will be easier to answer, if I know.

Stay healthy and strong. Greetings from my wife.

With the best greetings, Shafir Efriom

* * *

Shafir Efriom writes from Israel. The *aliyah bet* and the ship "Exodus Europe" and the struggle in the country smothered his memory of certain events.

He briefly describes what the Christians have told him, that the Jews were killed near the Gilincer Woods with a total of 8,000 thrown into two large holes.

Shafir also provides the information that several Jewish families from Rakishok and from neighboring shtetlach remain in the shtetl. He lists their names.

A Letter from Henokh Blakher (now in Israel)

In a letter of May 11, 1951, he describes his wanderings and a history of martyrdom, as well as the deaths of some shtetlach:

To the distinguished people of the Rakishok Landsleit Union, much peace!

You wrote to me, a Lithuanian Jew, who survived the death march of the Hitlerist gangsters in Europe.

As I am in Israel, I have read your appeal in the Yiddish Israeli newspaper, Nei Welt [New World], in which you ask all who know something about Rakishok and vicinity to be of assistance with information for a Yizkor book that will be written by you. I was born in Kelme, lived in Memel from 1924 to 1938, and when in 1938 Hitler marched into Memel, I moved to Rasein [Raseiniai]. And as the war started in 1941, we escaped from our last residence, Rasein, with many hundreds of Jews, with the goal of distancing ourselves from the Hitlerist storm-troopers who streamed in so rapidly. The goal of our running was to reach the Lithuanian border and cross into Russia, and this was our area.

We escaped from our residence to Shavl [Siauliai]. A heavy German bombardment took place the same day in Shavl and we successfully escaped further to the small shtetl, Ligem [Lygumai]. From Ligem, we continued to travel and went through many small shtetlach, the names of which we do not clearly remember, to Birzh [Birzai] and from Birzh to Rakishok.

Rakishok was the last stop because the Lithuanian Hitler-partisans stopped us. And here begins the smallest bit of information that we can give you about the place. As soon as we reached Rakishok, we clearly saw that our situation was desperate. The Lithuanians had seized power before the Germans arrived, while the Russians were making a disorderly withdrawal. We saw that there was no point in continuing our refugee march, and all of the refugees began to return to their homes.

We saw how the Lithuanian partisans tortured local and non-local Jews to some extent. One of the sights was of the Lithuanian partisans stopping an entire trainload of refugees who were going from Rakishok to Birzh. On the road, when we wanted to return to our homes, there were full wagons with Jewish families, walkers who did not have any wagons and also many young Lithuanian partisans who rode on scooters.

They surrounded us all and robbed each of us of our possessions: rings, watches, gold and other valuables, as well as horses and wagons from our families. And I saw another ugly prank that showed us that we had to go further. This was when the partisans caught small children and hit their heads on the wheels.

Several Russian airplanes appeared in the heavens and began firing with machine guns. They saved us.

Then the partisans told everyone to run to the shtetlach, but only in the direction back to Lithuania, not forward.

They knew that Hitler was coming in today or tomorrow and that, therefore, they would have time to do what they wanted. And so some of the non-local Jews survived because we did not remain in the area but traveled back in an attempt to return home.

This is all information from the course of five days of the war.

When we woke up on Friday morning, the 26th of June 1941, we found ourselves in a village; we saw that the Germans were streaming en masse in the direction of Latvia.

What then happened to the Jews of Rakishok and vicinity? We only know that in the course of 3 to 4 weeks there were no longer any Jews, except for a few who saved themselves from the mass slaughter.

And after nine days of running through villages and many times through fields by day and several times at night, we reached Shavli.

And in Shavli we went through all of the hell that the Jews of Shavli went through and here I lost my entire family: wife, children, sisters and brothers and my old mother who was with me, except for my son who is now with me.

These are the common everyday events from a short time wandering. It is impossible to describe the day-to-day details because no matter how many times one writes about them, one cannot describe everything.

On and on, the same thing happened in all of Lithuania. Jews were murdered in the provinces through mass murder and they perished in agony. And in the large cities, the Jews were concentrated in ghettos: this was Vilna, Shavl, Kovno, where the largest number of Jews perished slowly from work, hunger and various deportations and concentration camps.

With this, I give the small bit of information about Rakishok and the Rakishok Jews.

Be successful in your benevolent work because there are few Lithuanian Jews remaining who can write about their history of pain and agony.

Stay healthy

With respect: Henokh Blakher

* * *

Although, Henokh Blekher knows a little information about Rakishok, he was an eyewitness of the large march of refugees – how Jews ran from and to Rakishok – and how the Lithuanian partisans stopped an entire train of refugees in Rakishok and how they were all robbed, murderously beaten and murdered before the Germans entered.

He resolutely states that in the course of 3-4 weeks there were no longer any Jews in Rakishok, except for those who saved themselves from the mass slaughter.

The Rakishker Landsleit Society received the following letter from Reuven Shreiberg in America
Dated June 30, 1951

While reading the Yiddish newspaper "Der Tog," which is published in New York, I came across your announcement concerning the plans you are making to publish a Yiskor Book, perpetuating the Jewish community of Rakishok, and those of her vicinity.

I hail from Ponedel, and if I am not mistaken, Ruch is a cousin of mine. I am the son of Mendel Shaklier (Mendel Shreiberg). We owned a mill, located just as you enter the town. I came to America in 1939 to visit my brother for the occasion of the 1939 World's Fair, and due to the outbreak of the Second World War, I remained in the U.S.

When I left Ponedel, the town had about 300 Jewish people and two synagogues. Close to 80% of the residents received financial aid from family members in America. Soon after I arrived here, we formed a Ponedeler Society and at each general meeting we would collect money and send it to our town. I am sure that you all remember life as it was under the rule of the Lithuanian government. You must surely remember Velvele Herring. He came here about the same time as I did. After the war ended, I corresponded with a number of our Lithuanian neighbors. When the Germans withdrew, they burned down three quarters of the town. They also wrote to me that they ordered the entire Jewish population to pack up a few belongings and be ready to be shipped to Poland where a Jewish state had been established for them. The entire group was taken to a wooded area not far from Rakishok, and there they all met a violent death. This was the end of our parents, relatives, and friends, brought about at the murderous hands of the Germans.

Right after the war was over, I received a letter from a Lithuanian neighbor in which he informed me that my brother had been exiled to Siberia. He also sent me my brother's address, but it took a long time before I finally made contact with him. My cousin Moshe Michel's son (his father was a tailor), who is now a judge in Vilna, has somehow succeeded in freeing him from his banishment in the Gulag and has brought him to Vilna. For five years I received frequent letters from him. Lately I haven't heard from him.

The house of Gecel Azrakh in Ponedel. On the porch is D. Dektar (now in Capetown), before departure for South Africa.

My brother's name is Yankel. His wife, their children, and my parents were all murdered by the Lithuanian Nazi murderers. My brother wrote to me that when he came to Ponedel, he didn't find any surviving Jews there. He stayed in Ponedel one day and left. The very same Lithuanian neighbors who carried on a correspondence with me had massacred the Jews.

He wrote that those who managed to escape and have survived are: Gershon Shtanaver's daughter; Motel Shmid's son and daughter, and Itzik Muluntze's son Arke; and Yankel Shizimovitz's also survived. There may be more, however, of whom I have no information. I will try to contact some Ponedeler and Rakishker Landsleit here in America. Perhaps they may have some information.

Please let me know what progress you are making with publishing the Yizkor Book.

With best regards, Your Landsman, Reuven Shreiberg

Yerachmiel Korb, after the Liberation

How the Shtetlach, Salok and Dukshty, Perished
(From My Diary)

(The Rakishok landsmanschaftn in Israel received a 1/6/1951 letter from Yerakhmeil Korb that was accompanied by notes from his diary that mainly cover the history of martyrdom and death of the Lithuanian shtetlach, Salok [Salakas] and Dukshty [Dukstas]. Although the shtetlach are not in the vicinity of Rakishok, it is necessary to publish this because in those frightful days – in the first weeks of the occupation – the majority of the Lithuanian shtetlach endured the same tortures and history of martyrdom and they perished *el kidush haShem* [died in the sanctification of God's name as martyrs] in the same savage way.)

1941. Friday, erev [the night before] Shabbos Nokhmu [the Shabbos after Tishe b'Av], the Christian who we had sent to Lygumai to determine if it is correct that the shtetl had perished came to me and he confirmed that all of the Jews (over 200 souls) were killed by the Lithuanians and also those in Kaltinenai. (Both shtetlach are 15 kilometers from our shtetl.) We were confused. There was nowhere to escape. There was one consolation; the messenger said that this was done by the Lithuanians and the Germans did not know about it and they were carrying out an investigation and the guilty would be punished.

In the picture: a family from Kaltinyani that perished. Right to left: Berl Tabakovitch, son of Yakov-Moishe and Rajza. He perished [at the hands of the] Lithuanians and Germans together with his father; Yosel and Dworale Axelrod, children of Nekha Tabakovitch-Axelrod and Berl Axelrod. The children perished in Auschwitz; Berl Axelrod – pedagogue and social worker – perished in the 9th Fort* in Kovno. [Translator's Note: *The place where thousands of Jews were held, tortured and murdered.]

It was almost Shabbos. Young Leibshtein came running to me and shouted: "Yerakhmeil! Young girls are coming to you!"

Why are young girls traveling at such a time? I thought, perhaps my friend from Utenai wants to come to me to save himself because my shtetl, Salok, belongs to Poland. And I kept on thinking and a wagon arrived at my house with five young girls. One of them gave me a letter written by well known Padrader merchants, in which they wrote in short: "Mr. Korb, help the five young girls to get to their homes." I learned who the young girls were: two from Salok, Hirsh Brava's daughters. I knew their father. One was a teacher in the Vilner Jewish Gymnazie, the second in a public school; three young girls were from Novo-Aleksandrovsk [Zarasai]. One was a bookkeeper at Shopn's brewery and two were students at Vilna University.

I led them into the house, gave them food and they told me that immediately after the outbreak of the war they tried to escape to Russia. They were captured entering Molodeczno and everything they had was taken from them; they were sent to Vilna. They had been hungry the entire time and they tried to obtain permission to travel home.

They told me the following:

"But how do we get home? Jews cannot travel by train, and a Jew cannot travel in a wagon because the Lithuanians are guarding the roads and when they see a Jew, they kill him. We went on foot and arrived in Padbradzi (50 kilometers). The Jews in Padbradzi took us in, arranged for a wagon and, also, a letter to you, and thank God, we came here safely. And now we ask you to help us get to Salok."

We arranged for a wagon with an old Lithuanian driver and decided that they would travel early on Shabbos because everyone said that Shabbos is the best time for safer travel because the gangsters do not travel on the roads, knowing that Jews are not allowed to travel on Shabbos.

Early Shabbos. The wagon arrived. We said goodbye to them. They traveled to Salok. Shabbos at night, the wagon returned with the young girls. I asked the Christian, "What is this? Why did you bring them back?" The Christian told me: "I had already brought the wagon to the village Akhres (eight km from Salok). A Christian helped me and asked, 'Where are you taking the young girls? You are taking them to be shot? The Jews are being shot in Salok!' I turned around and brought the young girls to you and you have to pay me for two trips; for going to Salok and for bringing them back." I took care of it with the Christian.

The young girls cried that they had no money to pay me. I calmed them. Do not cry, children, thank God that you have survived thanks to the peasant and are here with me. There is still food and what we eat, you will eat.

* * *

Sunday afternoon, we succeeded in sending a messenger to Salok. The young girls sent a letter to one respected Lithuanian named Kavaliuk. In the letter they asked him to write to them about what was happening in the shtetl and if their parents were there, he should give them their letter.

The Christian returned Tuesday at night bringing a letter from Hirsh Brava in which he writes: "Dear Children, we are alive, thank God, and we think about seeing you. Last week all of the Jews were taken away and not allowed to take anything with them. We were brought to Shigardi (Shingardi) and 120 men were taken to the village of Paezere (This is on the way to Taragini [Tauragnai]). They were held for two days without food; the 12 men were killed in the village of Paezere [Translator's note: the first number of men is given as 120 and the second as 12.] and we were brought back from Shigardi to our shtetl and everyone was taken to Plan Street where a ghetto was created for us in the empty ruined houses. During the two days, the houses were emptied, but thank God, we are alive."

A group of young people from Salok

On the 4th of September, a well known Leaniskhi estate owner came to me; he greeted me. He was frightened. I asked him, "Mr. Regner, why are you so frightened?"

He shouted, "I cannot speak!"

"Tell me, explain to me!"

His answer was, "I must not speak!"

I repeated that he should tell me and he began to speak:

"The farmhand of my sister-in-law, Maria, and I were chosen to take the Jews from Dukshty. We were not told where we would be taking the Jews, but the Jews were told that they were being driven to Rakishki [Rokiskis] to work. And the same day, the Jews were driven out of Salok, Rymshany [Rimse], Turmont [Turmantas] and other shtetlach. We came to a forest near Degutse [Deguciai] (this was on the Utena-Zarasai highway), on the road that goes down to Dusiaty [Dusetos]. We were told to remain standing, that the Jews should get out of the wagons, and there was an immediate cry: Everyone should take off all of their clothing. The victims immediately saw that they were standing next to long deep pits and surrounded by gangsters with machine guns. There was a lament, a scream to the heavens. The men got undressed and none of the women took off their clothing. And immediately – shooting from the machine guns and all were shot. We were told that if any of us told, we would be shot. Two of the drivers lost their minds. And I came to tell you and, perhaps, you would be able to see how to escape."

I knew that Virshinski of the Salok militia had given a letter for the Rabbi of the shtetl and for Gilinksi, Yitzhak Shnurat's son-in-law and for Bak, the son-in-law of Tuvia the butcher. The form of the letter: "[Name]...is a very respected man, he should be taken care of."

And thus was the shtetl Salok annihilated — one of the oldest shtetlach in Lithuania which had scholars, despite the fact that it was poor. In my time, when I was growing up in Salok, besides the few shops in the shtetl, there were many peddlers who lived in the villages [during the week] and only came home for Shabbos, many tradesmen: shoemakers, tailors, carpenters, seamstresses and, mostly, sock knitters. Despite the poverty, every Jew studied. The learned men, who knew the Gemara and the Mishnah, taught the others. Zalman Leib, the tailor, also read for a group.

The shtetl had two shochets [ritual slaughterers], four small synagogues. An old 300-year old pinkes [book of records] was in the old synagogue. I remember once in 1904, when I left the virtuous path and started to read non-religious books, the shamas of the old synagogue, Reb Yehuda Leib Gordon, said, "What do you get from the books? I will give you the pinkes to read and there you will find good things," and I was truly satisfied with reading the pinkes from the time that Napoleon marched through on the way to Moscow, about the Polish Rebellion and many other things. Today, only the ruins of the walls of the synagogues remain and the dilapidated houses. No Salok Jew survived, only two Jews who were in the Russian army came to Salok: one, Tzibl, the grandson of the Mordekhai Tzibl; and one Shimon Leib Epshtein, Kashal's grandson. I saw them in 1945.

One of the above mentioned young girls, the student Ruchl Kroiz, survived, and thanks to her, I survived.

* * *

In 1945 The Soviets opened the graves in Salok and it was confirmed that some were shot in their clothing and some were naked.

Dukshty

This shtetl belonged to Novo-Aleksandrovsk District (Zarasai) before the First World War. From 1918 it was under Poland. When the Soviets took Vilna during the First World War, Dukshty and several other shtetlach were given to the Zarasaier apskrites (county).

Dukshty is 13 km from Salok, but completely different from Salok. If Salok was an old shtetl with learned men and many poor people, Dukshty was one of the richest shtetlach, a young shtetl with many educated people. (The first Jewish houses were built 87 years ago, when the Petersburg-Warsaw train line was built.) Thanks to the trains, settlements arose near the train stations. There were many shtetlach, of which Dukshty became the main depot for all goods, starting with the wood trade – wooden poles, telegraph poles and wood pulp would be sent to Germany and England from the station. The area was richest in grains and all kinds of fruit and they were sent, too. The trade in flax which was developed by the rich Hilsfarb-Kabarski firm was the largest.

From its intelligencia, it is worthwhile to mention the names, Rapaport, one of the first fighters among the members of the People's Party. He is from Dukshty, but he lived in Paris; the painter Eidlman and still many more doctors, pharmacists, teachers.

In 1941, just as the Germans marched through, the regime took over Lithuania and immediately began to drive the Jews every day to hard labor and loading wooden beams and stones which the Soviets had prepared to be taken. Money also began to be extracted from the Jews, to prevent their killing as Bolsheviks. When the work was at an end, the Jews were driven to Ostrov (island) on the lake; they were not permitted to take anything with them. On Ostrov, the gangsters took care that the peasants did not provide the Jews with any food and many of the peasants who did give the Jews something were punished.

At the same time, all of the Jewish houses in the shtetl were cleared out, the ovens broken and searches were made for the gold and jewelry that the Jews had hidden (in many places, gold was actually found); the Jews were taken to the villages. Then they were brought back to the shtetl and the Jews again settled down in the empty ruins of the houses.

Three days later they were still in their houses. All of the Jews were driven out to the court of Antanov (Novihanshke), three kilometers from the shtetl where they lay in the street for several days and then were driven out with the people from the other shtetlach in Zarasai apskrites to the forests near Diegusti [Degučiai], where they all perished.

In the entire county in which the Jews were shot, only two men successfully escaped from the pit and hid temporarily with a Christian acquaintance; one was Ahron and the second was Vishigor.

They were with me in the ghetto in Sventsyan [Švenčionys] and, also, working in the camps. In 1943, Ahron fell into the hands of the gangsters and he took his own life.

That is how the beautiful youngest shtetl in the Zarasai area perished, the rich shtetl, Dukshty.

In short I have written how the two shtetlach of the Zarasai apskrite (Novo-Aleksandovsk district) perished.

I am responsible for its truthfulness.

Respectfully: Yerakhmeil ben Abraham Moshe Korb (Born in Salok and living in Ignalina since after the First World War, Sventsyan County).

Meilech Bakalczuk-Felin: Editor of the "Memorial Book of Rokiskis and Environs"; Editor of the journal "South Africa" – monthly [publication] of the S. A. Jewish Culture Federation

The descriptions of Yerakhmeil Korb explaining how the shtetlach of Salok and Dukshty perished are considerable contributions to the Holocaust material about these towns.

The Jews in these above mentioned shtetlach did not imagine that the Germans would kill them and many Christians.

In his work he remembers the names of several destroyed shtetlach and, also, that the Jews of Dukshty were told that they were being taken to work in Rakishki.

In addition to the course of the Holocaust, he provides details and facts about the life in the shtetlach before the Holocaust, remembering people and the full worth of communal matters as well as institutions that can be a definite contribution to a monograph about these shtetlach.

* * *

These letters present a collection of cruel facts and tragic, dramatic situations before, during and after the Holocaust, as well as rich physical material from the survivors. The entire tragedy of the Holocaust spins before our eyes in its full cruelty. From these lines and letters written in blood, emerge specters and pictures, tragic episodes, the history and facts of a people's cruel catastrophe.

[Page 452]

The *Landsmanschaft* of Rakishok
(1912-1952)
M. Rotholz-Kur

This work was written on the basis of record books, excerpts from minutes, information, materials and notices which were given to me by Yerakhmiel Arons – Arsh, the landsleit [people from the same town] worker; Yitzhak Ginzburg, Ahron Noach – Noachmanovitch and Shlomo Rubin. Thanks to the material provided, I was able to assemble this documented treatise about the Rakishoker Landsmanschaft [society of people from the same town].

A. Activities of the Society

The *Rakishoker Landsmanschaft* has been in existence for over 40 years and those from the neighboring *shtetlekh*, Abel [Obelial], Kamay [Kamajai], Svidoshc, Ponedel, Tibat, Skopishak, Poneminok, Sevenishak, Anushishok, Novo-Aleksandrovski=Ezsherni and others, are also included as *landsleit*.

Many significant and great changes took place in Jewish life over the course of time. A great deal of water flowed over the Jews in many lands; not least the Jewish people suffered from anti-Semitic persecutions and pogroms and slaughters, the First World War and a Second, when the savage destruction of the Jewish people under the rule of the Nazis took place and, finally, the rise of the State of Israel.

Without a doubt, all of the years and times lay their seal on organized Jewish society in general and on the Rakishok Society, which at the critical moment had to master and absorb all of the shadows and light in Jewish life, seeing the strengthening of the beliefs of our members and awakening in them the hope of better times that stimulated them to communal activities and to national actions.

The barely 40 years of the Rakishok *landsmanschaft* is an important communal event not only in its own area, but also for the entire local Jewish organized society and it is therefore necessary to very abundantly reflect its activities in the columns of the Yizkor Book.

The Founding of the Society

The first emigrants from the Jewish *shtetlekh* in Lithuania who began to wander to distant South Africa did so in the role of pioneers and among them were educated circles of *landsleit* who were mutually connected and were among themselves like family members and *brothers* who would come together to share the news of those scattered in various population areas of South Africa. Such frequent gatherings were the beginning of a *landsmanshaft*.

[Page 453]

The devotion of one toward the other was expressed in deeds; a new emigrant was met at the ship, he was offered hospitality, helped to look for work and given the initial financial aid, and care was also given to a sick *landsleit*, providing him with a doctor and medications, too.

The excerpt from N.D. Hofman's *Book of Memories*, published in *Jews of South Africa* by Leibl Feldman (a Rakishok *landsman*), can serve as a source of information:

"When a *griner* [newly arrived] Jew would arrive in Cape Town, he would look for distant relatives with the addresses he had brought with him from home. He would be received with pity, taken to a bath to destroy his third plague [lice], he would be led to a barber, given other clean clothing and held at home for weeks at a time until he was rested from the long trip and became a little assimilated. Then the *landsleit* would take him to a wholesale merchant where they had credit and provide him with several pounds of goods. They would help him pack his bag, writing the price on each piece of goods, what it cost, as well as the price for which he should sell it. Placing the heavy pack on his back and tightly binding it with two wide leather straps, they would wish him success and would send him into the countryside around Cape Town among the Boers."

Landsleit circles were organized entirely spontaneously after which a *landsmanschaft* was founded. *Landsleit* would come together monthly on *Shabbosim* [Sabbaths], *yomim-tovim* [religious holidays] and on Sundays in a hall or at the home of a *landsman* – a pioneer – who had immigrated with his family or was able to bring them here.

In general single people, individuals, without wives and children, came with the first storm of immigration to South Africa and it was a long time before they decided to urge their families [to come] and to create a new home in South Africa. Even young men, who left brides beyond the sea, also did not rush to ask them because the ideas were deeply sunk into them that they still would save a little money and they would return home.

There was too strong a nostalgia with each Lithuanian Jew and Jewish immigrant for the way of life in his *shtetl* or city. He also could not live a religious life as at home. During the early years there were only a few *khederim* [religious primary schools] for children, only a few synagogues, clergymen, *beli tefilus* [men who read the prayers on holidays], cantors, *shoykhetim* [ritual slaughterers] and preachers.

The climatic and economic conditions also were entirely different from those in Eastern Europe.

It was difficult to adjust with respect to the work. There was no sellers market for much of the local work and means of earning a living. In addition, the industry in South Africa was still undeveloped at that time.

The immigrants, not mastering the language, could not take positions of employment in various trade firms. They became *trayers* [peddlers], carrying goods on their backs, mainly to the Boer villages and farmers, or they received work places in *kaferites* [restaurants for the Africans].

[Page 454]

There were many cases when immigrants returned home – to their wife and children, to the relatives and those closest to them. There were also those who again returned to South Africa when they lost their saved money in trade. These facts were not an influence in such measure that Jewish immigrants would consider South Africa as their permanent home.

The *landsleit* joined more strongly and more firmly together in order to quiet their longing for family and home.

L. Feldman in his above-mentioned book talks about the reciprocal connection and strong friendship among the *landsleit*. I quote here that passage from his book:

"The thousand miles that separated him (the immigrant) from his home increased his longing and loneliness. After work, on holidays and days of rest, he felt his loneliness in fear and strongly longed for community, at least to pass time. The wish for community to quiet his loneliness and longing for his family and familiar environment drove him to the relationship with Lithuanian Jews from his town or city. As others were in a similar situation as he was, they strongly befriended each other. They would come together at the home of a landsleit *and they would talk about the old home, about the difficulties of the new life, about income; they would ask for advice and they were helpful to each other.*

"The coming together of the landsleit *or of just Yiddish speaking Jews took on a more communal character each time. They would meet more and more*

often. In addition to discussing their old home and daily economic questions, they would also speak about and discuss news and worldly matters.

"*This led to founding of* landsmanschaftn *and* khevras *[groups] that had as their purpose to give material support, (gmiles khesed kases [interest free loan fund], medical aid) to the* landsleit *and help the shtetlekh of the* landsmanschaftn *in question.*"

The extract provided above can serve as an argument for what was necessary for the rise of *landsmanschaftn*, including the Rakishoker *Landsmanschaft.*

* * *

The genesis and stages of progress of the Rakishok *landmanschaft* are not comprehensive, but are mirrored in the protocol books of the Society that were kept. It is regrettable that they are dryly written, in a banal style and in a Yiddish language that has a great deal of English and German words. It is indeed a fact that the first Jewish immigrants from Lithuania, not being in the country for long, used such a strange mixed language.

Yet, looking at all its drawbacks, the protocol books are for us a worthwhile source from which we can learn and be informed about the founding and activities of the Rakishok *Landsmanschaft* in various periods of time. First of all, we are informed that the official founding of the Society took place on the 14th of January 1912, that is, over 40 years ago. From that historic day I cite the full text of the first protocol without any changes:

[Page 455]

"*A general meeting was held on Sunday, the 14th of January 1912 in South Africa, Palmesten [Palmerston] Hotel, Commissioner Street to found a Rakishoker Sick Benefit Society. The following officers were elected, S. Shwartsberg as chairman, Zalman Sher, vice chairman, Gedelia Zakstein as treasurer. Hilel Eidelman and S. N. Yafa, trustee committee, Sh. L. Yafe, Josef Feldman, S. H. Abelovitz, W. Kahn, D. Shaibla Yisrael, N. Kahn, Z. Beinart and S. Shneider as secretary. Meeting closed.*

It is signed by Shimon Shwartsberg"

After this "general meeting" two committee sessions took place:

"*Sunday the 21st of January 1912 and Sunday the 28th of January 1912.*

At the session of the 28th of January 1912, it was decided:

"Letters shall be printed and a general meeting shall be called for the 4th of February.

"At the general meeting of the 4th of February, 1912 the particular rules and regulations of the constitution for the landsmanschaft were discussed and a decision was made that the society would arrange for a doctor who would provide medical help for the member, and his family would have the benefit of a doctor for half price and also medicine for half price. It was then decided: register books shall be printed and each committee shall have a register book and collect contributions."

The second general meeting, which took place on Sunday the 10th of March, at 3 o'clock in the afternoon, 1912, dealt with and approved the points of the proposed constitution for the landsmanschaft. And a banking account was opened.

I publish the adopted constitution as an historical document.

Constitution
Rules and Regulations
of the
Rakishoker Sick Benefit Society
Johannesburg
* * *

1 – The name of the Society will be: "Rakishoker Sick Benefit Society," so long as there are 10 members in the society.

2 – The purpose of the Society will be: a) without cost to give those members who need to have a doctor and medicine; all remaining claims and services of the doctor should be taken to the committee.

[Page 456]

b) To give the wife and children of a member who need to have a doctor and medicine for the society's price at their own expense.

3 – Candidates can only become members of the Society when they are not less than 18 and not more than 45 years old.

4 – Each candidate must be brought before the committee and must be supported by two full members and shall be elected by a majority of the general body.

5 – The candidate who wishes to become a member of the Society must be a respectable man. Whoever is connected to immorality, both directly and indirectly, cannot join the Society. If the committee learns that a member has or has had connections with immorality, it has the right to return the money he has paid in and to exclude him as a member of the Society.

6 – In case a vote is brought to the committee of the Society when a member is accused of bad behavior or the behavior of a member is harmful, when the accusations are found to be correct, the committee has the right:

a) To take away from the member all rights, benefits, such as the committee will find suitable.

b) To call on the member in writing to resign and, if he does not resign, then the committee can remove him from membership. The committee should give the member all rights to defend himself and to appeal in person or in writing to the general meeting and if he is found guilty by the general meeting, then he will be bound by the punishment and he cannot make a claim against the society.

7 – Everything that is considered by the committee must be in private and those who reveal anything publicly to a stranger shall be penalized the first time with 2 shillings/56, the second time with 5 shillings and the third time he will be removed from the committee.

8 – A candidate who has not married according the Laws of Moses cannot become a member of the Society.

9 – The contribution will be 2/6 per month.

10 – The secretary shall send a registered letter to a member who does not pay his contributions two months in a row and ask him to pay his contributions. If he does not pay for six months, he loses all of his benefits. When a member is not able to pay his contributions, he shall inform the committee of this and they will give him time to pay, but they can also declare him without benefits.

11 – When a member travels, he must notify the secretary of this.

He is permitted to discontinue his obligations for six months and he is without benefits during this time.

In case of illness, the national member may present a certificate from a doctor and he will have the right to receive the same benefits according to the rules of the Society for a local member.

12 – Each person who becomes a member of the Society shall pay entry money and he shall be considered entitled to benefits after six months, if he has paid all of his obligations.

[Page 457]

13 – A member can leave the Society for 12 months. Over 12 months, he can join the Society according to the rules for candidates for membership.

14 – A member of the Society who gets married should receive a present from the Society and it should cost not less than 30 shillings.

15 – The committee of the Society shall consist of 15 members: chairman, vice chairman, treasurer, secretary, assistant secretary, two trustees, two auditors, a door-keeper and two committee members. The officers should be elected at a general meeting.

16 – Duties of the chairman:

The chairman shall administer all meetings; if he finds it impossible to attend a meeting because of certain circumstances, he must then notify the secretary in writing a half hour before the meeting or he will be fined one shilling. He shall control everything that belongs to the Society and sign the minutes of every general meeting. When he finds it necessary, he can call a special meeting. At the time of the meeting he must maintain order among the brothers of the Society. If a brother is not obedient, he has the right to punish him. If the brother is not obedient after being called to order three times, the chairman then has the right to take away his right to vote at this meeting. If the brother does not obey the penalty, then he has the right to ask him to leave the hall for the meeting. If the brother is not obedient the chairman can take him to arbitration. The chairman shall have a casting vote.

17 – Duties of the vice chairman:

The vice chairman has the same duties and rights as the chairman, when the chairman is absent.

18 – Duties of the treasurer:

The treasurer must attend all meetings and shall receive all monies from the secretary of the Society and give him a receipt for them. He shall deposit all monies, checks and other documents. He deposits everything he receives in the bank in the name of the Society.

19 –Duties of the secretary:

The secretary shall have correct reports of all meetings and handle all of the correspondence and the books of the Society in good order. He should inform each member by letter about each meeting. He must attend all meetings and insure that all of the contributions are paid. All money that he receives for the Society must be given to the treasurer and he has the right to keep up to one pound for small payments.

20 – Duties of the assistant secretary:

The assistant secretary has the same duties as the secretary. He must perform all of the tasks that the secretary gives to him for the Society. However, he cannot sign any documents that belong to the Society.

21 – Duties of the trustees:

The trustees shall attend each meeting and when the committee decides to issue a check, it is the duty of the trustee to sign the check.

[Page 458]

22 – Auditors' duties:

The auditors shall review the books every six months before the election and sign the balance sheet if it is correct. They have the right to demand the books at that time and verify them. In case an auditor does not fulfill his duty when he is asked, the committee has the right to arrange an election in his place.

23 – Duties of the committee:

Each committeeman must attend the meeting promptly and carry out all of the business that is brought to the committee. A quorum of the committee must be seven committee members in addition to the chairman.

If a committeeman fails to attend three committee meetings in a row without an important reason, the chairman has the right to fine him up to 2 shillings and then the secretary shall write a letter to him and if he fails to attend a fourth meeting the committee may declare his seat vacant and designate a replacement unless he sends in an apology.

The committee has no right to make new or other rules; a special general meeting must be called for this purpose.

The committee shall compile a report for the general meeting about the work that it undertook. Committee meetings shall be held every month.

24 – Duties of the doctor:

The doctor's duty is to examine a member when he asks him and in such cases he must send a certificate to the secretary and set down if his illness is infectious. He must attend all sick members at least once a day when they are seriously ill. When the sick person can, he must go to the doctor. When the doctor thinks that an extra doctor's help is needed and provides a certificate, the society will permit the taking of another doctor.

52 [This should be 25] – Each member must attend a quarterly meeting; if not, he shall pay a fine of a shilling unless he sends an apology. When one brother is speaking a second one may not interrupt. He must ask permission from the chairman. And when the brother has finished speaking, he can then speak. If he does not obey the rules, he can be fined. When a member speaks unpleasant words or insulting words, or leaves without the permission of the chairman, he shall be fined a shilling.

When a member moves to a new residence he must give notice to the secretary with his new address not later than two weeks or he will pay a one shilling fine.

26 – A quorum at the general meeting shall be 25 members in addition to the chairman. No member can be elected to office unless he has belonged to the Society for six months.

The Landsmannschaft of Rakishok

Greetings

Translated by Bella (Aarons) Golubchik

[Translator's Note: Ethel (Schwartzberg) Aarons and Yerachmiel "Ralph" Aarons are my parents. I watched the book being brought to life by the members of the Rakishker Landsmanscaft in the dining room of my parents "palace" in Mayfair, Johannesburg.]

In conjunction with the 40th anniversary of the Rakishker Landsmanschaft and concurrent with the publication [appearance] of The Yizkor Book of Rakishok and Environs, we publish the greetings of the following Institutions:

Board of Deputies in South Africa

To the Honorable Secretary

The Landsmanschaft of Rakishok and Environs

Esteemed Friends:

It gives me great pleasure to send you greetings for your Yizkor and Jubilee [anniversary] Book; in honor of the 40th anniversary of your Landsmanschaft. Your Association, like others of the same character, which we have in this country, has the important dual task of upholding brotherly ties with *landsleit* and simultaneously to strengthen the consciousness and to feel the commitment to your fellow members as Jews and citizens of this country. You have achieved much in both these regards.

In the relatively short history of South African Jewry, a 40th Jubilee is certainly a remarkable achievement.

I wish you and your Landsmanschaft success and continued fruitful labor.

With friendly greetings,

J. A. Maisels, President Johannesburg, 5th May 1952

Zionist Federation of South Africa

To the Rakishker Landsmanschaft in South Africa:

In the last 40 years, there have occurred enormous changes in the political, economic and social life of humanity and in the life of the Jewish People. All of these changes are of such a scope and significance that they can be judged by us as the greatest in the history of the Jewish nation.

[Page 434]

The destruction of European Jewry, including the communities from which your members originate, has placed on the Jews of the whole world a great responsibility for the fate of the whole Jewish People.

The South African Jewish communities are mainly composed of immigrants who came from cities and shtetlach like Rakishok, and of their children who, thanks to the beautiful traditions which they brought from the old home, have acquired a high reputation in the Jewish world.

The South African Zionist Federation, stimulated by these vital powers and these exalted traditions, have made a substantial contribution to the realization of the Zionist Ideal and the establishment of the Jewish State of Israel.

We are therefore happy to identify with you in your anniversary celebration and wish your Landsmanschaft, together with other Landsmanschaften, to have continuity in upholding our old traditions and remaining active in practical aid for the good of Eretz Yisrael, for the People of Israel, and for our Jewish Community in South Africa.

S. M. Kuper Chairman of the South African Zionist Federation Johannesburg, 21st May 1952

South African Board of Jewish Education

To the Honorable Secretary

of the Rakishker Society in Johannesburg

Dear Friends:

In the name of the Board of Education in South Africa, I have the pleasure to express hearty greetings to the Rakishker Landsmanschaft on 40 years of their existence in South Africa. The exceptional achievements of these landsmanschaften, among whom you contributed a significant portion, are well known to us, and it is no doubt that landsmanschaften like your Society have contributed a great deal to the progress and well-being of the South African Jewish community.

Your publication of the Yizkor Book of Rakishok, in memory of the martyrs, etc., is specially significant.

We appreciate that in the Yizkor Book, your active landsmanschaft will tell the heroic actions of the Jews of Rakishok and Environs, as is appropriate.

Yours faithfully,

P. Porter, Chairman Johannesburg, 9th June 1952

[Page 435]

The South African Jewish Culture Federation

To the Rakishker Landsmanschaft:

It is with great pleasure that the South African Jewish Culture Federation takes upon itself the duty to greet you on the 40th anniversary of your landsmanschaft. The role of the landsmanschaften was very big in the years when the immigration from Eastern Europe into South Africa began. But even now these landsmanschaften can do important work, both for those remaining refugees in the various countries, and also for their present members.

Apart from practical help, cultural work should be an important task of every landsmanschaft organization. By spreading the Jewish word, the landsmanschaften can strengthen the continuity between the present generation and the cultural treasures, which were created in the countries from which local Jews originate.

In your decision to publish a yizkor book about Rakishok and Environs, there is an important sign that your landsmanschaft understands the duty that life places on all of us.

We hope that this book will perpetuate the life and activities of a significant part of the Lithuanian Jewish population.

We wish you success in your important work.

With 'Friendly-Culture' Greetings,

South African Jewish Kultur Federatziah R. Friedman, Secretary Johannesburg, 15th June 1952

Chevra Kadisha and Helping Hand

To the Secretary of the Rakishker Landsmanschaft

Dear Friends:

I express to your Landsmanschaft the most enthusiastic greetings of the Executive Committee and members of the Johannesburg Chevra Kadisha and Helping Hand on your 40th anniversary.

It is for me a great pleasure on this occasion to express our friendship, which always exists between both our organizations.

Together with you we mourn over the great national catastrophe and over the Holocaust in Rakishok and Environs, and we believe you will in the future continue your noble activities.

May your Landsmanscahft go from strength to strength and increase in size.

Oscar Getz, Chairman Johannesburg, 21st May 1952

[Page 436]

Organization of Lithuanian Jews in Philadelphia and Environs

To the Rakishker Landsmanschaft in South Africa:

We greet you heartily, active members and leaders of Lithuanian Jewry, Association of Rakishker Landsleit, in honor of your 40th year Jubilee.

Greetings for your brotherly aid work and cultural activities and for publishing the Yizkor Book.

In you there burns the spirit of eternal energy of Lithuanian Jewry. Be proud of your organization and achievements. We are very happy to know that we are not alone in the great welfare work.

Let us together work to help the kernel that has risen from Lithuanian Jewry, from which can and will begin to be spun, future generations of the Jewish spirituality that enriched Jewish life until now.

Let us with united strength perpetuate the past and help to build Jewish life in Israel and all parts of the world, being an example of industriousness, culture-creating and freedom-loving people.

Greetings to you all and may you have success in all your endeavours.

Michael Levin, President Jacob Davis, Chairman of the Board Lewis Sasman, Finance Secretary David L. Frensky, Accountant Gitteh Ferman, Secretary Philadelphia, 15th February 1952

Committee of Welfare Association of Shatt and Environs

Landsmanschaft of Rakishok and Environs

Esteemed Friends:

We express to you our deepest acknowledgement for your publication of the Yizkor Book in memory of Rakishok and Environs. In our opinion, this book should be found in every Jewish house in Africa and the Diaspora.

Your undertaking of the publication of the Yizkor book should be hailed by all Jews.

A. Ch. Gaddye, Secretary Johannesburg, 5th July 1952

[Page 437]
Fordsburg – Mayfair Gmiluth Chessed

Very Esteemed Secretary of the Rakishker Landsmanschaft:

We greet you in your undertaking, which is truly a mighty achievement.

With the Yizkor Book will be perpetuated the memory of the tragic annihilation and Holocaust of East European Jewry generally, and of Lithuanian Jews in particular. It will be a memorial for all future generations.

We greet you on the 40th anniversary of your existence, which in our young communal life in South Africa is a very unusual occasion. During this time, a number of landsmanschaften have already ceased to exist, but you were active and are still active in many areas of our communal life.

Without a doubt, your activities will be written down in the annals of history.

May the hands of all those who took part in this holy labour be strengthened and blessed.

With friendly greetings,

Y. Orkin Johannesburg, 12th May 1952

[Pages 438-451]

Monograph of Jewish Communities and Towns in Jewish Historiography

by Dr. Philip Friedman, America

Translated by Bella (Aarons) Golubchik

1. Introduction

Recording Jewish History in the modern meaning of the word is a very young science. It is understandable that Jews, being a people with an ancient history, always had certain literary creations that dealt with political happenings. Much historical material is to be found in the Tanakh [the Jewish Bible]. Certain books are dedicated simply to tell a story. Books with a historical content are also found in external books, in the Septuagint [the translation of the 70 scholars] and other creations of the Hellenistic Period.

Dr. Philip Friedman: well-known historian and scholar

The classic Jewish historian of the Hellenic-Roman Period was Josephus Falvius, but he was not the only one to describe the struggle with Rome. [Unfortunately, the writings of other historians, such as Justus from Tiberius, have been lost.] In the later periods, however, the significance and interest for recording history was lost. The learned Jews of the Middle Ages did not create historical works apart from those that depicted the development of Halakha [Jewish Religious Law], Rabbi Sh'rira Ga-on, etc. First, there was the period of the Spanish expulsion. Under the influence of outstanding [exceptional] suffering and the influence of the Italian Renaissance, there came into being a few works which dealt with historic research or local news [chronicles]. [Yosef Hakohein; Yehuda Ibn Vigra; Avraham Zechuta; Shmuel Ushki; Azariah Min Ha Adumim and others]. But the example of the Spanish and Italian historians found only a scant response from the Ashkenazi Jews, who really distanced themselves from such 'idle things' [idle words]. [This was the opinion about history books of Rabbi Ya'akov Emden, in the 18th century.] With only a few exceptions [e.g., David Gandz – 'Tzemach David']. It is understandable that during these many hundreds of years, many memoirs were written, diaries, memories; (e.g., The Scroll of Achimetz; The Memoirs of Gluekel of Hamelin, and many, many others); family chronicles; and chronicles and scrolls about decrees and persecutions [e.g., about the Crusades and the Decrees of the years Täch and T"at and so on]. But these are the fabric and raw material of historical research, and not historical monographs or studies.

Modern Jewish historiography traces its connection to two great Jewish intellectuals, who began to develop their great historical work around the middle of the 19th century, Mordechai [Markus] Jost and Tzvi [Heinich] Graetz. Their works were great synthetic essays which encompassed the whole story of the Jewish people in all eras and all countries.

Simultaneously with this Jewish universal history, studies began to appear from other researchers who embraced only one period or one problem. A further step was "national history," which dealt with the history of the Jews in one country e.g., Germany, Poland, Italy, Turkey, and so forth. Only later did an interest begin to develop in the history of Jews in particular towns, communities, and individual areas, i.e., local and regional history.

2. The Amateur Community Monographs

To begin with, this latest branch of the Jewish Story was principally in the hands of amateurs [lovers of Jewish History] and not in the hands of educated professionals, who wanted to engage themselves with the ways [high ways] of historical development, and regarded it below their dignity to busy themselves with such limited themes as local history. Only much later did there emerge an historiographical area [see Section 4], which showed that the regional and local investigations [researches] were precisely as important as the synthetic ones.

In the meantime, educated enthusiasts created a great deal in the area of community monographs. Among these amateurs there were also various levels. The best combination of amateur-historian in those days, particularly in Western and Central Europe, was represented by the 'Rav' [The Doctor-Rabbi]. He generally combined Jewish and general education, and completing a Rabbinic Seminary [or a Yeshiva] and a [secular] University. Scientifically and methodologically, however, he was more prepared [inclined] towards Tanakh [Bible] and Halakha [Jewish Law], Hebraic philology, and literature, rather than to history and sociological research. He had, however, at least an approach to both Judaic-Hebraic and non-Jewish sources.

The other types of amateurs were more one-sided. They had either secular or Jewish traditional education only.

Almost all the monographs written by the amateurs are one sided [biased], although among them were people of great education and ability. They occupied themselves mainly with the history of the communal institutions, charitable institutions, and biographies of renowned persons; describing or rewriting tombstones in old cemeteries, statements of accounts of congregations and account books, and giving long and detailed letters of the pedigree of well-known families. This one-sidedness [bias] is characteristic of monographs written by rabbis as well as ordinary learned people.

Other works suffer from another type of bias—that of people who have only a general secular education, with no access to the Hebrew and Jewish sources. They used mainly urban and national archives involving non-Jewish printed sources and research, and they occupied themselves mainly with the external organization, with legal questions, with by-laws [statutes] and privileges, with decrees, protests, and disagreements between Jewish and Christian townsfolk and so on.

In a word, all these monographs did not have a universal character. They were fragmentary in many aspects. Generally, they did not provide the economic and social development, the rich canvas of inner/internal life, language, cultural life and folk creativity, the national and social movements in the new era, and so on.

Nevertheless, amateur local researches have great value for the Jewish story. The history enthusiasts were the first to plough through the neglected field of community history. They saved for distant, future researchers, a great deal of important material, from notebooks, books, and tombstones, to oral tradition from elders and others--material that surely would have been lost without such dedicated labor. The blossoming period of these amateur monographs was the second half of the 19th century. However, this branch of our historiography has not died out totally with the awakening of the modern scientific and professional community monographics.

Even in our time a considerable amount of amateur-urban monographs are published. Aamong these hundreds of amateur communal descriptions [many of these are scattered in various periodicals and anthologies] are at least a few score that are exceptional, both due to the great expertise and skill of the compilers, as well as the significant and worthy material they bring. We will give here a short overview of the most important publications of this type.

Generally, the monographic works about the communities are written in Hebrew, the literary language of the educated in Eastern Europe. Most of the amateur monographs stemmed from Eastern Europe. The Hebrew monographs often carry their characteristic titles [names]. In the oratorical flowery language of these titles, we can already see the awe-filled, loving attitude of the compilers to their subject. We see that this is not simply a job for them--'a spade with which to dig'-- but a holy duty, a holy task. Here are a few titles of these books: *The Faithful City, The Exalted City, Totally Beautiful, City of Praise, City of Heroes, City of Righteousness, Monument of Holiness* and a few more 'neutral' titles; *City of Lesek and Her Wise Men, Rabbis of Minsk and Her Wise Men, Streets of the City, Memorial Tablets [lists], A Momento to the Great Men of Ostra, Rabbis of Dubno,* and so forth.

Now let us see which geographic areas these monographs covered and the tempo of their publication. [Next to each book we quote also the year of publication.] The first communities which attracted the consideration of the writers were the renowned ancient communities, with a great tradition of erudition. And here are the communities.

Krakow: G. M. Tzintz, *Ir Hatzedek [City of Righteousness]*, 1874.

Ancient Times from Various Notebooks, 1892 [Vitshtein].

And later *[various essays and notebooks with sources],* P. Ch. Vitshtein, 1982. Ch. D. Friedberg, *Memorial Lists [Tables],* 1897.

Vilna: Y. Finn, *Faithful City,* 1860. Noach Shtinschneider [Magid], *City of Vilna,* 1900.

Lemberg: G. Sochestov, *Holy Memorial* [four sections], 1863-1869. Ch. N. Dimbitzer, *Totally Beautiful,* 1888-1893. Shlomo Buber, *Famous People,* 1895. Dr. Yechezkiel Karo [Rabbi of the Lemberg Progressive Congregation], *History of the Jews in Lemberg,* 1894 [in German].

Sholkeveh: Shlomo Buber, *Exalted City* 1903.

Yaroslav: M. Shteinberg [Rabbi in Yaroslav], *The Jews in Yaroslav,* 1933 [in Polish].

Tchort'kev: Zunshin, Efraim [Rabbi in Torun, born in Tchort'kev], *Chapters from the Annals of the Lives of the Jews of Tchort'kov,* 1939.

Galina: *Scroll of Galina,* by Chanoch H. Halperin, 1950. [In Yiddish] *Community of Galina, 1473-1943,* by Asher Korach, 1950.

Dinau, Sanik, Dibetzk [Dubietzkah]: *The Destruction of Dinau, Sanik and Dibetzk,* by David Maritz, 1950 [Yiddish].

Mezeritch: *My Ravaged Life,* by Y. Horn 1946.

Karetz: *The Destruction of Karetz,* by Moshe Gildenman, 1949.

Lublin: Sh. B. Nissenboim, *History of the Jews of Lublin,* 1899. N. Sheman, *Lublin, City of Torah, Rabbinate and Chassidism,* 1951.

Piotr'kov: Feinkind, *The History of the Jews in Piotr'kov,* 1930 [in Polish]. *Lask and Its Wise Men,* P. Z. Gliksman, 1926.

Apta [Apatov]: Nochum Sokolov, *There Is No Harvest,* 1894.

Chelm: Shimon Milner, *There Is No Harvest,* 1902.

Dubnow: H. Sh. Margalit, *Rabbis of Dubnov,* 1910. P. Pessis: *City of Dubnov and Her Wise Men,* 1902. Ostrah [Ostrag] M. M. Bieber, *A Monument to the Great Men of Ostrah,* 1907.

Grodno: Sh. A. Friedshtein, *City of Heroes,* 1880. Shlomo Hurwitz, *Streets of the City,* 1881 [a critique of Friedenshtein's Book].

Brisk D'Litah [Brest-Litovsk]: A. L. Feinshtein, *City of Praise,* 1886.

Bialistok: A. Sh. Hershberg, *Bialistok Diary* [2 vols.], 1949-1950 [in Yiddish].

Minsk: Shmuel Tzitron, *Congregation of Israel in Minsk in Assembly of Israel,* 1886. Benzion Eizenshtadt, *Rabbis of Minsk and Her Wise Men,* 1898.

Novoradek [Novogradek]: D. Walberinsky – M. Markowitz, *History of the City of Novochrodek and Its Rabbis,* 1913.

Vitebsk: Zabizhinski, *History of the Jews of Vitebsk in 'Today,'* 1877.

Kovno: Tbilovski, *The Scroll of Kovno in Knesset Yisrael* [Congregation of Israel], 1886. D. M. Lipman: *History of the Jews of Kovno and Slovodkah* 1934.

Keidan: Ch. Kassel, *The City of Keidan,* 1930.

Kiev: A Kupernik, History of the Jews in Kiev, 1891.

3. The Historical Monographs

The historical monograph first appeared in Western Europe and German around the middle of the 19th century. In Eastern Europe, this new phase appeared approximately 50 years later on the crest between the 19th and 20th centuries.

Actually, there is no clear dividing line in Western Europe between the amateur and historical monograph. There were almost no erudite scholars of the Eastern European type among the community of historians. The first Jewish historians from the Western European community were mainly people with little Jewish education, or even without either Jewish or Hebrew education. This is a strong indication of the character and content of their books. There are also among them a few non-Jewish writers. However, with time, this area was overtaken, especially in Germany and Italy, by Rabbis or professionally schooled Jewish historians, and the historical monographs acquired a totally different aspect. In Poland the historical monograph [beginning in the 20th century], finds itself in the hands of Jewish historians with appropriate Jewish and general knowledge. The historical monographs were primarily written in the vernacular [French, Italian, German, Dutch, English, Polish, Russian, Hungarian, etc.]. In Eastern Europe, some works in Yiddish and Hebrew were also published.

Let us attempt to give a geographic overview of the main monographs, according to the countries and the communities that were being described.

France: [one of the oldest monographs]: Paris, Narbonne, Nice, Avignon, Bayonne, Metz, Strassbourg.

Spain: Seville.

Switzerland: Geneva.

Holland: Amsterdam.

England: London.

Italy: Rome [two classic works], Florence, Venice, Padua, and other communities.

Germany: Germany was the cradle of modern Jewish historical scholarship, and therefore it is no wonder that historical monographs blossomed here so strongly. There were almost no Jewish communities that lacked an attempt at such monographs. Here we will only concentrate on the most important works: The SHUM communities (Shpiera [Speyer], Warmiza [Worms], and Magentza [Mainz]), Keln, Bonn, Erfurt, Frankfort am Mein, Nurnberg, Fiorda [Firta], Wirtzburg, Regensburg, Augsburg, and Essen.

North Germany: the communities Ah'v [Altuna – Wandsbek, Hamburg], Libek, Danzig, Konigsberg.

Eastern Germany: Berlin [the classic work of man of letters and cultural historian Ludwig Geiger], Halberstadt.

The Provinces of Posen and Pomeren. These previously Polish provinces, which were a part of the German Reich from the end of the 18th century until 1918, were dealt with [treated] by German Jewish historians in a series of studies [some of these researches were published later, already in the period of independent Poland]. The historian and Rabbi, Dr. Lewis Levin, who described [related] the history of these communities, made great gains in this area: Kalish, Lisa [Leshno], Finah [P'riyoi] Inovrotzlav [Hohenzaltza] and Y. Hertzberg, who collaborated with A. Hefner in a lexicon of the communities in the region of Posen, apart from that written about the city of Posen and Bromberg-Biedgoshtch.

Of other communities it is significant to mention the studies about: Katowitz, Krotoshin, Ostroff, Ravitch and Shenlanka, [Tchshtch – Tch-shianka].

Balkan countries: Saloniki [two great monographs]. Yassi, Bucharest, Kishenov. Yitzchak Kron: *The Jews of Kishenov* 1950.

Hungary: Eizenshtadt [the monumental work of B. Wachshtein] Budapest.

Austria: A series of important works were published about Vienna, especially after the Historic Jewish Commission was founded in Vienna.

Czechoslovakia: [Behmen and Mehren]: The investigations [researches] were particularly intensive about how two publications were created: *The Periodical of the History of the Jews in Czechoslovakia* and *The Year Books of the History of the Jews in Czechoslovakia*. Regarding the former work, it is worth mentioning Frankel-Green's two volume work: *History of the Jews in Kremzir,* a community in Mehren.

[Editorial Note: Schedules from the bottom of page 443 to the middle of page 445 (France through Russia) were in English in the original and are included here verbatim without translation. An exception is the last line of the section on Poland, which was inserted in the original in Hebrew script and translated here into English.]

FRANCE: Theophil Malvezin: Histoire des Juifs de Bordeaux. 1875; Ad. Detcheverry:

Histoire des Israelites de Bordeaux. 1850; Leon Kohn; Histoire de la communaute juive de Paris 1886; idem: Les Juifs a Paris (various studies), 1889. 1894, 1892, 1898, etc.; Robert Anchel: Les Juifs a Paris à 18-e siecle. Bull de la Societe d'Histoire de Paris, xx LIX (1932); idem in *Jewish Social Studies*, II (1940) ; J. Régné: Les Juifs à Narbonne 1912; S. Kahn: Notice sur les Israélites de Nimes, 672-1808; Armand Mossé: Histoire des Juifs d'Avignon et du Comtat Venaissin , 1934; Henry Léon: Histoire des Juifs, de Bayonne. 1893; Nathan Netter: Vingt Siècles d'Histoire d'une Communauté Juive (Metz). 1938; Adolf Glaser: Geschichte der Juden in Strassburg. 1894. Alfred Levy: Notice sur les Israelites de Lyon. 1894.

SPAIN: M. Mendez Bejarano: Histoire de la juiverie de Sevilla; E. C. Girbal: Los Judios en Gerona. 1870: Jose Fiter y Ingles: Expulsion de los Judios de Barcelona. 1876.

SWITZERLAND: Achille Nordmann: Histoire des Juifs à Geneve de 1281 a 1780. *Revue des Etudes Juives*. LXXX (1925); idem: Geschichte der Juden in Basel, *Baseler Zeitschrift fuer Geschichte*, vol. XIII; Fritz Wyler: Die Entstehungder Schweizeischen Israelitischen Gemeinden. 1929.

HOLLAND: J. S. da Silva Rosa: Geschiedenis der Portugeesche Joden te Amsterdam, 1593-1925. 1925 Herbert I. Bloom: The Economic Activities of the Jews in Amsterdam in the 17th-18th Centuries. 1937; Henriquez Pimentel M.: De Portugeesche Israeliten in's Gravenhage (Hague), 1876; D S. van Zuiden: Geschiedenis der hoogduitsche Jode in's Gravenhage (Hague) 1914.

ENGLAND: Elkan Nathan Adler: London (Jew. Publication Soc. of America) 1930.

ITALY: Abraham (Adolph) Berliner: Geschichte der Juden in Rom. 2 vols. 1893; Hermann Vogelstein and Paul Rieger: Geschichte der Juden in Rom. 1895-96; H. Vogelstein: Rome (Je. Publ. Society of America); Umberto Cassuto: Gli Ebrei a Firenze. 1918; Cecil Roth: Venice (Jew. Publ. Soc. of A.) 1930; Antonio Ciscato: Gli Ebrei in Padova. 1901.

GERMANY: Schwab: Geschichte der Juden in Mainz. 1855; Max Levy: Geschichte der Wormser Gemeinde; Leopold Rotschild: Die Judengemeinden zu Mainz, Speyer und Worms. 1904; S. Rotschild: Aus Vergangenheit und Gegenwart der Israelit. Gemeinde Worms, 1909; E. Weyden: Geschichte der Juden in Koeln, 1867; C. Brisch: Geschichte der Juden in Koeln am Rhein, 1879-82; Adolf Kober: Cologne (Jew. Publ. Soc. of Amer.) 1940; Schreiber: Die Jeudische Gemeinde Bonn, 1879; Jaroczewski: Geschichte der Juden in Erfurt, 1868; Isidor Kracauer: Geschichte der Juden in Frankfurt a.M. 1150-1824. 2 vols. 1925-27; Hugo Barbeck: Geschichte der Juden in Nuernberg und Fuerth, 1878; Ziemlich: Die israelitische Gemeinde in Neurnberg. 1900; M. A. Szulwas: Die Juden in Wuerzburg Waehrend des Mittelalters, 1934; S. Samuel: Geschichte der Juden in Stadt und Synagogenbezirk Essen, 1913;

Fritz, Leopold Steinthal: Geschichte der Juden in Augsburg. 1911; Raphael Strauss: Regensburg and Augsburg. (Jew. Pub!. Soc. of Am.) 1939; Max Grunewald: Hamburgs deutsche Juden bis 1811. 1904; Jos. Carlebach: Geschichte der Juden in Luebeck, 1899; Jolowicz: Geschichte der Juden in Koenigsberg, 1867; Ludwig Geiger: Geschichte der Juden in Berlin. 2 vols. 1871; B. H. Auerbach: Geschichte der isr. Gemeinde Halberstadt. 1886; J. Perles: Geschichte der Juden in Posen. Breslau 1865; I. Herzberg: Posen I. Herzberg: Geschichte der Juden in Bromberg. 1903; Louis Lewin: Geschichte der Juden in Lissa, 1904; idem: Aus der Vergangen heit der jeud. Gemeinde in Pinne, 1903; dem: Beitraege zur Geschichte der Juden in Kalisch, in *Festschrift A. E. Harkavy* (1909); idem: Geschichte der Juden in Inowroclaw, *Zeitschr. der Historischen Gesellschaft feur die Provinz Posen*, 1900; J. Cohn: Geschichte der Synagogengemeinde Kattowitz, 1900; idem: Geschichte der Jeud. Gemeinde in Rawitsch, 1915; H. Berger: Zur Geschichte der Juden in Krotoschin, *Monatsschr.f.d. Geschichte u. Wissenschaf t des Judentums.* LI (1907); M. L. Bamberger: Geschichte der Juden in Schoenlanke (Trzianka), 1912; A. Freimann: Geschichte der Juden in Ostrow 1896; Jakob Jakobsohn: Geschichte der Juden in Rogasen, 1935.

THE BALKAN COUNTRIES: Joesph Nehama: Histoire des Israelites de Salonique. 4 vols. 1935-36; Isaac Samuel Emmanuel: Histoire des Israelites de Salonique. 1936; A. M. Halévy: Comunitatile Evreilor din Jassi si Bucuresti. 1931.

HUNGARY: Bernard Wachstein: Urkunden und Akten zur Geschichte der Juden in Eisenstadt und den Siebengemeinden Vienna 1926, 2 vols; Sandor Beuchler: A. Zsidok toertenete Budapesten (History of the Jews in B.) 1901; Miksa Pollak. A. Zsidok Toertenete Sopronban (History of the Jews in Sopron), 1896.

AUSTRIA AND CZECHOSLOVAKIA: Gerson Wolf: Geschichte der Juden in Wien, 1876; L. Bato: Die Juden im alten Wien, 1928; Siegmund Mayer: Der Wiener Juden 1700-1900. 1917; Leo Goldhammer: Die Juden Wiens, 1927; Alfred Pribram, ed.: Urkunden und Akten zur Geschichte der Juden in Wien 2 vols. 1917; Ignaz Schwarz and Max Grunewald: Geschichte der Juden in Wien, in Anton Meyer, ed.: *Geschichte der Stadt Wien*, 5 vols. 1914; Max Grunewald: Vienna (J. Publ. Soc. of Amer.) Adolf Frankl-Greun: Geschichte der Juden in Kremsier. 3 vols. 1896-1901.

POLAND: M. Schorr: Zydzi w Przemyslu do konca xvii wieku; I. Schipper: Zydzi w Tarnowie in *Kwartalnik Historyczny*, vol. xix idem: 700 lat gminy zydowskiej w Plocku. 1938ffi M. Balaban: Zydzi lwowscy na przelomie xvi i xvii wiekug. 1906 idem: Zydzi w Krakowie i na Kazimierzu 1304-1868. 2 vols. 1931-37; idem: Die Judenstadt von Lublin, 1919 (also in Yidd. translation, Buenos Aires, 1946); idem: Przewodnik po zabytkach zyd. Krakowa. 1935; D. Wurm: Z dziejow zydostwa brodzkiego do 1772, 1935; Lazar Estrin: Dzieje Zydow w Zamosciu (non publ); Mgr Getter: Dzieje Zydow w Sandomierzu (non publ); Sz. Gottlieb: Dzieje Zydow w Kolomyji (non publ); Emmanuel

Ringelblum : Dzieje Zydow w Warszawie do 1527.1932; Jacob Shatzky: Geshichte fun di Yidn in Varshe. 2 vols. 1947-48; Ph. Friedman: Tsu der geshichhte fun di Yidn in Lentchitz, in *Lodzer Visensh. Shriftn* vol. l.; idem: Dzieje Zydow w Lodzi do 1863.1935; J. Trunk: Plock 1237-1657 (in Yidd.) 1939; idem: A Jewish Community in Poland at the End of the XVIII Century (A Yidishe Khile in Polyn Tzum sof Fun XVIII Jaarhundert, in *Bleter for Geshichte* vol. I. (1934); El. Feldman: Geschichte fun di yidn in Kalish, in *Lodzer Visn. Shriftn* vol., and in *Landkentnish* (1934); Leo Streit: Dzieje Zydow w Stanislawowie (non publ); idem: Dzieje Synagogi Postepowej w Stanislawowie, 1939; idem: Dzieje wielkiej Synagogi miejskiej w Stanislawowie, 1936; idem: Ormianie a Zydzi w Stanislawowie 1936; Jakob Schall: Dawna Zolkiew i jej Zydzi. 1939; idem: Przewodnik po zabytkach zyd. Lwowa, 1936. The Polish Jewish Histiography has been extensively treated by this writer in his articles in Jew. Social Studies, vol. xi, no. 4 (1949) and in Miesecznik Zydowski vol. 5 (1935). Y. Haylperin, The History of the Jews in Tiktin, The Budapest Observer,1930.

THE BALTIC COUNTRIES: I. Joffe: Istoria Evreiev w Gor. Riga, in *Voskhod* 1885, A Buchholtz: Geschichte der Juden in Riga, 1899; S. Bershadsky: Istoria Evreiev v Vilne, in *Voskhod*, 1883, 1886, 1887, Israel Cohen: Vilno (Jew. Publ. Soc. of Amer.) 1943.

RUSSIA: M. Kulisher: Evrei v Kieve. in *Evreyskaya Starina* vi (1913).

Poland: The historical monograph achieved a very high level in Poland. The first great Jewish historians stemmed from Galitzia [Galicia], which was part of Austria until 1918, and part of Poland from 1918-1939. Professor Moshe Shur, Professor Meier Balaban, and Dr. Yitzchak Shipper laid the foundation of Jewish Historical Science in Galitzia, and also wrote monographs of communities; M. Shur about Pszemishel; Y. Shipper about Tarna, Plotzk and Drohovitch. [This last monograph has still not been published, it got lost at the time of the Nazi Holocaust.] M. Balaban, the classic monumental work about Lemberg and Krakov and the smaller monograph about Lublin.

Of the younger generation of historians, the following wrote monographs about communities:

Dr. Refael Mahler, Dr. Imamuel Ringelblum, [Warsaw, Kremenetz], Dr. P. Friedman [Lodz Lentshietz], Dr. Yaakov Shatzki [Warsaw], Dr. Ya'akov Shal [Zsholkeveh, Lemberg]. Of the latest [youngest] generation of historians it is worth mentioning, in particular, the group of students who came out of the Balaban Seminary for Jewish History in the University of Warsaw. Many from this group began to research the History of Particular Jewish communities [David Vaurm], Kalish [Elazar Feldman], Lublin [Bela Mandelsberg], Kutna and Plotzk [Y. Troonk],

Zamoshtch [Lazar Estrin], Tzuzmir [Getter], Kalamai [Sh: Gottlieb], etc. The last three monographs did not appear in print.

A basic monograph about Stanislav [in Polish], which was ready to be printed in the summer of 1939, also did not see the light. The compiler, Sholem Shtreit, expired in Nazi hands in his hometown. He did publish a few smaller studies about Stanislav in the earlier years.

The Baltic States: A few important monographs were published about Vilna itself. Beginning with Russian [not Jewish] historian Bershadsky, and the folk tales of Chaikel Lunsky [librarian of Strashun library and very knowledgeable about old and new Jewish literature]. Until the monographs of Dr. Yisroel Klausner: *The History of the Hebrew Community in Vilna 1938* and *Vilna in the Era of the Gaon* [The Gaon of Vilna], 1942, and Yisrael Cohen: Vilna [English], 1943. It is also worth mentioning two works about Riga [in German and in Russian].

Russia: We possess a notably small amount of historical monographs about the many communities in Russia and Ukraine, White Russia, Besserabia, etc. Since Dr. Mark Vishnitzer, contributed short lexicographic sections in the Jewish Encyclopedia in Russian [Yevrayskaya Entziklopedia] even before 1914, about these few Jewish communities [with Bibliography]. There was very little created in this area. It is worth mentioning a few smaller but methodical important works about Haradishtch [by Ya'akov Leshtchinsky in 1903]. Kiev [by M Kulisher in Yevrayskaya Starina], and about Odessa [B. Shuchtman, in *Cities and Mothers of Israel, Vol. 2*].

4. The Regional Area and the Post Holocaust Romantic-notsalgic Direction

The regional area is actually much older than the word 'regionalism' per se. Certain historians, already wrote in their style of writing, intuitively, in the spirit of regionalism, even before the coming into being of regionalism. They sought and found new ways, but they did not think about giving their new approach a new name, or a new theoretical foundation.

As the father of Regionalist History writing of the Jews, we can actually consider the Kovner-Jerusalemite, wise scholar, Avraham Moshe Luntz, who published a significant amount of work about Eretz Yisrael, and also among others, the 13 volumes of the Year Book *Yerushalayin,* 1882 – 1919. Many years later, with great regionalistic appeal, Nochum Sokolov published monographs of the Jewish communities [in *Ha Olam,* issues 9 and 10]. The writer of these lines, began larger studies of Regionalism in geographic lore:

Warsaw No 1-3, in *Miesientshnik Zshidovski,* 1935, Vol. 5, Nos. 3-4, and in *Future,* New York, December 1951.

Recording of Regional History by Jews developed remarkably after the year 1918, especially in Poland. Around the time of the First World War, Professor Meier Balaban developed his monographs about the Jews in Lemberg and Krakov. They served as an example for many regionalist researchers and writers.

Many regional monographs were written by Jews in the period between both World Wars. They described scores of Jewish populations, including large communities like, Krakov, Lodz, Vilna, Vienna, Frankfort am Mein, and smaller communities such as Szalkov, Brad, Kutna, Plotzk P'rushani, Eizenshtat, etc.

Then came the Second World War. The Nazi killing machine destroyed Jewish towns and shtetlach. After the war, the awful concept of the terrible destruction in all its horrible scope became clear. The tender feelings for the 'Alter Heim'–The Old Home--were renewed. It was no longer the lively shtetl, full of dear and beloved people, friends of one's youth and family. It now became a pain-filled memory of a world that had disappeared. Romantic feelings began to develop for 'Der Alter Heim' – The Old Home. People forgot that they left the 'Old Home' not because of prosperity, but because of troubles, deprivation, political oppression, and economic need. They saw the 'Old Home' with the dreamy eyes of someone in love. They remember the tender emotions of their childhood years and immerse themselves in the warmth of the past 'heimishe' [homely] Yiddish atmosphere. Romantic veils are cast over the past. The regionalistic muse plays out in high tones, not only in our historic literature, but also in our poetry and prose.

The 'Alter Haim' is sung about in poetic verses, in memoirs, in novellas and novels, in reportage and essays. The writer carries us with *Burning Footsteps* [Z. Segalowitch] in the *Courtyards of Warsaw [A. Teitelboim] and on T'lomatzkah – [main road in Warsaw] 13* [Z. Segalowitch; B. Y. Rozen] or in his *Destroyed Home* [Y. Groin].

Footnotes/References

It may be Dezikov (1) or Reishe (2) or Sokolov (3) or Teplik (4) or *In a House in Gzshibov* (5) or *A Little Street in Warsaw* (6). It carries us between *Ash and Fire* (7).

Between Terror and Hope (8). It shows *The Shabbos – Yom Tovdike Jews* [P. Bizberg]; *Between the Shine of Extinguished Stars* [Ch. Gradeh]; Sing about *Home and Homelessness* [Rochel Korn]; He sighs: *There Once Was a Life* [N. Meizel]; or he screams with pain *Not Here – Disappeared?]* [Z. Segalowitch]; He draws figures with an enamoured pen *In the Shadows of Generations* (9) or he is elevated/raised with awe to *Mount of Destruction* [Zerubavel].

The recording of regional history in our generation is, therefore, no more an isolated, clearly academic science; it is today inextricably bound with the feelings of the Jewish masses.

The conclusion: most of the general structure and content of regional historical literature is published by Landsmanschafts; and written, in the main, not by professionals or writers, but by simple 'Citizen Joes.' For the last 10-12 years, since the beginning of the Nazi Holocaust, quite a number of Yizkor Books have been published, as well as Almanacs, Notebooks and monographs. It is impossible to enumerate them all here.

We will therefore satisfy ourselves with giving a general overview, as we have done in the previous chapters.

5. The Regionalistic Works in Yizkor Literature

In their method of working and in their theme, most of the greater works about towns or regions written in the last 30 years were regionalistic. They were regionalistic, whether written knowingly or unknowingly. More often it was the latter [unknowingly regionalistic], because even when the authors had never heard of regionalism and its theory, they created in the spirit of our time, taking as an example, non-Jewish [and today even, famous Jewish] works, which were created on regionalistic foundations.

However, our regionalism is exceptional and not like all other nations. Since the great catastrophe of European Jewry, there has been a second much stronger emotional element added, to the scientific interest that we have explained above. This has brought more zest and internal warmth to our regional literature. Our record of regional history since about 1940 has also concurrently become a Yizkor Literature [e.g. the superb anthology, *A Thousand Years of Pinsk,* 1941; *The Lodzsher Book* [Book of Lodz], 1943, etc.

Characteristic of the recording of regional history is the inclination towards comprehensiveness and encyclopaedic completeness. Encyclopaedias were published about communities, or as a series of monographs, almanacs, and anthologies.

In earlier times, a monograph was the work of an individual [or rarely the work of two authors who together wrote one book]. Such are these Almanacs, Yizkor Books, Notebooks and other books of this type of anthology, where different authors created all aspects of Jewish Life. Characteristic of this creativity in approach and theme [subject] are, for example, such works as the above mentioned Pinsker Book, The Book *Litah* [Lithuania] [edit. M. Sudarsky], *The Jews of Tchenstochov* [Ed. Mahler], *Pinskas M'laveh* [Ed. Shatzky], numerous *Vilna Almanacs* [for exact details; see further], The Anthology about Pruszhaneh, Haravetz, Grieveh, Belchatov, etc. But let us revert to a systematic overview of the most important works, according to types.

Encyclopaedias and Series of Community Monographs

[Editorial Note: The following paragraph was in English in the original.]

A.M. Luncz, Jerusalem (Hebrew and German), 1882-1913; Henri Gross, Gallia Iudaica, 1897; Aron Friemann, Germania Iudaica, vol 1, 1917, vol 2, 1934; A. Heppner and J. Herzberg, Aus der Vergangenheit und Gengenwart der Juden und Juedischen Gemeinden in der Provinz Posen, 1904-1929; Hugo Gold, ed., Die Juden und Judengemeinden Maehrens in Vergangenheit und Gegenwart. Cf. also Gabrieli: Italia Iudaica, 1924; Fidel, La Espana Hebrea, 1891; Magyar Zsidok Lexikon 1929; Jacob Zineman, ed., Almanach gmin Zydowskich w Polsce.

Jewish Publication Society of America, Communities Series, Philadelphia.

Actually, the first community encyclopedias began appearing more than 50 years ago. The first, as far as I know, was *The Encyclopedia of French Communities,* by Henri Gross. Then came the unfinished *Encyclopedia of German Communities,* by Aharon Freiman, the *Encyclopedia of the Communities in the Province of Posen* [130 communities], by A. Heppner and Y. Hertzberg, and *Gold's Encyclopedia of the Jews of Mehren.*

A certain number have an encyclopedic character in their size. For the Jewish communities in Lithuania: The Book *Litah* [Ed. M. Sudarsky]. For Galitzia: *The Note Book of Galitzia* [Ed. N. Tzuker, 1945. For the Ukraine: *Towns and Shtetlach in the Ukraine,* by M. Asherowetch, 1948 [two volumes with monographs of more than 20 communities]. For Poland: *The Almanac of the Jewish Communities in Poland,* written in Poilish [Ed. Ya'akov Tzineman, not completed, deals with 34 communities].

A whole series of short community monographs have been printed since 1944 in the Hebrew Art Periodical *Gazit* about a few score of Polish and Ukrainian towns, as well as a few Lithuanian and Volinian towns. In the anthology *Cities and Mothers of Israel,* published by the Institute of Ha Rov Kook, under the editorship of Rabbi Y. L. Fishman [Mimon], in the five published volumes to date [1946-1952], there were printed an estimated 20 community monographs of various Western and Eastern European towns.

Another series of community monographs were published [in English] by the Yiddish Publishing Company in America regarding Koln (Cologne), Rome, Vilna, Vienna, Venice, Regensburg and Augsburg. A great achievement in this area includes the series of books from the Publishing House 'Polish Jewry' in Buenos Aires. Among the 80 books published by this publishing house in the last six years are found a series of historical descriptions of Jewish communities, mainly from the period of the Nazi Holocaust. A new, great undertaking of this genus is the *Encyclopedia of the Diaspora, Encyclopedia of the Dispersion* which is being prepared for publication under the editorship of Yitzchak Grinboim in approximately 25 volumes of exhaustive [intensive] compilation about the most significant Jewish communities in Europe. The first two volumes, about Warsaw and Lemberg, have already been printed. The editorial staff intend to publish their publications in Hebrew, Yiddish, and English. Meanwhile, the first two volumes are appearing in Hebrew.

A special place for anthologies and published material for regional history is occupied by the regional or landschafte [parochial] periodicals, for example: *The Polish Jew, The Besserabian Jew, The Ukrainian Jew, The Galitzianer, The Lithuanian Jew, Bialystok Life, Szhalechov Bulletin* [all in New York], *Vohlin Collection, News of the Organization of Immigrants from S'lonin, Immigrants from Dertzin, Immigrants from Grodno, News Sheet from the Organization of Central Europe* [all in Israel] and others. All the above mentioned landsmanschaft publications have, apart from historical [narrative] and memoir material, a lot of related chronicles, and have mainly a more popular than scientific character. The periodical *Landkentenish* had a more scientific regional character and was published in Warsaw in the years 1930-1934.

Outstanding scientific regional publications were *The Lodz Scientific Writings,* Vol. 1, Lodz, 1938 [Ed. Dr. P. Friedman]. A first scientific regional periodical was published in *Chapters from Bessarabia* Notebook 1 [Tel Aviv 1952], Eds. L Kupershtain and Yitzchak Kurn. The number of almanacs, notebooks, yizkor books and anthologies is very large.

The majority were published after the Holocaust of European Jewry; but there are also a significant number of earlier works. We will give an overview [summary] of the most important publications.

Vilna has the greatest number of significant publications: *The Vilna Collection* [anthology] [Ed. Dr. Tzemach Shabad, Vols. 1-2, Vilna, 1916-1918]; *Notebook of the History of Vilna,* [by Zalman Reizen, Vilna, 1922; *On the Ruins of Wars and Upheavels* [Ed. Moshe Shalit, Vilna, 1932]; and *Vilner Almanac* [Ed. A. Grodzenski, Vol. 1, Vilna ,1939]. It is also worthwhile here to mention the comprehensive *Jewish Vilner Correspondent: A Millennium/Thousand Years of Vilna,* by Zalman Shik, Vilna, 1939.

Pruszhana: there is the outstanding *Notebook of the Town of Pruszhana* 1930. Pinsk has the outstanding, monumental book, *A Thousand Years of Pinsk,* New York, 1941 [Ed. Dr. B. Hoffman (Tzivyon)]. And regarding Lodz, there is: *The Lodz Almanac,* New York, 1934 [Ed. Gustav (Getzel) Eizner], as well as *The Lodz Yizkor Book,* New York, 1943 [Ed. Zalman Zilbertzweig and others]. Berlchatov: *Belchatov Yizkor Book,* Buenos Aires 1951 [Ed. Mark Turkov]. Plotzk: *Plotzk, Pages of History,* Buenos Aires, 1945 [Ed. Y. Horn]. Tshenstochov: *Tshenstochover Jews,* New York, 1947 [Ed. Dr. R. Mahler and others]. M'laveh: *M'laveh Notebook,* New York, 1950 [Ed. Dr. Y. Shatzky]. Graieveh: *Graiever Yizkor Book,* New York, 1950 [Ed. Dr. G. Garin and others]. Stshegoveh; *Stshegover Yizkor Book,* New York, 1951. V'lotzlavek, Krushnewitz, Kutna: *Jubilee Book of Brentch* [611 Worker Squad], New York, 1951. Zaromb: [Zarombi-Kosh't'sheleneh]: *Zaromb,* New York, 1947 [Ed. Y. Dorfman]. Krasnitov: Krasnitov: Memoir [Yizkor] *in Memory of the Martyrs of Krasnitov,* Munich, 1948 [Ed. Aryeh Shtuntzeiger]. Radom: *Jewish Radom in Ruins,* Stuttgart, 1948 [Ed. Y. Rottenberg and others]. *The Friend from Radom,* Paris, 1950 – Editorial Board. Ostrovtzeh (Opatov, Aszharov and other surrounding towns): *Ostrovtzeh Yizkor Book,* Buenos Aires, 1949. Levertov: *The Destruction of Levertov,* Paris, 1947 [Ed. B. T'shubinsky]. Yavarov: *The Jewish Town of Yavarov* [Yiddish and English], New York, 950 [by Sh Druk]. Zablotov: *City of the Dead--Zablotov, Full and Destroyed,* Tel Aviv, 1948 [Ed. M. Henish and Getzel Kressel]. Volkovisk: *The Volkovisker Yizkor Book,* 2 Vols, New York, 1949 [in Yiddish and English] [Ed. Dr. Moshe Einhorn]. Bialystok: *Bialystok,* New York, 1951 [Ed. David Sohn] A monumental pictorial album. B'riansk: *B'rainsk: Memorial Book,* New York, 1948 [compiled by A. Truss and Sh. Cohen]. Horodetz: *Horodetz: A Story of a Shtetl,* New York, 1949 [Ed. E Ben Ezra]. Lachovitch: *Lachowitz Memorial Book,* Tel Aviv [1949] [Ed. Yisroel Rubin and others]. Aishishok: *Ishishok: Its History and its Destruction,* Jerusalem, 1950 [Ed. Dr. Shaul Barkoli and Peretz Alafi].

With the publication of this Rakishker Yizkor Book, one can also include: Rakishok: *The Yizkor Book of Rakishok and Environs,* Editor: Meilech Bakalczuk-Felin, published by the Rakishker Landsmanschaft in Johannesburg, South Africa.

Being prepared for printing are, among others, the following anthologies [collective works]: Chelm [in South Africa], Zamastch [in Israel], Kalish [in Paris], and Lomzshe [in Israel].

As far as we can see, the whole regionalistic literature is almost totally in Yiddish and Hebrew. Some books have English summaries [extracts]. Because of constraints of space, we have not given here any comment on these specific books. We have done this in another opus. [The Landsmanschaft – Literature in the United States for the Last Ten Years, in the Year Book of *Tashy?v* – 5712 [1951-1952] Tenth Volume, New York, 1951 [pages 81-96].

We have also not emphasized the literature that occupied itself specifically with the Nazi Destruction of the Jewish Communities in Europe because we have already published a whole series of works. [In Yiddish, in *Jewish Fighters,* Pesach Edition, 1950: Year Book 6710 and 5711 [1950-1951] 8th and 9th volumes; *Pages for Jewish Education 1949-1950,* New York Culture and

Education – April and May 1950, New York; *Bialistokker Voice*, September 1950 and September 1951; *Lita,* Volume 1. In English: *Jewish Social Studies*, New York, October 1949, January 1950, and October 1951. In Hebrew: *Dapim* [Pages], Book 1, 1950.

We have occupied ourselves in our work with the recording of the history of European Jewish Communities. The historiographical literature about Jewish settlements in Eretz Yisrael has a totally different character, as it reverts very often to the biblical and prehistoric period. It brings to bear, in part, an archaeological character and therefore must be dealt with separately. Also, these community monographs of new settlements that came into being or grew through the immigration of the last two or three generations [North and South America, South Africa, etc.] have a completely different set of problems than the old European settlements, and therefore merit another method of research [mainly sociological] and being dealt with separately.

6. A Short Summary

As we can see, the historical literature about the Jewish Communities and settlements is a rich one, but not homogeneous. In the 19th century it was, in Western and Central Europe, a rabbinic or professional literature, and in foreign languages. In Eastern Europe it was an amateur-bookish one [in Hebrew]. From the beginning of the 20th century, the monographic literature in Eastern Europe was dominated by historical professionals and went over mainly to the vernacular. First, with the growth of regionalist tendencies, monographic literature became emancipated from foreign influences and foreign languages. It now became concurrently scientific and the voice of the people. It is now exclusively Yiddish and Hebrew and finds a broad readership/circle, not only amongst the educated, but in the broad masses. The centre of gravity moves almost totally from Western and Central European communities to Eastern Europe. But in Eastern Europe as well, this literature is not evenly divided between certain geographic areas.

The Polish communities were the best adapted, in second place comes Lithuania, and far behind are the Ukrainian, Russian, White Russian, Vohlinian, and Bessarabian towns. There must still be many names to fill this conspicuous void [obvious emptiness].

[Page 452]

The *Landsmanschaft* of Rakishok

(1912-1952)

M. Rotholz-Kur

Translated by Gloria Berkenstat Freund

This work was written on the basis of record books, excerpts from minutes, information, materials and notices which were given to me by Yerakhmiel Arons – Arsh, the landsleit [people from the same town] worker; Yitzhak Ginzburg, Ahron Noach – Noachmanovitch and Shlomo Rubin. Thanks to the material provided, I was able to assemble this documented treatise about the Rakishoker Landsmanschaft [society of people from the same town].

A. Activities of the Society

The *Rakishoker Landsmanschaft* has been in existence for over 40 years and those from the neighboring *shtetlekh*, Abel [Obelial], Kamay [Kamajai], Svidoshc, Ponedel, Tibat, Skopishak, Poneminok, Sevenishak, Anushishok, Novo-Aleksandrovski=Ezsherni and others, are also included as *landsleit*.

Many significant and great changes took place in Jewish life over the course of time. A great deal of water flowed over the Jews in many lands; not least the Jewish people suffered from anti-Semitic persecutions and pogroms and slaughters, the First World War and a Second, when the savage destruction of the Jewish people under the rule of the Nazis took place and, finally, the rise of the State of Israel.

Without a doubt, all of the years and times lay their seal on organized Jewish society in general and on the Rakishok Society, which at the critical moment had to master and absorb all of the shadows and light in Jewish life, seeing the strengthening of the beliefs of our members and awakening in them the hope of better times that stimulated them to communal activities and to national actions.

The barely 40 years of the Rakishok *landsmanschaft* is an important communal event not only in its own area, but also for the entire local Jewish organized society and it is therefore necessary to very abundantly reflect its activities in the columns of the Yizkor Book.

The Founding of the Society

The first emigrants from the Jewish *shtetlekh* in Lithuania who began to wander to distant South Africa did so in the role of pioneers and among them were educated circles of *landsleit* who were mutually connected and were among themselves like family members and *brothers* who would come together to share the news of those scattered in various population areas of South Africa. Such frequent gatherings were the beginning of a *landsmanshaft*.

[Page 453]

The devotion of one toward the other was expressed in deeds; a new emigrant was met at the ship, he was offered hospitality, helped to look for work and given the initial financial aid, and care was also given to a sick *landsleit*, providing him with a doctor and medications, too.

The excerpt from N.D. Hofman's *Book of Memories*, published in *Jews of South Africa* by Leibl Feldman (a Rakishok *landsman*), can serve as a source of information:

"When a *griner* [newly arrived] Jew would arrive in Cape Town, he would look for distant relatives with the addresses he had brought with him from home. He would be received with pity, taken to a bath to destroy his third plague [lice], he would be led to a barber, given other clean clothing and held at home for weeks at a time until he was rested from the long trip and became a little assimilated. Then the *landsleit* would take him to a wholesale merchant where they had credit and provide him with several pounds of goods. They would help him pack his bag, writing the price on each piece of goods, what it cost, as well as the price for which he should sell it. Placing the heavy pack on his back and tightly binding it with two wide leather straps, they would wish him success and would send him into the countryside around Cape Town among the Boers."

Landsleit circles were organized entirely spontaneously after which a *landsmanschaft* was founded. *Landsleit* would come together monthly on *Shabbosim* [Sabbaths], *yomim-tovim* [religious holidays] and on Sundays in a hall or at the home of a *landsman* – a pioneer – who had immigrated with his family or was able to bring them here.

In general single people, individuals, without wives and children, came with the first storm of immigration to South Africa and it was a long time before they decided to urge their families [to come] and to create a new home in South Africa. Even young men, who left brides beyond the sea, also did not rush to ask them because the ideas were deeply sunk into them that they still would save a little money and they would return home.

There was too strong a nostalgia with each Lithuanian Jew and Jewish immigrant for the way of life in his *shtetl* or city. He also could not live a religious life as at home. During the early years there were only a few *khederim* [religious primary schools] for children, only a few synagogues, clergymen, *beli tefilus* [men who read the prayers on holidays], cantors, *shoykhetim* [ritual slaughterers] and preachers.

The climatic and economic conditions also were entirely different from those in Eastern Europe.

It was difficult to adjust with respect to the work. There was no sellers market for much of the local work and means of earning a living. In addition, the industry in South Africa was still undeveloped at that time.

The immigrants, not mastering the language, could not take positions of employment in various trade firms. They became *trayers* [peddlers], carrying goods on their backs, mainly to the Boer villages and farmers, or they received work places in *kaferites* [restaurants for the Africans].

[Page 454]

There were many cases when immigrants returned home – to their wife and children, to the relatives and those closest to them. There were also those who again returned to South Africa when they lost their saved money in trade. These facts were not an influence in such measure that Jewish immigrants would consider South Africa as their permanent home.

The *landsleit* joined more strongly and more firmly together in order to quiet their longing for family and home.

L. Feldman in his above-mentioned book talks about the reciprocal connection and strong friendship among the *landsleit*. I quote here that passage from his book:

"The thousand miles that separated him (the immigrant) from his home increased his longing and loneliness. After work, on holidays and days of rest, he felt his loneliness in fear and strongly longed for community, at least to pass time. The wish for community to quiet his loneliness and longing for his family and familiar environment drove him to the relationship with Lithuanian Jews from his town or city. As others were in a similar situation as he was, they strongly befriended each other. They would come together at the home of a landsleit and they would talk about the old home, about the difficulties of the new life, about income; they would ask for advice and they were helpful to each other.

"The coming together of the landsleit or of just Yiddish speaking Jews took on a more communal character each time. They would meet more and more often. In addition to discussing their old home and daily economic questions, they would also speak about and discuss news and worldly matters.

472   Rokiskis Yizkor Book

"This led to founding of landsmanschaftn and khevras [groups] that had as their purpose to give material support, (gmiles khesed kases [interest free loan fund], medical aid) to the landsleit and help the shtetlekh of the landsmanschaftn in question."

The extract provided above can serve as an argument for what was necessary for the rise of landsmanschaftn, including the Rakishoker Landsmanschaft.

* * *

The genesis and stages of progress of the Rakishok *landmanschaft* are not comprehensive, but are mirrored in the protocol books of the Society that were kept. It is regrettable that they are dryly written, in a banal style and in a Yiddish language that has a great deal of English and German words. It is indeed a fact that the first Jewish immigrants from Lithuania, not being in the country for long, used such a strange mixed language.

Yet, looking at all its drawbacks, the protocol books are for us a worthwhile source from which we can learn and be informed about the founding and activities of the Rakishok *Landsmanschaft* in various periods of time. First of all, we are informed that the official founding of the Society took place on the 14th of January 1912, that is, over 40 years ago. From that historic day I cite the full text of the first protocol without any changes:

[Page 455]

"A general meeting was held on Sunday, the 14th of January 1912 in South Africa, Palmesten [Palmerston] Hotel, Commissioner Street to found a Rakishoker Sick Benefit Society. The following officers were elected, S. Shwartsberg as chairman, Zalman Sher, vice chairman, Gedelia Zakstein as treasurer. Hilel Eidelman and S. N. Yafa, trustee committee, Sh. L. Yafe, Josef Feldman, S. H. Abelovitz, W. Kahn, D. Shaibla Yisrael, N. Kahn, Z. Beinart and S. Shneider as secretary. Meeting closed.

It is signed by Shimon Shwartsberg"

After this "general meeting" two committee sessions took place:

"Sunday the 21st of January 1912 and Sunday the 28th of January 1912.

At the session of the 28th of January 1912, it was decided:

"Letters shall be printed and a general meeting shall be called for the 4th of February.

"At the general meeting of the 4th of February, 1912 the particular rules and regulations of the constitution for the landsmanschaft were discussed and a decision was made that the society would arrange for a doctor who would provide medical help for the member, and his family would have the benefit of a

doctor for half price and also medicine for half price. It was then decided: register books shall be printed and each committee shall have a register book and collect contributions."

The second general meeting, which took place on Sunday the 10th of March, at 3 o'clock in the afternoon, 1912, dealt with and approved the points of the proposed constitution for the *landsmanschaft*. And a banking account was opened.

I publish the adopted constitution as an historical document.

Constitution
Rules and Regulations
of the
Rakishoker Sick Benefit Society
Johannesburg
* * *

The name of the Society will be: "Rakishoker Sick Benefit Society," so long as there are 10 members in the society.

The purpose of the Society will be: without cost to give those members who need to have a doctor and medicine; all remaining claims and services of the doctor should be taken to the committee. to give the wife and children of a member who need to have a doctor and medicine for the society's price at their own expense.

[Page 456]

Candidates can only become members of the Society when they are not less than 18 and not more than 45 years old.

Each candidate must be brought before the committee and must be supported by two full members and shall be elected by a majority of the general body.

The candidate who wishes to become a member of the Society must be a respectable man. Whoever is connected to immorality, both directly and indirectly, cannot join the Society. If the committee learns that a member has or has had connections with immorality, it has the right to return the money he has paid in and to exclude him as a member of the Society.

In case a vote is brought to the committee of the Society when a member is accused of bad behavior or the behavior of a member is harmful, when the accusations are found to be correct, the committee has the right:

To take away from the member all rights, benefits, such as the committee will find suitable.

To call on the member in writing to resign and, if he does not resign, then the committee can remove him from membership. The committee should give the member all rights to defend himself and to appeal in person or in writing to the general meeting and if he is found guilty by the general meeting, then he will be bound by the punishment and he cannot make a claim against the society.

Everything that is considered by the committee must be in private and those who reveal anything publicly to a stranger shall be penalized the first time with 2 shillings/56, the second time with 5 shillings and the third time he will be removed from the committee.

A candidate who has not married according the Laws of Moses cannot become a member of the Society.

The contribution will be 2/6 per month.

The secretary shall send a registered letter to a member who does not pay his contributions two months in a row and ask him to pay his contributions. If he does not pay for six months, he loses all of his benefits. When a member is not able to pay his contributions, he shall inform the committee of this and they will give him time to pay, but they can also declare him without benefits.

When a member travels, he must notify the secretary of this. He is permitted to discontinue his obligations for six months and he is without benefits during this time. In case of illness, the national member may present a certificate from a doctor and he will have the right to receive the same benefits according to the rules of the Society for a local member.

Each person who becomes a member of the Society shall pay7entry money and he shall be considered entitled to benefits after six months, if he has paid all of his obligations.

[Page 457]

A member can leave the Society for 12 months. Over 12 months, he can join the Society according to the rules for candidates for membership.

A member of the Society who gets married should receive a present from the Society and it should cost not less than 30 shillings.

The committee of the Society shall consist of 15 members: chairman, vice chairman, treasurer, secretary, assistant secretary, two trustees, two auditors, a door-keeper and two committee members. The officers should be elected at a general meeting.

Duties of the chairman: The chairman shall administer all meetings; if he finds it impossible to attend a meeting because of certain circumstances, he must then notify the secretary in writing a half hour before the meeting or he will be fined one shilling. He shall control everything that belongs to the Society and sign the minutes of every general meeting. When he finds it necessary, he can call a special meeting. At the time of the meeting he must maintain order among the brothers of the Society. If a brother is not obedient, he has the right to punish him. If the brother is not obedient after being called to order three times, the chairman then has the right to take away his right to vote at this meeting. If the brother does not obey the penalty, then he has the right to ask him to leave the hall for the meeting. If the brother is not obedient the chairman can take him to arbitration. The chairman shall have a casting vote.

Duties of the vice chairman: The vice chairman has the same duties and rights as the chairman, when the chairman is absent.

Duties of the treasurer: The treasurer must attend all meetings and shall receive all monies from the secretary of the Society and give him a receipt for them. He shall deposit all monies, checks and other documents. He deposits everything he receives in the bank in the name of the Society.

Duties of the secretary: The secretary shall have correct reports of all meetings and handle all of the correspondence and the books of the Society in good order. He should inform each member by letter about each meeting. He must attend all meetings and insure that all of the contributions are paid. All money that he receives for the Society must be given to the treasurer and he has the right to keep up to one pound for small payments.

Duties of the assistant secretary: The assistant secretary has the same duties as the secretary. He must perform all of the tasks that the secretary gives to him for the Society. However, he cannot sign any documents that belong to the Society.

Duties of the trustees: The trustees shall attend each meeting and when the committee decides to issue a check, it is the duty of the trustee to sign the check.

[Page 458]

Auditors' duties: The auditors shall review the books every six months before the election and sign the balance sheet if it is correct. They have the right to demand the books at that time and verify them. In case an auditor does not fulfill his duty when he is asked, the committee has the right to arrange an election in his place.

Duties of the committee: Each committeeman must attend the meeting promptly and carry out all of the business that is brought to the committee. A quorum of the committee must be seven committee members in addition to the chairman. If a committeeman fails to attend three committee meetings in a row without an important reason, the chairman has the right to fine him up to 2 shillings and then the secretary shall write a letter to him and if he fails to attend a fourth meeting the committee may declare his seat vacant and designate a replacement unless he sends in an apology. The committee has no right to make new or other rules; a special general meeting must be called for this purpose. The committee shall compile a report for the general meeting about the work that it undertook. Committee meetings shall be held every month.

Duties of the doctor: The doctor's duty is to examine a member when he asks him and in such cases he must send a certificate to the secretary and set down if his illness is infectious. He must attend all sick members at least once a day when they are seriously ill. When the sick person can, he must go to the doctor. When the doctor thinks that an extra doctor's help is needed and provides a certificate, the society will permit the taking of another doctor.

[This should be 25] – Each member must attend a quarterly meeting; if not, he shall pay a fine of a shilling unless he sends an apology. When one brother is speaking a second one may not interrupt. He must ask permission from the chairman. And when the brother has finished speaking, he can then speak. If he does not obey the rules, he can be fined. When a member speaks unpleasant words or insulting words, or leaves without the permission of the chairman, he shall be fined a shilling. When a member moves to a new residence he must give notice to the secretary with his new address not later than two weeks or he will pay a one shilling fine.

A quorum at the general meeting shall be 25 members in addition to the chairman. No member can be elected to office unless he has belonged to the Society for six months.

[Page 459]

The rules acquaint us with specific characteristics of that time and the active program of the *landsmanshaft*, as we read in these several points:

Point 1 says: "The name of the Society shall be a) 'Rakishoker Sick Benefit Society,' as long as there are 10 members in the Society." This point teaches us how strong the patriotism and connection to Rakishok was among the Rakishok *landsleit*, who wanted to make sure that the name "Rakishok Sick Benefit Society" would not be changed, "as long as there shall be 10 members of the Society."

Point 2 formalizes the purpose of the society as follows:

"The purpose of the Society shall be to give such members who shall need one a doctor and medicine for free. All remaining aid and services from a doctor shall be taken up by the committee.

To give the wife and children of a member who shall have need of a doctor and medicine the Society's price for their expenses."

Point 3 limits the age of the members of the *landsmanschaft* as follows:

"Candidates can only become members of the Society if they are not less than 17 and no more than 45 years old."

That a candidate could not be older than 45 was connected to financial calculations. In order not to carry the burden of medical help for members older than 45, because for the most part, older people become sick more often.

Points 5 and 6 are characteristic and instructive.

Point 5 relates to a candidate who acts immorally.

"The candidate who wishes to become a member of the Society must be a well-behaved man. Whoever has a connection to immorality, directly or indirectly, cannot be admitted to the Society. When the committee learns that a member is involved with immorality, the committee has the right to return the money he has paid in and to expel him as a member of the Society."

Point 6 has a close connection to point 5:

"If it is brought before the committee that a member is accused of bad behavior, or the behavior of a member is harmful to the will of the Society, the committee then has the right when the accusation is proved correct:
[Page 460]
"To take away all rights, benefits from a member that the committee shall find suitable."

"To call on the member in writing to resign. If he does not, then the committee can remove him from membership. The committee shall give the member all rights to defend himself and appeal in person or in writing to the general meeting and if he is found guilty at the general meeting, he will be bound to the punishment and has no right to complain to the Society.

Both rules were meant: to separate ourselves from such degenerate elements and not shame the name of the *landsmanschaft*, which must be a solid member of the Jewish societies and organizations in South Africa. The word "immorality" can be interpreted with a varied meaning, beginning with criminal offenses – such as robbery, swindling, as well as in the erotic area: houses of prostitution, trade in women, etc.

Point 8 has the object of protecting the purity of the Jewish race:

"A candidate who is not married according to the Laws of Moses may not be a member of the Society."

Finally I want to stress that Point 14 was intended to strengthen the brotherly approach among the *landsleit*:

"A member of the Society who is going to be married shall receive a present from the Society and it shall cost no less than 30 shillings."

The above mentioned, as well as many more points in the constitution, were consistent with that time when the Jewish community in South Africa was still young, taking its first steps.

Medical Help

The principle task of the *landsmanschaft* then was to give medical help to sick *landsleit*. The activities in the medical area figure prominently in the minute books.

The newly arrived immigrants went through more than a few illnesses – with their arrival in new climatic conditions and also because they lived in small rooms and were scattered over roads and detours, because they carried heavy packs of goods to the Boer customers who lived in faraway places among mountains and valleys and in the wilderness.

Taking into consideration that the immigrants were without families for the first time, they ate in cheap restaurants where the food was not fresh or they quickly cooked a little food and fed themselves with meals that were not nutritious.

There were extremely difficult working conditions in the cafeterias and other work places, which physically weakened the immigrants.

[Page 461]

Therefore, it is completely understandable that at first the Society cared about medical help for the *landsleit*. The most important task was in the foreground of its activities.

The Society drew experienced medical personnel to the medical work, such as Dr. Elson, Dr. Shapiro, Dr. Max Yafa, Dr. Reznik, Dr. A. Flaks, Mrs. Dr. M. Mendelev.

The Society had a standing committee, which was named the "Sick Committee." Its task was to follow the health condition of patients and they were in constant contact with the doctors and pharmacists.

In such cases, the chosen "Sick Committee" stood on watch and made sure that the patient would be treated conscientiously both by the doctor and by the apothecary. The "Sick Committee" would bring all of the disputes before the committee and the more severe conflicts would also be treated at a general meeting of the *landmanschaft*.

The patient, who in most cases lay lonely and solitary in his *rumke* [small room], would be tended to by *landsleit*. According to the determination of the committee, special attendants would sometimes be hired.

In connection with this it is worthwhile to illustrate with the account in the minutes:

"When a member becomes ill and he is alone in his room, we shall provide an attendant for the entire day and everything that the doctor orders shall be given to the member. This means: doctors, medicine and an attendant – in cases where we are not able to attend the patient with our own members from the society."

"A Sick Committee member, M. Nodel, gave his report for the committee: he hired a brother Yafa for one night for 8/3 [shillings/pence]. He served as an attendant for brother Press for three nights- 10 [shillings] a night and Mr. Press was attended to by several committee members for one night."

The primary connection to the sick *landsleit* can only be substantiated by the fact that at each meeting the health conditions of the sick brothers was first mentioned and, if they were all healthy, it was reported in this style:

"The Sick Committee reports that all brothers, thank God, are healthy."

Those patients who needed a hospital were connected by the *landsmanschaft* to the management of the hospitals and were provided with beds, frequent visits to the patient and the showing of a brotherly interest in the condition of that patient.

[Page 462]

The Society was also in contact with the Ladies Society, which provided the Jewish sick with kosher food in the hospital and also contributed on behalf of this purpose. To this day, the Rakishok *Landsmanschaft* is a member of the kosher kitchen at the hospital and pays a yearly taxation to the General Hospital.

The Loan Fund

After the Society normalized its activities in the area of medical help, a proposal was made to found a loan fund for its own *landsleit*. This was a necessity at that time. The immigrants in a strange land did not always have work and the income was sometimes not enough as a means of support and to send a few pounds to the family at home. There were also many cases where *landsleit* needed a little capital in order to open a small shop, to buy goods for peddling or to bring relatives across the sea.

The proposal to found a loan fund was filed on the 18th of May 1913. However, a few years passed before the loan fund was implemented.

It was decided on the 4th of April 1915 to open a loan account. The decision was accepted based on the following points:

The name of the interest free loan fund was chosen; it shall be called "the Rakishok Sick Benefit Loan Account."

The Fund shall consist of 75 pounds, which shall be taken from the sick benefit for the purpose of the interest free loan fund and with the hope for another 25 pounds to have a capital foundation of 100 pounds at the opening.

The purpose and aim is to lend to poor brothers in need of help in making a living and [in amounts] not higher than 10 pounds unless the committee finds it necessary and if it is possible. Each applicant must pay 2/6 [shillings/shillings] for the application no matter the amount of the loan and provide two guarantors whom the committee will recognize as worthy.

Those providing guarantees may be members as well as from outside and not members. To receive benefits members must be paid up in full. If from the outside, they must become a member. The financial committee cannot provide any guarantees.

A finance committee should be elected from the body, consisting of five people in addition to the treasurer and secretary, who are responsible for giving loans and investigating their security and they must attend meetings, unless a written excuse is sent to the secretary. Three members of the finance committee make a quorum. The applicants shall go to the secretary for an application. The applicant fills it out and returns it to the secretary. The secretary sets the meeting of the finance committee and the committee can come to a decision the day after the meeting.

[Page 463]

The treasurer must attend each meeting and give a report for which he is entitled to a receipt.

8)* The treasurer must attend each meeting and give a report according to the receipt book, as to the regularity of the payments. *[Translator's note: There are two entries with the number 8.]

The interest free loan [fund] shall have a separate banking account as well as a separate set of books. This all is recommended to the body and carried unanimously.

A financial committee was chosen at a meeting of the following people: Chaim Dovid Jafa, Morris Gordon, Kh. Sneig, Moshe Levin and Zakshtein.

A solemn gathering in honor of the opening of the loan fund was called on the 11th of April, which was attended by "brothers and friends." Everyone was seated at tablecloth covered tables and the chairman as well as the secretary clarified the significance and purpose of the founding of the interest free loan fund in short speeches that were received with applause.

Then a goblet, which cost one pound 10 shillings, was auctioned off and it was bought for seven pounds 10 shillings by J. Sneig, may he rest in peace, and for his entire life it was a dear memento for him of the founding of the loan fund of the society.

Organizing Work and Activities

The organizing work of the Rakishok *Landsmanschaft* went at a rapid tempo. All of the statutes were carried out exactly. Committee meetings took place regularly each week and general meetings were called often. Elections took place every half-year and then in the later years the terms of the committee were lengthened.

The duties of the members, of the chairman, of the committee members and the doorkeeper's duties were worked out in detail.

Because of the characteristic role which a doorkeeper had had and also because of the particular ceremony at the acceptance of a new member, I cite their duties according to the way it is followed in the minutes of the 22nd of September 1919.

Doorkeeper's Duty:

Is to remain in hall near the door and let in each member when the meeting is open for business and to stop him at the door and announce to the chairman the arrival of the member and his name so that when the new member appears in the middle of the hall, the chairman will greet him as necessary and he will quietly take his place. The doorkeeper must hold the registry book and record the members present or permit them to enter their names.

[Page 464]

The Greeting of A New Member:

"When the chairman gives notice of his initiation, it is the duty of everyone present in the hall to stand and greet him with enthusiasm, by clapping with the hands three times. Then the chairman or the secretary shall present him with his rulebook and address him about the worth of and obedience to the

482   Rokiskis Yizkor Book

Society, as well as his duties as a member and the duties to his brothers who shall end with hand-clapping."

According to the minutes we see that in general a discipline reigned and all decisions were carried out. Each one was commanded to carry out their duties. There was a strong reaction if a committee member or a member of the Society did not fulfill his obligations.

In addition the calendar showed many activities for the *landsmanschaft* to bring the members closer to each other. It was done at various opportunities.

The Society sent gifts: to a wedding of a *landsman* or to a wedding of his child; to a *Bar-Mitzvah*; at the birth of a child or to a *Bris* [ritual circumcision]. There were gifts for each member who showed activism at organizing balls and various undertakings on behalf of the society.

The Society took part in both the joys and the suffering of a *landsman*.

When a *landsman* died, it delegated its representative to the funeral and mourned with the family. In a case where the deceased was alone, the Society erected a headstone for him and photographed the headstone to send to his family. An obituary was also published in the press. There were cases in which the *yahrzeit* [anniversary of a death on which a memorial candle is lit and the memorial prayer is recited in the synagogue] was observed. There was also interest given to the situation of the orphaned family both the one in South Africa and the one beyond the sea, helping it financially and morally.

It also was concerned about the naturalization of the *landsleit* and supported those who endeavored to receive citizenship according to the proposal of Sh. Rubin, as follows:

Mr. Sh. Rubin proposed that the Society shall assist financially those who shall submit for naturalization. The chairman was instructed to offer support from the Society solicitor about the question of how to safely and inexpensively carry it out.

Such activities strengthened the connection among the *landsleit* and the leader, in which they saw brotherly interest and devotion.

[Page 465]

At various times an aid collection also was organized in behalf of Rakishok and its surroundings. They also helped to bring poor *landsman* or the family of a *landsman*, who did not himself have the money for travel expenses, to South Africa.

After the First World War the situation of the Jews in Lithuania was very sad. The returnees from the evacuation did not have any means to settle. Those who found themselves under the German occupation also had become very impoverished.

Although each *landsman* helped his closest family members and relatives, there were still many of those who had no relatives and friends in South Africa. Institutions also had to be supported.

At a meeting on the 14th of March 1920 it was decided to send 100 pounds for the Rakishok needy. The money was sent to the address of the Rakishok Rabbi, Reb Betzalel, of blessed memory. Fifteen pounds was also sent for the poor Jews in Abel [Obeliai].

Chaim Khit from Rakishok had – in the name of the Rabbi, Reb Betzalel - sent an accounting of the 100 pounds received, showing that it was divided in the following just manner: "One part for the orphans in the *Talmud Torah* [religious school for poor boys]; one part to buy wood for the poor and one part was given to repair the bathhouse and the *mikvah* [ritual bathhouse] in Rakishok."

A fire broke out in Luknik, a *shtetele* [small town]; the Rakishok *landsmanschaft* sent in its contribution in support of the victims of the fire.

The Rakishok Society accommodated all those in South Africa turning to it for help. It was in contact with all of the other *landsmanschaftn* and also contributed whenever a society turned to it.

Many levies were issued in support of various campaigns in South Africa, such as in support of the War Victims Fund and for the action to bring 250 Jewish orphans (after the First World War).

The beautiful *mitzvah* [commandment] of charity and aid for the home was adopted by the Rakishok *landsmanschaft* from the first day of its founding. The following can serve as an example:

"A donation was given for the Hebrew Orthodox synagogue and the members of the first committee – Sh. Shwartsberg, and Sh. Sher – were present at the laying of the cornerstone of the synagogue." Also they satisfactorily supported a Hasidic *minyon* [prayer group] with a letter when it turned for help to buy its own building. Thereby the society was guaranteed that it had the right to hold meetings in the building when it would need to at times when [the *minyon*] was not praying or themselves holding a meeting.

* * *

[Page 466]

There are two five-year money reports of the Society in the minute-books: from the 1st of January 1936 until the 31st of December 1940 and from the 1st of January 1941 until the 31st of December 1945. I find it necessary to write about the evolution of the "five-year report of the Society from the 1st of January 1936 to the 31st of December 1940," although it does not include the sums of money that the Rakishoker Society divided among various aid organization and campaigns:

Income		Expenses	
Membership	597 6 6	Doctors and Chemists	305 5 11
Loan repayments	118 7 6	Rent Jewish Guild	28 17 6
Entry fees	13 13 0	P.O. Box	6 5 0
Ball income	59 14 6	Post and revenue stamps	26 10 4
		Board of Deputies	25 4 0
		Donations and presents	25 6 0
		Bank costs	3 8 0
		Advertisements	11 0 6
		Secretary	146 9 6
		Income above expenses	210 14 9

£789 1 6		£ 789 1 6	

Loan Account

Balance on the 1st of January, 1936	780 9 6	Repayments	4587 8 3
Payments 108 loans	4755 0 0	Balance to 31 December 1940	948 1 3

£5535 9 6		£5535 9 6	

Balance Sheet
to the 31st of December 1940

Cash in Standard Bank	162 13 8	The Rakishoker Aid	
Loan Account	984 1 3	Society	60 0 0
Iron Safe	10 10 0	Doctors and Chemists	19 19 2
Paid to P.O. Box	1 5 0	Special Fund	38 15 6
P.O. Box	1 5 0	Capital on the 1st of January, 1936	739 0 6
		Added Income	210 14 9

£1122 9 11		£1122 9 11	

Collected capital £1042 10 9

A. Eidlman
Secretary

[Page 467]

Communal and Cultural Activities

On the face of it, we can add all of the money collections for institutions and on behalf of various funds to the bank account of communal activities. If the Rakishoker Society had not had any understanding and appreciation for communal work, it would not have developed such intensive activity, and who knows if it would have existed for as long as 40 years. Without an idea and without communal activities it would have long ago fallen apart or it would have been an organization without any color and hue, without a spiritual character.

We see that the Rakishok *landsmanschaft* [organization of people from the same town] responded warmly to all calls from the local central organizations and societies, When the Zionist Federation had turned, for example, to her, still before the First World War, to sell *shekels** and to make other commitments, she did so willingly.

*[Translator's note: The Zionist Organization sold membership certificates that were called *shekels*.]

We note in the minutes the participation of the Rakishok Society in all actions that the Board of Deputies organized in the interest of the Jewish community in South Africa and in the affairs of the Jewish people.

When the Board of Deputies, in partnership with the South African Zionist Federation, called a conference on the 12th of December 1917 that dealt with the plan from the British State about Palestine, the Rakishok Society was represented at the conference.

It also took part in the protest actions against the pogroms against the Jews in Ukraine and also on the 13th of July, 1919, with all the *landmanschaftn*, challenged the Board of Deputies to take steps against the terrible actions against the Jews in Poland. A representative of the Rakishok Society took part in the reception with General Smuts that took place on the 19th of October, 1919, when he declared to everyone that "Palestine belongs to the Jews."

However, a strong expansion of communal activities was noticed after the First World War, particularly when a new immigrant element arrived in South Africa that came to build a new home for themselves in South Africa and did not think of returning.

The newly arriving immigrants had left the war and revolution. Many of them also were witnesses to pogroms and endured maliciousness toward the Jews in the old home.

Deportations of the Jews from their homes by the Tsarist regime during the First World War and the forced labor by the Germans at that time, no doubt, changed the psychology of the Jews, who understood life differently before the First World War, when they had no idea of another kind of life besides the *shtetl* way of life.

The storm of immigrants to South Africa grew stronger every day. Each ship brought new transports of immigrants. Often, the mail brought requests to the Society from people who asked that we send them papers and travel expenses.

[Page 468]

The newly arriving immigrants brought a different spirit, the post-war spirit and the spirit of the revolution. They no longer carried their baggage in a sack or in a wicker basket like the first immigrant pioneers, but they came dressed in a modern way and with suitcases in their hands.

He, the newly arrived immigrant, already had an inkling of a party, of communal activity.

We note how in a short time, the literary union, the worker's club, the Zionist-Socialist Party were founded in Johannesburg. We transplanted the cultural organized society of the old home to African soil.

Almost all of the new Rakishoker immigrants became members of the Rakishok Society and saw its modernization. They were the first to fight the rules and regulations of the Society that were undemocratic and quaint.

Discussions about the rules and regulations developed at meetings and gatherings of the Society and new proposals and work projects emerged.

There was a new leadership for the Society in which representatives of the new storm of immigration were also elected: Z. Nafanovitz, M. Muskat, Yisroel Meikl, A. Noach, Sh. Rubin, H, Rubin, the Sher brothers and others. Dr. Maks Yafa, who was a progressive community man, was hired as a Society doctor.

The Society delegates on the Board of Deputies – Jakob Snieg, Shlomo Rubin and, later, Ahron Noach – also brought their influence to the work of the Board, that it should diversify and be in agreement with the interests of the [different] strata of the people of the South African Jewish community. They spoke Yiddish and demonstrated with this their love of the language of their people, negating the tendencies toward assimilation in Jewish society.

We read reports from the Board of Deputies in the minutes. A. Noach-Noachumovitz underlines that the Board needs to expand its work and asks for permission from the *landsmanschaft* that he propose to the Board a new activity plan.

Such *landsleit* [people from the same town] were also represented in the committee of the *landsmanschaft* who opposed each innovative measure, interpreting it as political activity. Khona Kohen, the chairman and one of the meritorious volunteers with the *landsmanschaft*, who was a member of the first generation of immigrants who were raised as territorialist-religious, opposed all of the new efforts. His attitude was: "No politics should be discussed." However, we note in the minutes from the later years that A. Noach-Noachumovitz was empowered to defend the direction of the progressive wing on the Board.

From the minutes, we notice that the Rakishoker *landsmanschaft* took part in all of the actions and measures organized by the Board of Deputies on behalf of the South African community and Jewish communities around the world.

[Page 469]

The Society was very active in all campaigns during the time of the Second World War.

Representatives of the Society took part in a conference which made a decision to send medical help to Russia, to help the Jews in Europe when the war ended and to all of the Jewish soldiers who would return to South Africa. There was also a decision to not take member dues and contributions from the Rakishok *landsleit* soldiers.

The *landsmanschaft* was active in Jewish war appeals, in the Kuybyshev* appeal and, in particular, with sending help to Russia and clothes to Russian Jews. In additon, it did not abandon the normal Society activities, such as aiding the sick and providing loans for the needy *landsleit*.

*[Translator's note: Kuybyshev is an industrial city in Russia that was chosen to be the Soviet Union's capital if Moscow were occupied by the Germans.]

It also stood on watch for local interests: the anti-Semitic-Nazi poison also spread in South Africa and there were Hilterist agents who spread a frightening hatred of the Jews. We find in the minutes that Mr. Avidov gave a report about the high importance of Jews protecting the synagogues in order to relieve the police who had other tasks at that time.

Rakishok Jews in South Africa engaged in the Rakishok work and there also were those who left South Africa and entered the ranks of the army in order to fight against the Germans who annihilated millions of Jews. Yerakhmiel Aront-Arsh, the chairman of the *landsmanschaft* who left his wife and children and voluntarily took part in the war against the Hilterist murderers and cannibals, can serve as a self-sacrificing example.

The communal activity of the Rakishok Society at the time of the war was especially devoted and very active. In order to accommodate various appeals and turns for help, a special war fund was created with the Society in 1940.

Shlomo Rubin proposed on the 8th of October 1940, "Whereas the Society is obliged to answer in support of all appeals from Russia, from the refugees in *Eretz-Yisroel*, from ORT-OZE [ORT - Jewish educational and vocational training organization; OZE - Society for the Protection of the Health of the Jews] and to help in general all of the needy, therefore, a special war fund needs to be created."

The proposal by Shlomo Rubin was approved and the following was recorded in connection with the war fund:

1.   The Society gives 50 pounds to the war fund;
2.   Every member is asked to provide as much as he can;
3.   A special sub-committee was created to arrange special offers on behalf of the fund.
4.   The Rakishok Aid Union was challenged to supply the war fund from its money, which could not now be used.

[Page 470]

Sh. Rubin, Y. Meikl, M Muskat, Sh. Shapiro and M. Wittz were chosen for the subcommittee.

In order to do communal work it was necessary to arrange for a report and to appropriately enlighten the members.

We remember that presentations by Ovidov, Sh. Bojarski, Mrs. Rabkin, M. Shur, M. Matis and others took place for the Society members.

A precise account from Mrs. Rabkin's lecture is here in the minutes of the 10th of May 1942, reporting about *ORT-OZE*:

"*ORT-OZE* endeavors to transform the Jewish masses from lacking a definite occupation into constructive workers. *ORT-OZE* works not only in ruined Europe where the Jews learned their earlier sources of livelihood and were forced to accept unpractical work, but even here, in a more fortunate land, *ORT-OZE* has much to do. The question of what our children should do when they finish school presents itself. Everyone now understands that they must learn a trade that has a future. Our youth know very well that they must forget about being a shopkeeper and, although we must have doctors, lawyers, who are often useful, not all of them can enter the mentioned professions. There are also other reasons. Anti-Semitism is more widespread among Christian shopkeepers than among Christian workers; in addition, the workers are protected by the government and trade unions and they have a more secure existence than shopkeepers. However, there are trades here and we must find a suitable trade for every young person. In America certain attempts are made with each young person to find out which trade is appropriate for him; here we only have to communicate and consider what to advise him. Then there is the question of where one learns a trade. Universities are not accessible for everyone and the trade school costs money, too. *ORT-OZE* hopes that with instruction, with special workshops, they will then find a place to work and in peacetime as well as wartime. Russia is strong not only with its strong army, but also with its highly qualified factory workers."

These reports were simultaneously an important cultural contribution for the Society members, although it cannot be concluded that they had a permanent effect.

However, based on the minutes, it can be seen that various entertainments took place, annual evening, picnics, which the Society arranged. These events included an artistic program with the participation of the artist and director, Shlomo Rubin, and of his wife, Genya Rubin – an actress with many years of service, of Yisroel Meikl – a folk singer, and of Kh. Katz and others. Noach-Noachumovitz would often read his own creations, mainly memories of the old home.

As an example we present an appreciation of the yearly performance that was written by "a Rakishoker" and was published in the *Afrikaner Yidishe Zeitung* [*African Jewish Newspaper*]:
[Page 471]

"Once a year the Rakishok *landsleit* in Johannesburg get together so that they not do become strangers to one another, to talk about and have greetings from survivors of the Holocaust.

Each time an event is carried out, it includes not only beautifully covered tables, but also a prepared program of Jewish folk songs, music, recitations and humor.

Mrs. Rubin made a strong impression with the recitation of Segalowicz's poem, *Dortn* [*There*] and Gotlib's *Lita* [*Lithuania*]. Her interpretations of the moving creations brought tears to the eyes of the crowd.

Another one who contributed with beautiful singing was Friend Meikl, from whose singing all present had a spiritual pleasure whenever he appeared. Rev. Sh. Kheitovitz also obliged the crowd with his voice and hearty singing of Yiddish folk songs.

The performance of Sholem Aleichem's *Oylem Habe* [Eternal Life] with the accompaniment of the well-known actor, Sh. Rubin, Mrs. Rubin. H. Miller and Mr. A. Seitovitz, who appeared on the stage for the first time, was very successful.

The chairman of the Society, H. Arons, and his wife deserve a *Yasha Koyekh* [may you have strength] for their devoted work, as well as the committee and the women who assisted in the success of the evening."

As we see, the program contained only Yiddish numbers and the Yiddish language. This is how all entertainments took place, in Yiddish, and the Rakishok Jews have not betrayed the Yiddish language and the national culture to this day, as well as the national Jewish way of life.

Only Yiddish is spoken at all gatherings. To this day they have a representative on the school managing committee of the Rakishoker *Folks-Shul* [public school]: earlier it was M. Witts, and then Shlomo Rubin.

When the census took place in South Africa, Brother Sh. Rubin declared at a meeting that was held on the 1st of May 1941 that they needed to inform the Jews that they should give Yiddish as their language. It is reported as follows in the minutes: "A statement by Brother Sh. Rubin also expressed the hope that every Jew will fulfill their duty and not deny their Jewish origins. The cost of spreading the leaflet about this was endorsed."

All of the above mentioned evidence as well as the fact that Yerakhmiel Arons, the present chairman of the *landsmanschaft*, turned to the Federation of the *Landsmanschaftn* to urge that they write letters in Yiddish, confirms the folksiness of the Rakishoker *Landsmanscaft* and their attachment to the Yiddish language and to Jewish communal work.

* * *

[Page 472]

The Rakishok Aid Society, founded a few years before the war, was exclusively focused on helping *landsleit* in the old home. It carried out its aid work very intensively after the war. However, the Rakishok *landsmanschaft* can say about this society: "bone of my bone, flesh of my flesh." The same workers in the *landsmanschaft* were also active workers in the Aid Society.

Here is further discussion about the activity of the Rakishok Aid Society. It later joined the Rakishok *landsmanschaft*.

With the unification it began a new fruitful phase under the chairmanship of Yerakhmial Arons-Arsh. Sh. Rubin stresses in his report: "In the time that I have been in the society, the work has never been as active as now."

The old home lay in ruins then, the earth was covered with the corpses, but the Jews throughout the world and, also including Rakishok, wrote on their flag: "No forgetting and no forgiving!" They did not forget the 6,000,000 Jewish martyrs and did not forgive the murderers and, at the same time, they turned their energy to helping the survivors of the Hitleristic hell. The arrival in South Africa of Gisa Levin, who told of the frightful Jewish martyrdom under the Nazi executioner and of her own survival in the Hilterist hell, made a strong impression. The *landsleit* greeted her warmly and movingly at a special welcome that was organized for her.

Because of the later emerging difficulties in provided help to the Jews in Russia, the work then concentrated only in the direction of helping the refugees from Rakishok and its surroundings who emigrated to Israel. Sums of money and food packages were sent for them. The Society taxed itself on behalf of the Lubavitcher Hasidim who wanted to build houses in Israel, for the Israeli Federation of Lithuanian Jews, for the *Mogen Dovid Adom* [Red Star or Shield of David – the Israeli emergency medical service] and for other purposes.

Communal contact was created with the *landsleit* through the Rakishok Jews travelling on a visit to Israel. First of all, they met with Rakishokers. Rakishok residents from Israel came to South Africa and there were ceremonial welcomes for each of them.

Yerekhmial Arons-Arsh, the chairman of the Society, traveled to Israel and he brought spirited greetings from the *landsleit* when he returned.

At a solemn welcome arranged in his honor by the Society on the 10th of August of that year, he spoke about life in Israel. He said to everyone the following:

"When one arrives in Israel, one can understand why the English, after being in Africa for dozens of years, still say 'home' when they remember England. Now after being in Israel for a short time, one can understand what such a thing as 'home' means. It can be felt just by being there."

Yerekhmial Arons-Arsh also had reported, "While he had seen everyone for whom he had an address and found out that the *landsleit* had organized themselves as well as all of the Jews in Israel. He emphasized that life in Israel is difficult, but bearable. In general,

[Page 473]

Dr. Michel Arelovitz

Israel made a good impression on him despite all of the backwardness and his belief is that what we do for Israel is too little and it is his belief that the Society needs to concentrate on helping Israel."

(Photo, caption: Dr. Mikhla Orleowitz)

In the minutes is noted that special evenings were held for all *landsleit* who came for a visit to South Africa.

A hearty welcome was arranged for *landsman* Baradovsky who came on a visit to South Africa. He, Kopl Baradowsky, is a chemist and accomplished a great deal in the chemical field for the good of the Givat Brenner communal settlement.

An impressive welcome was given to Dr. Mikhla Orlewitz and a beautiful farewell evening was arranged for Mrs. Shneiderman (Libke Ruch).

The cruel Jewish national tragedy has not been forgotten by the Rakishok Jews and every year a memorial day is organized in the Hasidic synagogue. A memorial service is carried out for all of the cruelly murdered Jews from Rakishok and the surrounding area and the Jews of Europe.

We publish the following eulogy by A. Noach-Noachumovitz that was given by him at the large memorial evening, which was arranged by the *Rakishoker Landsleit Farband* [Union] – at the Berea Synagogue, Johannesburg – in memory of the martyrs from Rakishok, for the neighboring *shtetlekh* and for the millions of fallen Jewish victims in Europe.

Year in and year out, generations will still come, we Jews will come together to deliver a eulogy, to cry and to lament the destruction of 1941-1945 and will not forget the victims, the martyrs, who perished in the sanctity of God's name and of the holy people.

The history of the Jewish people was always written in blood. However, this epoch is the bloodiest, the darkest.

Six million Jews perished – a third of the entire Jewish people.

The mourners were not yet born who would write the lamentations, the words that could express that for which every one of us feel [the need] to cry for the tragedy of the Holocaust. The words, *vakol nehi arimah* ["...for the sound of wailing [(is heard from Zion...)]" - Jeremiah 9:18], are not sufficient for the current third* destruction.

*[Translator's note: the destruction of the first and second temples in Jerusalem and the Holocaust.]

[Page 474]

New words had to be created that would express the terrible deeds, cruelty that our martyrs went through. The old lexicon did not know of all of the torture racks, such as gas, electrical currents, death factories.

Jewish history is rich in miracles, group miracles and individual miracles. In this present destruction there are no recorded miracles. Dark clouds covered the skies, the voices of the six million Jews, school children did not reach to the throne of honor.

Jewish children lay hidden in the dark cellars and lifted their hands, praying to God that the sun not shine in order that they not be seen.

Seven graves remained for us of our homes. Fate wanted Jewish Rakishok and the Jews from our neighboring *shtetlekh* to be destroyed with such a death. Everything that we built in the course of generations was swallowed by seven graves.

Eyewitnesses say: as soon as the Nazis entered Rakishok, all Jews were driven together to one place; each day Jews were taken to work; they would not return.

During the days of slaughter, all Jews were told to be ready. Everyone, young and old was driven together around the seven pits and machines guns were placed around them. The Jews understood that this was their end. The voices of women, children were head for distant, distant miles.

The rabbi of the city, the Rabbi, Reb Zelig Orelovitz, also was among the community of Jews. He begged the murderers that he be allowed to say several words to the Jews.

The rabbi could not call for an uprising in such circumstances. He cried out: "The will of God is from the heavens! Sanctify the name of God with love! We are not the first and we are not the last!"

After these words everyone became quiet. They no longer cried and they were ready to die calmly *al kiddush haShem* [in sanctification of the God's name].

Because of his words, the rabbi was the first to be shot.

Everyone was driven into the pits under a hail of bullets. Those Jews who were killed immediately by the bullets were fortunate; they did not have to be buried alive.

We, *landsleit,* who were left orphans, decided to write a yizkor [memorial] book in order to immortalize our martyrs of the third destruction. This would be a lament on the destruction of Rakishok and when the lamentations were read about the extermination of all of the Jewry in Europe, we would simultaneously read about the death of our *shtetlekh.*

The Rakishok book needs to be found in every one of our houses and be given as an inheritance from generation to generation.

We must always remember and must engrave in ourselves the words of Jeremiah in the Book of Lamentations that cried out: "Mine eyes have brought me grief over all of the daughters of my city." [3:51]. We must always feel the tragedy to be as great as if it were happening today.

[Page 475]

The graves must never be forgotten. We Jews must always remember our martyrs, our victims.

From generation to generation we always need to curse the murderers of our people; an eternal curse on those who annihilated a third of the Jewish people!

My eyes shed tears and will not be still. Our souls cry over the cruel extermination of millions of Jews and of my home *shtetl*, Rakishok.

* * *

Eulogies were made on the Society's days of mourning in memory of the Jewish martyrs and victims of the Nazi devils.

However, the Society wanted a monument for all of the tragically murdered *landsleit* to remain forever. Therefore, it decided to publish a yizkor book that

Rokiskis Yizkor Book   495

would sanctify Rakishok and its surroundings and there also would be a section dedicated to the Rakishok *landsmanschaft* for its 40 years of existence.

The decision to publish a yizkor book was accepted at a meeting on the 16th of June 1949. Taking part in this meeting were A. Levin, T. Orlin, Y. Miller, M. Muskat, Sh. Rubin, Ch. Rubin, B. Ruch, Mrs. Ruch, Mrs. Sura Klas, A. Orelovitz, A. Noach-Noachumovitz. The chairman was Yerakhmial Arons-Arsh.

The question was treated comprehensively and a commission of five people was chosen: Yerakhmial Arons-Arsh, A. Orelovitz, A. Noach-Noachumovitz, Sh. Rubin and B. Ruch. The commission needed to learn all of the details, select which format, choose an editor and learn the cost of printing.

At the general meeting of the 21st of August 1949, the question of a yizkor book was again discussed. Yerakhmial Arons-Arsh reported on the decision of the committee to publish a yizkor book and asked that it be accepted by the general meeting. He also emphasized that "The work had already begun with a letter in the Yiddish and Yiddish-English press and letters were sent overseas as well as to local individuals for material.

"After his report, the chairman was heartily greeted by applause by everyone present."

The question of the yizkor book was again considered at several committee meetings. Sh. Rubin reported "that material could be taken from the minutes for an interesting and historical work."

Pamphlets were sent out to request memorials for the book; there was a discussion about hiring an editor and about creating a fund to publish the book.

The question of the yizkor book was treated with more detail at a special session of the executive with the cooperation of Y. Ginzburg and Y. Meikle that took place at the home of Yitzhak Ginzburg.

[Page 476]

Through Shlomo Rubin and Yerakhmiel Arons we were informed that an understanding was reached that M. Bakalatshik-Felin was the editor of the book and this important and earnest work must immediately be undertaken because "the book must be a monumental work that should serve as an historic document, a source of material forever and ever."

All present accepted all of the resolutions in connection with the yizkor book.

Several appeals and notices were published in the *Afrikaner Yidisher Zeitung* [*African Jewish Newspaper*] in connection with the yizkor book.

These notices are published for the sake of historical documentation:

I. Rakishoker *Landsleit* in Johannesburg to Publish a Yizkor Book

It very soon will be 40 years since the Rakishok Society, which has maintained a close connection with all of the *landsleit* here and overseas during the course of 40 years, was founded in Johannesburg. The society also supported a *gmiles-khesed* [interest-free loan] fund and a fund for the sick, as well as an aid society for Rakishok *landsleit*, which did their good work by giving direct help to the *landsleit* across the sea during the time both before and after the war and which still carries on all of this work.

The committee decided to publish a book about Rakishok in which general Jewish life in Rakishok will be reflected and also will contain various pictures of Rakishok. Certain material is being collected and prepared for the book. It is the hope of the committee that the book will be not only a memorial (*a Sefer Zikhron* [memorial book]) to all of those martyrs who perished in Rakishok at the hands of the Nazi hangmen, but the book should also be of literary worth and of historical significance.

The committee also developed a certain plan to cover the costs of publishing the book – a plan in which all *landsleit* would have the opportunity to take part and it would not be a great burden. The members of the committee will promptly visit all *landsleit* in connection with the program. The committee hopes that all *landsleit* will respond sympathetically and take part in the important work and support and help the committee in publishing the book.

At this opportunity the committee asks all *landsleit* who have certain important material, such as official documents, papers from various institutions in Rakishok, *kehilus* [organized Jewish communities], the People's Bank and so on, biographies of historical worth, contact the secretary of the Society, P[ostal] B[ox] 3302, Johannesburg.

[Page 477]

II. *Landsmanschaft* of Rakishok and its Environs

P[ostal] B[ox] 3302, Johannesburg

Esteemed *Landsman,*

Our Society will be 40 years old in the near future. It is superfluous to describe here the role the Society has played in the life of the newly arriving emigrants to South Africa – this would take too much space. However, when we look at the activities of our Society during its existence – particularly during the recent years – we must say that we have no reason to be ashamed in relation to our Society.

Our Society not only helped our *landsleit* in Europe and Israel with money and with clothing, but also did important work in giving loans to *landsleit* here in this country, starting with a sum of several pounds and today reaching loans of a hundred pounds, as well as medical help for needy *landsleit*.

A large number of the founders of the *landsmanschaft* are already in the world of truth [died] and, thank God, several of them are still with us.

We believe that the names of all the workers on behalf of our *landsmanschaft* should be immortalized; the same with all of the names of the martyrs who came from Rakishok and its surroundings, who perished in the great catastrophe of our people.

In order to accomplish this we decided to publish a memorial book where everything would be recorded forever and ever. We want this book to be a sacred object in every house, of which our *landsleit* will be proud.

We appeal to you that if you have material that can be used in the publication of the above-mentioned book, such as descriptions, episodes, photographs and so on, you should send it to the address given.

The material needs to be of historical value.

If you want to immortalize the names of those closest to you, or an important personality, we will place the names in this book and it will remain a monument.

We also accept greetings to your surviving relatives or acquaintances, as well as for weddings, *Bar Mitzvus*, birthday celebrations and so on.

Please reply immediately.

With fraternal greetings, The Committee

[Page 478]

III. *Landsleit* Union of Rakishok and Its Surroundings Prepares a *Yizkor* Book

We announce to all *landsleit*, Yiddish writers, historians and scientists of Lithuania, both in the country and outside, that we are preparing to publish a memorial book about the life and death of Rakishok and its surroundings:

Anushishok, Kamajai Abel, Ponedel, Skopishok, Ponemunok, Sevenishok, Ezsherene [Ezerenai], Dusiat, as well as other surrounding *shtetlekh*.

We ask that you send us documents, letters and information, photographs, articles and monographs about the generations-long life of all of the above-mentioned Jewish *shtetlekh* in Lithuania.

Whoever knows should write to us with answers to the following questions:

How many residents (before the Holocaust and during the Holocaust) each *shtetl* had? How many institutions, associations or societies? What were their names and what purpose did they have? For what was each *shtetl* known? What is the number of surviving Jews who lived under the German occupation and in what manner did each one survive?

Every date and notice, document and writing is very important to us.

We will provide a place for lists of *landsleit* families that live in South Africa, Israel and other communities and also of those who perished in the Hitler catastrophe. Send us the names of families as well as photographic pictures. They can be of individuals, groups, societies or of buildings, streets and so on.

We also will publish memorials and short biographies of *landsleit*.

Material should be sent to this address: Rakishoker Society, Postal Box 3302, Johannesburg.

In the name of the *Rakishoker Landsleit Farein* [Rakishok *Landsleit* Union] in Johannesburg:

Yerakhmial Arons-Arsh (chairman) Berl Ruch (vice chairman) Yitzhak Ginzburg, Ahron Noachumovitz-Noach (committee members) Shlomo Rubin (secretary)

P.S. – We ask all Yiddish and Hebrew newspapers abroad to publish this appeal.

* * *

[Page 479]

This *yizkor book* and the actions of the *landsmanschaft* over 40 years are a reflection of the elevated and communal responsibility of the Rakishok Jews.

Today the society is represented in the majority of Jewish institutions and organizations in Johannesburg. Our representative, A. Noachumovitz-Noach, a delegate to the Board of Deputies, recently brought a proposal to banish Germany from the community [of nations] and absolutely demanded that they should ban the purchase of German goods. He also proposed that the Board create a People's Bank in order to assist the lowest and middle classes of the local Jewish population with loans.

B. Ruch also spoke about not buying German goods at a committee meeting and Yerakhmiel Arons (Arsh), the chairman, wrote an article in the *Afrikaner Yidishe Zeitung*.

The path of strong devotion to the Jewish people was maintained by the Rakishok *landsleit* with great, righteous enthusiasm and love during the course of the 40 years of existence of the society.

During the existence of the *Rakishoker Landsmanschaft* there were a great many commendable people who were in the leadership, for whom the work of the society was very dear.

We will record their names in the *Yizkor Book*:

Chairmen of the society were: Shimshon Shwarcberg, Shimshon Snieg, Yakov Snieg, Zarakh Beinart, Lou Herman, Yisroel-Naftali Kohen, Khona Kohen, Mendl Yoselovitz, Shmuel-Leib Yafa, Borukh Shadur, Betsalel Yafa, Mendl Muskat, Shlomo Rubin, Shlomo Shapiro. And Yerakhmiel Arons is now the chairman.

The vice chairmen were: Mendl Muskat, Moshe Sharp, Mendl Levin, Mendl Kuperman, Hirshl Sher, M. Witts, Zakshtein, Maurice Gordon, Zarakh Levin, Zalman Nodel, Shlomo Rubin. Berl Rukh is now the vice chairman.

The treasurers were: Eliason, Chaim Dovid Yafa, Mendl Kuperman. Mendl Muskat is now the treasurer.

The secretaries of the *landsmanschaft* were: Sh. Shneider, Leib Fogelovitz, Shlomo Silvershtein, Dovid Kuperman, A. Noach-Noachumovitz [Noachumovitz-Noach above]. Sh. Rubin is now the secretary.

I provide the following facts about the activities of several of them, who already are in the world of truth [have died]. It is possible that some have been omitted from the list, but this is because there are no biographical facts about them:

[Page 480]

Right to left: Shimshon Schwartzberg with his family

Shimshon Shwartsberg, of blessed memory

He was the first chairman. He laid the foundation for the long existence of the Rakishoker Society. The first constitution of the society was produced under his chairmanship and all of the rules were maintained with the greatest precision. Without a doubt, he spread love of the society's activities with his earnestness and responsibility as chairman.

Chaim-Dovid Yafa, of blessed memory

He was one of the Jews who felt it was a *mitzvah* [commandment or religious obligation] to do work for the Society. Even in his deep old age, it was not too difficult to go for miles to receive the signature from an endorser in order to ease the giving of loans for the needy. He was proud of his work for the Society and nothing was too difficult for him do on behalf of the welfare of the Society. He was the treasurer for years and at new elections no one ever thought of presenting another candidate in his place. He also was a member of the *khevre kadishe* [burial society].

Chaim-Dovid Yaffa

[Page 481]

Dovid Sheibl, may he rest in peace

He was among the first founders of the Society and helped a great deal so that the Society would stand on a strong foundation and was devoted to the Society until the last days before his departure from Johannesburg to Vryheid, Natal. He paid membership dues to the Society from his new place of residence until the last days of his life.

We find his name often in the minute books of the first years connected with his generous response to the needs of the Rakishoker Society.

Mendl Yoselevitz, may he rest in peace

Mendel Josselowitz and his wife Malka, departed from life

He was a fine Jew with a good reputation that he brought with him, thanks to his behavior in the old home. He became an active member of the Society from the first day of his arrival in South Africa. It was not at all difficult for him to go miles to recruit a new member and take on the duties of the Society. To his account we can add that he recruited a large number of members.

He was a committee member for many years and was chairman of the Society for a certain time.

He and his wife, Malka, were devoted to the Society with their hearts and souls.

Khona Kohen, may he rest in peace

He was a respected Jew, maintaining the middleclass behavior of the old home. He was the chairman of the Society for a great many years. Several years before his death, he was honored with the title, "President of the Society" as an expression of his devotion and energetic work on behalf of the Society. He required strict and exact adherence to the laws of the Society's constitution and took good care of each penny of the Society's treasury. He often supported the Society with his own payments when it was in need of money. When other societies called upon the Rakishoker Society for help, he was the first to take money out of his pocket and this stimulated other to follow his example. By providing funds himself he assured that the Society would not have to pay any money from its treasury.

[Page 482]

Yisroel Naftali Kohen, may he rest in peace

He was a brother of Khona Kohen. He also was a respected Jew with a beautiful patriarchal beard and was considered one of the most intelligent, enlightened types in the old home. He was the spokesperson for the Society to whose speech everyone always listened. He did a great deal for the Rakishoker Society from the day it arose.

He became the chairman of the Society at the resignation of the first chairman, Shimshon Shwartsberg.

Zalman Nadel, may he rest in peace

He was a Jew, a toiler, one of the original founders of the Society. With heart and soul he busied himself for the public good. He recruited members, collected debts for the Society and would provide a hall for general gatherings and banquets of the Society. Reading the minutes of the Society, we see his name often and it is noted how he did everything with dedication.

He was a committee member of the Society until the last day of his life.

Mendl Levin, may he rest in peace

He was one of the original founders of the Rakishoker Society. He had a warm, Jewish heart and strongly followed the religious way of life of the old home. He would lend money to the Society when it needed it.

He was a member of the committee of the Society for many years.

Borukh Shadur, may he rest in peace

He was the husband of the extraordinary communal worker, Chana Shadur, who was the mother of the Rakishok children's home and a sister of Zalman and Hilel Eidelson.

He was a Jew, unpretentious and very honest, being very devoted to the interest of the Society. Many nights he would watch over the sick and lonely *landsleit*.

He was a committee member for many years. The Society helped to erect a headstone on his grave.

[Page 483]

Mendl Vitts-Joselovitz, may he rest in peace

Mendl Vitts-Joselovitz

He was a Jew who lived here in South Africa through arduous labor. He was a committee member for many years and a vice president of the Society for a time.

Although he was far from a rich man, when the Society needed money, he would readily donate five pounds to support the needy *landsleit*.

He was a good brother of the Rakishoker Society, giving support to everyone who turned to him. He attended all meetings of the Society punctually.

He was a representative in the managing committee of the *Yidisher Folkshul* [Jewish People's School] in Johannesburg for a time.

* * *

In addition to the above mentioned people, there were outstanding workers who are now deceased: Yakov Sneig, Yosef Feldman, Charly Yafa, Zundl Seitovitz, Max Gordon, Lipa Shwartsberg, Leib Spak, Morris Gordon and, *eybodl lekhaim*,* Khetskl Obelovitz, Shlomo Sher, Betsalel Berger, Yosef Kuperman and his wife, Basheve, were capable workers.

*[Translator's note: May he be distinguished for life – a phrase used to separate the deceased from the living and differentiate between them.]

Jakob Snieg [Jacob Sneeg or Snegg], May He Rest In Peace
(The recently deceased chairman of the Society)

Jakob Snieg was born in 1878 in a small village, Bitsun, nine *verst* [a verst is a Russian measure equal to one kilometer or six-tenths of a mile] from Abele [Obeliai]. His father sent him to a *kheder* [religious primary school] in Abele, to Shmuel the *melamed* [religious primary school teacher] at the age of six. Then he studied with other *yeshiva* [religious secondary school stressing the study of Torah] students with a rabbi in the village of Pokipine, where a Jewish shopkeeper lived.

His father died [when Jakob was] nine years of age and he [Jakob] wandered to Riga during his young years, where he began heavy labor and also learned a trade.

He emigrated to South Africa in 1902, settling at first in Cape Town and he moved to Johannesburg a few years later, where he remained until his death.

* * *

The first years [after] immigration were difficult for everyone and J. Snieg also went through a difficult period of immigration. All of the *landsleit* [people from the same town] felt lonely and abandoned and everyone needed a close relative or friend, which could be found in the circle of his own *landsleit*. A central meeting point for the Rakishok and Abele *landsleit* was the home in Ferreira [Ferreirasdorf] of Shmuel Leib Yafa, whose family already was in South Africa. They created their own *minyon* [group of at least 10 men required for organized prayer] and because of the situation of Chaim Leib Bun, who became very ill and might have died of hunger, not having anyone to care for him, the idea of founding a society was born.

[Page 484]

Yakov Snieg

First, a *Bikur Kholim* [Society for Visiting the Sick] was created and then, in 1912, the *Rakishoker Landsmanschaft* [organization of people from the same town] was created with rules and reciprocal obligations.

The first chairman of the *Landsmanschaft* was Shimshon Shwartsberg. In 1915, Jakob Snieg was elected as chairman.

He organized events and raised money so that the interest-free loan fund would function well.

The First World War broke out in Europe. The Board of Deputies organized aid actions for the Jewish victims of war. A letter arrived from Rakishok in which great racks of torture and the poverty in the *shtetl* [town] was described. Jakob Snieg exhibited great activity in all areas and was tireless in his work, organizing various events. A silver goblet was auctioned at one such event and Jakob Snieg bought the goblet. The Society [engraved] an appropriate signature [on it] and he always felt the goblet was dear to him.

Jakob Snieg was connected to the *Rakishoker Landsmanschaft* for 41 years. He was elected chairman many times. Over the course of time he did not weaken in his interest for the work of the Society. He always stood watch over the interests of our society, being a great conciliator. He found a way to settle conflicts with wisdom.

The *Rakishoker Landsmanschaft* honored him with the title, lifelong chairman of the Society, in recognition of his important work on behalf of the *landsleit*.

He, Jakob Snieg, with his honest and devoted work, served as a distinguished person of honor.

Honor his memory!

[Page 485]

The management and the activists of the Rakishoker Society consisted of the following people:

Yerakhmiel Arons-Arsh

Yerachmiel Aarons-Arsh

He was born in Svadushch [Svedasai] in 1907 to rich, enlightened parents who planted in him love of the Zionist ideal.

After the First World War, arriving in Rakishok from evacuation to Russia, he decided to go through the work of *hakhshore* [agricultural preparation] so as to emigrate to *Eretz-Yisroel*. He was one of the most active *halutzim* [pioneers] in *Eretz-Yisroel*, taking upon himself the heaviest work of drying out swamps, agricultural work, etc.

He became ill with malaria, which endangered his life. The *Kupat Holim* [Sick Fund] issued a certificate for him that he had to leave the country for reasons of health.

[After] returning from *Eretz-Yisroel*, Yerakhmiel Arsh was active in various communal areas and simultaneously completed his general and Hebrew-Yiddish education.

He emigrated to South Africa and he was active in communal Jewish life. During the Second World War, he entered the army voluntarily to fight Nazi Fascism. Since the end of the war, he has been involved in the interests of the Rakishoker Society with his heart and soul. He was president of the Society for several years and, in addition to various important activities, he was the initiator and main worker in realizing the publication of the *Yizkor Book of Rakishok and its Environs*.

Etl Shwartsberg-Arons

Ethel Aarons-Schwartzberg

She was born in Subat, Courland in 1908. When the Lithuanian Jews in Courland were driven out in 1912, her father, Heshl Shwartsberg, who earlier had been a resident of Rakishok, returned to Rakishok with his family and in 1914, during the war, the Shwartsbergs remained there and lived under the German occupation.

She became a student at the compulsory school in Rakishok and later she studied at the Lithuanian *gymnazie* [secondary school].

In 1929 she emigrated to South Africa from Rakishok. Although she and her husband, Yerakhmiel Arons-Arsh, experienced a difficult time in the "golden" land, she learned to speak English and Afrikaans well.

After the Second World War, she joined the Rakishoker Aid Society and exhibited great activity. She carried out correspondences with various people to learn the addresses of *landsleit* and was the main force in organizing actions that were carried out by the Society. She was occupied with sending food and clothing packages to the *landsleit* and was one of the hardest working members of the Rakishoker Society.

[Page 486]

Arya Eidlman

He was born in 1895 in the *shtetle* Antalept [Antaliepte] that is located between Utiyan [Utena] and Rakishok. His father, Avraham-Yitzhak, was a Jew, a scholar, and because of a scarcity in income, he and his family moved to Dvinsk where he was involved with the teaching profession.

He, Arya, studied in *kheder* and then in the Mirer *Yeshiva*, where the head of the *yeshiva* was the famous *Gaon* [sage], Reb Eliyahu Borukh.

There, in the Mirer *Yeshiva*, he was influenced by the *haskala* [Enlightenment] movement and returned home. He joined the left [wing] of the Zionist movement and studied bookkeeping.

During the First World War, he traveled to Smolensk where he remained until and after the October Revolution.

In 1921 he came to Ponevezsh [Panevezys] from Russia and helped found the Zionist Socialist Party there. He was chosen as a delegate to the Ponevezsh *kehile* [organized Jewish community]. He moved to Mariampol [Marijampole] and there he also was active in the community, both in the Zionist Socialist Party and in other institutions.

He came to South Africa in 1930 and immediately became an active member of the Zionist Socialist Party. He joined the Rakishoker Society and, to this day, is its secretary.

Arya Eidlman is also active in the local Zionist institutions and also has been the secretary of the *kehile* in Mayfair, a suburb of Johannesburg.

Moshe Arlin

He was born in a *shtetele* near Vilkomir [Ukmerge]. His parents lived in Vilkomir during the German occupation during the First World War.

He, Moshe Arlin, studied in the Jewish Viklomir Real *Gymnazie* [secondary school] after the war and was active in *Makkabi* [international Jewish sports organization] and in other Jewish organizations.

He emigrated to South Africa in 1930. He joined the Rakishoker Society with his wife, Teyba Kyl-Arlin.

Moshe Arlin is an esteemed member of the Rakishoker Society.

Teyba Kyl-Arlin

Teyba Kyl-Arlin was a student of the German Compulsory School during the First World War. Then she studied in the *Tarbut* [secular, Hebrew language] school in Rakishok and in Kovno Hebrew Real *Gymnazie*. She was popular with the Rakishok young people who, in the 1920s, were seized by new ideas and by the national revival of the Jewish people.

[Page 488]

The national-Zionist young in Rakishok helped to create institutions such as the orphans house, the *Linet haTzedek* [society for visiting the sick] and the Hebrew school systems, *Tarbut* and *Yavne* [religious Zionist], the *Makkabi*, *HaHalutz* and the *Hashomer Hatzair* [The Youth Guard – Socialist-Zionists]. Teyba was very active in these institutions. She also was an active member of *Hashomer Hatzair*. Thanks to her talent, she took part in various spectacles and theatrical presentations.

In 1928 she left for South Africa and the young people of Rakishok considered her departure a great loss.

In South Africa she also was active in communal activities both in the Zionist Socialist Party and in *Histradrut Ivrit* [organization spreading the use of the Hebrew language]. She also helped with all Zionist campaigns.

Teyba Kyl-Arlin was active in the Rakishoker Society and helped the Aid Society in its work.

Yitzhak-Zorekh Beinart

He was born in 1981 [a typographical error – 1891]. When he was 10 years old, his parents – Moshe Feybish and Chava-Chaya – moved to Rakishok. At that time, they sent Yitzhak-Zorekh away to study at *OZE* [Jewish Health Society] in Kruk to his grandfather, who was a *shoykhet* [ritual slaughterer] there. There he studied a trade.

He escaped to South Africa from the Russian military draft in 1902. He worked at his trade in Cape Town during the first years and then he came to Johannesburg.

He was one of the first 12 *landsleit* who founded the Rakishok Society in 1912.

However, he was drawn home and in 1913 he came to Rakishok. He married there and when the war broke out, he and his wife evacuated deep into Russia.

In 1927 he again emigrated to South Africa. He was heartily welcomed by the Society and he was helped within the framework of its abilities so that he could establish himself financially.

Nakhum Blacher

He was born in Svadushch [Svedasai] in 1899 and, because his father, Aba, was burdened with many children, his grandmother in Dusiat raised him for a time.

He was separated from his parents at the beginning of 1915, during the expulsion from the cities and *shtetlekh* in Lithuania he traveled to Sventzion [Svencionys].

[Page 490]

After the war, in 1919, he wandered from one *shtetl* to another and, because he did not report for military service on time, he was sent away to a punishment battalion.

In 1936 he emigrated to Mexico and Cuba. From Cuba he emigrated as a sailor to France, where he remained for three years. He came from Paris to Rakishok and, after marrying Rywka Itsikman, they emigrated to South Africa, going through all of the phases of recent immigrants.

He has been an active member of the Rakishoker Society for many years.

Chaim Shual (Zev) Bacher

He was the son of Yitzhak (Alter) and Chaya-Sura-Ita Bacher. He followed in the steps of his parents, who gave him a traditional religious upbringing from childhood on and when he came to South Africa he kept to his beliefs and his views. He was and remained pious to God and honest to people.

Even the scope of his large businesses did not change a hair of his folksy, Jewish style and manner.

His businesses were closed on *Shabbos* [Sabbath] and holidays and he observed *Shabbos* and the holidays as in his old home.

He was known as a philanthropist, [giving] to all appeals and calls from various initiatives and distinguished himself with his anonymous help. There are many people who do not know that he helped them. He gave generously for the *yeshivus* [religious secondary schools] in Jerusalem, and was one of the pillars of the Johannesburg Chabad.

Chain Shual (Zev) Bacher joined many societies that he supported. He also supported the undertakings of our Rakishoker Society.

His farm near Germiston was the local place for *hakshora* [agricultural training for those hoping to emigrate to *Eretz-Yisroel*] of *Habonim* [Labor Zionist youth movement].

Kopl Bacher

Kopl Bacher, the brother of Chaim-Shual (Zev) Bacher, also served communally. He was the co-founder of the *Magen David Adom* [Red Shield of David – an emergency medical service] in South Africa and took part with activism and with financial help on behalf of the communal and Zionist funds.

The exercises of the South Africa *Haganah* [The Defense – paramilitary organization] took place on his farm.

The Rakishoker Society and other Jewish organizations would arrange cultural presentations and various undertakings on his farm. The institutions had the servants and goods at hand on the farm at their disposal without cost.

He is a devoted friend and member of the Rakishoker Society.

[Page 492]

Yitzhak Ginzburg

He was born in Rakishok in 1909. His grandfather, Artshik Ginzburg, was one of the fervid Hasidim in the city.

During the First World War, his father, Yosef–Rafal, evacuated to Melitopol, Russia, with his family and the family returned to Rakishok in 1919.

Yitzhak studied for several terms with Leib the *malamed* [religious teacher] and when the Rakishok *Talmud–Torah* [religious primary school for poor boys] opened, he studied at the *Talmud–Torah* and then in the Rakishok *yeshiva* [religious secondary school] and also was a student at the Slabodker *yeshiva* for a time.

The new times influenced Yitzhak Ginzburg. He came back to Rakishok and helped to found the youth organization named *Tiferet Bukherim* [Magnificent Young Men] at the *Agudah* [Orthodox political party]. Then he became a member of *Makkabi* [international Jewish sports association] and was also a co–founder of *HaNoar HaTzioni* [the Zionist Youth]. He was secretary of the Rakishok *Makkabi* for a time. He entered *Hahistadrut* and helped found *Al HaMishmar* [On Guard].

He emigrated to South Africa in 1936. He settled in Koppies where he founded a Zionist organization, serving as its vice chairman. From Koppies he moved to Vereeniging. He founded *Habonim* [the Builders] there.

Yitzhak Ginzburg settled in Johannesburg in 1930 and immediately became an active member of *Hitachdut* [Zionist–Socialists] and he helped carry out the unification of the Zionist Socialists with *Hitachdut*. He was a member of the central committee of the united party until 1948.

He also was one of the founders of the Rakishok Aid Society, serving as the president for many years. He was elected to the managing committee after the unification of the Rakishok Aid Society and the Rakishok Society and is a committee member for the Rakishok Society to this day.

Mota Gut

He was born in Dvinsk. He was evacuated to Russia during the First World War.

He came to Rakishok from distant Russia (Vologda) in 1919. He became the representative of the artisans on the council of the People's Bank, helped found the loan fund of the Artisans Union and was its treasurer until his departure from Rakishok.

He came to South Africa in 1928. He became the treasurer of the *Knesset Yisroel gmiles khesed* [the Jewish community interest–free loan]. He is now the life long president of this institution.

[Page 493]

Dovid Dektar

Dovid Dektar was an esteemed communal worker in Capetown. He was one of the initiators who, in 1944, organized an aid activity on behalf of Rakishok.

On the 3rd of December 1944, an initiating group was created that began to organize aid work. This group, which consisted of Dovid Dektar, Nakhum Sulkes–Kopelovitz and Mrs. Sheyna Davidovitz, called a meeting of Rakishok *landsleit*. Present at this meeting that took place in the Zionist Hall were 32 people who notably taxed themselves on behalf of Rakishok, knowing that if the war ended they would need to rebuild the Jewish community in Rakishok. No one yet imagined the size and cruelty of the destruction.

A short time later, when the scope of the national catastrophe became known, the collected money was utilized for help for the surviving Rakishok Jews.

The elected committee, under the chairmanship of Mr. Rabkin, was very active.

Dovid Dekter made a great contribution to this active work.

Avraham Levin

He was born in Rakishok in 1906. He studied in a kheder until the First World War. His father, Yona Levin, and his wife and children evacuated to Peski, Voronezh *Gubernia* [province] during the First Work War. There he attended a Russian school.

In 1918, the Levin family returned to Rakishok. They were the first refugees who returned from Russia, while the Germans were still in the shtetl.

Avraham Levin then studied in *khederim* of Chaim Eli the *melamed* and with Benish the *shoykhet*. Then he entered his father's businesses. He joined the Zionist youth at the same time. When the Zionist Socialist party was founded, he was one of its first comrades.

He emigrated to South Africa in 1925. He also signed up here [to work] for the Zionist ideal. He supports all Zionist campaigns and all Jewish institutions.

After the great tragedy for [our people] he joined the Rakishok *landsmanschaft* and was chosen as a member of the managing committee.

He is a devoted brother of the Rakishok Society.

[Page 494]

Mendl Moskat

He was born in 1898 in Halubets, Vilna *gubernia* [county]. He was orphaned when he was a few years old. He studied for several years in a *kheder* and thanks to his older brother he learned the tailor's trade.

The First World War broke out and then the revolution in Russia. He became swayed by the idea of equality and freedom, actively fighting against the White soldiers who wanted to restore the Czarist government.

In 1922 he came to Rakishok with his wife, Alta Cherelovitz, not having the right of residence in Lithuania.

The situation of a "foreigner" was then difficult, under the threat of being deported. Yet Mendl Moskat worked with great devotion in the Culture League and in the Rakishok Artisans' Union.

He emigrated to South Africa in 1926. He immediately became a member of the Rakishok *landsmanschaft*. Thanks to his activity he was chosen for the managing committee and also as its chairman. The *landsmanschaft* delegated him to the *Bikor Kholim* [organization for visiting the sick] and he often visits the sick in the hospital to this day.

He also helped found the Aid Society.

After this, when Khone Kohen, the long time chairman of the *landsmanschaft* resigned from the chairmanship, Mendl Moskat was the chairman for many years. Mendl has been treasurer of the society for many years.

Mendl Moskat is one of the most meritorious workers for the Rakishok *landsmanschaft*.

Yisroel Meikl–Mikhalevitz

He was born in Abel [Obeliai] in 1900. His Abel *melamdim* [religious school teachers] were Itse the hunchback and Aba the *melamed*, who strongly respected his learning abilities. His father, Mikhal Welwe, sent him to Vilna to the *yeshiva* [religious secondary school]. He left for Vilna and studied for three years in the *yeshiva*, which was located in Ramayles' synagogue.

In 1913 he left for Petersburg with his relative, Bertsik Shwarts. He threw away his studies and learned tailoring. He lived in Petersburg illegally and in 1915 he returned to Abel.

Shortly after his coming to Abel, the Germans occupied Lithuania. The Germans took him for heavy forced labor. He tried to escape from the German labor camp where he was captured and sent to a concentration camp. He finally escaped again from the Germans.

The Bolsheviks arrived after this, when the Germans left Lithuania. Then the Lithuanian Republic arose.

Yisroel Meikl–Mikhalevitz began to be interested in cultural communal work. He helped to create a dramatic circle in Abel and thanks to his beautiful voice he became one of the most successful amateurs in the ensemble.

[Page 495]

(Photos already included in past four pages)

[Page 496]

He and his wife emigrated to South Africa in 1927. He became a member of the Rakishok Society. For many years, he also was a member of *ORT–OZE.**

*[Translator's note: *ORT – Obshestvo Remeslenofo zemledelcheskofo Truda* – in Russian – is the Society for Trades and Agricultural Labor. *OZE – Obshchestvo okhraneniia zdorov'ia evreiskogo naseleniia* – in Russian – is the Society for the Protection of the Health of the Jewish Population.]

He participated often in concerts and undertakings of the Society and of other institutions.

He is an active member of the *landsmanschaft*.

A. Nach–Nochumovitz

He has been a member of the Rakishok Society since his arrival in South Africa in 1927.

He is also a representative of the Rakishok *landsmanschaft* on the Board of Deputies.

He is also one of the initiators who significantly worked to publish this yizkor book.

Ahron (Arke) Meitovitz

He was born in 1906 in Alukste, Courland [Ilutkste, Latvia]. His father, Shmerl Meitovitz, came from Varescine, a village near Rakishok. His father was sick and paralyzed for many years. The children had to help their mother to earn their means of support. Arke, too, while still very young, felt the yoke of life.

During the First World War, the Meitovitz family evacuated to Russia, to Balande and they returned to Lithuania, to Rakishok, in 1919. He studied to be a hairdresser in Rakishok and became active in communal life.

He emigrated to South Africa in 1929. In 1933, he joined the Rakishok Society in which he has been active the entire time. He also was a member of the managing committee of the Society for several years.

Sara Klass–Spivak

When we speak about the Rakishok Aid Society and its accomplishments we must remember Sara Klass who was the most active volunteer, corresponded with dozens of *landsleit*. She was among the founders of the Aid Society.

She was born in Rakishok in 1905 and lived in poverty from her earliest youth. Her mother was a widow and could not give her an education. She wanted to enter the Russian government school, but because of the financial allocations she was not accepted. She studied with Chaim Motien Panevez who was a modern teacher, studying Russian, Yiddish as well as Hebrew.

[Page 497]

(Photos already included in past four pages)

[Page 498]

The World War broke out and the Klass family evacuated to Borisoglebsk, Tambov *gubernia*. There, she attended the Jewish school of the OPE Society (Society to Provide Schooling). However, she was forced to interrupt her studies because she had to help her mother. She went to work and simultaneously studied at evening courses. She and her brother, Shmuel, who studied astronomy, supported the family.

In 1919 the family returned to Rakishok. She helped to found the Culture League and taught Yiddish to poor girls. She also was the letter-writer to friends in Africa. She actively took part in the journal, *Funken* [*Sparks*], a publication of the Culture League and was on the council of the Jewish *Folkshul* [people's school].

Sara Klass came to Africa in 1933. She has helped the Johannesburg Jewish *Folkshul* and is a member of its parents' council. During the last World War, she aided the campaigns for medical help for Russia.

She has been a member of the Rakishok Society for many years. She is a member of the managing committee.

Nakhum-Leib Kopelovitz (Sulkas)

He was born in Rakishok in 1906 and he was the oldest son of his parents, who gave him and his brother a traditional Jewish upbringing.

His father, Nakhman, was mobilized into the Czarist army during the First World War and his mother and their four children evacuated to Staraya-Russa, Novgorod *gubernia* and from there traveled to Petersburg (Leningrad).

He entered a *remesliene utshilishtshe* [craftsmen academy] in Petersburg where he acquired the trades of an electrical worker and a switchboard operator. At that time few Jews were interested in these trades. Graduating from this school, he left to work as a telephonist [operator of switchboard] at the telephone stations in Petersburg and Staraya-Russa. He became the only one to provide food for his household because his father was wounded on the battlefield in the Carpathian Mountains and lay for more than three years in a quarantine station, emerging a weak and sick man.

In 1933 the family returned to Rakishok from its evacuation.

Nachum-Leib Kopelowitz with his parents and brothers when they were in Russia, during the First World War.

Nakhum–Leib entered the Zionist Socialist Party and *Makkabi* [Jewish sports organization], showing active [participation] in these organizations and helping all Zionist undertakings. He was chosen for the managing committees of the Zionist Socialists and *Makkabi* and was trusted.

He was one of the first electrical–technicians in Rakishok and was an electrical–mechanic in the Rakishok movie theater.

[Page 499]

He emigrated to *Eretz–Yisroel* in 1929 where he at first worked at the telephone stations in Yaffa and in Tel Aviv and then he worked with Ahron Nach–Nochumovitz at the building.

Because the economic situation for his parents in Rakishok grew worse from day to day, he decided to emigrate to South Africa. He settled in Capetown where he was employed by a mobile movie theater over the course of three years.

In 1939 he established a movie theater for blacks and coloreds in Worcester. The giant undertaking was crowned with financial success that inspired him to open two more movie theaters for whites. In the course of time he reached an important financial position.

However, he remained the same simple and goodhearted Nakhum–Leib. He helps all of the cultural–social campaigns and appeals on behalf of Israel with even larger sums. He also actively took part in the aid work on behalf of the Rakishok *landsleit* who survived the great catastrophe for our people.

Moshe Klavir

He was born in Abel in 1905. His father, Zelig Dovid, was employed in trade and his mother, Eida, also understood how to conduct trade.

After the war he was called to military service in the Lithuanian army. Returning from the military, he entered the Abel Culture League. Then he helped to found the *Tzeiri–Zion* [Young Men of Zion] party, in which he was very active. He founded the Abel library and helped to organize lectures and reports. He also helped to create a dramatic section, which presented many productions, and he is also one of the best amateur actors.

Moshe Klavir also founded the first *haHalutz* [pioneer] group in Abel, being its chairman and also went to Kovno and Shavl for *hakhshara* [Zionist youth movement preparing members for emigration to *Eretz–Yisroel*].

He came to South Africa in 1928. He joined the Rakishok *landsmanschaft*. He was chosen for the managing committee many times and is an active and respected managing committee member.

[Page 500]

Kheikl Rubin

He was born in Rakishok in 1899. He studied in Abel with Aba the *Melamed* until his *Bar–Mitzvah*.

He went to Walk [Valga] (Estonia) with his parents during the First World War. He returned to Rakishok with his parents in 1918.

He emigrated to South Africa in 1929. He joined the Rakishok Society and became a member of the *Beis haMedrash d'Hasidim* [Hasidic House of Prayer] in Johannesburg.

It is already 20 years that Kheikl Rubin has been a member of the Society and he is always ready to do the most difficult work. He also is active in the Hasidic house of prayer with great dedication.

He is one of the rare perfect Jews who are here in South Africa. He observes Shabbos [the Sabbath] and the holidays as in the old home. He is a typical *tilim Yid* [Psalm Jew – one who recites Psalms] who observes all of the Jewish traditions and provisions.

Shlomo Rubin

He was born in Rakishok in 1894. He showed communal initiative at an early age. He founded the first Jewish library in Rakishok and played in and also directed various plays in the Yiddish language.

In 1926 he emigrated to South Africa. From the first day, even here on African soil, he showed his interest in communal work and performed with the Jewish theater ensemble in Capetown.

He became active in the Literary Union in Johannesburg and was the secretary of the Union and the library.

He acted in and directed plays in Johannesburg and he arranged many artistic undertakings on behalf of the Rakishok Society in which he has been a committee member since his arrival in the country. Today he is an honorary secretary of the *landsmanschaft*, one of the initiators who actively helped to publish the Yizkor Book.

He was delegated by the Society to the Board of Deputies and to this day he represents the Rakishok *landsmanschaft* on the managing committee of the Jewish *Folkshul* in Johannesburg.

He is a real and devoted man of the people, who deeply loves the Yiddish folk language and literature and is a devoted brother of the Society in word and deed.

[Page 501]

(Photos already included in past four pages)

[Page 502]

Genya Rubin

She was born in Kremenets, Wolyn, lived in Melitopol, Russia. She had a strong drive to perform in Yiddish theater.

She played her first role in 1918 in *Dovid's Firele* [*David's Wagon*]. She performed in a responsible role in Jakob Gordon's *Got, Mentsh un Tayvl* [*God, Man and Devil*] under the direction of the famous director and artist, Sokolow.

She came to Rakishok with her husband, Shlomo Rubin, and there produced *Di Brenendike Hoyz* [*The Burning House*].

She came to Africa in 1927. She acted with great success in the ensembles of [Yankev] Waislitz, Natan, Sarah Sylvia, Runitsh, Breitman, Niusia Gold, F. Zigelbaum.

Her love of Yiddish theater is great. And to this day she takes part in producing and appears with recitations at various small art evenings.

She greatly helps the Rakishok *landsmanschaft* in its cultural presentations.

Berl Ruch

He was born 1919 in a small village, Kurkletz, near Rakishok. His father Pesakh Ruch and his family moved to Rakishok at the time of the First World War.

Pesakh Ruch, an ardent Hasid and deeply religious man, raised all of his children in the religious spirit, including his son Berl, who went to *kheder* and to the *Talmud–Torah* and later studied for a time in the *yeshiva* with Reb Moshe Sidrin.

However, the new, modern ideas also penetrated the house of Pesakh Ruch. Berl left the *yeshiva* and became a student of the *Pre–Gymnazie* [preparatory school], *Yavneh*. He was an active member of the dramatic circle for a time.

The circumstances then of the Jews in Lithuania led to worry about the future, about a purpose and many young people began to learn a trade. Berl studied photography and, at the beginning of 1929, he emigrated to South Africa. He helped the Chabad [Lubavitch Hasidic] movement financially. He also helped the Yonishkel [Joniškėlis] Rabbi, Reb Yosef Sidrin, when he came to collect money for the Rakishok Yeshiva [religious secondary school].

At the same time, he was a Zionist and he was devoted to the Zionist movement heart and soul. He also was one of those who helped found the Rakishok Aid Society in Johannesburg and was its treasurer.

When the two societies merged – the Rakishok *Landsmanschaft* and the Rakishok Aid Society – he was chosen as and is to this day the vice chairman of the Rakishok *Landsmanschaft*.

[Page 503]

Liba Ruch

She was born in 1921 in Panevezys and, as a young person emigrated with her parents to South Africa, who settled in Muizenberg. Although she studied in the English schools, she still speaks Yiddish and is close to Jewish organizations, giving her help and contributions.

After her marriage to Berl Ruch, she became a devoted member of the Rakishok *Landsmanschaft*: helps to organize events, to send packages for *landsleit* and to gather funds.

She was chosen as a committee member of the Rakishok *Landsmanschaft* because of her activity.

Moshe Yisroel Sharf–Saltuper

He was born in Novo Alexandrovsk–Ezsherene in 1906. His father, Yerakhmiel, was an invalid without legs and his mother, Pesya–Malya, provided the income for her husband and children. The small Moshke, while still young, harnessed himself in the yoke of labor to make it easier for his parents.

His entire family evacuated to Saranks, Penza *Gubernia* [county] during the First World War. His mother was ill because of an accident. They returned to Novo Alexandrovsk in 1922.

Moshe became a peddler because of the bad economic situation in the home. He attempted to escape to Russia, but he was arrested in Latvia, sent back to Novo Alexandrovsk.

He then went to Kovno [Kaunas] where he studied tailoring. He also was active in the local "culture league," becoming an underground worker. He took an active part in YAK (Jewish Workers Club).

He emigrated to South Africa in 1926. After several difficult years as a *grinem* [one newly arrived], he succeeded in working himself up and is now the owner of an industrial enterprise.

He was active simultaneously in communal areas. He is an active member of the Mayfair Congregation and was its representative to the Board of Deputies. He was also a member and honorary treasurer of the interest loan fund in Mayfair–Fordsburg.

He also is an active member of the Rakishok *Landsmanschaft*, member of the managing committee and is also its vice chairman.

He helps with assessments on behalf of the local Jewish institutions and on behalf of various campaigns.

[Page 504]

(Photos already included in past four pages)

[Page 505]

Hirshl Sher

He was born in Antalept [Antalieptė]. Until his *Bar–Mitzvah*, he studied with Dowid Hirsh the *malamed*. When the First World War broke out, his entire family continued to live under the German occupation. Hirshl then learned a trade. He also was involved with smuggling goods. When the German occupation regime issued a decree that they must have licenses, Hirshl was delegated to go to Rakishok to purchase licenses for the traders in the *shtetl*.

This was his first communal mission that stimulated him to carry out activity in other communal areas, too.

He came to South Africa in 1927. He became an active member of the Rakishok Society. He is a member of the managing committee and also is the vice chairman of the Rakishok *Landsmanschaft*. He is also a member of the interest free loan fund of Bertrams.

[Page 506]

B. Aid Society

The Rakishok Aid Society in Johannesburg is an interesting and important chapter in itself and arose after the Rakishok *Landsmanschaft* in South Africa already had existed for 20 some years.

At first glance, we can examine the essential emergence of a separate aid society at the time when the Rakishok *Landsmanschaft* could fill the same functions, but when we comprehensively analyze the situation at that time, the economic and the political situation of the Jews of Europe, [the reason for] the rise of such an autonomous society that was founded a few years before the Second World War becomes understandable to us.

A depression had reigned over the world since 1932 and the fear of a second world war was very clear, primarily in Europe.

Letters often were received from Rakishok and from its surroundings, as well as from many other places in Lithuania and Poland, in which a fear of a second world war was expressed, emphasizing the growing social needs, the severe poverty of individuals and the financial crisis in the various institutions.

A special representative, the Joniskiai Rabbi, Reb Josef Sidrin from the Rakishok *yeshiva* [religious secondary school) came to Johannesburg, to South Africa in 1937 to collect money and he gave information about the bad situation in the Lithuanian towns. A committee was created then of the people: Mendl Muskat, Berl Ruch, Chaim–Moshe Gen, Shlomo Sher, Yitzhak Gruz, Shmerl Loubovitz and Sh. Rubin, which assisted him in his mission.

After his return home, various individuals and institutions in Rakishok and its surroundings appealed for support.

At first, individuals responded to the appeal, who themselves sent money to poor relatives and acquaintances and also to institutions. Thanks to the initiative of M. Muskat, a sum of money also was then collected for the Rakishok Culture League.

However, this was sporadic help and not significant.

It was necessary that the aid work be led by an organized body.

The Rakishok *Landsmanschaft*, in accordance with its constitution that was created during its first years, carried out its activities within the framework of local aid among the local *landsleit* and its main purpose was to distribute loans and give medical help to its members.

It should also be emphasized that there was a financial crisis in South Africa before the Second World War and the money reserves of the Society were very limited. This question always was on the agenda of the *Landsmanschaft* executive:

[Page 507]

how do we help the needy members who mostly belong to the poorest stratum of the local Jewish population? The richer *landsleit* rarely were Society members, believing that a society is an old–fashioned institution that they would not join.

For the reasons and facts mentioned above, the idea was born among several *landsleit* to found a special Aid Society.

This group of initiators – Avraham Orelovitz, Yitzhak Ginzburg, Mrs. Furman, Mendl Muskat, Mrs. Klein, Josl Kuperman, Mendl Vitz, may he rest in peace, M. Gut, Yitzhak Grin, Chaim–Moishe Gen, Shlomo Rubin, Berl Ruch, Shlomo Sher, Mrs. Shneider – had earlier distinguished itself and thanks to them the Aid Society was created that took on as its purpose the sending of financial help to the poor *landsleit* and institutions in the old home.

Josl Kuperman (chairman), Mendl Muskat (treasurer), Avraham Orelovitz (secretary), Yitzhak Ginzburg and Shlomo Rubin belonged to the presidium of the Aid Society.

An appeal to all *landsleit* in South Africa to contribute to the Aid Society was published.

A meeting was called at the end of 1937 at the Jewish Guild, Johannesburg. Among other things it was decided at this meeting to incorporate more women into the committee who would help organize various undertakings.

Entertainments were arranged often that brought in large sums of money to the treasury of the newly founded Society. At that time, if an entertainment provided income of several hundred pounds, it was a large sum considering that the pound was [equal to] 30 litai.

Mota Gut, the Mrs. Klein, Furman and Shneider, the Ruch family and Teyba Orlin–Kil demonstrated special activity in the work of the Society.

After the resignation of Josl Kuperman, the Aid Society was led by Yitzhak Ginzburg who became its chairman. The work intensified and many *landsleit* also took on obligations to pay regular monthly dues to be used by the Aid Society.

The financial help sent to the old home enabled the poor people to buy matzoh for Passover, buy wood for the winter and other necessities.

However, the Second World War broke out and, later, the Soviet–German War. Every contact with the old home was broken off from July 1941.

The Aid Society searched every path and byway to make contact with Rakishok and its surroundings, but all efforts were [unsuccessful]. Actually, there was then no one with whom to connect because the cruel Hitlerists had slaughtered [the residents of] Rakishok and its surroundings along with the great majority of Jewish *shtetlekh* in Lithuania during the first days of the occupation.

[Page 508]

Gathering of members of the Rokiskis Aid Society – Top row – right to left (standing) Mr. Pasvalski; Mrs. Pasvalski (Berkowitz); Mrs. Mervitch (Berkowitz); Mr. Mervitch; Shmerl Lubowitz. Second row – right to left (standing): Berl Ruch; unknown; Shlomoh Sher; Furman; Mendel Muskat. Third row – right to left: Heikl Rubin; Moishe Smit; Miss Muskat; Mrs. Furman; Mrs. Muskat; Mrs. Klein, Mrs. Shneider. Fourth row – Gordon; Shlomo Rubin and Yitzhak Ginzburg.

There was a sum of 100 pounds in the treasury of the Aid Society, which we supplied – as a deposit – to the treasury of the Rakishok *Landsmanschaft*, planning for the renewed activity ahead when the war would end, not anticipating that the Hitlerists had carried out the total slaughter of the Jews.

Various rumors reached us about German cruelty and also about the extermination of the Jews in Europe during the World War, but no one could believe that such slaughter could take place in our century. Others surmised that it was just gossip and not real facts. The human brain could not comprehend that such murders, mass exterminations of the Jews could occur and if it had happened, then it was nothing but the end of the world.

[Page 509]

A consultation was called to consider how we could learn the actual fate of our brothers and sisters. It was decided to send a letter to Kuibyshev, seat of the Moscow government at the time of the war, to obtain certain information.

It was also decided at the consultation to create a fund to be able to immediately help the surviving Jews when the storm of war had passed.

Everyone present at the consultation taxed themselves for a significant sum, underscoring that as soon as the first sad news came across the sea, everyone was ready to triple the sum they had given.

In 1944 the cruel truth already was known to us about the Jews in Europe and in all of the places occupied by the Germans. The radio announced that Kovno was freed from the Germans. Yitzhak Ginzburg, chairman of the Society, telegraphed the Anti–Fascist Committee in Moscow asking that it be announced in the local Jewish newspaper there, *Di Einikeyt* [*The Unity*] that if a *landsleit* had successfully escaped from the claws of death, he should contact the Rakishok Aid Committee. We also turned to the chairman of the Rakishok *Gorsoviet* (city council).

The first letter from the surviving *landsleit* arrived in 1945 in which the details and course of the slaughter were described and also that, alas, there were no longer any Jews in Rakishok because even those who did survive did not want to live in their ruined homes and would rather settle in Vilna, Kovno and in other cities.

Letters then arrived from the *landsleit* who were freed from the various concentration camps.

The secretarial work of the Aid Society from 1945 until its integration into the Rakishok *Landsmanschaft* was carried out by Yerakhmiel Arons (Arsh), who with his wife, Etl, took upon themselves the work of finding out the

Rokiskis Yizkor Book 539

residences of all surviving *landsleit* and to accomplish this they corresponded with various people in South Africa, Russia, Lithuania, Poland and with the refugee camps in Germany, Austria and Italy.

With great difficulty there was success in establishing the following names and addresses of 100 surviving *landsleit*, who were then in various places and nations:

Arsh, Melekh, lost his wife and children. Married in Vilna.
Arsh, Dr. Avraham and his wife Dr. Chaya Arsh and their two children, in Vilna.
Arsh, Dowid, with his wife and child (now in Israel).
Orelovitz, Zorekh, in Rakishok.
Abramovitz, Chaya Rywka, in Russia.
Abramovitz, Rywka, in Lithuania.

[Page 510]

Abramovitz, Hirshke, in Lithuania.
Baradovsky, Liba, in Givat Brener, Israel.
Baradovsky, Kh and wife, in Rakishok.
Bun, Etl (Yudl Kalman's daughter) in Lithuania.
Brinkman B., in Vilna.
A son of Shimshon Baradovsky, the rope maker, now in Lithuania.
Brik, Liba–Leah (née Meirovitz), in Israel.
Berz, S. (a grandson of Yisroel Yudl's), in Vilna.
Ginzburg, Avraham, in Murmansk, Russia.
Gelcer, Chaim, and his wife and son; his wife and son are now in Brazil and he is in Belgium.
Griz, Dwoyra (Shusiena), in Italy.
Gar, Ruchl (née Shpir), now in America.
German, Sonia, now in Israel.
Gafanovitz, Dwoyra (a daughter of Mendl the fisherman), in Lithuania.
Gordon, Elkhonen, in Riga.
Dulan, Shual Netska, from Radute (a grandson of Itshe Dulan), in Lithuania.
Two Dectar sisters, Yudl the miller's daughters, in Vilna.
Herckovitz, Dwoyra (née Ratner) and her husband, in Italy.
Weiner, Ida, in Russia.
Weiner, Y., (Mikhal's daughter), in Vilna.
Zakstein, Yehudas (daughter of Zalman Zakstein), in Vilna.
Zalcman, Avraham (Yakha Poplak's husband), in deep Russia.

Zager, Ruchl (Ruzner). (Now in Israel).
Chit, Avraham (Zorekh Meirim's nephew), in Lithuania.
Charit, Sara (née Griz), in Vilna.
Charmatz, Josef. (Now in Israel).
Charmatz, Dwoyra, now in Israel.
Turik, Breyna and son (Dore Ber's daughter), in Lithuania.
Jacobson, Zlata (a daughter of Yankl Jacobson), in Lithuania.v Yafa, Ida
and Shimeon, in Lithuania.
Yafa, Aba, now in Israel.
Yafa, Hirshl, Ruchl and Gnendl, in Kovno.
Mera Ita Chonen (Herce Yafa's granddaughter) in Lithuania.
A son of Hirshl Jakubovitz, in Lithuania.
Jalavecki and three children, in Lithuania.
Levin, Gisa, now in South Africa.
Levin, Ahron, in Vilna.
Levinzon, Dusya (née Zamet), now in Israel.
Levin, Altka (Yona Levin's daughter), in Lithuania.
Levin, Hinda (Berl Levin's daughter), in Lithuania.
Levin, Fanya (Layzer Levin's wife), in deep Russia.
Mekler, Sara (Bayla Jante's daughter), in Lithuania.

[Page 511]

A daughter of Pesakh Milkin, in Lithuania.
Maran, Sheyna, in Lithuania.
Meirovitz, Josef, now in Brazil.
Meirovitz, Berl, in Lithuania.
Meirovitz, Ahrik, in Lithuania.
Meller, Yudl, his wife and son, in Vilna.
Neymark, Sima, from the Weingrin family, now in Israel.
Sarver, Zorekh and his wife, in Vilna.
Segal, Sara–Mera (a daughter of the *Boba* [grandmother] Mariasha], in
Lithuania.
Seitovitz, Welwe (Zundl Yante's son), in Lithuania.
Sgieg, Shmuel Aba, in Munich, Germany.
Seitovitz, Chaya Henya (a grandchild of Avraham Seitovitz), in
Lithuania.
Seitovitz, Ruchl Leah (Yante's grandchild), in Lithuania.
Spivak, Leib, now in Israel.
Flach, Dovid (Etl's son), now in America.
Ferias, Beyla (Shmuel Baradovsky's daughter), in Lithuania.
Fein, Etl, in Vilna.

Citisky, Reyza (a grandchild of Shmuel the fisherman), in Lithuania.
Cindel, Breyna Leah and her husband and child, in Panavezys.
Kark, Eide (Yankl Kark's daughter), with a child, in Vilna.
A daughter of Notl Kruk (Azinkaia), in Lithuania.
Kark, Meir and his wife and child, in Vilna.
Kanan, Meir (from the Epshtein family), with a sister and her husband and child, in Vilna.
Kark, Relia, in Kovno.
Two Kur brothers (Yankl Hirshl's sons), in Vilna.
Koplansky, L. (son of Mariashka Prade), in Lithuania.
Kur, M, in Rakishok.
Krok, Chaim, now in Israel.
Kolworia, Ruchl (née Meirovitz), now in Israel.
Kanan, Rywka (née Epshtein) with a sister and her husband and child, in Vilna.
Ripiena (Yankl Kur's daughter) and child in Vilna.
Ruch, Leiba, in Vilna.
Feyga, a daughter of Basl Rif, in Lithuania.
Two Ribak brothers (Bunia's sons), in Lithuania.
Rudik, Leah, Yankl Rudik's friend, in Lithuania.
Basia and Breyna Rif (Meir Rif's daughters), in Lithuania.
Rozenkovic, Rywka (daughter of Feytl Rozenkovic), in Lithuania.
Pesakh, Leyba and Basheve Ruch, in Siberia.
Ratman, Moshe, in Vilna.
Ruch, Yerakhmiel and his wife Henya and son, in Riga.
Shruchisky (Yisroel the shoemaker's [son]), in Lithuania.

[Page 512]

Shatz, Khona, in Italy.
Shukhet, Leah, in Italy.
Spak, Berl, in Kovno.
Shreiberg, Nusan (a son of the candlemaker), in Lithuania.
Shamer, Khvalya, in Vilna.
Shamer, Leah, in Vilna.
Shamer, Khesia (now in Israel).
Shamer, Shmuel Yona, in Vilna.
Shpir, Efroim (Chaya the furrier's son). (Now in Israel).
Shmushkovitz, Welwl and family, in Vilna.
Sheinke, from Rakishok orphanage, in Lithuania.
Shubel, Nakhum and wife and a daughter, in Rakishok.
Chana Perl (Zelig Pesakh's daughter), and her husband, in Lithuania.

Chana Perl, in Rakishok.
A daughter of Meir Prades–Shimelovitz, in Lithuania.
Two daughters of Shaya–Josia the wagon driver, in Lithuania.
Food parcels, underwear, bedding and various kinds of clothing were sent by the Aid Society to the addresses found at that time. We also sent money. Several dozen blankets were sent through a Swedish firm to Vilna. The capable women of our *Landsmanschaft* knitted sweaters that were sent to the *landsleit* at the first opportunity.

A committee of those from Rakishok also was created in *Eretz–Yisroel* that solicited help, wanting to create an aid–fund for the new Rakishok immigrants who entered illegally and also for the refugees in the refugee camps in Germany, Austria, Italy and Lithuania.

We publish the full text of this letter from Israel as a historical document without stylistic and orthographic changes.

Tel Aviv

Esteemed Friend!

It is superfluous to write to you about the misfortune that all of Jewry and Lithuanian Jewry encountered. I know with certainty that we were orphaned and lost all of our closest and dearest ones.

The war ended and little by little the picture became clearer of what had happened there in our old home and we also learned about the fate of Rakishok, our former shtetl. Few survived through various miracles and remain alive. A few already have come to us in *Eretz–Yisroel*.

They gave us the bitter greetings, described the embittered hearts and also spoke about those who still remain in Lithuania.

[Page 513]

Therefore, we, those from Rakishok who live in *Eretz–Yisroel*, decided to found a fund and collect money to help the several survivors. We collected 20 pounds on the spot and already have sent two parcels to Lithuania (one to Chana–Ela Kruk, the second to Yenta's grandchild). We also gave a loan to one of those arriving [here].

We hope that our work will expand with the help of the Rakishokers who live in Africa. We are certain that you will do everything possible for this purpose. This is the only thing we can do for our unfortunate brothers who have suffered so much.

We have elected a council of three people: Rywka Dektor, Chaya–Rayzl Ponevezh–Dobicky and Chaya–Hinda Snieg–Urmel to be responsible for the money that is received and we will send you an account of our work. We ask each of you to contribute as much as you can and also awake others to do even more.

We only have addresses for some individuals; we ask you to send us the addresses of those from Rakishok with whom you meet. We hope that you will not let the idea rest that those close to us and with whom we are acquainted are still suffering today, after all of the troubles that they bore and you will help them and do everything for them, as we are doing here.

With best wishes, Chaya Snieg–Urmel, Rywka Dektor, Chaya–Rayzl Ponevezh–Dobicky.

We ask you to send money to the bank in the name of the three people mentioned above to the following address:

Anglo–Palestine Bank Tel Aviv

Chaya Urmel, Ben Yehuda 49; Rywka Dektor, Hebron 5; Shoshona Dobicky Bar Kochba 19.

It was agreed to help everyone and for that we needed larger amounts of money.

A meeting of the Rakishok *landsleit* was called then, which took place in the Jewish Guild in Johannesburg on the 27th of November 1945.

The times and the conditions were favorable for a large money collection. The women were reinvigorated by the letters they had received and the economic situation of the Jews in South Africa after the war was very good. Everyone responded with generosity.

A committee was chosen at the meeting with the following composition: Yitzhak Ginzburg (chairman), Mendl Muskat (treasurer), Avraham Orelowicz (honorary secretary), Yerakhmiel Arons–Arsh, Mrs. Sura Klas (vice chairman), Sh. Lubovitz, Sh. Sher, M. Smit, M. Gut, Sh. Rubin, H. Levin.

The first committee meeting took place on the 30th of January 1946 in Mendl Muskat's house. Important decisions were made about how to increase the aid work as well as the decision to add the *landsleit* Shaul Bacher, Zerakh Kosef and Berl Stein to the committee.

[Page 514]

There was an intensive exchange of letters with *landsleit* everywhere and the Aid Society did not refuse help for anyone, although the financial means – because of the widespread activity – were very limited.

Sura Klas, the vice chairwoman, corresponded with almost every surviving *landsleit* and she encouraged them with letters. The women, Toyba Orlin, Etl Arons–Arsh, Liba Ruch, Alta Muskat and others, also were active with diligence, with great responsibility and dedication. It was through them that various money collections were often organized.

When food parcels or clothing could no longer be sent to Russia, we concentrated on helping the refugees in the camps and above all we sent larger sums of money to Israel.

After Yitzhak Ginsburg resigned, the above–mentioned activity of the Aid Society was carried out under the chairmanship of Motl Gut. Later, Moshe Sharp, was chosen as chairman [and he] resigned. Then Mendl Muskat was chosen as chairman.

However, it was a suitable time for the question of merging the activities of the Aid Society with the work of the Rakishok *Landsmanschaft*.

At the general meeting of the Rakishok *Landsmanschaft* that took place on the 7th of July 1948, Yerakhmiel Arons (Arsh) strongly defended the idea that both administrative bodies merge. He also argued for his proposal in the following way:

We have two Rakishok Societies and the same people actually are active in both institutions. This is simply comical and unnecessary. The above–mentioned administrative bodies need to merge and, perhaps, we will succeed in showing more constructive and more substantial deeds. It should be understood that it will be necessary to change and modify the constitution of the Landsmanschaft. There must also be a change so that women can also be full members of the society.

Yerakhmiel Arons' proposal to integrate the Aid Society into the Rakishok *Landsmanschaft* was accepted after a debate with the stipulation that a special fund to carry on activities overseas would be created in the Rakishok *Landsmanschaft*.

A new constitution was put together then and many points were modified, such as:

According to the previous constitution in accordance with the paragraph in point 2:

"The purpose of the Society shall be: to give such members who are in need a doctor and medicines without cost, all remaining claims and services of the doctor shall be given to the committee."

[Page 515]

This paragraph was modified in the following manner:

a) *Aid to all needy landsleit here and oversees.*

The new constitution was adopted with the following points:

New Statute

Point 1.

The name of the Society (Landsmanschaft) is: **Rakishok Sick Benefit and Loan Society** *(Medicine and Loan Society).*

Point 2.

Tasks:

a) Help for all needy landsleit here and overseas. b) Interest free loans to all members of the Society. c) Medical help to all Benefit members.

[Translator's note: points 3, 17, 23, 24, 26 and 29 do not contain a clause b.]

Point 3.

a) All requests and letters need to be handled by the committee of the Society that makes the appropriate decisions.

Point 4.

a) Each member of the Society is entitled to receive a loan. b) For every loan of a pound, the borrower will pay six pennies to the Society. c) A member can receive a loan of up to 100 pounds.* d) The loans must be [undersigned] in such a manner: two endorsers are necessary for loans up to 25 pounds; three endorsers – for up to 50 pounds and four endorsers for 100–150 pounds. e) A husband and wife are entitled to receive only one loan from the Society.

_____ * Recently it was decided that the size of the loans can reach 150 pounds.*

f) One person can endorse only three loans. g) The loan must be repaid during the course of a year, but the committee can extend it to 18 months.

Point 5.

a) The Society distributes medical aid, treatment from its doctors and prescriptions to all of its Benefit members **without payment**. b) The family members of the Benefit member can also receive medical aid, but they have to pay according to the discount price of the Society. c) The Society does not give any medical aid in cases where the illness of the Benefit member is long–standing, a chronic [illness]. The interested person, in exceptional cases, must turn to the committee, which will decide about further free treatment of the sick person.

Point 6.

All expenditures for the medical aid provided and for other needs will be covered by dues.

Point 7.

The surplus which remains after paying all debts will be transferred to the general fund of the Society.

Point 8.

The capital of the Society, with the exception of the special aid fund, can be utilized for giving loans and not for other purposes.

[Page 516]

Point 9.

The distribution of aid to the needy will be covered by a special aid fund.

Point 10.

Monies from special undertakings will be given for general capital or to the aid fund at the decision of the committee.

Point 11.

a) Men and women not younger than 18 can become members of the Society and have voting rights if they have paid their member dues. b) A man or a woman who marries a non–Jew or not according to the laws of Moses and Israel cannot be a member of the Society. c) A person must have the recommendation of two members to become a member of the Society.

Point 12.

a) Men and women from 18 to 45 can become Benefit members if they have previously been examined by the Society doctor who must certify that they are healthy. b) The entry fee for a new member is 10 shillings and six pennies. c) The committee has the right not to accept new members. d) New members cannot receive benefits during the first six months [of their membership].

Point 13.

a) A Benefit member pays a member's dues of 48 shillings a year in advance. b) The member dues for a non–Benefit member is 30 shillings a year that must also be paid in advance. c) Member dues for a woman is 12 shillings a year, paid in advance. d) A member who [has not paid] member dues for six months is not entitled to receive benefits from the Society.

Point 14.

a) The Society (Landsmanschaft) is led by a committee that is elected at a general meeting. b) The committee is chosen only once a year. c) Only at the general meeting of the Society can members decide: if the election should take place openly or in secret. d) The general meeting elects its representatives – to represent the Society – in other unions or societies and designates the honorary officials and the editors. e) The legally [required] number of members at a general meeting must be no less than 20 members. In cases where the above–mentioned number of members are not present, a second meeting will be called where the legally required number will be present.

Point 15.

a) The committee consists of a chairman, vice chairman, honorary secretary, treasurer, three [financial] trustees (audit commission) and seven committee members. b) The committee has the right to add new committee members when it is necessary. c) The committee has the right to hire a paid secretary or bookkeeper.

[Page 517]

d) One must be a member of the Society for six months before becoming a member of the committee. e) One must be a committee member for not less than six months before becoming chairman or vice chairman of the Society.

Point 16.

a) The chairman is responsible for implementing the decisions of the committee and of the general meetings and directs all of the work of the Society. b) The chairman leads the general meetings and committee sessions. c) The chairman has the right to demand that a member leave the committee session or the general meeting in cases of a breakdown of discipline. d) The chairman sets the agenda for the meetings and committee sessions. e) The chairman calls the committee session that must take place no less than once a month. f) The chairman calls a general membership meeting no less than every six months.

Point 17.

a) The task of the vice chairman is to work with the chairman and represent him in his absence, carrying out his duties.

Point 18.

a) The treasurer is called upon to collect the member dues and the payment of loans punctually. b) He must give a receipt for all money given to him. c) The treasurer must immediately deposit the money he receives in the bank and is responsible for having the books audited at the end of each year and also having them certified by the audit commission of the Society (auditors).

Point 19.

a) The secretary of the Society is responsible for all of the written and *organizational work of the Society. b) The secretary is authorized to see that the work of a paid secretary or bookkeeper shall be carried out accurately. c) If the paid secretary or bookkeeper is absent, it is the duty of the honorary secretary to temporarily carry on the work. The secretary is obligated to take exact and precise minutes that need to be certified by the Society chairman.*

Point 20.

a) The duties of the trustees (audit commission) – to work in accord with the interests of the Society. b) The trustees have the right to audit the books and accounts of the Society at all times. c) In case the members of the audit commission are not satisfied with the state of the books or they find certain irregularities, they have the right to demand a general meeting. d) Ten members also have the right to demand a general meeting and the chairman must recognize the demand.

[Page 518]

Point 21.

a) The committee members are obligated to come to all committee meetings, take part in all deliberations and meetings of the Society and help in a practical way to carry out all of the decisions taken. b) The committee has the right to exclude a committee member if he does not attend three committee meetings in sequence without an appropriate reason. c) All committee members are authorized to hold certain negotiations, conversations and discussions in secret at the meetings if it could blemish the prestige of the Society.

Point 22.

a) The honorary president of the Society is a full member of the Executive. b) The honorary president leads the meetings at the time of voting.

Point 23.

a) Every member is obligated to submit to the points of the statute.

Point 24.

a) In case of the resignation of a committee member, someone must be elected by the general meeting to take his place.

Point 25.

a) A member can be excluded from the Society for refusing to pay member dues. b) In case a member refuses to carry out the decisions of the general meeting or he causes malevolent harm to the Society, he will be excluded from the Society.

Point 26.

a) Every member can personally appeal a committee decision to the general meeting when he is dissatisfied [with the decision].

Point 27.

The exclusion of a member must be accepted at a general meeting of the Society.

Point 28.

a) Only the general meeting can remove or add points to the statute or change them. b) Every change in the statute must be added in writing.

Point 29.

a) The statute enters in force only when it is accepted by the committee with a majority vote and then is accepted at a general meeting.

Point 30.

An agenda must be created for each general meeting that must be sent to each member of the Society [before the meeting].

A new committee was chosen with the following composition: Yerakhmiel Arons–Arsh – chairman; Berl Ruch – vice chairman; Shlomo Rubin – secretary; Mendl Muskat – treasurer; Etl Arons–Arsh, Tayba Orlin, Avraham Orelovitz, Yitzhak Niznburg, Motl Gut, Avraham Levin, Ahron Noach–Noachumovitz, Ahron Seitovitz, Moshe Klavir, Sura Klas, Liba Ruch, Kheikl Rubin, Hirsh Sher.

[Page 519]

Aid has been sent to the *landsleit* in the name of the Rakishok *Landsmanschaft* since the founding of the Aid Society [as part of] the Rakishok *Landsmanschaft*.

The most important activities of the Aid Society are reflected in the letters received from the *landsleit*.

We publish a series [of letters here].

From a letter from Chaim Kruk, dated the 12th of July 1946, Tel Aviv:

"At the start I can inform you that my family and I are all healthy. I have received the 50 pounds from you for which I sincerely thank you. I have received a residence as well as a place to work. I also have procured a few tools and I am working a little. I have the opportunity to begin to build my new home. The money from you should not be considered a donation. I hope that I will have the possibility of giving it back."

A letter from the Rakishok Committee in Israel, dated the 18th of October 1946:

"It is again possible to send parcels to Russia and we again are sending parcels to Russia, but we do not know how to proceed further and we are giving the matter to you for a decision. The issue is as follows: we think that you [should] take over the work directly because we have heard that parcels also are being sent to Russia from Africa and that it is not worthwhile to incur any additional costs with you sending things to us. We will send you all of the addresses that we have and you can send your help [directly] based on your decision."

From a letter from Leibl Spivak, Petar Tikvah, dated the 17th of March 1946:

"I have already written one letter to you and now I will need to thank you again for the 200 pounds that you sent to me and I send you my blessing for the duty you have felt to your tortured brothers and also wish you success in your work, that more Jews will answer and you will be able to help them. I cannot express my thanks to you and describe how much I needed [the help]. I was despondent and without hope. You know how we looked coming naked and barefoot from the concentration camps."

Mera Segal, from Vilna, in a letter of the 25th of November 1948, lets be known:

"I received a parcel of fabric and lining for a coat from you on the 9th of November. My daughter and I thank you sincerely. We wish you much success in your work."

Yoba Zalcman writes the following (the letter is from Yakutsk, dated the 4th of January 1949):

"I can write to you that we received your parcel today for which we thank you all, all those from Rakishok, for the good work you do for we few surviving Jews. We ask that you not forget us [in the future]."

[Page 520]

Yehudis Zakstein, wrote on the 28 of September 1948:

"This is written by Yehudis Zakstein, who received a parcel from you. I thank you very much for your effort and dedication. This is a joy for me because I do not know you at all. My dear one, write to me and tell me who you are and what drove you to send me the parcel. Do you, perhaps, know me? I am still a young girl and you have been in Africa for a long time."

The Aid Society received many such letters during the first years after the war. *landsleit* did, too – as telegrams or through postcards – thanking the Aid Society.

Recently the work has been concentrated on helping the survivors and those *landsleit* who already are settled in Israel because all contact with Russia and the refugee camps in Germany, Austria and Italy has been terminated as we mentioned earlier.

The letters from the *landsleit* in Israel were written with great approval and with a tremendous amount of warm feelings. We provide only summaries from several letters:

"We have received the parcel of food a few weeks ago. This was so kind and it arrived just in time; there is no doubt that it was given by our own people [people from Rakishok]."

(Shulamit Sarber–Frydman in Tel Aviv)

"We were very delighted to receive your letter, as well as the parcel. We thank you very much. We are not lacking for anything here and need nothing. However, we were moved by the attention and more than anything that somewhere in the world there still exist a few Jews with Rakishok names. It is superfluous to record how cherished and dear this is for us. We received a breeze of warmth and home from the distant past from your letter."

(Chana and Mikhal Orelovitz, Tel Aviv)

"A great, great thank you in our name and in the name of our childhood names for your beautiful gifts, the parcels that you sent us. We are all surprised that we were remembered in friendship by people who all lived together in our Rakishok and your attention to us made a terrific impression."

Pinkhas Patz (Hadera)

"First I want to thank you for the food parcel that I have received. Gratitude is due to you not only for sending the parcel; there is a feeling of concern, of family and this is worth a great deal and, therefore, I thank you again."

Tsipora Ziglbaum (Kril), Tel Aviv

"I received your parcel for which I wish you much luck in your further work. At this time you will be happy to hear that I am one of those who, thanks to your parcels during wartime, did not die of hunger. The thousands of people who fell in the streets like flies from hunger, many of them our closest friends, today still appear before my eyes."

(Chana Orelovitz, Tel Aviv)

"Several days ago I received a parcel of food and a letter from you. I was moved by your attention. I live in a *kibbutz* and all of us in the *kibbutz* were provided with a life. And I ask you not to send anything more. I imagine that there are many in the country [Israel] for whom the parcels are truly important. However, I will be thankful if you will keep in further contact with letters. Everyone carries his childhood in his heart, his home and of course his *shtetl*; and even if his life is rich in experiences and events, childhood and youth are the dearest, most intimate and sacred parcel of memories that everyone protects so strongly.

[Page 521]

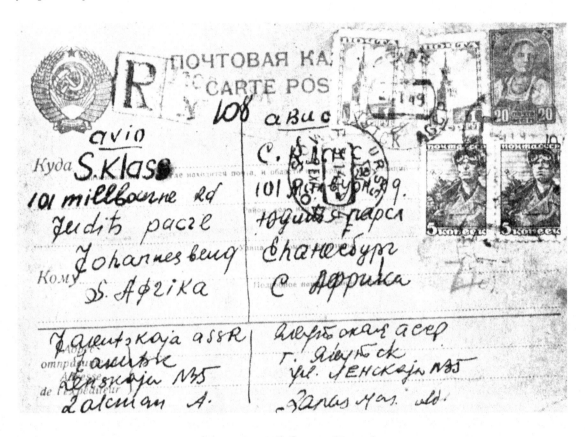

A postcard from Russia

A telegram from Russia

[Page 522]

(Nesya Urluvitz, Amir)

"I have received your extraordinarily good parcel for which I thank you very much. It was a splendid parcel. We wish you great success in your work."

(Darka Zelbovitz–Entin, Haifa)

"I can write to you that your parcel has been received. I send you my hearty thank you. We wonder greatly about how you knew my address. I really want to know who it is who is interested in us."

(Pesakh Inglin, Tel Aviv)

"This week I received a food parcel from the Rakishok Society. I do not know who the senders are. That they remembered me, it is enough that they are from Rakishok; they are our own, close, dear friends. I thank you very much for your friendship. The parcel is a very good one and very important for us but your friendship and dedication are more important than anything else to us. It is correct that we have left Lithuania with a curse on our lips because every stone there is covered with Jewish blood, with the blood of our parents, sisters and their children. However, I was born in Rakishok; my most beautiful childhood memories are connected with the accursed *shtetl*. And when I received your parcel – it suddenly awoke memories of my dear childhood years, [female] friends and [male] friends, school years. I went through the day as if in a dream. I would really like to know who you are, who did not forget your *landsleit* after so many years. Perhaps you were one of my girlfriends or boyfriends? Believe me that your friendly letter cheered me up no less than your parcel for which I thank you very much."

(Brik, Liba–Leah, Jerusalem)

"I send my lines to all of you from Israel with deep [friendship] and gratitude for the great consideration that you have shown me through your loving work. But it is not only the words (which are certainly beautiful and useful), but also the special feeling of belonging to a large family of people who hold you close. I can again only emphasize that the attention moved me greatly. With you are many people whom I knew well personally and several who were my good friends, but many I do not know personally – but we all have our roots in the Lithuanian shtetl named Rakishok. And each of has us dear ones and unforgettable ones who were left there – and this is a strong connection."

(Bluma–Lubia, Tel Aviv)

"First I want to thank you for your friendship; it is very pleasing to know that somewhere there are good friends and in addition the friendship is so real as is the respect [and it is accepted]. The second thank you is also really for the honor, as you refer to it. Everything was good and fine as from good friends who are close to them. It is a shame that you did not send us more details about your work and your activities.

[Page 523]

"Now about the addresses that you sent me to carry out a search and find. I have done everything possible and alas I have not heard from everyone because there are several here outside of Tel Aviv and I ceased [the search] there only after not yet receiving any answer. Therefore, I have decided to answer you with what I know and to send you the remaining in a second letter. Many addresses that you are unsure of actually are correct. I recorded everyone with certainty and I added several [city residents] who you did not include. Incidentally, where did you get all of the names and addresses? You truly are an address office!"

Chaya Urmel (Tel Aviv).

"The parcel that you sent to us a week ago was unexpected by us [and gives us great joy]. Until today [when we received the letter from you] we did not know who had sent it to us, but today it is clear to us that an 'angel from heaven' has brought it to us. We thank you heartily for the deep interest.

"We thank you again, many, many times."

Hinda Ginzberg (Ramat HaShofet)

"We acknowledge the parcel that you have sent to us, which we received today at the South African office on HaYarkon Street in Tel Aviv, with gratitude and thanks. We consider your special effort as a worthy, friendly, effective gift and what a good thing at the time.

Berl Sarver, Tel Aviv

Rokiskis Yizkor Book   557

In the end, we publish a letter from the Rakishok Rabbi, Reb Shmuel *haLevi* Levitin, who is in America and occupies an esteemed place at the Central Lubavitch [Chabad] *Tomchei Temimim* Yeshiva, in its full text:

25 Kislev 5712 [24 December 1951]

Brooklyn

In honor of my dear ones, honored, eminent habitants of the city of Rakishok now living in the State of South Africa. May God protect her!

Peace and blessings!

I already twice have had the opportunity of hearing a greeting from many of you through Rabbi Shai Weinberg.

I was very happy to receive a living greeting from a large number of the refugees from our city that the Lord God, the reason for everything, led to come to South Africa and as a result be protected from the hand of the oppressive enemy, may his name be erased.

I certainly remember the warm Jewish and Hasidic atmosphere that reigned in our city Rakishok and certainly you did everything possible so that your life in South Africa would be in the spirit in which you were raised and lived for many years.

[Page 524]

And may the Lord, God grant that your children born in Africa may also mirror this way of life.

I also was very satisfied to hear from Comrade Weinberg of your warm help to his sacred mission for the holy Lubavitch institutions that are disseminating Torah across the entire world.

I am making use now of the opportunity that Comrade Weinberg is traveling again to your country and send with him a hearty greeting to all those from Rakishok.

Simultaneously I want to ask you to help Rabbi Weinberg in his holy mission now even more than previously because, alas, our institutions find themselves in a very critical situation, particularly our institutions in *Eretz–Yisroel*.

The Rabbi, Shmuel *haLevi* Levitin, former rabbi of Rakishok, Lithuania.

In connection with this letter it is worthwhile to underline that in addition to help for the *landsleit*, the Aid Society helped various campaigns with sums of money: on behalf of the Israel Appeal; for the War Appeal; for the *Mogen*

Dovid Adom [Israeli emergency medical service – Red Shield of David]; for Chabad Lubavitch Fund.

In the course of its existence, the Rakishok Aid Society wrote a meritorious page in the history of our local *Landsmanschaft.*

[Pages 525-527]

Notes on the *Landsmanschaft* of Rakishok

by A. Eidelman

Translated by Gloria Berkenstat Freund

I was the secretary of the Rakishok *Landsmanschaft* [organization of people from the same town] during the years 1936-1948.

Although the *shtetl* Rakishok is little known to me, because I was there only a few times for a few hours, I write these notes of mine with great joy because the work of the Rakishok "Society" is well known to me and close to my heart.

The name "Rakishoker" is actually a nickname for all Lithuanian Jews who emigrated from Lithuania. The Rakishoker Society consisted not only of Jews from Rakishok and surrounding [towns] such as Abel [Obeliai], Kamei, Ponedel [Pandelys], Ezhereni [Ezeranai], Dusiat [Dusetos] and others, but even Latvian Jews were members of the Rakishok *landsmanschaft*.

Forty years ago, the founders of the Society foresaw the possibility of a foreign "invasion" and, therefore, installed a plank in the constitution that said as long as there were 10 Rakishokers in the Society, the name, "Rakishoker Society" should not be changed.

The first founders of the Society were very proud of the founding constitution and, to this day, the younger members have not brought in any great, substantial changes to the constitution.

* * *

Jews from Rakishok and its environs were among the first Lithuanian Jews who, 50 years ago, started "to go" to Africa. It was usually done not with the thought of remaining in the unknown land, far from God and from family, but they traveled to Africa only for a few years in order to "make" several hundred pounds and, coming home, to exchange them for several thousand rubles. It was thought that with the earned money, an unmarried older daughter could be married and a warehouse could be opened.

Many Jews did this. They returned to Lithuania and opened wholesale businesses and grain warehouses. But when the goods from the flour warehouses or other enterprises that were distributed through loans among the poor retailers and shops and the wholesale stores began to decrease, they bought a ship ticket with their last few rubles to travel again to far Africa.

The longing by the men for their families was very great. Therefore, in many cases, they returned to their families in Lithuania and then emigrated again to South Africa.

There were poor as well as rich among the Rakishok *landsleit* in South Africa, but at the same time, the wealth was not that great, so there was not much of a difference from the poor elements. However, there was a reciprocal connection and a readiness, and if someone lacked a few pounds to send home, to buy goods or was short of money, he was not ashamed to borrow from a landsman.

They would come together often and talk about matters from home. They maintained the religious *Yiddishkeit* [Jewish culture]: prayed three times a day and tried not to work on *Shabbos* [the Shabbat].

From coming together closely and often came the idea to found the Society. For a few shillings of membership dues a month, each member or "brother" had free medical help, received a "fiver" or a "tener" as a loan, and also had the opportunity to meet *landsleit* at meetings and gatherings, and hear news from home.

The older members, or "brothers," remember well how the Rakishok Society was created. They remember the first founding meeting of the Society and remember to this day all the details. A skyscraper now stands on the spot of the house where they met for the first time.

The activities of the Rakishok Society in the first years of its existence were already written about in an earlier article. I will only report certain characteristic details in connection with secretarial activities.

I took over the office of secretary in 1936, when the Society was already known in South Africa as one of the first *landsmanshaftn* that exhibited great aid activity on behalf of its members both materially and spiritually.

The first chairman of the society was also one of the first Rakishok pioneers: Reb Khona Kohan, of blessed memory. He was a devoted brother. He carefully watched the Society's every penny just as his own coins and, despite his poor health, he took an active part in the work until his last day.

There was then a member of the committee, Mendl Yoselowitch, of blessed memory, who was very active in regard to acquiring new members. I think that he was the only brother who tried to have all of his children and sons-in-law become members of the Rakishok Society.

One of the original founders of the Society was Yakov Snieg. Although he was also a member of other societies, he did the work of the Rakishok Society with dedication. He knew how to lead general meetings, bringing himself respect and trust.

Dr. Max Yaffe was very popular among the Rakishokers. In addition to being the Society doctor, he, as a Rakishoker, came to all of the Rakishoker events and entertainments.

Kuperman, the previous secretary of the Society, from whom I took over my secretarial post, was very devoted to the Society and always gave me encouragement in my work.

An extremely devoted and interesting worker for the Society was Reb Chaim Dovid Jaffa, of blessed memory. He was the treasurer, and according to the rules, those who needed to take loans had to come to the treasurer for endorsement and to sign the needed formalities. But Reb Chaim Dovid, despite his age and poor health would personally go to the interested people taking loans – in all parts of the city – and get their signatures.

I believe that the volunteers from Rakishok were an exception compared to the communal workers from other institutions. A member of the Rakishok Society never felt any dejection when he took a loan, but he thought that he was coming to a brother and taking money from a brotherly fund in which he was a member.

It is worthwhile to emphasize that in the course of my years in office as secretary, not one penny was lost or wasted by the Society. All lenders paid their debts with great punctuality. In the first years the Society would lend "fivers" or "teners." Recently, the Society has given loans as high as 150 pounds. Loans are given to *landsleit* to buy a [word is not fully visible in text], a house or even a motor-car. It is also a fact that there are *landsleit* who take a loan from the Society because they have the superstition that this money is "lucky."

The committee, it should be understood, primarily gave to the needy *landsleit*, but no one was ever refused a loan. If the fund lacked money, the committee members "found a way." The committee would turn to the *gmiles khesed* [interest-free loan] fund in such cases and help out its *landsleit.*

* * *

The Society also aided the *landsleit* in the area of medical help. It responded to various charity appeals and to the extent of its ability contributed to various funds. During the last World War, the Rakishok *landsleit* organized a special Aid Society.

The Society is represented on the Board of Deputies and in other central Jewish communal institutions.

[Page 528]

The Family Manne-Manelewitz

by S. Rubin

Translated by Michael (Jakubowics) Jackson and Ralph Weiner

Avraham Mendel and Judith Manelevitch

Rakisher Jews have contributed a fair amount to the development of commerce and industry in South Africa. Among the Rakisher community, the Manne-Manelevich family occupies a prominent place.

The Manelevitch family originates from a very distinguished background. The Grandfather, Yitzchak Manelevitch, was known in Rakishok as Reb Yitzchak Manelevitch, a dignified and respectable businessman. He dealt with flax and items that had to be smoked. He was well known in the area.

Avraham Mendel was the son of Yitzchak Manelevitch. He received a traditional Jewish upbringing and inherited his father's noble character. He married into a fine family. His wife, Judith Blond, was the daughter of Yitzchak Blond from Kreitzburg, who had a prominent place in the business world. His family background was known throughout the area, and he was also a respected Talmudist.

Avraham Mendel and his wife Judith became the parents of six children. The parents, being modern, gave their children a modern upbringing in parochial and secular schools in Panevich and Vilna.

Avraham Mendel took charge of his father's businesses and handled it honorably.

Sholem Manne Manelevitch

Avraham Mendel's oldest son, Moishe, was the first pioneer to settle in South Africa in 1910. He went through all the stages of a newcomer in a strange country. In 1922, he brought his brother Sholem to South Africa. In 1925 he brought his brother Eliahu to South Africa. To date, they have a chain of shoe stores.

Their parents and sisters arrived in 1929. With modest steps the brothers Manne-Manelevitch started a little shoe store in a suburb named Jeppestown.

The brothers worked their way up and now have a large shoe company named ABC. The company consists of 11 stores and 300 employees.

Sholem Manne Manelevitch, now deceased, had great talent and energy, and was responsible for the growth of the business. He was a person imbued with great knowledge and culture.

Sholem Manne was also well versed in Hebrew culture and literature. He and his brothers were very active in all types of causes, especially Jewish ones.

Sholem Manne passed away very suddenly at age 50, leaving behind a name for himself as a modern cultured intellectual who loved his people and his culture.

The brothers' parents passed away in 1937. The children honored their parents by upholding their traditions with great love and respect.

The Rakisher family Manne-Manelewitz is well known in South African Jewish circles as having good hearts and are highly respected.

[Page 530]

The Thorny Path of Jewish Immigration to South Africa

by J. M. Sherman

Translated by Rae Meltzer

It is truly a significant and important undertaking of the Jews of Rakishok to publish a Yizkor Book, which will be a memorial for the Jews of Rakishok whom the Nazi murderers annihilated. It will also be a memorial for the Jews who came here (South Africa) years and years ago. They struggled against harsh and severe conditions and obstacles that they found here. They persisted in their struggle and found a way to survive and preserve the Jewish way of life in South Africa. Their struggle and disappointments, their anguish and suffering, was that of new immigrants who come to a strange land and find a foreign language, with unfamiliar customs and economic conditions. Nevertheless, they persevered and cleared a path! All of their experiences from the very beginning are full of rich historical material and are of great significance and interest. They must be written down so that the children, grandchildren and future historians will learn how the Jews of South Africa, beginning as immigrants, achieved the status of citizenship in South Africa. It is good that the Jews of Rakishok are documenting all of their history. Let us hope their efforts will prove to be an example to others. The time is short. The generation of the first Jewish immigrants to South Africa is getting fewer in number and much important historical material is therefore being lost.

J. M. Sherman: well-known writer and journalist

Taking the example of Rakishok, (although I am not a landsman) I would like to write about some of the details of the life of the Rakishok immigrants to South Africa, as I knew them first hand from the period of the Boer War. The Jewish immigrant, whether he came from Rakishok or from Poshvitin (my shtetl) experienced a very similar situation, with only minor differences. I am describing the immigrant situation in Johannesburg, but there was very little difference in the Jewish immigrant's situation in Cape Town or the other large cities. It was the same process, with similar occupations and similar living situations.

Immediately after the Boer War ended in May 1902, Jewish immigration to South Africa increased. When the Boer war broke out in 1899, many Jews returned home and many went to Cape Town. After the war they came back to Johannesburg and there was a new strata of fresh immigrants: young men who ran away from "priziv" (military conscription in Czarist Russia), heads of families (young and older) forced to immigrate for economic reasons, political refugees, and also some adventurers. The stopping-off place for most of the immigrants was the Johannesburg suburb named Berea. The gentiles, who were the first to come rushing to South Africa after the discovery of gold there in 1886, slowly left Berea, and the immigrant Jews replaced them, occupying almost all the vacant houses and opening various businesses. They built synagogues, "houses of learning," and talmud torahs, supporting rabbis and "shokhtim" (ritual slaughterers), as well as quarreling about who would be warden of the synagogue, who would run community institutions, and other community issues. Generally they wanted, and they soon succeeded, in transforming Berea into a small Lithuanian or Polish shtetl.

A large number of both the new and the earlier immigrants were "single" individuals whose families remained in the old home. These "singles" lived:

In small rooms without air or light,

(There are two sleeping in that tiny room),

The walls are black; covered with growing

mosses, mushrooms and all kinds of grasses.

The windows are broken and covered with paper,

The door is full of holes and the floor is all cracked....

These little rooms were smaller than described in the above poem. They were all over Berea: in the sexton's yard, in Goldberg's yard, and in the small sexton's yard which was near the "green " house of learning (beth midrash)-- two stories up a room for a nap with a green balcony above so the tenants in the top rooms should not fall down. Such rooms to rent were also found in Fordsburg, Everton, and in other existing suburbs of Johannesburg. (Doornfontein was then an upscale suburb). The rent for one of these little rooms was two to three pounds per month, but the first and early immigrants did not have it in their power to pay so much rent. They would double-up two to a room and, in the larger rooms, three to a room. The walls were black from the smoke of the "primus cooking stove" which everyone had for cooking food, and boiling water for tea, etc. The food was prepared on the run, and men who in the old home never even boiled water for tea had to learn to cook here. The food did not always come out tasting superb, and one ate hurriedly, not wanting to waste time eating instead of earning money. The result was that many had stomach ailments. There were also some who simply denied themselves food in order to save the money. This was called "kishke- gelt" (intestine-money). There were very few of this kind, but they did exist, and if they survived, they paid dearly with their health.

What kind of occupation did the "greeners" (new immigrants) get? As I mentioned before, many Jews went to Cape Town at the outbreak of the Boer war and returned to Johannesburg immediately after the end of the war. Amongst them were storekeepers, dealers, merchants, and craftsmen. Due to the war, many of them were ruined financially, but knowing the conditions and situations of the country, they soon rehabilitated themselves. The new Jewish immigrants therefore found a more stable Jewish community and economy: butchers, tailors, shoemakers, restaurants, food-stores, etc. The "greener" who had a skill or trade made his way more quickly, but the majority were "luft-menschen" (air-people). What could they do? Their friends and landsleit advised them to try different things:

become a "tryer" (peddler) with "boser-kosher" (kosher meat), bread, and vegetables; buy old clothes, sacks, and bottles; go out with a basket of eggs, with a few chickens--and you have a business and you are a business man. There is no more available existence among local Jews; and if there is, it carries a different character and different "face." Even "tachen" is already historic. But let us go in order."

How does one become a peddler with "boser-kosher"? This is not an item that one can save from one day to the next, or weeks even, as one can with household items like pots or cloth. Therefore, the first task is to get customers who will be ready to buy meat from the peddler. The peddler had to enlist his friends and landsleit to commit themselves to buy meat from him, and to recruit their acquaintances who had families and even those who were "singles" to become customers. The customer that the peddler got was usually at the expense of another or even the butcher who sold the meat to the peddler. However, since there was a continuous stream of new immigrants arriving every month, no one worried or objected to the process. The butcher also did not object to this arrangement--he had his steady customers and the more peddlers he had coming to him to buy meat, the happier he was. Thus, instead of having to deal with 20 or more women customers, he deals with one customer who buys large quantities at one time. Of course, he has to sell to the peddler for a somewhat lower price so the peddler can earn a percentage profit for his livelihood.

Now that he has several customers, the peddler comes to the butcher shop every evening. In those years, between 1902-1907, all businesses and stores remained open until late in the evening. The peddler gives a list of his customer's orders: ribs, flanken, breast, soup-meat, tongue. etc. Having bargained energetically with the butcher for an extra bone or fat (which his customers warned him not to forget) he separates the portions on a table or board, puts a piece of paper with the name and address of each customer on each portion, and goes home. The following day, he will come to the butcher shop very early to wrap every portion of meat in paper, write down the name and address on each wrapped portion, and put all the packages of meat in his sack. If he also has customers for bread, he goes to the bakery after the butcher shop and chooses some white and dark bread and bagels.

The following morning he will carry two bags over his shoulder on his back--one bag of meat and one bag of bread. Thus, whether it was cold or burning hot, in dust or in rain, with two sacks over his shoulders, one with meat and the other with bread, the peddler went from customer to customer (often quite a distance from one another). When he returned home he was exhausted, hungry, and beaten. "The customer is always right." The women customers who gave him their orders and took them away made his life bitter and shortened his years with their complaints. One complained that he was too late, and the other that he was too early; one objected that the meat was too fat, and the other that it was too lean; one was angry that he did not bring more bones for her soup and another that he forgot to bring the "calf-hoofs" for her "petsha," etc. From these peddlers came some Jews who became rich. First of all, they bought a horse and wagon. This gave them the resources to enlarge their clientele by covering a larger area. Then they started taking orders for dry goods: handkerchiefs, tablecloths, bed linens, and blankets;

pots, oil, herring, knives, graters, and anything that a customer required or requested. When they were tired of driving around and had already amassed quite a good sum of capital, they sold their business for a good price and opened a clothing store or iron business in the center of the city's business section. They brought their families from home to South Africa and established themselves in their new country.

The Jewish population grew, spread out over the city, and began to settle in new suburbs. Butcher shops opened up in these new suburbs and the housewives took the trouble to go themselves to shop at the butcher shop. The peddlers were no longer economically profitable or viable and they slowly disappeared from the Jewish street. The butchers, who had customers some distance out, delivered the customers' orders by black messengers. Even today one can see blacks on bicycles with packages of meat and bread, rushing through the streets. The former peddlers went into other businesses. Some became butchers with their own shops. Others opened other types of shops and some transformed themselves in the province. Some traded in produce and other products, wool and leather, or even became "tachers."

The majority of the peddlers were married, and while some had their families with them, others had their families in the old homeland. These occupations did not appeal to the bachelors. They found occupations elsewhere, becoming waiters in restaurants, employees in taverns, bars ("soda-water stores"), and "kaferaiteh" (kafir-eating-houses restaurants for blacks), and the businesses around the gold and coal mines. The restaurants (kosher, of course) and the taverns and bars were clubs where friends met. The new arrivals ("greeners") came there to search for jobs and often did find work there. When a special event occurred, like the closing of a partnership, or a marriage proposal, there was a gathering in the restaurant or the tavern to "water it down" with a glass of tea, a flask of lemonade which one brought, or the tavern-owner volunteered a flask of whiskey. In the tavern, Jews also practiced playing cards until late into the night, discussed politics, talked about race issues, raised or lowered reputations, and considered who were the worthy people.

"Kaferaiteh" existed at every shop that was close to a gold mine or coal mine, but they also existed in places where there were no mines. Wherever they existed they were illegal for hygienic reasons. In and around the "kaferaiteh" (restaurant) there was always an odor of bad meat and dead cats. The place had neither floor nor ceiling. The tables were black and shiny from spilled fat soup, melted candle-wax, and syrup. In the summer, a multitude of flies lay siege to the walls, the tables, the meat, and bread; they fell into the hot soup, the hot tea, and the dough for meat-biscuits. The work shift in the kaferaiteh was very long, perhaps as long as 18 hours per day and even more. The shift might last all day and night--as long as 24 hours. Because the pay was much greater in the kaferaiteh than in the shop, many went to work in a kaferaiteh. But many others did not because it was considered a low level of work, and to be called a "kaferaitenik" was to be insulted and reviled. Probably this stems from the fact that the place was always dirty and smelly and the people who frequented the place, including the white people, went about unclean. There was no supervision about cleanliness, as exists today. But this was only about "kaffers," so who cares and what difference does it make?

In the gold and coal mining shops, the atmosphere was cleaner, but the working day was also very long--from six in the morning to seven or eight in the evening. (No unions of workers existed as yet). The pay for a "greener" was 10 pounds for three months, with free meals and lodging. It took quite a while to reach the pay of 10-15 pounds for three months. The boss of the concessions handled his workers according to his plan: they kept one or two experienced assistants, the rest were "half or all greener," who were being trained by the assistants to be salesmen. If one of the "greeners" became dissatisfied with his pay and was bold enough to ask for a raise, he was told (8 out of 10 times) to look for another place. In his place they employed someone else for 10 pounds for three months. If the employee showed signs of becoming a good clerk, then they gave him a raise with a pound or two, because a good clerk could easily get a position in one of the concessions.

Being one of those who earned the "princely" salary of 10 pounds for three months, I later became interested in these workers in the "kaferaitehs" and in the shops around the gold and coal mines. I wondered about their eventual fate. What was the pattern of their lives? I followed it for a long time. The results I found were that most of them continued to work until their late 30's. Then, exhausted from their hard work and way of life, they let themselves be courted by a small dowry, opened a grocery, and worked together with their wives. Others took over a kosher restaurant from someone, or a "soda water store" and went with the Jewish "flow." They became a member of a congregation or joined the Zionist organization. Others joined prophetic factions, while some became chairmen of their landsmanshaften and active in charitable institutions and organizations. Very few of the multitudes of working men became owners of a concession, but the Jews became conspicuous.

One of the occupations that the newcomers (greeners) chose was trading in old clothes. They continued in this occupation even after they were no longer newcomers, and were only "half-green". Having received a loan from a charitable society or from friends who helped, the immigrant bought some old coats and went out on the street to find customers:

All day from early in the morning until late,

You'll find him always on the street,

On his back he carries a large sack,

Full of old clothes.

He goes from house to house

And knocks on every door

And as with all humility for charity:

"Can you help me with something?"

He knocked on the doors of poor homes, and not necessarily of Jewish homes. Perhaps he avoided Jewish homes because he was ashamed of running into landsleit who knew him from home as a good teacher, student, or merchant. He was ashamed to write home to his family and tell them what he was doing. "I am doing 'business,'" he wrote home. He also went among the blacks, perhaps his best customers. They were dreadfully poor and old coats cost a lot less than new ones.

Later, some of the more experienced clothing-traders rented stores and conducted their business with more success; others went into businesses such as lumber, furniture, and glassware. Those who could not or did not want to deal in old clothes, constructed a wooden box to which they nailed leather straps, filled it with cigarettes, candles, matches and slung the straps over the neck and went out to earn a living. They went around to restaurants.

Some of them would push the wagon with vegetables and on their neck carry the box with merchandise over their heart, until their heart weakened and their feet gave out. Thus, exhausted and broken in health and spirit, they returned home. Those who were stronger and more energetic remained and struggled to find a way. From pushing a wagon with greens, one became a produce and fruit merchant, and from the chest with cigarettes, matches and candles, one became owner of a tobacco shop, or even owner of a candle factory. Or two Jews would meet in a restaurant or tavern, both looking for some kind of occupation or business. They began to talk and discovered that one of them was no longer a "greener." He was here during Paul Kruger's regime. The Boer War had disturbed and unsettled him. He has some money, he understands the language of the land, but not well enough to undertake "tochen." The other man is still "half-green." He does not have much money, but he thinks his friends will help him. He also wants to begin "tochen." He understands that it pays well. The result of this conversation is that they became partners.

They bought a covered wagon and stocked it with merchandise that they thought the Boers needed, and the Boers needed many things. After the war the Boers were ruined economically. With the several million pounds that the British government gave to the Transvaal, some of the Boers were helped to get back on their feet. The Boer needed everything, from a shirt to a needle. "Tocher" was a Yiddish transliteration of the Afrikaner word "toch," meaning to ride or travel, but the Boer called him "smous" (peddler), in Yiddish, "a village storekeeper." Thus the two Jews who met and talked it over established their partnership and began their "tochen." The "toch" often lasted several weeks. The province at that time was sparsely populated and farmers lived quite far apart from each other, so the "tocher" had to ride a good part of the day in order to reach a farm. If he did not reach a community before night fall, he had to sleep in the fields, either under his wagon or in "godly" rapture under the spacious, comfortable sky, looking with wonder at the huge stars hanging in great profusion in space. Perhaps he was lying in the open field in dread and fright, shaking with every clap of thunder and the fiery lightening that lit up the whole area. He was drenched from the storms and rainfall. After that he traveled more slowly.

The relationship between the "smous" (peddler) and the farmer was a friendly one. Of course, there were exceptions on both sides, but generally they lived peacefully and dealt honestly with each other. Their business with each other was based on giving one's word rather than on written contracts. The Boer's attitude and relations with the Jews was a friendly one--first, because the Jew believed in the Bible, like himself, and secondly, because the Jew was the "newspaper" and political source for the Boer farmer. The "smous" came loaded not only with merchandise but also with news from the city and the wide world. The farmer talked politics with him and the Jew naturally agreed with everything the farmer said. The Jew was the enabler between the farmer and the city market--he bought the farmer's products and delivered everything that the farmer needed and gave him long term credit. The "smous" brought with him a civilizing influence to the far-flung corners of the land. Sometimes it was in the form of a new type of knife with a corkscrew, sometimes a clock that chimed every quarter-hour, or a wristwatch. Perhaps another time it was a curious toy or plaything, etc.

When the "smous" arrived at the farm, even if it was his first visit, he was welcomed with friendship. His horses were cared for and a good bed was made ready for him. Food was prepared for him and the farmer did not let him leave until he bought something from the "smous." They always made purchases. The housewife had already prepared a list of items and articles that she wanted to purchase. In the morning, immediately after breakfast, everyone gathered on the veranda of the house: the farmer, his wife, children, neighbors, in-laws, daughter-in-law, son-in-law (if there were any), and asked the peddler to display his merchandise. The black man who traveled with him carries in two sacks with merchandise, takes the merchandise out of the sacks, and displays it on the floor of the veranda. Then the choosing and bargaining begins and lasts a couple of hours. In the end they purchase hammers, stockings, pants, linen, canvas, fabric for dresses, knives, spoons, and toys for children and grandchildren. The favorite toy was a mouth harmonica and a knife with two blades. The life of the "tocher" was not an easy one. For weeks and months he traveled around the land, never spending his nights in the place where he spent his days, often finding himself in the open fields in all kinds of weather. In addition he had to worry about collecting on the credit he gave his customers, not because his customers did not want to pay--they simply could not pay on time or even late. The scale of the farmer's production was small and there was no export market at that time. Even the "rich" farmer was not really rich enough, but on average, the loss was not big. By the time "tochen" went out of style, the economic situation of the country was much improved, and the province was also helped thereby. -

Why did "tochen" fade away as livelihood? Because railroads spread out over the land. This new network of railroads brought the farmers in the villages close to the cities. Before the railroads came, if a Boer farmer wanted to go to the city with his family to do some shopping, he would "waste" at a minimum several days. This was not practical. Therefore, he depended on the "smous" to bring the merchandise to his doorstep so he could shop on his own veranda. But when the railroad network brings the train almost to his doorway, he can board the train and in a few hours he is in the city, does his shopping and returns home by train, all in just a half-day. The "smous" could not compete with the great volume and variety of merchandise in the city stores, and so the farmer soon preferred to shop in the city stores and the custom of "tocheri" became unprofitable and ceased to exist.

The majority of former "tochers" did not give up hope: they started businesses at the train station and at cross-roads that led to the farms. Now, instead of traveling to the farmer, the farmer came to a specific "smous." Now the Jew carried a larger and more varied amount of merchandise, since he was in a stationary place and no longer had to transport heavy sacks of merchandise from farm to farm over long distances. In time a town developed around the train stations and many Jews settled in them.

I have only identified certain traits and features of Jewish immigrant life in South Africa in the beginning of this century. These are important because the daily life and people's employment pursuits of the past illuminate how their character has been transformed in the present. Jewish life as I knew it in Berea was varied and had many sides to it. It had two functioning Jewish theater groups, a weekly newspaper, and "cheders" where Yiddish was taught as the foundation language. It was populated with rabbis, "shoichtim" (ritual-slaughterers), cantors, schools, and small synagogues, "aptekers" (druggists), and doctors. There was no lack of tailors, shoemakers, tinsmiths, blacksmiths, watch-makers, and "turners." [The Yiddish word "tokers" means "turners." The English dictionary definition is, (1) "fashions or shapes objects on a lathe"; (2) "tumbler or gymnast." In the context used here it could be either one.] There were fierce arguments between Zionists and socialists, and Jewish book-sellers loaned out books on "prikot." ["Prikot" is not found in English or Yiddish dictionaries. Perhaps it is Slavic and in context used here may mean "on credit."] Even a Jewish missionary was not lacking. Several times a month on Sunday he appeared in Berea on a street-corner, and for the Jews who gathered around him, he would talk about the wonders of Jesus and the uplifting quality of the Christian religion. The Jews around him laughed and threw questions at him. Sometimes heated discussions developed, so heated that the missionary barely escaped from the group and vanished. But this did not deter him from coming back again.

The life of the Jewish immigrant was very hard because he did not find in South Africa any organization that was on his side and concerned with his situation, no organization to help him economically or spiritually. The immigrant Jew had to undertake everything on his own shoulders--shoulders that were not always strong or broad enough for that burden. Perhaps, therefore, the immigrant sometimes followed a crooked path and lost his way. In general though, the Jewish immigrants who came to South Africa have nothing to be ashamed of--not as Jews and not as citizens.

[Page 539]

In Remembrance

(In Memoriam)
Translated by Bella Golubchik

[Editor's Note: the original book was assembled on the dining room table of Bella Golubchik's parents in Mayfair, Johannesburg. Bella's father, Mr. R. Aarons-Arsch was a member of the Praesidium of The Rakishok Landmanschaft.]

[Page 540]

In Remembrance
[In Memoriam]

of our parents

Ya'akov Shimshon and

Esther Braina Schwartzberg

who died in

Kestell OFS

Orange Free State, South Africa

and were buried in
the Jewish Cemetery in
Bethlehem, Orange Free State

[from]

Sossel Rochel Abrams, husband and children

Moshe Schwartzberg, wife and children

Sheva Malk

Leah Gordon and Son

Ella Allen, husband and children

Stirel Cohen and husband

Yentel Gamsu and husband

[Page 541]

May these few lines serve as a memorial

in memory of our parents

David Yitzchak and

Soreh Beile Shusterman

[Aleihem Hashalom – may they rest in peace]

and of our sisters

Chyeneh [Chasyia]

Elkeh

Chanyeh

and their families

who were born in Antalept
and perished in the Great Jewish Destruction [Holocaust]
through the Hitler murder [extermination]

[from]

their sons and brothers:

**Shlomo, Hershel and Mottel Sher
and their families**

[Page 542]

**In honor of
and as an illuminated memory of**

our father **Leibe-Hirsch Yosselowitz**
who died in Rakishok in 1924,
of our mother **Beileh-Raiche** who died in Rakishok,
of our brother **Abraham Yosselowitz**,
wife, and children, who perished in Rakishok
of our brother **Mendel Witz [Yosselowitz]** who died in Johannesburg,
of our brother **Isaac Yosselowitz** who died in Rakishok in 1914
of our sister **Soreh Yellin** who died in Johannesburg.

We will remember you all forever.

[from]

Sachneh Lovitsch [Yosselowitz] and

daughters in Durban

Chaykel Yosselowitz, wife and children in Israel

Yechiel David Lovitsch [Yosselowitz], Durban

Gershon Witz [Yosselowitz] wife and children, Durban

Kalman Witz [Yosselowitz], Durban

**In Eternal Memory
of our father**

Beinash Nochumowitz

who died 18th Cheshvan 1918, Petrograd,

and of our mother
Rochel Gittel Nochumowitz-Bris [Barris]

who died 8th Kislev 1951
Giv'at Brenner, Israel.

We will always remember you!

[from]

Sonia and Koppel Barkai [Baradavka]

and children, Giv'at Brenner, Israel

Aharon Naki and wife Chaya, Cape Town

Moshe and Shalom Naki, Nochumowitz, Cape Town

[Page 543]

We perpetuate the memory of

our father

Michoel Lapp

who died in Johannesburg

14th September 1942

[from]

daughter Feige Rudnick
and her husband

For our parents,
brother and sister-in-law

David and Malkah Spivak

and brother, and nephew

Moshe

who perished in Rakishok.

May this be a Memorial

[from]

son Leib
and wife Luyba Spivak

and children
sister Soreh
and Leizer Klas and children

In memory

of our brothers and

sister and families

and the whole large family

who were massacred

by the Hitler murderers in Kurpletz,
a village near Rakishok

[from]

Henyeh and Asher Jacobson [Yakobowitz]
Kayleh Segal, husband and children

The memory is unforgettable

of our sister

Chayeh-Itah

and her husband

Shlomo Kuklavsky

and children

who perished in Rakishok

[from]

Leizer and Soreh Klas and children
Chasiyah Friedman and daughter

[Page 544]

For our father
Yudel Brinkman

for our mother
Hindeh-Matleh Brinkman

who perished in Yuzhint

for our brother
Binyamin Brinkman, his wife
Mushe and children who perished in Kamaiy

for our sister **Peiah**,
husband and **Alter Reve** and
their children who perished in Yuzhint

for our brother **Abraham Brinkman**,
wife and children
who perished in the Churban Rakishok –
the Destruction of Rakishok

for our brother **Zaleh [Zalman] Brinkman** and
his wife and children who perished in Yuzhint

for our brother **Ortchik [Aharon]**, wife **Chana** and
their children who perished in Yuzhint

for our uncle **Yisroel-Leib Snegg** and his wife **Freidel**
who perished in the Destruction of Rakishok

for our cousin **Binyomin** and his wife **Mineh-Tzibel** and
their ten children who perished in the Destruction of Rakishok

May these lines be an eternal Memorial

[from]

Yerachmiel and Mineh Brinkman and daughters in Israel

Sareh and Moshe Mandel and sons in Israel

Nathan and Leah Brinkman and children in South Africa

Yehoshuah Brinkman, wife, and sons in Israel

Miryam and Yosef Gefner and daughters in Israel

[Page 545]

We will never forget and always hold the memory dear [precious]
of
our father **Uri Leizer Hurwitz**
who died 23rd Kislev 1938
of
our mother **Ettel Hurwitz**
of
our brother **Efraim Yitzchok**,
wife
Bassel and children
of
our sister **Rivka-Dvora Shneider**
husband **Berel** and children
of
our brother **Avrohom Refael Hurwitz**
wife **Ita** and children
of
our brother **Leibe Hurwitz**,
wife and child

They were all martyred together with our mother in the Destruction of Rakishok in 1941.

We will remember you forever.

[from]

Yisrael Moshe and Batya Hurwitz
and children
Chayim Elyeh and Rivka Leah Hurwitz
and children and grandchild,
South Africa
Berel Hurwitz, America

Uri Leizer and Ettel Hurwitz

Berel and Rivka-Dvorah Shneider and children

[Page 546]

May this be an eternal memorial
[in everlasting remembrance] of our parents

Mendel Leib and Soreh Frumeh Levin

of our sister **Feige** and
husband **Ya'akov Levin**
and their little children
Pereleh and Maneh Leizer

of our sister **Henyeh**
and brother **Leivik**
who perished in Churban Rakishok
[Destruction of Rakishok]

and in memory of our brother **Shmuel** who fell
in the slaughter by the German murderers
while fighting in the ranks of the Red Army.

We will always remember you.

[from]

Ya'akov and Chana Levin and children

Chayim Yitzchak and Leah Levin and children

Shaiorka [Shaikeh] Levin and family

Gisa Levin

[Page 547]

May this Memorial [Hazkarah]

be an eternal light

in memory of the

husband and brother

Abraham-Aharon Orelowitz [z"l]

[may he rest in peace]
who died 23rd August 1950
in Johannesburg

[from]

his wife **Roseh Orelowitz** and
sister **Musel Lewis**

South Africa

[and from]

**sister Rodah and husband
Mordechai Beril and children**

sister Chana Orelowitz

**sister Dr. Michle Orelowitz
and Shlomo Leibel**

**sister Nesyeh and husband
Dov Reznik and children**

Israel

[Page 548]

We will always remember the tragic death of our unforgettable father

Shaul Gershon Klas

Who perished by the hands of the Nazi Beast. He found his rest in the common [communal, shared] grave, among 2,500 martyrs somewhere in the vicinity of Abel.

He was in America for a short while, but in order not to desecrate the Holy Shabbat [not to become secular] he traveled back 'aheim' [home], in order to be able to live in a traditional Jewish spirit [atmosphere].

Of our mother **Zviah [Zivyah]**
who died 21st Shevat 1935 in Abel.

May these few words serve as a memorial.

[from]

**David Moshe Klas, wife and daughter
Johannesburg**

[Page 549]

The unforgettable parents
Leizer and Rivka Zilber

the sister
Tzviah Zelikman, husband, and two children who perished in the Destruction of Dvinsk

The brother

Leibe Zilber

who fell as an heroic fighter with the Red Army in Stalingrad

May this be a memorial

[from]

Yehudit and Pineh [Pinyeh] Merkel and children

[Page 550]

We express our deep and great sorrow
over the death of our mother

Nechama-Sheine Mikel

who died in the Ponevezh hospital.
Prior to her death she sighed the following words:
"Where are you my far flung [flown far away] children?"
She was buried in the Jewish cemetery
[by Judaic rites] in Ponevezh on
Shemini Atzeret 1927.

Over the death of our brother

Choneh Mikel

who died in the 1st World War in the
Ukraine in the year 1916.

We will remember you forever!

[from]

**Yitzchak and Yisroel Mikel [Michalewitz], Johannesburg
Schimon Yosef Mikel-Michalewitz, Pretoria, with their wives and children**

[Page 551]

We, children and grandchildren, will remember you

forever dear and precious parents
Yerachmiel and Peseh Maliyeh Saltuper

We will remember our Father and Zaida, who lived all the years in agony,
as an invalid without legs. The image of our mother will always
appear before us. Even though she was also a sickly [weak] woman,
she looked after our father with great love and devotion,
and in the final minutes [moments] going to the
Nazi pyres [bonfires], to the slaughter, she never
abandoned him even for a moment, and together they underwent
the gruesome fate of their cruel death.

May their bones rest in the communal graves [brothers' graves]
of Ezhereni–Novo Aleksandrovsk.

[from]

**Moshe Israel and Mina Sharp-Saltuper and
children, Johannesburg.
Henye Silver, husband, and son, Vilna
Yehoshua Shal and Eli Sharp Saltuper and daughters in Nairobi, Kenya**

[Page 552]

Noach Zvi and Matleh Shapiro

and of my brother **Hertzl Shapiro** and his wife **Rocheh-Gittel** and their children,

who perished due to the Nazi Executioners [hangmen] in the Rakishok Holocaust.

In honour of their memory.

[from]

son and brother

Morris Shapiro
with his wife and children
Johannesburg, South Africa

In eternal remembrance of my parents

Noach-Zvi Shapiro

who died 4th Teivet 1935,

Matleh Shapiro

who died 7th Teivet 1915

Herzl and Rocheh-Gittel Shapiro and children

[Page 553]

We will remember and never forget
our father

Abba, the son of Ya'akov Sacks

who died in Johannesburg on 29th April 1941
2nd Iyar Tashä,

and our mother

Chana, daughter of Tzvi Sacks,

who died in Johannesburg 10th October 1938
the 2nd day of Sukkot Tartzät.

Your memory is holy and precious to us.

[from]

Soreh-Rochel and Yitzchak Reef and children

Yosheh Sacks and wife

Sheineh and Kalman Yudelowitz and children

Zalman [Solly] Sacks and children

Baruch [Benny] and Dolyeh Sacks

[Page 554]

In illuminated memory of
our father

Avraham-Koppel B'R Leib Ruch

who died in Rakishok 1st Tishrei Tarsäh,

of our mother

Liebeh Bat Ya'akov Wolf

who died in January, 26th Shevat Tarpäv,

for our brother

Michal-Yitzchak Ruch

who died in Johannesburg 27th Sivan 1942,

for our brother, husband and father

Yudel Ruch

who died in Cape Town 2nd day Adar Bet 1932.

We will not forget you and you will live forever in our hearts!

[from]

Toiveh Shneider and children

Asnah and Abraham Furman and children

Vitell and Faivush Klein and children

**Soreh Ruch [wife of Yudel Ruch] and
children Liebeh-Viteh and Chayim Leib**

[Page 555]

On the tombstone:

Our Dear Father

Reb Yitzchak Ben Shaul Halevi

died 1st Shevat Tarpäg

In memory of our father

Yitzchak [Alter] Bacher

who died 1st Shevat Tarpäg,

for our mother
Chayeh Soreh Ita
daughter of **Reb Abraham Koppel**

who died 29th Av Tashäg 28th August 1943.

We will remember you forever.

[from]

Chayim Shual [Ze'ev] Bacher, wife, and children
Koppel Bacher, wife, and children
Frieda Aron, husband, and children
Ella-Etel Scop, husband, and children
Meier-Moshe Bacher, wife, and children
South Africa
Debra Charney and husband and children, Bulawayo, Rhodesia

[Page 556]

May this be a holy sanctifying and unforgettable
remembrance for our extended family:

father **Dovid Moshe Beder**
who died Yom Kippur night 1937,
mother **Esther Rochel Beder**
perished [murdered] by the Nazis in Rakishok

sisters **Chaya Gofanowitz**, husband **Moshe Yitzchak**, and children, **Soreh**, **Reizeh**, **Taibeh**, **Frida**, and son **Aryeh Leib**

Rasiah – Beileh Abramowitz and husband, **Abraham**, originally from Antalept – a son of the famous Antalepter Maggid [preacher] and their children **Hershel**, **Zelig**, and **Yechiel**, who perished together with the Jewish population in Rakishok in 1941 by the hand of the German murderers,

brothers **Pinye Ya'akov Beder**, wife **Liebe**, and daughter **Asna**, perished in Posvel,

Chayim Beder, wife **Shifra**, and children, perished in Kovno,

Karpel Beder, wife **Soreh**, and children **Rivka**, **Ya'akov, Yechiel, Yehuda, Yitzchak and Dovid-Moshe**, perished in Rakishok.

Dovid Moshe and Esther Rochel Beder

And in memory of all the relatives and friends who perished
cruelly by the hand of the Germans in Lithuania,
we will remember you forever

[From]

**your children, brothers, sisters, and friends
Rivka and Ya'akov Miller and children
Shlomo Beder and family
Binyomin Beder and family
Yitzchak Beder and family**

[Page 557]

Our brother
the martyr

Nottel Gordon

Nottel Gordon

Who perished in Dachau together with 10,000 other Jews.

We erect hereby a memorial [headstone]

for his eternal memory.

[from]

**his brothers
Berel, Michal, and Yeshayahu Gordon
and their families**

[Page 558]

With these lines we erect an eternal memorial to
Necha, our dear one who passed away
at the age of 49 on 18 Sivan Tashyäg 1st June 1953.

Necha [Nechama] Bakalczuk –Tabachowitz

She devoted her best years and exceptional talents to teaching in the public primary schools in Poland, in the displaced persons camps after the Holocaust, and in South Africa. She was a wonderful personality, noble and aristocratic in her strength of character, in the beauty of her pure and innocent soul, and in her love of our nation and its culture.

You, dear Necha, were saved from the flames of the furnaces, from the inferno of the Nazis, but you enfolded into yourself the period of horrors that were stuck in your flesh like burning needles, and the tempest of nightmares that you experienced always floated before your eyes – together with the terrible tragedy that your children, **Yosseleh** and **Devoreleh**, were destroyed in the death chambers of Auschwitz. All these horrors, of the extermination camps, the tortures, the threats of death and conflagration that were organized by the wild animals, the accursed Germans, impoverished and weakened your health.

Those who remain are in sorrow and deep mourning.

**Your husband, your friend and companion
Meilach Bakalczuk
Your brothers Simon and Yosef Tabachowitz and families**

[Page 559]

On the fresh grave
of our
unforgettable father and brother

Ya'akov Snegg

who died on the first day of Chol
Ha Mo Eid Pesach the 12th April 1952.

May this be in
eternal remembrance.

[from]

wife Ita Snegg

son Abraham Snegg

**daughter Yenteh [Iris Josephine],
husband Peretz Blum, and sons**

daughter Leah and husband Zelig Blesovsky

**son Mottel Snegg, wife Yehudit, daughter
Beileh and Moshe Finger, and their
daughter Yehudit Chana Snegg**

**brother Mottel Leib and Chana Snegg,
children, and grandchildren [America]**

[Page 560]

To the everlasting and hallowed memory

of our parents

Yonah
and
Chaya-Leah Levin

Your children, who will remember you forever

[from]

**Avraham, Esther-Mineh, Moshe,
Nathan and Israel Levin and families**

[Page 561]

In memory of our dear parents:

father **Elchanan Arsh**,

the nationalist [patriotic] modern Jew,
who never abandoned the threshold of the shul;
aristocratic of spirit and wholeheartedly enthusiastic

mother **Nechama-Liebe**,

the quiet woman, overflowing with an
abundance of good manners [gentility],

who were slaughtered by Hitler and his cohorts
among the martyrs of Rakishok, Lithuania.

Beloved and pleasant in their lives, and
in their death they were not separated.

[from]

**Rochel, Meilach, Yerachmiel, Bluma,
Avraham and David Arsh**

and their families

[Page 562]

We will remember you forever

daughter and sister

Chaya-Ita Swartzberg

You will live in our hearts forever,
holy martyr.

[from]

**your parents
Hessel and Chana-Leah Swartzberg**

**your brother
Efraim Swartzberg, wife Soreh Yehudit,
and children**

**your sister Ethel and brother-in-law
Yerachmiel Aarons–Arsh, and children**

**your sister
Soreh Yehudit and brother-in-law Yosef Kark and family**

[Page 563]

It pains the heart and the wound will never be healed,
knowing how our whole family perished.
The memory is eternally unforgettable of:

our father **Menachem Mendel Krook**

who died in Varestzineh in 1922, 17th Tamuz Tarpäb

of our mother **Rochel Krook**

of the sisters **Reineh, Soreh, and Tzippeh**

of our brother **Abraham**, his wife, and children

of our brothers **Gershon, Shlomo, and Berel**

Who all perished in the Rakishok Holocaust [Destruction].
And of our brother **David**, wife, and child
who perished in Kupishok.
No-one was saved from this extended [large] family.
Your memory is holy to us.

[from]

**Sachneh and Leah Kruger and son
Menachem Mendel and Reuven**

[Page 564]

May this be a holy memorial for our sister and aunt

Miriam Farber [Gandelman]

with her husband and children
who committed suicide in Rakishok in order not
to be transported to the Nazi scaffolds – to the mass graves,

for our sister and aunt

Sheineh Farber [Epshtein]

for her husband **Chayim Yosef**
and their daughters,

who perished by the hand of the Nazi murderers
in S'vadosh.

[from]

**your brother
Nochum-Leib Farber, wife, and children,
your nieces and nephews:**

**Rochel, Meilach, Yerachmiel, Blumah,
Abraham, and David Arsh
and their families**

[Page 565]

May this be a light and eternal memory

for our father

Refael B"R Aharon Nachumowitz

who died 10th September 1937 – 5th Tishrei Tartzäh
in Johannesburg,

for our mother

Heniah-Malkah

who died 28th November 1944 – 13th Kislev Tashäh
in Johannesburg.

May this be a memorial.

[from]

Rivka, Naomi, Soreh-Liebeh and Aaron Nachumowitz

[Page 566]

We will forever hold the memory precious and holy

of our sincere and devoted [faithful] parents

Azriel-Yehuda and Toibeh Dektor

who perished tragically in Rakishok,

of our dear sister **Lyubeh Dektor**

who passed away in Moscow in 1943.

We, with our families, will never forget you.

[from]

**David Dektor
Shlomo Dektor
Meyer Dektor
Merah Dektor-Melamed
Ida Dektor-Kantan
Chaya Dektor-Gordon
and their families**

[Page 567]

A memorial for our father

Shlomo Hurwitz

who died on 5th Iyar Tarpäh,

and our mother
Soreh-Leah who perished in the massacre in Abel,

for our brother-in-law
Chatzkel Levin

who fell in the slaughter by the German cannibals, near Riga.

We will never forget you.

**Binyomin Michal and
Chaya Hurwitz and children
Freidel and Henech-Dovid Katz
Rochel Yaffe and her children
[South Africa]
Peretz Ze'ev and Liebe Hurwitz
Chayim Elia Hurwitz [America]**

Soreh-Leah Hurwitz

We hereby perpetuate [the memory] of our parents

Abba and Tcherneh-Liebe Blacher

who died in Ostrachan in the First World War,

and the martyrs **Ya'akov Ben-Zion Blacher**
who was the shochet [ritual slaughterer] in Visinti
and his wife, may she rest in peace [neé Behr] and children,

and the uncle, **Alter Shein 'Alav Ha Shalom'**
[May He Rest in Peace]
the Rosh Yeshiva in Slabodka, who perished by hand of the Germans,
in a tunnel, trying to hide the children of the Slabodker Ghetto in
sacks, wanting to save them from the German murderers.

Your memory is holy.

[from]

Nochum and Rivka Blacher and sons

[Page 568]

May this be a holy memorial
for our unforgettable parents

Meyer Berzack

born in 1883 and died 17th Iyar 1949

Yenteh-Beileh

born in 1889 and died 19th Adar 1948.

Both were buried in Cape Town, South Africa.

Your shining memory will never be forgotten.
Our ties to you are still very strong.
[The feelings of being connected to you are for us,
your children, still very strong.]

Their charity and good deeds have embedded themselves in the
hearts of Johannesburg Jewry and in us.

[from]

**Mordechai, Leibeh, Yehuda, Moshe and Heinech Berzack, wives,
and children in Johannesburg and Cape Town**

[Page 569]

May this be a holy memorial
for our unforgettable parents

Meyer Berzack

born in 1883 and died 17th Iyar 1949

Yenteh-Beileh

born in 1889 and died 19th Adar 1948.

Both were buried in Cape Town, South Africa.

Your shining memory will never be forgotten.
Our ties to you are still very strong.
[The feelings of being connected to you are for us,
your children, still very strong.]

Their charity and good deeds have embedded themselves in the
hearts of Johannesburg Jewry and in us.

[from]

**Mordechai, Leibeh, Yehuda, Moshe and Heinech Berzack, wives,
and children in Johannesburg and Cape Town**

[Page 570]

For our father **Sh'merel Saitowitz**
who died in Rakishok on 22nd Adar Tarpat.

and our mother **Soreh-Rasheh** who passed away in
Johannesburg 8th Shevat, 10th January 1946.

May these lines serve as a memorial.

[from]

Rochel-Tziviah and Yitzchak Zinman children and grandchildren
Genendel and Motteh Goott
Pinyeh and Pessiah-Gittel Saitowitz children and grandchildren
Dovid-Berel and Esther Saitowitz and children
Aharon and Soreh-Leah Saitowitz and children

May this be in memory of our parents

Avrohom-Ya'akov and Mineh Saitowitz

and brother **Gershon**, who was martyred [in sanctifying Hashem] in Rakishok
and brother **Zundel Saitowitz**, wife and children, who perished in Shavli [Shavel],
and sister **Rochel-Frumeh**, who died in Rakishok 14th Elul 1921
and sister **Genendel**, who died in Vilna.

[from]

Yisroel-Moshe and Tzipporah Saitowitz and children [in Kiryat-Chayim, Israel]
Soreh-Leah and Aharon Saitowitz and children [in South Africa]
Menucha-Rivka and Velvel Saitowitz and children [in South Africa]

We will always cherish the memory of our parents
Yosef and Chaya-Soreh Dublansky, who died in Abel.

and of our brother **Nottel** and his wife
Reizel Dubiansky and sons, who perished in Ezhereni,

of our sisters **Chana-Elkeh**, **Feigetshkeh** and
Merel, and her husband **Aharon Levin**,
of our brother **Sholem Dubiansky** and his wife
of our uncle and aunt **Hirsheh and Toibeh Yosselowitz**
who all perished in Abel.

Your memory is holy.

[from]

Esther and Dovid-Berel Saitowitz and children

[Page 571]

May this Hazkorah be an Eternal Light

for our father

Chayim-Itzeh Fulman

who died in S'vadoshtz on 21st March 1929,

for our mother **Ida-Feigeh Fulman**,

for our sister **Mereh**, husband **Leibeh** and children,

for our sister **Rivkah Fulman**,

who all perished in Sviadoshitz,

for our sister

Soreh-Leah, husband **Bentzieh Miller**, and

daughter **Chashkeh**, who perished in Rakishok.

The memory of all of you is holy!

We will never forget you!

Hindeh and Avrohom Merkel and children

[from]

Dinah Merkel, Chaya and Chayim
Lipschitz, and children [Cape Town]

Leibeh and Rochel-Leah Fulman and
children [Boston, America]

Avrohom-Gershon and Fenyah Fulman and
children [Boston, America]

Chana and Yisroel Fushner and
daughters [Boston, America]

[Page 572]

For our unforgettable parents

Reuven and Rochel Ruch

we, the sons and daughters, erect here
on this Yizkor Page, a memorial

in honour of your holy memory.

In sorrow, your children who remained behind:

[from]

Tuviah Ruch and family, Johannesburg, South Africa

Ahuva Ruch and family, Israel

Leah Ruch and family, Johannesburg

Latteh Ruch and family, Cape Town

Elchanan Ruch and family, Canada

Reizel Ruch and family, Canada

Sorrel Ruch and family, Canada

Avrohom Ruch and family, Canada

Ittel Ruch and family, America

Yerachmiel Ruch and family, Riga, Soviet Union

[Page 573]

Let this be a memorial and

an everlasting memory [remembrance]

for our Father and Zaida

Chayim Shimshon Swartzberg

who died in Worcester, America
24th Teivet Tartzā
13th January 1931,

for our mother

Riveh-Giteh Swartzberg
[Bat Reb Yisroel-Tzvi]

who died in Rakishok 26th Adar Tarsā.

[from]

**Hessel and Chana-Leah Swartzberg
children and grandchildren**

We, Moshe and Chaya-Soreh Klavier, express our great
sorrow over the cruel death

of our parents **Zelig-Dovid and Tileh-Ida Klavier**,

of our brother **Ya'akov Klavier**,

who were murdered by the German gangsters [bandits] in Abel.

May these lines be an eternal memorial light
for our father **Mendel Klatzkin**, who died in Yanishok in 1939,
for our mother **Chassel Klatzkin**,
for our brother **Avrohom Klatzkin** and wife,
for our sister **Rivka Galperin**, husband, and children,

who all perished in Yanishok.

We will never forget all of you.

Your names will be engraved in our hearts forever.

[from]

Moshe and Chaya-Soreh Klavier and children

[Page 574]

May this be
in everlasting memory

of our father
Mordechai-Peretz Berzack,

who perished in Bagoslavishok,

of our mother **Chaya Berzack**, who
died in Bagoslavishok in 1929,

of our brother Gedaliah Berzack,
who perished in Keidan,

of our sister **Gittel**,
who perished in Bagoslavishok.

[from]

**Reizel and Yisroel Michel-Michalewitz
and children, Johannesburg**

Yentel and Reuven Novick and children, Pretoria

May this be a memorial

for my husband and the father
of our children

Mendel Witz [Yosselowitz]

We will always remember you, who
are unforgettable.

[from]

**Malkah Witz and her children
Berel Witz and wife
Liebeh and David Kaplan
Binyomin Witz and wife
Beileh and Leah Witz**

[Page 575]

A hallowed memorial for our mother

Rikle Smilg

who died in Johannesburg 5th [Menachem] Av Tarsät, 31st July 1944

and for our sister and brother-in-law
Goldeh and Nottel Gordon, and children,
who perished in the Rakishok Holocaust,
and for all our relatives
who perished in the Holocaust of Lithuania.

[from]

Moshe and Leah Smiedt [Smilg] and children

May this be a memorial for my
beloved parents

Dovid and Sheineh Sabel

who passed away in Vryheid, Natal.
Your memory is holy and precious to me!

[from]

Sarah Jacobson

For **Katriel and Sheineh Sommer**
and
Beileh-Tzindel and her children,

who all perished by the hand of the
German murderers in Rakishok.

May this be an everlasting memorial for them!

[from]

Avrohom-Yisroel and Rochel Tzeredines
Miller, Oudtshoorn, Capetown

[Page 576]

On the new [fresh] grave of
my devoted wife and mother of our children

Soreh Moskowitz

who died suddenly
Shabbat 7th Teivet Tashyav 5th January 1952

May these lines be a hallowed and an
everlasting memory!

We will never forget her and always
remember her!

[from]

Chayim-Refael Moskowitz and
sons Shmuel [Sam] and Zalman [Zummy]
daugher Tamara and son-in-law Avraham [Arnold]
Tannenbaum and granddaughter Hayley

[Page 577]

I am deeply shattered by the gruesome murder
of my cousins

Mottel Katz and family

Hertzl Shapiro,

wife **Rochel-Gittel** and family,

and of the tragic deaths of all my friends
who were brutally murdered by the Nazi-cannibals
in Rakishok.

[from]

Rochel Herr [Shapiro]

In Memoriam
[remembrance]
of my beloved sister

Ida

with her husband and children,
son-in-law and grandchildren.

I will never forget you.

[from]

Mirch and Yudel Riback
Johannesburg

I will never forget and
always remember
my beloved sister

Soreh Tzadok,

brother-in-law, and three sons,

Pesach, Yankel and Lazar

[from]

Yudel and Mireh Riback

[Page 578]

Hereby, we erect a memorial
for our parents

Meyer-Leizer and Dobra Orelowitz

for our sisters

Freida, husband **Avraham**, and their children,

Rochel-Ita, husband, and children,

for our brothers

Pesach and his wife and children,
Choneh and his wife and children,
and for our brother **Ben Zion**.

Your memory is holy to us!

[from]

Chayim Leib and Beileh Orelowitz and children

May this be a memorial

for our parents

Chatzkel and Chaya Tzukernick,

for our sister
Reizel,

who perished tragically by the hand of the Nazi murderers.

We will never forget your tragic death!

[from]

Beileh and Chayim Leib Orelowitz and children

[Page 579]

And our brother

Moshe Zelig Karabuz

who died [serving] in the
South African Army
in the year 1944.

**We, Yossel Chayim
Ozer Yitzchak Bezalel
Liebeh Gordon
Mineh Medin
Slava Paul**

Will always remember you!

In hallowed memory of our sister

Reizel and her husband **Moshe Hesselkowitz**

who perished in the graves together with all the Rakishok Jews.
We will never forget you!

[From]

**Rivka, Naomi, Soreh-Leikeh
and Aaron Nochumowitz and their families**

We, daughters and sons,

perpetuate with this Hazkarah

[the memory] of our parents

Elieh-Leizer

and

Soreh Karabuz

who died in Cape Town

[Page 580]

We will never forget our parents

Moshe and Goldeh Zageh,

and our mother and mother-in-law

Tzviah Zageh and children,

who perished in Rakishok.

[from]

Reuven Zageh and family,
South Africa
Rochel Roszhner-Zageh,
Israel

May this be an everlasting
memory
[memorial]

for my sister

Soreh-Mineh and her husband

Shmuel Charmatz.

and for my sister

Feigeh-Rochel and her husband

Yisroel-Moshe Grif.

who perished in Rakishok.

[from]

Hindeh Koppelowitch
and family

In memory of
our father
brother
and grandfather,

the important [an illustrious] man,
exalted [very learned] in his knowledge of Torah,

**Moshe Ya'akov B"R Nochum Leib
Ha Kohein Farber**.

who passed away [was gathered to his people]
in Yerushalayim
on 2nd Kislev Tashyäg,

at a full age [a ripe old age] being
97 years old.

We erect this memorial to him.

[Page 581]

In memory of
our father
brother
and grandfather,
the important [an illustrious] man,
exalted [very learned] in his knowledge of Torah,

Moshe Ya'akov B"R Nochum Leib Ha Kohein Farber

who passed away [was gathered to his people]
in Yerushalayim
on 2nd Kislev Tashyäg,

at a full age [a ripe old age] being
97 years old.

We erect this memorial to him.

[from]

**Nochum Leib and Necha Farber, children and
Grandson,**
Port Elizabeth

Fanya Rubinshtein and daughters,
Leningrad

Zalman Michal and Matlah Cohen and family

**Rochel, Meilech, Yerachmiel, Blumah
Abraham and David Arsh
and their families**

[Page 582]

As an illuminated memorial

Of our father **Avraham Yitzchak Eidelman**

who died 12th Adar 1920 in Abel,

of our mother **Simeh Eidelman**

of our sister **Chyeneh** and brother-in-law

Tuvia Radeh, and children, **Yitzchak, Chaya-Henyeh, Leib, Peretz, Chana, and Ben-Zion,**

who perished in Abel together with our whole extended family.

[from]

**Aryeh and Rochel Eidelman and family
Rochel Hurwitz,**
San Francisco

May this be an unforgettable reminder of our brother

Yechezkel, his wife **Soreh,** and son **Immanuel Jacobson,**

who perished in Ezhereni.

[from]

sister and brother-in-law
Rochel and Aryeh Eidelman and sons

[Page 583]

I will never forget even to the
last minute of my life
that August dawn in 1942,
under the hail of the Hitler-Fascist bullets, at the ghetto
fences, that we parted finally
[fatally] and after that you
perished tragically in the
slaughter of Vohlin, Ukraine.

You my dearly loved

Devorah [Dora] Bat Shlomo Chayim

and

Rodel Eizenshtein from Pinsk.
and my only daughter

Feigeh [Felinkeh] Bat Eli Melech,

and **Devorah Bakalczuk.**

You are, for me, deeply engraved in my soul and spirit.

The memory is unforgettable and holy of my dear and quaint mother

Soreh Bat Meir

whose soul expired on the first day of Rosh Hashanah 1940
in Sernik [Palesia].

Until I go into eternity, I will
remember you in great holiness [I will remember you until I die].

[from]

Elimelech [Meilech] Bakalczuk

[Page 584]

We perpetuate hereby

our mother

Sarah-Riveh Bat Ettel Levin,

our father

Reb Aryeh B"R Yisroel Levin,

our mother

Chana-Riveh Bat Tzireh Kriel,

our father

Reb Yitzchak-Boruch B"R Zisheh Kriel

[from]

**Chana and Bunem-Idel Kriel
and their children**

For my brother

Chatziah-Leib Ashkenazi,

and his wife **Soreh-Leah,**

and their children **Chayim, Yishayahu, Chaikeh, Hirshel, and Bashkeh,**
who perished in the destruction of
Rakishok [the Rakishker Holocaust],

for our sister **Mersh**

with her husband **Eliyahu Segal**

who perished in Utian,

for their five children
who perished with their families in
the Kovno Ghetto,

May this be an eternal remembrance.

[from]

**Ittel and
Yerachmiel Genn and family**

May this be a memorial

for our husband and father

Michael Podlass,

who died in Johannesburg,
South Africa,

for my sister **Braineh**
with her five married children
and her grandchildren,

for my brother
Yankel, wife, children, and grandchildren,

who all perished in Melitopol
[Ukraine] by hand of the
Hitler murderers.

[from]

Leah Podlass and children

May this serve as a holy
memorial [rememberance] of

my mother **Rikleh,**

who died in Johannesburg
31st July 1941 5 days in Adar,

my sister **Goldeh Gordon** and her husband **Nottel,** and their
children **Yosef, Leib, Zeldeh and Itzik,**

my sister-in-law **Beileh Jacobson** and brother-in-law **Yankel,**
and their children,

and of all our relatives, who perished in the last Great Holocaust.

[from]

Taibie Gordon and children

[Page 585]

In holy remembrance

of wife and mother

Pereh-Ida Ruch,

who died in remote [far away] Siberia 16th Sivan 1952

of our son and brother

Elchanan Zelig Ruch

who died in Rakishok 14th Adar 1931,

and his wife **Chaya-Zeldeh** and daughter **Chana**
who perished in the Rakishker Holocaust,

of our son and brother

Meier and daughter **Soreh Ruch,**

of our brothers
David and Yissacher Ruch.

who were the first martyrs in Kovno, shot
by the Nazi executioners [hangmen] 21st June 1941,

of our daughter and sister
Tzipporah, who perished in the destruction
of Alita, with her husband **Yitzchak Krengel**
and their children, **Chana and Yisroel**.

for our brother and uncle **Shmuel Ruch**
and his wife **Leah** and their daughter **Michleh**,
who perished in Rakishok,

for our father, brother, and uncle,
the beloved Rosh Yeshiva, The Rabbi
Reb Yehoshuah Zelig Ruch,

with his wife **Esther**

and daughters **Chaitzeh and Pereleh,**
who perished in the Vilna Holocaust.

[from]

**Pesach Ruch, Leibeh, and Gitteh Ruch
Berel and Chaya-Laykeh Ruch
and children
Batya Ruch
Meier-Leib and Soreh Ruch and children**

[Page 586]

May this memorial page be a headstone

for our father **Yisroel Itzikman** who died
in Rakishok 10th Iyar, 13th May 1927,

for our mother **Chiyeneh Itzikman**

and sister **Liebeh Shulman** and husband **Yisroel**
and their two children, who were killed by a
bomb dropped from a German plane
as they were escaping from Kovno,

for our sister **Bassel Gamburg**, husband **Velveh**,
and children, who perished during the slaughter in Rakishok,

for our sister **Chaya-Devorah**, who died
suddenly in Worcester, America on the
5th Candle, Channukah, year 1928,

for our uncle **Yerachmiel Itzikman** and family,

and for our aunt **Mineh Wineberg**
who were massacred by the hand of the
German executioners.

We will be reminded and remember you.

[from]

**Rivka and Nochum Blacher and Sons
Yisroel and Abbo (Solly and Abe)**

Reichel and Avrohom Gordon and children

[Page 587]

**In memoriam
for our parents**

father **Shmerel**
died in Abel,
Lithuania, 1924,

mother **Soreh,**
murdered by the Germans,

our brother
Avrohom-Moshe,

our sisters
Dobbeh, Riveh, Mineh

Who perished tragically during the national catastrophe.
May Hashem avenge their blood!

[from]

Yosef Shneider and family

[Page 588]

For our father

Mendel Leib Griz

who died in Johannesburg 1930,

for our mother

Ella Griz

who perished in September 1941
in the Kovner Ghetto.

[from]

Yitzchk and Winfred Griz and sons, Mendel-Leib and Zossel

We mourn our parents,
Zaida and Bobba

Zalkeh and Soreh-Buneh Shapiro

who perished in the
Ponevezher Holocaust.

[from]

daughter Tzvia and
Hirshe-Michael Segal
Chaya-Liebeh and Berel Ruch
and children

May these lines stand
in eternal memory
of our parents, Zaide and Bobba,

Faivush Segal

died 23rd Tamuz 1941.

of our mother

Tziviah Segal

who died
in Kovno 29th Tishrei 1932.

[from]

Hirshe-Michoel and Tzivia Segal
Chaya-Liebeh and Berel Ruch
and children

We will always remember
our parents
Zaida and Bobba

Michoel and Tzeppeh Klug,

sister and aunt **Liebeh**,

husband **Chayim,** and children,

brothers and uncles

Nechemiah and Moshe Klug

who perished in Rakishok.

[from]

Chayah-Ettel and husband Tzemach Salomon, Pretoria

Leah Klug and family, Kovno
Feigeleh Lapp

[Page 589]

Liebe Blumah and Aharon Ginzburg

For our father **Aharon Ginzburg** [Artzik Pesachs], who died in Rakishok 28th Iyar 1941,

for our mother **Liebeh-Blumah**, who died in Rakishok 19th Kislev 1929,

for our brother **Yosef Rafael**, wife **Rochel** and children, who perished in the Rakishok Holocaust,

for our sister **Chana** and her husband **Herman Wagenheim** and four children,

who were murdered by the Germans in Dublin-Letland,

for our sister **Feigeh** and her husband who perished in Vilkomir,

and for all our relatives who perished.

For our brother:
Chayim Dov-Behr Ginzburg, who died in Parys, South Africa 7th Iyar – 13th May 1945,

and for our brother **Moshe Ginzburg**, who died 20th Teivet Tashyäg, 2nd December 1952.

May these lines [words] serve as a Memorial.

[from] Yisroel and Yenteh Ginsburg and family
Shmuel and Merel Ginsburg and family

Chayim Dov-Behr Ginzburg

[Page 590]

For our Parents

Shlomo
and
Tzippeh Friedman

who perished in Abel.

May this serve as an eternal
[everlasting] remembrance.

[from]

Abba Friedman and his wife

Johannesburg

[Page 591]

Not one of you has a tombstone, so I, who remained living, erect
a memorial, which will remember my father
Baruch B"R Aharon Bakalczuk,
who perished in the destruction of Sernik, a shtetl near
Pinsk, in the month of Av, 1941;

Rabbi Tzvi-Hirsh Bakalczuk

Rabbi Tzvi-Hirsh who was the Rosh Bet-Din
in Stolavitch and Deretshin, White Russia;
my brother **Rabbi [HaGaon] the genius Tzvi Hirsh Bakalczuk**,
who perished together with his wife **Chaya-Miriam**
in Treblinka, and his children **Malka, Simeh,** and **Moshe-Aharon**,
who were shot to death in the Holocaust in Deretshin;
my brother **Yehuda-Leib Bakalczuk**, his wife **Chaya**,
and their children **Berel** and **Aharon, Feigeh Malka,** and **Brocheh,
Sheineh-Yentel** and **Rochaleh**, who perished in the Serniker massacre;
my sister **Esther-Goldeh Lande**, who perished in the massacre
in Vohlin, and her husband **Abraham**, who died in Dambrowitz in the 1930s;
my sister **Riveleh** and her husband **Hershel Fishman** and their children **Aharon-Yitzchak,
Motteh,** and **Zeldeleh**, who perished in the
graves [pits] of the Morotshner Ghetto.

[from]
your son, brother, and uncle
Melech Bakalczuk

[Page 592]

May this be a hallowed memory

for our parents

Chayim-Yerachmiel and Chaya-Batya Ruch,

for our sisters

Heinieh, Iteh, Keileh, Liebeh, Gitteh-Zeldeh and
our brother **Hirsh,**

who all perished in the Rakishok Holocaust,

for our sister **Leah**

who perished in Vilna where she was studying,

for our aunt and uncle

Rochel and Zelig Zageh

who perished in Rakishok,

for my Zaida **Elieh Hirsheh**

and Bobba **Zeldeh Reef**

who died in Rakishok,

and for my whole extended family who perished
by hand of the Hitler murderers.

[from]

daughter and son-in-law

Ella and Leibe Osband and children
Reizeh and Asher Manne

[Page 593]

We will never forget you

our father and father-in-law

Itzik Baradavka

who died in Rakishok 21st February 1940,

our mother and mother-in-law

Ethel Baradavka,

our brother and nephew

Zalman Baradavka

who perished in the Rakishker Holocaust,

our sister and niece

Eidel and her child

who perished in the Kovno Ghetto,

our sister and aunt

Reizeh-Dobra Penkin [neé Ruch]

who died 28th February 1932,

our brother-in-law

Katriel Penkin

who died 24th June 1926 in Cape Town.

[from]

Koppel Barkai [Baradavka] wife and child in Israel
Leibeh Davkin [Baradavka] wife and child
Asna and Abraham Furman, children
and grandchildren

[Page 594]

May this be a memorial

Seated: father Hertzeh; mother Toibe-Riveh; brother Avrohom-Leib.
Standing: Chaya-Dvorah, Soreh, and Chasia.

For our unforgettable parents
Hertzeh Wingrin, who died in Rakishok 7th Elul 1936.
Toibeh-Riveh Wingrin, who perished in the Kovno Ghetto.

For our unforgettable brothers and sisters
Avrohom-Leib Wingrin and wife **Henieh**, who perished in Rakishok.

Chasia and husband **Naphtali Wolk** and son, who perished in Rakishok.

Chaya-Dvorah and husband **Shaul Lubowitz** and four children,
who perished in the massacre in Dvinsk.

Soreh Wingrin, who perished running away from
the Germans from the Kovno Ghetto.

We will remember you forever!

[from] Asnah Chait, husband and children, Pretoria
Malkah Levy and children, Johannesburg
Yisroel-Pesach Wingrin, wife and children, Johannesburg

[Page 595]

As an enlightened and eternal memory [memorial]

for our parents

Aharon-Natan and Irleh-Brochah Rubin,

who died in Philadelphia, North America.

Tombstones: Irleh-Brochah [Front] Aharon-Natan [Back] Rubin.

We and our families will always remember

and perpetuate your names in holiness.

[from]

Shlomo Rubin, Johannesburg, South Africa

Hertz Rubin, Philadelphia, USA

Gitteh Ferman, Philadelphia, USA

Abba Rubin, Dartmore [?], USA

[Page 596]

May this be an eternal memorial
of our mother **Soreh-Rivka Rubin**,
of our brother **Shlomo Rubin** and wife **Rochel**, and
their children **Dovid-Leizer** and **Leibeh**.

[from]
Chaikel and Soreh-Liebe Rubin, children and grandchild

We mourn the Destruction of Rakishok and Environs
and the demise [deaths]

of six million Jews

by the German Executioners.

[from]
Business: Bacher, Aron and Co.

May this be an eternal flame

for my father **Hirsh Baradavka**, who died
when I was a child,
for my mother **Etta**,
who perished 15th September 1941,
and my sister **Esther Baradavka-Shwartz**
and husband **Shlomo**,
who perished in the
Kovno Ghetto 15th July 1944.

[from] Liubah Baradavkah, Israel

[Page 597]

A memorial

for our father

Fishel Levin – Ha Levi,

and for our mother

Sheineh-Rochel,

who died in Uzbrkistan, having been evacuated [there]
during the Second World War.
We will remember you forever!

[from]

Chaya and Binyomin-Michal Hurwitz and children, South Africa
Ethel and husband Avrohom Nussbaum, Canada
Beileh and Mendel Lerman, Canada
Soreh and Yitzchak Shneidman and children, Canada
Meier-Natan Levin, wife, and children, Canada
Chaim Shimon Levin, wife, and children, Canada
Yosef and Feigeh Levin and children, Vilna

....

In memory of all those

who lie in the dust [sleep],

the departed of our family
and
landsleit.

H. Orelowitz
Parys, South Africa

[Page 598]

For the enlightened [illuminated] and dear memory of our
Father, Husband and Zaida

Menachem-Mendel B"R Yisroel Yosselowitz

who surrendered his hallowed soul on the
Holy Shabbat, Friday night, while performing the
Kiddush, 6th Candle Channukah 1948.

He observed Torah and Mizvot. He kept Torah laws
and was a lovable and friendly person. He took great
interest in everything and in the needs of the community.
In his home shtetl of Abel, he was a gabbai
[a Shul official] in the Chassidic Shul, and also
here in Johannesburg he was a committee member
of the Chassidic Minyan [Congregation].
He was also an important and capable worker
and member of the Rakishok Society.

Mainly, the love of Israel [the Jewish People]
was very precious and holy to him.

In sorrow, those who remain:

[his sorrowful widow]
his wife Zeldeh Malka Yosselowitz;
daughter Liebe, son-in-law Moshe David Fisher,
and children Soreh, Yonah, and Pinchas Hertzl;
daughter Elkeh, son-in-law Lipman Friedman,
and children Yehuda, Chaya-Musheh and Leah;
daughter Rivka, son-in-law Moshe Bunem Super,
and children Natan, Ya'akov, Zorach, D'vorah, and Rochel Leah;
daughter Sarah, son-in-law Ya'akov Lifshitz, and children;
daughter Henkeh, son-in-law Avrohom Yitzchak Yachad,
Ben Zion, Reuven and Leah
son Yisroel-Leib, daughter-in-law Esther,
and children Menachem-Mendel and Chayah Rochel.

[Page 599]

A Memorial

For my father

and mother

and the whole perished family.

[from]

Yitzchak Shneider and wife

Randfontein, South Africa

[Page 600]

For wife and mother

Chaya-Genendel Bat Shmuel-Micha Katz,

who died in Johannesburg

28th Nissan Tashyäb
26th April 1952.

She was very charitable [righteous] with
many beautiful qualities [attributes].

May her memory be hallowed!

[from]

her husband,

daughters,

sons,

sons-in-law,

daughters-in-law,

and grandchildren

[Page 601]

Herewith
we erect an everlasting memorial
in memory

of our dear father,

Yankel-Hirsheh Kur,

of our dear mother,

Soreh Kur,

of our beloved brother

Faiveh-Behr,

who were massacred by the
cursed Nazi Fascist animals.

We will always remember you!

[from]

Sho'al Kur
Braineh Kur-Rotholz
Yossel Kur
Leah Kur-Riback,
South Africa

Devorah Kur, Israel

Henech, Leib Mendel, and
Michoel Kur and families, Vilna

[Page 602]

In eternal memory of our parents

Standing: Moshe, Yisroel, Leah, Lana, and Chana-Rochel.
Seated: Abba Yehoshua, Latteh-Gittel and No'ach.

Abba Yehoshua and Latteh Gittel Visakolsky

Father died in Dusyat 3rd Tishrei 1931,
and mother perished in Utian, witnessing the murdering
of her children who were shot before her eyes.

Of our brothers **Yisroel, Moshe, and Noach.**

Yisroel perished in the Rakishok massacre.
Moshe fell in the [massacre] slaughter by the Germans in
the battles of the Red Army with the Germans.
No'ach perished with his wife in Utian.

We will never forget you and hold
your memory dear, forever!

[from] Leah and Nathan Brinkman and children, Johannesburg
Lana Visakolsky, Vilna

[Page 603]

May this be in everlasting
remembrance of our parents
Yitzchak and Chaya Davidowitz.
We will remember you forever.
[from] Abba-Leib and Sheineh Davidowitz and children
Malkah Witz and children.

For our dear and unforgettable parents:
father **Avrohom-Mendel Lubowitz,**
who died in Johannesburg 20th January 1939,
mother **Ettel Lubowitz,**
who died in Johannesburg 16th August 1947.
May this be a memorial.
[from] Toibeh-Riveh and Leib Levitzky and daughter, Charkov
Soreh-Leah and Mottel Yaffe and daughters, Johannesburg
Chana-Mereh and Zelig Mendel Penn and children, Johannesburg
Shmerel and Yenteh Lubowitz and daughter, Durban
Chaim and Beileh Reizeh Lubowitz and children, Vereeniging

[Page 604]

Menachem-Mendel Nachumowitz
and Chaya Nachumowitz

May these lines be in
everlasting memory

for our husband and father
**Menachem-Mendel B"R Aharon
Nachumowitz,**

who died in Johannesburg
12th Teivet Tashyá
20th December 1950,

for our aunt
Musieh Kalakur
with her children and grandchildren,

for our uncle
Chayim Yitzchak Nachumowitz
and his family.

for our aunt
Soreh-Dinah Shribnik
with her husband and daughter **Feige Rivkah**,
all of whom perished in the
Rakishok massacre.

[from]

wife Chaya Nachumowitz

sons Chloineh Nachumowitz, wife, and child
Aharon Nachumowitz
Moshe Nachumowitz, wife, and child
Avrohom-Yosef Nachumowitz, wife, and child

daughter Gessiah-Rivka Jonas,
husband, and daughter

[Page 605]

May this be a memorial

for our father

Moshe B"R Yitzchak Aires

who died in Sviadoshitz,

for our mother

Pessia Aires,

for our sister

Soreh-Leah Pakawitz
with her husband **Leizer**, and their
four children,

for our sisters

Taibeh and Yiskeh,

for our brother

Binyomin,

who all perished in Sviadoshitz.

[from]

Chaikel Aires and children

Yitzchak and Sheineh Aires and children

[Page 606]

We perpetuate hereby the name of our brother

Ya'akov Shmuskowitz

hero of the Soviet Union and Finland.

He was
Lieutenant General and Chief of the
Soviet Air Force.

He was the most capable in our family.
His parents loved him dearly as their
first born and gifted [able] son.

He completed a Russian 'middle school'
and for a certain time he studied at the
Yiddishe-Folkshul of the 'Kultur League.'

He went to Soviet Russia and studied law.
He then entered the ranks of the Russian Army and
returned an invalid from the Japanese front
missing a leg [foot].

Nevertheless, he still managed to establish
a great military career for himself
because of his great heroism and knowledge
of the art of flying, both as a pilot
and also as a theoretician. He became
Chief of the Soviet Air Force.

In honor of his enlightened memory!

[from]

his brothers

Aaron and Yerachmiel Moss [Shmuskowitz]
and their families

Durban, South Africa

[Page 607]

In the holiest of holy memories

of our parents

Ya'akov and Guteh-Leah Kark,

of our sisters

D'vorah, Yochkeh and Yehuidit,

and of our brother

Leizer,

who all perished in Rakishok,

and of our brother

Leib

who died in Rakishok in 1938.

[from]

Yosef and Yehudit Kark and children
in South Africa

Yitzchak Kark, wife, and child in Israel

Meier Kark, wife, and children in Vilna

Ida Kark, husband, and child in Vilna

[Page 608]

For our father

Dov-Behr Berelowitz

who died in Johannesburg 6th August 1935,

for our mother

Chasia Tzireh

who died 10th Sivan 1916 in Melitopol [Crimea],

for our father

Shmuel-Natan Muskat

who died in Chaluwetz Province of Vilna
12th Sivan 1900,

for our mother

Feiga Bat R'Yerachmiel

who died 22nd Teivet 1925 in Dakshutz,

for our nephew
Chatzkel Berelowitz
who fell in the struggle for the Independence
of Israel against the Arab countries.

He was the first of the South African
Jews who fell in the struggle for Israel.

For the whole family Ruskind,
who perished in the great Holocaust.

May these lines serve as an everlasting memorial for them all.

[from]

Menachem Mendel and Chaya Riveh Muskat
children and grandchildren

[Page 609]

For our father and brother

Meier Moss [Shmuskowitz]

who died suddenly in Durban
5th September 1943.

May this be an unforgettable memorial.

[from]

Children Zalman and Feigeh Moss,

brother Aharon Moss, wife and children,

and

brother Yerachmiel Moss, wife, and children
Durban, South Africa

[Page 610]

We present this Hazkarah [Memorial]

for our father

Refael Gringut

who died in Subat [Kurland] 8ᵗʰ Tamuz 1900,

for our mother

Esther Shlosberg-Gringut,

for our brother

Chayim-Yitzchak Gringut and wife **Matleh**
and their sons **Refael** and **Chone,**

for our sister

Mineh and her husband **Henach Rozenberg**
and children,

for our sister

Soreh-Veleh and **Dovid Rosenberg** and children,

for our brothers

Arkeh, Shimkeh, Motkeh Shlosberg

and
for all our relatives who so gruesomely
perished in the Destruction of Subat.

[from]

Hirsheh-Leib and Rochel Green [Gringut],
with their children Eleh and Refael

[Page 611]

An eternal memory for our
dear innocent parents

Yosel Raphael and Rochel-Rivka Ginsburg

who were killed by the murderers of our
people with all the Jews of Rakishok,

for our sister
Soreh-Pessah Bunimowitz
and for our sister
Chana-Musiah Ginsburg,
who expired in the concentration camps
of the Nazis [may their name be obliterated!]

Their memory is engraved in us forever!

May their memory be blessed!

[from]
Yitzchak Ginsburg and family, Johannesburg
Tzipporah Ginsburg and family [Kimchi], Chaderah
Hindah Ginsburg and family [Kutz], Ramat Hashofeit
Pesach Ginsburg and family [Petersen], America
Aharon Ginsburg and family, Vilna, Russia

[In Hebrew not Yiddish.]

[Page 612]

The illuminated memory of my parents
who are interred [who sleep] in the dust of Rakishok:
father
Moshe Beynart, who died in 1938,
mother
Chayah Beynart, who died in 1933,
brother
Ya'akov Zelig, who was killed in
Johannesburg by murderers who entered
his clothing business [shop].

[from] Zorach Beynart and family

In holy memory
of my father

Mendel Kuperman

who died five days after Pesach 1940 in
Johannesburg.
[from]
David [Dave] Kuperman and family

We stand in sorrow at the graves

of our brother **David** and his wife,
of our sisters
Reizeh, Leah and Beileh,
who perished by hand of
the Hitler murderers.

[from] Yossel and Elkeh Perkis

We will always remember the names of our parents:
Reb Yosef-Yitzchak Klein [Rosh Yeshivah]
of Rakishok, who died in Poneveszh 8th Sivan 1927,

and our mother **Mereh-Feigeh**, who died on the road
during the evacuation of Lithuania in the First World War,

our brother **Menachem-Mendel**, who died in Mexico,

our sister **Soreh-Leah** and her husband **Eliyahu Shneider**
and their child **Michoel**, who perished in Kurshan during the
Lithuanian Holocaust.

[from]
Shlomit and Yona Nanas and children, Israel
Shoshana and Yechiel Leib Mindel and
children, South Africa
Chana and Menachem Mendel Gandelman
and their children, Israel

[Page 613]

We express our deep and great sorrow over the
death of our Father

Michoel-Ze'ev
who perished by the hand of the Nazi
animals in the year 1941,

over the death of our brother **Moshe**
and over the death of Moshe's one and
only little daughter **Frumkeleh**
who perished by the hand of the
German cannibals [may their name be
obliterated] in the year 1941.

We will always remember you!

[from] Yitzchak and Yisroel Mikel [Michalewitz], Johannesburg
Shimon-Yosel Mikel-Michalewitz, Pretoria
with their wives and children

[Page 614]

For our father **Hirsheh-Yankel Wiener**
who died in Abel, 28th Teivet 1914,

for our mother **Dobra Weiner**,
who perished in the Rakishok Holocaust.

for our sister **Malkah Zamelan** [Weiner],
who perished in the Rakishok Holocaust.

for our brother **Yudel Weiner**,
who fell in the massacre on the Japanese Front, 13th September 1945.

for our brother-in-law **Leibel Zamelan**,
who fell as a partisan in the struggle against the Germans.

May this be an illuminated memory!

[from] Rivkah and Michael Feldman and sons
Dinah and David Katz and children

May this be an unforgettable memorial
for our cousins
Yosef and **Batya-Ettel Shwartz**
and their son **Yitzchak**,

and for all our relatives
and friends who perished
in Rakishok and Environs.

[from] Feldman brothers
and their families

For our parents
Mottel and **Musheh-Batya Katz**,
for our brother
Berel, wife and children,
for our brother **Yudel**,
and sister **Soreh-Ettel Sohn**, husband,
and children,
who perished in Sevenishok.

May this be a memorial.

[from] David and Dinah Katz
and children

[Page 615]

Chayim Ya'akov Zakshtein

Seated: Pessel Pogrund.
Standing: sister Chieneh, brother
Reuven Meier, sister Feigeh Bluma,
brother-in-law.

May this be a memorial for my husband

Hayim Ya'akov Zakstein
who died in Johannesburg
15th December 1943,

for my father-in-law
Leibeh
and my mother-in-law
Henieh Zakshtein,
who died in Abel,

for the parents
Nochum Nottel and **Pessel Pogrund**,
who died in Abel.

For sister
Feige Blumah,
husband and son,

for sister
Chieneh Pogrund,

for brother
Reuven Meier Pogrund,

who all perished in the
great Holocaust in Abel.

[from]

wife Tzippeh-Reizen Zakshtein

daughter Serah Yudelsohn,
husband, and children,

son Nochum-Nottel Zakshtein.

[Page 616]

Standing: brother Meier and [long may she live] Golda-Pogrund-Dick.
Seated: sister Tzileh, mother Henieh, father Yitzchak, brother Zalman.

May this be a memorial stone for my father,
Yitzchak Pogrund, who died at the age of 77 years.
He was a learned Jew, very religious, and very loved in his home shtetl
Abel and environs. He took part in the communal activity of the shtetl
and helped all the shtetl institutions. He married off all his children.
The youngest daughter married a young man from the Slabodker
Yeshiva, who lifted the spirit of the Jewish population in Abel.

For my mother **Henieh**, who died at the age of 77 years.
She was the daughter of Eliyahu Zvi Peres
from Kupishok and was an educated and respected woman.
For our brothers, **Meier** and **Zalman**, and sister **Tzileh**.

Apart from those from the Lithuanian communities who were saved
before the Holocaust, the children and the whole extended family
perished with all the Jews of Lithuania.

[from] Kalman and Nathan Pogrund and family, Cape Town
Goldeh and Chayim Dick and family, Johannesburg

[Page 617]

May this be a memorial for our father
Nachman Koppelowitch,
who died in Rakishok in 1928,

for our mother **Liebeh**,
who perished in the Rakishok Holocaust,

for our brother **Leizer Koppelowitch**,
who perished in the Rakishker Holocaust,

for our brother **Isser** with his wife **Henieh [Yaffe]**
and their son, **Nochemkeh**,
who perished in the destruction of Rakishok,

for our brother **Zalman Koppelowitch**,
who fell, 2nd November 1943, behind Oriel, while fighting
in the ranks of the Lithuanian Brigade.

[from] Nochum Leib and Rivka Koppelowitch and
children, Nachman Gittel and Pesach Koppelowitch.

Rokiskis Yizkor Book   653

[Page 618]

We will always remember
the tragic death
of

Berel Wingrin

and his wife

Rozeh.

[from]

Elia and Henyeh Wingrin
Johannesburg, South Africa

....

May these few words
be a memorial for

Avrohom Dovid Chaitowitz.

and his wife

Ettel,

their son **Rabbi Eliezer** and his son
Mottel and daughter
Hindeh and their families.

who perished in the last Great
Jewish World catastrophe.

[from]

Maryasha Palavin

In hallowed memory of
my father

Ya'akov Zak.

May he rest in peace.
Died in 1918.

And my mother,
Rivka Zak

May she rest in peace.
Died in 1892 in Abel,
Lithuania.

[from]
Binyomin Zak

....

In memory of my

brother **Yitzchak** and his

wife **Sonia**
and their children,
**Mendel, Henieh-Rochel,
and Zeldeh.**

who perished in Kavarsk in 1941.

They will always remain in my memory.

[from]

Shmuel Ichilchik [Hillel]

[Page 619]

We perpetuate herewith
our unforgettable

husband and father

Chayim Moshe Gen

who died in Johannesburg
2nd Shevat 1943.

[from]
Dina Genn and sons,
Yehoshua, Avrohom,
Yerachmiel, Gutman Sholem,
and Zelig and families

....

For our father

Dov Behr B"R Chayim Kremer
(nicknamed Berel Leah's)
who died in Rakishok
28th Iyar 1921,

and for our mother

**Chayah-Soreh Kremer
Bat Reb Meier,**

who died in Rakishok in 1941.

May this be an
everlasting memory!

[from]

Shneier Zalman and
Liebeh Kramer and family

May the memory of our
father be honored

Yisroel Seratzhik,

died the morning after Shavuot
in Vilna in 1915,

of our mother **Sheineh-Dobra,**
who died
10th Shevat 1948 in Malat,

of our sister **Soreh-Leah** and her
husband **Moshe Skurkewitch**
and their children who
perished in Malat,

of our sister **Malkah Seratzhik**
who perished in Malat.

We will never forget you!

Leibe and Esther Seratzhik, children and
grandchildren

....

May this be a memorial
for our father

Shlomo Yehudah Fleishman
of Subat-Kurland, who died in Darpat,
12th Teivet 1910.

for our mother
Frumeh Fleishman
of Subat-Kurland,
who died 23rd Sivan Tarsä.

[from]
Chana Leah and Hessel
Swartzberg and family

[Page 620]

May this be an everlasting remembrance
for our beloved husband and father

Avrohom Yudel Kiel

Born in Varestzineh, near Rakishok.
Died 15th Cheshvan, 22nd October 1945
in Johannesburg.

In sorrow [sorrowfully], those who
remained behind.

[from]

Riveh Kiel
Sheineh-Etteh, Yishayahu Levin and
their daughter, Johannesburg
Moshe-Behr and Gittel Kiel and daughter, Johannesburg
Ziseh and Meier Greenberg and daughter, France
Taibeh and Moshe Chayim Orlin and
children, Johannesburg

Rokiskis Yizkor Book   657

Rokiskis Yizkor Book

Appendices of Material Not Included in the Original Yizkor Book   App A - 1

Abel / Obeliai[1]

Obeliai native Abraham ("Abe") Dick drew this sketch from memory. It was contributed to the Obeliai KehilaLinks website by Ida Weinberg.

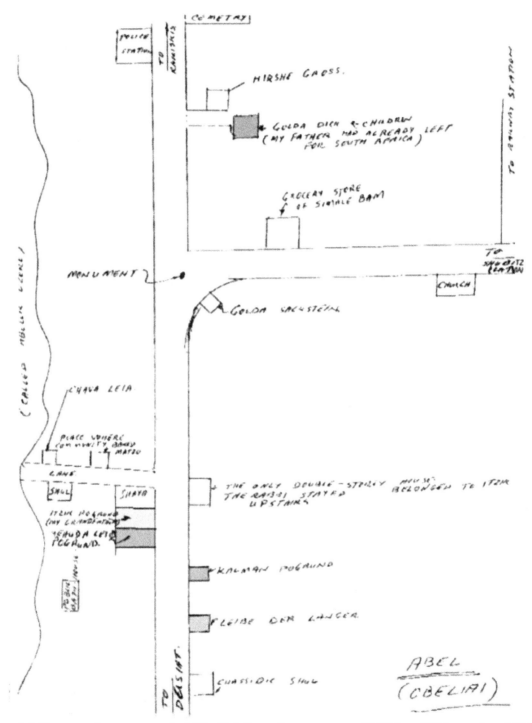

The Imperial German Army occupied Obeliai from the summer of 1915 until November 1918. The images on the following three postcards were created during that period.

---

[1] Note:

Abell Hauptstrasse [Abel Main Street]

Abeli, Russland [Abel, Russia]

Gruß aus Abeli – Bahnhof [Greeting From Abeli – Train Station]

Holocaust – August 1941

When Nazi Germany invaded Soviet Lithuania on June 22, 1941, many Jews from Abel tried to flee in the direction of Russia. However, Lithuanian partisans and some German paratroopers blocked the roads and forced the Jews to return home. Soon after the Germans took control, the Jewish men of Abel were sent to a temporary "ghetto" that had been established on the grounds of the Tyzenhaus manor in Rokiškis and the Jewish women and children under the age of eight years were sent to the grounds of the Antanašė manor, about 3 kilometers southeast of Abel, where they were confined to another temporary "ghetto." Each location held Jews from about ten communities in northeastern Lithuania.

The men who had been held at the Tyzenhaus manor were murdered on August 15 and 16, 1941, at the Velniaduobė woods, which is about five kilometers northeast of Rokiškis and just north of Bajorai village. The women and children who had been held at the Antanašė manor were killed on August 25, 1941.

App A - 4   Appendices of Material Not Included in the Original Yizkor Book

The Memorial at the Antanašė Killing Site

**The Memorial Stone dedicated to the murdered Jews of Obeliai
at the Ohel Jacob "Blue" Synagogue in Kaunas**

The Old Jewish Cemetery of Obeliai

Kamai / Kamajai

Market Square (undated)

Kamai Jewish Cemetery, July 2016   Cemetery Photo: Philip S. Shapiro

Appendices of Material Not Included in the Original Yizkor Book   App A - 7

Sussman Family Map and Photographs of Ponedel / Pandėlys

Dr. Samuel Sussman and Hirsh Laib Sussman were brothers whose family moved from Ponedel to Philadelphia before the First World War. In 1934, they began publishing a family newsletter that initially was called *Sussmania* and was later known as *Sussmanews*. The following hand-drawn map of Ponedel appearing on page 3 of the May 27, 1934, edition of *Sussmania*. Among other things, the map shows in the center-left the location of the Shul-Hof (synagogue square) and of the Bais HaMedrash and Neier Minyan buildings:

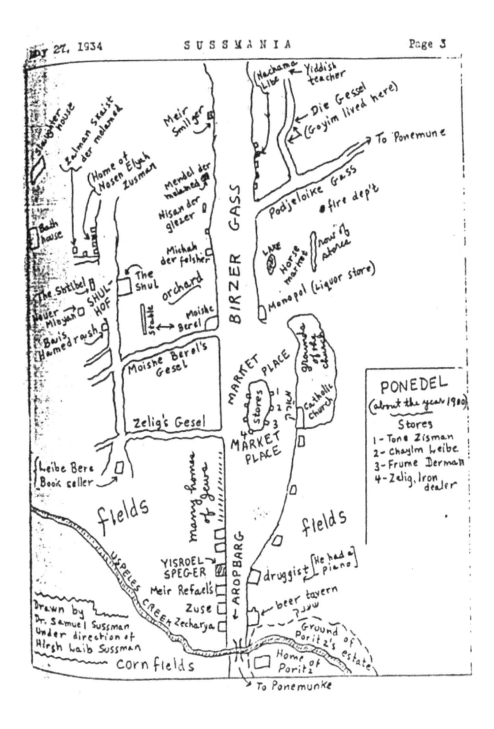

App A - 8   Appendices of Material Not Included in the Original Yizkor Book

From late May until early August 1935, Hirsh Laib Sussman visited his native Ponedel. In July he hired a photographer to take pictures of the town, including the following five images, which have been provided by Paula Sussman-Abrams of San Antonio, Texas. Her grandfather, Simon Sussman, was a brother of Dr. Samuel and Hirsh Laib Sussman.

The first two photographs show, respectively, the Bais HaMedrash and the Neier Minyan buildings in the Shul-Hof

Notation accompanying the photograph: "1935 In Ponedel, Lithuania Pictures brought by Hirsh Laib Sussman. Beis HaMidrash (larger than the Minyan. Stone foundation, Log walls. Tin Roof. Here, Tona Zisman and Yisroel Vengerin, pray."

Notation accompanying the photograph: " 'Neier Minyan' (old Synagogue). About 15 to 18 feet high. Ponedel 1935. Small building at the right is the Hebrew School."

The following three photos show buildings near the market place. The "town pump" was probably located near the place marked "lake" on the hand-drawn map.

Notation accompanying the photograph: "Store and Home of Meller and J. Flax (brother of Jacob Flax in South Africa). This is in the Ponedel market place, facing the town pump. Picture in 1935."

Notation accompanying the photograph: "Hirsh Laib Sussman had these pictures taken in Ponedel (Pandelys) Lithuania in 1935. Sarah Riva's home, on Birzer Street, 1935. She is the mother of Stella Glass in Philadelphia."

Notation alongside of the photograph: "Old booths in the 'mark' (market place). 1935. Now ordered to be torn down. Note → Horse and type of wagon."

Appendices of Material Not Included in the Original Yizkor Book   App A - 11

App A - 12   Appendices of Material Not Included in the Original Yizkor Book

Narrow-Gauge Railway Line

During the First World War, the Germans constructed a narrow-gauge railway line connecting Ponedel / Pandėlys to Skopishik / Skapiškis and Suvainishik / Suvainiškis. In this August 1932 photograph, members of a soccer team pose with an engine of the railway line. Yad Vashem Archives, Item 75328.

Appendices of Material Not Included in the Original Yizkor Book   App A - 13

1866 Rokiškis Map. This map shows the western half of Rokiškis' broad market square, which is dominated at the western end by St. Mathews Church (top, center). Entering the market square from the left is "Kamai Street" (Ulitza Kamaiskaya, today, Respublikos gatvė) On the extreme left are two "Jewish schools" ("yevreiskaya shkola").

The only words on this map are Russian, written in Cyrillic script. From 1864 until 1904, the Czarist government forbade the use of the Latin alphabet in Lithuania.

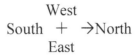

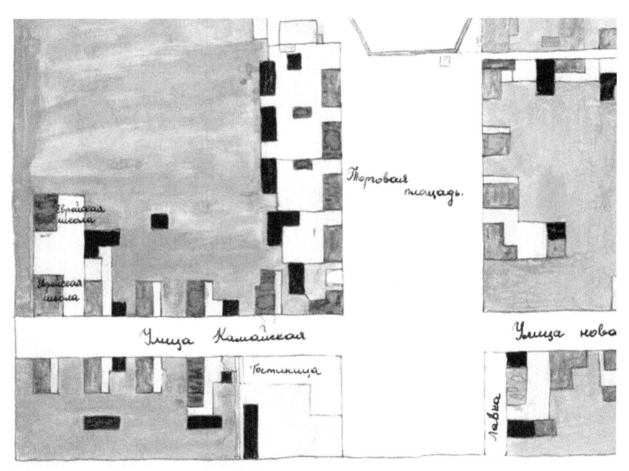

This map is from the archives of the Church of St. Matthew the Apostle and Evangelist in Rokiškis. Permission to use the map in this publication was graciously granted by the parish deacon, Father Eimantas Novikas. (Rokiškio Švento Mato apaštalo ir evangelisto bažnyčios archyvams priklausantis planas šiame leidinyje naudojamas gavus malonų minėtos bažnyčios klebono dekano Eimanto Noviko sutikimą.) All rights reserved.

App A - 14   Appendices of Material Not Included in the Original Yizkor Book

Eastern Entrance To The Old Jewish Cemetery in Rokiškis and Memorial Stone

In 2013, Remembering Rakisik Jewry, LLC, and its parent, Remembering Litvaks, Inc., (together, "RLI") commissioned the Rokiškis Machine Factory (Rokiškio mašinų gamykla, AB) to design and install a new gate and a section of fence along the eastern side of the Old Jewish Cemetery in Rokiškis. (The machine factory was founded by Rokiskis' prominent Zamet family.) RLI then commissioned Ponevezh sculptor Albertas Jasiūnas to create an engraved memorial stone, which was installed in May 2014 immediately outside of the new gate.

Credit: Hon. Amir Maimon

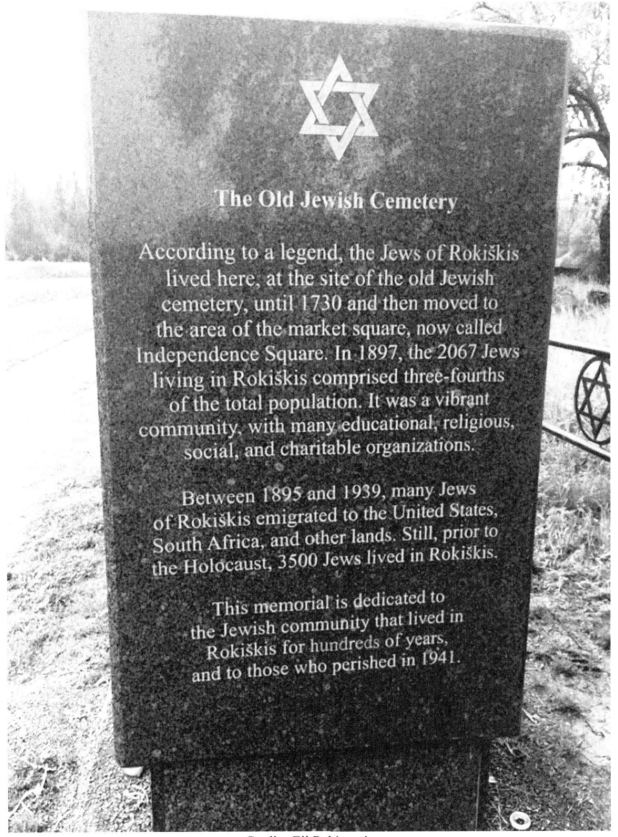

Credit: Eli Rabinowitz

App A - 16   Appendices of Material Not Included in the Original Yizkor Book

Credit: Philip S. Shapiro

Credit: Philip S. Shapiro

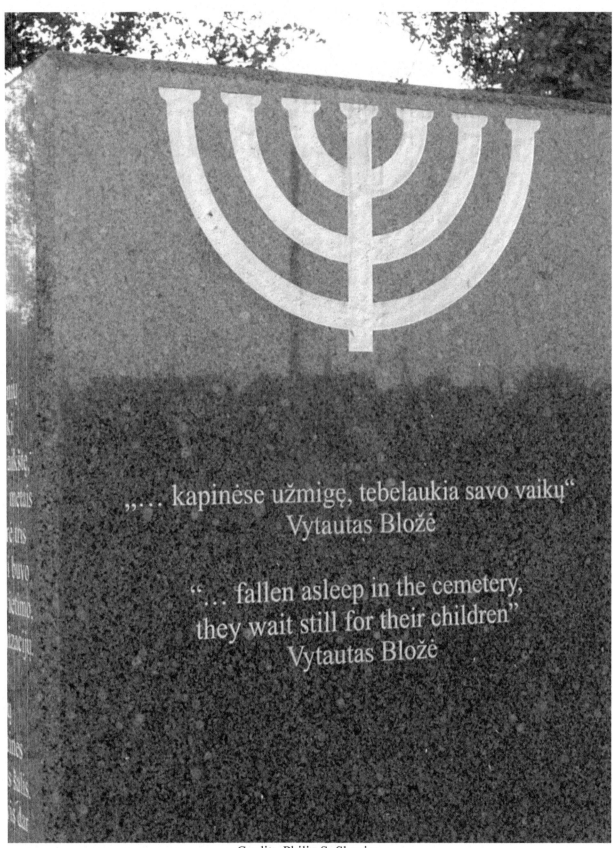

Credit: Philip S. Shapiro

Rokiškis' Synagogue Street – Images and Informational Sign

A 10 minute and 31 second collection of "home movie" segments taken during a trip to Lithuania before the Second World War has been posted by Hebrew University's Spielberg Jewish Film Archive at https://www.youtube.com/watch?v=Wv3CZSCdxXc. Scenes of Rokiškis appear between 04:15 and 06:20. The scenes include, among other things, a major market day on Independence Square, an outdoor wedding on the steps of the largest of the three houses of prayer on Synagogue Street (Sinagogų gatvė), a Lag Ba'Omer parade, the Tyzenhaus mansion, and a people bathing in Lake Vyžuona.

Three houses of prayer stood on the south side of Sinagogų gatvė. When Lithuania was independent, they were painted, respectively, in the colors of the national flag, namely, red, green, and yellow. The two-story Great Synagogue ("Graiseh Shul"), which stood at the corner of Sinagogų gatvė and Respublicos gatvė (Republic Street, formerly, Kamai Street), was painted red and was known as the red synagogue. It was also known as the "Alte Shul" (the "old" shul). All three were burned in July 1941.

In 2015, Giedrius Kujelis, the assistant director and historian of the Rokiškis Regional Museum, made the following several "still" pictures from the video segments showing the Synagogue Street area. Lithuanian architect Aurimas Širvys, a native of Obeliai / Abel, used the pictures to create three-dimensional images that were incorporated into an informational sign that was installed on Synagogue Street in September 2015.

Still Image 1 – Synagogue Street view, looking west-southwest. The Great Synagogue is on the left and the green synagogue is in the center background. The people are gathering for a wedding. A chuppah is seen in the middle of the picture.

App A - 20   Appendices of Material Not Included in the Original Yizkor Book

Still Image 2 – Synagogue Street view, looking east-southeast toward Republic / Kamai Street. The Great Synagogue is on right. The building on the left once housed the *Folksbank* (Jewish People's Bank) and was still standing in 2016. A wooden building on the northwest corner of the intersection (off camera) was the home of a rabbi.

Still Image 3 – Synagogue Street view, with the yellow synagogue in the background.

Appendices of Material Not Included in the Original Yizkor Book   App A - 21

From the still images, Lithuanian architect Aurimas Širvys created these representations of the three synagogues for the informational sign that now stands on Synagogue Street.

The Great Synagogue – for the general community

The Green Synagogue – for community leaders

The Yellow Synagogue – for scholars. It was also known as the "kleine" (small) shul.

App A - 22   Appendices of Material Not Included in the Original Yizkor Book

As noted above, in 2015, Giedrius Kujelis, the Rokiškis Regional Museum's historian, and architect Aurimas Širvys began work to design an informational sign that would describe the three synagogues that stood on Synagogue Street until 1941. The sign is written in Lithuanian, English, and Yiddish. Among those assisting with this project were Remembering Rakisik Jewry, LLC, and its parent, Remembering Litvaks, Inc.; Linda Cantor, the chairman of the Rokiškis Special Interest Group of Jewish genealogists; and American author Ellen Cassedy, who led a group of volunteers from Vilnius University's Yiddish Institute.

The sign was dedicated by Rokiškis Mayor Antanas Vagonis on September 6, 2015, which that year was the European Day of Jewish Culture.

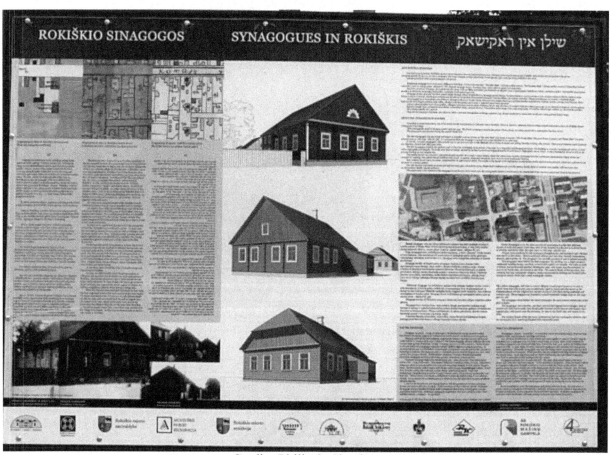

Credit: Philip S. Shapiro

Appendices of Material Not Included in the Original Yizkor Book   App A - 23

Speech of Mayor Antanas Vagonis
Upon the Dedication of the Informational Stand
On Synagogue Street in Rokiškis, Lithuania, September 6, 2015
(English Translation)

First of all, I would like to thank the coordinators of our [Rokiskis Regional] museum, who undertook this nice initiative. As you know, the process of reviving Jewish symbols began a very long time ago. And not long ago, when I myself was working for the municipal public works council, the sculptor, Albertas Jasiūnas, told me that he would need help in installing the memorial stone near the gates of the Jewish cemetery. And I told him that we would help, that it would not be a problem, that we could do it quickly, and that there would be no charge at all.

As you know, historically, and my advisor made some research, some time ago there was a large Jewish community [in this town], and the Jewish residents even outnumbered the Lithuanians.

It is very well said that we need to revive historical things. And today I want to touch upon the subject of bridges. Bridges serve not only for remembering and showing these [cultural] features but those bridges should also serve to invite people to come back over these bridges.

I know that our ethnic groups have been put into confrontation, and not just for one year. And for some things we should feel ashamed before your nation and some other nations. And we are constantly being put into confrontation with the Russians, and with the Poles, and even with our neighbors the Latvians, let alone the Jews.

We have to look at things the way they are now and think. There are no bad peoples, maybe only bad leaders of those peoples. It is not the fault of the Russians that they have such a leader as Putin, it is understood. Neither is it the fault of the Latvians or the Jews that they have been singled out. Indeed, every nation has an outstanding personality.

We are expressing our joy that you have not forgotten us. And I want to say more: Send a message to the whole world that if someone is longing for and would like to get back to their Motherland, we are looking forward to your coming back. ….

And I believe that, step by step, we have to come back. And, on my behalf, I promise, that our people will treat all nations with respect – with great respect.

And now, I thank you, all, and I thank everyone who worked to make this beautiful informational sign.

(Translated by Aldona Shapiro)

App A - 24   Appendices of Material Not Included in the Original Yizkor Book

Rokiškis Street Scenes

View of the Public Market Square (now Independence Square – Nepriklausomybės aikštė). From the 1920s "Naujiena" photographic study of Rokiškis, part of the photographic collection of the Rokiškis Regional Museum ("RKM"), RKM 7931. Turgus viešojoje (dabar Nepriklausomybės) aikštėje. Foto ateljė „Naujiena" Rokiškis XX a. 3 deš. RKM 7931. All rights reserved.

Another view of Rokiškis' Independence Square during the inter-war period. Yad Vashem Archives, Item 75199. All rights reserved.

During the First World War, the Imperial German Army occupied Rokiškis from the summer of 1915 until November 1918. This postcard picture, which is entitled, "Rakischki Markt u. Bahnhofstrasse" ("Rokiskis market place and rail station street), shows German soldiers posing near the public water fountain that stood in the Public Market Square (now Independence Square) near Kamai Street (now Republic Street). From the photographic collection of Aleksandras Samoilovas. (Iš Aleksandro Samoilovo kolekcijos.) All rights reserved.

The Zamet / Samet Family Home on Independence Square (now 10 Independence Square). This building was constructed in the 1920s, part of the RKM's photographic collection, RKM 2234. Zametų šeimos namas Nepriklausomybės aikštėje (dabar Nepriklausomybės a. 10). Pastatas statytas XX a. 3 deš. RKM 2234. All rights reserved.

View of the Jewish Peoples' Bank (now 17 Republic Street), 1930s, part of the RKM's photographic collection. Žydų liaudies Bankas (dabar Respublikos gatvė 17). XX a. 4 deš. RKM 50996. All rights reserved.

View of Respublikos gatvė from Independence Square, circa 1931-1932, from the photographic album of Count Jonas Pšezdzieckis (1877-1944), part of the RKM's photographic collection, RKM 52365/190. Rokiškio Respublikos gatvė (vaizdas nuo Nepriklausomybės aikštės pusės). Fotografija iš Grafų Pšezdzieckių albumo. 1931 – 1932 m. RKM 52365/190. All rights reserved.

Ironmonger's shop on Respublikos gatvė, seen from the Independence Square. Photograph from the album of Pranas Simanavičius, 1930s, part of the RKM's photographic collection, RKM 50995. Vaizdas iš Nepriklausomybės aikštės į geležies prekių krautuvę Respublikos gatvėje. Foto iš Prano Simanavičiaus albumo. XX a. 4 deš. RKM 50995. All rights reserved.

Two young women before they immigrated to Mandatory Palestine, Rokiškis, 1934. Yad Vashem Archives Item 73479. All rights reserved.

App A - 28   Appendices of Material Not Included in the Original Yizkor Book

The Ruch family home, at the corner of Independence Square and Vilnius Street (21 Nepriklausomybės aikštė), was built in 1921 by Pesach and Rachmiel Ruch on the lot identified as number 161 on the 1921 map of property owners and renters. It overlooks the part of the market square where horses were sold at the town's twice-annual great fairs. During the sixth Lebovitcher rebbe's only visit to Lithuania, in 1931, he stayed at the Ruch home for a week.

The Ruch family home in 2013   Credit: Philip S. Shapiro

Appendices of Material Not Included in the Original Yizkor Book   App A - 29

Two Interesting Group Photographs

November 1939 Gathering At the Home of Yudel Meller

Linda Cantor, the chairman of the Rokiskis Special Interest Group of Jewish genealogists, provided the following picture, which illustrates the fate of Jews who lived in independent Lithuania in the months after the Germans and Russians conquered Poland in September 1939.

The original photo is owned by Annette Apotheker Rosen. Her father, David Apotheker (1908-1995), the only survivor of eight siblings, was born in Bardejov, Slovakia (although his family had its roots in Nowy Sacz, Poland). David's family knew that he had escaped to Shanghai with a transit visa from Chiune Sugihara, the Japanese consul general in Kovno, Lithuania's inter-war capital. However, they did not know why David was in Rokiskis.

Fortunately, two of the people in the photo, Samuil Meller and his cousin Sana Meller Levin, recognized the photo as having been taken in November 1939 at the home of Yudel Meller to celebrate the bar mitzvah of Miron (Meir) Meller (born November 27, 1926). Not only were they able to identify many of those shown in the picture, but they also explained the fate of many in the following year and a half, a period marked by the Soviet annexation of Lithuania (June-August 1940), the Soviet deportation of tens of thousands of Lithuanian citizens (June 14, 1941), and the Nazi invasion of Lithuania (June 22, 1941):

App A - 30   Appendices of Material Not Included in the Original Yizkor Book

1 - **Yosef Milner**, dentist, murdered in Rokiskis, August 1941; 2 - **Bella Arsh**, daughter of the man who owned the house that Yudel Meller lived in, died in Israel; 3 - unknown; 4 - **Tsipora Levitin,** mother of Rashel (27) and Yacha (14), grandmother of Sana Meller (12), murdered in Lithuania, 1941; 5 - **Zorah Orelovich**, owner of a newspaper kiosk, was the only survivor of the Holocaust in Rokiskis and lived there after the Second World War before moving to Israel; 6 - **Chaim Reznikovich**, insurance agent, husband of Lisa (32), murdered in Rokiskis, August 1941; 7 - 8 Unknown; 9 - **? Vinokur**, wife of photographer (31), murdered in Rokiskis, August 1941; 10 - Unknown; 11 - **Yudel Meller**, co-owner of a factory, father of Sana (12) and Miron Meller (13), husband of Yacha (14), survived a Soviet concentration camp, died in Israel ; 12 - **Sana Meller**, daughter of Yudel (11) and Yacha (14), survivor of two Soviet exiles in Siberia and two prison terms in Vilnius, lives in Israel; 13 - **Miron (Meir) Meller**, son of Yudel (11) and Yacha (14), survivor of two Soviet exiles in Siberia, died in Israel; 14 - **Yacha Levitin Meller,** wife of Yudel Meller, survivor of two Soviet exiles in Siberia, died in Israel; 15 - **? Furmansky**, owner of a grist mill and a power station, murdered in Rokiskis, August 1941; 16 - **Mira Etingof**, wife of 17, murdered in Rokiskis, August 1941; 17 - **? Etingof**, doctor, escorted exiles to Siberia, died in Vilnius after the war; 18 - **Sarah Meller**, wife of Morduch (Mordechai) (34), survived Soviet exile in Siberia, died in Rubtsovsk, Russia; 19 - **Tsila Milner**, wife of Yosef (1), murdered in Rokiskis, August 1941; 20 - Unknown; 21 - **? Krasovsky**, refugee who dined with Fanya and Khona Meller's family; 22-24 - Unknown; 25 - **Samuil Meller**, son of Fanya (26) and Khona Meller, the cousin of Sana (12) and Miron (13), survived Soviet exile in Siberia, lives in US; 26 - **Fanya Rubanenko Meller**, wife of Khona, mother of Samuil (25), died in 1943 in Soviet exile in Siberia; 27 - **Rashel Levitin**, sister of Yacha Meller (14), survived in ghetto in Lithuania, died en route to Israel; 28 - Unknown; 29 - **Miriam Kan Meller**, wife of Samuil Meller (30), survived Soviet exile in Siberia, died in Krasnoyarsk, Russia; 30 - **Samuil (Shmuel Wolf) Meller**, co-owner of a factory, died in Soviet exile in Siberia; 31 - **? Vinokur**, photographer, husband of (9); 32 - **Lisa Meller Reznikovich**, wife of Chaim (6), murdered in Rokiskis, August 1941; 33 - **Tamar or Sana Meller**, daughter of Mordechai Meller (34) and Sarah Meller (18), murdered in Lithuania; 34 - **Morduch (Mordechai) Meller**, co-owner of a factory, husband of Sarah, died in Soviet concentration camp in Krasnoyarsk, 1942; 35 - **David Apotheker** (see story which follows).

Appendices of Material Not Included in the Original Yizkor Book   App A - 31

Samuil and Sana provided the following explanation of how David Apotheker and those who remain unidentified came to be at the celebration:

As for unknown people 3, 7, 8, 10, 20, 22, 23, and 24, we think that after Germany's invasion of Poland (in September 1939), Jewish refugees from Poland fled to Rokiskis. They were placed in detention camps, but were free to walk in the city. They used to dine with Jewish families. Every person was assigned to a family, which he or she visited every day, and shortly they became like members of the family.

David Apotheker, who saved this photo, was one of many such Polish refugees. He dined with the family of Yudel Meller.

As noted, David Apotheker was one of the fortunate who received a transit visa to travel to Shanghai. His daughter, Annette, tells the following story:

My father David, after having been in Siberia and after arrival in Vladivostok, was taken to Japan, beaten and expelled to Shanghai, where he lived for 4 years. After the war he made his way to Antwerp but didn't find any survivors. My father had a letter stating that he was a "persona non grata" in Belgium. He went to Holland, where he met a friend, Saul Braunhut, who had a weaving factory in Winterswijk, Holland, and joined him. While in Holland he met Reina Wijler-Kropveld, a war widow (of Lo Wijler), married her in 1948, and had two children. My brother Eli Apotheker and I both immigrated to Israel. My mother died in 1969 in Ruurlo, Holland, and my father died in 1995 in Tel Aviv, Israel.

App A - 32   Appendices of Material Not Included in the Original Yizkor Book

October 1934 Photograph

The following photograph is from files the Lithuanian State Central Archives (Lietuvos Centrinis Valstybės Archyvas). The information on the back (second image) indicates that the photograph was taken in Rokiskis on October 26, 1934, and provides some information about each person. Standing in the back are, from left to right, Ruvel Gafanovich ("tailor in Kaunas") and Yudel Weiner ("deported"). In the front, from left to right, are Yankel Chait "17 Kaunas Street in Rokiskis"), Motel Chaitovich ("deported"), Chaim Kruk ("watchmaker in Kaunas"), and Leibe Ruch ("hatmaker in Kaunas"). The photograph may have been taken for use by the Lithuanian government's security service.

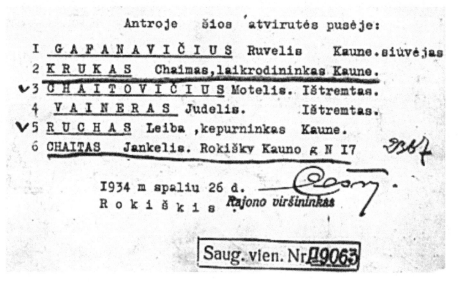

Appendices of Material Not Included in the Original Yizkor Book   App A - 33

Svėdasai Market Square Area

Prior to the Second World War, Svėdasai was in the Rokiškis region. In 2005, students at Svėdasai's J. Tumas-Vaižgantas high school made a study of the town's former Jewish community using available information and interviews with the town's older residents. The study found that before the war about 300 Jews (60 families) lived in Svėdasai, primarily on Tumas-Vaižgantas and Ežeras (Lake) streets, http://www.svedasai.lt/component/content/article/2-naujienos/39-zydai.html. The latter street, once known as Žydų (Jews') alley, had two Jewish religious buildings. As part of the project, the students prepared a map entitled, "Čia jų gyventa prieš karą" ("They Lived Here Before The War"). The map appears next (courtesy of Joana Gutmanienė) and a translation of the list of property owners appears on the page following the map.

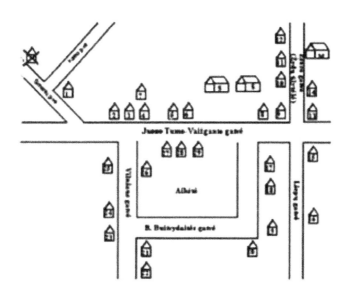

Čia jų gyventa prieš karą

1. Enokas (Emarkas Šmitas)
2. Elyčios krautuvė
3. Volfsono Leibos (Maušos) krautuvė
4, 7. Leizeris Pakovičius (gyvenamas namas, veltinių dirbtuvė)
5. Maušos ir Pakovičiaus restoranas
6. Žydaitės Cipkė ir Lipkė
8. Obromo krautuvė
12. Cilė Jevlov
13. A. Gero krautuvė
14. Jankelis
16. Rieznikas
17. Šermonų restoranas
18. Šachnavičių odų krautuvė
20. Misgankelio (Farbero) krautuvė
21. Rabinas
25. Kalvis Faifkė
26. Žydo krautuvė
27. Bercikas (kepė duoną)
28. Lietuvio Trečioko namas
29. J. Snolovo vaistinė
9, 10, 11, 15, 19, 22, 23, 24 - žydams priklausę namai

Building Icons in 2005 Map Created by Svėdasai's High School Students:

Sinagoga = Synagogue/Beis Medresh/"shkala"   Malūnas = Mill
Mokykla = School   Namas = Home

1   Enoch (Emark Shmit)
2   Alytshia's shop
3   Leibe Volfson's (Moshe's) shop shop
4, 7   Leizer Pakovitsh (living house, felt-boot workshop)
5   Moshe's and Pakovitsh's restaurant
6   The Jewish sisters Tsipke and Lipke
7   Abram's shop
12   Tsile Yevlov
13   A. Ger's shop home
14   Yankel

16   Rieznik
17   Sherman's restaurant
18   Shachnavitsh's leather-goods

20   Misiyankel's (Farber's) shop
21   Rabbi
25   The blacksmith Faifke
26   Jewish-owned shop
27   Bertzik (bread bakery)
28   The Lithuanian Tretshokas'

29   Y. Stolov's pharmacy

9, 10, 11, 15, 19, 22, 23, 24 – Jewish-owned homes

Selected Town Histories from Other Yizkor Books

Some of the other yizkor books being translated by JewishGen's Yizkor Book Project contain histories for individual shtetls (towns) within the area covered by the *Rokiskis and Environs* yizkor book. All of the histories that have been translated can be found at http://www.jewishgen.org/Yizkor/translations.html. Following are three translated histories, one for Abel / Obeliai and two for Rokiskis. These histories may not be reproduced in any form without the express permission of JewishGen, Inc. Rights may be reserved by the copyright holder.

"Abel" (from *Pinkas HaKehillot Lita*)

"Abel" was written by Raphael Julius and is included in *Pinkas HaKehillot Lita [Encyclopedia of the Jewish Communities of Lithuania]*, Editor Prof. Dov Levin and Assistant Editor Josef Rosin, Yad Vashem, Jerusalem, 1996, pp. 113-116, translated by Bob Kurtzman, http://www.jewishgen.org/Yizkor/Pinkas_lita/lit_00113.html. For this publication, several changes have been made to better align the translation with the original Hebrew text.

"Abel" - Encyclopedia of Jewish Communities in Lithuania (Obeliai, Lithuania)

55°56' / 25°48'

*   *   *

Obeliai (Lith.)

(Abel (Yiddish), Abeli (Russian))

*   *   *

A town in the Rokisok district

Year	Total Population	Jewish Population
1567	33 families	..
1897	975	652
1821	1,134	760*
1923	1,328	680**
1959	1,907	-

* 67% of the population
** 51% of the population, approximately 300 families

App A - 36   Appendices of Material Not Included in the Original Yizkor Book

Obeliai is a small village in the northeast of Lithuania near the Latvian border, located approximately 15 kilometers east of the district city, Rakishok, and very near the Dvinsk-Radvilishuk railway line. Obeliai is the first station on that line built on Lithuanian land. The village stands on the banks of a large lake whose name the same (Obeliai) and by the river Kriauna.

Obeliai is mentioned in the sources for the first time regarding the Lithuanian-Livony Treaty of 1529. In 1629 a church was built in the village. Every Thursday was market day. Farmers in the vicinity used to come to sell their products and to buy what they needed. Most days of the week the village was sleepy and quiet. So much so that the local residents earned the nickname "the dead ones of Obeliai." Every year in January there was a horse show that drew many visitors to the village. In 1828 a factory was opened for spinning cloth.

Many of the sons of Obeliai participated in the Polish revolt of 1831 against the Tzarist rule. After suppressing the revolt some of the local people were exiled to Siberia and in their place the Russian regime settled believers of the "yeshna" sect ("starovary"). The village began to develop in 1873 with the laying of the railway track there. In 1907 a factory for producing alcohol and spirits was established. On the eve of the 1905 revolution the revolutionists secretly gathered in the summer resort in the Stashon Forest to discuss and debate social issues. During the revolt the residents banished officials of the Tsar from the village. The Russian regime sent a punishment unit to Obeliai and in December of the same year the uprising was suppressed. Close to World War I [1899] a fire broke out in the village that destroyed half of the houses, which were built of wood and covered with thatch roofs. The village was divided by two streets and in the middle was the market place, with a large monument from which they used to announce notices or call attention to new regulations decreed by the authorities.

From December 19, 1918 until June 1919 Obeliai was under Soviet rule set up by Lithuanian Bolsheviks. In 1920 it served as a point of transfer and quarantine was founded for refugees that returned from Russia. Until 1950 it was a village district. Obeliai had a dairy farm, an electric power station, two flour mills, a lumber mill, a customs station and a work shop for repairing railway trains.

The Jewish Settlements Until World War I

There was a very old Jewish settlement in Obeliai. This is verified by tombstones in the Jewish cemetery. Some of them are 400 years old or more. Most of the Jews of Obeliai made a living from trade and commerce and the rest were tradesmen: sandlers, tailors, seamstresses, builders, slate roofers, a watch maker and some glaziers and also butchers bakers (including matza bakers) and gardeners who raised fruits that were marketed in Warsaw, Lodz, Riga and other cities. Similarly there were teamsters who brought passengers and their baggage to and from the train station. The big businessmen of Obeliai handled flax. The best quality merchandise was exported to Prussia. The seeds were sent to Dvinsk to an oil producing factory. But the richest merchants were wood merchants. One of them was the *gabbai*, head manager or treasurer of the chasidic synagogue.

In Obeliai there was a synagogue, a study hall, prayer hall ("minyan") for chasidim, and a burial society. In the great fire that broke out [in 1899] many buildings were destroyed but the old synagogue and study hall were not damaged.

Appendices of Material Not Included in the Original Yizkor Book   App A - 37

In the years prior to World War I there was hardly any cultural life in Obeliai. Some of the youth went to the big cities in search of enlightenment and knowledge. The main influence on the 300 families was in the hands of the rabbis. The adult Jewish residents were very pious observant Jews and feared the youth would abandon their heritage.

The Jewish children learned in institutions like the *cheder* that were dark, damp, filthy, and overcrowded. For many years there was no official community management that was concerned with improving education and matters of public Jewish concern. The Jews of Obeliai were divided between Chasidim and *misnagdim* that prayed separately. There were great hostilities between them. Not infrequently conflict broke out between the two camps that led to blows.

In 1915, the Russian authorities published an edict to exile all Jews from the border areas[2]. The Jews had been accused of spying for the enemy, in this case the Germans. Out of fear of the Cossacks three-quarters of the Jews of Obeliai left their *shtetl*. The rest hid in houses and cellars.

With the occupation of Obeliai by the Germans the Jews left their hiding places and soon adjusted to the new regime that appointed a civil authority and organized a civilian police force in the *shtetl*. The Germans appointed a Jew (Moshe Zakshtein) as the head of the local authority. Along with this, the Germans imposed forced labor on the Jews. Some Jews were even sent to a work camp where the conditions were very difficult: cruel treatment, limited food rations, blows, and very hard work - unloading and laying railroad tracks quarrying stones digging canals and so forth.

Among the rabbis who served in Obeliai were Rabbi Shlomo son of Gershon, who served in the rabbinate there at the end of the 18th Century. After him came Rabbi Chaim son of Shlomo from Grodno. In later generations there was Rabbi Zalman Segel (who was also a righteous teacher), Rabbi Shabtai-Chaim Shochet, author of the book *Zahav Shachut*, Rabbi Bunim Tzemach Silber (or Zilber, father of Rabbi Eliezer Silber), Rabbi Brilke (nicknamed Harav Ha'tzhov), and Rabbi Avraham Meirovitz (rabbi of Obeliai from 1928), who perished in the Holocaust.

Some other natives of Obeliai who achieved fame outside of the shtetl; among them Rabbi Eliezer L Silber son of Rabbi Bunim-Tzemach mentioned above. In the years 1908 to 1925 Rabbi Eliezer Silber was a rabbi in Harrisburg, Pennsylvania, in the USA and wrote a book on the *"Kedoshim"* book of the *Mishna*, and in 1929 was elected President of the Association of Rabbis of the United States and Canada. David Shochet, who lived in the Bronx in New York, wrote the book *The Jewish Court in the Middle Ages*; the author-journalist Benjamin Zak and the educator Abraham Chrit.

The Period of Independent Lithuania

After the German retreat a new period began, that of the independence of Lithuania (1918-1940). However, before that for a brief time, Obeliai was under Soviet rule. In 1919 the first cooperative was established in Obeliai, which helped the Jewish population that was impoverished during the

---

2 The decree required the expulsion of Jews living in the parts of central Lithuania and Latvia that were near the German-Russian front lines, specifically, areas "west of the line Kaunas, Jonava, Vilkomir (Ukmerge), Rogovo (Raguva), Panevezys, Pasvalys, Salata (Salociai), [and] Bauska." This decree did not apply to Jews living Abel or elsewhere in the Rokiškis. However, Jews did fear the approach of the front and the Russians' Cossack rear guard.

App A - 38   Appendices of Material Not Included in the Original Yizkor Book

German occupation. Membership in the cooperative allowed them to buy commodities and products at reasonable and fixed prices. In this period the Jewish youth displayed great activity.

After Lithuanian became independent Jewish refugees who were in the interior of Russia returned to their homes. The Lithuanian regime was suspicious of them and feared communist penetration. Those who wanted to return were forced to stay first in a kind of concentration camp, which was near the customs and duty station because Obeliai was the main point of entry for refugees from Russia. Sometimes Jews were incarcerated in this concentration camp for months until they were released. The sanitary conditions in the camp were poor and a typhus epidemic broke out which spread to all the shacks and bungalows despite the aid sent by the Jewish National Committee. Many Jews died and were buried in the old cemetery of Obeliai.

After the Jews returned, new winds began to blow in Obeliai that fostered expectations for achievements for cultural life and progress. In 1923 the Jewish community was established according to the Jewish autonomy law and the committee that was elected began to be concerned about Jewish matters in the *shtetl*. The first community committee was composed of representatives from the following parties: General Zionists - 2, Tzeirai Tzion - 1, Mizrachi - 1, Achdut - 1, Independent – 1. Among its members were Leib Zakshtein, Zalman Melech, Baruch Kadish and others.

Due to the attitude of the Lithuanian regime which worsened from year to year the youth began to feel that they had no future in the independent Lithuanian state. Many emigrated to countries overseas, such as South Africa and Eretz Yisrael [the Land of Israel]. Those who remained continued their social-cultural activities.

In this period there a school of the "Tarbut" network opened in Obeliai (under the direction of Michael Kuperman). A number of Jewish students studied in the Lithuanian school and some students from the "Tarbut" school continued their studies in high schools in the vicinity.

In the period between the two World Wars many Jews were shop keepers and home owners. Some maintained fruit and vegetable farms and marketed the yield abroad. Similarly there were flax and wood merchants who traded with foreign markets. According to a survey conducted by the Lithuanian government in 1931 there were 19 stores and business establishments, 15 of which were owned by Jews (79%). The distribution according to type of business is presented in the table below:

Branch or Type of Business	Total	Owned by Jews
Crops and flax	1	1
Butcher shops and meat trading	1	1
Restaurants and taverns	6	3
Food products	2	2
Drinks	1	1
Clothing, furs and textiles	3	2
Medicines, cosmetics	2	2
Radios, bicycles, sewing machines	1	1
Tools and iron products	1	1
Miscellaneous	1	1

In 1937, seven out of 23 houses were owned by Jews and the same number of Jews owned telephones. The same year the town had 18 Jewish craftsmen: 4 needle tradesmen, 3 shoemakers, 4 butchers, a baker, a pharmacist, and 5 other artisans (some of them worked in tanneries).

In 1920, there a branch of the Yiddish "Culture League" was established. They sponsored lectures on literature and attracted many young people. But the older members did not know how to bring youth closer to them and therefore the young people set up a new "Youth Branch." They founded a library and organized a night school. Almost all of the youth in the *shtetl* belonged to the *Yugent Abteilung* [Youth Branch].

In 1923, the Lithuanian authorities closed the "Culture League," which was considered leftist. In its place a Yiddish library was opened which, in time, was the cultural center of the *shtetl*. Next to it was a drama circle "The Dramatic Section of the Jewish Library." Members of the circle appeared before the public in a hut built by the German occupation authorities and the income was donated for the good of the library. In a short time the library was enriched with many Yiddish and Hebrews books that would meet the needs of the population of Obeliai.

In the years before World War II many of the Jews of Obeliai developed an active political awareness which is expressed by the number of participants in the elections to the Zionist congresses. In the town there were branches of Hapoel Hamizrachi, Tzierei Zion, the Socialist Zionists, and the General Zionists There was a Maccabee club with 50 members. Similarly there were branches of of Hashomer Hatzair and Bnei Akiva. The local youth were organized in the Scouts and in Hechalutz. The *chalutzim* were the most active group and many of its members went to agricultural training. A breakdown of the ballots of those in Obeliai who voted in the Zionist Congresses in the '20s and '30s is presented in the table below (in 1931 the elections were held in the Keren Kayemet L'Yisrael auditorium):

Congress no.	Year	Total "Shkalim"	Total votes	Working Eretz Yisrael		Revisi-onists	General Zionists		Politicals	Mizrachi	Leftists of Poalei Tzion
				S.Z.	Z.Z.		A	B			
14	1925	30	-			-	-	-	-	-	-
16	1929	26	17			-	2	-	-	3	-
17	1931	12	11			3	2	-	-	4	-
18	1933	-	30			-	4	-	-	2	-
19	1935	-	137			-	2	26	4	27	-
							National block				
21	1939	150	150	97			2		50		1

App A - 40   Appendices of Material Not Included in the Original Yizkor Book

During World War II

In the wake of the Ribbentrop-Molotov Agreement Lithuania, including Obeliai was under the rule of the USSR. During the period of the Soviet rule (1940-1941) the Zionist parties and movements were disbanded, the Hebrew School was closed, and in its place a school opened where the language of instruction was Yiddish and the program of study was acceptable to the Soviet Union. Similarly, businesses and economic life were adapted to what was practiced in the Soviet Union. The Soviet rule continued for about a year.

With the outbreak of war between Germany and the USSR on June 22, 1941, practically all the Jews abandoned the *shtetl*, fleeing east toward the Latvian border to escape to the Soviet Union following the retreating Red Army soldiers and the Soviet bureaucracy. But when they reached the border a bitter disappointment awaited them: the Soviet border guards did not allow to cross those who did not have in their hands proper transit permits and papers. Only a few had such papers. Meanwhile the Germans bombed the border area. With no choice Jews attempted to back track or seek refuge in the forests and nearby villages. The roads were full of Jewish refugees with children and movable property and given to the strafing of German planes and to the firing of German paratroopers and Lithuanian and Latvian nationalists. Tens of Jews found their death on their way back from the border and their bodies rolled to the side of the road. With difficulty some of them were able to return to their *shtetl*. With them came other refugees from the vicinity that joined them on the way. As they entered the *shtetl* they were attacked by incited farmers.

Immediately upon the entrance of the Germans into Obeliai on Thursday, June 26, 1941 the life of the Jews and their property was ownerless.[3] Local Lithuanian nationals seized the power and authority. They used to arrest Jewish men, supposedly for "investigations" and "explanations." None of them returned.

The Lithuanian authorities allowed the farmers to take Jews, men and women, for forced labor. Many Jews used the opportunity and went to work in the vicinity so that in this way they could get a little food. After a few weeks, at the end of July or the beginning of August 1941, the Lithuanian governor of the Rakishuk District, an officer named Žukas, publicized a decree regarding the employment of Jews. According to the decree there were citizens who did not exploit the Jews they employed; but instead of this and for money gave them comfortable conditions to idle away and waste time. The decree threatened that whoever behaved as cited above would be punished with maximal penalties as a saboteur and will be seen as a supporter of Jews.

The lives of the Jews became difficult from day to day. On August 25, 1941 (20 Elul 5701) their end came. On that same day armed Lithuanians took the local Jews together with refugees from the nearby towns to the village of Antanoshe (Antanašė), about 5 kilometers from Obeliai, and there, at a distance 100 meters to the left of the road, all were cruelly murdered and buried in a mass grave. According to a German source, 112 Jewish men, 627 Jewish women, and 421 Jewish children were murdered. All told, according to the above German report, 1,160 Jews were

---

[3] The "ownerless" is a literal translation of the Hebrew word "hefkar." As the German invasion began, a Lithuanian "Provisional Government" took power. Under their decrees, Jewish lives and property were beyond the protection of the law.

exterminated. The number includes Jews of Abel and the Jews of Rokishok who were murdered there 10 days earlier.

According to a Lithuanian source in the spring of 1944 the Germans arrested a Lithuanian named Vladas Andonas for the crime of giving a hiding place to Jews. A woman farmer named Vaičienenė from the village Kadeliai hid 5 Jews from Rakishok who were saved from the slaughter in Antanoshe (Benyamin Zak, Yossel Karebelnik, and three others). The woman farmer and the Jews were arrested by the Germans. Their fate is not known. After the war survivors of the community set up a monument on the mass grave in Antanošė.

[Footnotes omitted]

"Rokishok" (from *Pinkas HaKehillot Lita*)

"Rokishok" was written by Raphael Julius and is included in *Pinkas HaKehillot Lita [Encyclopedia of the Jewish Communities of Lithuania],* Editor Prof. Dov Levin and Assistant Editor Josef Rosin, Yad Vashem, Jerusalem, 1996, pp. 647-653, translated by Haim Pogrund, http://www.jewishgen.org/Yizkor/Pinkas_lita/lit_00646.html. For this publication, several changes have been made to better align the translation with the original Hebrew text.

"Rokishok" - Encyclopedia of Jewish Communities in Lithuania (Lithuania)

55°15' / 25°35'

*   *   *

Rokiškis (in Yiddish, Rakishok), (in Russian, Rokishki.)

A Provincial Town in Northeastern Lithuania.

Year	Total Population	Jews	Percentage
1824	200	"	"
1847	"	593	"
1859	460	"	"
1897	2736	2067	75
1914	3829	3000 approx.	78 approx.
1915	5000 approx.	"	45 approx.
1923	4325	2013	46.5
1939	9000 approx.	3500 approx.	40

App A - 42   Appendices of Material Not Included in the Original Yizkor Book

The town of Rokishok is situated on both sides of the Laukipe River, 22 km. from the Latvian border, and 3 km. from the railway line connecting Dvinsk, Leipaja, and Riga in Latvia with Ponevez, Shavli, and Kovno in Lithuania. Because of the distance from Kovno, Rokishok was called "Kamchatke."

The earliest reference to Rokishok by this name is found in records dating back to 1499 and belonged to the noble family of Kroshinski and later to the Count Tizenhaus. In 1780 Rokishok passed into the hands of the Pashdiatzki [Przezdziecki] family. The business manager of this family opened connections with the Jews in the vicinity, and invited them to settle in the area.

In the Nineteenth Century Rokishok changed from a country seat to the provincial center. A large market, which opened on Mondays, led to the expansion of economic ties from the town. In 1824 there were 28 houses in the town, and in 1825 more than 200 inhabitants were living there, the majority being tradesmen, while others were businessmen. By 1859, the numbers had doubled, beer being manufactured, flour mills, built and operated by wind and water, while woodcutting, a hotel, and an old people's home were established. In addition to the weekly markets, an annual trade fair was incepted. A hospital was opened in the middle of the nineteenth century, while in the second half, the town expanded rapidly, following the creation of a direct rail link in 1873. As a result of this wood exports increased tremendously as did that of wheat and linen. The town became the agricultural business hub of the district. The linen trade was especially successful with exports to foreign countries, including Holland and England via Riga.

By 1885 there were 187 houses in Rokishok. In 1908 the town boasted 100 shops mostly owned by Jews. A music school was created in the Tyzenhaus mansion.

Until the First World War Rokishok was a county capital in the Novo-Aleksandrovsk (in Lithuanian: Zarasai) District. [Note: The name of Zarasai was adopted in 1929. From 1919-1929, the town was known as Ezherenai (in Lithuanian: Ežerėnai).] During the German occupation (1915-1918) Rokishok became the provincial capital. When the Germans departed they burnt the railway station. On 13 December 1918, a Soviet government was installed which lasted until June 1919. Even during the period of an independent Lithuania after 1920 Rokishok retained its urban rights as well as its status as the provincial capital and continued to flourish. Roads and alleys were paved and sidewalks were completed. The number of houses increased and in 1923 there were 29 streets with a total length of 10 km., 551 houses (of which 48 were made of stone). There was a power station, three flour mills, a woodcutting mill, a dairy, a factory for starch production, a metal working factory, a hospital with 65 beds, and two pharmacies. The town boasted ten doctors. In 1918 a progymnasium was established which in 1919 became a full-fledged gymnasium (high school.)

The Jewish Settlement until the Second World War in Rokishok

According to local tradition, the Jewish settlement was originally a half kilometer from the present site, but was moved to its present position because of a tragic circumstance which involved the local countess by name Ishevna, her business manager, his son, and the son of a Jewish tailor, who was an only child. Due to an argument between the children in 1730, the countess, who hated Jews, decreed that when the Jewish boy marries, he and his bride should be burned on their wedding day. The Jews boycotted the place and moved their settlement some distance away. This place became the cemetery of Rokishok.

Once there was the threat of a pogrom against the Jews, many of whom heeded the advice of the local police chief and left the town. The wealthy members of the community hid their valuables as well as the Sifrei Torah of the community in the cellar of the home of the local priest, but the Cossacks discovered the hiding place as a result of information from the priest's servants, and stole the valuables and desecrated the Sifrei Torah.

In January 1885 a local farmer murdered a Jew named Zelig Krok while robbing him of three hundred rubles. The murderer was found and convicted and ordered to be deported to Siberia for seventeen years with hard labour. In addition, he was ordered to pay the widow one thousand rubles in compensation.

In 1889 a Bikkur Holim Society was established and one of its first tasks was to aid victims of the cholera epidemic in the early nineties.

In 1905 Hillel Idelson set up a loan fund which later became a bank. He also established a merchant bank. In 1906 a society for assistance to the poor was incepted.

During the First World War many of the Jews moved to Russia. Those who remained suffered from restriction of movement, confiscations and forced labor, which was imposed upon them by the Germans.

At the end of the war a portion of the Jews returned and amongst them were some from the surrounding districts. With the help of the Joint [the American Jewish Joint Distribution Committee] and the People's Bank (established in 1923 for the purposes of mutual loans; in 1927 it had 466 members, and in 1929 – 357), as well as relatives from abroad, the Jews rebuilt their homes and their businesses. This period was noted for rapid development and building projects. At the same time, many Lithuanians from the surrounding villages settled in Rokishok. They opened many businesses (before the war there were only 3 shops owned by non-Jews), as well as Lithuanian cooperatives. Lithuanian tradesmen and merchants came to the town, and one of them opened a shop for metal implements.

Most of the Jews made a living from small businesses and peddling. On market days they used to buy linen, beef, poultry, eggs, and other agricultural crops from the local farmers, and sold them groceries, cloth, machines, and haberdashery. In Rokishok there were a number of prominent merchants who controlled the trade in linen, grain, and cattle. Others had wholesale businesses in metal goods, textiles, agricultural machinery and so on. Before the First World War the merchants imported their goods from Dvinsk [today, Daugavpils, Latvia]. During the period of independent Lithuania (1918-1940), after the contact with Dvinsk stopped because of the creation of independent Baltic states, trade was done with Ponevez, Shavel, and Kovno.

After a number of years of development and building, a depression set in for the Jews. The reasons were the nationalization in trade of linen and grain, competition from the Lithuanian cooperatives, the burden of taxation and boycotting of tradesmen and Jewish merchants. Amongst others, a Catholic bank (or cooperative) was set up in order to undermine Jewish trade. Lithuanian merchants sold goods at especially low prices and caused substantial damage to Jewish tradesmen. This was done with the support and clandestine encouragement of the local government. After the Catholic bank went bankrupt, it burnt down and the Jews were blamed. In

App A - 44   Appendices of Material Not Included in the Original Yizkor Book

1925, there was a wave of bankruptcies of Jews, and many emigrated to South Africa and the U.S. Some went to Israel (in 1929-1930).

According to a government survey in 1931 there were 177 businesses in Rokishok Eighty- nine (76% were Jewish owned) as follows:

Type of Business	Total	Jewish owned
Grocery	5	4
Grain and Linen	15	14
Butcheries and stock	12	10
Restaurants and Bars	11	4
Foodstuffs	12	11
Liquor	1	1
Milk and Dairies	1	0
Clothing, furs and textiles	13	11
Skins and shoes	10	10
Haberdashery and household goods	8	7
Drugs and cosmetics	4	2
Radios, bicycles & sewing machines	3	3
Tools and Hardware	3	2
Building materials, wood, and furniture	3	0
Heating materials	1	1
Paper, books and writing materials	4	0
Miscellaneous	11	9

According to the same survey there were 33 light industries in Rokishok, of which 26 (79%) belonged to Jews as follows:

Type of Business	Total	Jewish owned
Metalwork, machinery and body work	5	2
Tombstones, glass and bricks	2	1
Chemical works: Soap and oils	2	2
Textiles, wool, linen and knitwear	2	2
Woodworking and sawmills	1	1
Paper industries: printing and binding	1	1
Food industries: flour mills, bakeries, liquor, and sweetmeats	9	8
Clothing and footwear, needlework	5	3
Leather industries, manufacture and tanning, felt making	3	3
Barbers and pig bristle preparation	3	3

Appendices of Material Not Included in the Original Yizkor Book   App A - 45

In 1937 there were 101 Jewish tradesmen: 33 shoemakers and leather stitchers, 24 butchers, 16 tailors and dressmakers, 7 metalworkers, 3 bakers, 3 barbers, 3 leatherworkers, 2 milliners, 2 knitters, 2 painters, 2 watchmakers, a carpenter, a photographer and two others.

A few hundred Jews made a living from small businesses -- tanning, flour milling, sausage making, metal casting, as well as from a factory for sweets and saccharine, a workshop for agricultural machinery, a wood mill, and a power station. A number of Jews were porters and and waggoners. Also under Jewish ownership were two hotels, two photography shops, and the cinema. Almost all the doctors and pharmacists in Rokishok were Jews. Although Rokishok developed rapidly, the Jews had stiff competition from the Lithuanians who were supported by the local authorities. In 1939, there were 130 telephones in Rokishok, 40 belonging to Jews.

The majority of Jews in Rokishok were Hassidim (Lubavitch, Bobroisk, and Lade.) Rokishok was one of the few places in Lithuania where there was a center for Hassidut Habad. The rabbi of Lade passed through Rokishok after his release from jail in Russia. Before the First World War there were two rabbis in Rokishok, one for the Hassidim and the other for the Mitnagdim, and two ritual slaughterers. One of these was a great scholar and a Talmud chaham. In February 1931, many visitors came to see the Lubavitcher Rebbe who was then visiting the town.

In the main street [note: Synagogue Street] there were three Batei Midrash, all belonging to Habad: The yellow Beit Hamidrash was for the scholars, the green was for property owners, and the red, which was the biggest, for the common people. (These colors were those of the Lithuanian national flag). In all of them Shiurim (studies) were held. The synagogue was at the edge of the town. Additional houses of worship were at the Talmud Torah of Rabbi Dober Zelkind, the Zionist Forum which gathered on festivals, and a minyan of youths which gathered throughout the year.

Before the First World War, most of the education was in heders or yeshivot. A few of the youth studied in the Russian gymansium. In 1910, a private progymnasium for girls was established (of the Misses Gurevitch and Rabinovitch.) During the period of independent Lithuania there was a yeshiva and a smaller one (of Rabbi Moshe Siderer,) where local youths also studied. An elementary school belonging to the Tarbut group (where 200 pupils studied); a school belonging to the Yavne group; and a Hebrew progymnasium (where 40 pupils studied), were also established. Pupils were accepted to the first three grades of the Hebrew progymnasium. Children from other shtetlach enjoyed substantial reductions in tuition fees here. Quite a number of Jewish boys studied at the Lithuanian Gymnasium. In Rokishok there was also a library and a drama club.

Rokishok had a very vibrant political life. In 1905 there was activity in the Revolutionary underground which distributed pamphlets and organized demonstrations against the regime of the Czar. In 1921 a communal committee was formed according to the autonomy granted to the Jews under the constitution for the independent Lithuania. It comprised 15 members, 4 General Zionists, 7 from Achdut, and 4 Poalim. The committee dealt with taxes as well as the maintenance of educational and charitable bodies. After the committee was disbanded, these functions were performed by private companies and societies.

At the beginning of the period of independent Lithuania, two Jews were appointed deputies to the mayor of the town at different times, (Itzhak Serber, and Wolpert.) In 1924, 7 Jews were

App A - 46   Appendices of Material Not Included in the Original Yizkor Book

elected to the town council, which comprised 14 members. At that time the mayor and his deputy were Jews. The Jewish faction on the council cooperated with the progressives. In 1931, 5 Jews and 7 Lithuanians were elected to the council.

Amongst the communal institutions were Linat Zedek, Bikkur Holim, an orphanage for 40 boys and girls (under the management of Hannah Shadur), and a Society of Pious Women that nursed the sick, aiding the poor, as well as bankrupts. In the summer of 1928, the Central Helping Committee distributed money to help the needy. The committee allocated 3,800 Lit. as non-interest loans. The distribution of the money was undertaken by the local branch of the Jewish People's Bank (*Folksbank*), which created a special committee for that purpose. One of the topics discussed by the central committee was how best to organize the charitable works in Rakishok. A local philanthropist, Hanoch Chmelnik, donated for this purpose 5000 Lit., which was also distributed by the People's Bank. The bank granted sums of 200 Lit. for three months and up to 300 Lit. for six days. The capital sum was held by the bank in trust for a period of one year. In recognition of the significant contribution of Hanoch Chmelnik, the management of the bank decided to call the fund by the name of Hanoch and Dvora (his wife) Chmelnik.

An American millionaire philanthropist by name Abraham Shapiro who stemmed from Radute, a nearby town, visited Rokishok and on his return to the US sent 19 boxes of clothing and shoes to be distributed to the needy, both Jewish and non-Jewish. He also requested to be involved in the construction of an old people's home and donated $500.00 for this purpose. Although the Rokishok town council hesitated to accept this donation for the intended purpose, the Jewish subcommittee established for this purpose, decided to use it for the building of a mikve (ritual bath) instead.

During the 1930s, branches of various General Zionist Movements including Zadik Zadik, Zadik Samech Jugend Verband, and Maccabi (which had 128 members), and Ha'Poel were active. There were 2 libraries and a reading room. In one library (belonging to the Liebhaber fun Wissen) [Seeker of Knowledge], there were housed 600 volumes, with only 50 readers. In the second library, belonging to the Zadik Samech Jugend Verband, there were housed only 300 volumes with an even smaller reading public. In the mid-1930s a literary trial took place for the first time in Rokishok by Zadik Samech. Besides the Zionist movements in Rokishok there was a branch of the Yiddish Culture League, as well as leftist organizations. In addition, the religious organizations had branches – Tiferet Bachurim, Young Mizrachi, Agudath Yisroel, and Young Agudath Yisroel. All the religious movements supported the settlement of Eretz Israel [the Land of Israel]. In 1935 a Yavneh group was active in Rokishok. In addition to the above, all the youth movements which were to be found in Lithuania were represented in Rokishok, *e.g.*, Hashomer Hatzair, Gordonia, and Betar

At the time that the agricultural fair ["yirid"] was held in March 1921 anti-Semitic pamphlets appeared, calling for Lithuanians to come out against the Jews. In April 1929, stones were thrown at Jews, windows were smashed and Jews were beaten. In October 1931 the opening of the Hebrew Gymnasium and the setting up of the Independence Monument were celebrated. The Lithuanian minister of defense praised the part taken by the Jews in the war for Lithuanian independence.

During the elections for the nineteenth Zionist Congress in 1935, the shtetl was at the center of a civil uprising. The Jewish inhabitants who until then had lived peaceably with each other became

Appendices of Material Not Included in the Original Yizkor Book   App A - 47

enemies, as if they had no other problems, such as earning a living, difficulties with the cotton monopoly, or indeed even being excluded from all sources of income.

On 19th June 1935 Yudel Mark (one of the leaders of the Peoples Party in Lithuania), appeared before the tradesmen's organization and urged them to set up a working committee to oppose the anti-Semitism which had reared up in Germany. The members of the organization asked for directives from Kovno.

Among the rabbis who served in Rokishok were: From the Mitnagdim, R. Eliahu Margaliot (who had served previously in Radin), and his son, R. Isser (Asher), the son-in-law of R. Isser, R. Shmuel Levitan, the founder of a yeshiva prior to the First World War. The yeshiva was reestablished afterwards by R. Dobar Zelkind. Amongst the heads of the yeshiva was R. Klein, and the junior yeshiva was headed by R .Moshe Siderer. The last rabbi of Rokishok was R. Zelig Orelowitz, who perished in the Holocaust. Among the Hassidic Rabbis, R. Bezalel the son of Yosef Katz, of the Lubavitcher Hassidim, who reached a good age and died at 96 years after he had worked at Rokishok for many years. His son-in-law R. Abraham Meyerowitz, a pupil of the yeshivas of Mir, Voloshen, and Slobodka and a founder of the Jewish People's Bank, went on to become the rabbi of Abel [Obeliai] in 1928.

Among the well-known communal personalities were Hillel Edelson and his sister Hannah Shadur, Ch. Ersh, David Rosenstein (the school principal), his wife Yaffa Rosenstein-Kaplan, Pesach Ruch, Harmatz, R. Dobar Zelkind, Moshe Westerman, and Avigdor Glombitzki, among the leaders of the Hebrew Scout Movement.

Some famous personalities who were born in Rokishok included: The Chief Military Rabbi of Lithuania, R. Shmuel-Abba Snieg, the industrialist Avraham Shapiro, who was mentioned previously, the journalist and writer Levi Shalit, the future Chief of the Soviet Airforce, Yaakov Smushkevich, who was born in 1902. He joined the Communist Party in 1918 and was amongst the founders of the Soviet government in Rokishok. When Soviet domination came to an end he traveled to Russia where he took part in the Civil War. He graduated from the Senior Aviation College and in 1936 took part in the Spanish Civil War. He distinguished himself in air battles and became known as "General Douglas." He returned to Russia in 1937, became chief of the air force, and distinguished himself in battle against the Japanese. In 1940 he was arrested, and in October of 1941, executed. Joseph Harmatz was one of the activists in the Vilna Ghetto and a partisan, and eventually became the General Director of World ORT.

On the eve of World War Two there were about 3,000 Jews in Rokishok, together with some hundreds of refugees from Poland. In June 1940 the Red Army occupied Lithuania and Rokishok came under Soviet control.

During the Soviet occupation (1940-1941) the authorities confiscated Jewish businesses and a number of shopkeepers and property owners, such as Harmatz and Klingman, were exiled to Russia. During this period in Rakishok, in the place of the Hebrew-language Tarbut school, a school was established in which teaching was in the Yiddish language. This school was founded with the help of "The Volks Hilf," the parents committee, and the Communist Party. This institution managed to produce two graduate classes, in all, 60 pupils.

App A - 48   Appendices of Material Not Included in the Original Yizkor Book

After the Germans invaded the Soviet Union in June 1941, the Red Army managed to hold out in the town until Friday, 27 June 1941. Even up until the day before, the Russians were preparing an attack against the German army and Jewish youth helped as well. Weapons were distributed to the latter and they were positioned and ready for defense and attack (it was not without good reason that the Jews of Rokishok attained the nickname of "The Rokishoker Tzimblers," in other words, ready to strike, or to be aggressive. However, on Friday morning the Red Army departed, taking with it the local government and party operatives. The Jews realized what fate awaited them and many attempted to flee with the departing Red Army to Russia. However, at the Latvian border the Russian Border Guards prevented them from crossing, and the majority had little alternative but to return to their homes. The few that managed to cross, found refuge in Uzbekistan and other places in Central Asia. The more able enlisted into the Lithuanian division of the Red Army, which was founded at the end of 1941.

With the entry of the Nazis into Lithuania in June 1941 an armed and organized unit was formed in northeast Lithuania, whose members were originally operatives in the Communist Party. Amongst them were many Jews from Rokishok. On 26th June, the unit attempted to push back the Lithuanian Nationalists who had infiltrated into the area (prior to the arrival of the Germans). About thirty members of the unit were killed and amongst them Yossel Shorper, a senior operative in the Communist party of Ponevezh. On the way to Rokishok, Lithuanian hooligans accosted the Jews and a number of the latter were killed. A few young men continued the fight with their weapons. A number of combatants fell on both sides.

The German army entered Rokishok on the evening of the same day but stopped in the middle of the town, because the official entry was supposed to have been on the following day, Shabbat, 28th June 1941. The next day the Germans marched through the streets of the town and were welcomed with cries of joy and flowers.

Amongst those who returned to Rokishok from the border were many Jews from the surrounding towns. One of the first decrees issued by the Germans was for the "foreigners" to return to their places of origin and so, on 30 June 1941, all of the latter were expelled from the town.

The first Jewish victim to fall immediately after the entry of the Germans was Jacob Jacobson who watched the marching Germans from a window and was shot. On the return from the funeral of the latter, a second Jew, Katriel Shomer, was shot and killed. This was the beginning of the suffering and humiliation which awaited the Jews of Rokishok.

The Germans separated the men from the women and children and delegated work to each group. Many farmers arrived to obtain Jewish workers. It is probable the Jewish males were held in the stone stables of the Count Pashdiatzki [Przezdziecki]. The women and the children up to the age of 8 years were gathered at Antanaše, the holiday resort of the inhabitants of Rokishok, not far from the town. The Lithuanian governor of the Rokishok area published a decree warning the farmers not to allow the Jews to be slack at their work and to curtail their movements. Those who violated this law were subject to punishment. The Lithuanian nationalists who collaborated with the Germans, physically and cruelly maltreated the Jews and even shot them. For a short time a Judenrat functioned in Rokishok with Ozinkovitz and Jacob Kark at its head.

The Jewish males were shot to death on Friday and Saturday the 15th and 16th August 1941. (Chaf Beth and Chaf Gimmel of Av Tash"a). They were assembled at a certain point and were even allowed to bring some personal belongings. They were then taken to a place 5 kilometers from Rokishok, near the village of Viziomka, where three-meter deep pits had been prepared. They were ordered to half undress. The men obeyed. R. Zelig Orelowitz spoke to them and called upon them to die with heads held high and with "Sheket Nafshi" for the Sanctification of the Name [the peace of mind of knowing that they were being martyred for their faith]. The women started wailing. The Jews were forced to jump into the pits and were shot by the murderers who surrounded the pits. According to another witness the Jews were made to lie down in the pits in groups of one hundred. Whoever raised his head was immediately shot. Following this, the rest were machine-gunned. Between every layer of victims 20 to 30 cms. of sand was scattered, prior to bringing the next group. On the first day some thousands of men were killed. A few days later, on Monday 25th August 1941 (Bet b'Elul Tash"a) the women, the elderly, and the children were murdered; the number was about 2000. According to other witnesses, this took place on 20th August. Besides the Jews of Rokishok, those from Abel, Suvinishok, Ponedel, Panemunek, Kamai, Raduta, and from surrounding smaller townlets were also killed. Doctor Gundelman poisoned his family and himself, and likewise did Ita Schwartzberg.

The one survivor, Rachel Zagai, happened to be in the Kovno Ghetto, and later received certification from the church that she was a gentile. With their help she drifted from village to village, later working in East Prussia. After the war she immigrated to Israel.

In the spring of 1944 the Gestapo arrested a Lithuanian by name Vladas Andonas, accusing him of giving shelter to Jews. A farmer's wife called Veisejiene from the town of Kadeliai hid 5 Jews who were ultimately saved from the slaughter. The farmer's wife and the Jews were captured by the Gestapo. It is not known what became of them. A Lithuanian woman named Šniokienė from the nearby village of Rudeliai hid four Jews in her home and cared for them. In 1942 she was arrested with the Jews and placed in Rokishok Prison. Leonardas Garzas from Rokishok hid Reznekov, who was a Jewish volunteer in the Lithuanian army, together with three members of his family, amongst them two children.

In the vicinity of Rokishok there are 4 communal graves (by another account 7): in Antanoše 5 km. from Abel, about 200 metres from the left side of the road are buried 1160 who were murdered on 25th August 1941; in the village of Vyzuonai about 200 metres to the left of the road leading to the settlement of Juodupė, are buried 67 who were murdered in July 1941; in the town of Steponiai 5 km. from Rokishok about 150 metres to the right of the road in the direction of Svedushch [Svėdasai] are 981 graves of those also murdered in July-August of 1941; in the forest of *Velniaduobe* 5 km. from Rokishok, not far from the village of Baiorai, 400 metres to the right of the road which leads to the road to Juodupė, are buried 3207 men, women, and children, who were killed on 25-26 August 1941. According to these facts the number of those murdered was between 4,700 and 4,800. After the war, those remaining from the surrounding villages erected monuments over the communal graves. On that in the Steponiai forest the following is inscribed: "At this spot are buried 981 citizens who were murdered by the fascist German occupiers and nationalist bourgeoisie between 27/6/1941 and 14/8/1941."

After the war a small number of Jews returned to live in Rokishok. In 1959 there were 36 Jews in the town. Over the years the numbers decreased. In 1989, only ten Jews remained in Rokishok.

"Rokishkis" (from *Lite, Volume I*)

"Rokishkis" was written by Yudel Gapanovitz and is included in *Lite* (vol. 1), Editors: Dr. Mendel Sudarsky, Uriah Katzenelenbogen, J. Kissin, and Berl Kagan, Jewish-Cultural Society, New York, 1951, pp. 1590-1592, http://www.jewishgen.org/yizkor/lita/Lit1589.html#Page1590. The article was translated by Judie Ostroff Goldstein and Dr. Sonia Kovitz.

Rokishkis
(Rakiskis, Lithuania)

55°58' / 25°35'

Our town Rakishok is located not far from the Latvian border, about 22 kilometers. We call Rakishok the Lithuanian *Kamchatka* [town in Siberia] because of its distance from our previous place of residence, Kovno. The population is over 5,000, of which 45% is Jewish.

Two hundred years ago Rakishok was located a half-kilometer away from present-day Rakishok, which began anew due to a sad incident. Rakishok belonged to a Count Titushevna. In the past the nobility had the right to punish their neighboring inhabitants. Count Titushevna had an administrator whose child was friendly with a local Jewish boy, a tailor's only son. And as it happens with children, the tailor's only son had a fight with the Christian boy and the Jewish boy was the victor. Then the administrator complained about the tailor and his son to the Count, who was an enemy of the Jews. The Count had the tailor come to see him and told the tailor of his decision. When the only son is about to be married, the tailor must let the Count know. If not, he will be punished.

The years went by and the young boy reached his thirteenth year. The father, afraid of punishment and not considering the evil intentions of the Count, told him the day and the hour of his only son's wedding. On that day, when the bride and groom were standing under the wedding canopy, the Count arrived with his people. He brought some dry willow branches, set fire to them, and burned the bride and groom in front of all the *town* residents.

The incident created many problems for the Jews and the town was under a ban. All the Jews had to leave. The more fortunate Jews left and the rest settled here, where the present day Rakishok exists, a half-kilometer from the place where the tragic event occurred. The site where the bride and groom were burned is the present Rakishok cemetery.

During the period of Lithuania's independence, our town was nicely built up. Before long our town was something to look at. The perpetual mud and the two deep ditches on each side of the street, towards which one had to run quickly in order to jump over them, have now disappeared. Finally even the back streets were paved, sidewalks were installed on both sides of the streets, and trees were planted. During the last ten years, dozens of new streets were laid from the railway station three kilometers from town. The railway station is one of the most beautiful in all of Lithuania. It was recently built and cost a half-million *lita*.

Appendices of Material Not Included in the Original Yizkor Book   App A - 51

Rakishok is located in a low area and there are swamps nearby. Therefore plenty of people become sick with tuberculosis. There is no lake or river here, but there are two hot springs that are pleasant to visit. From the large marketplace, around which all the businesses are clustered, the Town Council took a large piece to turn into a boulevard, where they erected a memorial to Lithuanian independence. On one side of the memorial is a statue dedicated to the freedom of the Lithuanian people, and on the other a statue of Dr. Basanavičius. This boulevard and the smaller streets make a fine impression.

As far as culture is concerned in our town, there is one Lithuanian high school with eight grades, a Lithuanian grade school that was recently built, and a Lithuanian library. There is also a movie theater and one *yavne* [Mizrakhi Zionist school] where all the children study. There is a Jewish library that is somewhat forlorn, since no new books arrive for the Rakishker readers to enjoy. Thus the Jewish youngsters order books from Kovno.

In 1931 Rakishok called on A. Shapiro from Boston for assistance. He sent to the Rakishok Town Council 1200 pairs of shoes, boots, and galoshes for the Jewish and Christian poor. Immediately afterward a letter from Shapiro arrived at the Rakishok *folksbank* stating that he is giving $500 towards building the old age home. But due to evil machinations of one of the town's powerful men, it never came about.

Tracing My Roots in *Rakishok*

By **Sorrel Kerbel, D.Phil.**

Editors' Note: Dr. Sorrel Kerbel's great-grandfather, Rabbi Bezalel Shlomo Ha-Cohen Katz (1843-1939), was a prominent Hasidic rabbi in Rokiskis and the story of his family provides a glimpse of Jewish life in that shtetl from the 19th Century until its destruction in 1941. This article first appeared in two instalments in *Shemot,* the journal of the JGS of Great Britain, March 2003, vol. 1.1, and June 2003, vol.II.2.

Dr. Kerbel is the editor of the *Routledge Encyclopedia of Jewish Writers of the Twentieth Century,* 2003 and 2010, a reference work providing essays on the "Jewishness" or not of some 350 Jewish novelists, poets and dramatists all around the world. She received a D.Phil. in English literature from the University of Cape Town. She taught English literature at the University of Port Elizabeth, where she and husband Jack lived for 24 years before immigrating to London. They, their three children, and eight grandchildren live in the UK, where she is an independent researcher and reviewer. She has also worked for some years in London with Holocaust survivors through Jewish Care.

The original version of Dr. Kerbel's article, "Tracing My Roots in *Rakishok*" was published on the Rokiskis Kehilalinks website at http://kehilalinks.jewishgen.org/rokiskis/sorrel.htm. For this publication, she has updated her article. Dr. Kerbel holds the copyright to this story, which may not be used without her permission.

Author's Introduction to the Updated Article. As a result of the publicity generated by the publication of my article in 2003, I discovered a very special relation in Cape Town, Attie Katz. This updated version is dedicated to him and to the honoured memory of all of my family who perished at the hands of a few Nazis and their willing Lithuanian collaborators in the Lithuanian Shoah. A new exhibition currently on show (2017) in Berlin about Litvak Jews for the first time acknowledges German responsibility for the "deaths by bullet" in Lithuania.

I would like to use here a quotation from Roger Cohen's essay, *The Girl From Human* Street, which was dedicated to his mother (*New York Times*, April 1, 2016). "Every Jew of the second half of the 20th century was a child of the Holocaust. So was all humanity. Survival could only be a source of guilt, whether spoken or unspoken. We bore the imprint of departed souls … I wanted to understand where I came from." This article, "Tracing My Roots in *Rakishok*," reflects my personal quest to understand where I came from and to remember so many names from the silenced past.

I am grateful to many for helping me update this article, including, but by no means limited to, *Shemot,* JewishGen's Yizkor Book Project, Philip and Aldona Shapiro in the USA, Giedrius Kujelis of the Rokiskis Regional Museum, and especially to my husband Jack, my children, and grandchildren who have nourished my interest in *Rakishok*, and to my many friends and other family members who have helped me organize genealogical details, namely (in alphabetical order), Cookie Epstein, Ada Gamsu, Dorothy Gelcer, Julia Segal-Holzer, Gerry Hornreich, Anne Martin, Ros Romem, Paul Teicher, the Todres brothers, and my Windisch family. One of our most amazing new links is to my favourite Yiddish playwright and novelist, Sholem Aleichem, and his daughter Bella.

Reb Bezalel Shlomo Ha-Cohen Katz (centre) with his son-in-law, Reb Avrom Meirowitz (left), and Reb Bezalel's nephew, Rabbi Shmuel Yalowetsky. The photograph was taken in *Rakishok* on the eve of Rabbi Yalowetsky's departure for the USA, where he would be known as Rabbi Samuel Yalow of Syracuse, New York. The two younger rabbis received *smicha* from Reb Bezalel. Rabbi Yalow is wearing a new straw hat to show off his role as a soon-to-be American.

Part 1

My mother's grandfather, Reb Bezalel Katz, "cheated" the Nazis by dying in July 1939, three months before the start of World War II. Reb Bezalel lived to the grand old age of 96. His 93-year-old wife Chaya Sora (nee Yalowetsky), for whom I am named, followed him a few weeks later to a peaceful grave. (She was affectionately known as *Rebbitzen "Sorke."*) But the family was not able to erect gravestones to their memory, as my mother, Nechama Meirowitz-Stein, explains in her essay in the *Rakishok Yizkor* book, "A Few Words in Place of a Tombstone."[1]

This is the only known surviving image of *Rebbetzin Sorke*, the wife of Reb Bezalel Katz, for whom I am named. She is shown here with her grandson, Israel Meirowitz, on the enclosed porch of their house, which stood facing the market square of *Rakishok*.

Rakishok, which is 13 miles from the Latvian border, was the largest shtetl in the northeastern region of Lithuania and was the district capital after 1915. It was a flourishing spiritual and business centre for Lithuanian Jewry. The Jewish population fluctuated in number according to the exigencies of the times. In 1847, the Jewish population was 593; in 1897, it was 2,067, constituting 75% of the general population; in 1914, on the eve of the First World War, it was about 3,000, out of a general population of 3,829. In 1923, following the upheavals of the First World War, 2,013 Jews lived there, constituting about half of the general population. In 1939, there were 3,500 Jews, constituting about 40% of the general population.[2]

Rakishok had excellent rail connections to Dvinsk, Riga, Panevezys (*Ponovezh*), Siauliai (*Shavli*), and Kaunas (*Kovno*) which facilitated trade. What contributed to its special development and stability were its long-standing and well-established markets for many kinds of products, such as flax, seeds, furs, grain, eggs, butter, fruit, poultry, lumber, and meat. During this era, there was also intensive trade by *Rakishker* Jewish merchants in raw hides and skins. Most Jews were traders and peddlers, but there were also artisans, such as tailors, shoemakers, hat-makers, butchers, bakers, metalworkers, and clockmakers. Several hundred Jews worked in small Jewish-owned industries like the tannery, flour mills, sausage factory, casting factory, and electric station. Most of the town's doctors and pharmacists were Jewish.[3]

Rakishok developed from an estate owned by the Polish house of Kroshinsky. The widowed Princess Helena, the last of that family, married Count Tizenhoff, and *Rakishok* passed to the family of the Counts Pshezdetsky. The impressive St. Matthew's Catholic Church, which overlooks the market square, was built between 1866 and 1885 upon the initiative of Count Reynold Tizenhoff. It is positioned to have a clear view beyond the market square to the front of the Tizenhoff manor house, one kilometer to the east. Then, as now, its towering spire dominates the landscape.

Reb Bezalel (1843-1939)[4] was born in *Rakishok* and lived "for as long as anyone could remember" on the *Kamayer Gasse* (now, Respublikos gatvė). This street originally led directly south from the market square to *Kamai,* which is 11 miles away. Across from *Kamayer Gasse* the market place would particularly bustle on Mondays, which were market days, on Sundays, when churchgoers would patronage Jewish shops, and especially on fair days, when thousands of peasants would come to town. Near his *Kamayer Gasse* house were the *Batei Midrashim* (houses of study) on Synagogue Street (now, Sinagogų gatvė).

From the time that Lithuania became an independent country, the synagogues were painted, respectively, the colours of the Independent Lithuanian flag – the yellow one was for scholars, the green one was for community leaders, and the red one, which was the largest, was for the general community. Prior to the First World War, there was a fourth synagogue nearby on Pirties gatvė (Bath Street) that had been built for use by *mitnagdim*. That synagogue had its own *mikveh* (ritual bath). During the First World War, the *mitnagid* synagogue was destroyed by a fire. Of the many Jews who fled either to Russia or Germany during the war, the relatively few *mitnagdim* who returned to *Rakishok* could not afford to rebuild their synagogue. As a result, it was agreed that the great ("red") synagogue would be used by everyone in the community.

Near this area were other buildings that were important for business, such as most of the larger shops for textiles and leather goods, flour storehouses, warehouses, a bank, and even a showroom of Singer's Sewing Machine Company.[5] The bank, which was known as the *Rakishker Yudishe Folkbank* (in Lithuanian, "Rokiškio Žydų Liaudies Bankas") was the *Rakishok* branch of the *Folkbank.* The *Folkbank* was established after the First World War with assistance from the Joint Distribution Committee ("Joint"), an American aid organization, and had several branches in Lithuania. (There were also branches in six Balkan countries).

Reb Bezalel was the "official" rabbi of *Rakishok*, and met the first President of Independent Lithuania, Antanas Smetona[6], on his visit to *Rakishok* on the occasion of the opening of the new railway station, circa 1920. He stood, a frail figure, on the festooned podium with the president and Graf Tizenhoff. Later that day; the President visited the synagogue complex.

Lithuanian President Antanas Smetona and Rabbi Betzalel Katz attending the inauguration of the new Rokiškis railroad station. Image was scanned by Barry Mann and Maurice Skikne from photos provided by Noami Musiker of the South African Jewish Board of Deputies' Archive in the Beyachad building in Johannesburg, ID 1443/3.

My great-grandfather Bezalel was a *Hasid* who gathered around him other rabbis of his persuasion, each with their own followings - *Lubavicher, Babroisker,* and *Ladier*. My mother describes her grandfather as a figure of great piety, modesty, and tolerance, who studied "*Yom ve'laila*" (day and night). He wrote many books and articles which regrettably have gone missing. He was also something of an expert in Hebrew, and once wrote a much praised letter in Hebrew to the director of education at the *Rakishok pro-gymnasium* (high school) which used Hebrew as the medium of instruction. This was the school where my mother and her sisters were educated. Reb Bezalel's granddaughter Feiga married Josef Caspi who served as the principal of both the *Tarbut Bet Sefer* and *Pro-Gymnasium*.[7]

Photo on left: My mother Nechama (centre), with her sister Liebe-Leike (Leah) far left (with fringe). Photo on right: Joseph Caspi (centre) with a pro-gymnasium class. To the right of Caspi is my mother Nechama and to the right of her is her sister Liebe-Leike. In the second row on the left, wearing a white collar, is Julia Segal Holzer.

The Graf Tizenhoff greatly admired my great-grandfather, who initially worked for him as an ironmonger and was for a short while his agent on the estate. In 1931, when the *Lubavicher Rebbe Yosef Yitzchak Shneersohn* honoured Reb Bezalel with a visit, Reb Bezalel met him at the railway station with a carriage and horses loaned by Graf Tizenhoff, and they drove through the town to the synagogue behind his house on *Kamayer* Street. According to an anecdote told by aunt, Rochel Kalwaria, a non-Jewish neighbour who was present proudly told my great-grandmother, *Rebbitzen Sorke,* "your Kaiser has arrived."

After working for the Count, Reb Bezalel received *smicha* (becoming ordained as a rabbi) from his father, Reb Yosef Ha-Kohen Katz, who was then the rabbi of *Rakishok.* Reb Bezalel served as a rabbi in *Karsevke* (now, Kārsava), Latvia, which is about 82 miles northeast of Dvinsk (now, Daugavpils), Latvia, where he had a "*guten nomen*" (good name/standing). (This is a reference to *Pirkei Avot* (*Ethics of Our Fathers*) 4:13, in which it is said that "there are three crowns: the crown of Torah, the crown of priesthood, and the crown of kingship. However, superior to all of these is the crown of a good name.") For his second rabbinic post he returned to *Rakishok,* inheriting the rabbinic "kisei" (seat) of his father, Rabbi Yosef HaKohen Katz.

My great-grandfather, Rabbi Bezalel, and his wife Sara had a daughter and three sons. Their daughter, Asne Rifke (1876-1941), married my grandfather, Rabbi Avrom (Abraham) Meirowitz (1875-1941), who is discussed below.

Reb Bezalel himself came from an important family. His father, Reb Yosef Ha-Kohen Katz, was born around 1814 in *Rakishok* and had six sons, some of whose descendants managed to escape to South Africa, Israel, Australia, and the USA. Avrom Leib, the eldest, was the great-grandfather of Dov Katz of Pardes Hanna (today, Pardes Hanna-Karkur), Israel, Attie and Sheilah Katz of Cape Town, and Ann Martin of Johannesburg. Bezalel, the second son and my great-grandfather, was also the great-grandfather of Thelma Windisch of London, Aharon Barak and Avi Keidar of Tel Aviv, and Riki Hirsowitz of Sydney, Australia. The descendants of Berzik, the third son, established the jewellery store Katz & Lurie in Johannesburg. The descendants of Shmuel, the fourth son, perished in Lithuania. The fifth son, Yaakov Katz (b. 1879 in *Rakishok*), married Reisa Galbershtat of *Rakishok* (1879-1939). Their son, Chaim Tuvia

App A - 58   Appendices of Material Not Included in the Original Yizkor Book

Katz (1909-1990), was a founding member of Dafna (3 May 1949), a kibbutz in the Upper Galilee of Israel. He and his wife Chaya Shein Czarka had two children, Tsofar Katz and Avigail, who live in Haifa. The sixth son, Shnuer Zalman (Shneyer Zalman) (b. 1881), died in Abel in 1941. Reb Yosef also had two daughters, one of whom, Raisa Devorah, married Reb Zecharya Alter Abrahams (whom my mother called called "Avromtzik Jossel"). Their son was Chief Rabbi Prof. Israel Abrahams of Cape Town, who was the father of Ros Romem of Jerusalem.

Reb Yosef, too, came from an illustrious family. He was the second of five sons born to Reb Meir Ha-Kohen Katz, who was born in *Linkuva* around 1790. Reb Meir was serving as a rabbi in *Rakishok* when his second son, Yosef, was born there. Thus, the Katz family served as rabbis in *Rakishok* for at least a hundred years.

According to family legend, generations of Ha-Kohen Katz rabbis served in communities in Lithuania for more than 300 years. The five sons of Reb Meir Ha-Kohen Katz are a genealogist's nightmare because they were each given different surnames at birth to avoid 25 years' conscription into the Czar's army. The eldest was Shmuel Leib Ha-Kohen Kaplan (b. 1808 in *Rakishok,* whose descendant Valerie Mathieson from the USA provided details of Shmuel and his wife Taube Kuperman of *Rakishok* and their six children, all of whom died in Lithuania). Tthe second son (my great-great-grandfather) was Yosef Ha-Kohen Katz. The third son's name was not known to my mother, though she notes that he later became a rabbi in *Linkuva*, taking his father's place (this may be the Rabbi Aharon Ha-Cohen who is mentioned on the Linkuva Kehilla website as having endorsed the collection of funds to assist distressed Jews after a large fire burned about 100 buildings, including the community's wooden synagogue). The fourth son was the eminent science populariser, Tzvi Hirsch Ha-Kohen Rabinowitz (1832-1889). The youngest son of Reb Meir was called Moshe Yaffe. (My mother notes simply that he was "a merchant," and therefore did not have much *"koved"* (prestige) in her eyes.)

The fourth son of Reb Meir Ha-Kohen Katz, Tzvi Hirsch Rabinowitz, showed an early inclination for mathematics and physics. From 1852, while studying in St. Petersburg, he began work on a comprehensive Hebrew-language project that was intended to encompass all the fields of physics. At length, one volume was published, in 1867, which was entitled, *Sefer ha-Menuchah ve-ha-Tnuah* ("The Book of Rest and Movement").

Tzvi Hirsch also wrote Hebrew-language books on mathematics, magnetism, chemistry, and steam-engines, thus enriching Hebrew terminology in these fields and bringing them to the attention of Hebrew readers. He also published many articles in *Ha-Meliz* ("The Ornamentation") and in several Russian periodicals which he edited and published, including *Russki Yevrei* (Russian Jews) from the late 1870s until 1885. All of his books were published in Vilna/Vilnius.

Title Page of Tzvi Hirsch Meir HaCohen Rabinowitz's *"Yisodei HaChachmat HaTeva HaKlalit,"* Vilna (1867).

As noted above, my great-grandparents, Rabbi Bezalel and *Rebbitzin Sorke* Katz, had a daughter Asne Rifke (1876-1941), who married my grandfather, Rabbi Avrom (Abraham) Meirowitz (1875-1941). Avrom Meirowitz was the fourth child of Moshe and Rifke Meirowitz of *Karelitz (Karelichi)*, a town 15 miles east of Novogrudek that was in the province of Minsk. Moshe and Rifke had 6 children, namely, Berl David, the eldest, whose family settled in Rhodesia and Israel; the second son Yaakov, who emigrated to the U.S., where there are many cousins; Ethel Cohen, who died in 1941; my grandfather Avrom; Yudel, who died in 1941; and the youngest, Meir, whom, they said, was killed by the Cossacks. Meir's wife Machle (nee Sachar) was from *Kupishok* and her brother, A. L. Sachar, was the founding president of Brandeis University. Her children settled in Israel.

Avrom Meirowitz studied at the yeshivas of *Mir, Slobodka, and Volozhin* (where his study-partner at one time was the renowned Hebrew poet, Chaim Nachman Bialik). When my mother, Nechama Meirowitz-Stein, was born in *Rakishok*, the couple lived in her grandfather's home because her father served in the nearby shtetl *Skimiahn* (Skemai, which is about 6 miles northeast of *Rakishok*).

App A - 60   Appendices of Material Not Included in the Original Yizkor Book

In early May 1915, during the First World War, the Czarist government ordered the Jews of central Lithuania exiled to the interior of Russia – on two days' notice. Although the order did not apply to Jews in northeastern Lithuania, many were concerned about the approach of the war front. The family, together with most of the Jewish inhabitants of *Rakishok*, fled into Russia for safety. Unfortunately, Russia experienced two revolutions in 1917, followed by a civil war. It was only after (Soviet) Russia and the new independent Lithuanian republic reached a peace agreement that the Jewish exiles could return to Lithuania. My mother recalls that as a child of ten, when her family returned to *Rakishok*, they were welcomed back by the Lithuanian townspeople with "flowers, love, and honour."

My mother Nechama wrote in the *Yizkor* book that her father, Rabbi Avrom Meirowitz, was a wise man who was no stranger to world affairs despite having lived in a relative backwater. He was a *mitnagid* who read many secular books. His command of Russian and German, acquired on his own, led him to read the great literature of those languages, including the works of Dostoevsky and Tolstoy. My grandfather's horizons went well beyond the confines of the narrow world of the shtetl. He was a founding member of the *Rakishok* branch of the *Folkbank* and served as the bank's director in *Rakishok*. In addition, he went often to *Ponovezh* (Panevėžys), where he sat on a rabbinical arbitration board to resolve disputes among litigants.

Rabbi Avrom Meirowitz was the chairman of the *Folkbank*. He is shown here, in the centre of the front row, with other members of the management board. First row, sitting right to left: Shloime Arelovits, Hillel Eidelson, Abba Leib Dovidovits, Avrom Meyerowitz, Leib Segal, Zalman Milner, Israel-Leib Snieg; Second row, right to left: Isaac Panets, Chaim-Moteh Lekach, Avrom Harmets, Yudel Gafanovits, Hertze Lang, Yosef Caspi; Third row, right to left: Velvel Lipovits, Mr. Bar, Nahum Katz, Solomon German.

The marriage of my grandfather, the *mitnagid* Rabbi Avrom, to my grandmother Asne, the daughter of the *hasidic* Rabbi Bezalel, reflects a good deal of tolerance on the part of the latter, who even permitted the young married couple to live in his household.

By the middle of the 1920s, with anti-Semitism growing in Lithuania, many Jews began to consider emigrating, especially to Palestine. The Balfour Declaration had promised the establishment there of a Jewish homeland. My grandfather, Rabbi Avrom Meirowitz, had a strong Zionist orientation (perhaps acquired at Volozhin Yeshiva, which was known for its espousal of Zionism). This inclination led him to join the *Mizrachi* - the National Religious Party - within the Zionist movement, and he appeared as a speaker at their meetings and rallies. As a result, understandably, he was less popular among the ultra-orthodox *Agudas Yisroel* circles.

Left photo: My grandfather, Reb Avrom Meirowitz, the last rabbi of *Abel*. Right photo: My grandmother, Asne Rifke Meirowitz, with her two grandchildren, Josef and Ester Michelson, the children of her eldest daughter Taube Mirkes. All were murdered in Abel in 1941.

In 1928 my grandfather became the rabbi in *Abel* (Obeliai), nine miles to the east. At a rabbinical conference in *Ponevezh* in the late 1930s, he warned his audience of the imminent dangers of Nazism, saying they were mistaken in thinking Hitler's objectives were confined to the destruction of only German Jews. This raised much criticism among the *Agudah* delegates, and his admonition fell on deaf ears.

Although Reb Avrom possessed immigration papers for America, his wife, Asne Rifke, refused to leave Lithuania without her grandchildren. Sadly, he met his death from an axe wielded by a Lithuanian collaborator while standing on the *bima* of the *shul* in *Abel,* where all of the Jews of the village were held in August 1941. He was thus the last rabbi in *Abel*. Because of my mother's delicate health, the truth of his death was kept from her, and the sanitized version she gives in her essay is not correct, according to my mother's last surviving sister, Rochel (Rachel) Kalwaria of Kiryat Ono, Israel (July 1995).

App A - 62   Appendices of Material Not Included in the Original Yizkor Book

In this photograph of the 1932 graduates from Vytautas Magnus University, my mother, Nechama Meirowitz, is shown in the next-to-bottom row, on the far left. Immediately to the right is her sister, Liebe-Leike Meirowitz.

Poor as they were, the Meirowitz family was enlightened and determined enough to send their children to college. My mother Nechama received a B.A. degree from Vytautus Magnus University in 1932. Her two sisters, Liebe-Leike and Rachel, became, respectively, a teacher and a pharmacist, while their brother Yisroel (Israel) became a medical doctor. They would go off by train from the nearby *Rakishok* railway station to the University in Kaunas where they boarded with *Rakishker landsleit*. My mother told me how, in winter, their landlady would be sent a frozen barrel of veal or beef by train, as partial payment for their board. (*Rakishok* was an important centre for the wholesale meat trade.)

Photo of my mother's brother, Dr. Israel Meirowitz (front row, second from the right), with his colleagues at a hospital in Kaunas. In 1944, while out on a medical call, he was shot dead.

In Lithuania, my mother's family and friends gave her the nickname "*die shvartze varona*" ("the black crow/raven") because she forewarned of a dismal future for Jews in Lithuania and tried to convince them to emigrate. After her graduation from Vytautas Magnus University she left for Jerusalem, where she married my father, Nathan Stein, and then migrated once more (with my sister Thelma) to Cape Town, South Africa.

A boating party in peaceful times on Lake Obeliai. Fourth from the right is Julia Segal Holzer, my mother's friend who was also saved in the *maline* in the Kovno ghetto. Third from the right is my mother's brother, Dr. Israel Meirowitz. Second from the right may have been Israel's fiancé, Miriam Jaffe, from *Kupishok*.

App A - 64   Appendices of Material Not Included in the Original Yizkor Book

Footnotes

[1] Nechama Meirowitz-Stein, "A Few Words in Place of a Tombstone" in *Yizkor-Book of Rakishok and Environs,* edited by M. Bakalczuk-Felin, Johannesburg, Yizkor Book Publishing Council, 1952, pp. 145-149. Most of the family information here was learned at my mother's knee or contained in her essay. I am indebted also to Alan Todres of Chicago and Raymond Karpelofsky of London who helped me with the Yiddish translation.

[2] Nancy Schoenberg and Stuart Schoenberg, *Lithuanian Jewish Communities*, New York, Garland Publishing, 1991, pp. 240-244.

[3] R. Aarons -Arsch, "Notes on the Economic Position of the Jews in Rakishok." in *Yizkor-Book of Rakishok and Environs,* pp. 19-29.

[4] The All-Russia Census of 1897 gives ages for Reb Bezalel and various members of the family which do not coincide with the ages presented here. For the purposes of this article, I have chosen to use the ages recorded by my mother in the *Yizkor-Book of Rakishok and Environs.*

[5] A. Orelowitz, "Rakishok Before and After World War I" in *Yizkor-Book of Rakishok and Environs,* pp. 7-18.

[6] Antanas Smetona (1874-1944) was the president of Lithuania from April 1919 to June 1920 and then from late 1926 until the end of the first Lithuanian republic. During most of the latter period, he ruled as an autocrat. Ostensibly and officially a "friend of the Jews," he surprised the British Consul in Kaunas by describing the Jews of Lithuania as "active Communists" and "dishonest traders." Masha Greenbaum, *The Jews of Lithuania: A History of a Remarkable Community 1316-1945,* Jerusalem, Gefen Publishing, 1995, p. 279. On June 15, 1940, as the republic succumbed to Soviet annexation, Smetona fled to Germany, and a year later moved to the USA.

[7] Feiga, my mother's cousin and the daughter of Aharon Katz, married Josef Caspi (Serebrovitz), who wrote as a Jewish journalist using the name "Caspi." He was born in *Rakishok*, worked first at *the Folkbank* (employed by Rabbi Avrom Meirowitz), then as principal of the Tarbut School and Pro-gymnasium in *Rakishok*. Because of his capitalist views, he was imprisoned in 1940 during the initial Soviet rule and released shortly after German occupation in late June 1941. He then threw in his lot with the Germans so that he could fight communism. He was exempted from wearing the yellow Star of David and allowed to live in Kaunas outside the ghetto and even to carry a gun. He was, in his own mind, "a living legend who will go down in Jewish history" (his words to the Council in the *Kovno* ghetto). He acted as an intermediary between the ghetto council and the Nazi commandant. In October 1941, he was sent to Vilnius. In June 1943, back in Kaunas, he was shot by the Nazis together with his wife and two daughters. Shortly before his death Caspi addressed the Jewish council of the Kovno ghetto, "You entertain illusions of survival. I know that if I survive, it will only be by chance." (He is shown in the photo above of the pro-gymnasium class with my mother and her sister Leibe. An account of this story appears in Avraham Tory's *Surviving the Holocaust: The Kovno Ghetto Diary*, Cambridge, Massachusetts, and London, Harvard University Press, 1990.

Tracing My Roots in *Rakishok*
Part 2

So it was with mixed feelings that my husband Jack and I drove to Rokiskis from Kaunas in September 2002, a pleasant two-hour drive through forested, fairly flat countryside. There was very little traffic on the roads, occasionally some cars and even the odd horse and cart. We were told that many poor Lithuanians had gone back to the days of the horse and cart because of the rising cost of petrol, now no longer subsidized by the Soviet state, but still half the price we paid in the UK.

I was armed with the details Julia Holzer (neé Segal) had given me in London some ten years before, kept in my diary all this time. Julia had been in the same class as my aunt Liebe-Leike at the Hebrew pro-gymnasium in *Rakishok*. She left Lithuania only in 1968, so she remembered it all clearly.

My reference points were the house of the Graf (now a hotel) and the imposing Catholic church. Counting left, the fourth house, a triple-storeyed narrow wooden building on a corner, with a wooden slatted roof and brick steps leading up to the front door, was where my mother grew up. It was unchanged. The garden in front, at the side, and in the back, is well-kept and planted with fruit trees and flowers. Reb Bezalel's house stood empty, for sale.

We peered through the windows into the front room. This was where *Rebbitzin Sorke* sold some household supplies, such as yeast and candles. She had the monopoly on selling yeast, an important perk for rabbi's wives at that time, bringing in a few *gruschen* to supplement their resources.

The *Batei Midrashim,* (synagogue and houses of study) were burned to the ground in July 1941.

In my mother's day, there were conveniently located on the market square a well and a large pump, surrounded by a low wall. Attached to the pump was a tin can, which passers-by could use to quench their thirst on a hot day. At the foot of the pump was a trough of water for cattle and horses. During my visit in 2002, there was on this site a Soviet-style memorial to the anonymous war dead, some twelve foot high in Soviet-style pink granite. Like many other Soviet-era monuments, it is has been removed.

We followed Julia's instructions to find the Russian Orthodox church (*tzerkve*); opposite it was the park (*bulvar*) where the horse market used to be. Still a park and children's playground. On the corner the large house facing the park was the Jewish orphanage, now a private dwelling. Turn left, and count three houses to a single-storeyed wooden house, the home of the Kruk (Kriger) family (See photo at http://kehilalinks.jewishgen.org/rokiskis/Kriger.htm), who left for Cape Town in 1931, despite a warning from the *Lubavicher* Rebbe not to go to this "*treife*" (unclean) country! (The Rebbe himself escaped to the USA in 1940, when the Soviets closed Jewish religious institutions.)

App A - 66   Appendices of Material Not Included in the Original Yizkor Book

It was all there, little changed. The small wooden houses of the Jews are occupied by more prosperous Lithuanians, mostly with double glazing, running water, and neat gardens. A van was delivering loads of firewood, so I guess they still depend on wood fires. The alternative type of dwelling today is a flat in one of the many ugly concrete Soviet-style blocks of flats situated on the outer perimeter of town. The Jewish houses are in the centre of town, so it is not surprising they are now highly desirable "bijou" townhouses.

I had carefully prepared a sentence from the Lithuanian dictionary asking the location of the Jewish cemetery, and asked a woman in the well-stocked bookshop on the relatively prosperous *Kamayer gasse* (now, Respublikos gatvė). I asked in English, showing my page, and a well-dressed couple responded. They were driving a newish German car and we followed them part of the way. Instead of leading us to the old Jewish cemetery, on the western edge of the town, they instead led us to the hamlet of *Bajorai,* which is northeast of *Rakishok*. There, an old woman with a drab headscarf and poor teeth (probably no more than my age) pointed us in the direction of a memorial with a sign written in Lithuanian that translated into "Memorial to the Fascist Martyrs of the Holocaust."

Continuing along a winding road into the deep and lovely birch woods beyond *Bajorai*, we reached a path, on the right, to the "killing field." It was here that more than 3,200 Jews died. They had been brought here from *Rakishok* and four hamlets, including *Abel* and *Skopishok*. They were rounded up shortly after the Germans arrived in late June 1941 and held for 6-8 weeks in a ghetto established for *Rakishok* area Jews in two barns of the estate owned by the Graf. A few escaped from the ghetto and fled to neighbouring farmers; they were mostly betrayed.

On August 15, 16, and 20, 1941, these Jews were marched some two miles from *Rakishok*, forced to dig their mass graves, and then shot and buried in seven large trenches, now concreted over. Today there is a simple memorial plaque in three languages. We were told that the post-Soviet Lithuanian State would not allow any mention of the fact that the Jews had been murdered with the willing collaboration of Lithuanians.

(See photo at http://kehilalinks.jewishgen.org/rokiskis/Holocaust.htm)

It was quite a day. Jack and I quietly said *Kaddish* in their names. There were a few tired red flowers at the memorial, and the remains of a few *Yahrzeit* candles. It was eerily quiet in the woods, with only a youngster walking to the forester's house further up the path.

The next day, having returned to Kaunas, we were met in the foyer of the Takioji Neris Hotel (now, the Park Inn by Radisson Kaunas) by the guide we had prearranged. Chaim Bargman is the Shlomo of Dan Jacobson's *Heshel's Kingdom*; an excellent guide who speaks five languages, including Hebrew.[1]

Also waiting in the foyer was Czeslovas Rakevicius, 84 years old, tall and well built. He is the son of the doughty peasant farmer whose wife (Czeslovas' mother) was a patient of my mother's brother, Dr. Israel Meirowitz. Czeslovas explained that before the war, his mother had had an operation in the hospital at Kaunas and became friendly with Jewish doctors there, including my uncle. The Rakevicius family wanted to help Jews and because their farm was very isolated, far off the beaten track, it was put on a list of safe houses. They hid my aunt, Liebe-Leike, who had

Appendices of Material Not Included in the Original Yizkor Book   App A - 67

escaped from the Kovno ghetto, and her son, then 11-year-old Aharon Barak, who had been smuggled out of the ghetto.

An article in the 23 July 1993 edition of the *Jerusalem Post* reported on the ceremony at *Yad Vashem* where they were honoured as righteous gentiles. It tells of how Zvi Brik (Barak) placed his son in a potato sack and smuggled him past a bribed guard out of the Kovno ghetto to a waiting wagon. In all, this tactic was used to save about 100 children. (The stories of some of those children is told in *Smuggled in Potato Sacks*, by Solomon Abramovich and Yakov Zilberg (Vallentine Mitchell 2011.) Those not smuggled out were murdered in the March 1944 *Kinderaktion.*

Left: Zvi Brik (Barak) was the deputy manager of a slave-labor shop in the Kovno ghetto where uniforms for Wehrmacht soldiers were sewn. He managed to get his son Aharon out of the ghetto in a sack that was thrown onto a horse-drawn cart. Right: Photo of Aharon Brik (Barak) at four years old.

Initially, Aharon was hidden on the farm of a righteous gentile, Jonas Mazuraitis. Later, he was hidden with his mother, Liebe-Leike Barak, on the farm of the Rakevicius family, who courageously saved 25 Jews. A remarkable and noble family.

Liebe-Leike told me that she had feared discovery at the Rakevicius farm because of her pronounced Jewish looks. So the family created a hiding space of one-and-a-half metres square behind a false wall in their living room and she lived in that confined space with her son for nearly two years. Food was passed to them and she used the time to teach her son everything she knew

Czeslovas agreed to show us the site of his family's farm, which is deep in the countryside, 84 miles west of Kaunas, near Paupys and Raseniai. Quite a trip on dirt roads. But we were pleased to do it because we heard from him, via the guide, the story of how the Rakevicius family became involved in hiding 25 Jews.

Before continuing, I would like to note the singular accomplishments of Aharon Barak, the rescued child. From 1975 to 1978, he was the Attorney General of Israel. In 1978 he was the principal drafter of the Israeli-Egyptian agreement at Camp David. In 1995 he became the Chief Justice of Israel – the head of the Supreme Court, a position he held until retiring in 2006. Since

App A - 68   Appendices of Material Not Included in the Original Yizkor Book

then, he has been a professor of law at the Herzlia Interdisciplinary Centre. Ari Shavit tells Aharon's story in *My Promised Land: The Triumph and Tragedy of Israel*, Spiegel & Gran, New York (2013), at pages 142-145, 155-157, and 162, where he describes Aharon as "a brilliant liberal jurist who has reshaped Israeli jurisprudence, and is admired worldwide."

It was only in 2005 that Aharon first spoke publicly about his escape from the Kaunas ghetto. At that year's Yom Hazikaron ceremony in Jerusalem, he began and ended his address by quoting from *Zechariya* 3:2 and *Amos* 4:1, "I am a brand plucked from the fire - in whom the spirit of man and of the people breathed life, a life of freedom and of the recognition of the dignity of every man, a life that aspires to achieve justice (righteousness) and the rule of law." He told of the 5,000 children of the ghetto who were taken from their parents and murdered in cold blood. "Few survived. I was among them. In the ghetto the high-pitched voices of children were no longer heard."

With reference to the two Lithuanian farming families who saved him, he said, "They were pious non-Jews who brought us to into their homes." Continuing, he said:

> In August 1944 we were freed by the Red Army. My father survived in one of the ghetto bunkers. ... We crossed Europe on a goods train that was carrying coal from Bucharest to Budapest. There we celebrated the end of the war. We crossed on foot the border from the Russian sector of Austria to the British sector, and continued on from there to Italy. In 1947 we came to Israel. Slowly Arik Brik became Aharon Barak."

> What lesson did I learn from all this? To what extent have these events formed my *Weltanschauung* [philosophical view of the world]? ... the Germans and their helpers sought to turn us into dust and ashes. They sought to take from us the human dignity that is within us. ... the Germans and their helpers succeeded in murdering many of us. They did not succeed in taking from us the image of man that is within us. ... in our state we must behave towards the non-Jew as we would expect them to behave toward us. We must not fail the minority group.

It was not easy to find the location of the Rakevicius' farm. After the Soviets had recaptured Lithuania, the farm was collectivised and the family relocated to Kaunas. A Soviet program to reduce the risk of flooding in the countryside had resulted in both the Rakevicius and Mazuraitis farms now being entirely under water - part of a lake for farming carp - and you could see nothing but lake. We lost our way a couple of times, but even that had its compensations. We visited a few of Czeslovas' former neighbours, who greeted him warmly. It is poor subsistence farming; small ramshackle wooden houses, with corrugated-metal or wooden roofs, outside loos replete with newspaper, hand or horse-drawn ploughs, covered wells, and small areas of land with just one or two cows. Mostly flat swampy land fringed by trees, and the odd cormorant diving for fish.

Then we visited the Ninth Fort outside Kaunas and the memorial to the "Killing Fields," where they marched the sick and elderly, and later everyone from the ghetto except for a few escapees. Aharon Barak's father, Zvi Brik, a well-known Zionist leader in prewar Kovno, was a member of

Matzok and manager of one of the large workshops in the ghetto. He was able to organise clandestinely the building of a *maline* (ghetto slang for bunker) near the river, outside the ghetto. Their *maline* saved eight people, including Rochel (Rachel), my mother's youngest sister and her husband Mendel Kalwaria, Mendel's brother and his wife, and Zvi Barak.

Toward the end of the ghetto's existence, the Germans searched for Jews in hiding, blowing up every stone house, and setting fire to every wooden one. The ghetto burned for several days until it was completely destroyed. Mendel, who was an engineer, had designed and constructed the *maline* with air vents. This crucial feature enabled those in the *maline* to avoid death by asphyxiation when the ghetto was burned. Twenty-five others survived in another *maline* inside the ghetto.

Rachel (youngest daughter of Reb Avrom Meirowitz) and her husband, Mendel Kalwaria, survivors of the Kovno ghetto, in Bari, Italy, awaiting a ship to Palestine, December 1945.

My uncle, Dr. Yisroel Meirowitz did not survive the war. In 1944 he had volunteered to go from the ghetto on a medical call and was then shot.

In the small museum at the Ninth Fort we saw the official list pinned up by the Nazis stipulating that the named persons were to report for duty as Yiddishe Ghetto Polizei. The 43rd and last name was "Meirowitz, Josef" (my mother's older brother who later settled in Brazil to avoid any enemies he might have made in the ghetto.) [2] [3]

My mother's brother, Josef Meyerowitz, who was ordered to be kapo number 43 in the Kovno ghetto, the last name on the list. He was freed when the Russians liberated the ghetto and later settled in São Paulo, Brazil, near our Gelcer, Zamet, Kagan, and Gorenstein cousins. This picture may have been taken aboard the ship to Brazil.

Then back to visit the Archives in Kaunas. They have the tax returns of various *shtetlach* from 1850-1915; but rabbinical families are no good because they were exempt from paying tax! The office was like something from Kafka – books with yellowed pages piled high up to the ceiling, in cupboards, and on rickety chairs and tables.[4]

In researching this article, I came across a tiny box-Kodak photograph from the 1930s of my great-grandfather, Rabbi Bezalel Katz, his son-in-law (and my grandfather) Rabbi Avrom Meirowitz, and Bezalel's nephew, Rabbi Shmuel Yalowetsky (later, Samuel Yalow). (A copy of the photo appears on the first page of this article.) Rabbi Yalow received *smicha* from Reb Bezalel and shortly thereafter emigrated to live and serve the community in Syracuse, New York.

I also discovered a newspaper article from the 7 June 1943 edition of the Syracuse *Post-Standard*, which reported on the wedding of Rabbi Yalow's son Aaron to Rosalind Sussman of New York. (As a result of her work in the field of radio-immuno-assays of peptide hormones, in 1977 she became the first woman in the USA to receive a Nobel prize in Medicine). The 1943 article quotes Rabbi Yalow expressing the following hope to the bride and groom, "I have neither wealth nor wisdom to bequeath to you. I can pass on to you but one thing, *mispor hayomim* - the continuity of the generations, your link with the immortal history of Israel."

Footnotes

[1] Dan Jacobson, *Heshel's Kingdom,* London, Penguin, 1999. Chaim Bargman lives at P. Lukšio gatvė 37-22, Kaunas LT-49391, Lithuania.

[2] See a record of their names in Sir Martin Gilbert's *The Righteous: the Unsung Heroes of the Holocaust,* New York and London, Doubleday, 2002.

[3] Avraham Tory, *Surviving the Holocaust: The Kovno Ghetto Diary*, Cambridge, Massachusetts, and London, Harvard University Press, 1990, p. 522.

[4] The archives are open to the public daily, 10-1 and 2-5, for information on the towns and villages of Kaunas province. If you need her, the archivist Vitaliya Girčytė is very helpful and speaks excellent English, v.gircyte@archyvai.lt. For information contained in Lithuania's historical archives (in Vilnius), use Istorijos.archyvas@centras.lt.

The following is a previously unpublished story of the family of Ray Kriger Katz, the mother of the author, Amanda Katz Jermyn. Although the family had deep roots in Rokiškis and other communities in northeastern Lithuania, in the early 1930s they chose to immigrate to South Africa. Amanda Katz Jermyn holds the copyright to this story, which may not be used without her permission.

Amanda Katz Jermyn was born in Cape Town, South Africa, and has lived in London and Montreal. Since 1980, she and her family have lived in Massachusetts, USA. She has published short fiction in various magazines, including Cosmopolitan, Mademoiselle, New Woman, Spotlight and Woman's Day. She currently writes astronomy articles for a Massachusetts newspaper and online publication. She is also writing a book on her family history.

RAY KRIGER KATZ

By Amanda Katz Jermyn

My mother, who was known in South Africa as Ray Katz, was born in the town of Rokiškis (Rakishik), Lithuania, on March 10th, 1929. Her Yiddish name was Rocha Frieda Kruk. Her first name "Rocha" reflects how Jews in northeastern Lithuania pronounced the name known in Hebrew as Rachel. Since she was born during the time of the independent Lithuanian republic, her legal name had to conform to the grammatical rules of the Lithuanian language. For this reason, her legal name was Rachelia Krukaitė.[1] She was the youngest of the five children of Rivka Kavalsky and Pesach Tzvi Kruk. Her older siblings were her sister Leah (born in 1913), brother Sam (born in 1914), brother Solly (born in 1919), and sister Anne (born in 1926).

Pesach Tzvi Kruk (later, Philip Kriger) and his wife Riva Kavalsky Kruk (later, Riva Kriger), the parents of Rocha Frieda Kruk (later, Ray Kriger Katz).

Appendices of Material Not Included in the Original Yizkor Book   App A - 73

The family had lived in Lithuania for as long as anyone knew. The surname Kruk probably comes from one of the two Lithuanian towns called Kriukai.[2] The surname Kavalsky probably comes from the Polish word kowal, which means a blacksmith or someone who forges metal.[3] This is not surprising given the history of Poland and Lithuania. Between 1659 and 1795 the Kingdom of Poland and the Grand Duchy of Lithuania constituted the two parts of a single state, the Commonwealth of Poland and Lithuania. When an estate was owned by a Polish-speaking nobleman, it would not be uncommon for people living on the estate to speak Polish. Our family's long association with Lithuania is also confirmed by recent DNA studies[4] that appear to show that we have "DNA relatives" from lands that today are in Lithuania, Latvia, Poland, and Belarus, all direct neighbors.

Ray's mother Riva was born in 1889 in the Lithuanian town of Utena (Utyan in Yiddish) and was the daughter of Vita and Shabse Kavalsky. The Kavalskys were Levites. True to his surname, Shabse Kavalsky was a poor blacksmith[5] who lived in Utena, and at one time, on a farm in Kazliškis, which is about midway between Rokiškis and Pandėlys (Ponidel in Yiddish). Though poor, he was ahead of his time, and wanted his five daughters, as well as his three sons, to receive a good education. Since there were no schools for girls at that time in Utena, he employed a tutor to teach them. My grandmother Riva thus grew up to be a well-educated woman. Among other things, she spoke several languages fluently and without trace of an accent, including Russian, German, Yiddish, Lithuanian and Polish. She was also practical and capable. I am told she spun the flax and wove the linen for her own trousseau.[6]

Utena had one of the earliest Jewish communities in Lithuania, dating from the 16th Century, and its first Jewish cemetery had tombstones dating from that time. The cemetery was located at what is now the end of Stoties Street, next to the Vilnius-Utena highway. However, the cemetery was completely destroyed in 1963 when the Utena City United Manufacturing Base facilities were built on its site, using the gravestones as building material. All that is left today is one mound bearing a memorial plaque. The other Jewish cemetery in the area is in the Šiline Forest, on a small hill quite far from town. It was abandoned during the Soviet era and desecrated by vandals who believed that gold would be found in the graves of Jews. In 1994 this cemetery was renovated and a commemorative plaque erected.

Most of the town's houses were built of wood, and in 1879 and 1890 the town was ravaged by fires that destroyed up to half of the wooden houses. The 1890 fire also destroyed the prayer houses and a beautiful synagogue that had been built in 1862. Afterwards, the houses, businesses, and synagogue were rebuilt using brick and stone.[7]

According to the All-Russia Census of 1897, when my grandmother Riva was eight years old, Utena had 2,405 Jewish residents, comprising about 74% of the population. Most of the Jews were shopkeepers, craftsmen, taverners, and peddlers. They also dealt in timber and money lending.[8] The main source of income was trade in flax, skins, and boar bristles.[9] Utena's main thoroughfare, later named J. Basanavicius Street, was intersected in 1899 by a railroad line that was established to connect Panevezys to Svencionys.

As noted, Shabse Kavalsky at one time had a farm near Pandelys, which the Rokiškis Yizkor Book describes as "a muddy and neglected little town"[10] with 150 Jewish families and 50 to 60 Christian families. The surrounding landscape was said to be very beautiful, with orchards and gardens.

App A - 74   Appendices of Material Not Included in the Original Yizkor Book

The family of my grandmother Riva Kavalsky's sister, Vita Leah, lived on a farm, and were murdered by their Polish landlord, a gambler who was unable to repay a substantial amount of money that he had borrowed from Vita Leah's family. My aunt, Leah Todres, told me how one night their house was set on fire and Vita, her husband Shmuel Ger, and their son and daughter were burned to death. Another son, Yeshia, had been sent back to the yeshiva,[11] where he was studying just before Shabbat, although he'd asked to stay for the weekend. His father had told him that he had no way to transport him back on the Monday, so off he went. Yeshia thus avoided this catastrophe.

Yeshia survived the First World War by fleeing to Russia. He also survived the Second World War, and afterwards went to Rokiškis where he stayed in the house of his relative, Pesach Ruch. Eventually, he couldn't stand the growing atmosphere of anti-Semitism and the fact that all his friends and family were gone, so he moved to a bigger town. His sons went to Israel and live there now.

Auntie Leah was named "Vita Leah" after her mother's sister. She described how every year her mother's family would go back to the farm where the murder took place to pay homage to the dead, just as one would visit a cemetery. One day when she was sixteen my grandmother Riva went there on her own and saw the Polish landlord who had murdered her family there. She courageously said to him: "You must be here because you're guilty." The landlord was charged with arson. At the trial, however, the defense argued that because Vita's husband, Shmuel, had been found dead with a lamp in his hand at the door, he could have caused the fire. Of course, this confirmed that Shmuel had not opened the door to a stranger but to someone he knew. Nonetheless, the Polish landlord was acquitted. According to Auntie Leah, "What chance did Jews have against Christians in court?"

Ray's father, Pesach Tzvi Kruk, was born in 1884 in Radutka (Radute), a small hamlet one verst (.66 of a mile) west of Rokiškis. He was the fourth of six children, three girls and three boys, born to Henna Reisa Gross, born in 1848 in Rokiškis, and Zalman Behr Kruk, born that same year in Radutka. Zalman Behr was a poor shopkeeper who sold tar in Radutka. His father Zelig had been a poor shopkeeper there too. There were only ten Jewish families in the hamlet. It had a synagogue and a Jewish cemetery, but was really a suburb of Rokiškis.

Auntie Leah told me that her mother had lived in a small village near Rokiškis, but shortly before she was married, the local Lithuanians had decided to get rid of the Jews and had torched all their homes. It is possible that this was Radutka since it is close to Rokiškis and was where her husband-to-be came from. Radutka was known to have burned down in 1913 but by then my grandparents were already married, so perhaps there were two separate occasions where homes were destroyed by fire.

According to Auntie Leah, our family had relatives all over the area, and we now know, through census, tax, and other records, that in addition to Pandelys and Utena, Kavalsky family members also lived in Anyksciai, Debekiai, Suvainiskis, and Svencionys. Rokiškis is in the north east corner of Lithuania, near the Latvian border, and Utena (65 km south of Rokiškis), Pandelys and these other towns are all close by. Before World War I Ray's parents had a general store and lived in Radutka. Utena, Pandelys, and Rokiškis were in Kovno Gubernia, the northern province of Lithuania under the Russian Empire (until 1918). The Kovno Gubernia was divided into seven districts and Pandelys and Rokiškis were in the Novo-Aleksandrovsk District. In 1929, the town of Novo-Aleksandrovsk was renamed Zarasai. Jews, however, called the town Ezherenai, which is derived from the Lithuanian word meaning "lakes." Utena was in the Ukmerge district. After the First World War, Pandelys was assigned to the new Rokiškis district and Utena was in its own district.

Life was difficult enough with the natural disasters that could periodically descend upon the shtetls. These included the famines that struck in the 1840s and between 1869 and 1871 as a result of great crop failures, as well as epidemics of cholera and other diseases. There were also man-made disasters associated with war. In the early 19th Century Napoleon's forces marched in, only to be routed by the Russians. The 20th Century brought the Russo-Japanese War and two world wars. My mother Ray told me that her mother Riva kept a diary both in Lithuania and in South Africa in which she wrote in Yiddish about her eventful life and that of her family. Unfortunately, after Riva passed away, the diary disappeared, and no one has been able to find it since.[12] I am saddened that this wealth of knowledge and memories has simply vanished, and one of my motivations in writing this family history is to insure that something like this never happens again. For now, all we have left are snippets of the past.

Auntie Leah told me that the area around Rokiškis was flat, with many lakes and forests. It was mainly a farming community with small villages and occasional larger towns. The winters were dark and cold. In spring the roads were muddy. During the summer my grandmother would swim in the lakes and in the Nemunėlis River with her children on her back. She witnessed the sky light up when the Tunguska meteoroid exploded over Siberia in the summer of 1908.

In the family home in Rokiškis there was a samovar, a large copper vessel used to heat water to provide a constant supply of hot tea.[13] My sister Joanne now has it in her home. It was traditional to drink tea out of a special glass with a metal holder, without milk, sometimes with a lump of sugar held between one's teeth. The house was heated by a large wood-fired oven and the family slept under perinas, duvets filled with soft goose feathers or down. On top of the oven was a space where younger children liked to sleep in order to keep warm.

In Rokiškis there were four synagogues. Three smaller shuls were on Synagogue Street and belonged to the Hasidim. During the period of Lithuania's independence, they were painted, respectively, in the colors of Lithuania's flag, red, green, and yellow, and each was referred to by its color. The yellow one was for scholars; the green one was for community leaders, professionals, successful business owners, and property owners; and the red one was for the general community.[14] A larger synagogue at one time stood on the edge of town.
My grandfather, who was a religious man and a Hasid, belonged to the Green Shul. While most Lithuanian Jews were Mitnagdim, followers of a more intellectual form of Judaism, Hasidim predominated in Rokiškis, and were of the Chabad Lubavitch branch. Hasidism emphasized the spiritual side of life, and its followers believed religion should be less scholarly and more accessible to the common man. Before World War I there were two rabbis, one for the Mitnagdim,[22] the other for the Hasidim.[23]

A few years ago I obtained a copy of the Rokiškis Yizkor Book, a memorial book written in Yiddish by former residents of the town who had survived the war, and published in South Africa in 1952. I had some chapters translated into English[15] and posted on the JewishGen website as part of the Yizkor Book Project. Subsequently the rest of the book has been translated

App A - 76   Appendices of Material Not Included in the Original Yizkor Book

and posted. Though they are no compensation for the loss of my grandmother's diary, for me these translations brought to life a world I had thought forever lost. I will never forget the thrill of the first words I read which described the beauty of the town's trees.

It is said that the name Rokiškis (pronounced Rok-ish-kis) comes from a legend about a man called Rokas who hunted for hares ("Kiškis" in Lithuanian) in this area. The town was founded in 1499, and developed from the estate of the Kroshinski princes, who settled there in 1523.

The nobility was interested in developing the economy of the estate and invited Jews to settle in Rokiškis. The Jewish community thrived for hundreds of years, though early records are not available. A survey conducted in 1784, toward the end of the Grand Duchy of Lithuania, listed 21 Jewish families as taxpayers. A subsequent survey in 1847 reported that there were 593 Jews in the town.

From 1715 Rokiškis belonged to the Tyzenhaus (Tyzenhof) family. In 1770 they moved their main residence from Postavy in what is now Belarus to Rokiškis.[16] Reynold Tyzenhaus died in 1880 and his sister Maria inherited the property. When she married Count Aleksander Pshedietsky the residence became known as Pshedietsky Manor.

There is a local legend that the Jewish settlement was originally located on the present site of the old Jewish cemetery, a half kilometer from the market square, and moved to the market square area due to a tragic incident. In 1730 the son of Count Titushevna's business manager and the only son of a Jewish tailor were friends. They had a fight, and the Jewish boy won. The business manager complained to the Count (or Countess Ishevna, in another version of the story), and the Count decreed that when the Jewish boy came to marry, he and his bride should be burned on their wedding day. The couple was set alight under the Chupah,[17] and the Jews moved away from this place, which later became the Jewish cemetery.

Development accelerated with the opening of a rail link in 1873. By 1897 there were 2,067 Jews in the town, 75% of the total population.[18] In 1914 there were about 3,000, and in 1921 1,900. Shortly before the Holocaust, 3,500 Jews lived in Rokiškis, about 40% of the population.[19]

Between August 15th and 16th, 1941, 3,207 Jews were murdered by the Nazis and their Lithuanian collaborators. Today (2017) there no Jews left in the immediate Rokiškis area (population 16,700) or in the Rokiškis region (population 42,000).

In the early 1900's, most Jews in the town were poor traders, craftsmen, and peddlers. The main business district was on Kamayer Street (today, Respublikos gatve), and the center of the town was the market place. At the western end of the market place is the grand Catholic Church of St. Matthias, which was built by the nobility in the second half of the 19th Century.

Deep ditches ran along the sides of the roads for drainage and waste. At the time, a water pump stood at the intersection of Kamayer Street and the market square that passersby would use to quench their thirst with the aid of a tin can attached to a chain. Below was a trough that cattle and horses could drink from.[20]

The square was surrounded by stores with small apartments above them. There was also the state bank, the post office, police station and jail, and the house and iron goods business of Pesach

Ruch. Monday was market day when the square was filled with peasant wagons and temporary wooden stalls. Jewish traders would buy farm produce such as flax, cattle, hides, and eggs from the peasants and sell them fabrics, machines, and grocery items.[21]

In June 2011 my cousin Stephen Kriger, son of my mother's brother Solly, visited Rokiškis and the house where our family lived. The house is at 7 Biliuno Street, near a field for horses and across the street from the former orphanage, which is now a school. Describing his visit to his siblings he wrote: "We struggled but found Daddy's home,[25] and the poor occupants got the fright of their lives when they found us walking around taking photos of their home. However, after an initial hostile reaction, they warmed and were very nice. We were invited in for coffee. These people have lived in the house since 1967. The inside has been substantially upgraded but you can see that the rooms are very small. (The house has a steep roof which looks like it has a loft but all the rooms are on the ground floor.)"

Ray's father Pesach Tzvi Kruk was conscripted by the Russian army to fight in the Russo-Japanese War (February 1904 - September 1905), and again in the First World War (1914 - 1918). During the First World War, Ray's mother Riva moved her family into Rokiškis because where they were living was too close to the Front. As explained next, many people from Rokiškis had fled to Russia in 1915. As a result, there were a number of vacant houses in the town. Riva moved into one of these houses because, with her two young babies, Leah and Sam, she was not able to flee anywhere.

On September 13th, 1915, troops of the reserve corps of the German army occupied Rokiškis while on their way towards Dvinsk/Daugavpils in Latvia.[26] In May of that year the Czar of Russia had issued a decree requiring all Lithuanian Jews living to the west of the railway line between Kovno, Yanove, Ponovezh, and Boisk to evacuate to designated districts in Russia on the false grounds that the Jews were collaborating with the invading Germans. Although the Jews in the Rokiškis area were not subject to this order, many of them fled the town to escape the fighting and also because Cossacks serving as a rearguard force for the retreating Russian forces terrorized the Jews living in these parts. On July 27th, 1915, the Cossacks instigated a pogrom in Rokiškis. Fortunately, the local police commissar gave an advance warning to the Jews who had not yet left. Wealthy Jews of the town hid their valuables in the courtyard cellar of the local priest and the Torah scrolls were hidden there, too. However, the Cossacks found the hiding place, stole the valuables, and destroyed the Torahs.[27] How this pogrom affected our family we do not know.

During the German occupation of Rokiškis, with her husband at war, Riva had a household full of relatives to support. She had two small children, only twenty-one months apart, her father, her deaf sister Beila, her husband's parents, and his sister Chana Kruk. Still another member of her wartime household was her niece Janie Kavalsky, who had got separated from her father after he remarried and fled to Russia during the war.[28]

The Russian soldiers were not paid for their military service, so Pesach could not support his family during this time. To make ends meet Riva ran an inn or "trattor" where she served meals and apple cider from the family's apple orchards. She did whatever she could because the currency was unstable and the situation was constantly changing.

App A - 78   Appendices of Material Not Included in the Original Yizkor Book

Riva spoke fluent German without an accent, and got on well with the Germans who were her main customers at the inn. With her Slavic features they never thought she was Jewish. They brought her flowers and scarce food supplies such as flour and sugar. Her Polish was also fluent and without an accent, so when she went to the marketplace and spoke Polish with the peasants they took her to be one of them.

She said that during the German occupation, things were not so bad for the Jews because they were adaptable and learned German, which was similar to Yiddish, whereas the peasants couldn't communicate with their new masters. Riva also worked as a nurse, transporting wounded soldiers by train back from the front and to and from the hospitals in Ponevezh and other towns. There were no lights in the trains so she would bring along a candle and read by its light. To make extra money she bought scarce black-market goods such as soap, cheese, butter, and eggs in Ponevezh from people she knew there to sell in Rokiškis. This was very risky as it was forbidden, and if you were caught you could be shot. So she hid the goods in the deep pockets of the long black coat she wore and in the clothing of the patients she was transporting back to Rokiškis. When the Germans inspected the trains, she would sometimes tell them that the patients had cholera or typhoid, knowing that, being paranoid about germs, the Germans would not investigate too closely.

Towards the end of the war, in 1918, Riva met a Polish doctor who had returned from the front who told her that her husband had been shot in the arm and had lost an eye. Riva showed him a picture of seven men in his regiment at a seder, and he picked out Pesach as the man who had been shot. She was naturally very upset.

Shortly thereafter, while on a train returning from escorting a patient, she overheard two men talking, and asked if they had news of her husband. They mentioned a soldier home from the front, a man called Margolis, who had heard that Riva was upset, and said he had seen Pesach and that he was well. Riva asked them where she might find this man, and they told her Ponevezh. She went there, but had no address for him, so she went from house to house asking after him. She eventually found a man who'd come home from the front and asked him if anyone in Pesach's regiment had been wounded. He said no. Then she told him who she was. He confirmed that her husband was well, but told her that Pesach wanted to wait until he was sure it was safe to return.

Pesach Tzvi Kruk finally reached Rokiškis six months later. Upon arriving, he stood in the central square at the fountain, not knowing where to find his family. A woman saw him and asked for the mitzvah of telling Riva that he was back. Although he had returned safely, during the war his regiment had been surrounded by Germans and he suffered severe starvation for eight days. This contributed to his weak heart and hence his early death.

When the Armistice took effect in November 1918, the Germans retreated and Lithuania was able to exercise its independence, which had been declared in February 1918 during the German military occupation. Almost immediately, a struggle began among Soviet Russia, Poland, and the newly independent Lithuanian republic. Rokiškis came under Soviet rule until Lithuanian forces dislodged them in July of 1919.

My grandparents, Pesach Tzvi and Riva, continued to live there with their children, Leah and Sam. Riva continued running her "Trattor," described in a 1931 list of Jewish businessmen in

Rokiškis as a "canteen" where tea and patisseries were served. Pesach Tzvi had his apple orchards with his brother Nottel. In 1919 Pesach and Riva's son Solly was born. In 1926 their daughter Anne arrived, followed by my mother Ray in 1929. A woman called Bassa was employed to look after the children, and my mother became very attached to her. According to my cousin Philip Todres, Bassa was an abandoned wife. Her husband had left for America and she never heard from him again. Without a "get" (religious divorce requiring the husband's consent), she could not remarry, and was left in limbo.

From left to right, Rivka, a cousin named "Chanelke," Anne, Solly, Ray, and Leah Kruk and the children's nanny Bassa. This photo taken in Rokiškis before Rivka and her children left in May 1931.

My grandmother was highly intelligent, enlightened, and ahead of her time. She kept a kosher home because it was important to my grandfather but she did not believe in it herself. She sent her daughter Leah to the secular Lithuanian gymnasium because she thought Leah would receive a better education there than at the local Jewish school. According to my Uncle Solly, while attending a court case in Lithuania, my grandmother noticed from the way a tree was cut (from examining its cross-section) that it could not have occurred naturally. In this way she changed the course of the trial. She also knew about home remedies for medical ailments, for instance, that using the juice of the aloe plant, known as stoletnik, would help heal wounds. She developed a reputation for being a wise woman, and many townspeople sought out her advice.

After the war the local count had a lot of war taxes to pay, which he financed by selling off some of his land. Normally, he wouldn't sell to Jews but because our grandmother spoke perfect Polish and Lithuanian, and looked Slavic, he didn't know she was Jewish, and sold her two plots of land. When my grandfather returned from the war my grandmother sold one plot and they used the money to build a house on the other plot. She wisely settled on the price for the building before construction began, thereby avoiding the effects of post-war inflation on the cost of housing materials.

App A - 80   Appendices of Material Not Included in the Original Yizkor Book

As nightfall does not come at once, neither does oppression. In both instances there is a twilight when everything remains seemingly unchanged. And it is in such twilight that we all must be most aware of change in the air – however slight – lest we become unwitting victims of the darkness.[29]

As noted before, during the inter-war period, various governmental programs were implemented to marginalize Jewish businesses. Among other things, cooperatives were established under the control of ethnic Lithuanians, and ethnic Lithuanians from surrounding areas opened stores in Rokiškis, both of which created competition for Jewish shop owners. In addition, trade in flax and produce was nationalized. These factors, as well as incitement against Jewish traders and artisans, led to a severe economic decline and bankruptcies among the Jews. As a result, many began to emigrate to America, Palestine, and South Africa.

A number of political organizations arose, including the Bund, the Labor Zionists, and the revolutionary Culture League. These groups espoused socialist ideals of equality of all peoples and freedom from discriminatory treatment, ideals which appealed to many discouraged Jews.

There was much political turmoil in Rokiškis, and the Lithuanian police became obsessed with identifying communists and socialists. For example, they would pick up discarded pamphlets from political meetings to see what was in them. The Culture League was shut down but continued to function as an underground movement.

Many young people were arrested at political meetings, and my grandmother Riva became concerned because her son Sam had begun to attend them. She did not want her children to go through another war, and she sensed another one was brewing. She was more concerned about the turmoil arising from the suppression of socialism than about the intentions of the Germans. In the First World War they had behaved like gentlemen, especially compared to the Russians, and it was initially hard to conceive that the problems ahead could have been devised by Germans. Many Lithuanians were anti-Semitic, and were sympathetic to the Nazi ideology and program. Lithuanians, like the Nazis, opposed communism, and also envisaged a state that was ethnically "pure" – free of Jews. (Indeed, according to Prof. Alfonsas Eidintas, nationalistic Lithuanians, who were largely Catholic, did not consider Jews to be people but rather thought that, like animals, Jews did not have souls.[30])

Much later, my grandmother recognized the rise of Hitler for what it was, but in the late 1920's, she just knew it was time to leave Europe. Originally, she wanted to go to America but by then, thanks to the Johnson Act of 1924, the doors to immigration there were closed. She therefore tried to persuade my grandfather that the family should immigrate to South Africa, where they had relatives. However, he had soldiered through two wars and was only too happy to settle down in the new house they had built, tending his apple orchards with his brother Nottel. He did not want to have to start out all over again in a strange land. People told my grandmother that before making such a momentous decision she should consult the Lubavitche Rebbe.[31] According to our cousin Russell Todres, the Lubavitche Rebbe would not meet women, so my grandmother must have got a message to him asking him his opinion on emigrating from Lithuania to South Africa. The message she received from him was that it would be safe to stay, that everything would be fine in Lithuania, and that she should not go to a "treife land."[32] (In 1940, the Lubavitche Rebbe himself left for America.)

From left to right: Alec Poplak, the son of Rivka's sister Ethel Kavalsky Poplak, Pesach Tzvi Kruk (later, Philip Kriger), and Pesach Tzvi's son, Shmuel Kruk (later, Samuel "Sam" Kriger). Alec moved to South Africa, where he lived with Pesach Tzvi and Rivka Kruk. The rest of Alec's family were killed in Lithuania in 1941. This photo was taken in Rokiškis in 1930.

Despite the Rebbe's advice, my grandmother was determined that her family should leave, and immediately set about making arrangements to do so. At that time, it was necessary to be sponsored by someone already living in South Africa. While there were already Kavalsky relatives living there, they were reluctant to sponsor our family and tried to discourage them from coming to South Africa, saying that life was hard there, and it would be better for them to stay in Lithuania. Luckily for us, my grandparents' good friends David and Reggie Decktor, then living in Cape Town but originally from Rokiškis, agreed to sponsor our family. My grandparents sold their home, which had been built only seven years earlier, and used the proceeds to pay for the boat tickets. In 1930 my grandfather came out to Cape Town, South Africa with his eldest son Sam. The rest of the family followed a year later in June of 1931.

Because of my grandmother's foresight and determination, our branch of the family was saved, and her descendants are alive today. About ninety-six percent of Lithuania's 200,000 Jews perished in the Holocaust, as did many members of our extended family.

It is not the strongest of the species that survive, nor the most intelligent, but the ones most responsive to change.[33]

On May 16th, 1931, my mother, together with her mother and her siblings Leah, Solly, and Anne, set sail from Hamburg on the German ship *Tanganyika*,[34] arriving in Cape Town on June 15th, 1931. They were originally scheduled to go via England. However my grandmother chose to travel via Hamburg instead because she knew German but not English, and figured that if anything happened, at least there she'd be able to communicate.

My mother's sister Leah recalled that traveling by train from Lithuania to Hamburg, though it was already May, there were still patches of snow and ice in the fields. My mother was then two years old, and has few memories of life in Lithuania. What she does remember is that she did not want to leave her nanny Bassa behind. When her mother tried to distract her with toys she said in Yiddish: "Tsatskes vill ich nicht. Ich vill Bassa!" – "I don't want toys. I only want Bassa!"

My grandmother did take her precious samovar. However, most of the family photographs were destroyed in a fire at some time in Lithuania so there were very few photos to bring along.

The Kriger family's Tula-made samovar

The journey was long and stressful. Almost everyone on the boat was seasick. At one point Riva sent Anne to fetch her some water, but when she arrived with it my grandmother suddenly thought: Where did she get it? She's too small to reach the faucet. Her daughter had reached into the toilet, of course! The only one in the family who did not get seasick was Solly. He strolled about the boat and became friends with the captain,[35] who, when he heard that Solly would soon have his bar mitzvah, gave him a photograph album as a present.

Leah's memories of the trip include stopping in Luderitz and Swakopmund in South West Africa (now Namibia). As the harbors there were too small, tugs transported passengers and goods to shore, with passengers transferred to the tug via a basket. At these stops, my aunt first encountered black people, other than in geography books.

In the family's immigration documents, which were issued upon arrival in Cape Town, reference is made to the "Immigration Quota Act, 1930," which severely restricted entry by Jews from Eastern Europe from that year on. This Act was passed shortly after my grandfather Pesach Tzvi and Uncle Sam had already immigrated in 1930, prompting my grandfather to immediately apply for the rest of the family to join him.[36] The experience of immigrants in America had been bad after the Johnson Act, and he was concerned that the family might not be reunited. Fortunately, since he had arrived in South Africa before the act's passage, our family was permitted entry.

As noted earlier, the surname Kruk most likely was the Yiddish name for two towns called Kriukai in Lithuanian, so perhaps our ancestors came from one of these. On arriving in South Africa they were told that the name "Kruk" sounded like the English word "crook," which had a bad connotation. For this reason, they changed their surname to "Kriger." It is not clear why they chose this specific surname, for while it does occur amongst Lithuanian Jews, I'm not aware that our family had any Kriger relatives. My mother's name had been Rachelia in Lithuanian and Rocha Frieda in Yiddish. It now became Ray. Her sister Henna Reisa became Anne, Leah remained Leah, Zalman Ber became Solly, and Shmuel became Sam. Her mother, Rivel or Rifka became Riva, and her father Pesach Tzvi became Philip. So it was that our family began new lives in Cape Town with new names.

Acknowledgement: I am most grateful to the following for their help with this article: Ray Kriger Katz, the late Leah Kriger Todres, Philip Todres, Stephen Kriger, Philip and Aldona Shapiro, and JewishGen's Yizkor Book Project.

Footnotes

[1] In Lithuanian, a female given name ends either with "a" or "ė" and a male given name ends with "s." The suffix of a surname indicates gender and, for women, marital status. For example, if a family in the Czarist era had the surname of Kruk, during the period of independent Lithuania the surname of male members of the family would be Krukas, the surname of the wife of a man named Krukas would be Krukienė, and the surname of an unmarried daughter of a man named Krukas would be Krukaitė. The spelling of a given name as Rachelia suggests that the name was pronounced ra-chel-a.

[2] There is a town called Kruk (Kriukiai) in Sakiai province and another in Siauliai.

[3] "Kaval" is the root word for horse in Polish, so "Kavalsky" relates to the shoeing of horses.

[4] The Family Tree DNA Family Finder Autosomal DNA test which confidently identifies relationships on both maternal and paternal sides for five generations.

[5] Shabse Kavalsky is listed in the 1885 Pandelys box tax list as a "poor blacksmith."

App A - 84   Appendices of Material Not Included in the Original Yizkor Book

[6] My cousin Philip Todres told me this. He has some of our grandmother's linens.

[7] "Utena," p. 1, article by Yosef Rosin and Dov Levin for JewishGen Kehilahlinks website.

[8] "Utena," p. 2, article by Yosef Rosin and Dov Levin for JewishGen Kehilahlinks website.

[9] Jewish Virtual Library, *Yahadut Lita 3*, 1967, pp. 284-285 (Yehuda Slutsky)

[10] "Ponedel" by R.H. Berchowitz-Peisachovitz, T. Katz, Jokl Evans, *Yizkor Book of Rakishok and Environs*, ed. M.Bakalczuk-Felin, p. 331

[11] Religious school

[12] My mother speculates that the diary may have been removed by a family member unhappy with something my grandmother had written about her.

[13] The family samovar was made in Tula, a town famous for its fine samovars. The word samovar is derived from the Russian words for "self" and "boiling."

[14] According to my cousin, Reuben Ruch, the religious Jews in Rokiškis could be divided into three general groups, namely, the Lubavitch Chassidim, the Mitnagdim (traditional rabbinic Jews who opposed the Chassidim), and the "regular" Orthodox. In addition, there were some "non-believers" – probably Jews who were secular and non-observant. Reuben also made the point that the red, green and yellow shuls were generally not differentiated by religious denomination.

[15] Translations by the late Rabbi Ezra Boyarsky and by Mrs. Rae Meltzer

[16] *Lithuanian Jewish Communities*, by Nancy and Stuart Schoenberg, Jason Arons, 1996

[17] Jewish wedding canopy

[18] Wikipedia article on Rokiškis

[19] *Lithuanian Jewish Communities*, by Nancy and Stuart Schoenberg, Jason Arons, 1996

[20] "Rakishok – Before and after World War I," by A. Orelowitz, Yizkor Book of Rakishok and Environs, 1952

[21] *Lithuanian Jewish Communities*, by Nancy and Stuart Schoenberg, Jason Arons, 1996

[22] Movement that stressed knowledge of and observance of the Torah

[22] Movement that stressed direct religious experience of God over traditional learning

[24] *Lithuanian Jewish Communities*, by Nancy and Stuart Schoenberg, Jason Arons, 1996

[25] This was the new home the family had built seven years before leaving Lithuania.

[26] "Rokiskis 1919-1921," Vitautas Doniela, Lithuanianphilately.com

[27] "The Exile of the Lithuanian Jews during the Fervor of the First World War (1914-1918)," by Louis Stein, translated by Judie Goldstein, http://www.jewishgen.org/yizkor/lita/lita.html, at 89

[28] Janie's mother was Riva Gita Kruk, a sister of my grandfather, Pesach Tzvi Kruk. Her father, Yehuda Laibe Kavalsky, was also my grandmother's first cousin.

[29] William O. Douglas, United States Supreme Court Justice, 1898 - 1980

[30] *Jews, Lithuanians and the Holocaust*, by Alfonsas Eidintas, pp. 40-47, translation by Vijole and Advardas Tuskenis, Vilnius, Versus Aureus, 2003. Translation of *Zydai,lietuviai ir holokaustas*, 2002

[31] The sixth Lubavitche Rebbe

[32] Non-kosher land

[33] Charles Darwin, 1809 - 1882

[34] The *Tanganyika* was operated by Hapag (Hamburg American Packet Ship Company), now Hapag-Lloyd. My cousin Russell Todres obtained copies of the ship's manifest with the family names listed, with incorrect ages for the children. The reason for this is unclear.

[35] According to my cousin Philip Todres, it was the ship's photographer he befriended.

[36] According to Philip Todres, many years later an attorney at the firm Abrahams & Gross gave Solly a copy of the application made by our grandfather.

The original version of Amanda Katz Jermyn's story "The Ruch Family" was published on the Rokiskis Kehilalinks website, http://kehilalinks.jewishgen.org/rokiskis/krigerstory.htm. For this publication, she has updated the story. Amanda Katz Jermyn holds the copyright to this story, which may not be used without her permission.

THE RUCH FAMILY

By Amanda Katz Jermyn

Reuben Ruch was born in 1927 in Rokiskis (Rakishok), Lithuania, the son of Henna-Rocha Gurvitch and Yerachmiel (who was known as Rachmiel) Ruch. Reuben is my second cousin since his grandmother, Rochel Kavalsky, was a sister of my grandmother, Riva Kavalsky. However, he is affectionately known to me as Uncle Ruvka. In January of 2005 Uncle Ruvka sent me the first part of his memoirs, written in Russian, regarding the tragedy that befell the Jews of Rokiskis during the Holocaust. He knew that I was writing a book on our family history and wanted me to include his story to make sure that the fate of the Jews of Rokiskis would be known and their memory honored. I am currently writing this book.

Left: Photo taken in 1935. Back row, from left to right: Sasha Ruch, Liebke (Ahuva) Ruch, Chanan (who was also known as "Honeh") Schneiderman, and Sonya Ruch. Front row: Henna-Rocha Ruch, Reuben Ruch, and Yerachmiel Ruch. Sasha, Sonya and Reuben were the children of Henna-Rocha and Rachmiel Ruch. Liebke (known later in Israel as Ahuva) was Yerachmiel's sister, and her husband was Henach Schneiderman. Right: Reuben Ruch.

The Ruchs were a prominent Jewish family in Rokiskis. Reuben's father was a photographer. His cousin Pesach Ruch had an iron goods store, and their two families lived in a large house over the Ruch businesses. Before the Second World War, Reuben's father Rachmiel used most of his money to send his siblings to safety in South Africa, so he didn't have enough left for his own family to leave. In 1938, at the age of 17, Reuben's sister Sonya developed tuberculosis and was sent to a sanatorium in Switzerland for treatment. She remained there throughout the war.

App A - 86   Appendices of Material Not Included in the Original Yizkor Book

On June 15th, 1940, the Soviets occupied Lithuania. At this time the population of Rokiskis was about 7,500, of whom about 4,000 were Jews. A year later, on June 14th, 1941, over 17,500 Lithuanian citizens were deemed to be enemies of the Soviet occupiers and deported to Siberia. Some members of the Ruch family were among them.

In accordance with the terms of the August 23, 1939, "German-Soviet Non-Aggression Pact," also known as the Molotov-Ribbentrop Agreement, in September 1939 the Germans seized the western half of Poland and the Soviets seized the remainder. In the German-held area, Jews (and Poles) were considered "untermenschen" (sub-humans) and subjected to highly discriminatory laws that were enforced with severe punishments. In June of 1941, two Jews who had escaped from Poland came to Rokiskis with first-hand accounts of the Nazis' atrocities against Jews in Poland. On June 22nd, Germany attacked the USSR, which included Lithuania. That same day Radio Kaunas proclaimed an interim Lithuanian government and announced that the Soviet regime had been deposed. The new pro-Nazi government made it known that 100 Jews would be shot for each dead German soldier. The next day the government ordered Jews to turn in all radios to the police. On the evening of June 24th, 1941, the Soviets began to depart from Rokiskis and panic erupted amongst the Jews.

Almost half of the Jews tried to leave, including Rachmiel Ruch, his wife Henna-Rocha, and their sons Reuben, 14, and Sasha, 17. They were among the few who succeeded in reaching the comparative safety of Russia. The decision to flee was heart-wrenching for the Ruchs because it meant leaving behind three close relatives who lived with them in Rokiskis, namely, Reuben's maternal grandparents, Hinda-Racha and Motel Gurvitch, and his aunt, Beile Kavalsky. They were elderly and could not have survived the arduous journey. Reuben told me he remembered that Beile, who was deaf, had come to live with their family after her father Shabse Kavalsky, died. She was also my mother's aunt. She had her own room and talked to herself. Rachmiel told Reuben to be nice to his aunt because she had no one in the world except them. He remembered that she sewed gloves and other items, and wore a long apron. Hinda-Racha and Motel Gurvitch and Beile Kavalsky perished in the Holocaust.

When the Ruch family set out on their journey, they had no horse and cart, only two bicycles, a couple of trunks, backpacks with food, and a jug of water. Initially they planned to walk to Dvinsk. However, when they reached the Obeliai train station they found a train there about to depart for Dvinsk, and they, along with many other Jews, were able to board it. The Jews hoped that from Dvinsk they could transfer to a train heading east.

At the time, the Russians were using the train to send KGB documents and officials out of Lithuania and they cynically assumed that if the Germans saw that there were many civilians on the train the Germans would be less likely to bomb it. When the train arrived in Dvinsk, however, the KGB plan became clear to the Jews: Only Russian officials and documents were allowed to leave the train, which was then sent back with the Lithuanian Jews on board. This happened three times.

As it became apparent that the KGB did not want the Jews to cross the Russian border, the Jews disembarked and began to walk to Russia. During this time, the German troops were advancing toward the major Russian cities of Leningrad (now, St. Petersburg) and Moscow. As a result, the Jews traveled on foot through the forests, When they heard bombs drop in the distance, they felt temporarily assured that the German soldiers were not nearby; but when the forests were quiet they were worried because they never knew where the German soldiers would strike next.

Reuben told me it took him and his family three weeks to walk to Russia. En route, one of their trunks was stolen and one of their bicycles taken. During this time his mother fell three or four times, asking the family to leave her there because she couldn't walk any further, but each time she got up and started to walk again. Reuben said he tried to think of a way to make a wheelchair for her out of the remaining bicycle but he couldn't.

Fortunately for the Ruchs, when they came close to the Russian border they encountered a retreating Soviet army unit that let them follow them across the border along an unguarded side path. The Ruchs were so grateful to those soldiers for saving their lives that they gave them all of the cigarettes they had, along with their two pens.

The Ruch family was lucky to escape. Most Jews who fled were stopped by Lithuanian or Soviet soldiers at the borders and forced to return to Rokiskis and almost certain death. As those Jews made their way back, they were shot at by Lithuanian partisans and German soldiers.

On July 9th, 1941, the Nazis, together with Lithuanian collaborators from the area, rounded up all of the Jews of Rokiskis and imprisoned them in a temporary "ghetto" that was created on the grounds of Count Tyzenhof's estate. According to a secret SS report for the Kaunas area known as the Jäger Report, between August 15th and 16th, 1941, 3,207 men, women, and children were murdered in the Velniaduobė woods near the village of Bajorai and on August 25th, 1941, 1,160 men, women, and children were murdered in the Antanašė forest.

Meanwhile, the Ruch family continued their eastward flight, finally settling in a small village in Uzbekistan near Tashkent, where they felt it would be easier to survive. There they remained until the end of the war. The village experienced terrible starvation during the war and many people died. Rachmiel and his family managed to find some way to obtain a little bread, and were thus able to save both themselves and many in the village. Reuben notes that during those tough times his mother, Henna-Rocha, fed her children at the expense of her own hunger, dropping from a weight of 154 pounds at the start of the war to 86 pounds at the end. She was also imprisoned for three years for attempting to make some extra money for her family by exchanging money on the black market. While she was in jail, Reuben would visit her every two or three days to give her some food and other necessary supplies.

Reuben told me that during the war his mother bribed the authorities in Uzbekistan to change the dates of birth on her two sons' passports, making them appear younger than they really were. So Sasha's date of birth was changed from 1923 to 1926, and Reuben's from 1927 to 1928. She did this in order to delay or avoid their conscription into the Red Army, as she was concerned for their survival. Nevertheless, in 1944 Sasha enlisted in the Red Army. He did so because he was grateful to the Soviets for saving him from the Nazis, and also because the early communists, under Lenin, were against pogroms and the anti-Semitism of the Czar. While traveling with the Red Army Sasha met his future wife, Maria (Masha) Spector.

As noted above, Sonya Ruch spent the war in the sanatorium in Switzerland. While her father was still in Rokiskis, he was able to send money for her care and she was well-treated. However, once the family fled Rokiskis and the money dried up, she was moved to an inferior part of the sanatorium and poorly treated. My parents visited her there in 1953. Later, she moved to South Africa. In 1962 she married an engineer from England and they moved to Manchester.

App A - 88   Appendices of Material Not Included in the Original Yizkor Book

Since Sonya's parents and brothers lived behind the Iron Curtain, she never saw them again. From 1962 to 1973, her mother, Henna-Rocha, was bedridden, partially paralyzed from a stroke, but managed to write letters to Sonya by attaching a pen with Scotch tape to her left hand because she couldn't use her right hand to write.

After the war, Sasha chose to continue in the military, where he served for seven years. In 1945 he was posted to Riga, Latvia, and all the family who had survived the war in the Soviet Union joined him, including his parents and brother Reuben. Sasha later became a marine engineer. The family was very close, and each year they spent holidays together on the Black Sea. Their parents, Rachmiel and Henna-Rocha, died in Riga. In 1972, when the Soviets allowed Jews to emigrate, Sasha and his family moved to Israel. Sasha and his wife Masha have both passed away. Their children and grandchildren all live in Israel, and their daughter Bella has become my friend.

In Riga Reuben first worked in a factory. Then he trained to become an electrician. After that he studied for a Ph.D. in electrical engineering at a university in Leningrad. However, when his brother applied to immigrate to Israel, Reuben was no longer allowed to study because the government said, in essence, "you'll just follow your brother, so there's no point in educating you." In Riga he worked for the government railway company. In 1977 he too left for Israel, where he worked in a similar field. His wife didn't want to leave Riga, and divorced him when he left for Israel. In 1980, she and their daughter and her family immigrated to Sydney, Australia, and in 1984 Reuben moved there too. He has lived there ever since. In December 2007, I finally got to meet Reuben when our family visited Sydney. He turned out to be just as wonderful as I had imagined.

After the war, some Lithuanians who had collaborated with the Nazis were identified. Among those was Andrushka, who had been employed by Reuben Ruch's uncle, the bagel-maker Chaim-Yerachmiel Ruch (not to be confused with Yerachmiel Ruch). Chaim-Yerachmiel and his whole family, except for one daughter, perished in the Holocaust. Andrushka had worked for Jews all his life and spoke fluent Yiddish. Reuben Ruch remembers him but says that he was not the worst. In his view the worst were the Lithuanian SS Einsatzgruppen who traveled from town to town each day killing thousands of Jews. In 1954 a number of Lithuanians who collaborated in executing Jews in Rokiskis were put on trial, having been named by Jonas Pupenis, the sole survivor of the massacre. Of the many involved, only eight were convicted and sentenced to 15 years in prison. They were released in 1980 and became honored citizens of Lithuania.

The greatest number of the town's Jews were murdered in a wooded area just north of the village of Bajorai, about 3 miles north of Rokiskis. Each year from 1965 to 1975, on the anniversary of the massacre, August 15 and 16, about 60 or more of the surviving Jews from Rokiskis met at the monument at that site for a memorial service at which Kaddish was recited and speeches were made. About 50 came by bus from Vilnius, including a rabbi, and Reuben and Sasha Ruch and their families came from Riga. The group would also visit similar sites near Obeliai, Miliūnai, and "Vyžuonai" (probably the village of Vyžuona, just north of Bajorai). These gatherings ended once the last Jewish residents of Rokiskis left Vilnius for Israel.

In Israel, Reuben Ruch joined a Landsman Society of Jews from Rokiskis. This group raised money for survivors, helped them re-establish themselves in Israel, and created a memorial in Holon. Each year, on the anniversary of the mass murders, they meet there to commemorate the tragedy that befell their community during the Holocaust.

Volunteer Private Ruvin Bun (Rufka Bun)

Ruvin Bun(as), the son of Abraham and Chaya Dina Bun(as), was born on May 11, 1902, in the hamlet of Pasubatė, in the Rokiškis region, Zarasių Uyezd, and later lived in nearby Aleksandravėlė, which is about 8 kilometers southeast of Obeliai / Abel. On July 11, 1919, during Lithuania's Wars of Independence, Ruvin volunteered to serve in the Lithuanian army. He died in battle near Giedraičiai on November 21, 1920, the last day of the Lithuanian-Polish War.

The battle monument at Giedraičiai lists his name (as "Bun Rufka") on the memorial plaque to those who fell in that battle. At the bottom of the plaque are the words, "Tėvynė nepamirš jūsų darbų, kuriuos padarėt jos laisvei ir garbei," meaning, "The Motherland will not forget the sacrifice you have given for her freedom and glory."

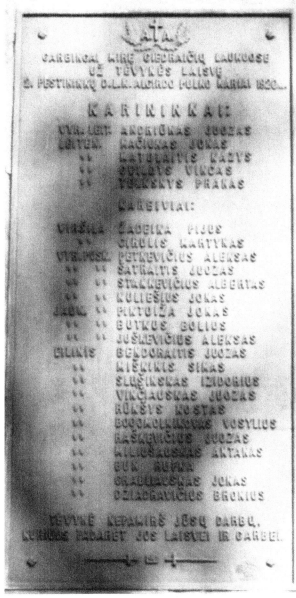

Volunteer Private Ruvin Bun was buried in the Ukmergė Jewish cemetery.

App A - 90   Appendices of Material Not Included in the Original Yizkor Book

In 1937, Private Bun posthumously received Lithuania's Volunteer Service Medal. The following three pages constitute the certificate of his service. Lithuanian Central State Archives, Liudymo Nr. 10018 (F. 930, ap. 4, b. 694, 1.12, 13a. p., 22).

This second page of the certificate (below), states:

Appendices of Material Not Included in the Original Yizkor Book   App A - 91

Certificate

This certifies that the killed soldier Ruvin Bun, the son of Abram, 18 years of age, from the town of Dusetos, Zarasai County, was a volunteer private in the Second Battalion of the Grand Duke of Lithuania Algirdas Infantry Regiment from July 11, 1919, until November 21, 1920. In November 1920 he perished honorably in combat against Polish forces at Giedraičiai. During the period of his military service he was never charged with a violation or desertion. This is certified by these signatures and the state seal. This certificate is issued to prove that a medal should be granted.

The diagonal signature on this page is that of Colonel J. Bobelis. His signature also appears on the following page.

L i u d i j i m a s .

Šiuo liudijama, kad žuvęs kareivis B u n   Ruvinas, sūn. Abromo, I8 met.amžiaus, kilęs iš Zarasų apskr., Dusėtų m., įstojo savanoriu eiliniu į 2-rą pėst. D.L.K.Algirdo pul ką I9I9 mt. liepos mėn.11 d. ir tarnavo iki 1920 mt. lapkričio mėn. 2I d.

1920 mt. lapkričio mėn. garbingai žuvo mušiuose su lenkais prie Giedraičių .

Laike tarnavimo kariuomenėje teismu baustas bei pabėgęs nebuvo, kas parašais ir valstybiniu antspaudu tvirtinama.

Šis liudijimas išduotas kūrėjo savanorio medaliui gauti.   M a j o r a s

Kapitonas

L.s.raštvedžio p.

6 rugpiučio

M.b. I2 .

Yakov Smushkevich

Yakov Smushkevich was born in Rokiškis in 1902. When the Czarist regime in May 1915 ordered the Jews of central Lithuania into internal exile, his family relocated to Russia. He joined the Red Army in 1918 and in 1922 transferred to the Soviet Air Force, where he rose to the rank of lieutenant general. In the 1936-1937 Spanish Civil War he shot down several Nazi aircraft and was an acquaintance of Ernest Hemingway. He also fought in the 1939 battle of Khalkin Gol in Mongolia and in the 1940 Soviet invasion of Finland. He was twice honored as a Hero of the Soviet Union and served from 1939 to 1941 as commander of the Soviet Air Force.

Smushkevich was arrested on June 7, 1941, and executed without trial on October 28, 1941, on the personal order of Lavrenti Beria. In 1954, a year after Stalin's death, he was rehabilitated. A bust of Smushkevich was created by the renowned Lithuanian sculptor Konstantinas Bogdanas. For many years it stood in Smushkevich Square in Rokiškis (a park immediately south of Laivės gatvė, between Vilniaus gatvė and Kauno gatvė). After Lithuania effectively regained its independence, in 1991, many Soviet-era statues were removed from public spaces. The Smushkevich sculpture was removed from this park around 2015.

Appendices of Material Not Included in the Original Yizkor Book   App A - 93

App A - 94   Appendices of Material Not Included in the Original Yizkor Book

June 14, 1941, Deportations to Siberia

The Soviet Union occupied Lithuania in the summer of 1940 and transformed it into a Soviet state. Strict censorship was imposed, many non-governmental organizations were disbanded, and large estates and businesses were confiscated. Sometime between February and early June 1941, General Ivan Serov, a Soviet state security official, issued top-secret instructions for the coordinated, sudden arrest and deportation to Siberia of "enemies of the Soviet people" in the Baltic states. ("Regarding the Procedure for Carrying Out the Deportation of Anti-Soviet Elements from Lithuania, Latvia, and Estonia")

The "Serov Instructions" were executed without warning on June 14, 1941. Whole families were arrested, taken together to collection points. There, in many cases, the family members would be separated, with the heads of families sent to Gulag labor camps and other family members sent to settlements in "distant" areas. [4]

The Lithuanian government's special archives of the Soviet secret police, such as the NKVD and KGB, contain the records of many of those deported to Siberia from Lithuania. In 2016 the archives provided a list of the names of the Jewish deportees from the Rokiskis region. Following is an English translation of part of the information from that list. (Courtesy of Litvak Special Interest Group. All rights reserved.) One of the deportees, Samuil Meller, reviewed the information from the list and provided corrected and additional information, as did a witness who was not deported. The corrected and additional information is provided within brackets ("[ ]").

Rokiskis-Region Jews Deported To Siberia

Surname	Given Name	Father	Family Position	Sex	Birth Year	Town [of Arrest]	Notes
MELERIS / [MELLER]	Motelis [Mordechai]	Abramas-Icikas	Head of household	M	1885 [1892]	Rokiskis	Sent to the NKVD Gulag [Krasnoyarsk Krai, station Reshoty, died there in 1942]
MELERIENE / [MELLER]	Sara [received a doctorate from the Sorbonne]	Abramas	Wife	F	1889	Rokiskis	Exiled to Altai Krai [Tiumentsevo village, and after World War II moved] to Rubtsov [where she died in 1976]
MELERIS / [MELLER]	Amnon	Motelis	Son	M	1927	Rokiskis	Exiled to Altai Krai [Tiumentsevo village, and after World War II moved] to Rubtsov. [Survived, later moved to Israel. He died there in 1997.]

---

[4] Approximately 17,500 Lithuanian citizens were deported. Of this number, about 1,700 were Jews. "Multidirectional memory and the deportation of Lithuanian Jews," by Violeta Davoliūtė, *Ethnicity Studies*, 2015/2 (Lithuanian Social Research Centre, June 2015), pp. 131, 134.

App A - 96   Appendices of Material Not Included in the Original Yizkor Book

MELERIS / [MELLER]	Judel	Abramas -Icikas	Head of household	M	1899 [1902]	Rokiskis	Sent to the NKVD Gulag [Krasnoyarsk Krai, station Reshoty. After World War II, returned to Lithuania. In 1952, exiled to Biysk in Altai Krai. In 1972, moved to Israel. He died there.]
MELLER	Jacha [Jakha]	Moisei	Wife	F	1904	Rokiskis	Exiled to Altai Krai to Biysk (Tiumentsevo according to some other documents) district [Exiled in 1941 to Vilkovo village in Tiumentsevo district. After World II, returned to Lithuania. In 1952, exiled to Biysk in Altai Krai. In 1972, moved to Israel. She died there.]
MELLER	Miron	Judel	Daughter [Son]	F [M]	1927 [1926]	Rokiskis	Exiled to Altai Krai to Biysk (Tiumentsevo according to some documents) district. [Exiled in 1941 to Vilkovo village in Tiumentsevo district. After World II, returned to Lithuania. In 1952, exiled to Biysk in Altai Krai. In 1974, moved to Israel. He died there in 2004.]
MELLER	Zuzana [Shoshana]	Judel	Daughter	F	1928	Rokiskis	Exiled to Altai Krai to Biysk (Tiumentsevo according to some other documents) [Exiled in 1941 to Vilkovo village in Tiumentsevo district. After World II, returned to Lithuania. In 1952, exiled to Altai Krai, Vilkovo village in Tiumentsev district and later transferred to Krasnoyarsk. In 1972 moved to Israel, where she lives now (2017).]
KLIGMANAS / [KLINGMAN]	Jankelis [Moshe ?]	Smuelis / [Shmuel]	Head of household	M	1895	Rokiskis	Sent to the NKVD Gulag [survived, later moved to Israel]
	Chaja	SERAS / [SHER] Chaimas	Wife	F	1894	Rokiskis	Exiled to Altai Krai to Barnaul; in 1942 transferred to Yakutia (not specified); in 1951 transferred to Krasnoyarsk Krai to

Appendices of Material Not Included in the Original Yizkor Book   App A - 97

KLIGMANIENE / [KLINGMAN]							Abansky district [survived, later moved to Israel]
KLIGMANAITE / [KLINGMAN]	Sima	Jankelis	Daughter	F	1922	Rokiskis	Exiled to Altai Krai to Barnaul; in 1942 transferred to Yakutia (not specified); in 1951 transferred to Krasnoyarsk Krai to Abansky district [survived, later moved to Israel]
VOLOVIC / [VOLOVICH]	Jakov	Judel	Head of household	M	1890	Rokiskis	Exiled to Altai Krai to Barnaul; in 1942 transferred to Yakutia to Yakutsk
VOLOVIC / [VOLOVICH]	Liza	Abram	Wife	F	1900	Rokiskis	Exiled to Altai Krai to Barnaul; in 1942 transferred to Yakutia to Yakutsk
VOLOVIC / [VOLOVICH]	Rasel / [Rashel]	Jakov	Daughter	F	1936	Rokiskis	Exiled to Altai Krai to Barnaul; in 1942 transferred to Yakutia to Yakutsk
VOLOVIC / [VOLOVICH]	Zelik	Jakov	Son	M	1922	Rokiskis	Exiled to Altai Krai to Barnaul; in 1942 transferred to Yakutia to Yakutsk
MELERIS / [MELLER]	Chona [Khona]	Abramas -Icikas	Head of household	M	1887 [1895]	Rokiskis	Sent to the NKVD Gulag [Krasnoyarsk Krai, Reshoty station, and died there in 1942]
MELERIENE / [MELLER]	Faina	Samuelis	Wife	F	1900	Rokiskis	Exiled to Altai Krai to [Vilkovo village in] Tiumentsevo district [He died there in 1943]
MELERIS / [MELLER]	Samuelis	Chona [Khona]	Son	M	1927	Rokiskis	Exiled to Altai Krai to [Vilkovo village in] Tiumentsevo district. [Conscripted into Russian military, fought in the Russo-Japanese War of 1945, later lived in Leningrad / St. Petersburg, Russia, and in 2000 moved to the USA]
PENTUSEVICIUS / [PENTUSEVICH]	Samuelas	Zelinas	Head of household	M	1889	Pandelys	Exiled to Altai Krai (not specified)
PENTUSEVICIENE / [PENTUSEVICH]	Reza	Pilchas	Wife	F	1900	Pandelys	Exiled to Altai Krai (not specified)

App A - 98   Appendices of Material Not Included in the Original Yizkor Book

Surname	Given name	Patronymic	Relationship	Sex	Birth	Place	Notes
RUCHAS / [RUKH]	Peisach	Michail	Head of household	M	1871 [1878]	Rokiskis	Exiled to Altai Krai to Pavlovsky district [died in Siberia]
RUCHIENE / [RUKH]	Pera [Pera-Aida]	Mendelis	Wife	F	1880	Rokiskis	Exiled to Altai Krai to Pavlovsky district [died in Siberia in 1952]
RUCHAS / [RUKH]	Leiba	Peisach	Son	M	1908	Rokiskis	Exiled to Altai Krai to Pavlovsky district [survived, later moved to Israel. He died there in 1982.]
RUCHAITE / [RUKH]	Basia	Peisach	Daughter	F	1920	Rokiskis	Exiled to Altai Krai to Pavlovsky district [survived, later moved to Israel, where she was known as Batya. She died there in 1999.]
MELERIS / [MELLER]	Samuelis / [Shmuelis Wolf]	Abramas	Head of household	M	1895 [1887]	Rokiskis	Exiled to Altai Krai to Barnaul district; in 1942 transferred to Yakutsk [Information is incorrect. Exiled to Rasskazikha village in Pavlovsky district; transferred in 1942 to Kazach'ye village in Yakutia, near the shore of the Arctic Ocean. He died in there in 1943]
MELERIENE / [MELLER]	Mariana [Mira]	Mejeris	Wife	F	1895	Rokiskis	Exiled to Altai Krai to Barnaul district; in 1942 transferred to Yakutia [Information is incorrect. Exiled to Rasskazikha village in Pavlovsky district; in 1942 transferred to Kazach'ye village in Yakutia, near the shore of the Arctic Ocean. In 1959 moved to Krasnoyarsk. She died there in 1970.]
MELERIS / [MELLER]	Abramas Icikas	Smuelis Vulfas	Son	M	1938	Rokiskis	Exiled to Altai Krai to Barnaul district; in 1942 transferred to Yakutia. [Information is incorrect. Exiled to Rasskazikha village in Pavlovsky district; in 1942 transferred to Kazach'ye village in Yakutia, near the shore of the Arctic Ocean. Moved to Krasnoyarsk in 1959 and lives there now (2017).

Appendices of Material Not Included in the Original Yizkor Book   App A - 99

LEVINAITE / [LEVIN][5]	Chana Leja	Josel	Head of household	F	1915	Rokiskis	Exiled to Guryev region (not specified)
FISERIS / [FISHER]	Sendaras /[Shendar]	Matelis	Head of household	M	1882	Pandelys	Exiled to Krasnoyarsk Krai (not specified)

In addition to the names above, which were provided by the Lithuanian special archives, the following individuals were also deported:

ZALCMAN	Avraham		Head of household	M	Rokiskis	Survived, later moved to Israel
ZALCMAN	Yacha		Wife	F	Rokiskis	Survived, later moved to Israel
ZALCMAN	Michael	Avraham	Son	M	Rokiskis	Survived, later moved to Israel
ZALCMAN	Basia	Avraham	Daughter	F	Rokiskis	Survived, later moved to Israel
ZALCMAN	Yudite	Avraham	Daughter	F	Rokiskis	Survived, later moved to Israel
ZALCMAN	Rachel	Avraham	Daughter	F	Rokiskis	Survived, later moved to Israel
LEVIN	Faina		Head of household	F	Rokiskis	Survived, later moved to Israel
LEVIN	Joseph		Son	S	Rokiskis	Survived, later moved to Israel
LEVIN	Dvora		Daughter	F	Rokiskis	Survived, later moved to Israel
LEVIN	Yudite		Daughter	F	Rokiskis	Survived, later moved to Israel

---

[5] According to one witness, although Chana Leja Levin's name was on the list of those to be arrested, she may have been spared arrest. In this regard, it should be noted that Yad Vashem's database of Holocaust victims includes two murdered individuals from Rokiskis with the name of "Khana Levin."

App A - 100   Appendices of Material Not Included in the Original Yizkor Book

The Meller families that were deported to Siberia in June 1941 consisted of the four sons of Abramas-Icikas Meller and their wives and children. Samuil Meller was born in Klaipeda 1927. He lives now (2017) in California. His grandfather, Abramas-Icikas, lived at 2 Vytauto gatve in Rokiskis.

Holocaust-Related Materials

On June 22, 1941, Nazi Germany attacked Lithuania, which the Soviet Union had ruled the country since July 1940. The *Rokiškis and Environs* yizkor book contains accounts of Holocaust survivors describing how the Jews in the Rokiškis region were attacked, gathered into temporary "ghettoes," humiliated, starved, and subsequently shot by Lithuanian nationalists and special German detachments. Jewish property having useful value was distributed by the nationalists. The three synagogues on Rokiškis' Synagogue Street, which had been patriotically painted, respectively, red, green, and yellow, were burned, as were many other Jewish houses of prayer in other shtetls throughout Lithuania.

Most official accounts indicate that the Jews of the Rokiškis region were killed at four locations, specifically, the Steponiai forest (July 1941), the Vyžuonai forest (July 1941), the Velniaduobė woods near the village of Bajorai (August 15 and 16, 1941 – 3,207 men, women, and children), and the Antanašė forest (August 25, 1941 – 1,160 men, women, and children).[6]

Excerpts from the Holocaust Atlas of Lithuania

In 2010 the Vilna Gaon State Jewish Museum and the Austrian association *Gedenkdienst* (Memory Service) launched initiated an on-line website, "Holocaust Atlas of Lithuania," which is intended to present comprehensive information regarding each mass-murder site in Lithuania, http://holocaustatlas.lt/EN/#about-project/. Following are the Atlas' descriptions of the massacre sites at (1) Velniaduobė, http://holocaustatlas.lt/EN/#a_atlas/search//page/1/item/75/, and (2) Antanašė, http://holocaustatlas.lt/EN/#a_atlas/search//page/1/item/76/.

1. Velniaduobė (Bajorai)

THE MASS MURDER OF THE JEWS OF ROKIŠKIS AND SURROUNDING AREAS AT VELNIADUOBĖ FOREST

ABOUT MASSACRE

The temporary Jewish ghetto in Rokiškis was set up in July, 1941. It didn't last long: all ghetto prisoners were shot on August 15 and 16, 1941. Soviet POWs were brought to Velniaduobė forest near Bajorai village about 4.5 kilometers from Rokiškis a few days before the mass

---

[6] This list of mass-murder sites in the Rokiškis region is by no means all-inclusive. For example, some of the more well-to-do Jews of Svėdasai, which was part of the Rokiškis region before the Second World War, were transported with their possessions in the direction of the temporary detention center in Rokiškis. En route, near the Trakas-Pempiškis forest, between Kamajai and Rokiškis, their captors murdered them and plundered their property. On June 21, 2017, the Rokiškis Regional Museum announced that it had documented this killing site and was working with two other groups to document another killing site where the young poetess Matilda Olkinaitė, her family, and other Jews were murdered. (An English language translation of the announcement appears below.) The Rokiškis Museum's documentation has been forwarded to Lithuania's Genocide Commission, to Lithuania's Holocaust Museum (the "Green House"), Yad Vashem, and the U.S. Holocaust Memorial Museum.

App A - 102   Appendices of Material Not Included in the Original Yizkor Book

murders and were forced to dig several large pits. Heads of auxiliary police units, subordinate to the commandatura in Rokiškis, were summoned there the night before the mass murder operation. They were ordered to assemble their units secretly at the Rokiškis manor that evening. The next day, August 15, the commander told the units assembled in the manor courtyard they must go to the ghetto and bring Jews in groups to the killing site. About 25 men from the Rokiškis Guard Unit went to Bajorai village in a truck. The remaining white armbanders went to the ghetto and began lining up Jews in long lines of about 100 people each. Most Jews were marched on foot but the elderly and small children were taken by truck and cart. The columns were marched toward Juodupė and then turned onto a road on the right at Bajorai village leading into the forest. They ordered their victims to undress before they shot them. They ordered groups of half-naked Jews into the pits and shot them from the edge of the pits. On the first day Rokiškis Guard Unit people and German Gestapo did the shooting. The site was surrounded by white armbander units from Rokiškis, Juodupė, Kamajai, and Svėdasai. A mobile unit (*Rollkommando* Hamann) of the Gestapo, about 12 SS troops armed with machine guns from Kaunas, commanded the shooting. After they shot one group of victims, Soviet POWs laid down a thin covering of earth over the corpses and the next group of victims was brought down into the pit. The sound of a nearby tractor engine drowned out the sound of gunfire.

On the first day approximately half of the Jews in the Rokiškis ghetto were murdered. The mass murder operation continued the next day. The shooting was performed in the same manner except that the Rokiškis Guard Unit did less shooting and auxiliary police from the rural districts and Gestapo did more shooting. Soviet POWs covered the pits over with dirt. The Jäger Report says 3,207 people were killed on August 15 and 16, 1941, at Bajorai village, including 3,200 Jews, 5 Lithuanian Communists, 1 Pole and 1 partisan.

Jäger on December 1 reported on the mass murder of the Jews of Rokiškis as a successful example of cooperation between the German mobile unit and Lithuanian white armbanders. Members of the Rokiškis Guard Unit each received a 150 ruble reward for their part in the mass murder of Jews. Several hundred Jews from Pandėlys, 6 Jewish families from Južintai, 70 Jews from Panemunėlis, 70 elderly, women and children from Svėdasai, 117 people from Kamajai, some of the Jews from Obeliai, 17 Jews of Maneivai village and 20 Jewish families from Onuškis were put in the Rokiškis ghetto .

*   *   *

Perpetrators

Rollkommando Hamann/1st Battalion 3rd Unit;
Rokiškis Guard Unit;
white armbanders from Rokiškis, Juodupė, Kamajai and Svėdasai

Velniaduobė (Bajorai) Memorial Plaques

In 1958, a memorial was erected at the Velniaduobė site with the following plaque, which states in Russian, Lithuanian, and Yiddish, "Here rest those killed on August 15-16, 1941, by Lithuanian-German nationalists." The Yiddish text provides the Hebrew calendar dates, and thus, the yahrzeit dates, as Av 22-23 [5701].

The following photograph was taken in 1997 of a metal sign that also marked the Velniaduobė massacre site. The sign stated, in Lithuanian and Yiddish, "In this place Hitlerists and their local helpers on August 15 and 16, 1941 cruelly killed 3207 Jews - children, women, men. Let the memory of them be blessed."

App A - 104   Appendices of Material Not Included in the Original Yizkor Book

2. Antanašė

MASS MURDER OF THE JEWS OF THE ROKIŠKIS REGION NEAR THE ANTANAŠĖ MANOR

ABOUT MASSACRE

Some of the Jews of the Rokiškis region (mainly women and children) were held in the summer of 1941 at Antanašė manor near Obeliai. On August 25, 1941, about 30 Rokiškis Guard Unit troops and several German Gestapo officers arrived at Antanašė manor from Rokiškis. The night before the mass murder operation, Soviet POWs dug two large pits at the edge of Degsnė forest (about 1.5 kilometers from the manor). Obeliai municipal and railway station auxiliary police were placed as guards on the road from Antanašė manor to the killing site. Other Obeliai white armbanders marched the Jews in large groups (of about 100 people). In total, about 120 to 160 Rokiškis Guard Unit troops and Obeliai rural district auxiliary police perpetrated the mass murder (including transporting and guarding Jews as well as shooting them). They ordered Jews to undress before they shot them. Executioners from Rokiškis and several Gestapo did the shooting. The mass murder operation lasted an entire day. The Jäger Report says 1,160 Jews were killed at Antanašė, including 112 men, 627 women and 421 children. Thirty policemen from Obeliai, 23 from Obeliai railway station, 13 from Aleksandravėlė and 12 from Kriaunos auxiliary police unit received rewards of 100 rubles each for the mass murder operation.

*   *   *

Perpetrators

German Gestapo;
Rokiškis Guard Unit;
Obeliai municipal and railway station auxiliary police;
Obeliai white armbanders;
Aleksandravėlė and Kriaunos auxiliary police

<u>Antanašė Memorial Plaque</u>

Yad Vashem Archives, Photo Collection No. 4043

Appendices of Material Not Included in the Original Yizkor Book   App A - 105

Professor Alfonsas Eidintas' Description of the Murders at Velniaduobė (Bajorai)

Professor Alfonsas Eidintas, a historian, served as ambassador to the United States from 1993 to 1997 and later served as Lithuania's ambassador to Israel. His book entitled *"Jews, Lithuanians, and the Holocaust,* [English translation of *Žydai, lietuviai ir holokaustas,* Leidykla Vaga (2002)], Versus Aureus (Vilnius 2003), includes the text of his 2002 address to the Lithuanian Seimas (parliament),[7] which described the murder of the Jews in Rokiškis as follows:

> The story of witness Brunius, recorded by Secretary General of the Lithuanian Nationalist Party Zenonas Blynas in 1941 testifies what the massacre in Rokiškis looked like – and it was exceptional, because observers were allowed to watch it, "Half naked Jews had to jump into a three-meter deep trench. They were shot at by killers walking around the trench. Brains and blood spattered everywhere. The killers were soaked in blood. [...] People from the area came to watch. At first they laughed and smiled and were satisfied, but later, women (Lithuanian)[8] began screaming in horror. A slaughter, how vile. The [administrative] governor of the district is Judas.[9] I had said that if Germans made us do it, everything had to be done quietly, in secret and without any scandal. That degenerate did quite the opposite."

-- Jews, Lithuanians, and the Holocaust, p. 500.

In the same book, Eidintas noted that in November 1965, the Soviets put on trial five individuals who were "parties to the killings in Rokiškis," specifically, Kazimier[a]s Dagys. Steponas Lašas, Stasys Varnas, and Petras Strumskis.[10] He added that news articles at the time observed that four other "members of the Rokiškis command company" who fled to the West after the Second World War, namely, "in the United States – Henrikas Dūda and Andrius Abarius, in Australia – Balys Milaknis, and in Canada – Vladas Erslovas. [footnote 54: S. Laurinaitis, "Kaltina nužudytieji, smerkia gyvieji" (Those who were murdered accuse, those who survived condemn), *Tiesa,* 7 November 1965.][11]

As of 2017, post-Soviet Lithuania had not successfully prosecuted any perpetrator.[12]

---

[7] "Presentation by Prof. Alfonsas Eidintas at the September 21, 2002, Lithuanian Seimas "Parliament' Special Session in Respectful Commemoration of the 60th Anniversary of the Holocaust in Lithuania," Supplement No. 3, *Jews, Lithuanians, and the Holocaust,* pp. 497-503.

[8] Elsewhere in his book, Eidintas translates the description as "Aryan women." *Jews, Lithuanians, and the Holocaust,* p. 289.

[9] In the original Hebrew text of the "Abel" [Obeliai] article in *Pinkas Hakehillot Lita* [*the Encyclopedia of Jewish Communities in Lithuania*], the name of the Lithuanian who was the governor of the Rokiskis District in July and August 1941 is written as זשוקאס (Žukas). *Pinkas Hakehillot Lita,* at 116 (third paragraph from the end of the article). According to another source, Žukas held the rank of lieutenant.

[10] *Jews, Lithuanians, and the Holocaust,* p. 355.

[11] *Id.*

[12] In January 1999, the names of 83 ethnic Lithuanians were included in a "Partial List of Lithuanian murderers of the Jews of Rokiskis and its district" that was published by the Lithuanian-born Israeli attorney Joseph Melamed in his publication *Lithuania: Crime and Punishment,* Volume 6, p. 113.

App A - 106   Appendices of Material Not Included in the Original Yizkor Book

The Jäger Report

Well in advance of the German invasion of Lithuania, various Lithuanian paramilitary groups were organized secretly in Lithuania to prepare for an "uprising" against the Soviet occupation administration and other "enemies," including Lithuania's Jewish civilian population. When the German invasion began, on June 22, 1941, the leaders of the Lithuanian nationalist forces seized the Kaunas radio station. They announced that a "Provisional Government" had been established and that Jewish lives and property were beyond legal protection. With this cue, nationalist cells throughout the country began their "uprising." [13] Violence against Jews and the looting of their property began before German troops arrived. SS paramilitary units soon arrived who systematized and oversaw the arrest, concentration, and murder of Lithuania's Jewish citizens. On December 1, 1941, Karl Jäger, the commander of SS Einsatzkommando 3 ("EK3"), issued a secret report detailing, by date and location, and the number and classification of the people killed in the zone assigned to his unit.

In the following English translation of the "Jäger Report," the names of the towns in and near the geographical area covered by the 1952 *Rokiskis and Environs* yizkor book are indicated in **bold** type.

Philip S. Shapiro

The Commander of the Security Police and the SD Einsatzkommando 3
Kauen [Kaunas, Kovno] 1 December 1941

=====================

Secret Reich Business

=====================

5 copies
——————— 4th copy —————-

Complete List Of Executions Carried Out In The Einsatzkommando 3 Zone Up To December 1, 1941

Security police duties in Lithuania taken over by Einsatzkommando 3 on 2 July 1941. (The Wilna [Vilnius] area was taken over by EK 3 on 9 Aug. 1941, the Schaulen [Šiauliai] area on 2 Oct. 1941. Up until these dates EK 9 operated in Wilna and EK 2 in Schaulen.) On my instructions and orders the following executions were conducted by Lithuanian partisans:

---

[13]   As noted by Lithuanian historian Dr. Arūnas Bubnys, the "participants" in the "uprising" in northeastern Lithuania went into action once they received word that the German invasion had begun. "The main organizers and future participants in the uprising were the *šauliai*, members of the *Šaulių sąjunga* (Riflemen's Association), officers and non-commissioned officers of the Lithuanian army, policemen, local government officials, teachers and patriotically inclined farmers. ... An important impulse was given by the news broadcast by Kaunas radio that the Provisional Government of Lithuania was being formed and Lithuania's independence was being restored. ... Before the arrival of the German army the uprising participants had essentially freed northeast Lithuania from the Soviet occupation and ruled the area for several days." "1941 m. Birželio Sukilimas Šiaurės Rytų Lietuvoje" ("The Uprising of June 1941 in Northeast Lithuania"), *Lietuvių katalikų mokslo akademijos metraštis*. T. 29. Vilnius, 2006, ISSN 1392-0502, 140, 168-169.

Appendices of Material Not Included in the Original Yizkor Book   App A - 107

Date Location   **Totals**
4.7.41 Kauen-Fort VII 416 Jews, 47 Jewesses 463
6.7.41 Kauen-Fort VII Jews   2,514

Following the formation of a raiding squad under the command of SS-Obersturmfuhrer Hamman and 8-10 reliable men from the Einsatzkommando the following actions were conducted in cooperation with Lithuanian partisans:

Date	Location		Totals
7.7.41	Mariampole	32 Jews	32
8.7.41	Mariampole	14 Jews, 5 Comm. officials	19
8.7.41	Girkalinei	Comm. officials	6
9.7.41	Wendziogala	32 Jews, 2 Jewesses, 1 Lithuanian, (f.), 2 Lithuanian Comm., 1 Russian Comm.	38
9.7.41	Kauen-Fort VII	21 Jews, 3 Jewesses	24
14.7.41	Mariampole	21 Jews, 1 Russ., 9 Lith. Comm.	31
17.7.41	Babtei	8 Comm. officals (inc. 6 Jews)	8
18.7.41	Mariampole	39 Jews, 14 Jewesses	53
19.7.41	Kauen-Fort VII	17 Jews, 2 Jewesses, 4 Lith. Comm., 2 Comm. Lithuanians (f.), 1 German Comm.	26
21.7.41	Panevezys	59 Jews, 11 Jewesses, 1 Lithuanian (f.), 1 Pole, 22 Lith. Comm., 9 Russ. Comm.	103
22.7.41	Panevezys	1 Jew	1
23.7.41	Kedainiai	83 Jews, 12 Jewesses, 14 Russ.Comm., 15 Lith. Comm., 1 Russ. O-Politruk	125
25.7.41	Mariampole	90 Jews, 13 Jewesses	103
28.7.41	Panevezys	234 Jews, 15 Jewesses, 19 Russ. Comm., 20 Lith. Comm.	288
29.7.41	Rasainiai	254 Jews, 3 Lith. Comm.	257
30.7.41	Agriogala	27 Jews, 11 Lith. Comm.	38
31.7.41	Utena	235 Jews, 16 Jewesses, 4 Lith. Comm., 1 robber/murderer	256
31.7.41	Wendziogala	13 Jews, 2 murderers	15
1.8.41	Ukmerge	254 Jews, 42 Jewesses, 1 Pol.Comm., 2 Lith. NKVD agents, 1 mayor of Jonava who gave order to set fire to Jonava	300
2.8.41	Kauen-Fort IV	170 Jews, 1 US Jewess, 33 Jewesses, 4 Lith. Comm.	209
4.8.41	Panevezys	362 Jews, 41 Jewesses, 5 Russ. Comm., 14 Lith. Comm.	422
5.8.41	Rasainiai	213 Jews, 66 Jewesses	279
7.8.41	**Utena**	483 Jews, 87 Jewesses, 1 Lithuanian (robber of corpses of German soldiers)	571

App A - 108   Appendices of Material Not Included in the Original Yizkor Book

8.8.41	Ukmerge	620 Jews, 82 Jewesses	702
9.8.41	Kauen-Fort IV	484 Jews, 50 Jewesses	534
11.8.41	Panevezys	450 Jews, 48 Jewesses, 1 Lith. 1 Russ.	500
13.8.41	Alytus	617 Jews, 100 Jewesses, 1 criminal	719
14.8.41	Jonava	497 Jews, 55 Jewesses	552
15-16.8.41	**Rokiskis**	3,200 Jews, Jewesses, and Jewish Children, 5 Lith. Comm., 1 Pole, 1 partisan	3207
9-16.8.41	Rasainiai	294 Jewesses, 4 Jewish children	298
27.6-14.8.41	**Rokiskis**	493 Jews, 432 Russians, 56 Lithuanians (all active communists)	981
18.8.41	Kauen-Fort IV	689 Jews, 402 Jewesses, 1 Pole (female), 711 Jewish intellectuals from Ghetto in reprisal for sabotage action	1,812
19.8.41	Ukmerge	298 Jews, 255 Jewesses, 1 Politruk, 88 Jewish children, 1 Russ. Comm.	645
22.8.41	**Dunaburg [Dvinsk]**	3 Russ. Comm., 5 Latvian, incl. 1 murderer, 1 Russ. Guardsman, 3 Poles, 3 gypsies (m.), 1 gypsy (f.), 1 gypsy child, 1 Jew, 1 Jewess, 1 Armenian (m.), 2 Politruks (prison inspection in Dunanburg	21
22.8.41	Aglona	Mentally sick: 269 men, 227 women, 48 children	544
23.8.41	Panevezys	1312 Jews, 4602 Jewesses,1609 Jewish children	7,523
18-22.8.41	Kreis Rasainiai	466 Jews,440 Jewesses, 1020 Jewish children	1,926
25.8.41	**Obeliai**	112 Jews, 627 Jewesses, 421 Jewish children	1,160
25-26.8.41	Seduva	230 Jews, 275 Jewesses, 159 Jewish children	664
26.8.41	**Zarasai**	767 Jews, 1,113 Jewesses, 1 Lith. Comm., 687 Jewish children, 1 Russ.Comm. (f.)	2,569
28.8.41	Pasvalys	Comm., 687 Jewish children, 1 Russ.Comm. (f.) 402 Jews, 738 Jewesses, 209 Jewish children	1,349
26.8.41	Kaisiadorys	All Jews, Jewesses, and Jewish children	1,911
27.8.41	Prienai	All Jews, Jewesses, and Jewish Children	1,078
27.8.41	Dagda and Kraslawa	212 Jews, 4 Russ. POW's	216
27.8.41	Joniskis	47 Jews, 165 Jewesses, 143 Jewish children	355
28.8.41	Wilkia	76 Jews, 192 Jewesses, 134 Jewish children	402
28.8.41	Kedainiai	710 Jews, 767 Jewesses, 599 Jewish children	2,076
29.8.41	Rumsiskis and Ziezmariai	20 Jews, 567 Jewesses, 197 Jewish children	784
29.8.41	**Utena** and Moletai	582 Jews, 1,731 Jewesses, 1,469 Jewish children	3,782
13-31.8.41	Alytus and environs	233 Jews	233
1.9.41	Mariampole	1,763 Jews, 1,812 Jewesses, 1,404 Jewish children,	5090

Appendices of Material Not Included in the Original Yizkor Book   App A - 109

		109 mentally sick, 1 German subject (f.), married to a Jew, 1 Russian (f.)	
28.8-2.9.41	Darsuniskis	10 Jews, 69 Jewesses, 20 Jewish children	99
	Carliava	73 Jews, 113 Jewesses, 61 Jewish children	247
	Jonava	112 Jews, 1,200 Jewesses, 244 Jewish children	1,556
	Petrasiunai	30 Jews, 72 Jewesses, 23 Jewish children	125
	Jesuas	26 Jews, 72 Jewesses, 46 Jewish children	144
	Ariogala	207 Jews, 260 Jewesses, 195 Jewish children	662
	Jasvainai	86 Jews, 110 Jewesses, 86 Jewish children	282
	Babtei	20 Jews, 41 Jewesses, 22 Jewish children	83
	Wenziogala	42 Jews, 113 Jewesses, 97 Jewish children	252
	Krakes	448 Jews, 476 Jewesses, 97 Jewish children	1,125
4.9.41	Pravenischkis	247 Jews, 6 Jewesses	253
	Cekiske	22 Jews, 64 Jewesses, 60 Jewish children	146
	Seredsius	6 Jews, 61 Jewesses, 126 Jewish children	193
	Velinona	2 Jews, 71 Jewesses, 86 Jewish children	159
	Zapiskis	47 Jews, 118 Jewesses, 13 Jewish children	178
5.9.41	Ukmerge	1,23 Jews, 1849 Jewesses, 1737 Jewish children	4,709
25.8-6.9.41	Mopping up in:		
	Rasainiai	16 Jews, 412 Jewesses, 415 Jewish children	843
	Georgenburg (Yurburg)	All Jews, all Jewesses, all Jewish children	412
9.9.41	Alytus	287 Jews, 640 Jewesses, 352 Jewish children	1,279
9.9.41	Butrimonys	67 Jews, 370 Jewesses, 303 Jewish children	740
10.9.41	Merkine	223 Jews, 640 Jewesses, 276 Jewish children	854
10.9.41	Varena	541 Jews, 141 Jewesses, 149 Jewish children	831
11.9.41	Leipalingis	60 Jews, 70 Jewesses, 25 Jewish children	155
11.9.41	Seirijai	229 Jews, 384 Jewesses, 340 Jewish children	953
12.9.41	Simnas	68 Jews, 197 Jewesses, 149 Jewish children	414
11-12.9.41	Uzusalis	Reprisal against inhabitants who fed Russ. partisans; some in possesion of weapons	43
26.9.41	Kauen-F.IV	412 Jews, 615 Jewesses, 581 Jewish children (sick and suspected epidemic cases)	1,608
2.10.41	Zagare	633 Jews, 1,107 Jewesses, 496 Jewish children (as these Jews were being led away a mutiny rose, which was however immediately put down; 150 Jews were shot immediately; 7 partisans wounded)	2,236
4.10.41	Kauen-F.IX	315 Jews, 712 Jewesses, 818 Jewish children (reprisal after German police officer shot in ghetto)	1,845
29.10.41	Kauen-F.IX	2,007 Jews, 2,920 Jewesses, 4,273 Jewish children (mopping up ghetto of superfluous Jews)	9,200

App A - 110   Appendices of Material Not Included in the Original Yizkor Book

Date	Place	Description	Total
3.11.41	Lazdijai	485 Jews, 511 Jewesses, 539 Jewish children	1,535
15.11.41	Wilkowiski	36 Jews, 48 Jewesses, 31 Jewish children	115
25.11.41	Kauen-F.IX	1,159 Jews, 1,600 Jewesses, 175 Jewish children (resettlers from Berlin, Munich and Frankfurt am main)	2,934
29.11.41	Kauen-F.IX	693 Jews, 1,155 Jewesses, 152 Jewish children (resettlers from from Vienna and Breslau)	2,000
29.11.41	Kauen-F.IX	17 Jews, 1 Jewess, for contravention of ghetto law, 1 Reichs German who converted to the Jewish faith and attended rabbinical school, then 15 terrorists from the Kalinin group	34

EK 3 detachment in Dunaberg [Dvinsk]

Date	Place	Description	Total
13.7-21.8.41:		9,012 Jews, Jewesses and Jewish children, 573 active Comm.	9,585

EK 3 detachment in Wilna:

Date	Place	Description	Total
12.8-1.9.41	City of Wilna	425 Jews, 19 Jewesses, 8 Comm. (m.), 9 Comm. (f.)	461
2.9.41	City of Wilna	864 Jews, 2,019 Jewesses, 817 Jewish children (sonderaktion because German soldiers shot at by Jews)	3,700
12.9.41	City of Wilna	993 Jews, 1,670 Jewesses, 771 Jewish children	3,334
17.9.41	City of Wilna	337 Jews, 687 Jewesses, 247 Jewish children and 4 Lith. Comm.	1,271
20.9.41	Nemencing	128 Jews, 176 Jewesses, 99 Jewish children	403
22.9.41	Novo-Wilejka	468 Jews, 495 Jewesses, 196 Jewish children	1,159
24.9.41	Riesa	512 Jews, 744 Jewesses, 511 Jewish children	1,767
25.9.41	Jahiunai	215 Jews, 229 Jewesses, 131 Jewish children	575
27.9.41	Eysisky	989 Jews, 1,636 Jewesses, 821 Jewish children	3,446
30.9.41	Trakai	366 Jews, 483 Jewesses, 597 Jewish children	1,446
4.10.41	City of Wilna	432 Jews, 1,115 Jewesses, 436 Jewish children	1,983
6.10.41	Semiliski	213 Jews, 359 Jewesses, 390 Jewish children	962
9.10.41	Svenciany	1169 Jews, 1840 Jewesses, 717 Jewish children	3,726
16.10.41	City of Wilna	382 Jews, 507 Jewesses, 257 Jewish children	1,146
21.10.41	City of Wilna	718 Jews, 1,063 Jewesses, 586 Jewish children	2,367
25.10.41	City of Wilna	1,776 Jewesses, 812 Jewish children	2,578
27.10.41	City of Wilna	946 Jews, 184 Jewesses, 73 Jewish children	1,203
30.10.41	City of Wilna	382 Jews, 789 Jewesses, 36 Jewish children	1,553
6.11.41	City of Wilna	340 Jews, 749 Jewesses, 252 Jewish children	1,341
19.11.41	City of Wilna	76 Jews, 77 Jewesses, 18 Jewish children	171

Appendices of Material Not Included in the Original Yizkor Book   App A - 111

19.11.41	City of Wilna	6 POW's, 8 Poles	14
20.11.41	City of Wilna	3 POW's	3
25.11.41	City of Wilna	9 Jews, 46 Jewesses, 8 Jewish children, 1 Pole for possession of arms and other military equipment	64

EK 3 detachment
in Minsk
28.9-17.10.41:

	Pleschnitza	620 Jews, 1,285 Jewesses,	
	Bischolin	1,126 Jewish children and 19	
	Scak	Comm.	
	Bober		
	Uzda		3,050
			———
		Prior to EK 3 taking over security police duties, Jews liquidated by pogroms and executions (including partisans)	4,000
			———
			–
		Total	137,346

Today I can confirm that our objective, to solve the Jewish problem for Lithuania, has been achieved by EK 3. In Lithuania there are no more Jews, apart from Jewish workers and their families. The distance between from the assembly point to the graves was on average 4 to 5 Km.

I consider the Jewish action more or less terminated as far as Einsatzkommando 3 is concerned. Those working Jews and Jewesses still available are needed urgently and I can envisage that after the winter this workforce will be required even more urgently. I am of the view that the sterilization program of the male worker Jews should be started immediately so that reproduction is prevented. If despite sterilization a Jewess becomes pregnant she will be liquidated.

(signed) Jager
SS-Standartenfuhrer [an SS rank that was equivalent to a full colonel]

App A - 112   Appendices of Material Not Included in the Original Yizkor Book

Forensic Reports for the Rokiškis-Area Massacre Sites Noted in the Jäger Report

The Jäger Report and several other sources identify four mass-killing sites in the Rokiškis region, specifically, the Steponiai forest (July 1941), the Vyžuonai forest (July 1941), the Velniaduobė woods near the village of Bajorai (August 15 and 16, 1941 – 3,207 men, women, and children), and the Antanašė forest (August 25, 1941 – 1,160 men, women, and children).[14]

In the summer of 1944, the Soviet army drove the forces of Nazi Germany out of the Rokiškis area and most of the eastern half of Lithuania. In October 1944, a special forensic commission exhumed and examined the bodies at each of the four Rokiškis-area sites. The commission was assisted by local medical authorities and medical experts from the Soviet army. Crowds of local residents were also present and some of the exhumed bodies were identified.

For each of these examinations, a hand-written report was created, written in the Lithuanian language. The reports are kept in the Manuscript Section of the Vrublevski Library of the Lithuanian Academy of Sciences ("VL-MS") in Vilnius. Following are summaries of the reports.

a.   Steponiai Forest Site Examination Report (VL-MS F159-51-1R and F159-51-1V)

The examination was conducted on October 26, 1944. The site is located 5 kilometers from Rokiškis on the Rokiškis-Čedasai road, 150 meters to the right, in the Steponiai Forest. The commission found 6 mass graves.

In the first grave, which measured 10 meters long, 3 meters wide, and 2 meters deep, 180 corpses were found. They were mostly Jews, lying neatly in rows. In the second grave, which measured 5 meters long, 2 meters wide, and 1.5 meters deep, 28 bodies were found, consisting of Lithuanian and Russian men. They were lying in the grave in a disorderly manner, so it is believed that they were killed on the edge of the graves and thrown in. Ten bodies were identified.

In the third grave, which measured 5 meters long, 2 meters wide, and 2 meters deep, 18 corpses were found. They were Jewish people of different sexes and ages, lying in rows. In the fourth grave, which measured 4 meters long, 2 meters wide, and 2 meters deep, 10 corpses were found. They were Jewish people of different sexes and ages, lying neatly in rows. In the fifth grave, which measured 5 meters long, 2 meters wide, and 2 meters deep, the bodies of 50 Jews were found. They were of different sexes and ages, lying neatly in rows.

In the sixth grave, which measured 10 meters long, 3 meters wide, and 2 meters deep, 100 bodies were found of different nationalities, Lithuanians, Russians, and Jews, of both sexes, thrown chaotically into the grave. Thirteen bodies were identified.

All of these murders occurred in the middle of July 1941.

---

[14] As noted below, however, there are other massacre sites in the Rokiškis region.

b. <u>Vyžuonai Forest Site Examination Report</u> (VL-MS F159-51-2R and F159-51-2V)

The examination was conducted on October 24, 1944. Among those present was a representative of the Catholic Church, parish priest Mykolas Juodelė and a numerous crowd of local residents. The site is located in the Rokiškis area, at a distance of 9 kilometers from Rokiškis, on the Rokiškis-Juodupė road, about 200 meters to the left of the road in marshes within the boundary of the forest.

There are two mass graves at this site, each of which is 4 meters long and wide and 1.5 meters deep. A total of 67 bodies of both sexes were found in these graves. In the first grave, 27 bodies were found, of which 12 were identified. In the second grave, 40 bodies were found, of which 9 were identified.

Experts from the commission stated that the condemned were killed on the edge of the graves and were thrown in in a chaotic manner. Next to the corpses were found ordinary items of life, such as combs, mirrors, toothbrushes, and wallets that first were emptied and then tossed on top of the bodies.

Most of those killed were Lithuanians or Russians but there were also the bodies of two Jews. Local people testified that German conducted these cruel killings in the first days of July 1941.[15]

c. <u>Velniaduobė (Bajorai) Woods Site Examination Report</u> (VL-MS F159-51-3R and F159-51-3V)

The examination was conducted on October 21, 1944. Among those present was a representative of the Catholic Church, parish priest Mykolas Juodelė and a numerous crowd of local residents.

The site is located in the Rokiškis area, in the village of Bajorai, 5 kilometers from Rokiškis, 400 meters to the right of the left of the Rokiškis-Juodupė road, on a sandy elevation.

There are eight mass graves at this site, each of which is 20 meters long, 3 meters wide, and 2 meters deep. Each grave contained about 600 corpses. The bodies were not lying in order but rather were lying on upon another. They were killed either by a bullet to the back of the head or by being struck with a heavy object. Some had been shot in the back and some of the children had broken legs.

Among those killed were men, women, children, youngsters, babies, and elderly people. Most of them were holding hands. Mothers were found who, horrified by knowledge of their coming deaths, were holding their children close to their chests waiting to be shot by a killer. Next to the bodies were found books of prayer, various household items, such as dishes, and

---

[15] Rokiškis native Joseph Harmatz noted that later in that month, on July 27, 1941, 493 people from Rokiškis, consisting of "mainly Lithuanians and Jews who had cooperated with the Soviets," were "shot near Lake Vižunka, by the main road close to the forest." *From the Wings, A Long Journey: 1940 – 1960* (Bath, England, 1998; ISBN 1-85776-392-0), at page 13. This larger massacre may have occurred near this location where the forensic examination found the bodies of 67 victims.

App A - 114   Appendices of Material Not Included in the Original Yizkor Book

documents. Here is one example: A security soldier's certificate, number 123124, issued in 1915 to Stolov Jahomas.[16]

Experts from the commission stated that all of those killed here were Jews, possibly as many as 5,000. Judging by the civilian summer clothing, the commission states that they were killed in the summertime.

According to local area witnesses, the cruel killings were performed by the Germans in August 1941.

According to local resident witnesses, those condemned to perish were escorted in groups of 100 to 200 people who were carrying bundles and kitchen and other items. This shows that they were escorted as if going to a place for work or to live. But they were taken alive to the place where mass graves had been prepared in advance and they were cruelly killed by Germans and local bandits.

d. <u>Antanašė Forest Site Examination Report</u> (VL-MS F159-51-4R)

The examination was conducted on October 28, 1944.

The Antanašė massacre site is in the Rokiškis area, near Obeliai, 5 kilometers from Obeliai on the Obeliai-Aleksandravėlė road, 100 meters to the left of the road. Two mass graves were found.

The first grave is 15 meters long, 3 meters wide, and 2.5 meters deep. In this grave were found 550 bodies of different ages, males, females, and children. They were laid in order in 3 rows. Nearly all were only wearing underwear. With a few exceptions, all were Jews.

The second grave is 30 meters long, 3 meters wide, and 2 meters deep. In this grave were found the bodies of 1,100 Jews of different ages and sexes. The bodies were laid in rows. They were killed in the graves.

According to peoples' testimony the murders occurred on August 19 to 20, 1941. The condemned were escorted to the killing place in groups.

Other Rokiškis-Area Massacre Sites

In 2017, the Rokiškis Regional Museum announced that it was in the process of documenting two previously unmarked massacre sites, one near the Trakas-Pempiškis forest and the other near the border between the villages of Šeduikiškis and Kavoliškis. Below is the English version of the museum's announcement. In time, other sites may come to light.

---

[16] As noted earlier, in 2005 students at Svėdasai's J. Tumas-Vaižgantas high school created a map showing where Jews lived in Svėdasai before the Second World War. A building on J. Tumas-Vaižgantas Street (number 29) is identified as "J. Stolovo vaistinė" – the pharmacy of J. Stolov. It is possible that the certificate found at the Velniaduobė site belonged to this pharmacist.

English Translation of June 21, 2017, Annoucement of Rokiškis Regional Museum Regarding Two Previously Undocumented and Unmarked Holocaust Killing Sites in the Rokiškis Region

ROKIŠKIO KRAŠTO MUZIEJUS

Biudžetinė įstaiga, Tyzenhauzų al. 5, LT-42115 Rokiškis, Tel. (8 458) 52 261, (8 458) 31 512, faks/tel. (8 458) 52 835, el. p.: muziejus@rokiskyje.lt. Duomenys kaupiami ir saugomi Juridinių asmenų registre, kodas 190263920

2017 06 21

On June 21, Phil and Aldona Shapiro, who are friends and sponsors of the Rokiškis Regional Museum, visited from the USA. Phil and his brother David founded a non-profit organization called Remembering Litvaks, Inc., which is dedicated to preserving and fostering the Litvak cultural heritage of Lithuania.

* * *

During the June 21 meeting, the visitors discussed several new projects, including those in which the Museum might be a partner. They also received the results of new historical research that the Museum recently conducted.

On May 8, 2017, Marijona Mieliauskiene, the Museum's Deputy Director of the Rokiškis Regional Museum, and Giedrius Kujelis, the Director of the Museum's History Department, visited Jonas Rudokas in Skrebiskis village (who was born in 1934 in the village of Skrebiškis in the Kamajai eldership). The purpose of the visit was to determine the place of killing and burial of a group of Svėdasai Jews.

Mr. Rudokas remembered that in 1941 July or August (he could not recall the precise date) more prosperous Jewish families from Svėdasai were shot on the outskirts of Trakas-Pempiškis forest, near the road leading from Kamajai northward to Rokiškis.

The Museum's staff, together with Mr. Rudokas and his wife, Aldona Rudokienė, went to the site of the Jewish shooting and burial, which is approximately one kilometer from their home. Mr. Rudokas pointed to the site at the edge of the Trako-Pempiškis forest close to the Kamajai-Rokiškis road.

Mr. Rudokas explained that the Jewish families from Svėdasai were being transported in the direction of Rokiškis with their possessions in horse-drawn carts. Their captors then decided to benefit themselves by killing their captives. When the massacre began,

App A - 116   Appendices of Material Not Included in the Original Yizkor Book

several of the victims tried to escape, but were attacked and shot.

Mr. Rudokas heard from other neighbors that 28 people were shot dead during the incident. Among the massacre perpetrators were men from the Bekintis family who lived in Svėdasai.

Museum Deputy Director M. Mieliauskienė (who was born in 1952 in Pašilės village in the Kamajai eldership) remembers that her parents and grandmother talked about these killings. Her grandmother, Anelė Jasiūnienė (1883-1965) had shown her the place where the murdered Svėdasai Jews were buried.

Jonas and Aldona Rudokas and Marijona Mieliauskienė explained that in the 1960s diggings occurred at the massacre site but they did not know who did the digging or the reason it was done. M. Mieliauskienė had also heard about this from his mother, Liudvika Jasiūnienė (1920-1987).

The Museum coordinators have recorded the specific location, documented the testimony of the witnesses, and drafted an official document regarding the massacre site. The Museum will present this information to the Genocide and Resistance Research Center of Lithuania for further actions. In the opinion of the Museum coordinators, the next steps should be to search for documents in archives, particularly any concerning a possible transfer of the victims' remains, archaeological research, protecting the site, building a memorial sign, and installing a road sign.

There are several mass murder sites in the Rokiškis area, where between June and August 1941 the Nazis killed Jews who were residents of the region. Four of these places have been documented. At Velniaduobė, near the village of Bajorai, 3207 people were killed. They were residents of the town of Rokiskis and residents from other Jewish towns in the area. More than 1160 victims are buried near Antanašė village, south of Obeliai. There are 70 people buried in a mass grave in the village of Vyžuonai and 981 people were killed in the Steponiai woods.

However, there are other massacre places, like the one near the Trakas-Pempiškis forest, that are not marked and have been forgotten by many people. One such location is on the border of the Šeduikiškis and Kavoliškis villages, just west of Rokiškis on the right side of a small field road. It was there that the Jofe and Olkin families from Panemunėlis were murdered and buried. Among those shot dead there was the young poet, Matilda Olkinaitė.

The tragedy of Matilda Olkinaitė has been immortalized by the play of the Theatre of Rokiškis company entitled, "Mute Muses," which was directed by Neringa Danienė. The theater company did not limit themselves to the performance to preserve the memory of the Olkin family. The theatre company, together with the volunteers from the Lithuanian Army's 506th National Guard unit, which is based in Rokiskis, undertook an expedition to identify the location of the massacre and burial site. There is a plan to mark the boundary of the site and build a commemorative plaque. The association also plans to publish a book of M. Olkinaitė's poetry.

Appendices of Material Not Included in the Original Yizkor Book   App A - 117

App A - 118   Appendices of Material Not Included in the Original Yizkor Book

Appendix of Rokiskis Shoah Victims

Yad Vashem maintains and continually updates a searchable Central Database of the names of Shoah victims. The following list was prepared from the results of a search in the database performed on November 23, 2016, seeking the names of victims associated with the town of Rokiskis. It is suggested that readers go to the Yad Vashem web site listed below and search for the names of people they are interested in, using Rokiskis as the town name and the last name of the individual.

There is much more information available on this web site, including the Pages of Testimony, etc.

http://yvng.yadvashem.org

Please note that in each row of the following list, the fifth column, which is entitled "Source," shows codes referencing the source of the information provided in that row. The following table explains those codes.

Source Codes	
Census	Census list
Deport	Deportation list
Dep-FR	List of deportation from France
Evac	List of evacuated persons
HLBV	List of Hungarian labor battalion victims
Jew Res	List of Jewish residents
Murd	Record of murdered persons
Persecut	List of persecuted persons
PT	Page of Testimony
PT Ds	Page of Testimony (digital signed)
PT D	Page of Testimony (digital)
Per Doc	Personal documents
Residen	List of residents
Yzkr Bk	List of murdered Jews from Yizkor books

APP-2   Appendix of Rokiskis Shoah Victims – not in the original Yizkor Book

First Name	Last Name	Birth Year	Place of Residence	Source	Fate from Source
Edel	Abir	1912	Slobodka, Poland	PT	murdered
Leib Lev	Abir	1888	Slobodka, Poland	PT	murdered
Hermann	Abraham	1913	Maramarossziget, Romania	HLBV	murdered
Pinchas Pinkhas	Abramovic Abramovitz	1886	Rakishik, Lithuania	PT	murdered
Badana	Abramovich		Rokishkis, Lithuania	PT D	murdered
Avraham	Abramovitz		Rokiskis, Lithuania	Yzkr Bk	murdered
Beile Rakhel	Abramovitz		Rokiskis, Lithuania	Yzkr Bk	murdered
Freda Frida Freida	Abramovitz	1878	Rokiskis, Lithuania	PT	murdered
Frida	Abramovitz	1887	Kowno, Lithuania	PT	murdered
Hirshel	Abramovitz		Rokiskis, Lithuania	Yzkr Bk	murdered
Itzhak Yitzkhak Mordekhai	Abramovitz	1917	Kowno, Lithuania	PT	murdered
Rasya	Abramovitz		Rokiskis, Lithuania	PT D	murdered
Slomo Shlomo	Abramovitz	1873	Rokiskis, Lithuania	PT	murdered
Tovie Tuvia	Abramovitz	1913	Kowno, Lithuania	PT	murdered
Yekhiel	Abramovitz		Rokiskis, Lithuania	Yzkr Bk	murdered
Yitzkhak Izak Mordekhai	Abramovitz	1914	Kaunas, Lithuania	PT	murdered
Zelig	Abramovitz		Rokiskis, Lithuania	Yzkr Bk	murdered
First name unknown	Abramovitz Abramovic		Rokiskis, Lithuania	PT	murdered
Abram Avraham Dov Ber	Abramowicz Abramovitz	1896	Rokiskis, Lithuania	PT	murdered
Schlom Leib	Abramowitsch	1872	Daugavpils, Latvia	Census	not stated
Schlom Leib	Abramowitsch	1872	Daugavpils, Latvia	Jew Res	murdered
Chia Zerika	Abramski		Kamajai, Lithuania	PT	murdered
Stera Lea	Abramski		Kamajai, Lithuania	PT	murdered
Yitzak	Abramski		Kamajai, Lithuania	PT	murdered
Sima	Adelman		Rokiskis, Lithuania	PT D	murdered
Eisik	Adler	1916	Nagybocsko,	HLBV	murdered
Hersh	Afromowic Efromovitz		Rakishik, Lithuania	PT	murdered
Leib	Afromowic Efromovitz	1906	Rakishik, Lithuania	PT	murdered
Risl Rakhel	Afromowic Efromovitz	1891	Rakishik, Lithuania	PT	murdered
Shlomo Sloma	Afromowic Efromovitz	1889	Rakishik, Lithuania	PT	murdered
Yitzkhak	Agulneek Agulnik	1899	Posvol, Lithuania	PT	murdered
Aharon	Agulnik	1898	Ostrów Mazowiecka, Poland	PT	murdered
Icchak Yitzkhak	Agulnik	1900	Posvol, Lithuania	PT	murdered
Icikas Yitzkhak	Agulnikas Agulnik		Pasvalys, Lithuania	PT	murdered
Beniamin	Airesh		Rokiskis, Lithuania	Yzkr Bk	murdered
Pesia	Airesh		Rokiskis, Lithuania	Yzkr Bk	murdered
Tauba	Airesh		Rokiskis, Lithuania	Yzkr Bk	murdered
Yiska	Airesh		Rokiskis, Lithuania	Yzkr Bk	murdered
Izrael	Altmann	1917	Klacsano, Czechoslovakia	HLBV	murdered
Avraham Moshe	Amdur	1890	Rokishkis, Lithuania	PT	murdered
Itzik	Amdur	1898	Kowno, Lithuania	PT	murdered
Itzik	Amdur	1898	Kowno, Lithuania	PT	murdered
Khanan Yokhanan	Amdur	1900	Kaunas, Lithuania	PT	murdered
Tevie	Amdur	1925	Rokishkis, Lithuania	PT	murdered
Yaakov Iakele	Amdur	1902	Rokiskis, Lithuania	PT	murdered
Yitzkhak Itzik	Amdur	1923	Rokishkis, Lithuania	PT	murdered
Kanoriya	Amdyur	1923	Kamai, Lithuania	Evac	not stated
Fruma	Anciski Antziski		Abeliai, Lithuania	PT	murdered

Appendix of Rokiskis Shoah Victims – not in the original Yizkor Book   APP-3

First Name	Last Name	Birth Year	Place of Residence	Source	Fate from Source
Yehuda Jidel	Anszyszek Anshishek	1865	Ponodol, Lithuania	PT	murdered
Fruma	Antziski		Abel, Lithuania	PT	murdered
Elkhanan	Arsh	1879	Rokiskis, Lithuania	PT	murdered
Elkhanan	Arsh		Rokiskis, Lithuania	Yzkr Bk	murdered
Khanan	Arsh	1881	Rokishok, Lithuania	PT	murdered
Liba	Arsh	1880	Rokiskis, Lithuania	PT	murdered
Libe Nekhama	Arsh		Rokiskis, Lithuania	Yzkr Bk	murdered
Aira	Aruliansky Arolanski	1922	Ponemon, Lithuania	PT	murdered
David	Aruliansky Arolanski	1920	Ponemon, Lithuania	PT	murdered
Batia	Ashkenazi		Rokiskis, Lithuania	Yzkr Bk	murdered
Hirshel	Ashkenazi		Rokiskis, Lithuania	Yzkr Bk	murdered
Khaia	Ashkenazi		Rokiskis, Lithuania	Yzkr Bk	murdered
Lea Sara	Ashkenazi		Rokiskis, Lithuania	Yzkr Bk	murdered
Yekhezkel Leib	Ashkenazi		Rokiskis, Lithuania	Yzkr Bk	murdered
Yeshiyah Chaim	Ashkenazi		Rokiskis, Lithuania	Yzkr Bk	murdered
Jakob	Atlas	1901	Rokiskis, Lithuania	Persecut	not stated
Male	Awerbuch	1896	Riga, Latvia	Jew Res	not stated
Male	Awerbuch	1896	Riga, Latvia	Residen	not stated
Ester	Bader Beder	1866	Rokiskis, Lithuania	PT Ds	murdered
Aharon	Bakalchuk		Rokiskis, Lithuania	Yzkr Bk	murdered
Aharon Moshe	Bakalchuk		Rokiskis, Lithuania	Yzkr Bk	murdered
Baruch	Bakalchuk		Rokiskis, Lithuania	Yzkr Bk	murdered
Ber	Bakalchuk		Rokiskis, Lithuania	Yzkr Bk	murdered
Brakha	Bakalchuk		Rokiskis, Lithuania	Yzkr Bk	murdered
Chaia	Bakalchuk		Rokiskis, Lithuania	Yzkr Bk	murdered
Dore Dora Dvora	Bakalchuk		Pinsk, Poland	Yzkr Bk	murdered
Dvora	Bakalchuk		Rokiskis, Lithuania	Yzkr Bk	murdered
Feiga	Bakalchuk		Rokiskis, Lithuania	Yzkr Bk	murdered
Feiga Malka	Bakalchuk		Rokiskis, Lithuania	Yzkr Bk	murdered
Hirsh Tzvi	Bakalchuk		Rokiskis, Lithuania	Yzkr Bk	murdered
Leib Yehuda	Bakalchuk		Rokiskis, Lithuania	Yzkr Bk	murdered
Malka	Bakalchuk		Rokiskis, Lithuania	Yzkr Bk	murdered
Miriam Chaia	Bakalchuk		Rokiskis, Lithuania	Yzkr Bk	murdered
Rakhel	Bakalchuk		Rokiskis, Lithuania	Yzkr Bk	murdered
Sara	Bakalchuk		Rokiskis, Lithuania	Yzkr Bk	murdered
Sime	Bakalchuk		Rokiskis, Lithuania	Yzkr Bk	murdered
Yenta Sheine	Bakalchuk		Rokiskis, Lithuania	Yzkr Bk	murdered
Yosef Josele	Bakalchuk		Rokiskis, Lithuania	Yzkr Bk	murdered
Beryl	Bakaltshuk		Rokiskis, Lithuania	PT D	murdered
Bracha	Bakaltshuk		Rokiskis, Lithuania	PT D	murdered
Chaya Miriam	Bakaltshuk		Rokiskis, Lithuania	PT D	murdered
Malcha	Bakaltshuk		Rokiskis, Lithuania	PT D	murdered
Moshe	Bakaltshuk		Rokiskis, Lithuania	PT D	murdered
Rechela	Bakaltshuk		Rokiskis, Lithuania	PT D	murdered
Sarah	Bakaltshuk		Rokiskis, Lithuania	PT D	murdered
Yehudi Leib	Bakaltshuk		Rokiskis, Lithuania	PT D	murdered
Frida	Bank	1890	Shantz, Lithuania	PT	murdered
Riva	Bank	1882	Riga, Latvia	Jew Res	not stated
Riva	Bank	1882	Riga, Latvia	Residen	not stated
Riva	Bank	1882	Riga, Latvia	Residen	not stated

APP-4   Appendix of Rokiskis Shoah Victims – not in the original Yizkor Book

First Name	Last Name	Birth Year	Place of Residence	Source	Fate from Source
Riva	Bank	1882	Riga, Latvia	Residen	not stated
Frieda Frida	Bankiene Bank	1890	Lithuania	PT	murdered
Henek	Bar Ber		Rakishik, Lithuania	PT	murdered
Chaim Khaim	Barba Bravo	1906	Kaunas, Lithuania	PT	murdered
Khaim	Barilkin	1895	Abeliai, Lithuania	PT	murdered
Sara Serl	Barilkin	1900	Abeliai, Lithuania	PT	murdered
Haja	Barkan	1903	Riga, Latvia	Jew Res	murdered
Haja	Barkan	1903	Riga, Latvia	Residen	not stated
Haja	Barkan	1903	Riga, Latvia	Residen	not stated
Haja	Barkan	1903	Riga, Latvia	Residen	not stated
Haja	Barkan	1903	Riga, Latvia	Residen	not stated
Haja	Barkan	1903	Riga, Latvia	Residen	not stated
Batia	Barolski	1909	Kowno, Lithuania	PT	murdered
Elka	Barolski	1907	Abel, Lithuania	PT	murdered
Folke	Barolski		Skapiskis, Lithuania	PT	murdered
Jda Ida	Barolski	1897	Skapiskis, Lithuania	PT	murdered
Khana	Barolski		Skapiskis, Lithuania	PT	murdered
Mosze Moshe	Barolski	1897	Skapiskis, Lithuania	PT	murdered
Nekhama	Barolski		Skapiskis, Lithuania	PT	murdered
Rachel Rakhel	Barolski	1916	Skopiskis, Lithuania	PT	murdered
Ruwen Reuven	Barolski	1926	Skopishok, Lithuania	PT	murdered
Sara	Barolski		Ponivez, Lithuania	PT	murdered
Tzvi	Barolski	1916	Ponivez, Lithuania	PT	murdered
Yehuda	Barolski	1919	Ponivez, Lithuania	PT	murdered
Fania	Baron Brun	1906	Kaunas, Lithuania	PT	murdered
Genia Genya	Baron Brun	1907	Ostrog, Poland	PT	murdered
Gitl Gitel	Baron Brun	1896	Skapiskis, Lithuania	PT	murdered
Jakov Yaakov Eliezer	Baron Brun	1927	Skapiskis, Lithuania	PT	murdered
Jakov Yaakov Eliezer	Baron Brun	1927	Skopishki, Lithuania	PT	murdered
Josef Mendel Yosef	Baron Brun	1933	Skapiskis, Lithuania	PT	murdered
Lev Yehoshua	Baron Brun		Skapiskis, Lithuania	PT	murdered
Menakhem Mendel	Baron Brun		Skapiskis, Lithuania	PT	murdered
Mendel Yosef	Baron Brun	1933	Skapiskis, Lithuania	PT	murdered
Mendel Yosef	Baron Brun	1933	Skapiskis, Lithuania	PT	murdered
Meyer Meir	Baron Brun	1901	Kaunas, Lithuania	PT	murdered
Mordchaj Mordekhai	Baron Brun	1894	Skapiskis, Lithuania	PT	murdered
Motelis Mordekhai	Baron Brun		Skapiskis, Lithuania	PT	murdered
Natanel	Baron Brun		Skapiskis, Lithuania	PT	murdered
Netanel Natanel	Baron Brun	1929	Skapiskis, Lithuania	PT	murdered
Netanel Natanel	Baron Brun	1929	Skapiskis, Lithuania	PT	murdered
Rivka Gitel	Baron Brun	1896	Skapiskis, Lithuania	PT	murdered
Yaakov Eliezer	Baron Brun		Skapiskis, Lithuania	PT	murdered
Yitzkhak Leib	Baron Brun		Skapiskis, Lithuania	PT	murdered
Chaim Khaim	Barukh		Vilkomir, Lithuania	PT	murdered
Mozes	Basch	1917	Irhoc, Czechoslovakia	HLBV	murdered
David	Bedek	1915	Kowna, Lithuania	PT	murdered
David	Bedek	1916	Pandelys, Lithuania	PT	murdered
Gershon	Bedek		Ponidel, Lithuania	PT	murdered
Gershon Gerszon	Bedek	1888	Ponodol, Lithuania	PT	murdered
Sara	Bedek	1894	Ponodol, Lithuania	PT	murdered

Appendix of Rokiskis Shoah Victims – not in the original Yizkor Book   APP-5

First Name	Last Name	Birth Year	Place of Residence	Source	Fate from Source
Sera Sara	Bedek		Ponidel, Lithuania	PT	murdered
Zecharia Zakharia	Bedek	1920	Pondel, Lithuania	PT	murdered
Asnat	Beder		Rokiskis, Lithuania	Yzkr Bk	murdered
Chaim	Beder		Rokiskis, Lithuania	Yzkr Bk	murdered
Chaim	Beder		Rokiskis, Lithuania	PT D	murdered
Itzchak	Beder		Rokishkis, Lithuania	PT D	murdered
Karpel	Beder		Rokiskis, Lithuania	PT D	murdered
Libe	Beder		Rokiskis, Lithuania	Yzkr Bk	murdered
Moshe David	Beder		Rokiskis, Lithuania	Yzkr Bk	murdered
Pinchas Pinya	Beder		Rokiskis, Lithuania	PT D	murdered
Polikarp	Beder		Rokiskis, Lithuania	Yzkr Bk	murdered
Rachel Esther	Beder		Rokiskis, Lithuania	Yzkr Bk	murdered
Rivka	Beder		Rokiskis, Lithuania	Yzkr Bk	murdered
Sara	Beder		Rokiskis, Lithuania	Yzkr Bk	murdered
Shifra	Beder		Rokiskis, Lithuania	Yzkr Bk	murdered
Yaakov	Beder		Rokiskis, Lithuania	Yzkr Bk	murdered
Yaakov Pinkhas	Beder		Rokiskis, Lithuania	Yzkr Bk	murdered
Yehuda	Beder		Rokiskis, Lithuania	Yzkr Bk	murdered
Yekhiel	Beder		Rokiskis, Lithuania	Yzkr Bk	murdered
Yitzkhak	Beder		Rokiskis, Lithuania	Yzkr Bk	murdered
Aide Ide	Beilic Beilitz	1882	Kowno, Lithuania	PT	murdered
Aharon Zelig	Beinart	1892	Paris, France	PT	murdered
Soruch	Beinert	1879	Asares, Latvia	Census	not stated
Soruch	Beinert	1879	Riga, Latvia	Jew Res	not stated
Soruch	Beinert	1879	Riga, Latvia	Residen	not stated
Soruch	Beinert	1879	Riga, Latvia	Residen	not stated
Naumas	Beinertas	1884	Rokiskis, Lithuania	Deport	murdered
Sara	Beniamin Binjamin	1905	Krakenovo, Lithuania	PT	murdered
Breina	Beniaminowic Beniaminovitz		Rakishik, Lithuania	PT	murdered
Feiga	Beniaminowic Beniaminovitz		Rakishik, Lithuania	PT	murdered
Jakow Yaakov	Beniaminowic Beniaminovitz	1905	Rakishik, Lithuania	PT	murdered
Matla	Beniaminowic Beniaminovitz		Rakishik, Lithuania	PT	murdered
Avram Avraham Meir	Beniatovitz	1904	Eisziszok, Poland	PT	murdered
Rivka	Beniatovitz		Eisziszok, Poland	PT	murdered
Tzvia	Beniatovitz		Eisziszok, Poland	PT	murdered
Dov	Berelovic Berlovitz	1893	Rokishok, Lithuania	PT	murdered
David	Berelovitz		Rakiszki, Lithuania	PT	murdered
Lipot	Berger	1918	Kassa,	HLBV	murdered
Farkas	Berkovics	1916	Lipcse, Czechoslovakia	HLBV	murdered
Mendel	Berkovics	1916	Dombo,	HLBV	murdered
Salamon	Berkovics	1917	Oroszmokra, Czechoslovakia	HLBV	murdered
Meir	Berkovicz Berkovitz	1871	Rakisok, Lithuania	PT	murdered
Chaske Khaska	Berkowitz Berkovitz		Riga, Latvia	PT	murdered
Gershon	Berlovitz	1938	Rokiskis, Lithuania	PT	murdered
Erno	Bernath	1919	Bercssovaja,	HLBV	murdered

APP-6 Appendix of Rokiskis Shoah Victims – not in the original Yizkor Book

First Name	Last Name	Birth Year	Place of Residence	Source	Fate from Source
Sara	Berolski Barolski	1886	Panevezys, Lithuania	PT	murdered
Berl Boris Berel	Bers	1883	Riga, Latvia	PT	murdered
Berl	Berz Brez	1884	Riga, Latvia	PT	murdered
Berl	Berzak		Rokishok, Lithuania	PT	murdered
Gedalia	Berzak		Rokiskis, Lithuania	Yzkr Bk	murdered
Gedalya	Berzak		Rokiskis, Lithuania	PT D	murdered
Gitel	Berzak		Rokiskis, Lithuania	Yzkr Bk	murdered
Peretz Mordekhai	Berzak		Rokiskis, Lithuania	Yzkr Bk	murdered
היווס Hevus	Berzin Berezin	1886	Rakishok, Lithuania	PT	murdered
Liba	Berzon		Joniskelis, Lithuania	PT	murdered
Reuben	Berzon		Rokiskis, Lithuania	PT Ds	murdered
Rosa	Berzon		Rokiskis, Lithuania	PT Ds	murdered
Sosa	Berzon		Rokiskis, Lithuania	PT Ds	murdered
Rivka	Berzun Berezin		Rokishkis, Lithuania	PT	murdered
Zoosman Gershon Zusman	Bitzik Bichik	1870	Gilvan, Lithuania	PT	murdered
Gitl Gitel	Blacher Blekher	1893	Nacioniskis, Lithuania	PT	murdered
Izchag Moshe Yitzkhak	Blacher Blekher	1891	Nacioniskis, Lithuania	PT	murdered
Rakhel	Blakher		Skaistkalne, Latvia	PT	murdered
Nachmanas Nakhman	Blatas Blat	1907	Kaunas, Lithuania	PT	murdered
Sara	Blecher	1911	Riga, Latvia	Jew Res	not stated
Sara	Blecher	1911	Riga, Latvia	Residen	not stated
Khaim	Blum	1886	Rakishok, Lithuania	PT	murdered
Fruma Malka	Blumenthal	1911	Riga, Latvia	Jew Res	not stated
Fruma Malka	Blumenthal	1911	Riga, Latvia	Residen	not stated
Fruma Malka	Blumenthal	1911	Riga, Latvia	Residen	not stated
Isak	Bodnev	1886	Rokiskis, Lithuania	PT	murdered
Yaakov	Bodnev	1916	Rokishkis, Lithuania	PT	murdered
Zalman	Bodnev	1910	Rokiskis, Lithuania	PT	murdered
Khaya	Bodneva	1912	Rokishkis, Lithuania	PT	murdered
Rakhil	Bodneva	1888	Rokishkis, Lithuania	PT	murdered
Feibush	Boras Barash		Rekishok, Lithuania	PT	murdered
Malka	Boras Barash		Rekishok, Lithuania	PT	murdered
Mejeras Meir	Boras Barash		Rekishok, Lithuania	PT	murdered
Rafael	Boras Barash		Rekishok, Lithuania	PT	murdered
Yehoshua	Boras Barash		Rekishok, Lithuania	PT	murdered
Rafael	Boras Bor		Solzartow , Lithuania	PT	murdered
Yisrael Rafael	Boras Bor	1910	Moliat, Lithuania	PT	murdered
Feibush	Boras Borash		Rakishki, Lithuania	PT	murdered
Malka	Boras Borash		Rakishki, Lithuania	PT	murdered
Yehoshua	Boras Borash		Taurage, Lithuania	PT	murdered
Fruma Dveire Dvora	Borodafke Borodavka		Rokishkis, Lithuania	PT	murdered
Edel	Borodavka		Rakishik, Lithuania	PT	murdered
Eidel	Borodavka		Rokiskis, Lithuania	Yzkr Bk	murdered
Ester	Borodavka		Rokiskis, Lithuania	Yzkr Bk	murdered
Eta	Borodavka	1890	Rokiskis, Lithuania	PT	murdered
Etel	Borodavka		Rokiskis, Lithuania	Yzkr Bk	murdered
Rakhel	Borodavka		Rakeshik, Lithuania	PT	murdered
Rasel Rassel Rakhel	Borodavka	1895	Rokishkis, Lithuania	PT	murdered
Shaia	Borodavka		Rokiskis, Lithuania	PT	murdered
Yitzkhak	Borodavka		Rakishok, Lithuania	PT	murdered

Appendix of Rokiskis Shoah Victims – not in the original Yizkor Book   APP-7

First Name	Last Name	Birth Year	Place of Residence	Source	Fate from Source
Zalman	Borodavka		Rokiskis, Lithuania	Yzkr Bk	murdered
Zalmen	Borodavka Borodovka		Rokiskis, Lithuania	PT D	murdered
Eta	Borodawka Borodavka	1900	Rokiskis, Lithuania	PT	murdered
Smuel Shmuel	Borodov Borodavka	1892	Rokiskis, Lithuania	PT	murdered
Idel	Borodovka		Rokiskis, Lithuania	PT D	murdered
Serel Charles	Borodvka Borodavka	1896	Rokiskis, Lithuania	PT	murdered
Schaja	Bovodawka	1914	Rokishki, Lithuania	Persecut	not stated
Khaim	Brauman	1886	Rakishok, Lithuania	PT	murdered
Dov Avraham	Bravo		Rakishik, Lithuania	PT	murdered
Dvora	Bravo		Rakishik, Lithuania	PT	murdered
Eta	Bravo		Rakishik, Lithuania	PT	murdered
Zheni	Bravo		Rakishik, Lithuania	PT	murdered
Avraham Dov	Bravo Brua		Rokishkis, Lithuania	PT	murdered
Dvora	Bravo Brua		Rokishkis, Lithuania	PT	murdered
Elka	Bravo Brua		Rakishik, Lithuania	PT	murdered
Eta	Bravo Brua		Rokishkis, Lithuania	PT	murdered
Eugenia	Bravo Brua		Rokishkis, Lithuania	PT	murdered
Lipman	Bravo Brua	1896	Rokishkis, Lithuania	PT	murdered
Lipman	Bravo Brua	1896	Rekishok, Lithuania	PT	murdered
Rahel Mikha Rakhel	Bravo Brua		Rakishik, Lithuania	PT	murdered
Rakhel Mira	Bravo Brua		Rokishkis, Lithuania	PT	murdered
Sara	Bravo Brua		Rakishik, Lithuania	PT	murdered
Sara	Bravo Brua		Rokishkis, Lithuania	PT	murdered
Cerne Tserne Charna	Bregstein Bergshtein	1865	Panemune, Lithuania	PT	murdered
Chaim Zvi Hersch Khaim Tzvi Hersh	Bregstein Bergshtein	1860	Panemune, Lithuania	PT	murdered
Chaim Zvi Hirsch Khaim Tzvi Hirsh	Bregstein Bergshtein	1866	Ponemon, Lithuania	PT	murdered
Chana Khana	Bregstein Bergshtein	1893	Ponemon, Lithuania	PT	murdered
Chana Khana	Bregstein Bergshtein	1900	Panemune, Lithuania	PT	murdered
Joshua Yehoshua	Bregstein Bergshtein	1890	Panemune, Lithuania	PT	murdered
Herz	Breitbord	1892	Riga, Latvia	Jew Res	not stated
Herz	Breitbord	1892	Riga, Latvia	Residen	not stated
Aharon Elizabeta	Brikman	1911	Juzintai, Lithuania	PT D	murdered
Aharon Ortzik	Brikman		Rokiskis, Lithuania	Yzkr Bk	murdered
Asna Riva Rive Asnat	Brikman	1929	Kamajai, Lithuania	PT	murdered
Avraham	Brikman	1911	Yozint, Lithuania	PT D	murdered
Avraham	Brikman		Rokiskis, Lithuania	Yzkr Bk	murdered
Beniamin	Brikman	1892	Juzintas, Lithuania	PT D	murdered
Beniamin	Brikman		Rokiskis, Lithuania	Yzkr Bk	murdered
Chana	Brikman		Rokiskis, Lithuania	Yzkr Bk	murdered
Faia	Brikman	1898	Yozint, Lithuania	PT D	murdered
First name unknown	Brikman		Rokiskis, Lithuania	Yzkr Bk	murdered
First name unknown	Brikman		Rokiskis, Lithuania	Yzkr Bk	murdered
Iudl	Brikman		Rokiskis, Lithuania	Yzkr Bk	murdered
Iudl	Brikman		Yozint, Lithuania	PT D	murdered
Khana	Brikman		Yozint, Lithuania	PT D	murdered
Lea Ela	Brikman	1927	Kamajai, Lithuania	PT	murdered
Matilda Hinde	Brikman		Rokiskis, Lithuania	Yzkr Bk	murdered
Meir	Brikman	1923	Kamajai, Lithuania	PT	murdered

APP-8   Appendix of Rokiskis Shoah Victims – not in the original Yizkor Book

First Name	Last Name	Birth Year	Place of Residence	Source	Fate from Source
Moshe	Brikman		Rokiskis, Lithuania	Yzkr Bk	murdered
Motel Khaim	Brikman	1900	Kamajai, Lithuania	PT	murdered
Reuven Ruven	Brikman	1921	Kamai, Lithuania	PT	murdered
Ruvim Reuven Khaim	Brikman	1919	Kamajai, Lithuania	PT	murdered
Ruvin Reuven	Brikman	1920	Kamajai, Lithuania	PT	murdered
Shore Sara	Brikman	1905	Kamajai, Lithuania	PT	murdered
Zalman	Brikman	1908	Juzintai, Lithuania	PT D	murdered
Zalman Zelig	Brikman		Rokiskis, Lithuania	Yzkr Bk	murdered
Getzel	Brikmann	1891	Riga, Latvia	Jew Res	murdered
Getzel	Brikmann	1891	Riga, Latvia	Residen	not stated
Getzel	Brikmann	1891	Riga, Latvia	Residen	not stated
Hirsch	Brikmann	1888	Riga, Latvia	Jew Res	not stated
Hirsch	Brikmann	1888	Riga, Latvia	Residen	not stated
Isak	Brikmann	1891	Riga, Latvia	Jew Res	murdered
Isak	Brikmann	1891	Riga, Latvia	Residen	not stated
Isak	Brikmann	1891	Riga, Latvia	Residen	not stated
Isak	Brikmann	1891	Riga, Latvia	Residen	not stated
Isak	Brikmann	1891	Riga, Latvia	Residen	not stated
Charles	Brilkin		Abel, Lithuania	PT	murdered
Khaim Yitzkhak	Brilkin	1897	Obeliai, Lithuania	PT	murdered
Khaim Yitzkhak	Brilkin		Abeli, Lithuania	PT	murdered
Sara	Brilkin	1897	Obeliai, Lithuania	PT	murdered
Nechama	Brinkmann	1925	Kamajai, Lithuania	Persecut	not stated
Gitel	Brizman		Vilnius, Poland	PT	murdered
Shimon	Brodawka Borodavka	1886	Rokiskis, Lithuania	PT	murdered
Eta	Brodovka		Rakiski, Lithuania	PT	murdered
Khaim	Bron Braun Veinshtein	1914	Vilkomir, Lithuania	PT	murdered
Feigel	Bronman		Skopiski, Lithuania	PT	murdered
Fania	Broon Brun	1875	Kowno, Lithuania	PT	murdered
Mordchaj Mordekhai	Brun	1894	Skapiskis, Lithuania	PT	murdered
Frida	Bun	1888	Rakishok, Lithuania	PT	murdered
Hana Riveka Khana Rivka	Bun	1909	Rakishok, Lithuania	PT	murdered
Iudl	Bun	1875	Rokiskis, Lithuania	PT	murdered
Yitzkhak	Bun	1911	Rakishok, Lithuania	PT	murdered
Asher	Bun Nan		Abel, Lithuania	PT	murdered
Feibush	Bun Nan		Abel, Lithuania	PT	murdered
Moshe	Bun Nan		Abel, Lithuania	PT	murdered
Pesia	Bun Nan	1901	Abel, Lithuania	PT	murdered
Pesa Sara	Bunimovitz		Rokiskis, Lithuania	Yzkr Bk	murdered
Tibor	Burg	1919	Debrecen, Hungary	HLBV	murdered
Chone Leib	Burin		Suvainiskis, Lithuania	PT D	murdered
Sara	Burshtein	1876	Kowno, Lithuania	PT	murdered
Sarah Sara	Burstein Burshtein		Aleksat, Lithuania	PT	murdered
Mordechai Mordekhai	Buselevitz Bushelevitz	1909	Abeliai, Lithuania	PT	murdered
Pesia	Buselevitz Bushelevitz	1912	Abeliai, Lithuania	PT	murdered
Alter	Cados	1891	Rakishok, Lithuania	PT	murdered
Alter	Cados Tzades		Rokiskis, Lithuania	PT	murdered
Chaim	Carnick	1870	Lithuania	PT	murdered
Chana	Carnick	1870	Lithuania	PT	murdered
Hovel	Carnick		Rakishok, Lithuania	PT	murdered

Appendix of Rokiskis Shoah Victims – not in the original Yizkor Book   APP-9

First Name	Last Name	Birth Year	Place of Residence	Source	Fate from Source
Libby	Carnick		Rakishok, Lithuania	PT	murdered
Meyer	Carnick		Rakishok, Lithuania	PT	murdered
Mirl Mirel	Carnick		Rokiskis, Lithuania	PT	murdered
Moshe	Carnick		Rakishok, Lithuania	PT	murdered
Rivka	Carnick		Rakishok, Lithuania	PT	murdered
Sonia	Carnick		Rakishok, Lithuania	PT	murdered
Tamara	Carnick	1870	Rakishok, Lithuania	PT	murdered
Dvore Dvora Gitel	Cemachovic Tzemakhovitz	1880	Rakishik, Lithuania	PT	murdered
Notel Nutel	Chajetovit Kheitovitz	1890	Rakisok, Lithuania	PT	murdered
Asher	Chajetoviz Kheitovitz	1884	Rakisok, Lithuania	PT	murdered
Miryam Miriam	Charchas Kharkhas		Rokiskis, Lithuania	PT	murdered
Shmuel	Charmatz		Rokiskis, Lithuania	PT D	murdered
Chaim Khaim	Chasman Khasman	1902	Rokiskis, Lithuania	PT	murdered
Hendale Hinda	Chasman Khasman	1934	Rokiskis, Lithuania	PT	murdered
Khaim	Chasman Khasman	1886	Rakishik, Lithuania	PT	murdered
Rivka	Chasman Khasman	1904	Rokiskis, Lithuania	PT	murdered
Rochale Ruchla	Chasman Khasman		Rokiskis, Lithuania	PT	murdered
Yosale Yosef	Chasman Khasman	1936	Rokiskis, Lithuania	PT	murdered
Avraham	Chaytoviz		Rokiskis, Lithuania	PT D	murdered
Libe Sure	Chazan		Rokiskis, Lithuania	PT	murdered
Pessie	Chazan		Rokiskis, Lithuania	PT	murdered
Bere Leib	Chein Khan	1871	Rokishok, Lithuania	PT	murdered
Mordekhai	Chertok	1887	Panemune, Lithuania	PT	perished beyond Nazi occupation lines
Rivka	Chidekel		Daugavpils, Latvia	PT	murdered
Chaja Khaia	Chirurg Khirurg		Kamajai, Lithuania	PT	murdered
Khanania	Chirurg Khirurg		Kamajai, Lithuania	PT	murdered
Khanania	Chirurg Khirurg		Kamajai, Lithuania	PT	murdered
Meir	Chirurg Khirurg	1914	Kamajai, Lithuania	PT	murdered
Sonia	Chirurg Khirurg	1916	Kamajai, Lithuania	PT	murdered
Chava Debora Khava Dvora	Cibuliene Tzibul		Uspol, Lithuania	PT	murdered
Mina	Cibuliene Tzibul		Rokiskis, Lithuania	PT	murdered
Benjaminas Beniamin	Cibulis Tzibul		Rokiskis, Lithuania	PT	murdered
Moshe	Cimerman Tzimerman		Plungian, Lithuania	PT	murdered
David	Cin Tzin	1901	Rokiskis, Lithuania	PT	murdered
Iudl	Cindler Tzindler	1891	Rakishok, Lithuania	PT	murdered
Beila Bila	Cinman Tzinman	1905	Rokiskis, Lithuania	PT	murdered
Sheina	Cirt Tzirt		Nacioniskis, Lithuania	PT	murdered
Fanya Fania	Codikov Tzodikov	1902	Panemune, Lithuania	PT	murdered
Nachman Nakhman	Codikov Tzodikov	1897	Panemune, Lithuania	PT	murdered
Nathan Natan	Codikov Tzodikov	1923	Panemune, Lithuania	PT	murdered
Reizl	Cukernik Tzukernik	1914	Rokiskis, Lithuania	PT	murdered
Nachum Nakhum	Cveigorn Zweihorn	1900	Kowno, Lithuania	PT	murdered
Abrakham Avraham	Daitz Doich	1865	Genichesk, Ukraine (USSR)	PT	murdered
Mina	Daitz Doich	1865	Genichesk, Ukraine (USSR)	PT	murdered

APP-10   Appendix of Rokiskis Shoah Victims – not in the original Yizkor Book

First Name	Last Name	Birth Year	Place of Residence	Source	Fate from Source
Liba Libke Libe	Davidovic Davidovitz	1904	Iwje, Poland	PT	murdered
Itel	Davidovich Davidovitz	1895	Rokiskis, Lithuania	PT	murdered
Yosef	Davidovitz		Ponedel, Lithuania	PT	murdered
Chaia	Davidovitz Davidovich		Rokiskis, Lithuania	Yzkr Bk	murdered
Yitzkhak	Davidovitz Davidovich		Rokiskis, Lithuania	Yzkr Bk	murdered
Chaim Khaim	Davidoviz Davidovitz Davidovich	1902	Rokiskis, Lithuania	PT	murdered
Aba	Davidson	1895	Posvol, Lithuania	PT	murdered
Michla Mikhla	Davidson	1874	Rokiskis, Lithuania	PT	murdered
Mikhla	Davidson		Rokiskis, Lithuania	PT	murdered
Yehuda	Davidson	1908	Rokiskis, Lithuania	PT	murdered
Yehuda	Davidson		Rokiskis, Lithuania	PT	murdered
Zakharia	Davidson		Birzai, Lithuania	PT	murdered
Sacharjahu Zakhariahu	Davidzon Davidson	1906	Rokiskis, Lithuania	PT	murdered
Yehuda	Dawidon Davidon	1908	Kamajai, Lithuania	PT	murdered
Elle Ele	Dawidowitz Davidovitz		Ponidel, Lithuania	PT	murdered
First name unknown	Dawidowitz Davidovitz			PT	murdered
First name unknown	Dawidowitz Davidovitz			PT	murdered
First name unknown	Dawidowitz Davidovitz			PT	murdered
Izrael Yehuda Azriel	Decktor Dektor	1877	Rokiskis, Lithuania	PT	murdered
Tova	Decktor Dektor	1876	Rokiskis, Lithuania	PT	murdered
Azriel Yehuda	Degtiar		Rokiskis, Lithuania	Yzkr Bk	murdered
Liube	Degtiar		Rokiskis, Lithuania	Yzkr Bk	murdered
Toibe	Degtiar		Rokiskis, Lithuania	Yzkr Bk	murdered
Toibe	Degtiar		Rokishki, Lithuania	PT	murdered
Yehuda	Degtiar		Rakishki, Lithuania	PT	murdered
Tova	Dekter	1873	Rokishki, Lithuania	PT	murdered
Yehuda	Dekter	1869	Rakishik, Lithuania	PT	murdered
Luba Lea	Dektor		Rokiskis, Lithuania	PT	murdered
Mendelis Menakhem Mendel	Dektoras Dektor	1875	Rokiskis, Lithuania	PT	murdered
Beile Beila	Dektoriene Dektor	1880	Rokiskis, Lithuania	PT	murdered
Erno	Deutsch	1919	Puspokladany Foldos,	HLBV	murdered
Lipka	Diamand		Ponedel, Lithuania	PT	murdered
Sofiya	Diner	1914	Rokishkis, Lithuania	Evac	not stated
Faivel Phyvel	Domovich Domowitz	1905	Lasday, Lithuania	PT Ds	murdered
Pesia	Domoviciene Domovich	1920	Rokiskis, Lithuania	PT	murdered
Pesia	Domovitsh Domovich		Rokiskis, Lithuania	PT	murdered
Szneur Shneiur	Dori	1889	Aleksanderski, Lithuania	PT	murdered
Sora Eide	Drujan	1895	Riga, Latvia	Jew Res	not stated
Sora Eide	Drujan	1895	Riga, Latvia	Residen	not stated
Elke Chana	Dubianski		Rokiskis, Lithuania	Yzkr Bk	murdered
Feiga	Dubianski		Rokiskis, Lithuania	Yzkr Bk	murdered
First name unknown	Dubianski		Rokiskis, Lithuania	Yzkr Bk	murdered
First name unknown	Dubianski		Rokiskis, Lithuania	Yzkr Bk	murdered
Natl Notl	Dubianski		Rokiskis, Lithuania	Yzkr Bk	murdered
Reizl	Dubianski		Rokiskis, Lithuania	Yzkr Bk	murdered
Shalom	Dubianski		Rokiskis, Lithuania	Yzkr Bk	murdered
Motel	Dubinsky		Rokiskis, Lithuania	PT D	murdered
Reyzel	Dubinsky		Rokiskis, Lithuania	PT D	murdered

Appendix of Rokiskis Shoah Victims – not in the original Yizkor Book   APP-11

First Name	Last Name	Birth Year	Place of Residence	Source	Fate from Source
Shalom	Dubinsky		Rokiskis, Lithuania	PT D	murdered
Shalom	Dubov	1917	Pandelis, Lithuania	PT	murdered
Yehuda Moshe	Dunai	1922	Rakishok, Lithuania	PT	murdered
Aharon	Duviansky Dubianski	1896	Panemun, Lithuania	PT	murdered
Rachel Rakhel	Duviavsky	1905	Panemune, Lithuania	PT	murdered
Izia Yitzkhak	Eckdesh Ekdisz	1931	Shavli, Lithuania	PT	murdered
Sime	Edelman		Rokiskis, Lithuania	Yzkr Bk	murdered
Muschka	Edelstein	1875	Riga, Latvia	Jew Res	murdered
Muschka	Edelstein	1875	Riga, Latvia	Residen	not stated
Chana Gittel Khana Gitel	Edges Edzhes	1925	Pandelys, Lithuania	PT	murdered
Elke Elka	Edges Edzhes	1899	Pandelys, Lithuania	PT	murdered
Fiva Nossen Feiva Nusen	Edges Edzhes	1920	Pandelys, Lithuania	PT	murdered
Sarah Sara	Edges Edzhes	1923	Pandelys, Lithuania	PT	murdered
Yancov Yaakov	Edges Edzhes	1899	Pandelys, Lithuania	PT	murdered
Menakhem Mendel	Egdish		Ponidel, Lithuania	PT	murdered
Avraham	Egdish Hekdesh		Ponedel, Lithuania	PT	murdered
Mosze Moshe	Egdisz Hekdesh	1911	Shavli, Lithuania	PT	murdered
Rachil	Egtus	1894	Riga, Latvia	Jew Res	not stated
Rachil	Egtus	1894	Riga, Latvia	Residen	not stated
Rachil	Egtus	1894	Riga, Latvia	Residen	not stated
Rachil	Egtus	1894	Riga, Latvia	Residen	not stated
Zalman	Eidelman	1891	Rakishok, Lithuania	PT	murdered
Sheva	Eidelman Idelman	1885	Uzpalis, Lithuania	PT	murdered
Chana Khana	Eidelson		Rokiskis, Lithuania	PT	murdered
Hilel	Eidelson	1861	Rokiskis, Lithuania	PT	murdered
Hilleil Hilel	Eidelson		Lithuania	PT	murdered
Hilleil Hilel	Eidelson		Lithuania	PT	murdered
Schimen	Eischischki	1917	Suvainiskis, Lithuania	Persecut	murdered
Izidor	Eisdorfer	1919	Szuszko, Czechoslovakia	HLBV	murdered
Miklos	Eisdorfer	1919	Tiszabezded, Hungary	HLBV	murdered
Shimen	Eishishki		Suvainiskis, Lithuania	Persecut	murdered
Ignac	Eisikovics	1913	Botfalva,	HLBV	murdered
Goda	Elperin Alperin	1903	Leningrad, Russia (USSR)	PT	murdered
Berl	Epshtein	1910	Rokishok, Lithuania	PT	murdered
Heselis Yehoshua Heshil	Epsteinas Epshtein	1876	Kelme, Lithuania	PT	murdered
Asna Asnat	Erman	1900	Abel, Lithuania	PT	murdered
Dvora	Erman	1920	Abel, Lithuania	PT	murdered
Dvora	Erman	1920	Abel, Lithuania	PT	murdered
Faivl Faivel	Erman	1921	Abel, Lithuania	PT	murdered
Haia Khaia Dvora	Erman	1918	Abel, Lithuania	PT	murdered
Khanokh	Erman	1926	Abel, Lithuania	PT	murdered
Lipa	Erman	1920	Abel, Lithuania	PT	murdered
Mina	Erman		Abel, Lithuania	PT	murdered
Miriam	Erman		Abel, Lithuania	PT	murdered
Moshe	Erman	1890	Abel, Lithuania	PT	murdered
Nekhama	Erman		Abel, Lithuania	PT	murdered
Sara	Erman	1890	Abel, Lithuania	PT	murdered
Slava	Erman		Abel, Lithuania	PT	murdered
Yeshayahu	Erman		Abel, Lithuania	PT	murdered
Isaak	Eros	1913	Svedasai, Lithuania	Evac	not stated

APP-12   Appendix of Rokiskis Shoah Victims – not in the original Yizkor Book

First Name	Last Name	Birth Year	Place of Residence	Source	Fate from Source
Mira	Etingof	1899	Rokiskis, Lithuania	PT	murdered
Rima	Etingof	1922	Rokiskis, Lithuania	PT	murdered
Rima	Etingofayte	1923	Panevezhis, Lithuania	PT	murdered
Fania	Etingoff Etingof	1910	Rakishok, Lithuania	PT	murdered
Bathia Batia	Evin Avin	1927	Ponidel, Lithuania	PT	murdered
David	Evin Avin	1925	Panedel, Lithuania	PT	murdered
Feibosh Feibush	Evin Avin		Pandelys, Lithuania	PT	murdered
Leaa Lea	Evin Avin		Ponidel, Lithuania	PT	murdered
Yehudit	Evin Avin	1933	Ponidel, Lithuania	PT	murdered
Ciril Tzira	Ewen Even	1890	Pandelys, Lithuania	PT	murdered
Fruma	Ewen Even	1906	Pandelis, Lithuania	PT	murdered
Rachel Rakhel	Ewen Even	1900	Pandelys, Lithuania	PT	murdered
Henie Henia	Ezrachiene Ezrakh	1860	Pandelys, Lithuania	PT	murdered
Hena	Ezrah Ezrakh	1890	Ponedel, Lithuania	PT	murdered
Aba	Fabricovic		Kupishki, Lithuania	PT	murdered
Zalman	Fabricovic	1900	Pandelis, Lithuania	PT	murdered
Malka	Fabricovich	1898	Pandelis, Lithuania	PT	murdered
Meyer	Fabricovich	1888	Kupishki, Lithuania	PT	murdered
Shenka	Fabricovich	1894	Pandelis, Lithuania	PT	murdered
Sore Riva	Fabricovich	1857	Pandelis, Lithuania	PT	murdered
Abram	Fain	1878	Riga, Latvia	Jew Res	murdered
Abram	Fain	1878	Riga, Latvia	Residen	not stated
Abram	Fain	1878	Riga, Latvia	Residen	not stated
Bene	Fain Fein		Skapiskis, Lithuania	PT	murdered
Gershon Gerson	Fain Fein		Skapiskis, Lithuania	PT	murdered
Khainkh	Falber	1883	Komai, Lithuania	Evac	not stated
Robert	Falkin	1923	USSR	PT	killed in military service
First name unknown	Farber		Rokiskis, Lithuania	Yzkr Bk	murdered
Miriam	Farber		Rokiskis, Lithuania	Yzkr Bk	murdered
Sheine	Farber		Rokiskis, Lithuania	Yzkr Bk	murdered
Sheyna	Farber		Rokiskis, Lithuania	PT D	murdered
Yosef Chaim	Farber		Rokiskis, Lithuania	Yzkr Bk	murdered
Efraim	Farber Ferber	1920	Kamajai, Lithuania	PT	murdered
Ida	Farber Ferber	1900	Rokiskis, Lithuania	PT	murdered
Ida	Farber Ferber		Rakishki, Lithuania	PT	murdered
Israel Yisrael	Farber Ferber	1930	Obeliai, Lithuania	PT	murdered
Israil Yisrael	Farber Ferber	1927	Obeliai, Lithuania	PT	murdered
Joske Yosef Ioske	Farber Ferber	1932	Obeliai, Lithuania	PT	murdered
Khaia	Farber Ferber	1870	Rokiskis, Lithuania	PT	murdered
Khaimale Khaim	Farber Ferber	1931	Obeliai, Lithuania	PT	murdered
Mikhle Mikhla	Farber Ferber	1901	Obeliai, Lithuania	PT	murdered
Mikhle Mikhla	Farber Ferber		Obeliai, Lithuania	PT	murdered
Moisei Moshe	Farber Ferber	1870	Rokiskis, Lithuania	PT	murdered
Nekhama	Farber Ferber		Rekishka, Lithuania	PT	perished beyond Nazi occupation lines

Appendix of Rokiskis Shoah Victims – not in the original Yizkor Book   APP-13

First Name	Last Name	Birth Year	Place of Residence	Source	Fate from Source
Rafael	Farber Ferber	1900	Obeliai, Lithuania	PT	murdered
Rafael Rafail	Farber Ferber	1897	Obeliai, Lithuania	PT	murdered
Rivka	Farber Ferber	1935	Obeliai, Lithuania	PT	murdered
Yehuda	Farber Ferber	1923	Rokiskis, Lithuania	PT	killed in military service
Hava	Feigin	1890	Riga, Latvia	Census	not stated
Hava	Feigin	1890	Riga, Latvia	Jew Res	not stated
Hava	Feigin	1890	Riga, Latvia	Residen	not stated
Rosa Rebecka	Feigin	1913	Riga, Latvia	Census	not stated
Rosa Rebecka	Feigin	1913	Riga, Latvia	Jew Res	not stated
Tibor	Fein	1920	Baranya Magocs, Hungary	HLBV	murdered
Schepsel	Feinberg	1902	Skapiskis, Lithuania	Persecut	murdered
Hava	Feldmann	1923	Riebini, Latvia	Jew Res	not stated
Zive	Feldmann	1924	Riebini, Latvia	Jew Res	not stated
Michla Mikhla	Ferber	1905	Obeliai, Lithuania	PT	murdered
Lea	Ferber Farber		Rakishki, Lithuania	PT	murdered
Moshe Aharon	Ferber Farber		Rakiski, Lithuania	PT	murdered
Mera	Ferd	1893	Riga, Latvia	Jew Res	not stated
Mera	Ferd	1893	Riga, Latvia	Residen	not stated
Mera	Ferd	1893	Riga, Latvia	Residen	not stated
Mera	Ferd	1893	Riga, Latvia	Residen	not stated
Mera	Ferd	1893	Riga, Latvia	Residen	not stated
Leizer	Fidler	1914	Rokiskis, Lithuania	PT	murdered
Riwka Rivka	Fingerbren	1909	Rokishok, Lithuania	PT	murdered
Shara Sara	Finkel	1906	Utian, Lithuania	PT	murdered
Natan	Finkelstein Finkelshtein	1891	Rokiskis, Lithuania	PT	murdered
Lea	Fishelevich	1913	Kowno, Lithuania	PT	murdered
Reuven	Fishelevich		Kovne, Lithuania	PT	murdered
Rut	Fishelevich		Kowno, Lithuania	PT	murdered
Adashe Edsha	Fishman		Panevezys, Lithuania	PT	murdered
Hirsh	Fishman		Rokiskis, Lithuania	Yzkr Bk	murdered
Matia	Fishman		Rokiskis, Lithuania	PT D	murdered
Motie	Fishman		Rokiskis, Lithuania	Yzkr Bk	murdered
Rivka	Fishman		Rokiskis, Lithuania	Yzkr Bk	murdered
Yitzkhak Aharon	Fishman		Rokiskis, Lithuania	Yzkr Bk	murdered
Zelda	Fishman		Rokiskis, Lithuania	Yzkr Bk	murdered
Hana	Flack	1888	Riga, Latvia	Jew Res	not stated
Hana	Flack	1888	Riga, Latvia	Residen	not stated
Hana	Flack	1888	Riga, Latvia	Residen	not stated
Hana	Flack	1888	Riga, Latvia	Residen	not stated
Hana	Flack	1888	Riga, Latvia	Residen	not stated
Dusia	Flaks		Ponidel, Lithuania	PT	murdered
Shneiur	Flaks		Ponidel, Lithuania	PT	murdered
Sneuris Shneiur	Flaksas Flaks		Pandelys, Lithuania	PT	murdered
Dusia	Flaksiene Flaks		Pandelys, Lithuania	PT	murdered
Chaim	Flax		Ponedel, Lithuania	Persecut	murdered
Chana	Flax		Ponedel, Lithuania	Persecut	murdered
First name unknown	Flax		Ponedel, Lithuania	Persecut	murdered
First name unknown	Flax		Ponedel, Lithuania	Persecut	murdered

APP-14   Appendix of Rokiskis Shoah Victims – not in the original Yizkor Book

First Name	Last Name	Birth Year	Place of Residence	Source	Fate from Source
First name unknown	Flax		Ponedel, Lithuania	Persecut	murdered
Musha	Flax		Ponedel, Lithuania	Persecut	murdered
Schneur	Flax		Ponedel, Lithuania	Persecut	murdered
Yizchak	Flax		Ponedel, Lithuania	Persecut	murdered
Dusia	Flax Flaks		Ponidel, Lithuania	PT	murdered
Hana Hena	Flax Flaks		Ponidel, Lithuania	PT	murdered
Ytzkhak Yitzkhak	Flax Flaks		Ponidel, Lithuania	PT	murdered
Mikhl	Fon		Panedel, Lithuania	Murd	murdered
Tzipora	Fon		Panedel, Lithuania	Murd	murdered
Rocha Nesa	Fradkin	1880	Riga, Latvia	Jew Res	murdered
Rocha Nesa	Fradkin	1880	Riga, Latvia	Residen	not stated
Rocha Nesa	Fradkin	1880	Riga, Latvia	Residen	not stated
Baruc Barukh	Franc Frank	1886	Rakisok, Lithuania	PT	murdered
Sandor	Freimann	1913	Kassa,	HLBV	murdered
Majer Meir	Fridman	1910	Lithuania	PT	murdered
Moishe	Fridman	1890	Abeliai, Lithuania	PT	murdered
Moshe	Fridman	1925	Obeliai, Lithuania	PT	murdered
Moska	Fridman	1922	Obeliai, Lithuania	PT	murdered
Musya	Fridman	1927	Abeliai, Lithuania	PT	murdered
Perel	Fridman	1893	Obeliai, Lithuania	PT	murdered
Shlomo	Fridman		Rokiskis, Lithuania	Yzkr Bk	murdered
Tzipe	Fridman		Rokiskis, Lithuania	Yzkr Bk	murdered
Yitzkhak	Fridman	1893	Obeliai, Lithuania	PT	murdered
Yuda	Fridman	1929	Abeliai, Lithuania	PT	murdered
Mira Miriam	Fridmanaitl Fridman	1911	Rokiskis, Lithuania	PT	murdered
Meir	Fridmanas Fridman	1912	Rakiski, Lithuania	PT	murdered
Marton	Fried	1918	Tekehaza, Czechoslovakia	HLBV	murdered
Fanny	Friedmann	1892	Riga, Latvia	Jew Res	not stated
Fanny	Friedmann	1892	Riga, Latvia	Residen	not stated
Fanny	Friedmann	1892	Riga, Latvia	Residen	not stated
Fanny	Friedmann	1892	Riga, Latvia	Residen	not stated
Fanny	Friedmann	1892	Riga, Latvia	Residen	not stated
Mosus	Friedmann	1877	Riga, Latvia	Jew Res	not stated
Mosus	Friedmann	1877	Riga, Latvia	Residen	not stated
Mosus	Friedmann	1877	Riga, Latvia	Residen	not stated
Mira	Froman Fruman	1932	Wilkomir, Lithuania	PT	murdered
Aba Yona	Frumkin		Skopishki, Lithuania	PT	murdered
Elieser Eliezer	Frumkin	1891	Skapiskis, Lithuania	PT	murdered
Kejla Keila	Frumkin	1896	Skopishki, Lithuania	PT	murdered
Reuven	Frumkin		Skopishki, Lithuania	PT	murdered
Yisrael	Frumkin		Skopishki, Lithuania	PT	murdered
Hana Khana	Frydman Fridman	1906	Rokiszki, Lithuania	PT	murdered
Miriam	Frydman Fridman	1909	Rokiszki, Lithuania	PT	murdered
Hadasa	Frydman Shtein Fridman Shulman	1908	Rokiszki, Lithuania	PT	murdered
Menachem Mendel	Fulda	1848	Siauliai, Lithuania	PT	murdered
Sarah Malka	Fulda	1921	Siauliai, Lithuania	PT	murdered
Aide Feige	Fulman		Rokiskis, Lithuania	Yzkr Bk	murdered
Rivka	Fulman		Rokiskis, Lithuania	Yzkr Bk	murdered
Gregor Grisha	Furmansky		Rokiskis, Lithuania	PT	murdered

Appendix of Rokiskis Shoah Victims – not in the original Yizkor Book   APP-15

First Name	Last Name	Birth Year	Place of Residence	Source	Fate from Source
Jefim	Furmansky		Rokiskis, Lithuania	PT	murdered
Misha	Furmansky		Rokiskis, Lithuania	PT	murdered
Polia	Furmansky		Rakiski, Lithuania	PT	murdered
Tonia	Furmansky	1922	Rokiskis, Lithuania	PT	murdered
Reuven	Gafanovic Gafanovitz	1888	Rakishok, Lithuania	PT	murdered
Yisrael	Gafanovic Gafanovitz	1886	Rokiskis, Lithuania	PT	murdered
Devarah	Gafanovich	1909	Memel, Lithuania	PT	murdered
Mendel Minachem	Gafanovich	1873	Rokiskis, Lithuania	PT	murdered
Ruvan	Gafanovich	1905	Rokiskis, Lithuania	PT	murdered
Zalmen Zamke	Gafanovich	1903	Rokiskis, Lithuania	PT	murdered
Zalman	Gafanovich Gafanovitz	1891	Rakishok, Lithuania	PT	murdered
Chona Haimke	Gafanovitch	1933	Rokiskis, Lithuania	PT	murdered
Feyga Rocha	Gafanovitch	1906	Rokiskis, Lithuania	PT	murdered
Moshe Leibe	Gafanovitch	1931	Rokiskis, Lithuania	PT	murdered
Sara Dina	Gafanovitch	1937	Rokiskis, Lithuania	PT	murdered
Roza	Gafanovitz גאפאנאוויץ		Rokiskis, Lithuania	Yzkr Bk	murdered
Feiga	Gafanoviz Gafanovitz	1904	Rakishik, Lithuania	PT	murdered
Khaimke Khaim	Gafanoviz Gafanovitz		Rakishik, Lithuania	PT	murdered
Moshe	Gafanoviz Gafanovitz		Rakishik, Lithuania	PT	murdered
Sarale Sara	Gafanoviz Gafanovitz		Rakishik, Lithuania	PT	murdered
Chaya	Gafenovich		Rokiskis, Lithuania	PT D	murdered
Awraham Avraham	Gafinowic Gafinovitz		Skapiskis, Lithuania	PT	murdered
Yitzkhak Mose Ithac Moshe	Gafnovit Gafanovitz		Rakiski, Lithuania	PT	murdered
Rivka	Galperin		Rokiskis, Lithuania	PT D	murdered
Miriam	Gandelman	1898	Rokishki, Lithuania	PT	murdered
Moris	Gandelman	1896	Rakishok, Lithuania	PT	murdered
Avsey	Gar	1882	Kamai, Lithuania	Evac	not stated
R	Gar	1884	Kamai, Lithuania	Evac	not stated
Riva	Gar	1917	Kamai, Lithuania	Evac	not stated
Khaia	Garbar Graber	1913	Rakishok, Lithuania	PT	murdered
Shlomo	Gec Gatz	1895	Rakishok, Lithuania	PT	murdered
Sarah	Geffenovitz		Rokiskis, Lithuania	PT D	murdered
Fyodor	Gegner	1908		PT	killed in military service
Oszkar	Gelbmann	1919	Balmazújváros, Hungary	HLBV	murdered
Gitel	Gelburt Gelbard	1913	Panimon, Lithuania	PT	murdered
Yisrael	Gelburt Gelbard		Panimon, Lithuania	PT	murdered
Mose Moshe	Gelcer Geltzer	1891	Rakishok, Lithuania	PT	murdered
Beniamin	Gelfer	1938	Obeliai, Lithuania	PT	murdered
Icik Itzik Zelig	Gelfer	1928	Obeliai, Lithuania	PT	murdered
Mordekhai	Gelfer	1908	Wilno, Poland	PT	murdered
Motel Mordekhai	Gelfer	1908	Obeliai, Lithuania	PT	murdered
Sonia	Gelfer	1910	Obeliai, Lithuania	PT	murdered
Sonia	Gellermann	1915	Daugavpils, Latvia	Census	not stated
Sonia	Gellermann	1915	Daugavpils, Latvia	Jew Res	not stated
Jeguda	Gelzer	1927	Rokishkis, Lithuania	Persecut	not stated
Khana	Gen		Birz, Lithuania	PT	murdered
Masza Moshe	Gendl Gendel	1901	Kamai, Lithuania	PT	murdered
Beba	German		Kalvaria, Lithuania	PT	murdered

APP-16   Appendix of Rokiskis Shoah Victims – not in the original Yizkor Book

First Name	Last Name	Birth Year	Place of Residence	Source	Fate from Source
Aviva	Gersater Gershator		Rokishkis, Lithuania	PT	murdered
Sara	Gersateriene Gershator	1907	Rokishkis, Lithuania	PT	murdered
Scheine Sheina	Gerschon Gershon		Kovno, Lithuania	PT	murdered
Zorach Jcchok Zerakh Yitzkhak	Gerschon Gershon		Rakiskai, Lithuania	PT	murdered
Haja Rachel Khaia Rekhel	Gersenovitz Gershonovitz	1875	Ponidel, Lithuania	PT	murdered
Refael Benedikt Rafael B	Gersenovitz Gershonovitz	1875	Kvatki, Lithuania	PT	murdered
Chaia Rekel Khava Rekhel	Gershenovitz Gershonovitz	1883	Ponidel, Lithuania	PT	murdered
Musha Moshe	Gershon		Rakiski, Lithuania	PT	murdered
Simon Shimon	Gershon	1898	Rakiski, Lithuania	PT	murdered
Refael Beinysz Rafael Beniamin	Gershonovitz		Ponidel, Lithuania	PT	murdered
Ben Zion Bentzion	Gerszuni Gershuni	1888	Suwailiszki, Lithuania	PT	murdered
Pirl Perel	Gerszuni Gershuni	1899	Suwailiszki, Lithuania	PT	murdered
Bat Sheva Sonia	Geseleviciute	1910	Birzai, Lithuania	PT	murdered
Girsh	Getz	1904	Rokishkis, Lithuania	PT	murdered
Razel Razele	Getz		Rokiskis, Lithuania	PT	murdered
Sara Khasia	Getz	1913	Rokishkis, Lithuania	PT	murdered
Sora Khasa	Getz	1908	Rokishkis, Lithuania	PT	murdered
	Ghefnovici Gafnowitz Gafanovitz		Rakiski, Lithuania	PT	murdered
Josef Yosef	Gilevic Gilevitz	1922	Kovne, Lithuania	PT	murdered
Avraham	Ginsburg		Suvainiskis, Lithuania	PT	murdered
Leizer	Ginsburg		Suvainiskis, Lithuania	PT	murdered
Musia Chana	Ginsburg		Rokiskis, Lithuania	Yzkr Bk	murdered
Rachel	Ginsburg		Rokiskis, Lithuania	Yzkr Bk	murdered
Rafael Yosef	Ginsburg		Rokiskis, Lithuania	Yzkr Bk	murdered
Rafael Yosef	Ginsburg		Rokiskis, Lithuania	Yzkr Bk	murdered
Rivka Rachel	Ginsburg		Rokiskis, Lithuania	Yzkr Bk	murdered
Musia	Ginsburgaite Ginsburg	1922	Rokiskis, Lithuania	PT	murdered
Rakhel Rivka	Ginzbirgiene Ginsburg	1885	Rokiskis, Lithuania	PT	murdered
Feyga	Ginzburg		Rokiskis, Lithuania	PT D	murdered
Musia	Ginzburg Ginsburg	1924	Rokiskis, Lithuania	PT	murdered
Rakhel	Ginzburg Ginsburg	1877	Rokiskis, Lithuania	PT	murdered
Yosef Rafael	Ginzburg Ginsburg	1875	Rokiskis, Lithuania	PT	murdered
Yosef Rafael	Ginzburgas Ginsburg	1885	Rokiskis, Lithuania	PT	murdered
Jacov Yaakov	Givovski		Rakiski, Lithuania	PT	murdered
Raia	Givovski		Rokiskis, Lithuania	PT	murdered
Rakhel	Givovski	1929	Rokishkis, Lithuania	PT	murdered
Yaakov	Givovski	1898	Rokiskis, Lithuania	PT	murdered
Yehudit	Givovski	1900	Rokiskis, Lithuania	PT	murdered
Ghita Gita	Giwowski Givovski		Rokishkis, Lithuania	PT	murdered
Erno	Glanzmann	1915	Munkacs, Czechoslovakia	HLBV	murdered
Khaim	Glick Glik	1886	Rokiskis, Lithuania	PT	murdered
Khane	Glik		Rokishkis, Lithuania	PT	murdered
Neyekh	Glik		Rokishkis, Lithuania	PT	murdered
Eizig Aizig	Gluch Glukh		Nemenzin, Poland	PT	murdered
Rywka Rivka	Gluch Glukh		Nemencine, Poland	PT	murdered
Golda	Gofanowicz Gafanovitz	1896	Kupiskis, Lithuania	PT	murdered

Appendix of Rokiskis Shoah Victims – not in the original Yizkor Book   APP-17

First Name	Last Name	Birth Year	Place of Residence	Source	Fate from Source
Alte	Golan	1896	Rokiskis, Lithuania	PT	murdered
Shaul	Golan	1893	Rakishok, Lithuania	PT	murdered
Zoltan	Gold	1915	Budszentmihaly, Hungary	HLBV	murdered
Chaja Khaia	Goldberg	1904	Kovno, Lithuania	PT	murdered
Reizl	Goldberg	1901	Dvinsk, Latvia	PT	murdered
Sarah Riva Sara	Goldin	1876	Dvinsk, Latvia	PT	murdered
Orel Michel	Goldschmidt	1876	Sesava, Latvia	Census	not stated
Orel Michel	Goldschmidt	1876	Riga, Latvia	Jew Res	not stated
Orel Michel	Goldschmidt	1876	Riga, Latvia	Residen	not stated
Beniamin	Goldshtein		Pandelys, Lithuania	Murd	murdered
Chaia	Goldshtein		Pandelys, Lithuania	Murd	murdered
Khaia	Goldshtein	1910	Ponidel, Lithuania	PT	murdered
Levi Yitzkhak	Goldshtein		Pandelys, Lithuania	Murd	murdered
Rivka	Goldshtein		Pandelys, Lithuania	Murd	murdered
Laszlo	Goldstein	1919	Hajdunadudvar, Hungary	HLBV	murdered
Mozes	Goldstein	1913	Palosremete, Romania	HLBV	murdered
Chaya Khaia	Goldstein Goldshtein	1911	Pandelis, Lithuania	PT	murdered
Musia	Gordin		Ponivez, Lithuania	PT	murdered
Natan	Gordin	1897	Rakishik, Lithuania	PT	murdered
Beniamin	Gordon	1894	Obeliai, Lithuania	PT	murdered
Beniamin	Gordon		Obeliai, Lithuania	PT	murdered
Benjamin Beniamin	Gordon	1890	Abeli, Lithuania	PT	murdered
Charles	Gordon		Rokishkis, Lithuania	PT	murdered
David	Gordon		Birzai, Lithuania	PT	murdered
Elchonon	Gordon	1894	Riga, Latvia	Jew Res	not stated
Elchonon	Gordon	1894	Riga, Latvia	Residen	not stated
Ella Freidella	Gordon	1870	Akniste, Latvia	Jew Res	not stated
Gita	Gordon		Rokiskis, Lithuania	PT	murdered
Golda	Gordon	1899	Rakishik, Lithuania	PT	murdered
Golda	Gordon		Rakishik, Lithuania	PT	murdered
Golda Golde	Gordon		Rokiskis, Lithuania	Yzkr Bk	murdered
Golda Golde	Gordon		Rokiskis, Lithuania	Yzkr Bk	murdered
Itzik	Gordon		Rokiskis, Lithuania	Yzkr Bk	murdered
Khaia	Gordon	1875	Sabile, Latvia	PT	murdered
Khaia	Gordon	1891	Obeliai, Lithuania	PT	murdered
Khaia	Gordon	1894	Obeliai, Lithuania	PT	murdered
Khaia	Gordon		Obeliai, Lithuania	PT	murdered
Leib	Gordon		Rokiskis, Lithuania	Yzkr Bk	murdered
Leiba	Gordon	1927	Rokiskis, Lithuania	PT	murdered
Leibe Leib	Gordon		Rakishik, Lithuania	PT	murdered
Michael Mikhael	Gordon	1895	Rakishok, Lithuania	PT	murdered
Mowscha	Gordon	1888	Daugavpils, Latvia	Census	not stated
Mowscha	Gordon	1888	Daugavpils, Latvia	Jew Res	not stated
Natl	Gordon		Rokiskis, Lithuania	Yzkr Bk	murdered
Natl Notl	Gordon		Rokiskis, Lithuania	Yzkr Bk	murdered
Natl Notl	Gordon		Rokiskis, Lithuania	Yzkr Bk	murdered
Notel Nutel	Gordon		Rakishik, Lithuania	PT	murdered
Reoven Reuven	Gordon	1921	Lithuania	PT	murdered
Sara	Gordon	1878	Riga, Latvia	PT	murdered
Shmuel	Gordon		Rokishki, Lithuania	PT	murdered

APP-18   Appendix of Rokiskis Shoah Victims – not in the original Yizkor Book

First Name	Last Name	Birth Year	Place of Residence	Source	Fate from Source
Simka	Gordon	1917	Kaunas, Lithuania	PT	murdered
Yosef	Gordon	1925	Rekishka, Lithuania	PT	murdered
Yosef	Gordon		Rokiskis, Lithuania	Yzkr Bk	murdered
Yosef	Gordon		Rakishik, Lithuania	PT	murdered
Zelda	Gordon	1929	Rakishok, Lithuania	PT	murdered
Zelda	Gordon		Rokiskis, Lithuania	Yzkr Bk	murdered
Zelde Zelda	Gordon		Rakishik, Lithuania	PT	murdered
Joske	Gordon Smilg		Rokiskis, Lithuania	PT	murdered
Leibke	Gordon Smilg		Rokiskis, Lithuania	PT	murdered
Notel	Gordon Smilg	1899	Rokiskis, Lithuania	PT	murdered
Zeldkle	Gordon Smilg		Rokiskis, Lithuania	PT	murdered
Mendel	Goron	1870	Daugavpils, Latvia	Census	not stated
Mendel	Goron	1870	Daugavpils, Latvia	Jew Res	not stated
Josef Yosef	Grabowiecki Grabovetzki	1898	Suwailiszki, Lithuania	PT	murdered
Khaim	Grabowiecki Grabovetzki		Suwailiszki, Lithuania	PT	murdered
Erno	Greger	1919	Balmazújváros, Hungary	HLBV	murdered
Abram Zalman Avraham	Greis	1875	Daugavpils, Latvia	PT	murdered
Faitel	Greis	1931	Rokiskis, Lithuania	PT	murdered
Feiga	Greis	1923	Rokiskis, Lithuania	PT	murdered
First name unknown	Greis		Abeil, Lithuania	PT	murdered
First name unknown	Greis		Abeil, Lithuania	PT	murdered
Itel	Greis	1881	Obeliai, Lithuania	PT	murdered
Mordekhai Ber	Greis		Abeil, Lithuania	PT	murdered
Zelda	Greis	1926	Rokiskis, Lithuania	PT	murdered
Mera Riva	Gribov	1907	Riga, Latvia	Jew Res	not stated
Mera Riva	Gribov	1907	Riga, Latvia	Residen	not stated
Mera Riva	Gribov	1907	Riga, Latvia	Residen	not stated
Mera Riva	Gribov	1907	Riga, Latvia	Residen	not stated
Mera Riva	Gribov	1907	Riga, Latvia	Residen	not stated
Mera Riva	Gribov	1907	Riga, Latvia	Residen	not stated
Israel Moshe	Grif		Rokiskis, Lithuania	Yzkr Bk	murdered
Rachel Feige	Grif		Rokiskis, Lithuania	Yzkr Bk	murdered
Liuba	Grinblo	1913	Pandelys, Lithuania	PT	murdered
Chona	Gringut		Rokiskis, Lithuania	PT D	murdered
Esther	Gringut		Rokiskis, Lithuania	PT D	murdered
Matele	Gringut		Rokiskis, Lithuania	PT D	murdered
Hana Khana	Grinshpan		Pultusk, Poland	PT	murdered
Yehuda	Grinshpan		Pultusk, Poland	PT	murdered
Jeuda Yehuda	Grinspan Gruenspan Grinshpan	1901	Pultusk, Poland	PT	murdered
Moshe Leib	Gris	1920	Abel, Lithuania	PT	murdered
Tzvia	Gris	1885	Abel, Lithuania	PT	murdered
Yitzkhak Yona	Gris	1880	Abel, Lithuania	PT	murdered
Ela	Griz	1886	Rokishok, Lithuania	PT	murdered
Ela	Griz		Rokiskis, Lithuania	Yzkr Bk	murdered
Meise	Grodzin	1915	Lazdijai, Lithuania	PT	murdered
Mor	Groszmann	1914	Satoraljaujhely, Hungary	HLBV	murdered
Sabetay Shabtai	Gruen Grin	1912	Suwailiszki, Lithuania	PT	murdered
Shulamit	Gruen Grin		Suwailiszki, Lithuania	PT	murdered
Mozes	Grunspan	1913	Borsa,	HLBV	murdered

Appendix of Rokiskis Shoah Victims – not in the original Yizkor Book   APP-19

First Name	Last Name	Birth Year	Place of Residence	Source	Fate from Source
Chana Khana	Grunspan Gruenspan Grinshpan	1903	Poltosk, Poland	PT	murdered
Menucha Menukha	Grupp Grof	1879	Oszmiana, Poland	PT	murdered
Khaim	Gurevitz		Rokishki, Lithuania	PT	murdered
Tzvia	Gurevitz		Rokishki, Lithuania	PT	murdered
Leiba	Gurvic Gurevitz	1895	Rokiskis, Lithuania	PT	murdered
Naftaly Naftali	Gurvic Gurevitz	1901	Rakishok, Lithuania	PT	murdered
Rashel Hinda	Gurvic Gurwitz		Rakisok, Lithuania	PT D	murdered
Sara	Gurviciene Gurvic Gurevitz	1889	Obeliai, Lithuania	PT	murdered
Gershon Gerson	Gurvicius Gurevitz	1911	Obeliai, Lithuania	PT	murdered
Icchak Yitzkhak	Gurvicius Gurevitz	1904	Obeliai, Lithuania	PT	murdered
Jakov Yaakov	Gurvicius Gurevitz	1913	Obeliai, Lithuania	PT	murdered
Mendel	Gurvicius Gurevitz	1905	Skopiski, Lithuania	PT	murdered
Mose Moshe	Gurvicius Gurevitz	1886	Obeliai, Lithuania	PT	murdered
Jehuda Yehuda	Gurwitz Gurevitz	1880	Riga, Latvia	PT	murdered
Yoseph Yosef	Gurwitz Gurevitz	1883	Pushelat, Lithuania	PT	murdered
Motell Mordechai	Gurwitz Gurvic		Rakeshik, Lithuania	PT D	murdered
Khaika Khaia	Gutman		Svyainishok, Lithuania	PT	murdered
Dezso	Guttmann	1919	Velete, Czechoslovakia	HLBV	murdered
Sara	Hackal Khatzkel	1890	Ponidel, Lithuania	PT	murdered
Batya Batia	Hackel Khatzkel	1920	Kowno, Lithuania	PT	murdered
Zalman	Hackel Khatzkel	1878	Ponidel, Lithuania	PT	murdered
Zelig Hirsh Zelik	Hackel Khatzkel	1924	Ponidel, Lithuania	PT	murdered
Hinda	Hahass Harhass Kharkhas		Rokiskis, Lithuania	PT	murdered
Mosus Mowscha	Hain	1871	Akniste, Latvia	Jew Res	not stated
Rivka	Halperin	1896	Yanishki, Lithuania	PT	murdered
First name unknown	Halpern		Rokiskis, Lithuania	Yzkr Bk	murdered
Rivka	Halpern		Rokiskis, Lithuania	Yzkr Bk	murdered
Batia	Hamburg		Rokiskis, Lithuania	Yzkr Bk	murdered
Tibor	Hamburg	1900	Pecs, Hungary	HLBV	murdered
Volf	Hamburg		Rokiskis, Lithuania	Yzkr Bk	murdered
Mari Meri	Harhas Kharkhas		Rokiskis, Lithuania	PT	murdered
Moshe	Harhas Kharkhas		Rokiskis, Lithuania	PT	murdered
Moshe	Harhas Kharkhas		Rokiskis, Lithuania	PT	murdered
Leije Lea	Heckal Khatzkel	1922	Ponidel, Lithuania	PT	murdered
Rivka	Hekdesh Egdish	1907	Ponedel, Lithuania	PT	murdered
Asnat	Herman		Abeil, Lithuania	PT	murdered
Avraham Shlomo	Herman		Obeliai, Lithuania	PT	murdered
Chaia Dvora	Herman		Abeil, Lithuania	PT	murdered
Chana	Herman		Obeliai, Lithuania	PT	murdered
Faitel	Herman		Obeliai, Lithuania	PT	killed in military service
First name unknown	Herman		Obeliai, Lithuania	PT	murdered
Khanokh Henikh	Herman		Obeliai, Lithuania	PT	murdered
Moshe	Herman		Obeliai, Lithuania	PT	murdered
Solomon Shalom	Herman	1897	Rakiski, Lithuania	PT	murdered
Sonia	Herman		Abeil, Lithuania	PT	murdered

APP-20   Appendix of Rokiskis Shoah Victims – not in the original Yizkor Book

First Name	Last Name	Birth Year	Place of Residence	Source	Fate from Source
Yehuda	Herman	1913	Rokishki, Lithuania	PT	murdered
Yeshayahu	Herman		Abeil, Lithuania	PT	murdered
Yitzkhak Joseph	Herman		Abeil, Lithuania	PT	murdered
Miklos	Hermann	1919	Szolnok, Hungary	HLBV	murdered
Ferentz	Herskovics	1919	Dolha,	HLBV	murdered
Selda	Herzberg	1913	Riga, Latvia	Jew Res	not stated
Selda	Herzberg	1913	Riga, Latvia	Residen	not stated
Selda	Herzberg	1913	Riga, Latvia	Residen	not stated
Moshe	Heselkovitz		Rokiskis, Lithuania	Yzkr Bk	murdered
Moshe	Heselkovitz		Rokiskis, Lithuania	PT D	murdered
Reizl	Heselkovitz		Rokiskis, Lithuania	Yzkr Bk	murdered
Samuel	Hilkin	1886	Ludza, Latvia	Census	not stated
Samuel	Hilkin	1886	Ludza, Latvia	Jew Res	murdered
Etel	Horovitz		Rokiskis, Lithuania	Yzkr Bk	murdered
First name unknown	Horovitz		Rokiskis, Lithuania	Yzkr Bk	murdered
Ite	Horovitz		Rokiskis, Lithuania	Yzkr Bk	murdered
Khasl	Horovitz		Rokiskis, Lithuania	Yzkr Bk	murdered
Lea Sara	Horovitz		Rokiskis, Lithuania	Yzkr Bk	murdered
Leibe	Horovitz		Rokiskis, Lithuania	Yzkr Bk	murdered
Rafael Avraham	Horovitz		Rokiskis, Lithuania	Yzkr Bk	murdered
Yitzkhak Efraim	Horovitz		Rokiskis, Lithuania	Yzkr Bk	murdered
Etel	Horowitz		Rokiskis, Lithuania	PT D	murdered
Hinde Rasa Hinda Rakhel	Hurvic Horovitz	1881	Kamai, Lithuania	PT	murdered
Motel Hirs Hirsh	Hurvic Horovitz	1876	Kamai, Lithuania	PT	murdered
Max	Hurwitz Gurwitz Hurvitz Gurevitz	1890	Kaunas, Lithuania	PT	murdered
Rachel Rakhel	Hurwitz Gurwitz Hurvitz Gurevitz	1892	Kaunas, Lithuania	PT	murdered
Max	Hurwitz Hurvitz	1890	Kowno, Lithuania	PT	murdered
Rachel Rakhel	Hurwitz Hurvitz	1892	Ponemon, Lithuania	PT	murdered
Ala	Iafe		Pandelys, Lithuania	Murd	murdered
Arie Leib	Iafe	1869	Ponidel, Lithuania	PT	murdered
Khanokh	Iafe	1891	Rakishok, Lithuania	PT	murdered
Rivka	Iafe	1914	Ponidel, Lithuania	PT	murdered
Yehuda Leib	Iafe		Pandelys, Lithuania	Murd	murdered
Yitzkhak	Iafe	1920	Ponidel, Lithuania	PT	murdered
Tova Taiba Dvora	Iafe Iofe	1917	Rokiskis, Lithuania	PT	murdered
Beila	Iakobson	1893	Rakishik, Lithuania	PT	murdered
Beile	Iakobson		Rokiskis, Lithuania	Yzkr Bk	murdered
Boris Khaim Ber	Iakobson	1918	Rokishki, Lithuania	PT	murdered
Hana	Iakobson	1904	Rekishok, Lithuania	PT	murdered
Iena Rivka	Iakobson	1926	Rakishik, Lithuania	PT	murdered
Levik	Iakobson	1875	Rakisok, Lithuania	PT	murdered
Misa	Iakobson	1878	Rokiskis, Lithuania	PT	murdered
Nekhama	Iakobson	1920	Rokishok, Lithuania	PT	murdered
Nekhemia	Iakobson	1906	Rakisok, Lithuania	PT	murdered
Yaakov	Iakobson	1885	Jakobstadt, Latvia	PT	murdered
Yaakov	Iakobson	1885	Yakovshtat, Latvia	PT	murdered
Yaakov	Iakobson	1910	Rekishka, Lithuania	PT	murdered
Yaakov	Iakobson		Rokiskis, Lithuania	Yzkr Bk	murdered

Appendix of Rokiskis Shoah Victims – not in the original Yizkor Book   APP-21

First Name	Last Name	Birth Year	Place of Residence	Source	Fate from Source
Yosef	Iakobson	1922	Rakishik, Lithuania	PT	murdered
Emanuel	Iakobson Iokobson		Rokiskis, Lithuania	Yzkr Bk	murdered
Sara	Iakobson Iokobson		Rokiskis, Lithuania	Yzkr Bk	murdered
Yekhezkel	Iakobson Iokobson		Rokiskis, Lithuania	Yzkr Bk	murdered
Fania	Ibedas Ibedes	1912	Vilkomir, Lithuania	PT	murdered
Lea	Ibjan Ibian	1907	Ponedel, Lithuania	PT	murdered
David	Ibjan Ibian Ebin		Ponedel, Lithuania	PT	murdered
Henia Sara	Icgal Itzgal	1866	Kamajai, Lithuania	PT	murdered
Rachmiel Yerakhmiel Rakhmiel Rakhmil	Icgal Itzgal	1898	Kvatki, Lithuania	PT	murdered
Rachmiel Yerakhmiel Rakhmil	Icgal Itzgal	1898	Kvatki, Lithuania	PT	murdered
Mendl	Ikhilchik		Rokiskis, Lithuania	Yzkr Bk	murdered
Rachel Khana	Ikhilchik		Rokiskis, Lithuania	Yzkr Bk	murdered
Sonie	Ikhilchik		Rokiskis, Lithuania	Yzkr Bk	murdered
Yitzkhak	Ikhilchik		Rokiskis, Lithuania	Yzkr Bk	murdered
Zelda	Ikhilchik		Rokiskis, Lithuania	Yzkr Bk	murdered
Hirshel	Iofe	1895	Dusiat, Lithuania	PT	murdered
Aviva	Ioffe	1937	Rokiskis, Lithuania	PT	murdered
First name unknown	Ioffe		Rokiskis, Lithuania	PT	murdered
Genekh	Ioffe	1900	Rokishkis, Lithuania	PT	murdered
Rina	Ioffe	1940	Rokishkis, Lithuania	PT	murdered
Sonya	Ioffe	1914	Rokishkis, Lithuania	PT	murdered
Avraham	Ioselovitz		Rokiskis, Lithuania	Yzkr Bk	murdered
First name unknown	Ioselovitz		Rokiskis, Lithuania	Yzkr Bk	murdered
Hirsh	Ioselovitz Ioselevitz		Rokiskis, Lithuania	Yzkr Bk	murdered
Toibe	Ioselovitz Ioselevitz		Rokiskis, Lithuania	Yzkr Bk	murdered
Mendl	Ioselovitz Veitz		Rokiskis, Lithuania	Yzkr Bk	murdered
Chayne	Isaakman		Rokiskis, Lithuania	PT D	murdered
Yerachmiel	Isaakman		Rokiskis, Lithuania	PT D	murdered
Feyga Leya	Isemina	1901	Latvia	Per Doc	not stated
Feiga Fanny	Isjemin	1902	Riga, Latvia	Jew Res	murdered
Feiga Fanny	Isjemin	1902	Riga, Latvia	Residen	not stated
Feiga Fanny	Isjemin	1902	Riga, Latvia	Residen	not stated
Khana	Itzikman		Rokiskis, Lithuania	Yzkr Bk	murdered
Yerakhmiel	Itzikman		Rokiskis, Lithuania	Yzkr Bk	murdered
Batya	Ivyan		Pandelis, Lithuania	PT	murdered
Chazkel	Jacobson		Rokiskis, Lithuania	PT D	murdered
Emmanuel	Jacobson		Rokiskis, Lithuania	PT D	murdered
Ovsey Nechamia	Jacobson	1869	Kupiskis, Lithuania	PT Ds	murdered
Nachama Nekhama	Jacobson Iakobson		Rakishik, Lithuania	PT	murdered
Yaakov	Jacobson Iakobson	1888	Rakishok, Lithuania	PT	murdered
Batia	Jafe Iafe	1885	Panedel, Lithuania	PT	murdered
Mosse Moshe	Jafe Iafe	1917	Ponodol, Lithuania	PT	murdered
Oga	Jafe Iafe	1914	Ponodol, Lithuania	PT	murdered
Shalom Salom	Jafe Iafe	1886	Rakishik, Lithuania	PT	murdered
Yitzkhak Icchak	Jafe Iafe	1880	Ponodol, Lithuania	PT	murdered
Kasreel	Jaffe	1905	Rakishok, Lithuania	PT	murdered
Leibe	Jaffe		Lithuania	PT	murdered
Velvel Velva	Jaffe	1906	Rakishok, Lithuania	PT	murdered

APP-22   Appendix of Rokiskis Shoah Victims – not in the original Yizkor Book

First Name	Last Name	Birth Year	Place of Residence	Source	Fate from Source
Civja Tzvia	Jaffe Iafe	1917	Pandelis, Lithuania	PT	murdered
Izchak Yitzkhak	Jaffe Iafe	1921	Pandelys, Lithuania	PT	murdered
Erno	Jakabovics	1920	Pecs, Hungary	HLBV	murdered
Beile Beila	Jakobson Iakobson	1893	Rakishik, Lithuania	PT	murdered
Chaim Khaim Ber	Jakobson Iakobson		Rakishik, Lithuania	PT	murdered
Hane Hena Khana	Jakobson Iakobson		Rakishik, Lithuania	PT	murdered
Hene Rive Hena Riva	Jakobson Iakobson		Rakishik, Lithuania	PT	murdered
Jakob Yaakov	Jakobson Iakobson		Rakishik, Lithuania	PT	murdered
Jokov Yaakov	Jakobson Iakobson		Rakishik, Lithuania	PT	murdered
Josef Yosef	Jakobson Iakobson		Rakishik, Lithuania	PT	murdered
Leivik Leib Lev	Jakobson Iakobson		Rakishik, Lithuania	PT	murdered
Meijer Meir	Jakobson Iakobson		Panevezys, Lithuania	PT	murdered
Musa Musia Moshe Muse	Jakobson Iakobson		Rakishik, Lithuania	PT	murdered
Nechemie Nekhemia	Jakobson Iakobson		Rakishik, Lithuania	PT	murdered
Sora	Janikun	1912	Riga, Latvia	Jew Res	not stated
Sora	Janikun	1912	Riga, Latvia	Residen	not stated
Sora	Janikun	1912	Riga, Latvia	Residen	not stated
Chana Khana	Jankilievicine Iankelovitz	1905	Rokishkis, Lithuania	PT	murdered
Mozes	Jeremias	1913	Halmi, Romania	HLBV	murdered
Meir	Jofe		Rokiskis, Lithuania	PT	murdered
Ette	Joffe	1915	Riga, Latvia	Jew Res	not stated
Ette	Joffe	1915	Riga, Latvia	Residen	not stated
Ette	Joffe	1915	Riga, Latvia	Residen	not stated
Frida	Joffe	1891	Akniste, Latvia	Jew Res	not stated
Leib	Joffe	1897	Riga, Latvia	Jew Res	murdered
Leib	Joffe	1897	Riga, Latvia	Residen	not stated
Leib	Joffe	1897	Riga, Latvia	Residen	not stated
Arie Leib	Joffe Iafe	1880	Pandelys, Lithuania	PT	murdered
Arie Leib	Joffe Iafe	1886	Latvia	PT	murdered
Chaja Khaia	Joffe Iafe	1912	Pandelys, Lithuania	PT	murdered
Chana Khana	Joffe Iafe	1880	Pandelys, Lithuania	PT	murdered
Ella	Joffe Iafe	1885	Pandelis, Lithuania	PT	murdered
Lea	Joffe Iafe	1910	Pandelys, Lithuania	PT	murdered
	Jofin Iofin		Panemune, Lithuania	PT	murdered
Ginda	Jorsch	1907	Ludza, Latvia	Census	not stated
Ginda	Jorsch	1907	Jekabpils, Latvia	Jew Res	not stated
Avraham	Joselevicz Ioselevitz	1886	Rokiskis, Lithuania	PT	murdered
Arie	Joselewicz Ioselevitz		Rakishki, Lithuania	PT	murdered
Awraham Avraham	Joselewicz Ioselevitz	1897	Rakishki, Lithuania	PT	murdered
Bilha	Joselewicz Ioselevitz		Rakishki, Lithuania	PT	murdered
Bluma	Joselewicz Ioselevitz	1898	Rokishki, Lithuania	PT	murdered
Khaia	Joselewicz Ioselevitz		Rakishki, Lithuania	PT	murdered
Moshe	Joselewicz Ioselevitz		Rakishki, Lithuania	PT	murdered
Chana Khana	Joselowic Ioselovitz	1914	Rakiski, Lithuania	PT	murdered
Sara	Josman Iosman	1900	Obeliai, Lithuania	PT	murdered
Avraham	Josman Veisman	1897	Obeliai, Lithuania	PT	murdered
Sara	Judin Iudin	1894	Dnepropetrovsk, Ukraine (USSR)	PT	murdered
Scholom Scholem	Judkowitsch	1892	Riga, Latvia	Jew Res	not stated
Scholom Scholem	Judkowitsch	1892	Riga, Latvia	Residen	not stated

Appendix of Rokiskis Shoah Victims – not in the original Yizkor Book   APP-23

First Name	Last Name	Birth Year	Place of Residence	Source	Fate from Source
Scholom Scholem	Judkowitsch	1892	Riga, Latvia	Residen	not stated
Hinda	Kac Katz	1890	Pandelys, Lithuania	PT	murdered
Zelda	Kacaite Katz	1922	Rokiszki, Lithuania	PT	murdered
Yeshayahu Yosef	Kacas Katz	1894	Rokiszki, Lithuania	PT	murdered
Slava	Kaciene Katz	1897	Rokishkis, Lithuania	PT	murdered
Gena	Kadischewitsch	1900	Riga, Latvia	Jew Res	not stated
Gena	Kadischewitsch	1900	Riga, Latvia	Residen	not stated
Nachman Leiser	Kadischewitsch	1860	Livani, Latvia	Census	not stated
Nachman Leiser	Kadischewitsch	1860	Livani, Latvia	Jew Res	murdered
Chaike	Kagan		Rokishkis, Lithuania	PT Ds	murdered
Dvora	Kagan		Rokishkis, Lithuania	PT Ds	murdered
Elke	Kagan	1914	Kaunas, Lithuania	PT Ds	murdered
Faigetzke	Kagan		Rokishkis, Lithuania	PT Ds	murdered
Mirke	Kagan		Rokishkis, Lithuania	PT Ds	murdered
Stirke	Kagan		Rokishkis, Lithuania	PT Ds	murdered
Yankel	Kagan		Rokishkis, Lithuania	PT Ds	murdered
Lipa	Kagan Kohen	1906	Kaunas, Lithuania	PT	murdered
Musha Moshe	Kahn Cohen Kan Kohen		Memel, Lithuania	PT	murdered
Aharon	Kalikur Kalikor	1881	Rakishok, Lithuania	PT	murdered
Gutel Gitel	Kalinkovitch Klinkovitz	1880	Panemun, Lithuania	PT	murdered
Hirsh	Kalinkovitch Klinkovitz	1906	Panemun, Lithuania	PT	murdered
Jakov Yaakov	Kalinkovitch Klinkovitz	1900	Kovna, Lithuania	PT	murdered
Menachem Menakhem	Kalinkovitch Klinkovitz	1906	Panemun, Lithuania	PT	murdered
Rafael Ber	Kalinkovitch Klinkovitz		Panemun, Lithuania	PT	murdered
Sarah Sara	Kalinkovitch Klinkovitz	1904	Kovno, Lithuania	PT	murdered
Shalom	Kalinkovitch Klinkovitz	1896	Panemun, Lithuania	PT	murdered
Aaron	Kalkoor		Rokiskis, Lithuania	PT Ds	murdered
Herschel	Kalkoor		Rokiskis, Lithuania	PT Ds	murdered
Israel Moses	Kalkoor		Rokiskis, Lithuania	PT Ds	murdered
Musa	Kalkoor		Rokiskis, Lithuania	PT Ds	murdered
Hermann	Kalla	1918	Nagydobos, Hungary	HLBV	murdered
Gyorgy	Kallos	1917	Szeged, Hungary	HLBV	murdered
Yaakov	Kalton	1891	Rakishik, Lithuania	PT	murdered
Yaakov Yankel	Kaltun Kalton	1891	Rakishok, Lithuania	PT	murdered
Sara	Kanaite	1904	Panemunes, Lithuania	Jew Res	not stated
Mendel	Kapelius Kapelush	1881	Rakishik, Lithuania	PT	murdered
Tovja Tuvia	Kapeliusch Kapelush	1910	Kaunas, Lithuania	PT	murdered
Pese Pesia	Kapelush	1874	Ponedel, Lithuania	PT	murdered
Abram Avraham Khaim	Kapilowitz Kapilovitz		Skapiskis, Lithuania	PT	murdered
Golda	Kapilowitz Kapilovitz			PT	murdered
Halina	Kapilowitz Kapilovitz			PT	murdered
Mendel	Kapilowitz Kapilovitz		Rezica, Latvia	PT	murdered
Yisrael Eliezer	Kapilowitz Kapilovitz			PT	murdered
Ajzik Aizik	Kaplan		Panemune, Lithuania	PT	murdered
Baruch Reuben Reuven Barukh	Kaplan	1907	Raseinai, Lithuania	PT	murdered
Ester	Kaplan		Panemune, Lithuania	PT	murdered
Isak	Kaplan	1903	Riga, Latvia	Jew Res	murdered
Itzchok Itzik	Kaplan	1877	Riga, Latvia	Jew Res	not stated
Itzchok Itzik	Kaplan	1877	Riga, Latvia	Residen	not stated

Appendix of Rokiskis Shoah Victims – not in the original Yizkor Book

First Name	Last Name	Birth Year	Place of Residence	Source	Fate from Source
Miriam	Kaplan		Panemune, Lithuania	PT	murdered
Moisei	Kaplan	1901	Kaunas, Lithuania	PT	murdered
Nachum Nakhum	Kaplan	1913	Rasseine, Lithuania	PT	murdered
Rachel Rochel	Kaplan	1890	Riga, Latvia	Jew Res	not stated
Rachel Rochel	Kaplan	1890	Riga, Latvia	Residen	not stated
Rachel Rochel	Kaplan	1890	Riga, Latvia	Residen	not stated
Rochel	Kaplan	1890	Riga, Latvia	PT	murdered
Semyon	Kaplan		Abeliai, Lithuania	PT	murdered
	Kaplan		Panemune, Lithuania	PT	murdered
Mera Yese	Kaplanski	1894	Rokiskis, Lithuania	PT	murdered
Gita Gitel	Karabelnik	1882	Panemune, Lithuania	PT	murdered
Ida	Karabelnik	1909	Ponemunek, Lithuania	PT	murdered
Mendel	Karabelnik	1872	Riga, Latvia	Jew Res	not stated
Mendel	Karabelnik	1872	Riga, Latvia	Residen	not stated
Mendel	Karabelnik	1872	Riga, Latvia	Residen	not stated
Shmuel	Karabelnik	1909	Ponemunek, Lithuania	PT	murdered
Josef Yosef	Karas	1887	Suwailiszki, Lithuania	PT	murdered
Liba	Karas	1890	Suwailiszki, Lithuania	PT	murdered
Bella Bela	Kark		Rakiski, Lithuania	PT	murdered
Bercik Ber	Kark		Pondel, Lithuania	PT	murdered
Chaia Idke Khaia	Kark	1903	Kamajai, Lithuania	PT	murdered
Dvora	Kark		Rokiskis, Lithuania	Yzkr Bk	murdered
Heniek Yisrael	Kark		Pondel, Lithuania	PT	murdered
Jacov Yaakov	Kark		Rakiski, Lithuania	PT	murdered
Lea Gute	Kark		Rokiskis, Lithuania	Yzkr Bk	murdered
Leizer	Kark		Rokiskis, Lithuania	Yzkr Bk	murdered
Meisel Moshe	Kark	1900	Kamajai, Lithuania	PT	murdered
Nisan	Kark	1928	Kamajai, Lithuania	PT	murdered
Sender	Kark	1891	Riga, Latvia	Jew Res	not stated
Sender	Kark	1891	Riga, Latvia	Residen	not stated
Sender	Kark	1891	Riga, Latvia	Residen	not stated
Yaakov	Kark		Rokiskis, Lithuania	Yzkr Bk	murdered
Yehudit	Kark		Rokiskis, Lithuania	Yzkr Bk	murdered
Yochka	Kark		Rokiskis, Lithuania	PT D	murdered
Yokheved Iokhke	Kark		Rokiskis, Lithuania	Yzkr Bk	murdered
Yekhezkel	Karpuz Karpus	1871	Rakishok, Lithuania	PT	murdered
Jardena	Kaschpi Kaspi	1927	Kaunas, Lithuania	PT	murdered
Miriam	Kaschpi Kaspi	1924	Kaunas, Lithuania	PT	murdered
Chaina Khana	Kastan Kashtan	1918	Rakishik, Lithuania	PT	murdered
Leah Lea	Kastan Kashtan		Rakishik, Lithuania	PT	murdered
Pesia Lea	Kataniene Katan		Rokiskis, Lithuania	PT	murdered
Alter	Katc Katz	1900	Panemun, Lithuania	PT	murdered
Hinda	Katc Katz		Panemun, Lithuania	PT	murdered
Judeska Yudeske	Katc Katz	1903	Panemun, Lithuania	PT	murdered
Judeska Yudeske	Katc Katz	1903	Panemun, Lithuania	PT	murdered
Nachum Nakhum	Katc Katz	1921	Panemun, Lithuania	PT	murdered
Avraham	Katz	1922	Rakiski, Lithuania	PT	murdered
Avraham	Katz		Rokiskis, Lithuania	PT	murdered
Batia Moshe	Katz		Rokiskis, Lithuania	Yzkr Bk	murdered
Benzion Bentzion	Katz	1900	Kovno, Lithuania	PT	murdered

Appendix of Rokiskis Shoah Victims – not in the original Yizkor Book   APP-25

First Name	Last Name	Birth Year	Place of Residence	Source	Fate from Source
Ber	Katz		Rokiskis, Lithuania	Yzkr Bk	murdered
Berel	Katz	1905	Kraukli, Latvia	Census	not stated
Berel	Katz	1905	Kraukli, Latvia	Jew Res	not stated
Betzalel	Katz	1860	Rakishok, Lithuania	PT	murdered
Chaia Sarah Khaia Sara	Katz	1901	Panemun, Lithuania	PT	murdered
Eli Berl	Katz	1896	Panemun, Lithuania	PT	murdered
Eliahu	Katz	1927	Panemune, Lithuania	PT	murdered
Elka	Katz	1925	Rokiskis, Lithuania	PT	murdered
Ester	Katz	1891	Rakishok, Lithuania	PT	murdered
Ethel Otilia	Katz		Rokiskis, Lithuania	PT	murdered
Etl Etel	Katz	1926	Obeliai, Lithuania	PT	murdered
Faivel	Katz		Panemune, Lithuania	PT	murdered
First name unknown	Katz		Rokiskis, Lithuania	Yzkr Bk	murdered
Gyula	Katz	1917	Debrecen, Hungary	HLBV	murdered
Hermann	Katz	1919	Szeleslonka, Czechoslovakia	HLBV	murdered
Ida	Katz	1921	Rokiskis, Lithuania	PT	murdered
Ilona	Katz		Rokiskis, Lithuania	PT	murdered
Isak	Katz	1909	Rezēkne, Latvia	Census	not stated
Isak	Katz	1909	Riga, Latvia	Jew Res	not stated
Isak	Katz	1909	Riga, Latvia	Residen	not stated
Isak	Katz	1909	Riga, Latvia	Residen	not stated
Itzik	Katz	1892	Riga, Latvia	Jew Res	not stated
Itzik	Katz	1892	Riga, Latvia	Residen	not stated
Itzik	Katz	1892	Riga, Latvia	Residen	not stated
Khaim	Katz	1924	Obeliai, Lithuania	PT	murdered
Khava	Katz	1897	Panemune, Lithuania	PT	murdered
Lea	Katz	1900	Obeliai, Lithuania	PT	murdered
Leiba	Katz	1885	Riga, Latvia	Jew Res	murdered
Leiba	Katz	1885	Riga, Latvia	Residen	not stated
Leiba	Katz	1922	Obeliai, Lithuania	PT	murdered
Matl Motl	Katz		Rokiskis, Lithuania	Yzkr Bk	murdered
Menachum Menakhem	Katz	1866	Rokishki, Lithuania	PT	murdered
Merka	Katz	1891	Daugavpils, Latvia	Census	not stated
Merka	Katz	1891	Daugavpils, Latvia	Jew Res	not stated
Motl Matl	Katz		Rokiskis, Lithuania	Yzkr Bk	murdered
Motl Mordekhai Motel	Katz	1900	Kaunas, Lithuania	PT	murdered
Nakhum	Katz		Rakishik, Lithuania	PT	murdered
Rakhel	Katz	1895	Rokiskis, Lithuania	PT	murdered
Sali Shmuel	Katz	1878	Altona, Germany	PT	murdered
Shaja Yeshayahu Yosef	Katz	1885	Lithuania	PT	murdered
Shmuel	Katz	1917	Rakishik, Lithuania	PT	murdered
Shmuel	Katz	1918	Rokiskis, Lithuania	PT	murdered
Shmuel	Katz	1918	Rokiskis, Lithuania	PT	murdered
Shmuel Samuel	Katz	1910	Rokiskis, Lithuania	PT	murdered
Shneiur	Katz	1881	Rakishok, Lithuania	PT	murdered
Shneiur	Katz		Rokiskis, Lithuania	PT	murdered
Sneiur Shneiur	Katz		Rokiskis, Lithuania	PT	murdered
Sonia	Katz		Rakishok, Lithuania	PT	murdered
Sprinza	Katz	1865	Riga, Latvia	Jew Res	not stated

APP-26   Appendix of Rokiskis Shoah Victims – not in the original Yizkor Book

First Name	Last Name	Birth Year	Place of Residence	Source	Fate from Source
Sprinza	Katz	1865	Riga, Latvia	Residen	not stated
Sprinza	Katz	1865	Riga, Latvia	Residen	not stated
Yosef	Katz		Panemun, Lithuania	PT	murdered
Yosef Leib	Katz		Rokiskis, Lithuania	PT	murdered
Zelda	Katz		Lithuania	PT	murdered
יסף Leib	Katz	1920	Rokishok, Lithuania	PT	murdered
Sara	Katz Kac	1905	Lithuania	PT	murdered
Raschel	Katzowitsch	1897	Daugavpils, Latvia	Census	not stated
Raschel	Katzowitsch	1897	Daugavpils, Latvia	Jew Res	not stated
Aba	Kaufman Kofman		Skopiskis, Lithuania	PT	murdered
Riva Rivka	Kaufman Kofman	1912	Skopiskis, Lithuania	PT	murdered
Mozes	Kaufmann	1916	Disznopataka, Romania	HLBV	murdered
Khaykel	Kaval	1907	Rakishki, Lithuania	Evac	not stated
Menachem Mendel	Kavalsky	1861	Pusalotas, Lithuania	PT	murdered
Feiga	Kaz Katz	1860	Lietava, Czechoslovakia	PT	murdered
Jozef Yosef	Kaz Katz	1860	Lithuania	PT	murdered
Nachum Nakhum	Kaz Katz	1881	Rakisok, Lithuania	PT	murdered
Sara	Kelman	1918	Vilno, Poland	PT	murdered
Aba	Kesel		Kelem, Lithuania	PT	murdered
Chava Khava	Kesel		Skopiskis, Lithuania	PT	murdered
Lea	Kez Kaz	1915	Kowno, Lithuania	PT	murdered
Aba Bina	Khaiat	1911	Kowna, Lithuania	PT	murdered
Esther	Khaiat		Rokishkis, Lithuania	PT	murdered
Yaakov Gershon	Khaiat	1912	Rokishkis, Lithuania	PT	murdered
Rakhil Rakhel	Khait Khaiat		Kharkov, Ukraine (USSR)	PT	murdered
Eliezer	Khaitovitz Kheitovitz		Rokiskis, Lithuania	Yzkr Bk	murdered
Efraim	Kharmatz	1927	Vilno, Poland	PT Ds	murdered
Leib Mikhael	Kharmatz		Rokiskis, Lithuania	PT Ds	murdered
Mina Sara	Kharmatz		Rokiskis, Lithuania	Yzkr Bk	murdered
Shmuel	Kharmatz		Rokiskis, Lithuania	Yzkr Bk	murdered
Chaim Khaim	Khasid Chosid	1941	Kovno, Lithuania	PT	murdered
David Avraham	Kheitovitz Khaitovitz		Rokiskis, Lithuania	Yzkr Bk	murdered
Etel	Kheitovitz Khaitovitz		Rokiskis, Lithuania	Yzkr Bk	murdered
Hinde	Kheitovitz Khaitovitz		Rokiskis, Lithuania	Yzkr Bk	murdered
Matl Motl	Kheitovitz Khaitovitz		Rokiskis, Lithuania	Yzkr Bk	murdered
Feiga	Kil		Panemunelis, Lithuania	PT	murdered
Khasya	Kil		Panemunelis, Lithuania	PT	murdered
Berta	Kili	1894	Kamai, Lithuania	Evac	not stated
Ester	Kili	1929	Kamai, Lithuania	Evac	not stated
Izrail	Kili	1885	Kamai, Lithuania	Evac	not stated
Liza	Kili	1926	Kamai, Lithuania	Evac	not stated
Jeno	Kind	1919	Visooroszi, Romania	HLBV	murdered
Roza	Kirzhner		Luknik, Lithuania	PT	murdered
Esteir Ester	Klar Klor	1907	Kamajai, Lithuania	PT	murdered
Berl	Klas	1899	Rokiskis, Lithuania	PT	murdered
Gershon Shaul	Klas		Rokiskis, Lithuania	Yzkr Bk	murdered
Shaul	Klass		Obeliai, Lithuania	PT D	murdered
Asna Asnat	Klasz Kles Kallós		Obeliai, Lithuania	PT	murdered
Sayle Shulamit	Klasz Kles Kallós		Obeliai, Lithuania	PT	murdered
Zelda	Klasz Kles Kallós		Obeliai, Lithuania	PT	murdered

Appendix of Rokiskis Shoah Victims – not in the original Yizkor Book   APP-27

First Name	Last Name	Birth Year	Place of Residence	Source	Fate from Source
Bessel	Klatskin		Rokiskis, Lithuania	PT D	murdered
Avraham	Klatzkin		Rokiskis, Lithuania	Yzkr Bk	murdered
Chasja Khana Dvora	Klatzkin	1860	Janischki, Lithuania	PT	murdered
First name unknown	Klatzkin		Rokiskis, Lithuania	Yzkr Bk	murdered
Khasl	Klatzkin		Rokiskis, Lithuania	Yzkr Bk	murdered
Aide Tehila	Klaver		Rokiskis, Lithuania	Yzkr Bk	murdered
David Zelig	Klaver		Rokiskis, Lithuania	Yzkr Bk	murdered
Yaakov	Klaver		Rokiskis, Lithuania	Yzkr Bk	murdered
David Zelig	Klavir Klevir	1882	Abeliai, Lithuania	PT	murdered
Eida Ida	Klavir Klevir	1883	Pandelis, Lithuania	PT	murdered
Jakubas Yaakov	Klavir Klevir	1916	Abeliai, Lithuania	PT	murdered
Esther Ester	Kleiman	1889	Riga, Latvia	PT	murdered
Armin	Klein	1919		HLBV	murdered
Markus	Klein	1918	Budapest, Hungary	HLBV	murdered
Miksa	Klein	1905	Ungvar, Czechoslovakia	HLBV	murdered
Vilmosh	Klein	1919	Nyiradony, Hungary	HLBV	murdered
Ita	Kletzmer	1911	Komai, Lithuania	Evac	not stated
Mikhail	Kletzmer	1937	Komai, Lithuania	Evac	not stated
Yenden	Kletzmer	1940	Komai, Lithuania	Evac	not stated
Eda Ede	Klevir Klaver		Abel, Lithuania	PT	murdered
Zelig	Klevir Klaver		Abel, Lithuania	PT	murdered
Ana	Klingman	1907	Rokiskis, Lithuania	PT	murdered
Basia Batia	Klingman	1892	Abeli, Lithuania	PT	murdered
Gitel	Klingman	1870	Rokishki, Lithuania	PT	murdered
Gitel	Klingman	1872	Rokishok, Lithuania	PT	murdered
Izchak Yitzkhak	Klingman	1903	Rokiskis, Lithuania	PT	murdered
Rakhel	Klingman		Rokiskis, Lithuania	PT	murdered
Rita	Klingman		Rokiskis, Lithuania	PT	murdered
Yitzkhak	Klingman	1891	Rakishik, Lithuania	PT	murdered
Yitzkhak	Klingman	1905	Rokiskis, Lithuania	PT	murdered
Leib Arie	Klinkovitz		Penimonik, Lithuania	PT D	murdered
Lipe Lipa	Klocas Klotz		Panemune, Lithuania	PT	murdered
Azriel	Klor		Kamajai, Lithuania	PT	murdered
David	Klor		Kamajai, Lithuania	PT	murdered
Khava	Klor		Kamajai, Lithuania	PT	murdered
Kopel	Klor		Kamajai, Lithuania	PT	murdered
Lea	Klor		Kamajai, Lithuania	PT	murdered
Pesia	Klor		Kamajai, Lithuania	PT D	murdered
Yisrael	Klor		Kamai, Lithuania	PT	murdered
Azriel	Kloras Klar Klor	1903	Kamajai, Lithuania	PT	murdered
Dov	Kloras Klar Klor		Kamajai, Lithuania	PT	murdered
Khava	Kloras Klar Klor		Kamajai, Lithuania	PT	murdered
Kopel	Kloras Klar Klor		Kamajai, Lithuania	PT	murdered
Lea	Kloras Klar Klor		Kamajai, Lithuania	PT	murdered
Pesa	Kloras Klar Klor		Kamajai, Lithuania	PT	murdered
Yisrael	Kloras Klar Klor		Kamajai, Lithuania	PT	murdered
Chaim	Klug		Rokiskis, Lithuania	Yzkr Bk	murdered
Chaim	Klug		Rokiskis, Lithuania	PT D	murdered
Chana Khana	Klug	1907	Rokiskis, Lithuania	PT	murdered
Henrik	Klug		Rokiskis, Lithuania	PT	murdered

APP-28   Appendix of Rokiskis Shoah Victims – not in the original Yizkor Book

First Name	Last Name	Birth Year	Place of Residence	Source	Fate from Source
Libe	Klug		Rokiskis, Lithuania	Yzkr Bk	murdered
Michael	Klug		Rokiskis, Lithuania	Yzkr Bk	murdered
Moshe	Klug		Rokiskis, Lithuania	Yzkr Bk	murdered
Nekhemia	Klug		Rokiskis, Lithuania	Yzkr Bk	murdered
Sara	Klug		Rokiskis, Lithuania	PT	murdered
Tzipe	Klug		Rokiskis, Lithuania	Yzkr Bk	murdered
	Klug		Rokiskis, Lithuania	PT	murdered
	Klug		Rokiskis, Lithuania	PT	murdered
Beila Bila Frida	Klumel		Rokiskis, Lithuania	PT	murdered
Beinis	Klumel		Lithuania	PT	murdered
Frida	Klumel		Lithuania	PT	murdered
Liuba	Klumel		Rokishkis, Lithuania	PT	murdered
Zalman	Klumel		Rakishki, Lithuania	PT	murdered
Rachmiel Rakhmiel	Klumiel Klumel		Rakisok, Lithuania	PT	murdered
Shmulis	Klyukos	1912	Rakishki, Lithuania	Evac	not stated
Aron	Koblikowsky	1929	Panemune, Lithuania	Persecut	not stated
Henach Khanokh	Kodesh	1916	Kupishkis, Lithuania	PT	murdered
Zenia Zhenia	Kodesh	1918	Rokishkis, Lithuania	PT	murdered
Laszlo	Kohn	1919	Debrecen, Hungary	HLBV	murdered
Aharon Naftali	Komraz		Oshpol, Lithuania	PT	murdered
Musia	Kontorovitz		Kharkov, Ukraine (USSR)	PT	murdered
Aharon	Kopelanski	1898	Rokiskis, Lithuania	PT	murdered
Frida	Kopelanski	1927	Rokiskis, Lithuania	PT	murdered
Leib Arie	Kopelanski	1925	Rokiskis, Lithuania	PT	murdered
Mariasha	Kopelanski	1898	Rokiskis, Lithuania	PT	murdered
Beryl Beril David	Kopelovitiz Kopelovitz	1925	Rokiskis, Lithuania	PT	killed in military service
Mushel Moshel	Kopelovitiz Kopelovitz	1896	Panemune, Lithuania	PT	murdered
Khaia	Kopelovitz	1890	Utena, Lithuania	PT	murdered
Isser	Kopelovitz Kopelovich		Rokiskis, Lithuania	Yzkr Bk	murdered
Leizer	Kopelovitz Kopelovich		Rokiskis, Lithuania	Yzkr Bk	murdered
Libe	Kopelovitz Kopelovich		Rokiskis, Lithuania	Yzkr Bk	murdered
Nakhumke	Kopelovitz Kopelovich		Rokiskis, Lithuania	Yzkr Bk	murdered
Yafa Khana	Kopelovitz Kopelovich		Rokiskis, Lithuania	Yzkr Bk	murdered
Zalman	Kopelovitz Kopelovich		Rokiskis, Lithuania	Yzkr Bk	not stated
Lorincz	Kopolovics	1919	Beregnagyalmas, Czechoslovakia	HLBV	murdered
David	Korabelnik		Utian, Lithuania	Yzkr Bk	murdered
First name unknown	Korabelnik		Utian, Lithuania	Yzkr Bk	murdered
Reizl	Korabelnik		Utian, Lithuania	Yzkr Bk	murdered
Reizl	Korabelnik		Utian, Lithuania	Yzkr Bk	murdered
Shmuel	Korabelnik		Utian, Lithuania	Yzkr Bk	murdered
Yehudit	Korabelnik		Utian, Lithuania	Yzkr Bk	murdered
Izia	Korabelnik Karabelnik		Panemunelis, Lithuania	PT	murdered
Samuel Shmuel	Korabelnik Karabelnik	1908	Panemunelis, Lithuania	PT	murdered
Khaia Gita	Korcher	1903	Ospul, Lithuania	PT	murdered
Musia Rashi Moshi	Kork Kark		Pondel, Lithuania	PT	murdered
Jakobas Yaakov	Kotonas Katan	1900	Kaunas, Lithuania	PT	murdered
Miksa	Krakauer	1916	Tallos, Czechoslovakia	HLBV	murdered

Appendix of Rokiskis Shoah Victims – not in the original Yizkor Book   APP-29

First Name	Last Name	Birth Year	Place of Residence	Source	Fate from Source
Rivka	Kramer		Rokiskis, Lithuania	PT	murdered
Chaja Ita Khaia	Krasnikoviciene Krasnikovitz		Kupiskis, Lithuania	PT	murdered
Rakhel Etel	Kravic Kravitz	1925	Ponidel, Lithuania	PT	murdered
Ester Rakhel	Kravicas Kravitz		Pandelys, Lithuania	PT	murdered
Icikas Yitzkhak	Kravicas Kravitz	1870	Pandelys, Lithuania	PT	murdered
Ruvinas Reuven	Kravicas Kravitz	1921	Pandelys, Lithuania	PT	murdered
Reizl	Kravicene Kravitz	1890	Ponidel, Lithuania	PT	murdered
Reizl Shoshana Reizel	Kraviciene Kravitz	1887	Pandelys, Lithuania	PT	murdered
Aharon Yitzkhak	Kravicus Kravitz	1885	Rokiskis, Lithuania	PT	murdered
Rakhel Natel	Kravicus Kravitz	1925	Rokiskis, Lithuania	PT	murdered
Reuven	Kravicus Kravitz	1921	Rokiskis, Lithuania	PT	murdered
Reuven	Kravitz	1921	Ponidel, Lithuania	PT	murdered
Yitzkhak	Kravitz	1880	Rakishok, Lithuania	PT	murdered
Rakhel	Kravitz Kravetz	1925	Rakishik, Lithuania	PT	murdered
Reoven Reuven	Kravitz Kravetz	1920	Rakishik, Lithuania	PT	murdered
Riezel Rizel	Kravitz Kravetz	1880	Rakishik, Lithuania	PT	murdered
Lea	Krell	1889	Daugavpils, Latvia	Census	not stated
Lea	Krell	1889	Daugavpils, Latvia	Jew Res	not stated
Eidel	Kremer	1878	Rakishok, Lithuania	PT	murdered
Eidel	Kremer		Rokiskis, Lithuania	PT	murdered
Haim	Kremer	1879	Daugavpils, Latvia	Census	not stated
Haim	Kremer	1879	Daugavpils, Latvia	Jew Res	not stated
Haim	Kremer	1879	Riga, Latvia	Residen	not stated
Samuel Hirsch	Kremer	1877	Riga, Latvia	Jew Res	not stated
Samuel Hirsch	Kremer	1877	Riga, Latvia	Jew Res	not stated
Samuel Hirsch	Kremer	1877	Riga, Latvia	Residen	not stated
Samuel Hirsch	Kremer	1877	Riga, Latvia	Residen	not stated
Samuel Hirsch	Kremer	1877	Riga, Latvia	Residen	not stated
Samuel Hirsch	Kremer	1877	Riga, Latvia	Residen	not stated
Samuel Hirsch	Kremer	1877	Riga, Latvia	Residen	not stated
Baruch Yaakov	Kril		Rokiskis, Lithuania	Yzkr Bk	murdered
Rivka Chana	Kril		Rokiskis, Lithuania	Yzkr Bk	murdered
Akiva	Krivitzki		Kobylnik, Poland	Yzkr Bk	murdered
Kivka	Krivitzky Krivitzki	1910	Kobylnik, Poland	PT	murdered
Bayla Beila	Krok		Skopishki, Lithuania	PT	murdered
Dvora	Krok	1884	Rokiskis, Lithuania	PT	murdered
Grunia Dvora	Krok		Rokiskis, Lithuania	PT	murdered
Hana Hena	Krok	1936	Rokiskis, Lithuania	PT	murdered
Henia	Krok	1936	Rokiskis, Lithuania	PT	murdered
Hilel	Krok	1881	Rokiskis, Lithuania	PT	murdered
Hilel	Krok	1883	Rokiskis, Lithuania	PT	murdered
Hillel Hilel	Krok		Rokiskis, Lithuania	PT	murdered
Hinda	Krok	1908	Rokiskis, Lithuania	PT	murdered
Hinda	Krok		Rokiskis, Lithuania	PT	murdered
Hirsh Harold	Krok		Skopishki, Lithuania	PT	murdered
Hirsh Harold	Krok		Skopishki, Lithuania	PT	murdered
Michal Mikhael	Krok	1933	Rokiskis, Lithuania	PT	murdered
Mihael	Krok	1931	Rokiskis, Lithuania	PT	murdered
Motel Tata	Krok		Skopishok, Lithuania	PT	murdered

APP-30   Appendix of Rokiskis Shoah Victims – not in the original Yizkor Book

First Name	Last Name	Birth Year	Place of Residence	Source	Fate from Source
Musia	Krok		Rokiskis, Lithuania	PT	murdered
Mussel	Krok	1885	Rokiskis, Lithuania	PT	murdered
Mussel Miriam	Krok		Rokiskis, Lithuania	PT	murdered
Shprinca Shprintza	Krok	1936	Rokiskis, Lithuania	PT	murdered
Shprintza Sprinza	Krok	1936	Rokiskis, Lithuania	PT	murdered
Volf	Krok	1881	Rokiskis, Lithuania	PT	murdered
Yacob Yaakov	Krok	1881	Rokiskis, Lithuania	PT	murdered
Yacob Yaakov	Krok		Rokiskis, Lithuania	PT	murdered
Zalman	Krok	1906	Rokiskis, Lithuania	PT	murdered
Zalmen Zalman	Krok		Rokiskis, Lithuania	PT	murdered
Hilelis Hilel	Krokas Krok		Rokiskis, Lithuania	PT	murdered
Rivka Rifka	Krokas Krok		Skopishok, Lithuania	PT	murdered
Reesa Gleea	Krokas Krok Karukes		Lithuania	PT	murdered
Avraham	Kruk		Rokiskis, Lithuania	Yzkr Bk	murdered
Ber	Kruk		Rokiskis, Lithuania	Yzkr Bk	murdered
David	Kruk		Rokiskis, Lithuania	Yzkr Bk	murdered
First name unknown	Kruk		Rokiskis, Lithuania	Yzkr Bk	murdered
First name unknown	Kruk		Rokiskis, Lithuania	Yzkr Bk	murdered
Gershon	Kruk		Rokiskis, Lithuania	Yzkr Bk	murdered
Pessa Paulina	Kruk	1894	Riga, Latvia	Jew Res	murdered
Pessa Paulina	Kruk	1894	Riga, Latvia	Residen	not stated
Pessa Paulina	Kruk	1894	Riga, Latvia	Residen	not stated
Pessa Paulina	Kruk	1894	Riga, Latvia	Residen	not stated
Rachel	Kruk		Rokiskis, Lithuania	Yzkr Bk	murdered
Reina	Kruk		Rokiskis, Lithuania	Yzkr Bk	murdered
Sara	Kruk		Rokiskis, Lithuania	Yzkr Bk	murdered
Shlomo	Kruk		Rokiskis, Lithuania	Yzkr Bk	murdered
Tzipe	Kruk		Rokiskis, Lithuania	Yzkr Bk	murdered
Khaya	Krukos	1921	Rakishki, Lithuania	Evac	not stated
Natalis	Krukos	1877	Rakishki, Lithuania	Evac	not stated
Rano Anis	Krukos	1886	Rakishki, Lithuania	Evac	not stated
Khaia	Krupat Kruft		Kamai, Lithuania	PT	murdered
Khana	Krupat Kruft		Kamajai, Lithuania	PT	murdered
Khana	Krupat Kruft		Kamajai, Lithuania	PT	murdered
Miriam	Krupat Kruft		Kamai, Lithuania	PT	murdered
Yokhanan	Krupat Kruft		Kamai, Lithuania	PT	murdered
Yokhanan Iudl	Krupat Kruft		Kamai, Lithuania	PT	murdered
Zundel	Krupat Kruft		Kamai, Lithuania	PT	murdered
Moshe	Krupatva Kruft		Kamai, Lithuania	PT	murdered
Sara	Krupit	1875	Ponovez, Lithuania	PT	murdered
Pera Dweira	Krut	1874	Daugavpils, Latvia	Census	not stated
Pera Dweira	Krut	1874	Daugavpils, Latvia	Jew Res	not stated
Chana Khana Dvora	Krywicki Krivitzki	1880	Kobilnik, Poland	PT	murdered
Faivus Feibush	Kuk Kok	1917	Rakishik, Lithuania	PT	murdered
Hinda	Kunin	1909	Riga, Latvia	Census	not stated
Hinda	Kunin	1909	Riga, Latvia	Jew Res	not stated
Mirl Sara Mirel	Kuperman	1885	Rokiskis, Lithuania	PT	murdered
Zalman	Kuperman	1891	Rakishok, Lithuania	PT	murdered
Abraham Ycchak Avraham Yitzkhak	Kur	1890	Rakishik, Lithuania	PT	murdered

Appendix of Rokiskis Shoah Victims – not in the original Yizkor Book   APP-31

First Name	Last Name	Birth Year	Place of Residence	Source	Fate from Source
Avraham	Kur	1891	Rakishok, Lithuania	PT	murdered
Ber Feibush	Kur		Rokiskis, Lithuania	Yzkr Bk	murdered
Bronya	Kur	1923	Lithuania	Evac	not stated
Feivus	Kur	1912	Rekishok, Lithuania	PT	murdered
Feiwel Faivel	Kur	1915	Rakiski, Lithuania	PT	murdered
Feyva Baer	Kur		Rokishkis, Lithuania	PT D	murdered
Hirsh Yaakov	Kur		Rokiskis, Lithuania	Yzkr Bk	murdered
Jakob Yaakov	Kur		Rakishki, Lithuania	PT	murdered
Khaim	Kur	1891	Rokiskis, Lithuania	PT	murdered
Khasia	Kur	1893	Rokiskis, Lithuania	PT	murdered
Kreina Kreindel	Kur	1895	Rakishik, Lithuania	PT	murdered
Matel	Kur	1895	Rakishik, Lithuania	PT	murdered
Matl	Kur	1886	Rakishok, Lithuania	PT	murdered
Rivka Ele	Kur	1898	Rakishok, Lithuania	PT	murdered
Sara	Kur	1879	Rakiski, Lithuania	PT	murdered
Sara	Kur		Rokiskis, Lithuania	Yzkr Bk	murdered
Sara Glika	Kur	1880	Rokiskis, Lithuania	PT	murdered
Sender	Kur	1896	Zarasai, Lithuania	PT	murdered
Yaakov Hirsh	Kur	1875	Rokiskis, Lithuania	PT	murdered
Faives Feibush	Kuras Kurs	1913	Rakishik, Lithuania	PT	murdered
Sara	Kuras Kurs	1885	Rakishik, Lithuania	PT	murdered
Yankel Hirsh	Kuras Kurs	1880	Rakishik, Lithuania	PT	murdered
Liba	Kuritzky	1863	Daugavpils, Latvia	Census	not stated
Liba	Kuritzky	1863	Daugavpils, Latvia	Jew Res	not stated
Vera	Kushnirova	1912	Aleksandrobolis, Lithuania	Evac	not stated
Haja	Kutschgal	1875	Daugavpils, Latvia	Census	not stated
Haja	Kutschgal	1875	Daugavpils, Latvia	Jew Res	not stated
Berel	Kveski		Viliai, Lithuania	Persecut	murdered
Berol	Kveski	1906	Viliai, Lithuania	Persecut	murdered
Riva	Kvin Kevin	1877	Riga, Latvia	PT	murdered
Khaia Sara	Kwartowsky Kvartovski	1902	Wilna, Poland	PT	murdered
Feiga	Lachmann	1898	Riga, Latvia	Jew Res	not stated
Feiga	Lachmann	1898	Riga, Latvia	Residen	not stated
Feiga	Lachmann	1898	Riga, Latvia	Residen	not stated
Fruma	Lafer	1900	Pondel, Lithuania	PT	murdered
Fruma	Laffer Lepar	1900	Ponidel, Lithuania	PT	murdered
Yitzkhak	Lan		Rokiskis, Lithuania	PT	murdered
Golde Golda Esther	Landa		Rokiskis, Lithuania	Yzkr Bk	murdered
Izidor	Landau	1919	Debrecen, Hungary	HLBV	murdered
Hershel	Lap	1895	Pandelys, Lithuania	PT	murdered
Lipka	Lap	1895	Pandelis, Lithuania	PT	murdered
Andor	Lase	1911	Bilke, Czechoslovakia	HLBV	murdered
Frida	Latt	1909	Riga, Latvia	Jew Res	not stated
Frida	Latt	1909	Riga, Latvia	Residen	not stated
Scheine	Latz	1925	Jelgava, Latvia	Census	not stated
Scheine	Latz	1925	Jelgava, Latvia	Jew Res	not stated
Sneier Zalman Shneiur	Latz	1885	Ponidel, Lithuania	PT	murdered
Sorra Malla Sara Mala	Latz	1865	Ponidel, Lithuania	PT	murdered
Bernat	Lebovics	1914	Szeklence, Czechoslovakia	HLBV	murdered

Appendix of Rokiskis Shoah Victims – not in the original Yizkor Book

First Name	Last Name	Birth Year	Place of Residence	Source	Fate from Source
Mihaly	Lebovics	1916	Alsoneresznice, Czechoslovakia	HLBV	murdered
Moric	Lebovics	1904		HLBV	murdered
Chaim	Leeman Liman	1890	Birdz, Lithuania	PT	murdered
Hinda	Leiboviciene Libovitz	1878	Pasvitinys, Lithuania	PT	murdered
Hilel	Leibovicius Libovitz	1878	Pasvitinys, Lithuania	PT	murdered
Chaya Devora	Leibowitz		Dvinsk, Latvia	PT	murdered
Iudl	Lekach Lekakh		Rokiskis, Lithuania	PT	murdered
Awraham Avraham	Lerner	1905	Ponemunek, Lithuania	PT	murdered
Beniamin	Lerner		Ponemunek, Lithuania	PT	murdered
Beniamin	Lerner		Panemunek, Lithuania	PT	murdered
Dov	Lerner		Panemunek, Lithuania	PT	murdered
Etel	Lerner		Ponemunek, Lithuania	PT	murdered
Mendl Mendil	Lerner	1904	Panemunek, Lithuania	PT	murdered
Moshe	Lerner		Panemunek, Lithuania	PT	murdered
Peretz	Lerner		Panemunek, Lithuania	PT	murdered
Hirshel	Levi	1891	Rakishok, Lithuania	PT	murdered
Fishel	Levi Levinas Levine	1862	Kamai, Lithuania	PT Ds	murdered
Aharon	Levin		Rokiskis, Lithuania	Yzkr Bk	murdered
Arie	Levin		Rokiskis, Lithuania	Yzkr Bk	murdered
Berul	Levin		Vilnius, Poland	PT	murdered
Breina	Levin	1918	Rokishok, Lithuania	PT	murdered
Chasie Khasia	Levin		Panemunelis, Lithuania	PT	murdered
Chune Khona	Levin		Nemencine, Poland	PT	murdered
Feiga	Levin	1896	Rakishik, Lithuania	PT	murdered
Feige	Levin		Rokiskis, Lithuania	Yzkr Bk	murdered
Fraidel Freidel	Levin		Panemunelis, Lithuania	PT	murdered
Fruma	Levin	1878	Rokiskis, Lithuania	PT	murdered
Frumet Sara	Levin		Rokiskis, Lithuania	Yzkr Bk	murdered
Girsho	Levin	1892	Kamajai, Lithuania	Evac	not stated
Guta	Levin	1931	Rekishok, Lithuania	PT	murdered
Hana Khana	Levin	1904	Rokiskis, Lithuania	PT	murdered
Isser	Levin	1871	Rokiskis, Lithuania	Dep-FR	murdered
Khana	Levin	1920	Rokiskis, Lithuania	PT	murdered
Khana	Levin		Rokiskis, Lithuania	Yzkr Bk	murdered
Lea Chaia	Levin		Rokiskis, Lithuania	Yzkr Bk	murdered
Leah Lea	Levin		Panemunelis, Lithuania	PT	murdered
Leib	Levin		Panemunelis, Lithuania	PT	murdered
Leib Mendl	Levin		Rokiskis, Lithuania	Yzkr Bk	murdered
Leizer Maria	Levin		Rokiskis, Lithuania	Yzkr Bk	murdered
Lev	Levin		Rokiskis, Lithuania	Yzkr Bk	murdered
Leya	Levin		Panemunelis, Lithuania	PT	murdered
Menahem Menakhem	Levin	1900	Rokiskis, Lithuania	PT	murdered
Mendel	Levin	1870	Rakishok, Lithuania	PT	murdered
Mendel	Levin	1876	Rakishok, Lithuania	PT	murdered
Mendel	Levin	1906	Rokiskis, Lithuania	PT	murdered
Merl	Levin		Rokiskis, Lithuania	Yzkr Bk	murdered
Mikhail	Levin	1932	Rakishki, Lithuania	Evac	not stated
Olka Olga	Levin	1907	Rokishok, Lithuania	PT	murdered
Perel	Levin		Rokiskis, Lithuania	Yzkr Bk	murdered

Appendix of Rokiskis Shoah Victims – not in the original Yizkor Book   APP-33

First Name	Last Name	Birth Year	Place of Residence	Source	Fate from Source
Pesakh	Levin	1886	Rakishki, Lithuania	PT	murdered
Rivka	Levin	1920	Kaunas, Lithuania	PT	murdered
Rivka Sara	Levin		Rokiskis, Lithuania	Yzkr Bk	murdered
Rufka Ruvim	Levin	1896	Rokishkis, Lithuania	PT Ds	murdered
Sara	Levin	1921	Rokiskis, Lithuania	PT	murdered
Shmuel	Levin		Rokiskis, Lithuania	Yzkr Bk	not stated
Yaakov	Levin	1894	Rakishik, Lithuania	PT	murdered
Yaakov	Levin		Rokiskis, Lithuania	Yzkr Bk	murdered
Yekhezkel	Levin		Rokiskis, Lithuania	Yzkr Bk	murdered
Yona	Levin		Rokiskis, Lithuania	Yzkr Bk	murdered
	Levin	1891	Rakishok, Lithuania	PT	murdered
Haskel	Levine		Kamai, Lithuania	PT Ds	murdered
Shayna	Levine	1865	Kamai, Lithuania	PT Ds	murdered
Reevl	Levinson	1880	Slobodka, Lithuania	PT	murdered
	Levinson		Slobodka, Lithuania	PT	murdered
Ester	Levit	1906	Kowno, Lithuania	PT	murdered
Ester	Levit	1906	Kovna, Lithuania	PT	murdered
Iudl	Levit	1887	Rakisok, Lithuania	PT	murdered
Iosif	Levitos	1885	Rokishkis, Lithuania	Evac	not stated
Frida	Levitt Levit	1876	Rokiskis, Lithuania	PT	murdered
Henia	Levitt Levit	1928	Rokiskis, Lithuania	PT	murdered
Taybe Yonina Taiba Yanina	Levitt Levit	1930	Rokiskis, Lithuania	PT	murdered
Riva Sara	Lewanawitsch	1911	Riga, Latvia	Jew Res	not stated
Riva Sara	Lewanawitsch	1911	Riga, Latvia	Residen	not stated
Riva Sara	Lewanawitsch	1911	Riga, Latvia	Residen	not stated
Riva Sara	Lewanawitsch	1911	Riga, Latvia	Residen	not stated
Riva Sara	Lewanawitsch	1911	Riga, Latvia	Residen	not stated
Riva Sara	Lewanawitsch	1911	Riga, Latvia	Residen	not stated
Riva Sara	Lewanawitsch	1911	Riga, Latvia	Residen	not stated
Riva Sara	Lewanawitsch	1911	Riga, Latvia	Residen	not stated
Riva Sara	Lewanawitsch	1911	Riga, Latvia	Residen	not stated
Genenda	Lewin	1910	Riga, Latvia	Jew Res	not stated
Genenda	Lewin	1910	Riga, Latvia	Residen	not stated
Eliezer	Lewin Levin		Rakiszki, Lithuania	PT	murdered
Nachmen Nakhman	Lewin Levin	1922	Rokiskis, Lithuania	PT	murdered
Sara	Lewin Levin	1908	Rakiszki, Lithuania	PT	murdered
Yitzkhak	Lewin Levin		Rakiszki, Lithuania	PT	murdered
Abramas Avraham	Libermanas Liberman	1909	Lithuania	PT	murdered
Hinda	Libovich Libovitz	1875	Poshvitin, Lithuania	PT	murdered
Khaim Hilel	Libovich Libovitz	1875	Poshvitin, Lithuania	PT	murdered
Breina	Liman	1880	Pandelis, Lithuania	PT	murdered
Chaim Khaim	Liman	1880	Birzai, Lithuania	PT	murdered
David Ber	Liman	1885	Birzai, Lithuania	PT	murdered
Israel Michal Yisrael Mikhael	Limon	1875	Ponedel, Lithuania	PT	murdered
Jozef Yosef	Limon	1901	Pondel, Lithuania	PT	murdered
Shoshana Roza	Limon	1908	Ponodol, Lithuania	PT	murdered
Asna	Liokman Goldberg	1898	Daugavpils, Latvia	Census	not stated
Asna	Liokman Goldberg	1898	Daugavpils, Latvia	Jew Res	not stated
Avraham	Lipovich Lipovitz		Rakishik, Lithuania	PT	murdered

APP-34   Appendix of Rokiskis Shoah Victims – not in the original Yizkor Book

First Name	Last Name	Birth Year	Place of Residence	Source	Fate from Source
Ester	Lipovich Lipovitz		Rakishik, Lithuania	PT	murdered
Rachel Etel Rakhel	Lipoviciene Lipovitz	1879	Rakishik, Lithuania	PT	murdered
Rachel Rakhel	Lipoviciene Lipovitz	1873	Rokiskis, Lithuania	PT	murdered
Aria Arie	Lipovicius	1875	Rakishik, Lithuania	PT	murdered
Bela	Lipovitz	1918	Rokishki, Lithuania	PT	murdered
Leiba	Lipoviz Lipovitz	1876	Rakisok, Lithuania	PT	murdered
Chaia Dvora	Liubovitz		Rokiskis, Lithuania	Yzkr Bk	murdered
Shaul	Liubovitz		Rokiskis, Lithuania	Yzkr Bk	murdered
Albert	Lobl	1918	Debrecen, Hungary	HLBV	murdered
Leya	Lopides	1900	Rokishkis, Lithuania	Evac	not stated
Miriam	Lotz	1905	Pandelys, Lithuania	PT	murdered
Snayer Zalman Shneiur	Lotz	1907	Pandelys, Lithuania	PT	murdered
Jozsef	Lowinger	1911	Ujfeherto, Hungary	HLBV	murdered
Saul	Lubovitz		Rokiskis, Lithuania	PT D	murdered
Libe Luba	Luri Lurie	1908	Utena, Lithuania	PT	murdered
Chawiwa Khaviva	Lurie	1890	Kowna, Lithuania	PT	murdered
Breina Brandel	Majofis	1901	Panimon, Lithuania	PT	murdered
	Majofis Mayofis	1880	Panimon, Lithuania	PT	murdered
	Majofis Mayofis Maiofis	1880	Panemune, Lithuania	PT	murdered
Lea Ita	Malatzky	1885	Daugavpils, Latvia	Census	not stated
Lea Ita	Malatzky	1885	Daugavpils, Latvia	Jew Res	murdered
Khanan	Maler	1915	Rakishok, Lithuania	PT	murdered
Aharon Shlomo	Maltzer	1881	Siauliai, Lithuania	PT	murdered
Feiga	Margolis	1885	Riga, Latvia	Jew Res	not stated
Feiga	Margolis	1885	Riga, Latvia	Residen	not stated
Feiga	Margolis	1885	Riga, Latvia	Residen	not stated
Haimas Khaim	Margolis	1903	Skopishki, Lithuania	PT	murdered
Jechuda Yehuda	Margolis	1909	Daugavpils, Latvia	PT	murdered
Judel	Margolis	1909	Daugavpils, Latvia	Census	not stated
Judel	Margolis	1909	Daugavpils, Latvia	Jew Res	murdered
Pinchas Dov Pinkhas	Margolis	1882	Daugavpils, Latvia	PT	murdered
Reuven	Margolis	1913	Daugavpils, Latvia	PT	murdered
Ruben	Margolis	1913	Daugavpils, Latvia	Census	not stated
Ruben	Margolis	1913	Daugavpils, Latvia	Jew Res	killed in military service
Samuel Schmuel	Margolis	1912	Daugavpils, Latvia	Jew Res	murdered
Sara	Margolis	1905	Skapiskis, Lithuania	PT	murdered
Gershon Gerson	Markel Merkel		Rokiskis, Lithuania	PT	murdered
Hoda Liebe Liba	Markel Merkel	1871	Subate, Latvia	PT	murdered
Chankin Khana	Markin Markeninya	1922	Rokiszki, Lithuania	PT	murdered
Rivka	Maron		Lithuania	PT	murdered
Shmuel	Maron		Rokiskis, Lithuania	PT	murdered
Matke	Matenzon	1926	Rokiskis, Lithuania	PT	murdered
Noime Noima	Matenzon	1930	Rokiskis, Lithuania	PT	murdered
Rachel Hena Rakhel	Matenzon	1905	Rokiskis, Lithuania	PT	murdered
Seinke Sheina Szainka	Matenzon	1925	Rokiskis, Lithuania	PT	murdered
Taibe Taiba	Matenzon	1923	Rokiskis, Lithuania	PT	murdered
Zusman	Matenzon	1886	Rakisok, Lithuania	PT	murdered
Zusman	Matenzon	1897	Rokiskis, Lithuania	PT	murdered

Appendix of Rokiskis Shoah Victims – not in the original Yizkor Book   APP-35

First Name	Last Name	Birth Year	Place of Residence	Source	Fate from Source
Rosa	Matlin	1886	Panemunes, Lithuania	Jew Res	not stated
Schmuel	Matlin	1883	Panemunes, Lithuania	Jew Res	not stated
Meyer	Matuson	1892	Memli, Lithuania	PT	murdered
Leale Lea	Matuson Matuzon	1931	Rokiskis, Lithuania	PT	murdered
Malka	Matuson Matuzon		Rokiskis, Lithuania	PT	murdered
Meyer Meir	Matuson Matuzon	1892	Memel, Lithuania	PT	murdered
Rivkale Rivka	Matuson Matuzon	1933	Rokiskis, Lithuania	PT	murdered
Shmuel Leib Samuel	Matuson Matuzon	1895	Shavel, Lithuania	PT	murdered
Yentale Yenta	Matuson Matuzon	1935	Rokiskis, Lithuania	PT	murdered
Zusman	Matuson Matuzon		Rokiskis, Lithuania	PT	murdered
Alta Alte Masha	Matz	1890	Utena, Lithuania	PT	murdered
Raya	Mebelste	1915	Lithuania	Evac	not stated
Majer	Mechlovits	1901	Keselymezo, Czechoslovakia	HLBV	murdered
Avraham	Meierovitz		Obeliai, Lithuania	Murd	murdered
Osnat Asnat Rivka	Mejeroviciene Meierovitz		Obeliai, Lithuania	PT	murdered
Abram Avraham	Mejerovicius Meierovitz		Obeliai, Lithuania	PT	murdered
Israel Yisrael	Mejerowicz Meierovitz	1912	Linkova, Lithuania	PT	murdered
Meir	Mekler	1886	Rakisok, Lithuania	PT	murdered
Dwora Dvora	Meler Maler		Rokiskis, Lithuania	PT	murdered
Gutel Guta	Meler Maler		Ponidel, Lithuania	PT	murdered
Gutel Guta	Meler Maler		Ponidel, Lithuania	PT	murdered
Josef Yosef	Meler Maler		Rakiski, Lithuania	PT	murdered
Keile Keila	Meler Maler		Rokiskis, Lithuania	PT	murdered
Smuel Shmuel	Meler Maler		Rokiskis, Lithuania	PT	murdered
Khava Elka	Melkin Milkin	1917	Rokishok, Lithuania	PT	murdered
Ben Tsiyon	Meller	1900	Ponedel, Lithuania	PT	murdered
Boris	Meller		Ponedel, Lithuania	Persecut	murdered
Gitel	Meller		Ponedel, Lithuania	Persecut	murdered
Bentzion	Meller Maler		Ponidel, Lithuania	PT	murdered
Eta Elka	Meller Maler	1935	Ponidel, Lithuania	PT	murdered
Sore Sara Rivka	Meller Maler	1930	Ponidel, Lithuania	PT	murdered
Riwka Rivka	Melner Milner	1918	Rokishok, Lithuania	PT	murdered
Henje Henia	Mendelewitz Mendelovitz	1912	Rassejn, Lithuania	PT	murdered
Gershon	Merkel		Rakeshik, Lithuania	PT	murdered
Ida	Merkel		Rakisok, Lithuania	PT	murdered
Khaia	Merkel		Rakisok, Lithuania	PT	murdered
Mano	Mermelstein	1901	Munkacs, Czechoslovakia	HLBV	not stated
Israel Yisrael	Meyerovich Meierovitz	1912	Linkuva, Lithuania	PT	murdered
Osnat Asnat Rivka	Meyerovitz Meierovitz		Rokiskis, Lithuania	PT	murdered
Khana	Michaleviz Mikhalovich	1891	Rakishik, Lithuania	PT	murdered
Bluma	Michalewicz Mikhlevitz	1908	Panedel, Lithuania	PT	murdered
Masza Moshe Masha	Michalewicz Mikhlevitz	1895	Pondel, Lithuania	PT	murdered
Mendel	Michalewicz Mikhlevitz	1890	Pondel, Lithuania	PT	murdered
Towa Tova	Michalewicz Mikhlevitz	1915	Ponodol, Lithuania	PT	murdered
Michel Velva Mikhael Velvel	Michelevitz Mikhlevitz	1867	Abeliai, Lithuania	PT	murdered
Chaim Khaim	Michelson Mikhelson		Rokiskis, Lithuania	PT	murdered
Ester	Michelson Mikhelson		Rokiskis, Lithuania	PT	murdered
Pinchas Pinkhas	Michelson Mikhelson		Rokiskis, Lithuania	PT	murdered
Tauba Tova Miriam	Michelson Mikhelson	1900	Rokiskis, Lithuania	PT	murdered

APP-36   Appendix of Rokiskis Shoah Victims – not in the original Yizkor Book

First Name	Last Name	Birth Year	Place of Residence	Source	Fate from Source
Yosef	Michelson Mikhelson		Rokiskis, Lithuania	PT	murdered
Zoltan	Mihaly	1918	Kunhegyes, Hungary	HLBV	murdered
Fruma	Mikhalovich	1922	Rakishok, Lithuania	PT	murdered
Bentzion	Miler		Rokiskis, Lithuania	Yzkr Bk	murdered
Khashke	Miler		Rokiskis, Lithuania	Yzkr Bk	murdered
Lea Sara	Miler		Rokiskis, Lithuania	Yzkr Bk	murdered
Pesakh	Milkin	1881	Rakishik, Lithuania	PT	murdered
Roza	Milkin	1886	Rakishok, Lithuania	PT	murdered
Schmerl	Miller	1901	Rokishkis, Lithuania	Persecut	murdered
Chanan Khanan	Milner	1920	Rokishki, Lithuania	PT	murdered
First name unknown	Milner	1928	Rokiskis, Lithuania	PT	murdered
Frida	Milner	1915	Onuskis, Lithuania	PT	murdered
Frida	Milner	1915	Rokiskis, Lithuania	PT	murdered
Frida Freidel	Milner	1915	Rokishkis, Lithuania	PT D	murdered
Iosif	Milner	1895	Rokiskis, Lithuania	PT	murdered
Iosif	Milner		Rokishki, Lithuania	PT	murdered
Khanan Khona	Milner	1924	Rokishkis, Lithuania	PT	murdered
Khaya	Milner		Rokishki, Lithuania	PT	murdered
Khona	Milner		Rokishki, Lithuania	PT	murdered
Mirjam Miriam Mera	Milner	1923	Rokishki, Lithuania	PT	murdered
Mirra	Milner	1929	Rokishki, Lithuania	PT	murdered
Riva	Milner	1918	Rokishkis, Lithuania	PT	murdered
Rivekka	Milner	1918	Rokishki, Lithuania	PT	murdered
Roche Zilya Cirele	Milner		Rokishok, Lithuania	PT D	murdered
Tzilya	Milner	1895	Rokishkis, Lithuania	PT	murdered
Yosef	Milner	1881	Rakishok, Lithuania	PT	murdered
Yosef	Milner	1890	Rokishok, Lithuania	PT	murdered
Zilya	Milner		Rokishok, Lithuania	PT Ds	murdered
David	Moldovan	1908	Bartfalva, Romania	HLBV	murdered
Bela	Moskovits	1911	Mezoladany, Hungary	HLBV	murdered
Chajim Khaim David	Mudrik		Panemune, Lithuania	PT	murdered
Chiena Khina	Mudrik	1895	Panemune, Lithuania	PT	murdered
Liuba	Mudrik		Panemune, Lithuania	PT	murdered
Rivka	Mudrik	1922	Panemune, Lithuania	PT	murdered
Rivka	Mudrik	1922	Panemune, Lithuania	PT	murdered
Samuelis Shmuel	Mudrik	1890	Panemune, Lithuania	PT	murdered
Shlomo	Mudrik	1919	Panemune, Lithuania	PT	murdered
Shlomo	Mudrik	1919	Panemune, Lithuania	PT	murdered
Yoel	Mudrik		Panemune, Lithuania	PT	murdered
Beila	Mugermann	1883	Daugavpils, Latvia	Census	not stated
Beila	Mugermann	1883	Daugavpils, Latvia	Jew Res	not stated
Bentzion	Muler	1891	Rokiskis, Lithuania	PT	murdered
Khasia	Muler Miler	1920	Rakishok, Lithuania	PT	murdered
Mala	Munits Munitz	1885	Skopishok, Lithuania	PT	murdered
Yehudit Yehuda Iudas	Munits Munitz	1901	Skopishki, Lithuania	PT	murdered
Zalman Moshe	Munits Munitz		Skopishki, Lithuania	PT	murdered
Yenta	Munitz	1923	Pandelis, Lithuania	PT	murdered
Yenta Yenthe	Munitz Monitz	1923	Skopishok, Lithuania	PT	murdered
Yosef Zalman	Munitz Monitz	1925	Skopishki, Lithuania	PT	murdered
Gersha	Munitzas	1901	Skapiskis, Lithuania	Evac	not stated

Appendix of Rokiskis Shoah Victims – not in the original Yizkor Book   APP-37

First Name	Last Name	Birth Year	Place of Residence	Source	Fate from Source
Khopel	Munitzas	1927	Skapiskis, Lithuania	Evac	not stated
Sara	Munitzas	1902	Skapiskis, Lithuania	Evac	not stated
Zalman	Munitzas	1924	Skapiskis, Lithuania	Evac	not stated
Zalman	Munitzas	1925	Lithuania	Persecut	killed in military service
Zeida	Munitzas	1921	Skapiskis, Lithuania	Evac	not stated
Baruch Barukh	Musel Mosel	1905	Abeli, Lithuania	PT	murdered
Baruch Barukh	Musel Mosel		Abel, Lithuania	PT	murdered
Lajb Arie Leib	Musel Mosel		Obeliai, Lithuania	PT	murdered
Rachel Rakhel	Musel Mosel		Abeli, Lithuania	PT	murdered
Rachel Rakhel	Musel Mosel		Obeliai, Lithuania	PT	murdered
Yankel Laib Iankel Leib	Musel Mosel		Abeli, Lithuania	PT	murdered
Chana Fryda Khana Frida	Mychalewicz Mikhlevitz	1875	Panedel, Lithuania	PT	murdered
Mendel	Mychalewicz Mikhlevitz	1898	Pandelis, Lithuania	PT	murdered
Ester	Nachamovic Nekhamovitz	1886	Rakishok, Lithuania	PT	murdered
Yitzkhak Chaim	Nakhumovitz		Rokiskis, Lithuania	Yzkr Bk	murdered
Etel	Nasatir	1898	Dvinsk, Latvia	PT	murdered
Eta Lea	Naschatir	1895	Daugavpils, Latvia	Census	not stated
Eta Lea	Naschatir	1895	Daugavpils, Latvia	Jew Res	murdered
Batia Hena Rakhel	Natanzon	1891	Rokiskis, Lithuania	PT	murdered
Aaron	Nochomovitz		Rokiskis, Lithuania	PT Ds	murdered
Eva	Nochomovitz		Rokiskis, Lithuania	PT Ds	murdered
Itzik Chaim	Nochomovitz		Rokiskis, Lithuania	PT Ds	murdered
Mottel	Nochomovitz		Rokiskis, Lithuania	PT D	murdered
Mottel	Nochomovitz		Rokiskis, Lithuania	PT D	murdered
Musa	Nochomovitz		Rokiskis, Lithuania	PT D	murdered
Rive	Nochomovitz		Rokiskis, Lithuania	PT Ds	murdered
Berl	Ogenc Ogentz	1906	Pandelys, Lithuania	PT	murdered
Pesja Pesia	Ogenc Ogentz	1876	Pandelys, Lithuania	PT	murdered
Reisel Reizl	Ogenc Ogentz	1909	Pandelys, Lithuania	PT	murdered
Golda	Orelovic	1870	Panevezys, Lithuania	PT	murdered
Roza	Orelovic	1896	Rokiskis, Lithuania	PT	murdered
Meir Leizer	Orelovic Orlovitz	1866	Rakishok, Lithuania	PT	murdered
Pesach Pesakh	Orelovic Orlovitz	1896	Rakisok, Lithuania	PT	murdered
Shabtai	Orelovic Orlovitz	1897	Rokiskis, Lithuania	PT	murdered
Zelig	Orelovic Orlovitz	1895	Rokiskis, Lithuania	PT	murdered
Zelig	Orelovic Orlovitz	1895	Rokiskis, Lithuania	PT	murdered
Khanan	Orelovich Orlovitz	1894	Rokishok, Lithuania	PT	murdered
Bentzion	Orelovitz		Rokiskis, Lithuania	Yzkr Bk	murdered
Dobre	Orelovitz		Rokiskis, Lithuania	Yzkr Bk	murdered
First name unknown	Orelovitz		Rokiskis, Lithuania	Yzkr Bk	murdered
First name unknown	Orelovitz		Rokiskis, Lithuania	Yzkr Bk	murdered
Khona	Orelovitz		Rokiskis, Lithuania	Yzkr Bk	murdered
Leizer Meir	Orelovitz		Rokiskis, Lithuania	Yzkr Bk	murdered
Pesakh	Orelovitz		Rokiskis, Lithuania	Yzkr Bk	murdered
Zelig	Oreloviz Orlovitz	1886	Rekishok, Lithuania	PT	murdered
Avraham	Orlovitz		Rokiskis, Lithuania	PT D	murdered
Dobra	Orlovitz		Rokiskis, Lithuania	PT D	murdered

APP-38   Appendix of Rokiskis Shoah Victims – not in the original Yizkor Book

First Name	Last Name	Birth Year	Place of Residence	Source	Fate from Source
Roza	Orlowits Orlovitz	1904	Rakiski, Lithuania	PT	murdered
Moshe	Orlowitz Orlovitz		Rakiski, Lithuania	PT	murdered
Zelig	Orlowitz Orlovitz	1898	Rakiski, Lithuania	PT	murdered
Bailie Chana	Padkarsky Radkarsky	1890	Lithuania	PT	murdered
Luba	Padkarsky Radkarsky	1923	Rakishok, Lithuania	PT	murdered
Haikel	Pakempners	1910	Panemunes, Lithuania	Jew Res	not stated
Kreine	Pakempners	1881	Panemunes, Lithuania	Jew Res	not stated
Meier	Pakempners	1913	Panemunes, Lithuania	Jew Res	not stated
Jozsef	Pal	1919	Berettyoujfalu, Hungary	HLBV	murdered
Ryvka Rivka	Pelz Peltz		Bircza, Poland	PT	murdered
Binjamin Beniamin	Pen		Rokiskis, Lithuania	PT	murdered
Golda	Pen		Rokiskis, Lithuania	PT	murdered
Iudl	Pen	1886	Rakishok, Lithuania	PT	murdered
Juda Yehuda	Pen		Rokiskis, Lithuania	PT	murdered
Jaakov Tzvi Yaakov	Peres	1917	Svedasai, Lithuania	PT	murdered
Josef Yosef Eliezer	Peres	1883	Svedasai, Lithuania	PT	murdered
Shalom Salom	Peres	1920	Svedasai, Lithuania	PT	murdered
Ester	Peres Pres		Svedasai, Lithuania	PT	murdered
Esther Ester	Peres Pres		Svedasai, Lithuania	PT	murdered
Henne Rochel Hena Rakhel	Peres Pres	1893	Svedasai, Lithuania	PT	murdered
Joseph Lazer Yosef Lazar	Peres Pres	1883	Svedasai, Lithuania	PT	murdered
Shulem Shalom	Peres Pres		Svedasai, Lithuania	PT	murdered
Yankel Hirsh Iankel	Peres Pres		Svedasai, Lithuania	PT	murdered
Bella	Perkim		Rokiskis, Lithuania	PT D	murdered
David	Perkim		Rokiskis, Lithuania	PT D	murdered
Pesa	Perlmann	1904	Bauska, Latvia	Census	not stated
Pesa	Perlmann	1904	Riga, Latvia	Jew Res	not stated
Pesa	Perlmann	1904	Riga, Latvia	Residen	not stated
Pesa	Perlmann	1904	Riga, Latvia	Residen	not stated
Schemuel Shmuel	Pik	1880	Pondel, Lithuania	PT	murdered
Batia	Pintuseviciene Pintusevitz		Ponidel, Lithuania	PT	murdered
Abramas Avraham	Pintusevicius Pintusevitz		Ponidel, Lithuania	PT	murdered
Jcchakas Yitzkhak	Pintusevicius Pintusevitz		Pandelys, Lithuania	PT	murdered
Zalmanas Zalman	Pintusevicius Pintusevitz		Ponidel, Lithuania	PT	murdered
Etel	Pintuseviciute Pintusevitz		Ponidel, Lithuania	PT	murdered
Ida	Pintuseviciute Pintusevitz		Pandelys, Lithuania	PT	murdered
Avraham	Pintusevitz		Ponidel, Lithuania	PT	murdered
Batia	Pintusevitz		Utian, Lithuania	PT	murdered
Etel	Pintusevitz		Ponidel, Lithuania	PT	murdered
Ida	Pintusevitz		Ponidel, Lithuania	PT	murdered
Yitzkhak	Pintusevitz		Ponidel, Lithuania	PT	murdered
Zalman	Pintusevitz		Ponidel, Lithuania	PT	murdered
Etel	Pintusewits Pintusevitz		Pandelis, Lithuania	PT	murdered
Batia	Pintusewitz Pintusevitz		Pandelis, Lithuania	PT	murdered
Ida Yehudit	Pintusewitz Pintusevitz		Pandelis, Lithuania	PT	murdered
Yitzkhak Izchak	Pintusewitz Pintusevitz		Pandelis, Lithuania	PT	murdered
Avraham	Pintushevitz	1910	Pandelis, Lithuania	PT	murdered
Doba	Pintushevitz	1885	Pandelis, Lithuania	PT	murdered
Zalman	Pintushevitz	1880	Pandelis, Lithuania	PT	murdered
Bryna	Podlas		Rokiskis, Lithuania	PT D	murdered

Appendix of Rokiskis Shoah Victims – not in the original Yizkor Book   APP-39

First Name	Last Name	Birth Year	Place of Residence	Source	Fate from Source
First name unknown	Podlas		Rokiskis, Lithuania	Yzkr Bk	murdered
Yaakov	Podlas		Rokiskis, Lithuania	Yzkr Bk	murdered
Yehudah Loeb Yehuda Leib	Pogrund		Abel, Lithuania	PT	murdered
Feice Feicha Tzipora	Polonski	1900	Rageliai, Lithuania	PT	murdered
Khaim	Pomeranc Pomerantz	1886	Rokishok, Lithuania	PT	murdered
Yisrael	Ponivez	1896	Rakisok, Lithuania	PT	murdered
Abram	Poplak	1892	Riga, Latvia	Jew Res	murdered
Mura	Portnaya	1900	Rakishki, Lithuania	PT	murdered
Avigdor	Portnoi	1925	Rakishki, Lithuania	PT	murdered
Itzek	Portnoi	1927	Rakishki, Lithuania	PT	murdered
Izrail	Portnoi	1898	Rakishki, Lithuania	PT	murdered
Yudel	Portnoi	1895	Voronezh, Russia (USSR)	PT	killed in military service
Becalel Betzalel	Portnoj Portnoi	1874	Riga, Latvia	PT	murdered
Chaim Khaim	Portnoj Portnoi	1870	Riga, Latvia	PT	murdered
First name unknown	Portnoj Portnoi	1882	Riga, Latvia	PT	murdered
Malka	Portnoj Portnoi	1873	Riga, Latvia	PT	murdered
Haim Leib	Portnoy	1880	Riga, Latvia	Jew Res	murdered
Ruvin	Portnoy	1884	Daugavpils, Latvia	Census	not stated
Ruvin	Portnoy	1884	Daugavpils, Latvia	Jew Res	not stated
Slowa Slawa	Portnoy	1900	Daugavpils, Latvia	Census	not stated
Slowa Slawa	Portnoy	1900	Daugavpils, Latvia	Jew Res	not stated
Zalel Nechemia	Portnoy	1879	Riga, Latvia	Jew Res	murdered
Zalel Nechemia	Portnoy	1879	Riga, Latvia	Residen	not stated
Becalel Betzalel	Portnoy Portnoi	1875	Riga, Latvia	PT	murdered
Hana Khana	Portnoy Portnoi	1897	Panevezhis, Lithuania	PT	murdered
Smuel Shmuel	Preid Freid	1881	Rakishok, Lithuania	PT	murdered
Aharon	Pres		Kupishok, Lithuania	PT	murdered
Arie Zakharia Leib	Pres		Kupishok, Lithuania	PT	murdered
Berta	Pres	1923	Kamai, Lithuania	Evac	not stated
David	Pres		Kupishok, Lithuania	PT	murdered
G	Pres	1887	Kamai, Lithuania	Evac	not stated
Khaike Khaika	Pres		Kupishok, Lithuania	PT	murdered
Kheina Khiena	Pres		Kupishok, Lithuania	PT	murdered
Tzella	Pres	1928	Kamai, Lithuania	Evac	not stated
Zelman	Pres	1886	Kamai, Lithuania	Evac	not stated
Lea	Press Pres		Kamai, Lithuania	PT	murdered
Moshe	Prozer		Rokishkis, Lithuania	PT	murdered
Tema Basia	Prozer		Pandelis, Lithuania	PT D	murdered
Yerukhim Yefim	Pulde	1910	Moskva, Russia (USSR)	PT	killed in military service
Leib	Pulman		Rokiskis, Lithuania	PT D	murdered
Mira	Pulman		Rokiskis, Lithuania	PT D	murdered
Michael Mekhael	Pun	1879	Ponidel, Lithuania	PT	murdered
Tzipora	Pun	1903	Ponidel, Lithuania	PT	murdered
Yosef	Pun		Ponidel, Lithuania	PT	murdered
Barukh	Purva Purwe		Kowna, Lithuania	PT	murdered
Mina	Purva Purwe		Kowna, Lithuania	PT	murdered

APP-40   Appendix of Rokiskis Shoah Victims – not in the original Yizkor Book

First Name	Last Name	Birth Year	Place of Residence	Source	Fate from Source
Mordekhai	Purva Purwe		Kowna, Lithuania	PT	murdered
Mordekhai	Purva Purwe		Kowna, Lithuania	PT	murdered
Baruch	Purwe Purva	1936	Kowna, Lithuania	PT	murdered
Mikhael Michal	Purwe Purva		Kowno, Lithuania	PT	murdered
Mordchai Motele Mordekhai	Purwe Purva	1934	Kowna, Lithuania	PT	murdered
Tauba	Rabinovich	1904	Zaporozhia, Ukraine (USSR)	Evac	not stated
Lotta Lote	Rabinovitz	1870	Riga, Latvia	PT	murdered
Hilel	Rabinoviz Rabinovitz		Panevezys, Lithuania	PT	murdered
Benzel	Rabinowitsch	1863	Riga, Latvia	Jew Res	murdered
Benzel	Rabinowitsch	1863	Riga, Latvia	Residen	not stated
Benzel	Rabinowitsch	1863	Riga, Latvia	Residen	not stated
Benzel	Rabinowitsch	1863	Riga, Latvia	Residen	not stated
Benzel	Rabinowitsch	1863	Riga, Latvia	Residen	not stated
Luba	Rabinowitsch	1904	Ludza, Latvia	Census	not stated
Luba	Rabinowitsch	1904	Ludza, Latvia	Jew Res	not stated
Chana Khana	Racemoriene Ratzimora		Pandelys, Lithuania	PT	murdered
Shlomo	Rachman Rakhman	1886	Rokiskis, Lithuania	PT	murdered
Bentzion	Rade		Rokiskis, Lithuania	Yzkr Bk	murdered
Chana	Rade		Rokiskis, Lithuania	Yzkr Bk	murdered
Khana	Rade		Rokiskis, Lithuania	Yzkr Bk	murdered
Khana Chaia	Rade		Rokiskis, Lithuania	Yzkr Bk	murdered
Leib	Rade		Rokiskis, Lithuania	Yzkr Bk	murdered
Peretz	Rade		Rokiskis, Lithuania	Yzkr Bk	murdered
Tuvia	Rade		Rokiskis, Lithuania	Yzkr Bk	murdered
Yitzkhak	Rade		Rokiskis, Lithuania	Yzkr Bk	murdered
Josif Yosef	Radin	1892	Panevezys, Lithuania	PT	murdered
Debora	Rakhman		Rakishki, Lithuania	PT	murdered
Leyb	Rakhman	1923	Rakishki, Lithuania	PT	murdered
Shlyoma	Rakhman	1895	Rakishki, Lithuania	PT	murdered
Vikhne	Rakhman	1916	Rakishki, Lithuania	PT	murdered
Yenta	Rakhman	1918	Rakishki, Lithuania	PT	murdered
Zyama	Rakhman	1921	Rakishki, Lithuania	PT	murdered
Scheina	Rapeiko	1898	Griva, Latvia	Jew Res	not stated
Sara Lea	Ratman Retman	1875	Rokiskis, Lithuania	PT	murdered
Shimshon	Ratman Retman	1908	Rokiskis, Lithuania	PT	murdered
Khana	Ratzemor		Birdz, Lithuania	PT	murdered
Zira	Rauchmann	1905	Riga, Latvia	Jew Res	not stated
Zira	Rauchmann	1905	Riga, Latvia	Residen	not stated
Alter	Rebe		Rokiskis, Lithuania	Yzkr Bk	murdered
Pua	Rebe		Rokiskis, Lithuania	Yzkr Bk	murdered
Hana Khana	Reef Rif		Kovne, Lithuania	PT	murdered
Meir	Reif Rif	1890	Rokiskis, Lithuania	PT	murdered
Seine Sheina	Reif Rif	1898	Rakiski, Lithuania	PT	murdered
Zelig	Reif Rif	1916	Komai, Lithuania	PT	murdered
Zelig	Reif Rif		Rokiskis, Lithuania	PT	murdered
Roza	Remez	1888	Wilna, Poland	PT	murdered
Moshe	Reznikovic Reznikovich	1891	Rokiskis, Lithuania	PT	murdered
Chaim	Reznikovich	1900	Rokiskis, Lithuania	PT Ds	murdered
Liza	Reznikovich	1903	Rokiskis, Lithuania	PT Ds	murdered

Appendix of Rokiskis Shoah Victims – not in the original Yizkor Book   APP-41

First Name	Last Name	Birth Year	Place of Residence	Source	Fate from Source
Mirla	Reznikovich	1932	Rokiskis, Lithuania	PT Ds	murdered
Yanina	Reznikovich	1929	Rokiskis, Lithuania	PT Ds	murdered
Chaim Khaim	Reznikowitz Reznikovich		Rokiskis, Lithuania	PT	murdered
Liza	Reznikowitz Reznikovich		Rakiski, Lithuania	PT	murdered
Avraham	Ribac Ribak	1896	Rokiskis, Lithuania	PT	murdered
Batshewa Batsheva	Ribak		Rakeshik, Lithuania	PT	murdered
Betzalel Charles	Ribak	1934	Rokiskis, Lithuania	PT	murdered
Sofia Batsheva	Ribak	1897	Rokiskis, Lithuania	PT	murdered
Yehuda	Ribak		Rokiskis, Lithuania	PT	murdered
Yehuda	Ribak		Rakishok, Lithuania	PT	murdered
Yitzkhak Volf	Ribak	1932	Rokiskis, Lithuania	PT	murdered
Yosef Dzho	Ribak	1936	Rokiskis, Lithuania	PT	murdered
	Ribak		Lithuania	PT	killed in military service
Avram Avraham	Rif		Rokiskis, Lithuania	PT	murdered
Daniel	Rif	1925	Rokiskis, Lithuania	PT	murdered
Daniel	Rif		Rokiskis, Lithuania	PT	murdered
Dora	Rif	1920	Rokiskis, Lithuania	PT	murdered
Matl	Rif	1871	Rokiskis, Lithuania	PT	murdered
Mayer Meir	Rif		Rokiskis, Lithuania	PT	murdered
Meir	Rif	1871	Rakisok, Lithuania	PT	murdered
Meir	Rif		Rokiskis, Lithuania	PT	murdered
Seina Sheina Riva	Rif		Rokiskis, Lithuania	PT	murdered
Shaina Riva Sheina	Rif	1886	Rokiskis, Lithuania	PT	murdered
Shulamit	Rif		Rokiskis, Lithuania	PT	murdered
Surra	Rif	1876	Rakishik, Lithuania	Evac	not stated
Zelig	Rif	1916	Rokiskis, Lithuania	PT	murdered
Zelig Zelik	Rif		Rokiskis, Lithuania	PT	murdered
	Rif		Abeliai, Lithuania	PT	murdered
Scheine	Rimer	1924	Skapiskis, Lithuania	Persecut	not stated
Schloma	Ringo	1877	Daugavpils, Latvia	Census	not stated
Schloma	Ringo	1877	Daugavpils, Latvia	Jew Res	not stated
Jakuba Yaakov	Ritz	1893	Vilkomir, Lithuania	PT	murdered
Leiba Bascha	Ritz	1880	Riga, Latvia	Jew Res	not stated
Leiba Bascha	Ritz	1880	Riga, Latvia	Residen	not stated
Leiba Bascha	Ritz	1880	Riga, Latvia	Residen	not stated
Leiba Bascha	Ritz	1880	Riga, Latvia	Residen	not stated
Dina	Riz Ritz	1886	Rokiskis, Lithuania	PT	murdered
Leiba	Riz Ritz	1881	Rakiski, Lithuania	PT	murdered
Braina Breina	Rob Robs Rav	1900	Lithuania	PT	murdered
Brejna Breina	Rob Rub	1905	Riga, Latvia	PT	murdered
Aharon David	Rodnicki Rodnitzki	1910	Kamai, Lithuania	PT	murdered
Batia	Roh Rokh		Rokishki, Lithuania	PT	murdered
David	Roh Rokh		Rokiskis, Lithuania	PT	murdered
Isoshar Issakhar	Roh Rokh		Rokishki, Lithuania	PT	murdered
Leibel Libel	Roh Rokh		Rakishik, Lithuania	PT	murdered
Perl Perel	Roh Rokh		Rokishki, Lithuania	PT	murdered
Pesah Pesakh	Roh Rokh		Rakishki, Lithuania	PT	murdered
Tipora Tzipora	Roh Rokh		Rokiszki, Lithuania	PT	murdered

APP-42   Appendix of Rokiskis Shoah Victims – not in the original Yizkor Book

First Name	Last Name	Birth Year	Place of Residence	Source	Fate from Source
	Roh Rokh		Rokiskis, Lithuania	PT	murdered
	Roh Rokh		Rekishok, Lithuania	PT	murdered
Meir	Roh Rub		Rakiski, Lithuania	PT	murdered
Batia Chaia	Rokh		Rokiskis, Lithuania	Yzkr Bk	murdered
Chana	Rokh		Rokiskis, Lithuania	Yzkr Bk	murdered
David	Rokh		Rokiskis, Lithuania	Yzkr Bk	murdered
Esther	Rokh		Rokiskis, Lithuania	Yzkr Bk	murdered
Gite	Rokh		Rokiskis, Lithuania	Yzkr Bk	murdered
Hirsh	Rokh		Rokiskis, Lithuania	Yzkr Bk	murdered
Issakhar	Rokh		Rokiskis, Lithuania	Yzkr Bk	murdered
Ite	Rokh		Rokiskis, Lithuania	Yzkr Bk	murdered
Keile	Rokh		Rokiskis, Lithuania	Yzkr Bk	murdered
Khaiatze	Rokh		Rokiskis, Lithuania	Yzkr Bk	murdered
Khana	Rokh		Rokiskis, Lithuania	Yzkr Bk	murdered
Lea	Rokh		Rokiskis, Lithuania	Yzkr Bk	murdered
Lea	Rokh		Rokiskis, Lithuania	Yzkr Bk	murdered
Libe	Rokh		Rokiskis, Lithuania	Yzkr Bk	murdered
Makhla	Rokh	1930	Rakishok, Lithuania	PT D	murdered
Makhla	Rokh		Rokiskis, Lithuania	Yzkr Bk	murdered
Meir	Rokh		Rokiskis, Lithuania	Yzkr Bk	murdered
Meir	Rokh		Rokishkis, Lithuania	PT	murdered
Perel	Rokh		Rokiskis, Lithuania	Yzkr Bk	murdered
Rachel	Rokh		Rokiskis, Lithuania	Yzkr Bk	murdered
Reuven	Rokh		Rokiskis, Lithuania	Yzkr Bk	murdered
Sara	Rokh		Rokiskis, Lithuania	Yzkr Bk	murdered
Shmuel	Rokh		Rokiskis, Lithuania	Yzkr Bk	murdered
Shmuel	Rokh		Rakiski, Lithuania	PT D	murdered
Yehoshua Zelig	Rokh		Łomża, Poland	PT D	murdered
Yerakhmiel Chaim	Rokh		Rokiskis, Lithuania	Yzkr Bk	murdered
Zelda	Rokh		Rokiskis, Lithuania	Yzkr Bk	murdered
Zelda	Rokh		Rokiskis, Lithuania	PT	murdered
Zelda Chaia	Rokh		Rokiskis, Lithuania	Yzkr Bk	murdered
Zelig Yehoshua	Rokh		Rokiskis, Lithuania	Yzkr Bk	murdered
Sara	Rokh Rok	1938	Rokishkis, Lithuania	PT	murdered
Anna Ana	Rosenbaum Rozenbaum		Kowno, Lithuania	PT	murdered
Ishtvan	Rosenberg	1920	Barcs Dravaeroopuszta,	HLBV	murdered
Izsak	Rosenfeld	1912	Huszt, Czechoslovakia	HLBV	murdered
Aliza	Rosenstein Rozenshtein		Rokiskis, Lithuania	PT	murdered
Seine Chaja Sheina Khaia Yafa	Rosenstein Rozenshtein	1908	Rokiskis, Lithuania	PT	murdered
Tzipora	Rosenstein Rozenshtein		Rokiskis, Lithuania	PT	murdered
Aliza	Rosensteinas Rozenshtein		Rokiskis, Lithuania	PT	murdered
Dovydas David	Rosensteinas Rozenshtein	1906	Rokiskis, Lithuania	PT	murdered
Tzipora	Rosensteinas Rozenshtein		Rokiskis, Lithuania	PT	murdered
Deena Dina	Rosental	1926	Panemune, Lithuania	PT	murdered
Perel Pnina	Rosental	1928	Panemune, Lithuania	PT	murdered
Raizl Gitl	Rosental	1890	Panemune, Lithuania	PT	murdered

Appendix of Rokiskis Shoah Victims – not in the original Yizkor Book   APP-43

First Name	Last Name	Birth Year	Place of Residence	Source	Fate from Source
Jozsef	Rosner	1912	Kolcseny, Czechoslovakia	HLBV	murdered
Ita	Rotenshtein	1896	Rakishok, Lithuania	PT	murdered
Samuel	Roth	1918	Hajdudorog, Hungary	HLBV	murdered
Zunia	Rothberg Wisniak Rotberg Vishniak	1925	Skalat, Poland	PT	murdered
Evelina Sara	Rozenberg		Rokiskis, Lithuania	Yzkr Bk	murdered
First name unknown	Rozenberg		Rokiskis, Lithuania	Yzkr Bk	murdered
Henokh	Rozenberg		Rokiskis, Lithuania	Yzkr Bk	murdered
Mina	Rozenberg		Rokiskis, Lithuania	Yzkr Bk	murdered
Isaakas Mose Yitzkhak Moshe	Rozenholc Rozenholtz	1910	Aleksandravele, Lithuania	PT	murdered
Judit Yehudit	Rozenkowicz Ruzankovitz	1901	Wilno, Poland	PT	murdered
Liba	Rozenkowicz Ruzankovitz	1880	Aleksanderski, Lithuania	PT	murdered
Welwl Volf	Rozenkowicz Ruzankovitz	1905	Wilna, Poland	PT	murdered
David	Rozenstein Rozenshtein	1896	Rakishok, Lithuania	PT	murdered
Sonia	Rozenstein Rozenshtein	1898	Rokiskis, Lithuania	PT	murdered
Dina	Rozental	1925	Lithuania	PT	murdered
Pnina	Rozental	1928	Lithuania	PT	murdered
Ela	Rozinkowitz Rozinkovitz		Rokiskis, Lithuania	PT	murdered
Mendel	Rozinkowitz Rozinkovitz		Rokiskis, Lithuania	PT	murdered
Nechama Nekhama	Rozinkowitz Rozinkovitz		Rokiskis, Lithuania	PT	murdered
Wulf Zeev	Rozinkowitz Rozinkovitz		Rokiskis, Lithuania	PT	murdered
Motel	Rozovich		Nowy Borek, Poland	PT	murdered
Hanna Khana	Rozovski		Panemune, Lithuania	PT	murdered
Kele	Rubanenko	1865	Rakiski, Lithuania	PT	murdered
Leibe	Rubin		Rokiskis, Lithuania	Yzkr Bk	murdered
Leizer David	Rubin		Rokiskis, Lithuania	Yzkr Bk	murdered
Lina	Rubin	1911	Panemunes, Lithuania	Jew Res	not stated
Meier	Rubin	1908	Panemunes, Lithuania	Jew Res	not stated
Rachel	Rubin		Rokiskis, Lithuania	Yzkr Bk	murdered
Rakhel	Rubin	1896	Rokishkis, Lithuania	PT	murdered
Rivka Sara	Rubin		Rokiskis, Lithuania	Yzkr Bk	murdered
Shlomo	Rubin	1891	Rokiskis, Lithuania	PT	murdered
Shlomo	Rubin		Rokiskis, Lithuania	Yzkr Bk	murdered
Zila	Rubin	1871	Panemunes, Lithuania	Jew Res	not stated
Zila	Rubin	1906	Panemunes, Lithuania	Jew Res	not stated
Chaim Jerachmiel Khaim Yerakhmiel	Ruch	1888	Rakishik, Lithuania	PT	murdered
Hanna Henny Khana Heni	Ruch Green Rokh Grin	1913	Rokiskis, Lithuania	PT	murdered
Abram Avraham	Ruch Rokh	1876	Rokishok, Lithuania	PT	murdered
Chaya Basha Khaia	Ruch Rokh	1890	Rokiskis, Lithuania	PT	murdered
Gitta Gita	Ruch Rokh	1930	Rokiskis, Lithuania	PT	murdered
Itta Ita	Ruch Rokh	1917	Rokiskis, Lithuania	PT	murdered
Itze Hirsch Icie Hirsh	Ruch Rokh	1925	Rokiskis, Lithuania	PT	murdered
Keila	Ruch Rokh	1919	Rakishik, Lithuania	PT	murdered
Leah Lea	Ruch Rokh	1921	Rakishik, Lithuania	PT	murdered
Libby Liba	Ruch Rokh	1923	Rakishik, Lithuania	PT	murdered
Zelda	Ruch Rokh	1930	Rokiskis, Lithuania	PT	murdered
Abram Avraham	Rybak Ribak	1916	Rakishik, Lithuania	PT	murdered
Asnat Asne	Rybak Ribak	1912	Rakeshik, Lithuania	PT	murdered

APP-44   Appendix of Rokiskis Shoah Victims – not in the original Yizkor Book

First Name	Last Name	Birth Year	Place of Residence	Source	Fate from Source
Ber	Rybak Ribak		Rakeshik, Lithuania	PT	murdered
Jdes Yehudit	Rybak Ribak	1917	Rakishik, Lithuania	PT	murdered
Bune Buna	Rybek Rovek	1900	Rakeshik, Lithuania	PT	murdered
David	Sachs	1915	Aknaszlatina, Czechoslovakia	HLBV	murdered
Haja	Sack	1864	Riga, Latvia	Jew Res	not stated
Haja	Sack	1864	Riga, Latvia	Residen	not stated
Lea	Sack	1896	Riga, Latvia	Jew Res	not stated
Lea	Sack	1896	Riga, Latvia	Residen	not stated
Lea	Sack	1896	Riga, Latvia	Residen	not stated
Lea	Sack	1896	Riga, Latvia	Residen	not stated
Lea	Sack	1896	Riga, Latvia	Residen	not stated
Lea	Sack	1896	Riga, Latvia	Residen	not stated
Gershon	Sagel		Suvainiskis, Lithuania	PT	murdered
Haia Khaia Rakhel	Sagel		Rakishok, Lithuania	PT	murdered
Avraham	Sagel Segal		Rokiskis, Lithuania	PT	murdered
Barel Berl	Sagel Segal		Rokiskis, Lithuania	PT	murdered
Meir	Sagel Segal		Rokiskis, Lithuania	PT	murdered
Natan	Sagel Segal		Rokiskis, Lithuania	PT	murdered
Sandor	Sager	1917	Tecso,	HLBV	murdered
Faiga Feiga Mira	Sagl Segal		Rekishok, Lithuania	PT	murdered
First name unknown	Saitovitz		Rokiskis, Lithuania	Yzkr Bk	murdered
Gershon	Saitovitz		Rokiskis, Lithuania	Yzkr Bk	murdered
Mina	Saitovitz		Rokiskis, Lithuania	Yzkr Bk	murdered
Yaakov Avraham	Saitovitz		Rokiskis, Lithuania	Yzkr Bk	murdered
Zundel	Saitovitz		Rokiskis, Lithuania	Yzkr Bk	murdered
Haim	Saitowitsch	1884	Subata, Latvia	Census	not stated
Haim	Saitowitsch	1884	Subate, Latvia	Jew Res	not stated
Ela	Sak Elkishok Zak	1882	Pondel, Lithuania	PT	murdered
Rosa Roza	Sak Zak	1912	Pandelys, Lithuania	PT	murdered
Mirjassa	Salagaler Zalegaler		Oknist, Latvia	PT	murdered
Awraham Izchak Avraham Yitzkhak	Salitan Shliten	1910	Rokiskis, Lithuania	PT	murdered
J Yakob Yaakov	Salitan Shliten		Rokiskis, Lithuania	PT	murdered
Marjascha	Sallegaller	1876	Akniste, Latvia	Jew Res	not stated
Liuba	Samuolis Samolis	1913	Kaunas, Lithuania	PT	murdered
Etel Sara	San		Rokiskis, Lithuania	Yzkr Bk	murdered
First name unknown	San		Rokiskis, Lithuania	Yzkr Bk	murdered
Hirsch	Sandler	1894	Bauska, Latvia	Census	not stated
Hirsch	Sandler	1894	Bauska, Latvia	Jew Res	not stated
Ida	Sandler	1907	Panemunes, Lithuania	Jew Res	not stated
Rebecka	Sandler	1913	Panemunes, Lithuania	Jew Res	not stated
Sara	Sandler	1909	Panemunes, Lithuania	Jew Res	not stated
Sheier	Sapira Shapira		Rokiskis, Lithuania	PT	murdered
Henia	Sapiriene Shapira	1912	Kaunas, Lithuania	PT	murdered
Hertzel	Sapiro	1891	Rokiskis, Lithuania	PT	murdered
Herzel	Sapiro		Rokiskis, Lithuania	PT	murdered
Matle	Sapiro	1933	Rokiskis, Lithuania	PT	murdered
Rahel Git	Sapiro	1905	Rokiskis, Lithuania	PT	murdered
Sneier	Sapiro	1934	Rokiskis, Lithuania	PT	murdered

Appendix of Rokiskis Shoah Victims – not in the original Yizkor Book   APP-45

First Name	Last Name	Birth Year	Place of Residence	Source	Fate from Source
Moshe	Sapiro Shapiro	1888	Rokishok, Lithuania	PT	murdered
Moshe	Sapiro Shapiro	1888	Rokishok, Lithuania	PT	murdered
Arie	Sapoznik Sapozhnik	1910	Juzintai, Lithuania	PT	murdered
Dina	Sapoznik Sapozhnik	1885	Juzintai, Lithuania	PT	murdered
Herszl Juidl Tzvi Yehuda	Sapoznik Sapozhnik	1900	Juzintai, Lithuania	PT	murdered
Josef Yosef	Sapoznik Sapozhnik	1878	Juzintai, Lithuania	PT	murdered
Jthak Yitzkhak	Sapoznik Sapozhnik	1880	Juzintai, Lithuania	PT	murdered
Tziwia Tzivia	Sapoznik Sapozhnik	1900	Juzintai, Lithuania	PT	murdered
Zwi Tzvi	Sapoznik Sapozhnik	1900	Juzintai, Lithuania	PT	murdered
David	Sarber Serber		Rakishki, Lithuania	PT	murdered
Chajim Khaim	Sarkas Sharakas		Panemune, Lithuania	PT	murdered
Lea	Sarkas Sharakas		Panemune, Lithuania	PT	murdered
Mendel	Sarkas Sharakas		Panemune, Lithuania	PT	murdered
Rejzale Roza	Sarkas Sharakas		Panemune, Lithuania	PT	murdered
Ruven Reuven	Sarkas Sharakas		Panemun, Lithuania	PT	murdered
Sender	Sarkas Sharakas		Panemune, Lithuania	PT	murdered
Henie Eidel Hena	Sarver Serber	1890	Lithuania	PT	murdered
Salmon	Sawelewitsch	1927	Rokiskis, Lithuania	Persecut	not stated
Boris	Sawilewitz	1926	Rokishkis, Lithuania	Persecut	not stated
Taube Rochel Rael Tolbe	Schadchin	1867	Daugavpils, Latvia	Census	not stated
Taube Rochel Rael Tolbe	Schadchin	1867	Daugavpils, Latvia	Jew Res	not stated
Abba Tuvia	Schames		Panemune, Lithuania	PT Ds	murdered
Avigdor	Schames		Panemune, Lithuania	PT Ds	murdered
Beryl Dov	Schames		Panemune, Lithuania	PT Ds	murdered
Rachel Devorah	Schames		Panemune, Lithuania	PT Ds	murdered
Sarah	Schames		Panemune, Lithuania	PT Ds	murdered
Yaacov David	Schames		Panemune, Lithuania	PT Ds	murdered
Alter	Schames Shemesh	1892	Panemune, Lithuania	PT	murdered
Avigdor	Schames Shemesh		Panemune, Lithuania	PT	murdered
Avigdor	Schames Shemesh		Panemune, Lithuania	PT	murdered
Chajene Khina	Schames Shemesh	1900	Panemune, Lithuania	PT	murdered
Libale	Schames Shemesh		Panemune, Lithuania	PT	murdered
Libale	Schames Shemesh		Panemune, Lithuania	PT	murdered
Zalman	Schames Shemesh		Panemune, Lithuania	PT	murdered
Zalman	Schames Shemesh		Panemune, Lithuania	PT	murdered
Mendel	Schavlik Shavlik	1863	Ponemunok, Lithuania	PT	murdered
Hirsch	Scher	1895	Riga, Latvia	Jew Res	not stated
Hirsch	Scher	1895	Riga, Latvia	Residen	not stated
Hirsch	Scher	1895	Riga, Latvia	Residen	not stated
Hirsch	Scher	1895	Riga, Latvia	Residen	not stated
Hirsch	Scher	1895	Riga, Latvia	Residen	not stated
Nechama	Schiff	1880	Antwerp, Belgium	PT	murdered
Mera	Schlachter	1896	Riga, Latvia	Jew Res	murdered
Mera	Schlachter	1896	Riga, Latvia	Residen	not stated
Bela	Schlesinger	1919	Debrecen, Hungary	HLBV	murdered
Yentl Gentil	Schmukler Shmukler	1890	Panimon, Lithuania	PT	murdered
Aron	Schneider	1908	Panemunes, Lithuania	Jew Res	not stated
Base	Schneider	1898	Panemunes, Lithuania	Jew Res	not stated
Hanna	Schneider	1910	Bauska, Latvia	Census	not stated
Hanna	Schneider	1910	Bauska, Latvia	Jew Res	not stated

APP-46   Appendix of Rokiskis Shoah Victims – not in the original Yizkor Book

First Name	Last Name	Birth Year	Place of Residence	Source	Fate from Source
Jocheweda	Schneider	1933	Panemunes, Lithuania	Jew Res	not stated
Male	Schneider	1877	Panemunes, Lithuania	Jew Res	not stated
Simon	Schneider	1917	Bauska, Latvia	Census	not stated
Simon	Schneider	1917	Riga, Latvia	Jew Res	not stated
Simon	Schneider	1917	Riga, Latvia	Residen	not stated
Leibe	Schochat	1907	Rokishki, Lithuania	Persecut	not stated
Eta Jetta	Schochen	1876	Bauska, Latvia	Census	not stated
Eta Jetta	Schochen	1876	Kundzini, Latvia	Jew Res	murdered
Meria	Schochen	1902	Bauska, Latvia	Census	not stated
Meria	Schochen	1902	Kundzini, Latvia	Jew Res	not stated
Ruvel Ruven Rufke	Schochen	1874	Bauska, Latvia	Census	not stated
Ruvel Ruven Rufke	Schochen	1874	Kundzini, Latvia	Jew Res	murdered
Berel	Schochen Sochen	1891	Bauska, Latvia	Census	not stated
Berel	Schochen Sochen	1891	Bauska, Latvia	Jew Res	not stated
Esther	Schochen Sochen	1914	Bauska, Latvia	Census	not stated
Esther	Schochen Sochen	1914	Bauska, Latvia	Jew Res	not stated
Haje	Schochen Sochen	1928	Bauska, Latvia	Census	not stated
Haje	Schochen Sochen	1928	Bauska, Latvia	Jew Res	not stated
Hirsch	Schochen Sochen	1906	Bauska, Latvia	Census	not stated
Hirsch	Schochen Sochen	1906	Bauska, Latvia	Jew Res	not stated
Ita	Schochen Sochen	1918	Bauska, Latvia	Census	not stated
Ita	Schochen Sochen	1918	Bauska, Latvia	Jew Res	murdered
Lina	Schochen Sochen	1898	Bauska, Latvia	Census	not stated
Lina	Schochen Sochen	1898	Bauska, Latvia	Jew Res	not stated
Meier	Schochen Sochen	1882	Bauska, Latvia	Census	not stated
Meier	Schochen Sochen	1882	Bauska, Latvia	Jew Res	murdered
Muscha Rocha	Schostak	1875	Daugavpils, Latvia	Census	not stated
Muscha Rocha	Schostak	1875	Daugavpils, Latvia	Jew Res	not stated
Schmuil Nosel	Schreberk	1890	Daugavpils, Latvia	Census	not stated
Schmuil Nosel	Schreberk	1890	Daugavpils, Latvia	Jew Res	not stated
Frida	Schreiberg Shreiberg	1905	Pandelys, Lithuania	PT	murdered
Lea	Schreiberg Shreiberg	1890	Pandelys, Lithuania	PT	murdered
Moshe Mozes	Schreiberg Shreiberg	1885	Pandelys, Lithuania	PT	murdered
Reizl Roza Reizel	Schreiberg Shreiberg	1860	Pandelys, Lithuania	PT	murdered
Schamuel Shmuel	Schreiberg Shreiberg	1860	Pandelys, Lithuania	PT	murdered
Taibe Taiba	Schreiberg Shreiberg	1910	Pandelis, Lithuania	PT	murdered
Schimion Shimon	Schreibergas Shreiberg	1895	Pandelys, Lithuania	PT	murdered
Chawa Khava	Schulman Shulman	1872	Shavel, Lithuania	PT	murdered
Nathaniel Natanel	Schulman Shulman	1867	Savli, Lithuania	PT	murdered
David	Schuster	1910	Bauska, Latvia	Census	not stated
David	Schuster	1910	Bauska, Latvia	Jew Res	not stated
Dina	Schuster	1871	Bauska, Latvia	Census	not stated
Dina	Schuster	1871	Bauska, Latvia	Jew Res	murdered
Hirsch	Schuster	1895	Bauska, Latvia	Census	not stated
Hirsch	Schuster	1895	Bauska, Latvia	Jew Res	not stated
Scheine	Schuster	1902	Bauska, Latvia	Census	not stated
Scheine	Schuster	1902	Bauska, Latvia	Jew Res	not stated
Chaim Khaim	Schvarcberg Shvartzberg	1903	Shavl, Lithuania	PT	murdered
Ester	Schwarc Shvartz	1916	Rakishki, Lithuania	PT	murdered
Icchak Yitzkhak	Schwarc Shvartz	1919	Rakiski, Lithuania	PT	murdered

Appendix of Rokiskis Shoah Victims – not in the original Yizkor Book   APP-47

First Name	Last Name	Birth Year	Place of Residence	Source	Fate from Source
Yosef Iosef	Schwarc Shvartz	1894	Rakishik, Lithuania	PT	murdered
Gyorgy	Schwarcz	1920	Pecs, Hungary	HLBV	murdered
Vilmosh	Schwarcz	1917	Iglinc, Czechoslovakia	HLBV	murdered
Samu	Schwartz	1913	Alsoverecke, Czechoslovakia	HLBV	murdered
Sandor	Schwartz	1910	Buj, Hungary	HLBV	murdered
Chaya Ita	Schwartzberg		Rokiskis, Lithuania	PT	murdered
Ester	Schwarz Shvartz	1915	Kowna, Lithuania	PT	murdered
Idel	Schwarzberg	1878	Taurkalne, Latvia	Census	not stated
Idel	Schwarzberg	1878	Riga, Latvia	Jew Res	not stated
Idel	Schwarzberg	1878	Riga, Latvia	Residen	not stated
Idel	Schwarzberg	1878	Riga, Latvia	Residen	not stated
Bencion Bentzion	Scklar Shklar	1910	Kamajai, Lithuania	PT	murdered
Amalia	Segal	1889	Rokiskis, Lithuania	PT	murdered
Amalia	Segal		Rokiskis, Lithuania	PT	murdered
Arie	Segal		Rokiskis, Lithuania	PT	murdered
Avrom Avraham	Segal	1933	Rokiskis, Lithuania	PT	murdered
Berl	Segal	1886	Rakishok, Lithuania	PT	murdered
Brana	Segal	1936	Rokiskis, Lithuania	PT	murdered
Don	Segal	1915	Janova, Lithuania	PT	murdered
Don	Segal	1916	Rokiskis, Lithuania	PT	murdered
Donia	Segal		Rokishki, Lithuania	PT	murdered
Eliahu	Segal		Rokiskis, Lithuania	Yzkr Bk	murdered
Feibush	Segal		Rokiskis, Lithuania	Yzkr Bk	not stated
Itzik	Segal	1939	Rokiskis, Lithuania	PT	murdered
Khava	Segal	1909	Rokiskis, Lithuania	PT	murdered
Leib	Segal	1900	Rokiskis, Lithuania	PT	murdered
Leib	Segal		Rokiskis, Lithuania	PT	murdered
Leib	Segal		Rokiskis, Lithuania	PT	murdered
Leib Leon	Segal	1900	Rokiskis, Lithuania	PT	murdered
Miriam	Segal		Rokiskis, Lithuania	Yzkr Bk	murdered
Rafael	Segal	1928	Janova, Lithuania	PT	murdered
Raphael Rafael	Segal	1928	Rokiskis, Lithuania	PT	murdered
Rivka	Segal		Suvainiskis, Lithuania	PT	murdered
Sheina Feiga	Segal		Suvainiskis, Lithuania	PT	murdered
Sholom Shalom	Segal	1909	Rokiskis, Lithuania	PT	murdered
Sonia	Segal	1904	Rokiskis, Lithuania	PT	murdered
Sonia	Segal	1905	Rokiskis, Lithuania	PT	murdered
Sonia	Segal		Rokiskis, Lithuania	PT	murdered
Golda	Segaliene Segal	1878	Kaunas, Lithuania	PT	murdered
Mendel	Segelis		Svedasai, Lithuania	PT D	murdered
Haim Berka	Selbowitsch	1888	Riga, Latvia	Jew Res	not stated
Haim Berka	Selbowitsch	1888	Riga, Latvia	Residen	not stated
Haim Berka	Selbowitsch	1888	Riga, Latvia	Residen	not stated
Haim Berka	Selbowitsch	1888	Riga, Latvia	Residen	not stated
Haim Berka	Selbowitsch	1888	Riga, Latvia	Residen	not stated
Haim Berka	Selbowitsch	1888	Riga, Latvia	Residen	not stated
Israel	Selbowitsch	1888	Riga, Latvia	Jew Res	not stated
Israel	Selbowitsch	1888	Riga, Latvia	Residen	not stated
Mortchel Morduch Mortel	Selbowitsch	1868	Riga, Latvia	Jew Res	murdered

APP-48 Appendix of Rokiskis Shoah Victims – not in the original Yizkor Book

First Name	Last Name	Birth Year	Place of Residence	Source	Fate from Source
Mortchel Morduch Mortel	Selbowitsch	1868	Riga, Latvia	Residen	not stated
Mortchel Morduch Mortel	Selbowitsch	1868	Riga, Latvia	Residen	not stated
Mowscha	Selbowitsch	1891	Riga, Latvia	Jew Res	not stated
Mowscha	Selbowitsch	1891	Riga, Latvia	Residen	not stated
Mowscha	Selbowitsch	1891	Riga, Latvia	Residen	not stated
Samuel	Selbowitsch	1881	Auce, Latvia	Census	not stated
Samuel	Selbowitsch	1881	Auce, Latvia	Jew Res	not stated
Samuel	Selbowitsch	1881	Riga, Latvia	Residen	not stated
Sundel Salaman	Selbowitsch	1895	Riga, Latvia	Jew Res	murdered
Sundel Salaman	Selbowitsch	1895	Riga, Latvia	Residen	not stated
Sundel Salaman	Selbowitsch	1895	Riga, Latvia	Residen	not stated
Abram Avraham	Seraber Serber		Rakishki, Lithuania	PT	murdered
Enia Edel Henia Etel	Seraber Serber		Rakishki, Lithuania	PT	murdered
Jacov Yaakov	Seraber Serber		Rakishki, Lithuania	PT	murdered
Hirsh	Shabshevitz	1911	Rokishkis, Lithuania	PT	murdered
Lea	Shabshevitz	1940	Rokishkis, Lithuania	PT	murdered
Zlata	Shabshevitz	1938	Rokiskis, Lithuania	PT	murdered
Khana	Shadur	1880	Rakishok, Lithuania	PT	murdered
Elkhanan	Shakhnovitz		Svedasai, Lithuania	PT	murdered
Rakhel	Shakhnovitz		Sviadoshz, Lithuania	PT	murdered
Yosef	Shakhnovitz		Svedasai, Lithuania	PT	murdered
Feiga Chaia	Shalit	1906	Ponevezh, Lithuania	PT	murdered
Haya Khaia Feiga Feige	Shalit		Panevezys, Lithuania	PT	murdered
Avraham	Shapira	1889		PT	murdered
Bune Sara	Shapira		Rokiskis, Lithuania	Yzkr Bk	murdered
Frida Freida Libke	Shapira	1928	Rokiskis, Lithuania	PT	murdered
Hertzel	Shapira		Rakishik, Lithuania	PT	murdered
Khaia	Shapira	1890	Lithuania	PT	murdered
Lea	Shapira	1909	Panimon, Lithuania	PT	murdered
Sara Rivka	Shapira	1920	Rakisok, Lithuania	PT	murdered
Zalkind	Shapira		Rokiskis, Lithuania	Yzkr Bk	murdered
Gitel Rachel	Shapira Shapiro		Rokiskis, Lithuania	Yzkr Bk	murdered
Hirsh	Shapira Shapiro		Rokiskis, Lithuania	Yzkr Bk	murdered
Hirsh	Shapira Shapiro		Rokiskis, Lithuania	Yzkr Bk	murdered
Rakhel	Shapira Shapiro		Rokiskis, Lithuania	Yzkr Bk	murdered
Lazar	Shapiro	1903	Moskva, Russia (USSR)	PT	killed in military service
Libska	Shapiro	1912	Rokishkis, Lithuania	PT	murdered
Mina	Shapiro		Panemun, Lithuania	PT	murdered
Yakov	Shapiro		Panemun, Lithuania	PT	murdered
Zalka	Shapiro		Rokiskis, Lithuania	PT D	murdered
Alter	Shapiro Shapira	1909	Rokiskis, Lithuania	PT	murdered
Ber Berele	Shapiro Shapira	1921	Rokiskis, Lithuania	PT	murdered
Gotman Guta	Shapiro Shapira	1931	Rokiskis, Lithuania	PT	murdered
Hershel	Shapiro Shapira	1913	Rokiskis, Lithuania	PT	murdered
Herzel Hertzel	Shapiro Shapira		Rokiskis, Lithuania	PT	murdered
Jaakov Yaakov	Shapiro Shapira		Panemune, Lithuania	PT	murdered
Matelle Matla	Shapiro Shapira		Rokiskis, Lithuania	PT	murdered
Matla	Shapiro Shapira	1931	Rokiskis, Lithuania	PT	murdered

Appendix of Rokiskis Shoah Victims – not in the original Yizkor Book   APP-49

First Name	Last Name	Birth Year	Place of Residence	Source	Fate from Source
Minna Mina	Shapiro Shapira		Panemune, Lithuania	PT	murdered
Mordechai Mordekhai	Shapiro Shapira	1932	Rokiskis, Lithuania	PT	murdered
Pearl Perl Perel	Shapiro Shapira	1925	Rokiskis, Lithuania	PT	murdered
Rachel Rakhel	Shapiro Shapira	1927	Rokiskis, Lithuania	PT	murdered
Rachel Rakhel	Shapiro Shapira		Rokiskis, Lithuania	PT	murdered
Rachel Rakhel Gitel	Shapiro Shapira		Rokiskis, Lithuania	PT	murdered
Rayzel Reizl	Shapiro Shapira	1890	Rokiskis, Lithuania	PT	murdered
Rivka	Shapiro Shapira	1914	Rokiskis, Lithuania	PT	murdered
Toybe Toibe	Shapiro Shapira	1917	Rokiskis, Lithuania	PT	murdered
Yechiel Benjamin Yekhiel Beniamin	Shapiro Shapira	1880	Rokiskis, Lithuania	PT	murdered
Shalom Moshe	Shapoznikow Shapoznikov	1892	Shavli, Lithuania	PT	murdered
Eliahu	Sharakas		Panemun, Lithuania	PT	murdered
Golda	Sharakas	1908	Panemun, Lithuania	PT	murdered
Hana Khana	Sharakas	1920	Panemun, Lithuania	PT	murdered
Jehuda Yehuda	Sharakas	1913	Panemun, Lithuania	PT	murdered
Lea	Sharakas	1887	Panemun, Lithuania	PT	murdered
Menahem Menakhem	Sharakas	1881	Panemun, Lithuania	PT	murdered
Reuwen Reuven	Sharakas	1911	Panemun, Lithuania	PT	murdered
Rivka	Sharakas	1915	Panemun, Lithuania	PT	murdered
Sender	Sharakas	1919	Panemune, Lithuania	PT	murdered
Shmuel Leib	Sharakas		Panemun, Lithuania	PT	murdered
Shosanah Shoshana	Sharakas	1915	Panemun, Lithuania	PT	murdered
Tzipora	Sharakas		Panemun, Lithuania	PT	murdered
Feigale Feiga	Sharakas Sarkas		Panemune, Lithuania	PT	murdered
Aron	Sheimelsky	1889	Panemunes, Lithuania	Jew Res	not stated
Bluma	Sheimelsky	1895	Panemunes, Lithuania	Jew Res	not stated
Israel	Sheimelsky	1934	Panemunes, Lithuania	Jew Res	not stated
Lea	Sheimelsky	1925	Panemunes, Lithuania	Jew Res	not stated
Sena	Sheimelsky	1923	Panemunes, Lithuania	Jew Res	not stated
Eliezer Leizer	Sher	1918	Rokiskis, Lithuania	PT	murdered
Fruma	Sher	1907	Ponewez, Lithuania	PT	murdered
Moshe	Sher	1891	Rokishkis, Lithuania	PT	murdered
Pesa	Sher	1918	Rokiskis, Lithuania	PT	murdered
Sonia	Sher	1910	Ponewez, Lithuania	PT	murdered
Avraham	Shimanovitz	1925	Rakishik, Lithuania	PT	murdered
Hirshel	Shimanovitz		Rokiskis, Lithuania	PT	murdered
Khaia Rakhel	Shimanovitz	1895	Rekishok, Lithuania	PT	murdered
Yisrael	Shimanovitz	1930	Rekishka, Lithuania	PT	murdered
Chaja Khaia	Shimelevich Shimelevitz		Lithuania	PT	murdered
Chasia Khasia Bela	Shimelevich Shimelevitz		Lithuania	PT	murdered
Ehudit Yehudit	Shimelevich Shimelevitz		Lithuania	PT	murdered
Eliezer	Shimelevich Shimelevitz		Lithuania	PT	murdered
Meir	Shimelevich Shimelevitz		Lithuania	PT	murdered
Nechama Nekhama	Shimelevich Shimelevitz		Lithuania	PT	murdered
Sara	Shimelevich Shimelevitz		Lithuania	PT	murdered
Meer Meir	Shimeleviz Shimelevitz	1881	Rakishok, Lithuania	PT	murdered
Avraham	Shklar		Kemai, Lithuania	PT	murdered
Bentzion	Shklar		Kamajai, Lithuania	PT	murdered

APP-50   Appendix of Rokiskis Shoah Victims – not in the original Yizkor Book

First Name	Last Name	Birth Year	Place of Residence	Source	Fate from Source
Ida Eida	Shklar		Kemai, Lithuania	PT	murdered
Khaia	Shklar		Kemai, Lithuania	PT	murdered
Maor	Shklar		Kamajai, Lithuania	PT	murdered
Mira	Shklar	1871	Komajai, Lithuania	PT	murdered
Noakh	Shklar		Kemai, Lithuania	PT	murdered
Sheina	Shklar		Komajai, Lithuania	PT	murdered
Eidel	Shklyar Shklar	1938	Kamajai, Lithuania	PT	murdered
Khaia	Shklyar Shklar	1901	Kamajai, Lithuania	PT	murdered
Meyer Meir	Shklyar Shklar	1927	Kamajai, Lithuania	PT	murdered
Riva	Shklyar Shklar	1931	Kamajai, Lithuania	PT	murdered
Faitel	Shlep	1914	Obeliai, Lithuania	PT	murdered
Josef Yosef	Shlep	1900	Abel, Lithuania	PT	murdered
Sara Dvora	Shlep	1912	Obeliai, Lithuania	PT	murdered
Sara Dvora	Shlep	1912	Obeliai, Lithuania	PT	murdered
Yosef	Shlep	1881	Obeliai, Lithuania	PT	murdered
David	Shliman	1900	Kovno, Lithuania	PT	murdered
Iosif Yosef	Shliman	1895	Kaunas, Lithuania	PT	murdered
Aharon	Shlosberg		Rokiskis, Lithuania	Yzkr Bk	murdered
Arke	Shlosberg		Rokiskis, Lithuania	PT D	murdered
Esther	Shlosberg		Rokiskis, Lithuania	Yzkr Bk	murdered
Khona	Shlosberg		Rokiskis, Lithuania	Yzkr Bk	murdered
Matilda	Shlosberg		Rokiskis, Lithuania	Yzkr Bk	murdered
Motke Mordekhai	Shlosberg		Rokiskis, Lithuania	Yzkr Bk	murdered
Rafael	Shlosberg		Rokiskis, Lithuania	Yzkr Bk	murdered
Shimon	Shlosberg		Rokiskis, Lithuania	Yzkr Bk	murdered
Yitzkhak Chaim	Shlosberg		Rokiskis, Lithuania	Yzkr Bk	murdered
Aba	Shmit		Riga, Latvia	PT	murdered
Alter	Shmit	1876	Rokiskis, Lithuania	PT	murdered
Eliahu	Shmit		Pondel, Lithuania	PT	murdered
Ester	Shmit	1925	Ponidel, Lithuania	PT	murdered
Khaim	Shmit	1911	Dusiat, Lithuania	PT	murdered
Khava Lea	Shmit		Ponidel, Lithuania	PT	murdered
Mordekhai	Shmit		Ponidel, Lithuania	PT	murdered
Shlomo Moshe	Shmit		Pompeuan, Lithuania	PT	murdered
Tzvi	Shmit	1922	Ponidel, Lithuania	PT	murdered
Yitzkhak	Shmit		Ponidel, Lithuania	PT	murdered
Barukh	Shmukler		Panimon, Lithuania	PT	murdered
Yentl	Shmukler		Panemun, Lithuania	PT	murdered
Zundel זונדלה Zundl	Shmukler Schmukler	1928	Panimon, Lithuania	PT	murdered
Baruch Barukh	Shmukler Smukleras		Panemunes, Lithuania	PT	murdered
Yaakov	Shmuskovitz		Rokiskis, Lithuania	Yzkr Bk	not stated
Ber	Shneider		Rokiskis, Lithuania	Yzkr Bk	murdered
Dobra Dobe	Shneider		Rokiskis, Lithuania	Yzkr Bk	murdered
Dvora Rivka	Shneider		Rokiskis, Lithuania	Yzkr Bk	murdered
Eliahu	Shneider		Rokiskis, Lithuania	Yzkr Bk	murdered
First name unknown	Shneider		Rokiskis, Lithuania	Yzkr Bk	murdered
Lea Sara	Shneider		Rokiskis, Lithuania	Yzkr Bk	murdered
Michael	Shneider		Rokiskis, Lithuania	Yzkr Bk	murdered
Mina	Shneider		Rokiskis, Lithuania	Yzkr Bk	murdered
Moshe Avraham	Shneider		Rokiskis, Lithuania	Yzkr Bk	murdered

Appendix of Rokiskis Shoah Victims – not in the original Yizkor Book   APP-51

First Name	Last Name	Birth Year	Place of Residence	Source	Fate from Source
Rivka	Shneider		Rokiskis, Lithuania	Yzkr Bk	murdered
Sara	Shneider		Rokiskis, Lithuania	Yzkr Bk	murdered
Reizl	Shneiderman		Rakishok, Lithuania	PT	murdered
Abraham Avraham	Shneiur Zalewicki Zelvitzki		Pondel, Lithuania	PT	murdered
Max	Shnerson Shneierson	1891	Rokiskis, Lithuania	PT	murdered
Nekhama	Shokhet	1892	Petrashon, Lithuania	PT	murdered
Rakhel	Shokhet		Kaunas, Lithuania	PT	murdered
Katriel	Shomer		Rokiskis, Lithuania	Yzkr Bk	murdered
Sheine	Shomer		Rokiskis, Lithuania	Yzkr Bk	murdered
Braina Breina	Shomer Shumer	1901	Riga, Latvia	PT	murdered
Katriel	Shomer Shumer	1880	Rokiskis, Lithuania	PT	murdered
Sheina	Shomer Shumer		Rokiskis, Lithuania	PT	murdered
Sheina	Shomer Shumer		Rokiskis, Lithuania	PT	murdered
Etka	Shon		Suvainiskis, Lithuania	PT	murdered
Hirsh	Shon		Suvainiskis, Lithuania	PT	murdered
Khava	Shon		Suvainiskis, Lithuania	PT	murdered
Yerakhmiel	Shon		Suvainiskis, Lithuania	PT	murdered
David	Shpivak		Rokiskis, Lithuania	Yzkr Bk	murdered
David	Shpivak		Rokiskis, Lithuania	PT	murdered
David	Shpivak		Rakishok, Lithuania	Murd	murdered
Malka	Shpivak		Rokiskis, Lithuania	Yzkr Bk	murdered
Malka	Shpivak		Rokiskis, Lithuania	PT	murdered
Moshe	Shpivak		Rokiskis, Lithuania	Yzkr Bk	murdered
Moshe	Shpivak		Rokiskis, Lithuania	PT	murdered
Aba	Shrier Shreier	1902	Rokishki, Lithuania	PT	murdered
Mendel Menakhem	Shrier Shreier	1874	Uspol, Lithuania	PT	murdered
Dobale	Shtamler	1924	Rekishok, Lithuania	PT	murdered
Feiga	Shtamler	1930	Rakiszki, Lithuania	PT	murdered
Mikhael	Shtamler	1895	Rokiskis, Lithuania	PT	murdered
Nakhum	Shtamler	1905	Rakishok, Lithuania	PT	murdered
Yehudit	Shtamler	1897	Rakishik, Lithuania	PT	murdered
Yitzkhak	Shtamler	1860	Rekishka, Lithuania	PT	murdered
Lea Miriam	Shtein Stein	1868	Dwinsk, Latvia	PT	murdered
Moisey	Shtern		Rokiskis, Lithuania	PT	murdered
Vulf	Shtern		Rokiskis, Lithuania	PT	murdered
Khana	Shternblitz		Panemunelis, Lithuania	PT	murdered
Lea	Shternblitz		Panemune, Lithuania	PT	murdered
Mendel Mendi Menakhem	Shternblitz		Panemune, Lithuania	PT	murdered
Yaakov	Shternblitz		Panemunes, Lithuania	PT	murdered
Yosef	Shternblitz		Panemune, Lithuania	PT	murdered
Khashka Khana	Shtoler	1918	Imbradas, Lithuania	PT	murdered
Bonya	Shtroynen	1923	Kamai, Lithuania	Evac	not stated
Rokhla	Shtroynen	1923	Kamai, Lithuania	Evac	not stated
Tzemakh	Shub	1886	Rokiskis, Lithuania	PT	murdered
Israel	Shulman		Rokiskis, Lithuania	Yzkr Bk	murdered
Khaim Zalman	Shulman	1886	Kowna, Lithuania	PT	murdered
Libe	Shulman		Rokiskis, Lithuania	Yzkr Bk	murdered
Liube	Shulman	1908	Kovno, Lithuania	PT	murdered
Shmuel	Shulman	1868	Kovno, Lithuania	PT	murdered

Appendix of Rokiskis Shoah Victims – not in the original Yizkor Book

First Name	Last Name	Birth Year	Place of Residence	Source	Fate from Source
Yisrael	Shulman	1905	Kowno, Lithuania	PT	murdered
	Shulz Shultz		Rushinka, Lithuania	PT	murdered
Berl	Shur	1900	Antalept, Lithuania	PT	murdered
Mendel	Shuster	1871	Rakisok, Lithuania	PT	murdered
Shmuel	Shuster	1906	Rakishki, Lithuania	PT	murdered
Zelda Zoia	Shuster	1913	Alitus, Lithuania	PT	murdered
Zelda Zoya	Shuster	1910	Kaunas, Lithuania	PT	murdered
Shmuel	Shuster Suster	1886	Rakishok, Lithuania	PT	murdered
Beile Sara	Shusterman		Rokiskis, Lithuania	Yzkr Bk	murdered
Chayna Chasia	Shusterman		Rokiskis, Lithuania	PT D	murdered
Elke	Shusterman		Rokiskis, Lithuania	Yzkr Bk	murdered
Hanie	Shusterman		Rokiskis, Lithuania	Yzkr Bk	murdered
Khasia Khaia	Shusterman		Rokiskis, Lithuania	Yzkr Bk	murdered
Yitzkhak David	Shusterman		Rokiskis, Lithuania	Yzkr Bk	murdered
Chaim Khaim	Shvarcberg Shvartzberg	1905	Lithuania	PT	murdered
Batia Etel	Shvartz		Rakishik, Lithuania	PT	murdered
Esther	Shvartz		Rokiskis, Lithuania	Yzkr Bk	murdered
Etel Batia	Shvartz		Rokiskis, Lithuania	Yzkr Bk	murdered
Shlomo	Shvartz		Rokiskis, Lithuania	Yzkr Bk	murdered
Yitzkhak	Shvartz	1913	Rakishik, Lithuania	PT	murdered
Yitzkhak	Shvartz		Rokiskis, Lithuania	Yzkr Bk	murdered
Yosef	Shvartz		Rokiskis, Lithuania	Yzkr Bk	murdered
Yosef	Shvartz		Rakishik, Lithuania	PT	murdered
Ite Chaia	Shvartzberg		Rokiskis, Lithuania	Yzkr Bk	murdered
Khaim	Shvartzberg	1905	Rakishok, Lithuania	PT	murdered
Khaia Ita	Shvarzberg Shvartzberg	1915	Rakisok, Lithuania	PT	murdered
Zelda	Shvaytzbergaite	1921	Rokishkis, Lithuania	Evac	not stated
Iosel	Shvorinas	1889	Skopishki, Lithuania	Evac	not stated
Pesya	Shvorinas	1901	Skopishki, Lithuania	Evac	not stated
Ruvin Bera	Shvorinas	1927	Skopishki, Lithuania	Evac	not stated
Samuil	Shvorinas	1925	Skopishki, Lithuania	Evac	not stated
Shorobla	Shvorinas	1930	Skopishki, Lithuania	Evac	not stated
Ester	Shwartz Shvartz	1912	Kowno, Lithuania	PT	murdered
Jozsef	Sichermann	1919	Csarnato, Czechoslovakia	HLBV	murdered
Baruch Barukh	Siegmann Zigman	1912	Mariampol, Lithuania	PT	murdered
Chaja Khaia Tova	Siegmann Zigman	1888	Panjemunya, Lithuania	PT	murdered
Dow Dov	Sigar		Kamajai, Lithuania	PT	murdered
Frida	Sigar		Kamajai, Lithuania	PT	murdered
Hayim	Sigar		Yurburg, Lithuania	PT D	murdered
Abram Avraham	Simanovic Shimanovitz Shimonovitz		Rakishik, Lithuania	PT	murdered
Chaja Rochel Khaia Rakhel	Simanovic Shimanovitz Shimonovitz		Rakishik, Lithuania	PT	murdered
Hirshel	Simanovic Shimanovitz Shimonovitz		Rakishik, Lithuania	PT	murdered
Israel Yisrael	Simanovic Shimanovitz Shimonovitz		Rakishik, Lithuania	PT	murdered
Nichama Nekhama	Simelowitz Simelovitz		Rokiskis, Lithuania	PT	murdered
Yudit Iudit	Simelowitz Simelovitz		Rokiskis, Lithuania	PT	murdered
Chaja Khaia	Similovitz Shmilovitz		Rokiskis, Lithuania	PT	murdered

Appendix of Rokiskis Shoah Victims – not in the original Yizkor Book   APP-53

First Name	Last Name	Birth Year	Place of Residence	Source	Fate from Source
Eliezer	Similovitz Shmilovitz		Rakishki, Lithuania	PT	murdered
Meir	Similovitz Shmilovitz		Rakishki, Lithuania	PT	murdered
Sara Guta	Similovitz Shmilovitz		Rakishki, Lithuania	PT	murdered
Izsak	Simon	1916	Bustyahaza Falu, Czechoslovakia	HLBV	not stated
Jeno	Simon	1916	Bustyahaza Falu, Czechoslovakia	HLBV	murdered
Malcha	Siratsik		Rokiskis, Lithuania	PT D	murdered
Feiga	Sitkin	1923	Riga, Latvia	Jew Res	murdered
Feiga	Sitkin	1923	Riga, Latvia	Residen	not stated
Feiga	Sitkin	1923	Riga, Latvia	Residen	not stated
Feiga	Sitkin	1923	Riga, Latvia	Residen	not stated
Feiga	Sitkin	1923	Riga, Latvia	Residen	not stated
Schneier Salmen	Sitkin Setkin	1922	Riga, Latvia	Jew Res	not stated
Schneier Salmen	Sitkin Setkin	1922	Riga, Latvia	Residen	not stated
Schneier Salmen	Sitkin Setkin	1922	Riga, Latvia	Residen	not stated
Zundel	Skaist Briss Skeist Bris		Skuodas, Lithuania	PT	murdered
Abraham Menakhem Avraham	Sklar Shklar	1883	Kamai, Lithuania	PT	murdered
Benzion Bentzion	Sklar Shklar		Kamajai, Lithuania	PT	murdered
Chaia Khaia	Sklar Shklar		Lithuania	PT	murdered
Hesl Hes	Sklar Shklar	1869	Lithuania	PT	murdered
Meika Maia	Sklar Shklar	1926	Kamajai, Lithuania	PT	murdered
Senie Shania	Sklar Shklar	1891	Kamai, Lithuania	PT	murdered
Rivka	Skluer		Kamajai, Lithuania	PT	murdered
Bentzion	Skolower Shklaver		Kamajai, Lithuania	PT	murdered
Menachem Menakhem	Skolower Shklaver	1896	Komai, Lithuania	PT	murdered
Rakhel	Skolower Shklaver		Kamajai, Lithuania	PT	murdered
Seine Sheina	Skolower Shklaver	1900	Kamajai, Lithuania	PT	murdered
Moshe	Skorkevits		Rokiskis, Lithuania	PT D	murdered
Szymon	Slawenczynski Slavenchinski	1875	Lodz, Poland	PT	murdered
Khava	Slep		Abeil, Lithuania	PT	murdered
Yaakov	Slep		Abeil, Lithuania	PT	murdered
Josef Yosef	Slimanas Shliman	1895	Kaunas, Lithuania	PT	murdered
Sabs Shabtai	Slimanas Shliman	1906	Panemune, Lithuania	PT	murdered
Sara	Slimaniene Shliman	1875	Panemune, Lithuania	PT	murdered
Zina	Slimaniene Shliman	1900	Panemune, Lithuania	PT	murdered
Ester	Slosberg Shlosberg	1891	Rokiskis, Lithuania	PT	murdered
Gita	Slova	1908	Obeliai, Lithuania	PT	murdered
Ida	Slovo	1915	Obeliai, Lithuania	PT D	murdered
Raquel	Slovo		Obeliai, Lithuania	PT D	murdered
Wolf	Slovo		Obeliai, Lithuania	PT D	murdered
Feige	Smilga	1874	Panemunes, Lithuania	Jew Res	not stated
Gersch	Smilga	1905	Panemunes, Lithuania	Jew Res	not stated
Haja	Smilga	1908	Riga, Latvia	Jew Res	not stated
Haja	Smilga	1908	Riga, Latvia	Residen	not stated
Haja	Smilga	1908	Riga, Latvia	Residen	not stated
Haja	Smilga	1908	Riga, Latvia	Residen	not stated
Sore	Smilga	1910	Bauska, Latvia	Census	not stated

APP-54   Appendix of Rokiskis Shoah Victims – not in the original Yizkor Book

First Name	Last Name	Birth Year	Place of Residence	Source	Fate from Source
Sore	Smilga	1910	Bauska, Latvia	Jew Res	not stated
Boruch Barukh	Smukler Shmukler	1880		PT	murdered
Yentel Yenta	Smukleriere Shmukler		Panemun, Lithuania	PT	murdered
Bella	Smushkevich	1914	Rakishki, Lithuania	Evac	not stated
Grigoriy	Smushkevich	1918	Rakishki, Lithuania	Evac	not stated
Sara	Smuskovics Shmushkovitz		Riga, Latvia	PT	murdered
Sonia	Snejor Shneiur Zamet	1899	Rokishki, Lithuania	PT	murdered
Yenta	Snejor Shneiur Zamet		Rokishki, Lithuania	PT	murdered
Beniamin	Snieg		Rokiskis, Lithuania	Yzkr Bk	murdered
Freidel	Snieg		Rokiskis, Lithuania	Yzkr Bk	murdered
Leib Israel	Snieg		Rokiskis, Lithuania	Yzkr Bk	murdered
Mina	Snieg		Rokiskis, Lithuania	Yzkr Bk	murdered
Samuel	Snieg	1898	Rokiskis, Lithuania	Persecut	not stated
Chaimas Slomo Khaim Shlomo	Sniegas Snieg		Rokiskis, Lithuania	PT	murdered
Hoda	Sniegas Snieg	1926	Rokiskis, Lithuania	PT	murdered
Isakas Rubinas Yitzkhak Reuven	Sniegas Snieg		Kupiskis, Lithuania	PT	murdered
Israelis Leibas Yisrael Leib	Sniegas Snieg	1864	Rokiskis, Lithuania	PT	murdered
Jsakas Eliezeris Yitzkhak Eliezer	Sniegas Snieg	1918	Rokishki, Lithuania	PT	murdered
Jsakas Eliezeris Yitzkhak Eliezer	Sniegas Snieg		Panevezys, Lithuania	PT	murdered
Freida Frida	Sniegiene Snieg	1874	Rokiskis, Lithuania	PT	murdered
Jda Ida	Sniegiene Snieg		Rokiskis, Lithuania	PT	murdered
Iudl	Sochad Shokhet	1891	Rokiskis, Lithuania	PT	murdered
Michel Mendel	Sochen	1867	Daugavpils, Latvia	Census	not stated
Michel Mendel	Sochen	1867	Daugavpils, Latvia	Jew Res	not stated
Yehoshua Yaakov	Sofer		Obeliai, Lithuania	Murd	murdered
Gitel	Soloweitschik	1881	Riga, Latvia	Jew Res	not stated
Gitel	Soloweitschik	1881	Riga, Latvia	Residen	not stated
Breina	Someras Shumer			PT	murdered
Katriel	Someras Shumer	1883	Kamai, Lithuania	PT	murdered
Raela	Son	1889	Riga, Latvia	Jew Res	murdered
Raela	Son	1889	Riga, Latvia	Residen	not stated
Blyuma	Sonis	1880	Rokishkis, Lithuania	Evac	not stated
Grigoriy	Sonis	1937	Rokishkis, Lithuania	Evac	not stated
Tatiyana	Sonis	1941	Rokishkis, Lithuania	Evac	not stated
Ester	Sorbinski	1882	Rokishok, Lithuania	PT	murdered
Luba	Sorbinski	1918	Rokishok, Lithuania	PT	murdered
Aba Yehoshua	Spak Shpak		Pandelis, Lithuania	PT	murdered
Aba Yehoshua	Spak Shpak		Pandelis, Lithuania	PT	murdered
Khana	Spak Shpak		Pandelis, Lithuania	PT	murdered
Khana	Spak Shpak		Pandelis, Lithuania	PT	murdered
Leib	Spak Shpak		Kowno, Lithuania	PT	murdered
Miriam	Spak Shpak		Kowno, Lithuania	PT	murdered
Nachum Nakhum	Spak Shpak		Pandelis, Lithuania	PT	murdered
Pesia Rivka	Spak Shpak		Pandelis, Lithuania	PT	murdered
Shalom	Spak Shpak		Pandelis, Lithuania	PT	murdered

Appendix of Rokiskis Shoah Victims – not in the original Yizkor Book   APP-55

First Name	Last Name	Birth Year	Place of Residence	Source	Fate from Source
Shalom	Spak Shpak		Pandelis, Lithuania	PT	murdered
Marton	Spiegel	1913	Kassa,	HLBV	murdered
Miklos	Spiegel	1912	Nagycsongova, Czechoslovakia	HLBV	murdered
Gelda	Spielmann	1900	Riga, Latvia	Jew Res	murdered
Gelda	Spielmann	1900	Riga, Latvia	Residen	not stated
Gelda	Spielmann	1900	Riga, Latvia	Residen	not stated
Ignac	Spielmann	1910	Ilonca, Czechoslovakia	HLBV	murdered
Riva	Spielmann	1915	Krustpils, Latvia	Jew Res	not stated
Riva	Spielmann	1915	Riga, Latvia	Residen	not stated
Riva	Spielmann	1915	Riga, Latvia	Residen	not stated
Samuel	Spielmann	1912	Krustpils, Latvia	Census	not stated
Samuel	Spielmann	1912	Riga, Latvia	Jew Res	killed in military service
Samuel	Spielmann	1912	Riga, Latvia	Residen	not stated
Samuel	Spielmann	1912	Riga, Latvia	Residen	not stated
Samuel	Spielmann	1912	Riga, Latvia	Residen	not stated
Samuel	Spielmann	1912	Riga, Latvia	Residen	not stated
Gyula	Spitz	1919	Torokszentmiklos, Hungary	HLBV	murdered
Marton	Spitzer	1916	Hajdunanas, Hungary	HLBV	murdered
Malka	Spivak		Rokiskis, Lithuania	PT D	murdered
Moshe	Spivak		Rokiskis, Lithuania	PT D	murdered
Dawid Selig David Zelig	Spiwak Shpivak	1898	Rokiskis, Lithuania	PT	murdered
Ryfka Rivka Malka	Spiwak Shpivak	1892	Rokiskis, Lithuania	PT	murdered
Yisrael Moshe	Spiwak Shpivak		Rokiskis, Lithuania	PT	murdered
Aba Leib	Sreier Shreier		Joniskelis, Lithuania	PT	murdered
Nechama Nekhama	Sreier Shreier		Joniskelis, Lithuania	PT	murdered
Dina	Sribnik		Rokiskis, Lithuania	PT Ds	murdered
Faiga Rivka	Sribnik		Rokiskis, Lithuania	PT Ds	murdered
Solomon	Sribnik		Rokiskis, Lithuania	PT Ds	murdered
Gitel	Srubinsky	1886	Rakishok, Lithuania	PT	murdered
David	Starobin	1868	Rakiski, Lithuania	Jew Res	not stated
Mera	Stein	1866	Daugavpils, Latvia	Census	not stated
Mera	Stein	1866	Daugavpils, Latvia	Jew Res	not stated
Alter	Stein Shtein	1904	Rakisok, Lithuania	PT	murdered
Nesia	Stein Shtein		Rokiskis, Lithuania	PT	murdered
Rivka	Stein Shtein	1906	Ljuta, Czechoslovakia	PT	murdered
Yaakov Khaim Jankelis Chaim	Steinas Shtein	1912	Rokiskis, Lithuania	PT	murdered
Reizl Roza	Steingrob Shteingrob	1888	Kobylnik, Poland	PT	murdered
Hadasa	Steiniene Shtein	1909	Rakishki, Lithuania	PT	murdered
Jozsef	Stepper	1919	Borszek, Romania	HLBV	murdered
Ignac	Stern	1910	Verece, Czechoslovakia	HLBV	murdered
Kalman	Stern	1912	Kemecse, Hungary	HLBV	murdered
Rohel Rakhel Lea	Stern Shtern	1886	Svedasai, Lithuania	PT	murdered
Avraham	Stolov	1924	Svedasai, Lithuania	PT	murdered
Golda	Stolov	1892	Svedasai, Lithuania	PT	murdered
Hana	Stolov	1941	Rokiskis, Lithuania	PT	murdered

APP-56 Appendix of Rokiskis Shoah Victims – not in the original Yizkor Book

First Name	Last Name	Birth Year	Place of Residence	Source	Fate from Source
Henia	Stolov		Rokiskis, Lithuania	PT	murdered
Rahel Rakhel	Stolov	1929	Svedasai, Lithuania	PT	murdered
Sima	Stolov	1915	Rokiskis, Lithuania	PT	murdered
Sima	Stolov		Rokiskis, Lithuania	PT	murdered
Yaaqov Yaakov	Stolov	1880	Svedasai, Lithuania	PT	murdered
Yohanan Yokhanan	Stolov	1915	Svedasai, Lithuania	PT	murdered
Yona	Stolov		Rokiskis, Lithuania	PT	murdered
Yonatan	Stolov	1916	Svedasai, Lithuania	PT	murdered
Jeta	Stoltzer	1904	Bauska, Latvia	Census	not stated
Jeta	Stoltzer	1904	Bauska, Latvia	Jew Res	murdered
Berl	Strait Shtreit		Kamajai, Lithuania	PT	murdered
Berl Berel	Strait Shtreit		Kamajai, Lithuania	PT	murdered
Chaim Khaim	Strait Shtreit		Kamajai, Lithuania	PT	murdered
Chaim Khaim	Strait Shtreit		Kamajai, Lithuania	PT	murdered
First name unknown	Strait Shtreit		Kamai, Lithuania	PT	murdered
First name unknown	Strait Shtreit		Kamai, Lithuania	PT	murdered
First name unknown	Strait Shtreit		Kamai, Lithuania	PT	murdered
First name unknown	Strait Shtreit		Kamai, Lithuania	PT	murdered
Kopel	Strait Shtreit		Kamajai, Lithuania	PT	murdered
Kopel	Strait Shtreit		Kamajai, Lithuania	PT	murdered
Nachum Nakhum	Strait Shtreit		Kamajai, Lithuania	PT	murdered
Nakhum	Strait Shtreit		Kamajai, Lithuania	PT	murdered
Necha Nekha	Strait Shtreit		Kamajai, Lithuania	PT	murdered
Nekha	Strait Shtreit		Kamajai, Lithuania	PT	murdered
Rachel Rakhel Lea	Strait Shtreit		Kamajai, Lithuania	PT	murdered
Ruchel Rakhel Lea	Strait Shtreit		Kamai, Lithuania	PT	murdered
Rachel Rakhel	Suchad Sukhad	1902	Kamai, Lithuania	PT	murdered
Baruch Barukh	Suel Shuel		Obeliai, Lithuania	PT	murdered
Fajga Feiga	Suel Shuel		Avle, Latvia	PT	murdered
Rakhel	Suel Shuel	1925	Avle, Latvia	PT	murdered
Aide	Surname unknown		Rokiskis, Lithuania	Yzkr Bk	murdered
Avraham	Surname unknown		Rokiskis, Lithuania	Yzkr Bk	murdered
Berl	Surname unknown		Rokishki, Lithuania	Murd	murdered
Bluma Feige	Surname unknown		Rokiskis, Lithuania	Yzkr Bk	murdered
Breina	Surname unknown		Rokiskis, Lithuania	Yzkr Bk	murdered
Feige	Surname unknown		Rokiskis, Lithuania	Yzkr Bk	murdered
First name unknown	Surname unknown		Rokiskis, Lithuania	Yzkr Bk	murdered
First name unknown	Surname unknown		Rokiskis, Lithuania	Yzkr Bk	murdered
First name unknown	Surname unknown		Rokiskis, Lithuania	Yzkr Bk	murdered
First name unknown	Surname unknown		Rokiskis, Lithuania	Yzkr Bk	murdered
First name unknown	Surname unknown		Rokiskis, Lithuania	Yzkr Bk	murdered
Freide	Surname unknown		Rokiskis, Lithuania	Yzkr Bk	murdered
Fruma	Surname unknown	1901	Svedasai, Lithuania	PT	murdered
Ite Rachel	Surname unknown		Rokiskis, Lithuania	Yzkr Bk	murdered
Leibe	Surname unknown		Rokiskis, Lithuania	Yzkr Bk	murdered
Liuba	Surname unknown		Rokishki, Lithuania	Murd	murdered
Miriam	Surname unknown		Rokiskis, Lithuania	Yzkr Bk	murdered
Rebecca	Surname unknown		Rokiskis, Lithuania	PT Ds	murdered
Ester	Svartz Shvartz	1915	Kovno, Lithuania	PT	murdered
Jehuda Yehuda	Svorn Shvoren	1906	Svedasai, Lithuania	PT	murdered

Appendix of Rokiskis Shoah Victims – not in the original Yizkor Book   APP-57

First Name	Last Name	Birth Year	Place of Residence	Source	Fate from Source
Malca Malka	Svorn Shvoren	1909	Svedasai, Lithuania	PT	murdered
Terna Charna	Svorn Shvoren	1911	Svedasai, Lithuania	PT	murdered
Seftel Shabtai	Svorn Shvoron	1914	Seda, Lithuania	PT	murdered
Avraham	Szaitowicz Sheitovitz		Kowna, Lithuania	PT	murdered
Gershon	Szaitowicz Sheitovitz		Rakiszki, Lithuania	PT	murdered
Khana	Szaitowicz Sheitovitz		Rakiszki, Lithuania	PT	murdered
Mona	Szaitowicz Sheitovitz		Rakiszki, Lithuania	PT	murdered
Zundel	Szaitowicz Sheitovitz		Rakiszki, Lithuania	PT	murdered
Hiena Khiena	Szajtowic Frydman Sheitovitz Fridman	1898	Rokishki, Lithuania	PT	murdered
Jehoszua Yehoshua	Szajtowicz Sheitovitz	1895	Rokiszki, Lithuania	PT	murdered
Gyorgy	Szanto	1907	Nagymuzsaly, Czechoslovakia	HLBV	murdered
Pinchas Pinkhas	Szejtowicz Sheitovitz	1924	Rokishki, Lithuania	PT	murdered
Musha Masha Moshe	Szpriregen Shpreiregen		Dolhinow, Poland	PT	murdered
Menyhert	Szrulovics	1915	Nyirbator, Hungary	HLBV	not stated
Chaim Jakob Khaim Yaakov	Sztajn Shtein	1911	Rokiszki, Lithuania	PT	murdered
Baruch Barukh	Szuelis Shuel	1915	Abeli, Lithuania	PT	murdered
Faige Feiga	Szuelis Shuel		Abeli, Lithuania	PT	murdered
Rachel Rakhel	Szuelis Shuel	1926	Abeli, Lithuania	PT	murdered
Mendel	Tabachovitz		Ponedel, Lithuania	PT	murdered
Beile Beila	Tarnegel Tarangel	1890	Svedasai, Lithuania	PT	murdered
Gita	Tarnegel Tarangel	1924	Subata, Latvia	PT	murdered
Hirsh Girsh	Tarnegel Tarangel	1936	Svedasai, Lithuania	PT	murdered
Khaim	Tarnegel Tarangel	1926	Svedasai, Lithuania	PT	murdered
Moshe	Tarnegel Tarangel	1938	Svedasai, Lithuania	PT	murdered
Sora Sara	Tarnegel Tarangel	1930	Svedasai, Lithuania	PT	murdered
Zalman	Tarnegel Tarangel	1892	Svedasai, Lithuania	PT	murdered
Beila	Tarnegol	1890	Svedasai, Lithuania	PT	murdered
Zalman	Tarnegol	1890	Svedasai, Lithuania	PT	murdered
Ella	Tawjev	1870	Riga, Latvia	Jew Res	not stated
Fajwel Feibush Meir	Torf	1870	Skopishki, Lithuania	PT	murdered
Fruma Gitel	Torf	1900	Skopishki, Lithuania	PT	murdered
Jehuda Yehuda	Torf	1897	Skapiskis, Lithuania	PT	murdered
Minka	Torf		Skopishki, Lithuania	PT	murdered
Hinda	Trapido	1935	Kupiskis, Lithuania	PT	murdered
Leibe	Trapido	1933	Kupishki, Lithuania	PT	murdered
Zalman	Trapido	1936	Kupishki, Lithuania	PT	murdered
Avraham	Trifskin		Rokishkis, Lithuania	PT	murdered
Izya	Trifskin		Rokishkis, Lithuania	PT	murdered
Nakhum Naum	Trifskin		Rokishkis, Lithuania	PT	murdered
	Trifsky Trifskin	1881	Rakishok, Lithuania	PT	murdered
Avraham	Troib		Utian, Lithuania	Yzkr Bk	murdered
Golda	Troib		Utian, Lithuania	Yzkr Bk	murdered
Itel	Trozky Davidovich Trotzki Davidovitz	1900	Rokiskis, Lithuania	PT	murdered
Chajale Chaja Khaia	Trozky Trotzki		Rokiskis, Lithuania	PT	murdered
Khaim	Trozky Trotzki	1890	Rokiskis, Lithuania	PT	murdered
Sarah	Tsadok		Rokiskis, Lithuania	PT D	murdered
Yankel	Tsadok		Rokiskis, Lithuania	PT D	murdered

Appendix of Rokiskis Shoah Victims – not in the original Yizkor Book

First Name	Last Name	Birth Year	Place of Residence	Source	Fate from Source
Bella	Tsindel		Rokiskis, Lithuania	PT D	murdered
Ajida Ida	Turkos	1924	Rekishok, Lithuania	PT	murdered
Etl Etel	Turkos	1923	Rakiski, Lithuania	PT	murdered
Eto	Turkus	1925	Rokiskis, Lithuania	PT	murdered
Eydel	Turkus	1932	Rokiskis, Lithuania	PT	murdered
Berl	Tzadikowich Tzadikovich	1928	Subacius (Town), Lithuania	PT	murdered
Eliezer	Tzadok		Rokiskis, Lithuania	Yzkr Bk	murdered
First name unknown	Tzadok		Rokiskis, Lithuania	Yzkr Bk	murdered
Pesakh	Tzadok		Rokiskis, Lithuania	Yzkr Bk	murdered
Sara	Tzadok		Rokiskis, Lithuania	Yzkr Bk	murdered
Yaakov	Tzadok		Rokiskis, Lithuania	Yzkr Bk	murdered
Dvora Gitel	Tzemakhovitz	1880	Rakishok, Lithuania	PT	murdered
Beniamin	Tzibul		Lithuania	PT	murdered
Moshe	Tzimerman	1902	Plunjen, Lithuania	PT	murdered
Beile	Tzindel		Rokiskis, Lithuania	Yzkr Bk	murdered
Betzalel	Tzirt	1918	Nacioniskis, Lithuania	PT	murdered
Khaim	Tzirt	1940	Nacioniskis, Lithuania	PT	murdered
Khona Khanan Mikhael	Tzirt		Nacioniskis, Lithuania	PT	murdered
Moshe	Tzirt		Nacioniskis, Lithuania	PT	murdered
Tzvi Yaakov	Tzirt		Nacioniskis, Lithuania	PT	murdered
Dina Khana	Tzirt Cirt		Nacioniskis, Lithuania	PT	murdered
Khaia	Tzirt Cirt		Nacioniskis, Lithuania	PT	murdered
Chaia	Tzukernik		Rokiskis, Lithuania	Yzkr Bk	murdered
Reizl	Tzukernik		Rokiskis, Lithuania	Yzkr Bk	murdered
Yekhezkel	Tzukernik		Rokiskis, Lithuania	Yzkr Bk	murdered
Israil	Ursanov	1923	Rakishki, Lithuania	Evac	not stated
Leiba	Urshon	1896	Rakishok, Lithuania	PT	murdered
Fruma	Urson			PT	murdered
Tzvi Zelig	Urson Ursonas		Rokishkis, Lithuania	PT	murdered
Chana	Vagenheim		Rokiskis, Lithuania	PT D	murdered
Herman	Vagenheim		Rokiskis, Lithuania	PT D	murdered
Chana	Vagnhaim		Rokiskis, Lithuania	Yzkr Bk	murdered
Herman	Vagnhaim		Rokiskis, Lithuania	Yzkr Bk	murdered
Alte	Vainer Veiner	1905	Rakiskai, Lithuania	PT	murdered
Malka	Vainer Veiner	1916	Rokishok, Lithuania	PT	murdered
Stirl Stirel	Vaintzimer Weinzimmer		Wilno, Poland	PT	murdered
Erikh	Varbar	1901	Rakishki, Lithuania	Evac	not stated
Tzal	Vastern	1868	Kamai, Lithuania	Evac	not stated
Leiba	Veger	1870	Rakishok, Lithuania	PT	murdered
Ita Cila	Veinberg	1885	Riga, Latvia	PT	murdered
Mina	Veinberg		Rokiskis, Lithuania	Yzkr Bk	murdered
Dvora	Veiner		Rokiskis, Lithuania	Yzkr Bk	murdered
Iudl	Veiner		Rokiskis, Lithuania	Yzkr Bk	not stated
Reisa Roza	Veiner	1899	Rakiski, Lithuania	PT	murdered
Rivka	Veiner		Rakiski, Lithuania	PT	murdered
Slava	Veiner		Panidielis, Lithuania	PT	murdered
Avraham Leib	Veingrin		Rokiskis, Lithuania	PT D	murdered
Ber	Veingrin		Rokiskis, Lithuania	Yzkr Bk	murdered
Ber Dov	Veingrin	1905	Rekishka, Lithuania	PT	murdered

Appendix of Rokiskis Shoah Victims – not in the original Yizkor Book   APP-59

First Name	Last Name	Birth Year	Place of Residence	Source	Fate from Source
Berl	Veingrin	1898	Rakishok, Lithuania	PT	murdered
Dov	Veingrin	1905	Vilna, Poland	PT Ds	murdered
Henya	Veingrin		Rokiskis, Lithuania	PT D	murdered
Khana	Veingrin		Rokiskis, Lithuania	Yzkr Bk	murdered
Leib Avraham	Veingrin		Rokiskis, Lithuania	Yzkr Bk	murdered
Riva	Veingrin		Rokiskis, Lithuania	PT D	murdered
Rivka Toibe	Veingrin		Rokiskis, Lithuania	Yzkr Bk	murdered
Roza Roze	Veingrin		Rokiskis, Lithuania	Yzkr Bk	murdered
Sara	Veingrin		Rokiskis, Lithuania	Yzkr Bk	murdered
Zelig Yoel	Veingrin	1880	Malat, Lithuania	PT	murdered
Fruma	Veinshtein	1878	Ludza, Latvia	PT	murdered
Moshele	Vekhter		Rokishki, Lithuania	Murd	murdered
Bayla	Venegerin		Ponedel, Lithuania	Persecut	murdered
Isroel	Venegerin		Ponedel, Lithuania	Persecut	murdered
Jakob	Venegerin		Ponedel, Lithuania	Persecut	murdered
Meir	Verebei	1896	Panimon, Lithuania	PT	murdered
Dvora	Verebei Vorbei		Panimon, Lithuania	PT	murdered
Dvora	Verebei Vorbei		Panimon, Lithuania	PT	murdered
Perel	Verman		Rakishki, Lithuania	PT	murdered
	Vinakur Vinokur	1886	Rakishok, Lithuania	PT	murdered
Ber Hirsh	Vingrin Veingrin	1866	Rokiskis, Lithuania	PT	murdered
Khaia	Vingrin Veingrin	1891	Rakishok, Lithuania	PT	murdered
Roza	Vingrin Veingrin	1898	Rakishok, Lithuania	PT	murdered
Lotte Gitel	Visokalsky		Rokiskis, Lithuania	PT D	murdered
Naftola Naftali	Volak	1910	Rokiskis, Lithuania	PT	murdered
First name unknown	Volakh		Rokiskis, Lithuania	Yzkr Bk	murdered
Khasia	Volakh		Rokiskis, Lithuania	Yzkr Bk	murdered
Naftali	Volakh		Rokiskis, Lithuania	Yzkr Bk	murdered
Moshe	Volfe Volpe	1903	Suvainiskis, Lithuania	PT	murdered
Chasya	Volk Volak		Rakishok, Lithuania	PT	murdered
Khasia	Volk Volak	1910	Rokiskis, Lithuania	PT	murdered
Naftali	Volk Volak		Rakishok, Lithuania	PT	murdered
Aron	Volpert	1880	Leningrad, Russia (USSR)	PT	perished beyond Nazi occupation lines
Isser	Volpert	1911	Rokiskis, Lithuania	PT	murdered
Dvora Dora	Vorbei		Panimon, Lithuania	PT	murdered
Meir	Vorbei	1885	Panimon, Lithuania	PT	murdered
Samuel	Wachter	1911	Munkacs, Czechoslovakia	HLBV	murdered
Musja	Wagenheim	1924	Dobele, Latvia	Census	not stated
Musja	Wagenheim	1924	Dobele, Latvia	Jew Res	not stated
Rebeka Rivka	Wainer Veiner		Rokiskis, Lithuania	PT	murdered
Roza	Wainer Veiner		Rokiskis, Lithuania	PT	murdered
Slava Slova	Wainer Veiner		Lithuania	PT	murdered
Fruma Haja	Wainstein	1878	Ludza, Latvia	Census	not stated
Fruma Haja	Wainstein	1878	Ludza, Latvia	Jew Res	murdered
Doba	Warum Varum	1886	Warszawa, Poland	PT	murdered
Ignac	Weber	1913	Bilke, Czechoslovakia	HLBV	murdered

APP-60   Appendix of Rokiskis Shoah Victims – not in the original Yizkor Book

First Name	Last Name	Birth Year	Place of Residence	Source	Fate from Source
Ita	Weinberg	1885	Riga, Latvia	Jew Res	not stated
Ita	Weinberg	1885	Riga, Latvia	Residen	not stated
Mendel	Weinberg	1853	Daugavpils, Latvia	Census	not stated
Mendel	Weinberg	1853	Daugavpils, Latvia	Jew Res	murdered
Jozsef	Weinberger		Tiszaszentmarton, Hungary	HLBV	murdered
Mihaly	Weinberger	1919	Szarvas,	HLBV	murdered
Anna	Weinblatt	1895	Riga, Latvia	Jew Res	not stated
Samuel	Weiner	1912	Maramarossziget, Romania	HLBV	murdered
Berkas Berl	Weiner Veiner	1900	Ponedel, Lithuania	PT	murdered
First name unknown	Weiner Veiner		Ponedel, Lithuania	PT	murdered
Lea	Weiner Veiner		Rokiskis, Lithuania	PT	murdered
Moshe	Weiner Veiner	1910	Rokiskis, Lithuania	PT	murdered
Rebeka Rivka	Weiner Veiner	1918	Rakishik, Lithuania	PT	murdered
Majer	Weingarten	1911	Miskarovica,	HLBV	murdered
Yoel Zelig	Weingerin Veingrin	1882	Malat, Lithuania	PT	murdered
Cila Tzila Betzalel	Weispap Veispap		Juzintas, Lithuania	PT	murdered
Perl Perel	Weiss Veis	1870	Ponivez, Lithuania	PT	murdered
Mozes	Weisz	1919	Alsoverecke, Czechoslovakia	HLBV	murdered
Pal	Weiszberger	1917	Kunhegyes, Hungary	HLBV	murdered
Sima Rivka	Werses Verses	1888	Vilnius, Poland	PT	murdered
Mihaly	Wieder	1912	Maramarossziget, Romania	HLBV	murdered
Gabor	Wiesel	1918	Radostyan, Hungary	HLBV	murdered
Avraham Leib	Wingrin		Rakishok, Lithuania	PT	murdered
Henye	Wingrin		Rakishok, Lithuania	PT	murdered
Sara	Wingrin		Rakishok, Lithuania	PT	murdered
Tauba Riva Taube	Wingrin		Rakishok, Lithuania	PT	murdered
Dobra	Wischnewsky	1893	Riga, Latvia	Jew Res	not stated
Dobra	Wischnewsky	1893	Riga, Latvia	Residen	not stated
Dobra	Wischnewsky	1893	Riga, Latvia	Residen	not stated
Dobra	Wischnewsky	1893	Riga, Latvia	Residen	not stated
Chayim Khaim	Wolfson Volfson	1910	Svedasai, Lithuania	PT	murdered
Bertha	Wulfowitsch	1900	Bauska, Latvia	Census	not stated
Bertha	Wulfowitsch	1900	Bauska, Latvia	Jew Res	not stated
Zelda	Yaffe Iafe	1914	Pandelys, Lithuania	PT	murdered
Nison Zalman Zalmen	Yalovetzki	1901	Shaulyay, Lithuania	PT	murdered
Gana Hana	Yalovetzkite	1905	Rokishkis, Lithuania	PT	murdered
Itchak	Yichiltshik Iekhilchik		Rokiskis, Lithuania	PT D	murdered
Zelda	Yishiltshik		Rokiskis, Lithuania	PT D	murdered
Chava	Yofe	1870	Rokiskis, Lithuania	PT	murdered
Dveire	Yofe	1910	Rokiskis, Lithuania	PT	murdered
Riva	Yofe		Rokiskis, Lithuania	PT	murdered
Khaim	Yofe Iofe		Vilnius, Poland	PT	murdered
Manchik Mantzik	Yofe Iofe		Kupiskis, Lithuania	PT	murdered
Musa	Yoselovitz Ioselovitz	1876	Kupreliski, Lithuania	PT	murdered
Sara	Yudin Iudin	1890	Dnepropetrovsk, Ukraine (USSR)	PT	murdered

Appendix of Rokiskis Shoah Victims – not in the original Yizkor Book   APP-61

First Name	Last Name	Birth Year	Place of Residence	Source	Fate from Source
Rakhel	Zager Zeger	1886	Rokiskis, Lithuania	PT	murdered
Zelig Zelik	Zager Zeger	1876	Rakishok, Lithuania	PT	murdered
Benyamin	Zak	1896	Obeliai, Lithuania	PT	murdered
Benyamin Beniamin	Zak	1898	Obeliai, Lithuania	PT	murdered
Chaim	Zak	1925	Obeliai, Lithuania	PT	murdered
Eta	Zak	1938	Obeliai, Lithuania	PT	murdered
Etel	Zak	1938	Obeliai, Lithuania	PT	murdered
Itzik	Zak	1868	Obeliai, Lithuania	PT	murdered
Izik	Zak	1870	Obeliai, Lithuania	PT	murdered
Khaim	Zak	1924	Obeliai, Lithuania	PT	murdered
Moisei Moshe	Zak	1903	Birzhay, Lithuania	PT	murdered
Moshe	Zak	1903	Birzai, Lithuania	PT	murdered
Rachel	Zak	1910	Obeliai, Lithuania	PT	murdered
Joszua Yehoshua Shaia	Zalbowicz Zelbovitz	1870	Ponodol, Lithuania	PT	murdered
Batsheva	Zalewicki Zelvitzki		Ponedel, Lithuania	PT	murdered
Israel Siman Yisrael	Zalewicki Zelvitzki	1897	Ponedel, Lithuania	PT	murdered
Khaia Sara	Zalewicki Zelvitzki		Ponedel, Lithuania	PT	murdered
Mina	Zalewicki Zelvitzki		Ponedel, Lithuania	PT	murdered
Roza Dobra Reiza	Zalewicki Zelvitzki		Ponidel, Lithuania	PT	murdered
Michael Mikhael	Zalivicki Zelevitzki	1912	Ponidel, Lithuania	PT	murdered
Jozef Yosef	Zalobowicz Zelbovitz	1900	Ponodol, Lithuania	PT	murdered
Lejb Leib Arie	Zalobowicz Zelbovitz	1902	Pondel, Lithuania	PT	murdered
Alte	Zamet	1896	Rokishki, Lithuania	PT	murdered
Besel Batia	Zamet	1870	Rokishok, Lithuania	PT	murdered
Besel Batia	Zamet		Rakishki, Lithuania	PT	murdered
Chanan Khanan	Zamet	1900	Rokishki, Lithuania	PT	murdered
Chune Khanan Khona	Zamet	1898	Rokishok, Lithuania	PT	murdered
Fania	Zamet	1900	Rokishki, Lithuania	PT	murdered
Henia	Zamet		Rokishki, Lithuania	PT	murdered
Israel Yisrael	Zamet	1900	Rokishok, Lithuania	PT	murdered
Khona	Zamet	1900	Rokiskis, Lithuania	PT	murdered
Nakhum	Zamet		Rokishki, Lithuania	PT	murdered
Sonia	Zamet	1901	Kovno, Lithuania	PT	murdered
Sonia	Zamet	1902	Rokiskis, Lithuania	PT	murdered
Zalman	Zamet	1937	Rokiszki, Lithuania	PT	murdered
Zalman	Zamet		Rokishki, Lithuania	PT	murdered
	Zamet		Rakishki, Lithuania	PT	murdered
Hena	Zametaite Zamet	1935	Rokiskis, Lithuania	PT	murdered
Batia	Zametas Zamet	1875	Rakishki, Lithuania	PT	murdered
Batia	Zametas Zamet	1875	Rakishki, Lithuania	PT	murdered
Khona	Zametas Zamet	1902	Rakishok, Lithuania	PT	murdered
Nakhum	Zametas Zamet	1932	Rakishki, Lithuania	PT	murdered
Yisrael	Zametas Zamet	1899	Rakishok, Lithuania	PT	murdered
Alte	Zametiene Zamet	1906	Rakishki, Lithuania	PT	murdered
Fania	Zametiene Zamet	1912	Rokiskis, Lithuania	PT	murdered
Fania	Zametiene Zamet	1912	Rokiskis, Lithuania	PT	murdered
Rivka	Zavitz		Kovna, Lithuania	PT	murdered
Golda	Zecstein Zekshtein		Rokiskis, Lithuania	PT	murdered
Golda	Zecstein Zekshtein		Rokishkis, Lithuania	PT	murdered
Malka	Zecstein Zekshtein		Rokiskis, Lithuania	PT	murdered

APP-62   Appendix of Rokiskis Shoah Victims – not in the original Yizkor Book

First Name	Last Name	Birth Year	Place of Residence	Source	Fate from Source
Meir	Zecstein Zekshtein		Rokiskis, Lithuania	PT	murdered
Nakhum Tzvi	Zecstein Zekshtein		Rokiskis, Lithuania	PT	murdered
Nakhum Tzvi	Zecstein Zekshtein		Rokishkis, Lithuania	PT	murdered
Yehudit	Zecstein Zekshtein		Rokiskis, Lithuania	PT	murdered
Zalman	Zecstein Zekshtein		Rokishkis, Lithuania	PT	murdered
Haia Khaia Sara	Zecztein Zekshtein		Rekishka, Lithuania	PT	murdered
Josef Yosef	Zelbovic Zelbovitz	1893	Pandelis, Lithuania	PT	murdered
Lea	Zelbovic Zelbovitz	1868	Pandelis, Lithuania	PT	murdered
Leibe Liba	Zelbovic Zelbovitz	1895	Birzai, Lithuania	PT	murdered
Faige Feiga Ester	Zelbovich Zelbovitz	1939	Pandelis, Lithuania	PT	murdered
Haim Khaim	Zelbovich Zelbovitz	1937	Pondel, Lithuania	PT	murdered
Izik Itzik Yitzkhak	Zelbovich Zelbovitz		Pandelis, Lithuania	PT	murdered
Lea	Zelbovich Zelbovitz		Pandelis, Lithuania	PT	murdered
Mendel	Zelbovich Zelbovitz	1938	Pandelis, Lithuania	PT	murdered
Henja Henia	Zelevicki Zelevitzki	1907	Ponidel, Lithuania	PT	murdered
First name unknown	Zeligman		Rokiskis, Lithuania	Yzkr Bk	murdered
Sara	Zeligman	1890	Ponivez, Lithuania	PT	murdered
Tzvia	Zeligman		Rokiskis, Lithuania	Yzkr Bk	murdered
Zalman	Zeligman	1886	Ponovez, Lithuania	PT	murdered
Arja Arie	Zelivicki Zelevitzki	1902	Ponidel, Lithuania	PT	murdered
Mose Moshe	Zelivicki Zelevitzki	1883	Ponidel, Lithuania	PT	murdered
Rivka	Zelivicki Zelevitzki	1889	Ponidel, Lithuania	PT	murdered
Lea	Zibulin	1887	Riga, Latvia	Jew Res	murdered
Lea	Zibulin	1887	Riga, Latvia	Residen	not stated
Leiba	Zigman	1912	Kowna, Lithuania	PT	murdered
Leibe	Zilber		Rokiskis, Lithuania	Yzkr Bk	not stated
Leizer	Zilber		Rokiskis, Lithuania	Yzkr Bk	murdered
Rivka	Zilber		Rokiskis, Lithuania	Yzkr Bk	murdered
Zelda	Zilber		Lithuania	PT	murdered
Tona	Zisman		Ponedel, Lithuania	Persecut	murdered
Chaim Khaim	Ziszle Zisle	1895	Panemun, Lithuania	PT	murdered
Hirsh	Ziszle Zisle		Panemun, Lithuania	PT	murdered
Sheina	Ziszle Zisle		Panemun, Lithuania	PT	murdered
Braina Breina	Zitlowski Zhitlovski		Skapiskis, Lithuania	PT	murdered
Henek	Zmuckin Zmutzkin	1886	Rakishik, Lithuania	PT	murdered
Henek	Zmuckin Zmutzkin	1886	Rakishok, Lithuania	PT	murdered
Sara Serl	Zrelman	1889	Kamai, Lithuania	PT	murdered
Zimelis	Zrelman	1891	Kamajai, Lithuania	Persecut	not stated
Khaim Yaakov	Zweihorn		Kovna, Lithuania	PT	murdered
David	אמדוראס	1902	Kaunas, Lithuania	PT	murdered
Betzalel	גאפאנאוויץ	1914	Shvunishok, Lithuania	PT	murdered
Khaikel	גאפאנאוויץ	1912	Kovno, Lithuania	PT	murdered
Libe Asnat	גאפאנאוויץ	1916	Rakeshik, Lithuania	PT	murdered
Moshe Reuven	גאפאנאוויץ	1878	Rokiskis, Lithuania	PT	murdered
Moshe Reuven	גאפאנאוויץ	1884	Rakishik, Lithuania	PT	murdered
Chaia	גאפאנאוויץ Gafanovitz		Rokiskis, Lithuania	Yzkr Bk	murdered
Freida	גאפאנאוויץ Gafanovitz		Rokiskis, Lithuania	Yzkr Bk	murdered
Leib Arie	גאפאנאוויץ Gafanovitz		Rokiskis, Lithuania	Yzkr Bk	murdered
Sara	גאפאנאוויץ Gafanovitz		Rokiskis, Lithuania	Yzkr Bk	murdered
Tauba	גאפאנאוויץ Gafanovitz		Rokiskis, Lithuania	Yzkr Bk	murdered

Appendix of Rokiskis Shoah Victims – not in the original Yizkor Book   APP-63

First Name	Last Name	Birth Year	Place of Residence	Source	Fate from Source
Yitzkhak Moshe	גאפאנאוויץ Gafanovitz		Rokiskis, Lithuania	Yzkr Bk	murdered
Frumet	מיכאלעוויץ		Rokiskis, Lithuania	Yzkr Bk	murdered
Moshe	מיכאלעוויץ		Rokiskis, Lithuania	Yzkr Bk	murdered
Zeev Michael	מיכאלעוויץ		Rokiskis, Lithuania	Yzkr Bk	murdered
Meir Mejer	מרקול Merkul	1881	Rakishok, Lithuania	PT	murdered
Khana	פאגרונד		Rokiskis, Lithuania	Yzkr Bk	murdered
Meir	פאגרונד		Rokiskis, Lithuania	Yzkr Bk	murdered
Meir Reuven	ונדפאגר		Rokiskis, Lithuania	Yzkr Bk	murdered
Tzila	פאגרונד		Rokiskis, Lithuania	Yzkr Bk	murdered
Zalman	פאגרונד		Rokiskis, Lithuania	Yzkr Bk	murdered
Chana	קרענגעל		Rokiskis, Lithuania	Yzkr Bk	murdered
Israel	קרענגעל		Rokiskis, Lithuania	Yzkr Bk	murdered
Tzipora	קרענגעל		Rokiskis, Lithuania	Yzkr Bk	murdered
Yitzkhak	קרענגעל		Rokiskis, Lithuania	Yzkr Bk	murdered
First name unknown	ראסקינד		Rokiskis, Lithuania	Yzkr Bk	murdered
Beile			Rokiskis, Lithuania	Yzkr Bk	murdered
David			Rokiskis, Lithuania	Yzkr Bk	murdered
Dina Sara			Rokiskis, Lithuania	Yzkr Bk	murdered
Doba			Ponidel, Lithuania	PT	murdered
First name unknown			Rokiskis, Lithuania	Yzkr Bk	murdered
First name unknown			Rokiskis, Lithuania	Yzkr Bk	murdered
First name unknown			Rokiskis, Lithuania	Yzkr Bk	murdered
Golda Golde			Rokiskis, Lithuania	Yzkr Bk	murdered
Helena			Rokiskis, Lithuania	Yzkr Bk	murdered
Israel			Rokiskis, Lithuania	Yzkr Bk	murdered
Ite Chaia			Rokiskis, Lithuania	Yzkr Bk	murdered
Lea			Rokiskis, Lithuania	Yzkr Bk	murdered
Lea			Rokiskis, Lithuania	Yzkr Bk	murdered
Lea Sara			Rokiskis, Lithuania	Yzkr Bk	murdered
Lea Sara			Rokiskis, Lithuania	Yzkr Bk	murdered
Leibel			Rokiskis, Lithuania	Yzkr Bk	not stated
Leizer			Rokiskis, Lithuania	Yzkr Bk	murdered
Lote Gitel			Rokiskis, Lithuania	Yzkr Bk	murdered
Malka			Rokiskis, Lithuania	Yzkr Bk	murdered
Malka			Rokiskis, Lithuania	Yzkr Bk	murdered
Malka Pesia			Rokiskis, Lithuania	Yzkr Bk	murdered
Moshe			Rokiskis, Lithuania	Yzkr Bk	murdered
Moshe			Rokiskis, Lithuania	Yzkr Bk	not stated
Moshe			Rokiskis, Lithuania	Yzkr Bk	murdered
Musie			Rokiskis, Lithuania	Yzkr Bk	murdered
Noakh			Rokiskis, Lithuania	Yzkr Bk	murdered
Rachel			Rokiskis, Lithuania	Yzkr Bk	murdered
Rachel Chana			Rokiskis, Lithuania	Yzkr Bk	murdered
Rivka Feiga			Rokiskis, Lithuania	Yzkr Bk	murdered
Roza			Rokiskis, Lithuania	Yzkr Bk	murdered
Shlomo			Rokiskis, Lithuania	Yzkr Bk	murdered
Tzvia			Rokiskis, Lithuania	Yzkr Bk	murdered
Yerakhmiel			Rokiskis, Lithuania	Yzkr Bk	murdered
Zalman Shneiur			Rokiskis, Lithuania	Yzkr Bk	not stated
Zelig			Rokiskis, Lithuania	Yzkr Bk	murdered

Appendix of Rokiskis Shoah Victims – not in the original Yizkor Book

First Name	Last Name	Birth Year	Place of Residence	Source	Fate from Source

Source Codes	
Census	Census list
Deport	Deportation list
Dep-FR	List of deportation from France
Evac	List of evacuated persons
HLBV	List of Hungarian labor battalion victims
Jew Res	List of Jewish residents
Murd	Record of murdered persons
Persecut	List of persecuted persons
PT	Page of Testimony
PT Ds	Page of Testimony (digital signed)
PT D	Page of Testimony (digital)
Per Doc	Personal documents
Residen	List of residents
Yzkr Bk	List of murdered Jews from Yizkor books

Partial List of Lithuanian murderers of the Jews of Rokiskis and its district

Adomavicius Kazys	Rokiskis+Obeliai	Kazanavicius Bronius	Skapiskis
Augulis Jonas	Skapiskis	Kaziauskas Petras	Rokiskis+Obeliai
Avizienis Antanas	Rokiskis	Klimas Balys	Rokiskis+Obeliai
Bagdonavicius Erslovas	Rokiskis+Obeliai	Krisciunas Jonas	Rokiskis+Obeliai
Balciunas Antanas	Skapiskis	Lauckas Pranas	Rokiskis+Obeliai
Balciunas Petras	Rokiskis+Obeliai	Lekavicius Matas	Rokiskis+Obeliai
Barstinskas Juozas	Rokiskis+Obeliai	Lepinaitis Vladas	Rokiskis+Obeliai
Berzelis Kazys	Rokiskis	Luksys Domazas	Rokiskis+Obeliai
Biebertas Albinas	Rokiskis+Obeliai	Lydeika Kazys	Rokiskis+Obeliai
Birbila Antanas	Rokiskis	Martinonis Petras	Kamajai
Brazenas Jurgis	Rokiskis+Obeliai	Martinonis Vladas	Kamajai
Butkauskas Pranas	Rokiskis	Medzevicius Kazys	Rokiskis+Obeliai
Cepukis Jonas	Kamajai	Mikusauskas Stepas	Rokiskis+Obeliai
Ciuksys Bronius	Rokiskis+Obeliai	Motuzas Jonas	Skapiskis
Danilevicius Antanas	Rokiskis+Obeliai	Okas Jurgis	Rokiskis+Obeliai
Domanauskas Petras	Obeliai	Packauskas Zigmas	Rokiskis+Obeliai
Dubinskas Jonas	Rokiskis+Obeliai	Paliusis Henrikas	Rokiskis+Obeliai
Gelezevicius Juozas	Kamajai	Paplauskas Leonas	Rokiskis+Obeliai
Greblikas Vladas	Rokiskis+Obeliai	Petrila Antanas	Rokiskis+Obeliai
Gricius Stasys	Rokiskis+Obeliai	Pietronas Juozas	Obeliai
Grigaliunas Vincas	Rokiskis+Obeliai	Pliskauskas Leonas	Rokiskis+Obeliai
Gudauskas Kazys	Rokiskis+Obeliai	Pupelis Ipolites	Rokiskis+Obeliai
Januskevicius Aleksas	Rokiskis+Obeliai	Puronas	Skapiskis
Judikevicius Jurgis	Kamajai	Repsis Juozas	Obeliai
Jurgelevicius Henrikas	Rokiskis+Obeliai	Rimavicius Bronius	Skapiskis
Jurgelevicius Leonas	Rokiskis+Obeliai	Samaturovas Leonidas	Rokiskis+Obeliai
Jurgelevicius Zenonas	Rokiskis+Obeliai	Samulionis Vincas	Rokiskis+Obeliai
Kalendra Stasys	Rokiskis+Obeliai	Scesna Mykolas	Rokiskis+Obeliai
Kapianis	Obeliai	Sciukauskas Jonas	Rokiskis+Obeliai
Katele Antanas	Skapiskis	Seveikis Antanas	Rokiskis+Obeliai
Simanavicius Petras	Obeliai		
Simukonis Bronius	Rokiskis+Obeliai		
Simukonis Feliksas	Rokiskis+Obeliai		
Sirocenko Vacys	Rokiskis+Obeliai		
Sirvinskas Stasys	Rokiskis+Obeliai		
Slefendorfas Jurgis	Rokiskis+Obeliai		
Stancikas Bronius	Skapiskis		
Stancikas Leonas	Skapiskis		
Stankaitis Juozas	Rokiskis+Obeliai		
Stepanas	Obeliai		
Sulinskas Vincas	Rokiskis+Obeliai		
Taparauskas Pranas	Rokiskis+Obeliai		
Unekas Juozas	Rokiskis+Obeliai		
Vaitonis Stasys	Rokiskis+Obeliai		
Vakrikas Vytautas	Rokiskis+Obeliai		
Varnackas Vincas	Rokiskis+Obeliai		
Vasaitis Jurgis	Rokiskis+Obeliai		
Vasiljevas Vitalgus	Rokiskis+Obeliai		
Vilutis Jonas	Kamajai		
Zagunas Jonas	Skapiskis		
Zekas Julius	Rokiskis		
Zokas Povilas	Skapiskis		
Zukas (Lt.)	Rokiskis		

May God punish these cowards. May they and their associates and collaborators and their closest, their descendants and offspring, stand defamed and cursed to all posterity.

The murder of young girls from Rokiskis, summer 1941

CPSIA information can be obtained
at www.ICGtesting.com
Printed in the USA
BVOW04*0728270917
495145BV00005B/4/P